JOHN CATT'S
Which School?
2021

Published in 2020 by
John Catt Educational Ltd,
15 Riduna Park,
Melton, Suffolk IP12 1QT UK
Tel: 01394 389850
Fax: 01394 386893
Email: enquiries@johncatt.com
Website: www.johncatt.com

© 2020 John Catt Educational Ltd

A CIP catalogue record for this book is available from the British
Library.

ISBN: 978 1 912906 97 0

Contacts

Editor
Jonathan Barnes
Email: jonathanbarnes@johncatt.com

Advertising & School Profiles
Tel: +44 (0) 1394 389850
Email: sales@johncatt.com

Distribution/Book Sales
Tel: +44 (0) 1394 389863
Email: booksales@johncatt.com

Website: www.schoolsearch.co.uk

2

Contents

How to use this guide

Which School? has been specifically designed with the reader in mind. There are clearly defined sections providing information for anyone looking at independent education in the UK today.

Are you looking for help and advice? Take a look at our editorial section (pages 5-40). Here you will find articles written by experts in their field covering a wide variety of issues you are likely to come across when choosing a school for your child. Each year we try to find a differing range of topics to interest and inform you about the uniqueness of independent education.

Perhaps you are looking for a school or college in a certain geographical region? Then you need to look first in the directories, which begin on page D271. Here you will find basic information about all the schools in each region complete with contact details. From this section you will be directed to more detailed information in the guide where this is available. An example of a typical directory entry is given below.

Are you looking for a certain type of school or college in your local area? Then you will need to look in the directories for your local area (see contents page for a list of all regions). Underneath each school you will find icons that denote the different types of schools or the qualifications that they offer.

Some of you may already be looking for a specific school or college. In which case, if you know the name of the school or college but are unsure of its location, simply go to the index at the back of the guide where you will find all the schools listed alphabetically. Page numbers prefixed with the letter D denote the directory section; those without, a detailed profile.

If, however, you need to find out more information on relevant educational organisations and examinations, then you can look in the appendices where you will find up-to-date information about the examinations and qualifications available (page 377). There is also a section giving basic details about the many varied and useful organisations in the education field (page 397).

The profile and directory information in this guide is also featured on **www.schoolsearch.co.uk**, which also includes social media links, and latest school news.

Key to directory

County

Name of school or college

Indicates that this school has a profile

Address and contact number

Head's name

Age range

Number of pupils.
B = boys G = girls VIth = sixth form

Fees per annum.
Day = fees for day pupils.
WB = fees for weekly boarders.
FB = fees for full boarders.

Wherefordshire

College Academy

For further details see p. 12

Which Street, Whosville,
Wherefordshire AB12 3CD

Tel: 01000 000000

Head Master: Dr A Person

Age range: 11–18

No. of pupils: 660 B330 G330 VIth 200

Fees: Day £11,000 WB £16,000 FB £20,000

Key to directory icons

Key to symbols:
- ⚥ Boys' school
- ⚥ Girls' school
- 🌐 International school
- ⑯ Tutorial or sixth form college

Schools offering:
- Ⓐ A levels
- ♨ Boarding accommodation
- ⓔ Bursaries
- ⑯ Entrance at 16+
- ⑱ International Baccalaureate
- ⊘ Learning support
- ✺ Vocational qualifications

The questions you should ask

However much a school may appeal on first sight, you still need sound information to form your judgement

Schools attract pupils by their reputations, so most go to considerable lengths to ensure that parents are presented with an attractive image.

Modern marketing techniques try to promote good points and play down (without totally obscuring) bad ones. But every Head knows that, however good the school prospectus is, it only serves to attract parents through the school gates. Thereafter the decision depends on what they see and hear.

When you choose a school for your son or daughter, the key factor is that it will suit them. Many children and their parents are instinctively attracted (or otherwise) to a school on first sight. But even if it passes this test, and 'conforms' to what you are looking for in terms of location and academic, pastoral and extracurricular aspects, you will need to satisfy yourself that the school does measure up to what your instincts tell you.

Research we have carried out over the years suggests that in many cases the most important factor in choosing a school is the impression given by the Head. As well as finding out what goes on in a school, parents need to be reassured by the aura of confidence which they expect from a Head. How they discover the former may help them form their opinion of the latter.

So how a Head answers your questions is important. Based on our research, we have drawn up a list of 24 points on which you may need to be satisfied. The order in which they appear below does not necessarily reflect their degree of importance to each parent, but how the Head answers them may help you draw your own conclusions:

- How accessible is the Head, whose personality is seen by most parents as setting the 'tone' of the school?

- Will your child fit in? What is the overall atmosphere?

- To which organisations does the school belong? How has it been accredited?

- What is the ratio of teachers to pupils?

- What are the qualifications of the teaching staff?

- How often does the school communicate with parents through reports, parent/teacher meetings or other visits?

- What is the school's retention rate? Do larger lower classes and smaller upper classes reflect a school's inability to hang on to pupils?

- What are the school's exam results? What are the criteria for presenting them? Are they consistent over the years?

- How does the school cope with pupils' problems?

- What sort of academic and pastoral advice is available?

- What is the school's attitude to discipline?

- Have there been problems with drugs or sex? How have they been dealt with?

- What positive steps are taken to encourage good manners, behaviour and sportsmanship?

- Is progress accelerated for the academically bright?

- How does the school cope with pupils who do not work?

- What is the attitude to religion?

- What is the attitude to physical fitness and games?

- What sports are offered and what are the facilities?

- What are the extracurricular activities? What cultural or other visits are arranged away from the school?

- What steps are taken to encourage specific talent in music, the arts or sport?

- Where do pupils go when they leave – are they channelled to a few selected destinations?

- What is the uniform? What steps are taken to ensure that pupils take pride in their personal appearance?

- What are the timetable and term dates?

- Is it possible to speak to parents with children at the school to ask them for an opinion?

Independent schools have proven their worth in lockdown

Barnaby Lenon, chair of the Independent Schools Council, says it's time to congratulate teachers for their hard work

In some respects independent schools in the UK had a good Covid-19. With lockdown in March they rapidly shifted to offering close to a full timetable online. Pupils were taught well and were assessed fully. Many schools felt that their pupils had learnt more than they might have done had the school operated normally. For the first time parents could actually see what was being taught in lessons. Some even learnt something!

This was in stark contrast to many state schools who, in the face of union intransigence, found it much harder.

So independent schools faced the academic year 2020-2021 with confidence. Their pupils had not fallen behind. Which is just as well because it is expected that GCSEs and A-levels will be set and sat in June 2021 with limited change in content and no change in level of difficulty.

Financially independent schools have faced three challenges: the understandable reduction in the number of overseas pupils because of the poor health record of the UK, the fact that some fee-paying parents have lost their jobs, and the decision taken by most governing boards to cut fees in the summer 2020 term. Many held fees down in autumn 2020 as well. As costs faced by these schools were little reduced (the main cost being teaching staff, most of whom carried on working), the budgets of schools were badly hit. Some schools closed, others merged or were sold to investors.

But the schools who closed were generally small and already facing financial difficulties. Most independent schools survived, although many had to cut costs. Many were able to help parents with bursary support.

The Independent School Council Census 2020 shows there are currently just over 58,000 non-British pupils at ISC schools with just under 30,000 having parents overseas

(5.5% of all ISC pupils). The loss of some of these overseas pupils will be acutely felt – particularly in boarding schools – and measures will be needed to build the confidence of overseas families about returning to the UK.

Most independent schools remained open during lockdown in order to look after the children of key workers or vulnerable children. Many worked to support state schools nearby.

Today the picture looks surprisingly good – better than expected in dreadful circumstances. Not only have academic standards been maintained but independent schools have done a brilliant job with the pastoral care of

Today the picture looks surprisingly good – better than expected in dreadful circumstances. Not only have academic standards been maintained but independent schools have done a brilliant job with the pastoral care of the children in their care.

the children in their care. Mental health has been a focus of all our schools since reopening. After all, the children had been confined to home for months and some lost relatives to the virus.

But it will take time to get back to normal. As I write there are no contact sports being allowed and there are restrictions on the normal activities in subjects like PE, drama and dance. Local lockdowns are expected so teachers have to cope with juggling teaching as normal with the possibility that tomorrow they may have to revert to online lessons. The testing system is failing schools badly.

Finally, let us congratulate both independent school teachers for their hard work and expertise during this crisis and the pupils for bearing up at a time which was hard for many. We must hope that soon the pandemic will seem a distant memory.

For more information about the Independent Schools Council see page 34

Our strength and resilience has shone through to meet new and unexpected challenges

Headteacher Mrs Paula Anderson reflects on the challenges created by Covid-19 on Bishop Challoner School, an all-through co-educational Catholic Independent establishment, and how the school has adjusted

During the unprecedented times of the Covid-19 pandemic, Bishop Challoner has risen to the challenge with a real sense of commitment and responsibility to ensure that we were able to adopt and implement a flexible learning approach; one that could be as effective as possible in the circumstances. The school is fortunate to have robust technology in place that has allowed us to interact with pupils and provide a learning platform across the whole age range of 3 to 18 years. When the announcement came that schools were likely to close in March 2020, the Senior Leadership Team began to put plans in place before the national lockdown had started. As a school we are forward thinking, highly organised and decisive to ensure that we are prepared for any crises that may arise.

Our staff have adapted amazingly well to online teaching, always seeking to 'go the extra mile' in order to maximise learning opportunities for our pupils. In the senior department, the introduction of Microsoft Teams has been used to provide quality remote learning and in the junior department, pupils have been using Purple Mash. The nursery has interacted superbly with the children and stayed connected using Tapestry which allowed photographs, videos and diary entries to be shared with parents.

During the period of lockdown, Bishop Challoner has further demonstrated that it is a kind and caring community where everyone looks out for each other. 'Community and Service' is one of our Catholic Christian values at Bishop Challoner. In a time like this, our NHS frontline workers and care workers deserve our utmost praise for the essential roles that they continue to carry out amid putting themselves and their families at risk. Throughout the pandemic, we have stepped up to ensure that we cared for any vulnerable pupils and looked after the children of key workers during term time and in the holiday period.

Collaboration, teamwork and a strong sense of community spirit are important aspects of our school and certainly have been magnified during this time. Our Heads of Sections and School Counsellor have enabled strong pastoral support to continue and to ensure that all children feel supported. We have had well-being at the heart of all that we have done and introduced a Challoner Channel simply aimed at the pupils to support their mental health and emotions (https://www.bishopchallonerschool.com/information/newsletter).

A month before the lockdown, Bishop Challoner had a Diocesan Denominational Inspection, and the school was judged outstanding. It was reported that;

"Pupils benefit greatly from being part of this outstanding Catholic school where the pastoral care of the pupils lies at the heart of the work of the school. As a result, pupils feel safe, secure and happy in a family environment where each person is welcomed, valued, respected and cared for".

I feel immensely proud of the way the pupils have acknowledged the significant changes. They have responded incredibly positively to the new 'normal' and learnt to be adaptable, flexible, show courage and resilience. The children have been using their initiative to develop a range of skills as well as being creative, curious and inquisitive. It has been wonderful to see how well the children have adapted to independent learning in their own spaces, ranging from learning British Sign Language, writing letters to support the lonely and making visors for care homes. This time away from the classroom has given the children the opportunity to explore and to develop their independent learning.

I too as Headteacher have had to adapt to the changes in technology and deliver online assemblies. This will become the expected way of delivering most of our assemblies until the situation changes.

I am proud to be the Head of Bishop Challoner and never have I been more proud than now, having seen so many generous acts of kindness, goodwill and professionalism from the whole school community and from my dedicated team of staff who pull together in true community style. The parent body at Bishop Challoner is amazing, highly supportive and keen to engage and one can never underestimate the huge sacrifices that parents make to send their children to our independent school and their faith in our Catholic Christian ethos, values and sense of purpose is so valued. Maintaining Bishop Challoner's strong, supportive community spirit is one of our many strengths and the school has responded so well at a time when this pandemic dictates our daily lives.

The new meaningful technologies that we have harnessed and adopted at Bishop Challoner will, no doubt, continue to be used to enhance our teaching and learning.

For more information about Bishop Challoner School see page 106

Our distance learning journey

David Boggitt, Deputy Head Academic, Cranleigh School, explains the transition from classroom to digital – and how the school's boarding community adapted to the challenge

Pupils at Cranleigh have enjoyed a full distance learning programme from the moment that the school took the view to close a week before the end of the Spring term. Fortunately, we were preparing for the restrictions well in advance, having been working closely with educators on the ground in China and seeing the pandemic unfolding. Changsha (Hunan Province) opened in Autumn 2020 and we're opening another in Chengdu (Sichuan Province) in September 2021 and are hugely grateful for the advice and support of our partners, Cogdel.

As a school we also introduced iPads into our teaching and learning three years ago along with Google's GSuite platform to facilitate collaboration. This involved training all teachers on the devices and tools in the preceding year and therefore gave us an advantage as staff and pupils already understood the place of technology and were used to many of the elements needed for successful distance learning; use of apps, workflows for the submission of work, online assessment methods and new creative possibilities. Pupils were already familiar with email for communication with teachers but we expanded this to include Instant Messaging and video calls to create a more timely and personal experience. The teaching staff also reimagined much of their content for distance learning, making interactive worksheets, video tutorials and online assessments to improve engagement and ensure the curriculum could continue to be delivered.

Having said this, even with this experience and excellent platform to build on, it remained a challenge to get five year groups with well over 300 individual classes up to speed and working successfully in a remote way. We made the decision early on that live teaching would be too intense for our younger pupils so our prep school has two live lessons per day, with the rest being available on our VLE, Firefly. However, we also took the view to conduct all lessons for the senior school (year 9 upwards) as live lessons. We shortened lesson length slightly to reduce screen time and give longer breaks between lessons, alongside adapting our timetable from six days to five to allow for a proper break at the weekend.

As a boarding community, the importance of keeping pupils engaged socially as well as in a co-curricular and cultural programme cannot be underestimated. We held online sport/fitness sessions and challenges, alongside art, music, drama; the co-curricular elements that pupils enjoy and that are so important as part of their day-to-day education. Our pastoral leaders and their tutor teams have been brilliant at keeping pupils engaged with fun and daily challenges, alongside regular 1-to-1 pastoral meetings to support our pupils all the way through this journey.

Naturally, we have had to significantly adapt various approaches to how we approach teaching and assessment, as well as successfully implementing our first virtual parents' meeting. Teachers have learned a huge amount about what is most effective, so we're prepared for a time when we may have to implement a distance learning programme in the future.

For more information about Cranleigh School see page 180

Reading – a gift to treasure

Sarah Kruschandl, Head of English at Burgess Hill Girls, reflects on a time when stories and books become more important than ever

The benefits of reading have long been extolled, but during lockdown novels became even more treasured; their ability to transport us to another world was a tonic to the stress and uncertainty of life during the pandemic. Burgess Hill Girls is a school with holistic aims: to achieve both academic excellence and positive wellbeing. In March 2020 we introduced a 'Book of the Week' campaign to support the pupils and wider school community during these unprecedented times.

The pupil who reads at home will have obvious advantages in English lessons. The more a child reads for pleasure, the better their reading will be at school. Additionally, readers are also better writers. Reading improves a pupil's grammar, composition and gives pupils a greater breadth of vocabulary. The benefits of reading spread further than the English classroom, however. Reading a book is akin to taking your brain to the gym: it improves your intelligence. The brain lights up like a firework display when observed reading under an ECG, which might explain why an enthusiastic reader will gain higher exam results than their peers, even in subjects such as Maths. Proven to be more influential than having well-educated parents, reading leads to achievements. This success is not limited to schools, for reading books is the only extra-curricular activity that has a positive correlation with obtaining a managerial or professional job.

Reading literature not only makes us smarter, it also makes us more philanthropic, for the art of the novel is to transport us into someone else's story. The reader cannot be rigid and insular; they are forced to expand their perspective and to empathise. As Harper Lee explains in To Kill a Mockingbird, 'You never really understand a person until you consider things from his point of view... until you climb in his skin and walk around in it.' As we read, we climb into a character's skin and walk around through their story. We are immersed in a new view of the world and thus, through reading a novel, we have an insight into other minds, which helps us to be more liberal, inclusive and to approach life with more creativity.

Literature is our way of reflecting our experience of the world, but while novels encourage diverse and ever

> Reading releases endorphins, our happy chemical. In addition, reading is a therapeutic escape from the trivialities which can consume us.

expansive understanding, they also nurture and comfort us. Dr Samuel Johnson, who suffered from severe bouts of depression, said in the 18th century, 'the only end of writing is to enable the reader better to enjoy life or better to endure it.' Novels can help us understand and cope with times of deep emotional strain. Coronavirus aside, the epidemic which has a grip on the modern world is the rising tide of mental health problems. Reading is restorative. While various studies have highlighted the curative benefits of reading on our wellbeing, the reasons for this recuperative influence are complex. Reading releases endorphins, our happy chemical. In addition, reading is a therapeutic escape from the trivialities which can consume us. We all face emotional challenges; relationships can be complex and life deals us a mixture of fortunes, some good and some bad. The realisation that this is a collective experience is both reassuring and healing. Thus novels unite us and define our humanity.

In an age when reading is in competition with so many other forms of communicational and technological stimulation, we aspire that pupils leave Burgess Hill Girls equipped and keen to read. Our library, called the Learning Resource Centre (LRC), is at the heart of our school, both physically and as a part of the girls' routine; it buzzes with pupils at break, lunch and afterschool. The English Department works alongside the LRC manager delivering dedicated reading lessons, reading rewards, clubs and events.

Our 'Book of the Week' campaign aims to foster reading at home, by recommending books which are both entertaining and stretching. From two-year olds to adults, we have novels for all age groups. More recently we have adapted our lists to reflect our times. We supported the Black Lives Matter campaign with a week of recommendations celebrating black authors and our summer holiday list transported readers around the world, for most, the only way to experience new foreign cultures during the summer. These lists are available on our social media sites and website, where we have also included a small synopsis and a link to buy the books.

Reading helps us academically, but also psychologically, spiritually and collectively. Shakespeare wrote in The Tempest, 'Books are the engines of change, windows on the world, a lighthouse erected on the sea of time.' Create a culture of reading in your home; it is a gift that your child will treasure forever.

For more information about Burgess Hill Girls, see page 174

The importance of an outstanding education in a changed world

William Brierly, Headmaster of Claremont Fan Court School, reflects on an a once-in-a-lifetime school year

I have fond memories of applying to become headmaster of Claremont Fan Court School back in January 2018. My three rounds of interviews and assessments were much as you might expect, but then they conducted a role play situational interview. I had to demonstrate how I might deal with an anxious pupil. On reflection, this allowed me to demonstrate empathy and kindness, even though I simply saw it as a task to be done. They didn't ask the key question: tell me, Will, could you give me an example of how you have successfully navigated a school through a global pandemic?

So there I was, telling teachers in late March that while our primary role is in educational excellence, we do so knowing we are a business, albeit a charity, for which the customer needs to know what they are getting for their money. Never would we be under more scrutiny of what we were delivering. A term on, I find every year in the middle school (and indeed the prep school) is fuller than it was when we closed. It is only spoken about quietly, because independent schools are the last out of a recession as well as the last in, but parents appear to be of the mind that even if they can hardly afford the fees, they cannot afford to not pay the fees, if it will deliver an excellent education.

As headmaster, it is at times of crisis that you most effectively see the strength, or otherwise, of the team of staff you work with. For me, their stoic determination to do the right thing for the children we teach has been the mark of our success. I should have known from the role play interview that I was joining a school that cared. In one week, we trained every teacher to use Google Classroom (where work is set and submitted using an online platform) and Google Meet (for face to face conference lessons). We introduced a quality assurance process from day one,

with senior colleagues including myself routinely calling the whole senior school parent body to help us evolve what we were doing, and not doing.

Initially feedback from non-exam-year parents was cautious. They were worried lockdown would simply involve lots of work being set, and their feedback helped to underline the social contact their children were missing – the teacher seeing them in person to understand what they didn't understand – which drove us to want to improve and evolve over a busy Easter break.

> Online lessons have enabled parents to see what does happen in the classroom as never before.

Perhaps having four children who study in four different schools (including one in Year 7 at Claremont) has given me perspective. It has certainly allowed me to recognise when we are getting it right. I do not have a wide enough vocabulary to convey how reassuring it is to know my son cannot fall behind with his learning because Claremont teachers would be rapidly on the case if he missed lessons or did not submit work, thanks to lessons simply following the timetable; he may not have been on site, but he was simply following the same 8.30am to 4pm school day model

and was talking to his teachers and classmates. The school day, week or even term entirely disappears when tasks are simply set online without the follow-up of human interaction, certainly with my teenagers. Pupil ratios are lower in an independent school, we afford more specialist teachers, our pupils and staff have laptops. This is not intended as an essay bashing maintained schools because these three factors have been key in our ability to be flexible.

Nevertheless, this has so far been an economic phenomenon like no other, with parents who are concerned for their own businesses and income levels applying and committing their savings, their debt or their disposable income to an independent school education with only the feedback of their friends, the glance at an online interactive open event and an online interview to guide their choice. I realise online lessons have enabled parents to see what does happen in the classroom as never before. I appreciate too we are just a school bus drive away from south west London, we have 100 acres of land, a beautiful learning environment and a growing reputation; stage one of the worst recession of our lifetime is focusing minds on the importance of an education with which their children can flourish, even under a global pandemic. We approach the new term with a confidence we can fully reopen and with a determination that we should do everything in our power to prevent schools ever needing to close again, but to have been able to recruit this term, in lockdown, more effectively than a few years ago when our doors were wide open says a great deal about the importance of a great education in this changing world.

For more information about Claremont
Fan Court School see page 178

A collective determination to learn, develop, improve and thrive

Giles Entwisle, Headmaster of Durston House, looks ahead to a future filled with promise amid global uncertainty

Having completed by far the most extraordinary term in my teaching career, facing unprecedented challenges, catching our collective breath at the beginning of the summer holidays has allowed time to reflect on Home Learning and my new post as Headmaster at Durston House from September. I have been involved in the Home Learning provision at Durston House as part of my handover and while these have been unprecedented times, it has also been heart-warming. Joining a school in such a period has allowed me to see how Durston has reacted and adapted to Home Learning successfully.

In the time BC or before-COVID-19, Durston House's Virtual Learning Environment was used for homework and sharing curriculum resources. The real learning still took place in person, with the teacher in the classroom, on the fields, or out on adventures. The move to the alternative classroom or Home Learning, came upon us incredibly swiftly and required a comprehensive and radical rethink of how Durston does things, and how to ensure that outcomes for pupils would not suffer. Reflecting on how our teachers responded to live video-conference lessons and remote task setting so quickly and so professionally was a humbling lesson in how important it is to retain the commitment to being a life-long learner. Pupils were quickly following a core subject focused timetable, receiving live, detailed tuition and immediate personalised remote feedback. Durston laid out a solid foundation with provision adapted as teachers continued to learn this new form of delivering the curriculum remotely. Pupils and staff established capabilities, expectations and adjusted to 'the new normal'. Pupil learning didn't suffer; the boys embraced the change and rapidly came to appreciate a whole lot more. Feedback from parents and pupils saw a pattern emerge, whereby pupils were enjoying greater family time and connection. They talked about enjoying the simple things, like going for a walk, playing a game with the family, enjoying their own gardens and appreciating more profoundly, the immediate world around them. Pupils spent more time developing their cooking, photography, art, design, building and musical skills following the Enrichment program.

The opportunity for greater numbers of pupils to come back into school following the phased re-opening was grasped (at a distance) with both hands, carefully washed for 20 seconds with soap and water. Durston had remained open for children of key workers but welcomed back additional year groups and divided them into 'pods'. Home Learning still continued for those who didn't return but staff managed to expertly juggle both being in the classroom and being online.

It was only after properly reconnecting and talking with pupils and parents on their return that the overarching message became so clear. Distance had brought us all much closer together. The admiration from the parent body for the teachers in how they continuously went the extra mile for the pupils was humbling. Parents also appreciated the balance of the curriculum; that the academic was blended with the co-curricular program allowing for a varied and interesting curriculum. Most importantly it was manageable. There were large disparities with what families could manage and it was important for everyone's well-being that the amount and type of work be engaging, challenging and most importantly, achievable.

Durston managed to host assemblies as well as some of our usual events like Sports Day and House Competitions. Durston's Got Talent was also a roaring success. The ability to come together and celebrate achievements and take part in something created a palpable spirit of community, as well as allowing pupils to find comfort in the normality and familiarity these events offer.

There is at Durston House, a collective determination to take all we have learned from this pandemic. While it has been difficult at times, there have been many positives; Pupils have become more self-motivated, organised, and accountable and intrinsically driven which will be helpful in the future. The insight our parents have gained into what great teaching looks like, and the vital way in which parents and teachers have collaborated for the benefit of the pupils, is not something we are willing to lose as we go into the new academic year.

I realise we will not see a return to complete normality by any means in the near future We will need to keep learning and developing the provision for our pupils and staff. We will need to adapt to changing circumstances energetically and with meticulous planning. At Durston House there is an understanding in the transformative power of education. It will be our pupils' personal qualities and values, not just exam results that will set them apart. It is critical to give young people the skills, confidence and capabilities to navigate their own paths through life – along with the unshakeable sense of self they need to influence the world around them for the better. I have no doubt that Durston House will continue to provide the highest quality education and finest pastoral care.

For more information about Durston House see page 128

Bethany School swaps classrooms for remote learning

Reflections on an education in lockdown – from pupils, parents and staff

The UK Government closed schools on Friday 20th March 2020 until further notice due to the continued spread of Covid-19. Thanks to the hard work of staff and pupils, Bethany was very well prepared for this announcement and pupils successfully swapped their classrooms at School for a classroom at home.

Bethany staff have been receiving in-depth training on using online learning systems, including Microsoft Teams, for over two years, therefore the School was well prepared to make the transition to remote learning seamlessly. The Bethany Science department tested metals and non-metals remotely, Food & Nutrition Studies pupils followed tutorials via Instagram and even PE and Games pupils were able to continue their learning by creating online activity diaries.

Proudly British, Bethany also has pupils from several different countries. Consequently, processes were put in place so that pupils could join lessons from anywhere in the world.

One pupil participated in a poetry class from Belgium, and another attended an English as an Additional Language class from China.

The feedback on our remote learning offering from parents and pupils alike was overwhelmingly positive:

"Although we're only a few hours in – both children have said, unprompted, 'this is working'. They are very much benefiting from the structure and visibility of their teachers and classmates and they are both feeling positive about this setup.

"I also wanted to say that in chatting with other friends about their children's respective school setups during this time, what Bethany is doing is far above what other children seem to be getting.

"The fact that all kids have laptops and online access to everything has made Bethany well placed to handle a crisis like this."
Parent of pupils in Years 7 and 9

"I am so impressed with Bethany. Today, my son has seamlessly transitioned to online learning. He is having virtual lessons, talking with his friends, completing work and loving it! His routine continues, and he is happy and engaged. It has also meant that I am able to continue working from home to support my clients."
Year 7 parent

"I have to say that I was really impressed with the system, my son was able to just get on with his schoolwork while my husband and I continued working from home.

"I have also heard extremely positive feedback from other Year 7 parents. Long may it continue."
Year 7 parent

"Both girls had such a positive experience with remote learning and didn't feel nearly as isolated with all their friends available. A huge thank you to you all – it takes a team, and the dedication required from the school to make this work, in such stressful times, and in the short period of time we had, is nothing short of amazing.

"Well done, and thank you, Bethany! It's a huge relief to know that the girls' education won't slip during these trying times."
Parent of pupils in Years 7 and 9

Headmaster Francie Healy said: "When I started teaching, I never thought for one minute that I would end up being Headmaster of a School that was delivering all of its lessons remotely. I would like to pay tribute to the amazing teaching staff who have worked incredibly hard on top of all their other commitments, so that they can deliver remote teaching excellently. I would also like to praise our pupils who have adapted to this enforced change so well.

"All of us here at Bethany really do appreciate the very complimentary emails that many parents have sent into the School praising the level of service that Bethany is providing."

Bethany are now well underway with making the necessary preparations to fully reopen the School at the start of the Autumn 2020 term.

For more information about Bethany School see page 172

"Although we're only a few hours in – both children have said, unprompted, 'this is working'. They are very much benefiting from the structure and visibility of their teachers and classmates and they are both feeling positive about this setup.

Defying distance: Keeping learning standards high

Kathryn Gorman, Head at Abbot's Hill School, explains how the challenges of the past few months has brought the school community closer together

Schools are reacting in a multitude of ways to the ever-changing demands of the Covid-19 pandemic. At Abbot's Hill, we reflect on the highly effective way we became a digital school almost overnight and maintained academic and pastoral excellence during lockdown.

At Abbot's Hill, we thought our great excitement of the year would be our 'Excellent' ISI report, which praised our high standards throughout all areas of school life. However, like the rest of the country's schools, only weeks later, we were forced to navigate complete closure. This required us to create and design a remote learning curriculum and pastoral programme from scratch, train pupils and staff to master online interaction, and utilise Google Meet and Google Classroom to sustain the day-to-day life of our community.

We were fortunate to be able to follow in the footsteps of schools overseas who were at the front line of the response to Covid-19 and we will be forever grateful to colleagues at the Kellett School in Hong Kong and Harrow Prep, Bangkok alongside others in Italy and elsewhere from whom we learnt so much. Nevertheless, nothing quite prepares you when faced with those challenges at such short notice!

Just before closure we were able to hold training sessions for staff to ensure that the Google suite was fully accessible to all Y3–Y11 pupils and the superb SeeSaw APP was understood by our Reception–Y2 pupils and parents. Tapestry continued to work well for Nursery parents and enabled live story time, arts and crafts and other fun activities to be shared with families. Remote learning was going to be tough and we were determined to ensure that all pupils were engaged, motivated and challenged and that staff had the resources to provide stimulating lessons

– all of this whilst pupils, parents and staff managed their work from home alongside suddenly becoming teachers and navigating the various other challenges that being in Lockdown brought.

Our plan was to begin every day with live pastoral sessions from tutor groups to assemblies. In Prep, we also had live pastoral sessions at the end of the day: a kind of virtual

> The year has been challenging for all involved on so many different levels: emotionally, financially, personally but we have been proud of the way we have come together.

circle time, if you will. Pupils' days were therefore framed with human interaction – something that became so essential as the term went on. Staff and pupils missed each other, missed the human contact and the spontaneity of conversation that had been taken for granted. In addition to whole class meetings for registration, tutors and class teachers provided small group support each week to ensure that the pupils had individual and personalised support along the way. In addition, we also provided tailored learning and emotional support for those most affected.

We re-wrote timetables from scratch and gave families something very important – time together that would usually have been spent commuting or dashing

to some club or activity. We were determined to find the silver linings in The Great Pause. As the term progressed, we solicited frequent feedback from pupils, staff and parents. With this feedback we were able to adapt our initial plans. Live lessons remained a priority as did the need to provide enriching and challenging extension tasks, clubs and as much 'normal' school life as possible. It was important that we regularly reviewed our programme to keep pupils and staff motivated and engaged.

We were able to loan out iPads and Chromebooks so that each pupil was able to have their own device at home. Our amazing IT department worked tirelessly supporting everyone with device issues, technical support and also provided training and guides to ensure that the very best could be delivered to our pupils.

The year has been challenging for all involved on so many different levels: emotionally, financially, personally but we have been proud of the way we have come together. It hasn't been a smooth ride but we have grown as a community, pulled together and supported each other. The power of positivity and perseverance: that's how we want to remember Lockdown. There are more challenges and changes to come, for that we are sure but we feel ready to face them head on.

We invite your nursery children and daughters to grow, change and flourish with us.

Abbot's Hill School was recently awarded 'Excellent' ISI ratings across all areas. We invite you to visit our school and see for yourself just how incredible it is. Visit www.abbotshill.herts.sch.uk

For more information about Abbot's Hill see page 64

Lockdown lessons

How Gordon's School staff and pupils responded when crisis hit

Medical and Keyworkers dubbed them 'Easter visors' as they donned the crucial PPE made by Gordon's teaching and support staff.

Nearly 2,000 visors with the distinctive canary-yellow band were made by the PPE production line soon after the start of lockdown for local hospitals, vet practices, supermarkets and charities.

Meanwhile kitchen and food technology staff at the school in West End, Surrey Heath were taking food; protective gloves and food containers – as well as raiding tuck shops across the school – for donations to the community's homeless.

Anxious to do their bit, Sixth Former Magnus Jackson produced ear savers from a 3-D printer at home, having watched tutorials on Instagram and YouTube. And fellow Sixth Former Toby Johnson joined frontline workers, collecting recently deceased from hospital morgues or their homes.

Boarder Elysee Spacie started baking each week for her local hospital, producing 30 cakes and biscuits for staff at St Peter's and her brightly coloured drawings with motivational messages were soon cheering up patients travelling in London ambulances. Also included in her messages of goodwill was a letter to Her Majesty the Queen, which to Elysee's delight, elicited a reply from the Queen's Lady in Waiting.

Across the school, students and staff put their skills to good use in whatever way possible.

Edwin Sutton, the school's Internal Fleet Manager, got back on his bike. The former traffic policeman delivered blood products and Covid-19 specimens across the country on his 'blood bike'.

Two of the school's Medical Centre nurses – Emma Light and Julie Unsworth volunteered for nursing duties at Frimley Park Hospital. And elderly Gordonians were touched to receive cheery calls from the Gordonian Officer Sue Parkin.

House Parent Ben Heathcote begun the first in a series of Lockdown Live music events at the school, which were heard in nearby West End and across the world via live-stream video. Adding their voices to the Gordon's chorus of talented Heads of Houses were Gary Knight with his mixture of classics and swing and former Fiji Rugby Sevens Team analyst and skills coach Chris Davies and his blend of modern rock and old favourites.

Pipers from Gordon's Pipes and Drums Band saluted the NHS every Thursday evening from their gardens, to the delight of neighbours. And the First XI Hockey Team set to work raising money for the NHS. Both their target of running 1,500 miles during the month of May and raising £500, were easily smashed and they nearly tripled their fundraising.

Robbed of their chance to take to the open water and compete, Boat Club students took to their ergos instead with borrowed equipment from school, carrying out a gruelling training regime and completing their Peak Week at home instead of their Easter camp.

Eleven of the group then took part in the British Rowing Virtual Championships, joining over a thousand entrants from 30 countries world-wide, competing in a real-time side-by-side race from the comfort of their own homes!

Head Teacher Andrew Moss described the academic year as "...more difficult than any of us has ever encountered". Paying tribute to students, their parents and staff, he said: "Teenagers often receive poor press nationally for their lack of resolve and thoughtless actions; a bright spot in this difficult term has been how well Gordon's students have risen to the challenge and many will have become better people as a result of this national crisis."

For more information about Gordon's School see page 184

For more information about Gordon's School see page 184

"Teenagers often receive poor press nationally for their lack of resolve and thoughtless actions; a bright spot in this difficult term has been how well Gordon's students have risen to the challenge and many will have become better people as a result of this national crisis."
Andrew Moss, Headteacher

Educational continuity during coronavirus

At Oakham School, there was a 'clarity of what was important'

In the blink of an eye, earlier this year, Coronavirus created a new era in education. Pupils found themselves at home without their peers. Schools found themselves changing their approach; adapting to use technology to deliver lessons. The change continued when schools returned in September – where safety and social distancing led to adapted timetables and alterations to school sites and buildings.

Oakham School in Rutland has successfully adapted to each phase of the coronavirus challenge. Having returned in September, there are rigorous measures in place to keep all of its pupils – of which 500 board and 500 are day students – as safe as possible. "The extensive plans and protocols that we have established are even more wide-ranging than the Boarding Schools' Association (BSA) COVID-Safe Charter that we, like other boarding schools across the country, have signed," says Mrs Sarah Gomm, Deputy Head Pastoral.

As well as the variety of practical measures to keep the Oakham community safe, including 170 sanitising stations and special quarantine provision and care for overseas boarders, the School has been carefully organising its 'new normal' curriculum.

"We have a variety of timetables to ensure the stability of our educational provision and to help pupils to feel confident and ready to engage in their academic studies," adds Mrs Gomm.

"We want the School to feel as *normal* as possible, but recognise that there will be a variety of different scenarios that we could face. We have therefore have three different timetables to ensure we can move and adapt should we need. There is our 'normal' timetable which sees all pupils moving freely about School, an enhanced social distancing timetable that reduces movement across campus, and a distance learning timetable in the event of a local lockdown and schools are instructed to close."

The distance learning timetable was successfully established back in March, and includes all lessons being delivered online, with pupils benefiting from a full daily timetable of two-way virtual teaching. "At times of crisis, such as these, there is clarity of what's important," says Dr Leo Dudin, Deputy Head Academic." For us, it is that human relationships are at the heart of education; that face-to-face interactions and relationships matter and bring learning to life." The School uses Microsoft Teams as this easily enables relationships and interactions to be at the heart of Oakham's approach to distance learning and social distancing. It allows effective video discussions between a whole class of pupils, for teachers to share their screens as they live-stream lessons and to incorporate their pre-recorded content. Oakham has always used the phrase 'learning isn't limited to the classroom'. Never has it been truer though, with their distance learning approach enabling pupils to continue to enjoy their specialist music lessons as well as even taking science lessons - conducting investigations and experiments in their 'home laboratories'!

Oakham has always been known for its continuous focus on the happiness and well-being of its pupils. Its pro-active pastoral care underpins life both in and beyond the classroom – enabling children to flourish at school and long into the future. The School's strong pastoral systems are fully embedded into the remote education timetable. During lockdown pupils met (virtually) every day with their House or their tutors and House spirit thrived through exciting activities, challenges and competitions. These were all designed to keep pupils connected and happy – and would continue again, should remote education come back into effect. Oakham's belief that school days are precious and should be enjoyable, memorable, and transformative will always be upheld, even if the community is apart or has to be socially distanced. Chapel remains at the heart of Oakham's daily life, albeit virtually, with pupils enjoying everything from 'thought for the day' messages to singing together whilst in lockdown, and virtual services continuing during social distancing.

Oakham is also renowned for having an innovative approach to education – having offered the IB Diploma and BTECs alongside A-levels for many years, as well as more recently developing the IB MYP for its youngest pupils. This same spirit of educational innovation saw the launch of a new Academic Cornerstone Course during lockdown for pupils whose examinations had been cancelled. This series of courses covered academic skills, life skills, and employability skills. Each strand was designed by a team of teachers selected from across several departments, to ensure the course was original and impactful, as well as drawing on the School's wide range of teaching expertise, experience and enthusiasm. At its heart, the course taught a variety of skills that are important to pupils' futures – showcasing, even during unprecedented times, how an Oakham education focuses on preparing pupils for life after school, equipping them to be intellectually ambitious thinkers, with the knowledge, skills and confidence needed to thrive and to make a difference in the world.

Prospective parents are encouraged to take either a 'Virtual Visit' to Oakham or to book an individual visit to see Oakham's wonderfully unique school community in action for themselves.

For more information about Oakham School, see page 102

Full STEAM ahead!

Jill Walker, Headmistress of Maltman's Green School, explains the importance of an innovative approach to STEAM

Maltman's Green has a rich history of preparing girls for the future and a strong reputation for being a school that is forward thinking. I believe that this approach will be more important than ever, with the Fourth Industrial Revolution already upon us! Characterized by a fusion of technologies that is blurring the lines between the physical, digital, and biological spheres, disruptive technologies and trends such as the Internet of Things (IoT), robotics, virtual reality (VR) and artificial intelligence (AI) are changing the way we live, work and communicate. Its impact is being felt in all disciplines, industries, and economies. At no time has this been more keenly felt than in the recent coronavirus crisis, with us all having to find new ways to work and connect.

It is against this rapidly changing and unpredictable backdrop, that the World Economic Forum Future of Jobs Report came up with the top 10 skills that are needed to drive success. Maltman's Green School is nurturing the female leaders of the future. Our girls will be the movers and shakers of tomorrow. So, along with promoting academic excellence, developing our girls' skills and aptitude in areas such as problems solving, critical thinking, people management, decision making, negotiation, flexibility, innovation, creativity and emotional intelligence, will all be more important than ever.

And this is where the STEAM curriculum (Science, Tech, Engineering, Art and Maths) comes in. Traditionally the arts and sciences have only been delivered in schools as separate subjects. But, increasingly the learning in school needs to reflect what is going on in the real-world - where scientists, engineers and mathematicians work collaboratively with designers and the creative industries, harnessing the power of technology to find innovative and novel solutions to problems. Children learn by doing. So, it is important for teachers to provide these active learning opportunities through a variety of approaches. Examples might include the girls sharing and exploring their ideas with others (both off and on-line) as they work together on a group project such as designing a new musical instrument or a house made out of recycled materials with a built in security system, or make connections between maths, art and science as they explore the symmetry of nature and create their own remote controlled aeroplanes in a special curriculum themed week, be offered the freedom to go off-piste and explore their own ideas independently through a variety of media in termly 'creative homework', as well as the school developing extra-curricular activities to include a DT and engineering programme with access to a specially designed 'Maker Space'. Of course, in these unprecedented times, where home learning has been an integral part of what we offer our pupils, we have seen how important it is to provide an evolving, innovative learning environment with ubiquitous access to technology. I believe that digital technology can transform learning – bringing it to life, making it relevant and fun. From using green screens, class blogs, micro bits, floor robots, or a virtual learning environment, it is important to empower the girls to move from being passive consumers of information and technology, to active creators and innovators.

As we reflect on what we have learnt during the lock-down period, we are recognising there are opportunities to promote the environmental agenda. New approaches can have a low financial impact and also benefit our world and make it more sustainable. The challenge for the young is to achieve economic wealth alongside environmental health. A vibrant and carefully crafted STEAM programme nurtures creativity and adaptability, builds self-confidence, the ability to work flexibly with others and fosters empathy and a socially responsible and outward looking mind-set. These are the key skills and attributes our children will need to rely upon in the future.

For more information about Maltman's Green School, see page 192

Maltman's Green School is nurturing the female leaders of the future. Our girls will be the movers and shakers of tomorrow. So, along with promoting academic excellence, developing our girls' skills and aptitude in areas such as problems solving, critical thinking, people management, decision making, negotiation, flexibility, innovation, creativity and emotional intelligence, will all be more important than ever.

Digital learning – what progress have we made?

David McClymont, Director of IT of Downe House School, reflects on the use of technology in schools during lockdown

In the wake of the Covid-19 pandemic and the resulting lockdown, technology played a crucial role in ensuring the continuity of teaching and learning for pupils who suddenly found themselves studying remotely at home with only virtual contact with their classmates. Not to mention the teachers who were faced with the challenge of adapting in just a few weeks to remote working, on-line collaboration and a whole plethora of new technologies to enable them to deliver the curriculum and support their pupils. All this at a time of huge anxiety and stress about the relentless spread of the Coronavirus across the globe.

In just a few weeks, schools and teachers were expected to switch from conventional face-to-face teaching in the classroom to livestreaming their lessons, creating video blogs and feedback, communicating via online chat, using new digital tools such as Flipgrid and Edpuzzle and attending Zoom or Microsoft Teams meetings.

However the pace at which this happened and its ultimate success was of course dependent on the existing digital framework in place, the level of IT support, availability of hardware and software and to what extent digital technologies and training had already been incorporated into teaching practice.

As a result, the outcomes for pupils varied enormously across schools in the UK as online learning was delivered with varying degrees of success and effectiveness. According to the social mobility charity, the Sutton Trust, a third of pupils were taking part in online lessons while schools were closed and pupils from independent schools were twice as likely as state school pupils to take part in online lessons every day. Crucial to the success of the transition to online learning were the availability of devices or pupils' access to broadband and the digital capability of the school and its staff.

At Downe House, we introduced our Digital Strategy four years ago based on the Microsoft Office 365 platform and implemented comprehensive staff training and a phased roll-out of the MS Surface programme to all year groups so that every pupil and teacher had their own Microsoft Surface. Never did we dream that our digital capabilities would become so critical or that we would have to take the whole School online and deliver entirely on-line teaching and learning due to a global pandemic!

> Now that pupils are back in school, there is an urgent need for debate about the way forward for digital teaching as the importance of equipping pupils with digital skills and tools for the workplace cannot now be disputed.

However, thanks to the work we had already done, the transition to virtual teaching proved relatively smooth as everyone was already very familiar with using online tools such as Teams and OneNote. So much so, we were able to continue to give our pupils a full timetable of lessons taught by their teachers and livestreamed to their homes across the globe both in real time, and as recorded lessons. Microsoft Stream provided a simple way for staff to record and share their lessons, which can now be used as a further resource for future pupils."

Of course, whether they were accustomed to using digital tools or not, most teachers were plunged into a very different approach to teaching and had to quickly master a whole range of digital skills. Teachers had to work hard to adapt to a completely new way of working and finding creative ways to engage pupils online whilst taking into account safeguarding issues. Whilst research is ongoing to assess the effectiveness of remote learning, anecdotal evidence shows that it does work and many pupils thrived on the alternative learning experience, enjoyed acquiring new digital skills or found it helpful to go back and watch a recorded lesson again.

Now that pupils are back in school, there is an urgent need for debate about the way forward for digital teaching as the importance of equipping pupils with digital skills and tools for the workplace cannot now be disputed. A cultural shift has already taken place in digital literacy and many teachers have embarked on their digital journey with more confidence than ever before. Investment is needed across the board in hardware, connectivity, staff training, dedicated support and resources as well as a careful approach to ensuring the perfect balance between face-to-face teaching and utilisation of digital technologies.

The lockdown and school closures were unprecedented as were the outstanding efforts of schools to ensure the continuity of teaching and learning online for the nation's children. Perhaps there could be a silver lining to the crisis in the form of a quantum leap forward for schools embracing digital learning and harnessing its power to transform education for everyone.

For more information about Downe House School, see page 48

100 years of Manor House School

The English Riviera to Little Bookham, Surrey

With the new academic year starting afresh this September, Manor House School was ready to open its gates to old and new staff and students, marking 100 years of Manor House history. Instead, with lessons and teaching moving online and into homes during much of 2020 and creating an alternative landscape for its school community, plans for the Centenary celebrations have been put on hold until 2021. Despite this, early September saw staff and girls reunite enthusiastically onsite, quietly celebrating a return to some normality.

Manor House School started its life in the seaside town of Sidmouth in Devon in September 1920 as the Beehive School. Founded by two visionary ladies, Miss Elizabeth Green and Miss Wheeler, their original motto "To love it to Live" is still central to the school's ethos today.

Looking back to that founding year, education for children had become compulsory only 39 years before in 1881. In the 19th century, schooling was seen as a passport to success for Victorian middle-class boys, who were educated "for the world", whilst middle-class girls were educated "for the drawing room". Most were taught at home, with only a minority attending boarding schools with a non-academic curriculum, with this pattern continuing until WW1.

Before then, changes had started to be seen with the founding of the North London Collegiate School in 1850, the first modern fee-paying day school offering girls a similar education to that given to boys, followed in 1877 by the first girls' public school in St Andrew's Scotland, Roedean in 1885 and Wycombe Abbey in 1896.

By 1921, the population of England and Wales had reached 37 million compared to 26 million in 1881, and the 1918 Representation of the People Act had enfranchised all men over the age of 21 and all women over the age of 30.

Many more middle-class British girls were attending school, studying a curriculum similar to boys' schools, although its ultimate purpose was still to prepare women for the role of wife and mother. The same period saw the opening of numerous girls' boarding schools fuelled by the demand from middle-class British parents based overseas during the days of the British Empire.

Miss White and Miss Wheeler grasped their opportunity to create a nurturing and academic environment for both girls and boys to thrive, whilst meeting the needs of overseas families and offering a haven after the hardships of WW1.

> Old girls remember staff with high standards for learning and behaviour, but above all a caring and nurturing community where girls were encouraged to be themselves.

At the time Beehive School was opening its doors, Sidmouth was known as a holiday destination, the northern edge of the "English Riviera", with the Sidmouth Guide of 1930 listing 17 hotels and 66 boarding houses. A visit by Queen Victoria's son the Prince Regent in 1856 had, for a time, made it "the most fashionable seaside resort in England".

By the late 1920s, Miss Green and Miss Wheeler felt that the school would benefit from moving closer to London and relocated to Little Bookham in 1937 when Miss Green acquired the Manor House. The School has occupied the same site ever since, even remaining open throughout WW2. The following decades saw further expansion with the building of the Sports Hall known as EGH (Elizabeth Green Hall) and Mason which houses the Science labs, followed in the 2000s with the Prep, Nursery and Art blocks.

Since its founding, the school has known 11 Headmistresses and was named Best Small School in 2007 in the Sunday Times Best UK School guide. When Alumni talk about what they remember of their time at the school, some clear trends emerge. Lasting friendships are always first to be mentioned, followed by memorable school trips, outdoor performances and games in the Dell (a natural amphitheatre in the school grounds), and of course the Marrow Uniform (for better or worse!) Equally, old girls remember staff with high standards for learning and behaviour, but above all a caring and nurturing community where girls were encouraged to be themselves. These are the foundations the school continues to aspire to today.

Through the active Alumni Society, old girls and boys are regularly in touch. One boy boarder during the Second World War recently shared copies of letters he'd sent from Manor House in 1942 to his father who had been captured and incarcerated in Saigon as a Japanese prisoner of war, thankfully surviving the war. More recently the school has had contact with fashion designers, nurses and medical researchers, journalists, civil servants with the Ministry of Defence, trial lawyers to name a few, all of which make up the rich legacy of the school.

As Manor House looks towards 2021, admission enquiries continue to rise, the outdoor swimming pool is calling for its summer games to resume and the school community looks forward to celebrating its Centenary with past and present staff and girls, including plans for a Centenary Ball and Summer Picnic in the coming months.

For more information about Manor House School, see page 194

Help in finding the fees

Chris Procter, joint managing director of SFIA, outlines a planned approach to funding your child's school fees

Average school fee increases between the last year 2 school years, according to the ISC census, were 4.1%. This is lower than expected given the increased cost of Teachers Pension Scheme which came in last year. There appears to have been a conscious effort by schools over the last 10 years to control fees. Since 2010 fee increases have averaged 3.9%. Between 2000 and 2010 they averaged 6.6%.

The latest Independent Schools Council (ISC) survey, conducted in January 2020 and completed by all 1,374 schools in UK membership, indicate that there are now a record 537,315 pupils being educated privately, the highest number since records began in 1974, rising 0.22% since 2019.

Pupils registered to board stands at 13.0% with weekly and flexi boarding becoming increasingly popular. The percentage of pupils attending single sex schools stands at 24.5%, marginally lower than last year.

The overall average boarding fee is £11,763 per term and the overall average day fee is £4,980 per term.

However, fees charged by schools vary by region – for example, the average boarding fee ranges from £9,292 per term in the North East to £13,372 per term in Greater London; the average day fee ranges from £3,725 per term in the North West to £5,993 per term in Greater London.

The overall cost (including university fees) might seem daunting: the cost of educating one child privately could well be very similar to that of buying a house but, as with house buying, the school fees commitment for the majority of parents can be made possible by spreading it over a long period rather than funding it all from current resources.

It is vital that parents do their financial homework, plan ahead, start to save early and regularly.

Grandparents who have access to capital could help out; by contributing to school fees they could also help to reduce any potential future inheritance tax liability.

Parents would be well-advised to consult a specialist financial adviser as early as possible, since a long-term plan for the payment of fees – possibly university as well – can prove very advantageous from a financial point of view and offer greater peace of mind. Funding fees is neither science, nor magic, nor is there any panacea. It is quite simply a question of planning and using whatever resources are available, such as income, capital, or tax planning opportunities.

The fundamental point to recognise is that you, your circumstances and your wishes or ambitions, for your children, or grandchildren are unique. They might well appear similar to those of other people but they will still be uniquely different. There will be no single solution to your problem. In fact, after a review of all your circumstances, there might not be a problem at all.

So, what are the reasons for seeking advice about education expenses?

- To reduce the overall cost
- To get some tax benefit
- To reduce your cash outflow
- To invest capital to ensure that future fees are paid
- To set aside money now for future fees
- To provide protection for school fees
- Or just to make sure that, as well as educating your children, you can still have a life

Any, some, or all of the above – or others not listed – could be on your agenda, the important thing is to develop a strategy.

At this stage, it really does not help to get hung up on which financial 'product' is the most suitable. The composition of a school fees plan will differ for each family depending on a number of factors. That is why there is no one school fees plan on offer.

The simplest strategy but in most cases, the most expensive option, is to write out a cheque for the whole bill when it arrives and post it back to the school. Like most simple plans, that can work well, if you have the money. Even if you do have the money, is that really the best way of doing things? Do you know that to fund £1,000 of school fees as a higher rate taxpayer paying 40% income tax, you currently need to earn £1,667, this rises to £1,818 if you are an additional rate taxpayer where the rate is 45%.

How then do you start to develop your strategy? As with most things in life, if you can define your objective, then you will know what you are aiming at. Your objective in this case will be to determine how much money is needed and when.

You need to draw up a school fees schedule or what others may term a cash flow forecast. So, you need to identify:

- How many children?
- Which schools and therefore what are the fees? (or you could use an average school fee)
- When are they due?
- Any special educational needs?
- Inflation estimate?
- Include university costs?

With this basic information, the school fees schedule/cash flow forecast can be prepared and you will have defined what it is you are trying to achieve.

Remember though, that senior school fees are typically more than prep school fees – this needs to be factored in. Also, be aware that the cost of university is not restricted to the fees alone; there are a lot of maintenance and other costs involved: accommodation, books, food, to name a few. Don't forget to build in inflation, I refer you back to the data at the beginning of this article.

You now have one element of the equation, the relatively simple element. The other side is the resources you have available to achieve the objective. This also needs to be identified, but this is a much more difficult exercise. The reason that it is more difficult, of course, is that school fees are not the only drain on your resources. You probably have a mortgage, you want to have holidays, you need to buy food and clothes, you may be concerned that you should be funding a pension.

This is a key area of expertise, since your financial commitments are unique. A specialist in the area of school fees planning can help identify these commitments, to record them and help you to distribute your resources according to your priorities.

The options open to you as parents depend completely upon your adviser's knowledge of these complex personal financial issues. (Did I forget to mention your tax position, capital gains tax allowance, other tax allowances, including those of your children and a lower or zero rate tax paying spouse or partner? These could well be used to your advantage.)

A typical school fees plan can incorporate many elements to fund short, medium and long-term fees.

Each plan is designed according to individual circumstances and usually there is a special emphasis on what parents are looking to achieve, for example, to maximise overall savings and to minimise the outflow of cash.

Additionally, it is possible to protect the payment of the fees in the event of unforeseen circumstances that could lead to a significant or total loss of earnings.

Short-term fees

Short-term fees are typically the termly amounts needed within five years: these are usually funded from such things as guaranteed investments, liquid capital, loan plans (if no savings are available) or maturing insurance policies, investments etc. Alternatively, they can be funded from disposable income.

Medium-term fees

Once the short-term plan expires, the medium-term funding is invoked to fund the education costs for a further five to ten years. Monthly amounts can be invested in a low-risk, regular premium investment ranging from a building society account to a friendly society savings plan to equity ISAs. It is important to understand the pattern of the future fees and to be aware of the timing of withdrawals.

Long-term fees

Longer term funding can incorporate a higher element of risk (as long as this is acceptable to the investor), which will offer higher potential returns. Investing in UK and overseas equities could be considered. Solutions may be the same as those for medium-term fees, but will have the flexibility to utilise investments that may have an increased 'equity based' content.

Finally, it is important to remember that most investments, or financial products either mature with a single payment or provide for regular withdrawals; rarely do they provide timed termly payments.

Additionally, the overall risk profile of the portfolio should lean towards the side of caution (for obvious reasons).

There are any number of advisers in the country, but few who specialise in the area of planning to meet school and university fees. SFIA is the largest organisation specialising in school fees planning in the UK.

This article has been contributed by SFIA and edited by Chris Procter, Managing Director.
Chris can be contacted at: SFIA, 29 High Street, Marlow, Buckinghamshire, SL7 1AU
Tel: 01628 566777
Fax: 0333 444 1550
Email: enquiries@sfia.co.uk
Web: www.schoolfeesadvice.org

The Independent Schools Council

The Independent Schools Council (ISC) works with its members to promote and preserve the quality, diversity and excellence of UK independent education both at home and abroad

What is the ISC?

The ISC brings together seven associations of independent schools, their heads, bursars and governors. Through our member associations we represent more than 1,350 independent schools in the UK and overseas. These schools are among the best in the world and educate more than half a million children each year.

The ISC's work is carried out by a small team of dedicated professionals in an office in central London. We are assisted by contributions from expert advisory groups in specialist areas. Our priorities are set by the board of directors led by our chairman, Barnaby Lenon. We are tasked by our members to protect and promote the sector in everything we do.

ISC schools

Schools in UK membership of the ISC's constituent associations offer a high quality, rounded education. Whilst our schools are very academically successful, their strength also lies in the extra-curricular activities offered – helping to nurture pupils' soft skills and encourage them to be self-disciplined, ambitious and curious. There are independent schools to suit every need, whether you want a day or boarding school, single sex or co-education, a large or a small school, or schools offering specialisms, such as in the arts.

Our schools are very diverse: some are selective and highly academic, while others have very strong drama or music departments full of creative opportunities in plays, orchestras and choirs. For children with special needs such as dyslexia or autism there are many outstanding independent schools that offer some of the best provision in the country.

Academic results

Typically, the ISC publishes a sector-wide analysis of Year 11 and Year 13 exam results for independent schools every August. However, due to the coronavirus pandemic, there was no sector-wide publication of results in 2020 because exams were temporarily replaced by an assessment process that Ofqual had to create in response to the crisis. Schools provided students with their grades in August as normal and the Department for Education is expected to publish results for all schools (state and independent) in January 2021.

Looking back at exam results in 2019, 45.7% of Year 13 exam entries at independent schools were graded A*/A, compared to the national average of 25.5%. That year also saw 95.6% of Year 11 exams at independent schools graded C/4 or higher, compared to the national average of 67.3%. Figures recorded in 2019 also demonstrated more students are following different pathways post-GCSE.

Fee assistance

Schools take issues around affordability very seriously and are acutely aware of the sacrifices families make when choosing an independent education. Schools work hard to remain competitive whilst facing pressures on salaries, pensions and maintenance and utility costs. They are strongly committed to widening access and have made strenuous efforts to increase the amount they can offer in bursaries. This year, £440m was provided in means-tested fee assistance for pupils at ISC schools. Currently a third of pupils at our schools benefit from reduced fees.

School partnerships

Independent and state schools have been engaged in partnership activity for many years, with the majority of ISC schools currently involved in important cross-sector initiatives. These collaborations involve the sharing of expertise, best practise and facilities, and unlock exciting new opportunities for all involved. To learn more about the partnership work taking place between state and independent schools, visit the Schools Together website: www.schoolstogether.org/

ISC Associations

There are seven member associations of the ISC, each with a distinctive ethos in their respective entrance criteria and quality assurance: Girls' Schools Association (GSA), Headmasters' and Headmistresses' Conference (HMC), Independent Association of Prep Schools (IAPS) Independent Schools Association (ISA), The Society of Heads, Association of Governing Bodies of Independent Schools (AGBIS), and the Independent Schools' Bursars Association (ISBA).

Further organisations who are affiliated to the ISC: Boarding Schools Association (BSA), Council of British International Schools (COBIS), Scottish Council of Independent Schools (SCIS) and Welsh Independent Schools Council (WISC).

The Independent Schools Council can be contacted at:
First Floor,
27 Queen Anne's Gate,
London,
SW1H 9BU
Telephone: 020 7766 7070
Website: www.isc.co.uk

independent schools council

Choosing a school initially

Educational institutions often belong to organisations that guarantee their standards. Here we give a brief alphabetical guide to what the initials mean

BSA

The Boarding Schools' Association

Since its foundation in 1965-66, the Boarding Schools' Association (BSA) has had the twin objectives of promoting boarding education and the development of quality boarding through high standards of pastoral care and boarding accommodation. Parents and prospective pupils choosing a boarding school can be assured that the 600+ plus schools in the UK and internationally that make up the membership of the BSA are committed to providing the best possible boarding environment for their pupils.

A UK boarding school can only be a full member of the BSA if it is also a member of one of the Independent Schools Council (ISC) constituent associations, or in membership of the BSA State Boarding Forum (SBF). These two bodies require member schools to be regularly inspected by the Independent Schools' Inspectorate (ISI) or Ofsted. Other boarding schools which are not members of these organisations can apply to be affiliate members. Similar arrangements are in place for international members. Boarding inspection of ISC-accredited independent schools has been conducted by ISI since September 2012, while Ofsted inspects boarding in state schools and non-association independent schools. Boarding inspections must be conducted every three years. Boarding in England and Wales is judged against the National Minimum Standards for Boarding Schools which were last revised for primary and secondary schools in England in 2015 and are set to be updated again soon.

In 2020, the Boarding Schools' Association became part of the BSA Group. BSA Group comprises BSA (Boarding Schools' Association), SACPA (Safeguarding and Child Protection Association) and BAISIS (British Association of Independent Schools with International Students). BSA Group champions excellence in boarding and safeguarding and delivers services for more than 600 members in 35 countries.

Relationship with government

The BSA is in regular communication with several government departments, including the Department for Education (DfE), Home Office, Foreign and Commonwealth Office and Ministry of Defence. The Children Act (1989) and the Care Standards Act (2000) require boarding schools to conform to national legislation and the promotion of this legislation and the training required to carry it out are matters on which the BSA and the DfE work closely.

Boarding training

Through the BSA Academy (training school), the association maintains the high standards expected as a consequence of that support and from the BSA's Commitment to Care Charter – which all member schools must abide by. The BSA organises five three residential conferences, six one day conferences and more than 90 seminars and webinars a year for governors, Heads, deputies, housemasters and housemistresses, and matrons and medical staff where further training takes place in formal sessions and in sharing good practice. The BSA provides the following range of training and information:

- Professional qualifications for teaching and non-teaching staff in boarding schools. The BSA Academy has developed a host of courses including: Certificates of Professional Practice in Boarding Education, Certificate in International Boarding, Certificate in Professional Practice for Nurses and Matrons, and a Diploma for senior leaders. A rolling programme of day seminars and webinars on current boarding legislation and good practice.

- Bespoke training, INSET, and consultancy on best boarding practice, particularly with regard to safeguarding.

- The Accredited Boarding Practitioner scheme, where individuals working in boarding can have their service and experience accredited by BSA.

- Centre for Boarding Education Research (CEBER) which brings together a wide variety of articles and research on all matters related to boarding.

State Boarding Forum (SBF)

The BSA issues information regards its 40 state boarding school members and the BSA should be contacted for details of these schools. In these schools, parents pay for boarding but not for education tuition.

60 St Martin's Lane
London WC2N 4JS
Tel: 020 7798 1580
Email: bsa@boarding.org.uk
Website: www.boarding.org.uk

bsa | BOARDING SCHOOLS' ASSOCIATION

GSA

The Girls' Schools Association, to which Heads of independent girls' schools belong

The Girls' Schools Association helps girls and their teachers to flourish. It represents the Heads of a diverse range of independent UK girls' schools (day & boarding), among which are some of the top-performing schools in the country.

The GSA encourages high standards of education and promotes the benefits of being taught in a largely girls-only environment. GSA schools are internationally respected and have a global reputation for excellence. Their innovative practice and academic rigour attract pupils from around the world. Students at GSA schools enjoy abundant extra- and co-curricular opportunities. Academically, they thrive in the humanities and do disproportionately well in 'difficult' modern languages and STEM (science, technology, engineering, maths) subjects. A high percentage – 96% – progress to higher education.

GSA schools share experience, specialisms, opportunities and facilities with state sector schools in a wide range of partnerships. Many also provide means-tested bursaries for families of limited financial means.

Twenty first century girls' schools come in many different shapes and sizes. Some cater for 100% girls, others provide a predominantly girls-only environment with boys in the nursery and/or sixth form. Some follow a diamond model, with equal numbers of boys but separate classrooms between the ages of 11 to 16. Educational provision across the Association offers a choice of day, boarding, weekly, and flexi-boarding education. Schools range in type from large urban schools of 1000 pupils to small rural schools of around 200. Many schools have junior and pre-prep departments, and can offer a complete education from age 3/4 to 18. Some also have religious affiliations. Heads of schools in the Girls' Day School Trust (GDST) are members of the GSA.

The Association aims to inform and influence national educational debate and is a powerful and well-respected voice within the educational establishment, advising and lobbying educational policy makers on core education issues as well as those relating to girls' schools and the education of girls. The Association liaises with the Department for Education, the Office for Standards in Education, the Qualifications and Curriculum Authority and other bodies.

The GSA also provides its members and their staff with professional development courses, conferences, advice and opportunities to debate and share best practice, ensuring that they have every opportunity to remain fully up-to-date with all aspects of their profession.

As the GSA is one of the constituent bodies that make up the Independent Schools' Council (ISC), its schools are required to undergo a regular cycle of inspections to ensure that these rigorous standards are being maintained. GSA schools must also belong to the Association of Governing Bodies of Independent Schools, and Heads must be in membership of the Association of School and College Leaders (ASCL).

The Association's secretariat is based in Leicester.

Suite 105, 108 New Walk, Leicester LE1 7EA
Tel: 0116 254 1619
Email: office@gsa.uk.com
Website: www.gsa.uk.com
Twitter: @GSAUK

President 2020: Jane Prescott, Portsmouth High School GDST
President 2021: Samantha Price, Benenden School
Chief Executive: Vivienne Durham (until December 2020); Donna Stevens (from January 2021)

HMC

The Headmasters' and Headmistresses' Conference, to which the Heads of leading independent schools belong

Founded in 1869 the HMC exists to enable members to discuss matters of common interest and to influence important developments in education. It looks after the professional interests of members, central to which is their wish to provide the best possible educational opportunities for their pupils.

The Heads of some 296 leading independent schools are members of The Headmasters' and Headmistresses' Conference, whose membership now includes Heads of boys', girls' and coeducational schools. International membership includes the Heads of around 56 schools throughout the world.

The great variety of these schools is one of the strengths of HMC but all must exhibit high quality in the education provided. While day schools are the largest group, about a quarter of HMC schools consist mainly of boarders and others have a smaller boarding element including weekly and flexible boarders.

All schools are noted for their academic excellence and achieve good results, including those with pupils from a broad ability band. Members believe that good education consists of more than academic results and schools provide pupils with a wide range of educational co-curricular activities and with strong pastoral support.

Only those schools that meet with the rigorous membership criteria are admitted and this helps ensure that HMC is synonymous with high quality in education. There is a set of membership requirements and a Code of Practice to which members must subscribe. Those who want the intimate atmosphere of a small school will find some with around 350 pupils. Others who want a wide range of facilities and specialisations will find these offered in large day or boarding schools. Many have over 1000 pupils. 32 schools are for boys only, others are coeducational throughout or only in the sixth form. The first girls-only schools joined HMC in 2006. There are now 39 girls-only schools.

Within HMC there are schools with continuous histories as long as any in the world and many others trace their origins to Tudor times, but HMC continues to admit to membership recently-founded schools that have achieved great success. The facilities in all HMC schools will be good but some have magnificent buildings and grounds that are the result of the generosity of benefactors over many years. Some have attractive rural settings, others are sited in the centres of cities.

Pupils come from all sorts of backgrounds. Bursaries and scholarships provided by the schools give about a third of the 240,000 pupils in HMC schools help with their fees. These average about £35,000 per annum for boarding schools and £15,000 for day schools. About 190,000 are day pupils and 45,000 boarders.

Entry into some schools is highly selective but others are well-suited to a wide ability range. Senior boarding schools usually admit pupils after the Common Entrance examination taken when they are 13.

Most day schools select their pupils by 11+ examination. Many HMC schools have junior schools, some with nursery and pre-prep departments. The growing number of boarders from overseas is evidence of the high reputation of the schools worldwide.

The independent sector has always been fortunate in attracting very good teachers. Higher salary scales, excellent conditions of employment, exciting educational opportunities and good pupil/teacher ratios bring rewards commensurate with the demanding expectations. Schools expect teachers to have a good education culminating in a good honours degree and a professional qualification, though some do not insist on the latter especially if relevant experience is offered. Willingness to participate in the whole life of the school is essential.

Parents expect the school to provide not only good teaching that helps their children achieve the best possible examination results, but also the dedicated pastoral care and valuable educational experiences outside the classroom in music, drama, games, outdoor pursuits and community service. Over 89% of pupils go on to higher education, many of them winning places on the most highly-subscribed university courses.

All members attend the Annual Conference, usually held in a large conference centre in September/October. There are ten divisions covering England, Wales, Scotland and Ireland where members meet once a term on a regional basis, and a distinctive international division.

The chair and committee, with the advice of the general secretary and membership secretary, make decisions on matters referred by membership-led sub-committees, steering groups and working parties. Close links are maintained with other professional associations in membership of the Independent Schools Council and with the Association of School and College Leaders.

Membership Secretary: Ian Power
Tel: 01858 465260

12 The Point
Rockingham Road
Market Harborough
Leicestershire LE16 7QU
Email: gensec@hmc.org.uk
Website: www.hmc.org.uk

Leading Independent Schools

IAPS

The Independent Association of Prep Schools (IAPS) is a membership association representing leading headteachers and their prep schools in the UK and overseas

With around 670 members, IAPS schools represent a multi-billion pound enterprise, educating more than 160,000 children and employing more than 20,000 staff. As the voice of independent prep school education, IAPS actively defends and promotes the interests of its members.

IAPS schools must reach a very high standard to be eligible for membership, with strict criteria on teaching a broad curriculum, maintain excellent standards of pastoral care and keeping staff members' professional development training up-to-date. The head must be suitably qualified and schools must be accredited through a satisfactory inspection. IAPS offers its members and their staff a comprehensive and up-to-date programme of professional development courses to ensure that these high professional standards are maintained.

Member schools offer an all-round, values-led broad education which produces confident, adaptable, motivated children with a passion for learning. The targets of the National Curriculum are regarded as a basic foundation which is greatly extended by the wider programmes of study offered. Specialist teaching begins at an early age and pupils are offered a range of cultural and sporting opportunities.

IAPS organises a successful sports programme where member schools compete against each other in a variety of sports. In 2019-20, over 17,000 competitors took part in 119 events across 7 sports.

Our schools are spread throughout cities, towns and the countryside and offer pupils the choice of day, boarding, weekly and flexible boarding, in both singe sex and co-educational schools. Most schools are charitable trusts, some are limited companies and a few are proprietary. There are also junior schools attached to senior schools, choir schools, those with a particular religious affiliation and those that offer specialist provision as well as some schools with an age range extending to age 16 or above.

Although each member school is independent and has its own ethos, they are all committed to delivering an excellent, well-rounded education to the pupils in their care, preparing them for their future.

IAPS
11 Waterloo Place
Leamington Spa
Warwickshire CV32 5LA
Tel: 01926 887833
Email: iaps@iaps.uk
Website: iaps.uk

Excellence in Education
The Independent Association
of Prep Schools

ISA

The Independent Schools Association, with membership across all types of school

The Independent Schools Association (ISA), established in 1879, is one of the oldest of the Headteachers' associations of independent schools that make up the Independent Schools' Council (ISC). It began life as the Association of Principals of Private Schools, which was created to encourage high standards and foster friendliness and cooperation among Heads who had previously worked in isolation. In 1895 it was incorporated as The Private Schools Association and in 1927 the word 'private' was replaced by 'independent'. The recently published history of the association, *Pro Liberis*, demonstrates the strong links ISA has with proprietorial schools, which is still the case today, even though boards of governors now run the majority of schools.

Membership is open to any Head or Proprietor, provided they meet the necessary accreditation criteria, including inspection of their school by a government-approved inspectorate. ISA's Executive Council is elected by members and supports all developments of the Association through its committee structure and the strong regional network of co-ordinators and area committees. Each of ISA's seven areas in turn supports members through regular training events and meetings.

ISA celebrates a wide-ranging membership, not confined to any one type of school, but including all: nursery, pre-preparatory, junior and senior, all-through schools, coeducational, single-sex, boarding, day and performing arts and special schools.

Promoting best practice and fellowship remains at the core of the ISA, as it did when it began 140 years ago. The association is growing, and its 541 members and their schools enjoy high quality national conferences and courses that foster excellence in independent education. ISA's central office also supports members and provides advice, and represents the views of its membership at national and governmental levels. Pupils in ISA schools enjoy a wide variety of competitions, in particular the wealth of sporting, artistic and academic activities at area and national level.

President: Lord Lexden
Chief Executive: Rudolf Eliott Lockhart

ISA House, 5-7 Great Chesterford Court, Great Chesterford, Essex CB10 1PF
Tel: 01799 523619
Email: isa@isaschools.org.uk
Website: www.isaschools.org.uk

ISA celebrates a wide-ranging membership, not confined to any one type of school, but including all: nursery, pre-preparatory, junior and senior, all-through schools, coeducational, single-sex, boarding, day and performing arts and special schools

The Society of Heads

The Society of Heads represents the interests of independent secondary schools

The Society of Heads represents the interests of independent, secondary schools. Established in 1961, The Society has as its members 125 Heads of well-established secondary schools, many with a boarding element, meeting a wide range of educational needs. All member schools provide education up to 18, with sixth forms offering both A and AS levels and/or the International Baccalaureate. Also some offer vocational courses. Many have junior schools attached to their foundation. A number cater for pupils with special educational needs, whilst others offer places to gifted dancers and musicians. All the schools provide education appropriate to their pupils' individual requirements together with the best in pastoral care.

The average size of the schools is about 350, and all aim to provide small classes ensuring favourable pupil:teacher ratios. The majority are coeducational and offer facilities for both boarding and day pupils. Many of the schools are non-denominational, whilst others have specific religious foundations.

The Society believes that independent schools are an important part of Britain's national education system. Given their independence, the schools can either introduce new developments ahead of the maintained sector or offer certain courses specifically appropriate to the pupils in their schools. They are able to respond quickly to the needs of parents and pupils alike.

Schools are admitted to membership of the Society only after a strict inspection procedure carried out by the Independent Schools Inspectorate. Regular inspection visits thereafter ensure that standards are maintained.

The Society is a constituent member of the Independent Schools Council and every full member in the Society has been accredited to it. All the Society's Heads belong to the Association of School and College Leaders (ASCL) (or another recognised union for school leaders) and their schools are members of AGBIS.

The Society's policy is: to maintain high standards of education, acting as a guarantee of quality to parents who choose a Society school for their children; to ensure the genuine independence of member schools; to provide an opportunity for Heads to share ideas and common concerns for the benefit of the children in their care; to provide training opportunities for Heads and staff in order to keep them abreast of new educational initiatives; to promote links with higher and further education and the professions, so that pupils leaving the Society's schools are given the best advice and opportunities for their future careers; and to help Heads strengthen relations with their local communities.

The Society of Heads Office,
12 The Point, Rockingham Road, Market Harborough,
Leicestershire LE16 7QU
Tel: 01858 433760
Email: info@thesocietyofheads.org.uk
Website: www.thesocietyofheads.org.uk

The average size of the schools is about 350, and all aim to provide small classes ensuring favourable pupil: teacher ratios. The majority are coeducational and offer facilities for both boarding and day pupils. Many of the schools are non-denominational, whilst others have specific religious foundations

School profiles

Channel Islands

St Michael's Preparatory School

St. Michael's Preparatory School is situated in a unique educational setting on Jersey in the Channel Islands. A forward thinking IAPS prep school preparing pupils for the rigours of secondary school education both on and off island. We place great emphasis upon the traditional values of care, consideration and courtesy.

The staff and pupils are justifiably proud of the School, and work together to create and maintain a high-achieving, well-organised and friendly environment in which every child is encouraged to do 'a little bit better' than anyone thought possible.

The curriculum is designed to give all children a broad, balanced and relevant education, which enables them to develop as enthusiastic, active and competent learners acquiring the knowledge, skills and understanding to allow them to grow up in today's world leading a full and active life. The school's ethos places emphasis on the individual and aims to encourage development in academic, physical, spiritual, moral and cultural aspects of the 'whole child'.

The teaching is multi-sensory, allowing children of all abilities and learning styles to be able to make progress in their learning. Differentiation is integral to the curriculum and children with special needs are well supported, as are the gifted and talented, who go on to achieve scholarship success.

The schemes of work are based upon the National Curriculum, the Jersey Curriculum and the requirements of the ISEB Common Entrance and Scholarship syllabuses. The curriculum is enriched and enhanced by numerous trips and visits as Jersey has an array of museums, cultural sites of interest and environmental locations.

The school prepares children for Common Entrance and Scholarships to English boarding secondary schools as well as entry to local Jersey establishments. We also offer a Shell Year (pre-GCSE) specifically to provide a bridging opportunity for Year 10 entry to our island state schools. Classes are small and there is a very low pupil to teacher ratio. All expected subjects are taught and there are flourishing and well-equipped Art, Music, Science, Design Technology and ICT departments as well as a custom built Sports Hall, Dance/Drama Studio, Gymnasium and indoor Swimming Pool.

As well as providing a wide range of academic subjects, the school seeks to introduce each child to a large variety of sports, performing arts, activities and challenges enabling him or her to discover, through experience, hidden talents and preferences with a view to future specialisation.

I hope St. Michael's pupils will leave us having achieved the very best they are capable of, having found out what it is that they love and are good at, having learned to challenge themselves and to value other people.

I.S.I. Inspection (Oct 2017) Key findings:
- The quality of the pupils' learning and achievements is excellent
- The quality of the pupils' personal development is excellent

"St Michael's makes ordinary children special, and special children extra-ordinary." A parent quote.

ST MICHAEL'S
PREPARATORY SCHOOL

(Founded 1949)

La Rue de la Houguette, St Saviour, Jersey JE2 7UG UK

Tel: 01534 856904

Email: office@stmichaels.je

Website: www.stmichaels.je

Head of School: Mr Mike Rees

Appointed: 2014

School type: Coeducational Day

Age range of pupils: 3–14

No. of pupils enrolled as at 01/09/2020: 315

Boys: 169 **Girls:** 146

Fees per annum as at 01/09/2020:

Day: £10,230–£16,080

Average class size: 18 max

Teacher/pupil ratio: 1:9

Central & West

Downe House School

Downe House is an exceptional boarding school for girls aged 11-18 years with family-friendly boarding and day places. The School offers a unique blend of traditional values and a forward-thinking approach on a secure 110-acre woodland estate in rural West Berkshire, only an hour from London.

Whoever you are...Whoever you want to be...Be a Downe House girl.

There is no such thing as a 'typical Downe House girl' because we understand that every girl is an individual with her own interests and talents. Whether she is an artist and a scientist, an actress and an historian, a coding whizz and a photographer – she will be equally valued, supported, stretched and encouraged at every step of the way. What girls do have in common however, is that they are expected to aspire to academic success and are given almost limitless enrichment and cocurricular opportunities to identify and develop their strengths to become accomplished musicians, actors, athletes, artists – wherever their talents and ambitions take them.

So what is it that makes a Downe House girl? The answer is rooted deep in the Downe House DNA and its seven key characteristics – Collaboration, Resilience, Creativity, Aspiration, Compassion, Communication and Outward Looking. No matter what the girls go on to do beyond Downe, and the sheer variety of the career paths of our alumnae is testament to our ethos, they all carry the enduring imprint of the Downe House DNA throughout their lives.

Being a Downe House girl means much more than a set of outstanding academic results but of course they matter, and we are immensely proud of our consistently impressive exam results. In 2020, 95% of the grades achieved were A* to B (or equivalent) at A Level with A* (or equivalent) remaining at 46%. At GCSE, 90% of grades were at 9-7 and over 71% were graded 9-8 (A** and A*). However, we place equal importance on equipping every girl with a well-established work ethic and a core set of traditional values, skills and beliefs that will allow her to flourish in today's rapidly changing world. With only girls in the classroom, in the science labs, on stage and on the sports field, both intellectual and physical confidence can grow without any stereotyping or gender-weighted expectations.

The gift of time provided by a full boarding education enables girls to develop their interests and take on new challenges. They might stretch their imaginations in the arts, give back by volunteering at local charities, take on leadership or mentoring roles or broaden their outlook through attending lectures and other activities.

What makes Downe House special?

So many things make the difference at Downe House. The term spent at our school in France. The opportunity to take part in our far-reaching Global Schools' Exchange Programme with 16 partner schools across six continents. Our Elective Programme that provides super-curricular academic enrichment to challenge and stretch able girls and encourage enquiring minds. Our holistic approach to wellbeing through the 'Learning for Life' programme that gives girls the tools for life to care for themselves as well as each other. Our DH LINKS programme connects girls' past and present with the alumnae network and our parents, who generously offer invaluable careers-based knowledge, guidance and practical support such as networking, internships and work shadowing opportunities.

We aim to ignite a lifelong love of learning and take each girl on an adventure in education to ensure that when the time comes to leave Downe House, she believes that there is nothing that she cannot achieve in the world.

Downe House

(Founded 1907)

Downe House, Cold Ash, Thatcham, West Berkshire RG18 9JJ UK

Tel: +44 (0)1635 200286

Email: registrar@downehouse.net

Website: www.downehouse.net

Headmistress: Mrs Emma McKendrick BA(Liverpool)

Appointed: September 1997

School type: Girls' Boarding & Day

Age range of girls: 11–18

No. of pupils enrolled as at 01/09/2020: 593

No. of boarders: 560

Fees per term as at 01/09/2020:

Day: £9,705 per term

Full Boarding: £13,050 per term

Average class size: 15-20

Headington School Oxford

Headington is a highly successful day and boarding school in Oxford for 800 girls aged 11-18 with a Preparatory School for 250 girls aged 3-11 occupying its own site just across the road. The School offers girls an unrivalled opportunity to pursue academic, sporting and artistic excellence in a caring and nurturing environment.

Founded in 1915 and set in 23 acres of playing fields and gardens, our superb facilities provide the perfect backdrop for teaching and learning that extends way beyond the classroom and curriculum. We encourage participation in all aspects of sport and culture, teamwork and leadership, challenging girls to discover and explore their own potential and achieve more than they thought possible.

Consistently in the premier league of academic schools in the UK, life at Headington is about much more than exam results. Through the sheer breadth of subjects and activities at Headington, we aim to educate the complete individual, giving girls the confidence and self-awareness to compete, contribute and succeed at school, university and in their adult lives.

Facilities

Headington offers a superb range of facilities to support and enhance learning.

These include a state-of-the-art Music School complete with recording studio, 240-seat professional theatre, light and airy Art School, Dance and Fitness Centre, Swimming Pool and award-winning Library. We recently completed an update to our Sixth Form Centre and a new Creativity and Innovation Centre will open in 2021.

Outside the classroom

Around 150 extra-curricular activities take place every week. A wide choice of subjects, sports, interests and hobbies including such diverse pastimes as Debating and Robotics, Cheerleading and CCF.

Headington offers a genuinely inclusive approach to sport and encourages each girl to enjoy sport at the level that suits her. Girls can choose from more than 30 different sporting activities, from Athletics to Zumba. The School enjoys national success in a wide range of sports including Fencing, Rowing, Cross Country, Swimming and Equestrian.

Around 450 individual music lessons take place each week while the School has four orchestras, three choirs and numerous ensembles.

There is a busy programme of productions in our Theatre each year and girls become involved in all aspects of theatre, from writing and producing their own plays, to lighting, costume and make up.

A huge range of dance options are on offer, from Ballet to Street Dance and Contemporary. As well as annual Dance Shows, the Headington Dance Company competes in local and national competitions.

Boarding

Headington has always been a boarding school and just over a quarter of the School board with us today. The five boarding houses provide the girls with a 'home from home' where, supported by a team of highly experienced staff, they learn to develop into mature and independent young people. Many of our boarders come from the UK and we are also very proud of our international boarding community, made up of more than 30 nationalities from all over the world. Girls can choose between full, weekly or half-weekly boarding.

(Founded 1915)

London Road, Oxford, Oxfordshire OX3 7TD UK

Tel: +44 (0)1865 759100

Fax: +44 (0)1865 760268

Email: admissions@headington.org

Website: www.headington.org

Headmistress: Mrs Caroline Jordan MA(Oxon)

School type: Girls' Day & Boarding

Age range of girls: 11–18

Fees per term as at 01/09/2020:

Day: £6,090–£6,635 per term

Full Boarding: £8,282–£13,395 per term

Prep: £3,205 – £4,880 per term

Average class size: Depends on age

Teacher/pupil ratio: 1:8

Shiplake College

Shiplake College is a thriving boarding and day school for boys aged 11-18, with girls joining in the Sixth Form. Overlooking the River Thames, two miles upstream of the famous Henley Royal Regatta stretch, students enjoy an inspirational 45-acre rural site. Flexi, weekly and full boarding is available from Year 7 (age 11).

Shiplake provides a friendly, supportive and structured environment to bring out the best in each and every pupil and aims to equip them with the skills they need to enter the next stage of their lives as confident, personable and talented young adults. Academically ambitious and renowned for outstanding pastoral care and personal development, the College welcomes pupils with wide-ranging skills and talents, who will make the most of the many opportunities offered to them.

Every pupil is placed at the heart of Shiplake life and the College's ethos is underpinned by the three Is – Inclusive, Individual and Inspirational. All pupils are valued regardless of academic prowess, artistic flair or sporting ability, with opportunities for all to join in and try new things.

We are a small community where every pupil becomes well-known to their House's pastoral team, especially the Housemaster, personal tutor and matron. Each pupil's best method of learning is identified and catered for by their teachers, with high-achieving pupils continually stretched while those requiring additional support can access it in a variety of ways. There is a wide range of A Level and BTEC subjects available, with all Sixth Formers also undertaking either the EPQ or CoPE as part of a bespoke PULSE (Personal Understanding, Learning Skills and Enrichment) programme.

Interpersonal skills, confidence and talents are also discovered outside the classroom. Two afternoons are reserved for an array of clubs and activities, including a comprehensive outdoor education programme, with pupils encouraged to extend their horizons and experience new challenges and responsibilities. Sports training takes place on three afternoons a week, with the majority of fixtures on Saturday mornings.

The College recruits highly motivated teaching staff with an ability and passion to inspire future generations and we ensure pupils have the best possible learning resources and facilities at their disposal. The environment we provide encourages pupils to take inspiration from their teachers, their surroundings, and each other.

In 2020 the College opened a Sixth Form Centre, with a café where Year 12 and 13 girls and boys can socialise and work independently and some additional classrooms. The Davies Centre was also opened in 2020. This exciting facility includes storage for rowing boats and other watersports, mountain biking and outdoor education, CCF and DofE equipment, and incorporates an indoor archery/rifle range, a climbing wall, weights room and an ergo room, which transforms into a function room with a balcony overlooking the river.

Academic, Art, Music, Drama and Sport Scholarships, and means-tested bursaries, are available. The College is also offering one 100% All-Rounder scholarship to a boy currently at a state-maintained primary school who would be looking to join Year 7 in September 2021, who would not be able to attend Shiplake without substantial financial support.

Entry points are normally at Year 7 (11+), Year 9 (13+) and Year 12 (16+). Prospective families are encouraged to arrange an individual visit or attend an open morning, which take place in the Autumn Term and March each year. Please go to www.shiplake.org.uk to book your attendance, complete a registration form and explore the whole site, which includes details of admissions processes, fees, bus routes and answers to most academic, co-curricular and pastoral questions that prospective parents may have.

SHIPLAKE COLLEGE
HENLEY-ON-THAMES

(Founded 1959)

Henley-on-Thames, Oxfordshire RG9 4BW UK

Tel: +44 (0)1189 402455

Fax: +44 (0)1189 405204

Email: registrar@shiplake.org.uk

Website: www.shiplake.org.uk

Headmaster: Mr T G Howe MA, MSt, MBA

Appointed: 2019

School type:
Boys' Boarding & Day, Co-educational Sixth Form

Religious Denomination: Church of England

Age range of boys: 11–18

Age range of girls: 16–18

No. of pupils enrolled as at 01/09/2020: 478

Boys: 423 **Girls:** 55 **Sixth Form:** 192

No. of boarders: 125

Fees per annum as at 01/09/2020:

Day: £18,985–£23,850

Weekly Boarding: £26,615–£33,280

Full Boarding: £35,470

Flexi Boarding (2 nights per week): £22,420 – £27,270

Average class size: 16

Teacher/pupil ratio: 1:6

St Mary's Calne

St Mary's (founded in 1873) is an independent boarding and day school for girls aged 11-18, a happy, purposeful and flourishing community of around 360 pupils with an 80% to 20% boarding-to-day ratio. St Mary's welcomes cultural diversity and around 15% of the students come from overseas.

The school is located in the market town of Calne and amidst the Wiltshire Downs, an area of stunning natural beauty and historical significance. The school is within easy reach of the university towns of Bath, Bristol and Oxford and just over an hour by train from London. This ideal location means that the girls benefit from a huge range of curriculum-enhancing opportunities as well as extra-curricular ones.

Focus on the individual

Small by design, St Mary's provides exceptional all-round education in a warm, nurturing environment. It is the individualised approach to every aspect of school life that makes St Mary's Calne special.

The pastoral care is outstanding. Every girl has a Tutor to support her through aspects of school life, from organisational skills and subject choices through to university application.

High Achievers

St Mary's Calne has a well-deserved reputation for academic excellence and is committed to providing an education that will challenge and inspire its pupils. In the Sunday Times Parent Power Schools' Guide 2020, St Mary's was ranked 1st independent school in Wiltshire and 2nd in the South West. St Mary's is also the first independent school in the UK to be awarded the Platinum Science Mark Award.

In 2020, 91% of the students secured their first choice of university and they will be studying a diverse range of subjects, ranging from Anthropology, Biochemistry, Computer Science, Economics, Engineering, English Literature, Geography, History, History of Art to Law, Liberal Arts & Sciences, Mathematics, Medicine and Modern Languages.

Outside the Classroom

Opportunities in sport, music, art and drama abound and the facilities are superb, including a £2.55 million sports complex and full-size astro, theatre, and a Sixth Form Centre with 120+ girls.

80% of girls play musical instruments and take part in a wide variety of ensembles. The girls perform at many events, both in the local community and further afield.

Drama productions in the purpose-built theatre are of the highest standard and have transferred to the London stage. The Drama Department has a unique relationship with RADA, offering a course in advanced communication skills and girls also perform annually at the Edinburgh Fringe.

In Art, in addition to holding a triennial exhibition in London, the girls have received numerous awards, including having artwork selected for the Young Artists' Summer Show at the Royal Academy of Arts. The girls are also very active in the community and volunteer at a local school on a regular basis. In 2019, the girls raised £10,000 in support of a local homeless charity and over £4,000 for military bursaries.

The girls excel at sport, and the school is represented at county level in several major sports and nationally in athletics and lacrosse, and internationally in horse riding, with all girls taking advantage of the superb sports facilities. The girls also enjoy many other sports, including tennis, hockey, horse riding, fencing and ski racing.

For further information, or to book onto one of our Open Days, please visit: www.stmaryscalne.org

ST MARY'S CALNE

(Founded 1873)

Curzon Street, Calne, Wiltshire SN11 0DF UK

Tel: 01249 857200

Fax: 01249 857207

Email: office@stmaryscalne.org

Website: www.stmaryscalne.org

Headmistress: Dr Felicia Kirk BA(University of MD), MA, PhD (Brown University)

Appointed: January 2013

School type: Girls' Boarding & Day

Religious Denomination: Church of England

Age range of girls: 11–18

No. of pupils enrolled as at 01/09/2020: 360

Sixth Form: 120

Fees per annum as at 01/09/2020:

Day: £30,045

Full Boarding: £40,275

Average class size: Max 17, smaller in the Sixth Form

Teacher/pupil ratio: 1:5

The Manor Preparatory School

'To challenge, cherish and inspire'

Situated in Abingdon, The Manor Preparatory School is an independent co-educational day school that welcomes children aged 2-11.

The school has a wonderfully happy, creative atmosphere where every individual is valued and nurtured to reach their potential. The Manor's most recent ISI Inspection awarded every area of school life receiving the highest possible rating of 'Excellent'. Inspectors commented that *"Pupils approach every day with an overwhelming passion to learn and develop."*

This is in part due to the exceptionally caring and invigorating tone of the school, where laughter is an essential part of the school day and children's personal development being further strengthened by staff who act as excellent role models.

Every child is encouraged to push themselves to new challenges and fulfil their own potential, resulting in outstanding results academically, on the sports field, and in creative and performing arts. Headmaster, Alastair Thomas, says *"Our job is to prepare children for life, not just secondary school."*

The school has an excellent record in ensuring leavers move on to the next school that is perfectly suited to each individual. Scholarships, awards and exhibitions feature highly in all areas.

Completion of a new Sports Hall in September 2018 underpins the exciting development programme that is underway, and extends even further the breadth of opportunities that are on offer to the children.

The school aims to simplify the logistics of family life as well, and so has created an extensive daily bus service covering Oxfordshire, Berkshire, Buckinghamshire and Wiltshire, as well as fully flexible wraparound care, much of which is free of charge.

For further information or a private tour, please visit our website www.manorprep.org or contact Mrs Karen Copson, Director of Admissions and Communications on 01235 858462 or admissions@manorprep.org.

The Manor
Preparatory School
Abingdon

(Founded 1907)

Faringdon Road, Abingdon, Oxfordshire OX13 6LN UK

Tel: 01235 858458

Email: admissions@manorprep.org

Website: www.manorprep.org

Headmaster: Mr Alastair Thomas

Appointed: January 2018

School type: Coeducational Day

Age range of pupils: 2–11 years

No. of pupils enrolled as at 01/09/2020: 370

Fees per annum as at 01/09/2020:
Please see website

Average class size: 14-20

Teacher/pupil ratio:
Pre-Prep 1:10, Pre Nursery 1:4, Nursery 1:6

Thornton College

Thornton College day and boarding school for girls, located between Milton Keynes and Buckingham, is set in 26 acres of beautiful grounds. The main school building is a manor house dating back to the 14th century and it became a school in 1917, founded by the Sisters of Jesus and Mary. The school is very proud of its rich history, exceptional pastoral care for the individual and its strong emphasis on core Christian values, though it is also proud of the fact that it is a forward looking school, with exciting opportunities both in and outside the classroom, and where girls of all faiths and no faith are equally welcome.

Thornton College is part of an international family of J&M schools in twenty eight countries around the world. This gives our students the best of opportunities for student international partnership programmes, celebrations, projects and exchanges, enabling each student to grow a unique global outlook and cultural intelligence.

Boarding is 'upstairs' in our main manor house offering a home from home experience. The boarding bedrooms and common areas are bright and spacious. We offer flexi, weekly and termly boarding for domestic and international students with a dense programme of exciting evening activities and weekend trips.

Our academic results are comparable with high achieving competitive schools whilst having a varied ability intake. Thornton co-educational nursery creates a sense of wonder making children's introduction to learning so exciting. Woodland walks, cookery, ballet, French, music and movement, library time and a host of other regular pursuits enhance the play and craft activities and excite their young minds. As a Forest School, girls at Thornton excel inside and outside the classroom with our prep school children enjoying our outdoor classroom in our woodlands and exploring and pond dipping in our eco habitat park. Thornton College is leading the introduction of robotics into prep school curriculum. Students in senior and Sixth Form enjoy overseas sporting tours, World Challenges, Duke of Edinburgh (with sixth formers achieving their Gold Awards); EPQs; partnership work with our heritage link school St Columba's School for boys such as STEAM events, UCAS and careers events and debating. Our Sixth Form, which opened in 2016, offers a wide subject choice, small class sizes and individual attention with future pathway support. Sixth Form students undertake the Oxbridge programme, gain competitive apprenticeships, and apply and receive Russell Group offers.

Our one site school ensures that the transition from early years into our pre-prep, prep, senior and sixth form is smooth and our older girls are role models for our younger students ensuring plenty of opportunities for mixed age group activities. At Thornton, EVERY GIRL is encouraged to develop her talents, not only in the classroom but through a broad co-curricular programme which makes use of our modern facilities and beautiful grounds. Thornton College is non-selective, recognising, in line with its ethos, that children develop at different rates and stages of their lives and in each one there is potential to excel. A strong work ethic, exceptional teaching and excellent pastoral care provides the secure environment where each girl is known and encouraged to develop her strengths, her social skills and her ability to pursue, with confidence, the next stage of life.

THORNTON

(Founded 1917)

College Lane, Thornton, Buckinghamshire MK17 0HJ UK

Tel: 01280 812610

Email: admissions@thorntoncollege.com

Website: www.thorntoncollege.com

Headteacher: Mrs Val Holmes

Appointed: November 2018

School type: Girls' Day & Boarding

Age range of boys: 2–4

Age range of girls: 2–18

No. of pupils enrolled as at 01/09/2020: 414

No. of boarders: 52

Fees per annum as at 01/09/2020:

Day: £10,035–£16,005

Weekly Boarding: £17,310–£21,900

Full Boarding: £21,525–£26,700

Average class size: 14

Teacher/pupil ratio: 1:20

Wycombe Abbey

Wycombe Abbey is a global leader in outstanding education and modern boarding. The School is committed to creating tomorrow's women leaders and has a long tradition of academic excellence, it is consistently one of the country's top performing schools.

Our learning environment is supportive, yet challenging, with a sense that pupils and their teachers are on an educational journey together. We pride ourselves on the outstanding teaching provided by our specialists who communicate a genuine love of their subject and serve to inspire the girls they teach.

We believe that education should not simply be about delivering a curriculum and examination syllabus, but that real learning stems from stimulating intellectual curiosity and nurturing a love for the subjects being taught, which will stay with our girls throughout their lives.

In all we do, boarding is the key to our continued success. The School has a culture that inspires throughout the day, seven days a week, empowering girls to achieve their best, academically and socially. Our happy and close community is a truly global one, with 29 countries represented. Each girl is known, and cherished, as an individual. Consequently, every girl's potential, whatever that might be, is explored and fulfilled.

Girls learn to be independent, to value and support others, and to develop the skills needed for future challenges in a global workplace. Given the nature of boarding life, girls are able to enjoy a wealth of co-curricular opportunities. Each and every girl carves out a unique learning path according to her interests and has the space to thrive within our magnificent grounds. Our approach to boarding is also sympathetic to the needs of today's families and pupils have the opportunity to go home regularly and parents are actively involved in the numerous School events and activities.

The School is an oasis of calm, set in 170 acres of magnificent, conservation-listed grounds and woodland. Modern, state-of-the-art facilities include the Sports Centre, with a 25-metre indoor pool, the Performing Arts Centre with a theatre and recital hall, an atrium café, dance and fitness studios, and extensive sports pitches. Two brand new Boarding Houses opened in September 2017 and a refurbishment of all the boarding accommodation will follow.

Wycombe Abbey is easily accessible with excellent transport links. It is about 35 miles west of London and 30 miles east of Oxford. It is a 30-minute journey from Heathrow Airport and a 90-minute journey from Gatwick Airport by road.

To find out more about gaining a place at Wycombe Abbey, please visit our website at www.wycombeabbey.com or contact our Admissions Team on (+44) (0) 1494 897008 or by emailing registrar@wycombeabbey.com.

WYCOMBE ABBEY

(Founded 1896)

High Wycombe, Buckinghamshire HP11 1PE UK

Tel: +44 (0)1494 897008

Email: registrar@wycombeabbey.com

Website: www.wycombeabbey.com

Headmistress:
Mrs Jo Duncan MA (St Andrews), PGCE (Cantab)

Appointed: September 2019

School type: Girls' Day & Boarding

Religious Denomination: Church of England

Age range of girls: 11–18

No. of pupils enrolled as at 01/09/2020: 649

Fees per annum as at 01/09/2020:

Day: £30,270

Full Boarding: £40,350

East

Abbot's Hill School

Abbot's Hill School is a happy and thriving community in which pupils aim high, grasp opportunities, enjoy learning and make lasting friendships. The Independent Schools Inspectorate awarded Abbot's Hill School the highest rating 'Excellent' across all areas of the schools. The nursery has also been recognised as 'Outstanding' in all areas of the EYFS frameworkl as well as receiving accreditation with Early Years Quality Standards by Herts for Learning.

The school offers an all-round education for girls aged 4-16 years, and the Day Nursery & Pre-School caters for girls and boys from 6 months. Our happy and united community gives each pupil the opportunity to shine.

The school is set within 76 acres of parkland only 10 minutes from St Albans, a 15 minute walk from the nearest stop on the Euston train line, and seven minutes' drive from junction 20 of the M25. Our first-rate facilities provide space for a wide range of sports and extra-curricular activities including swimming, golf, football and rugby alongside the traditional netball and lacrosse. The school runs an equestrian club and has a thriving ski team who enjoy the proximity of the Hemel Snow Dome. We are lucky enough to have a county standard cross-country course, a full orienteering route through our woodland and extensive tennis facilities including an on-site professional tennis facility. Our historic campus offers diverse opportunities in a magnificent country setting.

Abbot's Hill has a strong record of academic success. Throughout the school, pupils are taught in genuinely small classes. Excellent teaching and personalised support ensure that everyone is inspired to exceed their potential and to thrive.

The broad curriculum is enhanced by a wide range of trips and activities to stimulate learning. Extra-curricular clubs offer a lively balance of music, sports, languages, debating, drama and more. In short, there is something for everyone!

At Abbot's Hill, we pride ourselves on our pastoral care. The school's ethos is one which places the well-being and success of children at the heart of all it does, and this is reflected in many aspects of school life. We give individual attention to each girl so that she will discover her own, unique strengths, learn who she is and succeeds at whatever she sets her mind to. Abbot's Hill achieves something very remarkable as a result: we are truly a community of individuals where every pupil is known and celebrated.

In such a nurturing environment, pupils grow naturally in confidence, are happy to embrace new challenges and eagerly take on leadership roles and responsibilities. Authentic, not arrogant, Abbot's Hill pupils embody confidence and self-belief. They therefore leave fully equipped to take on the challenges and opportunities life has to offer.

We are proudly non-selective on entry. Therefore, our consistently excellent results at GCSE – with superb value-added scores for all pupils – are testament to our ethos: at Abbot's Hill, your daughter will achieve her very best because she is happy. Pupils gain access at 16+ to a wide variety of highly sought-after Sixth Forms, schools and colleges, frequently attracting scholarships to some of the most competitive courses.

Our approach and ethos was validated by the 2020 ISI report. Head, Mrs Kathryn Gorman, said *"The Independent Schools' Inspectorate understand our simple philosophy; that happy pupils learn and grow with confidence. We know that our pupils are celebrated as individuals and therefore develop into wonderful young adults ready to embrace the opportunities and challenges of life."*

Abbot's Hill

(Founded 1912)

Bunkers Lane, Hemel Hempstead, Hertfordshire HP3 8RP UK

Tel: 01442 240333

Email: registrar@abbotshill.herts.sch.uk

Website: www.abbotshill.herts.sch.uk

Headmistress: Mrs K Gorman BA, MEd (Cantab)

Appointed: January 2020

School type: Girls' Day

Age range of girls: 4–16

No. of pupils enrolled as at 01/09/2020: 502

Fees per term as at 01/09/2020:

Prep School: £3,714 – £4,683 per term

Senior School (Years 7-11): £6,395 – £6,434 per term

Average class size: 12–18

Brentwood School

Brentwood School shines out as a beacon of excellence. Our students are happy individuals who thrive on the high standards which are expected of them. They benefit from state-of-the-art facilities, set in the heart of Brentwood in Essex, and surrounded by 75 acres of green playing fields and gardens.

Academically, we sit comfortably alongside the best day and boarding schools in the country, and we enjoy an unparalleled local reputation.

We celebrate a 464-year history and take our heritage seriously. We are a Christian School with a chapel and a chaplain, and our School values, encapsulated in our motto "Virtue, Learning and Manners", have as much resonance today as they did when written by English poet John Donne in 1622. Our pupils are expected to have self-respect, to exhibit pride in their appearance and embrace values such as courtesy, consideration for others, kindness, looking after each other, honour, courage, sportsmanship, duty and selflessness.

Brentwood School pupils achieve excellent academic standards that rank among some of the best in the country. Our track record of exam results shows consistent high grades are achieved by all our pupils. They work exceptionally hard and are supported by highly professional and inspiring teachers to achieve excellent results at both GCSE level and in Sixth Form, whether studying A levels or the IB Diploma. An average of eight students per year are offered places at Oxford or Cambridge and over 80% of offers are from Russell Group universities.

We offer both GCSEs and IGCSEs; A levels and the IB Diploma. More recent curriculum developments include the introduction of a Human Universe course in the Fourth and Fifth Year, which examines critical thinking and global issues.

Brentwood was the first school in Essex, and one of the first in the country, to adopt the Diamond Model: single-sex classes from the age of 11-16 within an overall mixed gender environment. We believe this model helps our teachers to tailor their teaching to the different learning styles of boys and girls and provides the best of single gender teaching within a coeducational environment.

From an early age, we encourage pupils to aim high, think creatively and develop independence, so by the time they leave Sixth Form, they are well prepared for the expected, but can also tackle the unknowns. A flourishing Old Brentwoods community keeps thousands of alumni connected across the globe.

Our vast and exciting co-curricular programme enjoys national prominence, and we focus on providing opportunities for all to participate, as well as the pursuit of excellence for the most able.

Our Combined Cadet Force is one of the oldest and largest in the country, we offer The Duke of Edinburgh's Award to pupils who want to satisfy their taste for adventure, and a Voluntary Service in Action Unit which raises tens of thousands of pounds every year to help specific charitable organisations.

Our sports centre houses a 25-metre swimming pool, glass-backed squash courts, fencing salle and dance studio and pupils achieve top sporting honours both nationally and internationally.

We are proud to be a Steinway School, enabling our pupils to learn on the very best-made pianos in the world, as well as some rare instruments otherwise unavailable to them.

Our musicians have played in the National Youth Orchestra, and our actors have gained places in the National Youth Theatre, RADA and other top Drama schools.

The lessons pupils learn at Brentwood will last for a lifetime. Integrity, initiative, a spirit of enterprise and an international mind-set help our pupils to thrive in the twenty-first century.

Brentwood School

(Founded 1557)

Middleton Hall Lane, Brentwood, Essex CM15 8EE UK

Tel: 01277 243243

Fax: 01277 243299

Email: headmaster@brentwood.essex.sch.uk

Website: www.brentwoodschool.co.uk

Headmaster: Mr Michael Bond

Appointed: September 2019

School type: Coeducational Day & Boarding

Religious Denomination: Church of England

Age range of pupils: 3–18

No. of pupils enrolled as at 01/09/2020: 1800

Fees per annum as at 01/09/2020:

Day: £20,097

Full Boarding: £39,381

Average class size: 18 in Prep & Senior; 8 in Sixth Form

Teacher/pupil ratio: 1:9

Haileybury

Haileybury is an independent co-educational boarding school, located between London and Cambridge, in 500 acres of beautiful Hertfordshire countryside. Spectacular grounds are home to outstanding facilities, excellent teaching and superb pastoral care for its community of boarding and day pupils.

Founded in 1862, Haileybury is proud of its history, tradition and values, taking the best from the past whilst also looking to the future. Haileyburians leave as leaders and lifelong learners who can make a difference in the world beyond school.

Academic opportunity

The school offers a dedicated Lower School for Years 7 and 8, a wide range of GCSEs and IGCSEs and the choice of the International Baccalaureate (IB) Diploma or A levels in the Sixth Form.

As part of a commitment to innovation, the school uses artificial intelligence (AI) to help understand a pupil's learning profile. Classrooms are fitted with Apple technology and Google Suites.

Pupils select personal pathways, such as coding and global civilisations, based on their individual passions and in the Sixth Form, electives include criminology, geopolitics and music technology. Haileybury is ranked Top 10 in The Times league table for co-ed independent schools which offer the IB.

Boarding and day

More than two thirds of pupils are boarders with school life centred around 12 boarding houses and Lower School benefitting from having their own house. Pupils join at 11+, 13+, 14+ or 16+ entry points. Flexi-boarding is available in Lower School only, which means families do not have to commit to full boarding at this stage. From Year 9 onwards, there is the additional flexibility of pupils being able to return home after sporting commitments on Saturday afternoons.

Exceptional opportunities

Pupils benefit from professional sports coaching and the school regularly hosts speakers and performers from the arts, sporting and academic worlds.

There is a packed co-curricular programme of more than 130 options, from scuba diving and African drumming to bee-keeping, Mandarin and survival skills. The school's Model United Nations programme sees more than 700 international students invited to Haileybury each spring to debate global issues – one of the largest programmes of its kind in the UK. Throughout the year, there is an abundance of music concerts, drama productions and public performances while more than 30 visiting specialists teach hundreds of instrument lessons every week.

Supportive environment

At Haileybury, a caring environment is crucial to a pupil's happiness and fulfilment. There is an emphasis on pastoral care with round-the-clock support from housemasters and housemistresses, to the chaplain and tutors, and there is an onsite health centre. The school is a home-from-home, with a warm and friendly feel. Every child is given the confidence to find their identity on a personal journey of discovery.

A warm welcome

There is a busy programme of open days and taster events which take place throughout the year. Families are warmly invited to discover what life at Haileybury has to offer and why its pupils flourish.

For further information, please contact Registrar Michele Metcalfe, on either uk.admissions@haileybury.com or int.admissions@haileybury.com, depending on your location.

Haileybury

(Founded 1862)

Haileybury, Hertford, Hertfordshire SG13 7NU UK

Tel: +44 (0)1992 706353

Email: uk.admissions@haileybury.com

Website: www.haileybury.com

The Master: Mr Martin Collier MA BA PGCE

Appointed: September 2017

School type: Coeducational Boarding & Day

Age range of pupils: 11–18

(entry at 11+, 13+ and 16+)

No. of pupils enrolled as at 01/09/2020: 880

Boys: 481 **Girls:** 399 **Sixth Form:** 319

No. of boarders: 570

Fees per annum as at 01/09/2020:

Day: £17,712–£26,646

Full Boarding: £22,929–£36,141

Teacher/pupil ratio: 1:7

King's Ely

Shortlisted in the 2020 Independent Schools of the Year Awards, King's Ely is a leading independent co-educational day and boarding school built on a fascinating history stretching back over 1,000 years, making us one of the oldest schools in the world.

We serve the academic and pastoral needs of around 1,000 boys and girls from the age of 2 through to 18, with boarders from 7 years old. King's Ely is nestled in the picturesque cathedral city of Ely, which is just 15 minutes from Cambridge and 1 hour from London, with direct rail links to both. Our privately-run school buses stop at key locations around Cambridgeshire, Suffolk and Norfolk.

The adventure of a King's Ely education enables pupils of all ages to flourish, from the children in King's Ely Acremont and Nursery to the young men and women in our Sixth Form. Whether a student shines in a classroom or laboratory, on a stage, on a pitch or on a mountainside, our school promises an abundance of opportunity for personal development, both academically and socially.

King's Ely students are renowned for their energy, their courage and their integrity. Our pupils achieve excellent GCSE and A Level results and every year, 95-100% of students secure a place at their first-choice university or institution. However, our school is about much more than exam results and league tables. As reported in the Good Schools Guide, King's Ely is a "friendly, well-balanced, caring community valued for getting the best from a broad range of abilities".

We empower our young people to challenge themselves, to push beyond the boundaries of their own expectations and to achieve more than they ever believed possible. Innovative approaches to teaching and learning are the hallmark of every section of King's Ely. Through a broad and balanced curriculum, pupils develop the self-knowledge and inner resilience that will enable them to face the challenges of an ever-changing world.

Music, Drama, Art, Textiles and Dance are each embedded in the culture of King's Ely, with vast opportunities for pupils of all abilities and aspirations. Recent accolades include a 5* review for our original production, Ugly Youth, at the 2019 Edinburgh Fringe Festival, and our boys' a cappella group, the King's Barbers, being crowned National Champions. All major sports are offered, along with an impressive array of other activities, helping every pupil to realise their sporting potential. Rowing, athletics, golf, cricket, hockey, tennis, rugby, netball, equestrian and football – the choices are endless. Our 1st XV boys' rugby team have just had an unbeaten season, plus we enjoyed success at the British Rowing Senior Championships in 2019.

From the high peaks of the Himalayas to the gushing torrents of the rivers in the Alps, our unique Ely Scheme programme also offers boundless opportunities for pupils to learn through outdoor education. We give students the chance to undertake their Duke of Edinburgh's Award at all three levels.

King's Ely boasts some of the region's most historic buildings yet teaching facilities are modern and purpose-built. Our close links with Ely Cathedral – one of the finest cathedrals in the world – make the perfect setting for concerts and performances.

Boarders, including the Ely Cathedral Boy and Girl Choristers, live in picturesque and community-spirited boarding houses, well led by caring housemasters and housemistresses. A strong pastoral structure where childhood is respected and cherished is a key feature.

King's Ely is a school that can take each child on a seamless journey, travelling from one section to the next, whilst welcoming newcomers at key transition stages, giving support and adapting the offering to the needs of every child in our care. Only by visiting King's Ely can you feel the energy and warmth of our community.

(Founded 973)

Ely, Cambridgeshire CB7 4EW UK

Tel: 01353 660707

Fax: 01353 667485

Email: admissions@kingsely.org

Website: www.kingsely.org

Principal: Mr John Attwater MA (Oxon)

Appointed: September 2019

School type: Coeducational Boarding & Day

Age range of pupils: 2–18

No. of pupils enrolled as at 01/09/2020: 1016

Fees per annum as at 01/09/2020:

Day: £10,470–£31,005

Full Boarding: £23,580–£40,980

Average class size: Max 20

Teacher/pupil ratio: 1:9

Mander Portman Woodward – Cambridge

Cambridge is where the MPW success story began. Nearly 50 years ago, three Cambridge graduates – Messieurs Mander, Portman and Woodward came together with an ambition to create a unique secondary education experience. They focused on several elements, based on their great Alma Mater, which they considered significant to the overall learning experience. Amongst these were the following: small class sizes, a strong tutorial system and superb teaching – and all of these within an informal atmosphere, which would allow creative minds to flourish.

Move the clock forward to the present day and these elements are still very much the hallmark of an MPW education. With fewer than 10 students per class for GCSE and A level, (though in fact the college average is closer to 6 in a class), the learning experience is truly personalised. As well as simulating the small class size at Oxbridge our students experience the privilege of being treated as an individual and not a number. Small classes mean our students know their questions will be answered and that they will have genuine contact time with their tutors in every lesson. With more than 30 A level subjects on offer and no restrictions on combinations, our students can choose subjects that suit them. Whilst Maths, Business, Economics and of course the Sciences remain popular choices, less well known subjects such as Ancient History and Classical Civilisation are also available.

With a current cohort of 60% British and 40% International, MPW Cambridge offers a world-class education to all. Education, however, is much more than what happens in the classroom. The preparation for life after secondary education is important too. Students need to be especially well-informed when they begin their UCAS application. The daily help by the personal tutors to each tutee is immense. From initial, informal discussion on determining the most suitable university course, through several drafts of the personal statement, often through BMAT or other entrance tests, for some even through daunting interview prospects, the MPW Personal Tutor is there. Their mandate is to 'hold the student's hand' throughout, providing encouragement and support.

We're also proud to assist those who might not have done so well the first time around. Our weekly assessments provide diagnostics where we can see which elements require further support. They also ensure that all of our students are fully prepared for the actual exam and properly understand critical success factors such as timing and weighting.

We'll leave the final words to Ofsted, taken from our college report in 2019: *'Pupils and sixth-form students say that Mander Portman Woodward (MPW) is 'amazing' and a great place to study. They know what they want to get out of their studies and are exceptionally well motivated to learn. Staff have high expectations. Most pupils and students respond to these expectations by working hard, so they achieve very well. They are confident that the support they get from their teachers will help them to be 'the best that they can be'.'*

(Founded 1987)

3-4 Brookside, Cambridge, Cambridgeshire CB2 1JE UK

Tel: 01223 350158

Fax: 01223 366429

Email: cambridge@mpw.ac.uk

Website: www.mpw.ac.uk

Principal: Mr Tom Caston

School type: Coeducational Day & Boarding

Age range of pupils: 15–19

Average class size: 6

Teacher/pupil ratio: 1:5

Orwell Park School

Developing a life-long love of learning in a magical setting...

Orwell Park, established in 1868, is a co-educational prep school for day pupils and boarders from 2 1/2 to 13. The outstanding beauty of the grounds and the historic 18th century buildings contribute to an inspiring experience which combines the legacy and the traditions of the past with the dynamism and energy of the present and future. Outstanding facilities include a working Victorian observatory, a walled garden with outdoor pool, a nine-hole golf course, floodlit sports facilities, a library in the mansion house, as well as a new, state of the art outstanding Pre-Prep facility, which was opened in 2013, set in the shadow of the main building among woods full of opportunities for outdoor learning.

Boys and girls are given every opportunity to be the best they can be, both in and outside the classroom. High expectations, and learning strategies tailored to the individual child, lead to high levels of attainment. Pupils progress to a wide range of senior schools both local and national and our leaving year group in 2018 achieved 31 scholarships in art, academic, music, DT, sport and all-rounder.

Whilst we value greatly the past, we also embrace technology and, as such, every child in Years 3-8 has their own ipad in order to enhance learning in the classroom and beyond. The ipads allow pupils to learn in a way that they are used to, fostering collaboration between pupils, whilst providing portability.

In addition to the traditional curricular subjects, Orwell Park pupils are involved in a comprehensive activity programme, including: orchestra and various ensembles, chess, community service, skiing, equestrianism, climbing on the bouldering wall, OPS Challenge (a two-year mini D of E course), camping and campfire fun in the School's woodlands, Art and DT clubs, Goldies and Blueys (boys' and girls' clubs), as well as numerous large scale theatrical productions. The school achieves success in all the major sports and recently introduced cricket for all girls as the summer sport. In addition, Orwell Park is linked with Mayo College in Rajasthan, India and Year 7 pupils have the opportunity to visit India and sample the Taj Mahal, Jaipur and spend time at one of India's most famous boarding schools.

Boarding is extremely popular at Orwell Park and takes the form of flexible boarding, weekly boarding and full boarding, which incorporates a comprehensive programme of weekend activities. Pupils choose to board, driven by a desire to enjoy the company of friends once the normal school day is over. Dormitories are bright, spacious and clean and a dedicated team of boarding staff and school matrons are totally committed to the health and welfare of the boys and girls in their care.

Join us at an Open Event to see for yourself what makes Orwell Park such a special and inspirational place to be.

For more information contact our Registrar on 01473 653224 or email admissions@orwellpark.org.

ORWELL PARK SCHOOL | Celebrating 150 YEARS

(Founded 1868)

Nacton, Ipswich, Suffolk IP10 0ER UK

Tel: 01473 659225

Fax: 01473 659822

Email: admissions@orwellpark.org

Website: www.orwellpark.co.uk

Headmaster: Mr Adrian Brown MA(Cantab)

Appointed: September 2011

School type: Coeducational Boarding & Day

Religious Denomination: Interdenominational

Age range of pupils: 2–13

No. of pupils enrolled as at 01/09/2020: 248

Boys: 146 **Girls:** 101

No. of boarders: 98

Fees per term as at 01/09/2020:

Pre-Prep Day: £2,794 – £3,974 per term

Prep Day: £5,762 – £6,386 per term

Prep Boarding: £7,715 – £9,200 per term

Average class size: 12-14

Teacher/pupil ratio: 1:12

St Cedd's School

St Cedd's School is a co-educational 3-11 IAPS Charitable Trust School offering pupils the opportunity to aspire and achieve in a caring environment that nurtures talent and supports individual endeavour. This is a school in which every child matters. We value and celebrate their many diverse talents and qualities and the grounded confidence the pupils develop results in great personal achievement.

Individual Pupil Progress
The progress of pupils, of all abilities, throughout the school is rapid. Our standardised assessment results and 11+ scores far exceed national averages and annually we celebrate an unrivalled success rate to selective grammar and independent senior schools with an impressive track record of scholarship awards. This level of achievement is significant given that we are academically non-selective. Assessments on entry are designed to capture the strengths and areas for development of each child so that the education is tailored to the needs of the individual.

Centre of Excellence
The Independent Schools Inspectorate (ISI) placed St Cedd's School at the top level in every category of inspection in February 2013 which places the school amongst the very best 3-11 preparatory schools in the country. The accolade confirms what we witness every day; high academic achievement, outstanding records of attainment in music, an inclusive sporting ethos and successes at national tournaments, a sense of purpose and ambition that shows itself in the attitude and actions of the pupils and staff, and a very effective pastoral care system.

In December 2018, the academic excellence of the school, and our provision for the most able, was recognised by the National Association for Able Children in Education in the awarding of the NACE Challenge Award.

Broad and Balanced Curriculum
With over 70 after-school activities to choose from, extra study opportunities are balanced with a firm focus on academic work. This synergy supports the development of confident self-assured pupils ready for the challenges ahead. PE, music, art, French and science are taught by specialists with the teaching of PE, music and French starting in the Pre-School. Acknowledging the breadth of talents of pupils is an important aspect of life at St Cedd's School. To this end, our baccalaureate-style Year 6 curriculum, HOLDFAST, leads to awards in recognition of 'Holistic Opportunities to Learn and Develop, Furthering Achievement, Service and Talent'.

As a member of the Choir Schools Association our Choristers sing in the Cathedral Choir and the Junior and Senior Chamber Choirs sing at Evensong in Chelmsford Cathedral.

Nurturing the Future
For more than 85 years, boys and girls at St Cedd's School have been enjoying a quality of education that is among the very best you will find. We provide the best start in our recently refurbished Pre-School where the children thrive in a colourful and nurturing environment that widens their horizons and instils in them a love of learning.

Breakfast Club operates from 7:30am-8:00am and a wrap-around care programme is open until 6:00pm. Fees include curriculum-linked extra-curricular activities, 1-1 learning support, lunch and the majority of after-school clubs.

To attend an open day or to arrange an individual tour, please contact Mrs Abbott on 01245 392810 or email admissions@stcedds.org.uk.

St Cedd's School

(Founded 1931)

178a New London Road, Chelmsford, Essex CM2 0AR UK

Tel: 01245 392810

Email: info@stcedds.org.uk

Website: www.stcedds.org.uk

Head: Mr Matthew Clarke

Appointed: September 2018

School type: Co-educational Day

Age range of pupils: 3–11

No. of pupils enrolled as at 01/09/2020: 400

Boys: 200 **Girls:** 200

Fees per annum as at 01/09/2020:

Day: £8,550–£10,935

Average class size: Average 23; Max 24

St Columba's College

St Columba's College and Preparatory School is an independent Catholic day school for pupils aged 4-18 in the heart of St Albans, Hertfordshire. We provide a high-quality education to young people of all faiths and none.

Our Columban ethos and values guide all that we do, allowing us to provide an education of the Head and Heart that places happiness and confidence at the centre of its mission. We have created a nurturing environment where each student is challenged to achieve their own best academic standard, while becoming confident, resilient and compassionate individuals.

Teaching the Columban values of courage, courtesy and compassion enables our students to become confident and well-rounded individuals, with the skills to enter an ever-changing and complex world.

Our moral education is based on the Charism of the Brothers of the Sacred Heart. We support each student's development in a community where they are known, valued and treasured, through a well-structured pastoral system.

We strive for academic excellence whilst realising that it is well-rounded education that best prepares our young people for the world and workplace of tomorrow. As a result, our young people are academically successful, intellectually curious, happy and empathetic. The world needs leaders with these qualities, who can connect with people and respond wisely to the many complex challenges we face in an ever-changing society.

St Columba's College is moving to co-education! This exciting next step in our development means that from September 2021, we will welcome girls into Lower Sixth (Year 12) and Lower Prep (Reception, Year 1 and Year 2). This will be followed by a phased transition, which will eventually see St Columba's offering its unique, high-quality Catholic education to boys and girls from ages 4-18.

In recent years we have invested millions of pounds in new facilities including a fitness suite, science and D&T labs and a modern IT suite in the Prep School. We are currently upgrading our sports pitches, which will be completed by September 2021 for use by the whole school.

Our remote learning programme in 2020 was a great success with parents and pupils. Our dedicated staff utilised a range of resources, including Microsoft Teams, to deliver interactive and engaging lessons, following the normal timetables. We continued our provision of strong pastoral support through regular communication with parents and students. The Heads of House and Tutors maintained ongoing contact with the students and their families as they adapted to remote learning.

Here are some snippets of what some of our parents said about our remote programme:

'A big thank you for the excellent pastoral care for both boys. We are really fortunate that the school generally takes such an interest in their wellbeing. The teaching is excellent.'

'Thank you for the brilliant job you are doing. It must be extremely difficult. Our son is very happy and therefore so are we.'

St Columba's pupils continue to be recognised nationally for their academic and extra-curricular achievements, including the Big Bang Competition Finals and the British Education Awards 2020. They continue to be accepted onto prestigious programmes such as the Royal College of Music Junior Department.

(Founded 1939)

King Harry Lane, St Albans, Hertfordshire AL3 4AW UK

Tel: 01727 892040

Email: admissions@stcolumbascollege.org

Website: www.stcolumbascollege.org

Head: Mr David Buxton

Appointed: 2008

School type: Day (Coeducational from 2021)

Religious Denomination: Catholic

Age range of boys: 4–18

No. of pupils enrolled as at 01/09/2020: 760

Fees per annum as at 01/09/2020:

Reception, Prep 1, 2: £10,902

Prep 3: £12,783

Prep 4, 5, 6: £14,100

Senior: £16,326

Average class size: 6-24

St Faith's

Bright Beginnings – Exciting Futures

Judged UK Prep School of the Year in 2019 by the Times Educational Supplement, St Faith's is a Prep School for boys and girls aged 4-13 located in a green, spacious site in the heart of Cambridge.

We believe in providing a future-focused education, preparing our pupils for the needs of the modern world. Pupils need the skills of team work, an understanding of how a computer works and of the engineered world around them, and a strong grounding in Science and Maths, the Humanities and Languages as the foundation stones for virtually every path their future lives might take.

Across our curriculum each child is taught, developed and nurtured, to equip them well for life. Our teachers are passionate about sharing their knowledge, exploring new ideas, challenging the status quo and instilling a life-long passion for learning. Top-down excellence in all lessons ensures we continually stretch our pupils to achieve more than they thought possible. Owing to small class sizes, exceptional teachers and the above average ability of our children all subjects follow an accelerated curriculum and the vast majority of pupils work at a higher level commensurate with their age.

A leader in the early introduction of Computing to the curriculum, we now support over 25 schools in their development of Computing. In 2015 we became the first, and still only, Prep school to teach Engineering as a core curriculum subject for all children from age seven. Our curriculum explores all forms of engineering; chemical, mechanical, robotics, structural, civil, electrical and aeronautical. In 2018 The Times awarded us 'Strategic Education Initiative of the Year' for our introduction of Engineering to the curriculum. Furthermore, The Week Independent Schools Guide named us 'The Best of the Best' for STEM education in 2019.

Sport is a conduit for developing mental and physical fitness, team spirit and resilience. Twenty different individual and team sports are taught at St Faith's. Our 'Sport for All' culture ensures that all pupils, irrespective of ability, receive specialist sports teaching from the age of five. In 2018/19 11 team and 9 individual national titles were awarded to St Faith's in Gymnastics, Trampolining, Hockey and Athletics. The 2019/20 season was suspended but by March we held national titles in girls and boys hockey, netball and gymnastics. Drama, Music and Art are tools not only for teaching children a life-long love of the arts but for promoting self-belief and confidence.

Our green and spacious 9-acre site, located in the heart of Cambridge, together with extensive playing fields a two-minute walk away, provide some of the best facilities of any prep school in the UK. The shelves in our library are crowded with over 12,000 works of fiction and non-fiction. Engineering suites provide access to tools and equipment beyond many inventor's wildest dreams. Fully-equipped science laboratories and computer suites are used by all year groups. The Hub provides flexible large indoor spaces for interdisciplinary projects, a roof-top night sky viewing platform and a virtual reality suite allows all children to explore the universe around them in the most exciting ways.

St Faith's pupils are confident, articulate, grounded and courteous, attributes which will stand them in good stead for their futures. On average 28 scholarships are awarded to our Year 8 pupils as they move to senior schools, with over 90% of leavers gaining a place at their first choice school.

St Faith's
CAMBRIDGE

(Founded 1884)

Trumpington Road, Cambridge, Cambridgeshire CB2 8AG UK

Tel: 01223 352073

Email: admissions@stfaiths.co.uk

Website: www.stfaiths.co.uk

Headmaster: Mr N L Helliwell

Appointed: September 2011

School type: Coeducational Day

Age range of pupils: 4–13

No. of pupils enrolled as at 01/09/2020: 540

Boys: 305 **Girls:** 235

Fees per annum as at 01/09/2020:

Day: £13,170–£16,590

Average class size: 16-18

St Margaret's School, Bushey

St Margaret's School in Bushey, Hertfordshire, is an independent day and boarding school for pupils aged 3 to 18. Founded in 1749, we are one of the oldest independent schools in the UK. As well as day places for all ages, we offer a range of flexible boarding options for both UK and international pupils from the age of 11.

We are a school with a proven record of academic success in public examinations and our pupils move onto competitive courses at leading universities and institutions both here in the UK and around the world. In 2019, 70% of our A-Level results were A*-B grades, with 62% of all GCSE results at 9-7 (A*-A) grades.

Our outward looking ethos aims to encourage a genuine enthusiasm for learning and an ability to independently explore subjects beyond the classroom. Our curriculum addresses a rapidly changing world filled with complex challenges as well as exciting new possibilities.

In January 2020, we began our transition to co-education, with St Margaret's School starting the journey from being an all girls school to providing education to both girls and boys.

The pastoral care at St Margaret's is the central pillar upon which the success of the school is based and we are proud of the quality of care and opportunity given to every one of our pupils no matter what stage of their education. We offer a rich programme of extra-curricular activities and pupils are encouraged to find their talent whatever that may be.

There is no typical St Margaret's pupil; all are valued individually by our qualified and committed staff. However, they are all dedicated young people who strive to succeed in all that they do and are passionate about topics facing them today. The quality of care at St Margaret's School enables pupils to grow in an atmosphere of tolerance and understanding and leave equipped with the confidence, aptitude and skills they need for life and for work.

Our beautiful 60 acre site boasts a combination of superbly resourced historic and modern buildings and we are easily accessible from both London, the Home Counties and all the major London airports. If you have not yet visited us, please do and we will show you the love of learning, culture of achievement and relish of challenge that is the essence of St Margaret's.

St Margaret's School

(Founded 1749)

Merry Hill Road, Bushey, Hertfordshire WD23 1DT UK

Tel: +44 (0)20 8416 4400

Email: admissions@smbushey.com

Website: www.stmargaretsbushey.co.uk

Headteacher: Lara Péchard

Appointed: January 2020

School type: Coeducational Day & Boarding

Age range of pupils: 3–18 years

No. of pupils enrolled as at 01/09/2020: 445

Fees per term as at 01/09/2020:

Senior Day: £5,832 per term

Senior Full Board: £10,992 per term

Junior: £4,886 per term

Average class size: 20

The Leys School

Founded in 1875 The Leys School is Cambridge's only co-educational boarding school for children aged 11 – 18. Unusually for a city school, it is situated within a leafy 50 acre campus, close to the banks of the River Cam, yet only a 10 minute walk from the buzz of the city centre. Our ethos is simple – to provide an excellent, all-round education for our pupils, combining the traditional values of tolerance, respect and decency with a forward-looking and collaborative approach to teaching and learning.

Our Unique Location; the Cambridge Experience

The university of Cambridge provides the kind of enrichment opportunities most schools can only dream of. Links with the University are strong and we take full advantage of this; we host world-renowned speakers in our Great Hall and attend academic lectures within university departments. Our Chapel Choir regularly joins forces with the College choirs, singing in some of the most stunning College Chapels in the world. We share our award-winning Boathouse with 3 university colleges and compete in many of their sporting fixtures. Our superb location truly does offer a world of exceptional opportunities.

Academic Life

Through the provision of a broad and balanced curriculum Leys pupils develop into articulate, confident and well-rounded individuals. Their timetables are tailored to their aptitudes, needs and interests. As pupils move up through the school they take on increased responsibility for planning their workloads, with support from a coordinated tutorial system. Class sizes are small and the school's academic results reflect the expertise, vitality and enthusiasm of its teachers.

Beyond the Classroom

Pupils at The Leys are encouraged to take part in as many wider-curricular activities as they can realistically manage. Over 100 clubs, societies and groups take place every week. 26 sports are offered from Athletics to Water Polo, alongside CCF, Duke of Edinburgh and Community Service groups. The opportunities for outdoor pursuits are endless and, combined with first class performance facilities, the school exudes an air of purposefulness and busyness.

Support and Wellbeing

The Leys is a close-knit community, based on mutual respect and shared values. Its backbone is the House system where our pupils are assured of a supportive and caring environment. Their wellbeing is at the heart of what The Leys stands for; it is a happy, inspiring and unique place.

Joining The Leys

Girls and boys join The Leys in Years 7, 9 and 12 and may either sit the school's own tests, obtain places via pre-assessment in Year 7 or apply for one of a range of scholarships, bursaries or exhibitions. To find out what makes The Leys such a special place contact the Admissions Team to arrange a visit.

THE Leys
CAMBRIDGE

(Founded 1875)

Trumpington Road, Cambridge, Cambridgeshire CB2 7AD UK

Tel: 01223 508900

Fax: 01223 505303

Email: admissions@theleys.net

Website: www.theleys.net

Headmaster: Mr Martin Priestley

Appointed: September 2014

School type: Coeducational Boarding & Day

Age range of pupils: 11–18

No. of pupils enrolled as at 01/09/2020: 572

Fees per annum as at 01/09/2020:

Day: £16,545–£22,920

Full Boarding: £24,960–£34,245

Average class size: 15-20

Teacher/pupil ratio: 1:8

The Peterborough School

The Peterborough School is the city's only independent day school for boys and girls from Nursery to Sixth Form.

Situated on one beautiful, leafy campus in the heart of Peterborough, the Nursery, Prep and Senior Schools enjoy excellent transport links and shared facilities.

The combined campus means the School is a vibrant place with small classes providing boys and girls with the individual attention, opportunities, confidence and ability to exploit fully their natural potential within a happy, caring and friendly community.

The 56-place Nursery has been rated Outstanding in its last five ISI Inspections. It enjoys an excellent location in a separate building on the School site, with ample gardens and outside spaces, and is close enough to Peterborough station, with its high-speed train services to London, to make it highly attractive for working families.

In the Preparatory School (4 to 11 years), the children are encouraged to be independent and inquisitive learners and develop many important skills through the extended curriculum and many extra curricular clubs and activities available.

In the Senior School and Sixth Form, students' unique talents are identified and developed, whether they are in the classroom, in the creative arts or on the sports field. Closely monitored academic performance means students usually achieve levels higher than those originally expected.

The Sixth Form is going from strength to strength with consistently impressive A Level results and is an area of focus for development, with a new bespoke Sixth Form block now in place. This facility has a large, wi-fi enabled Study Room, including a student meeting space, offices and a large, well-facilitated Common Room with kitchen. This development has also created a new state-of-the art Senior Library.

Our pastoral support is extremely strong and we passionately believe that children cannot learn well unless they are happy.

Headmaster, Adrian Meadows, is proud that the long-standing traditions of the school, which was founded in 1895, remain but at the same time it is a forward-looking, progressive place where children continually surprise and delight him. *"I have seen students winning a national STEM award on the same day that the Reception Classes and Pre-schoolers enjoyed a Teddy Bear's Picnic. Being amongst children of such a wide age range is fascinating, entertaining and always interesting but overall it is incredibly rewarding and humbling to be part of such an amazing school and community."*

Visitors to the School and Nursery are very welcome. We have Open Days on Saturdays in September and May each year when appointments are not necessary. There is also a Sixth Form Open Evening in October. Alternatively, visits can be booked by calling the School on 01733 343357 or completing the Request A Visit form on our website www.thepeterboroughschool.co.uk.

The Peterborough School

(Founded 1895)

Thorpe Road, Peterborough, Cambridgeshire PE3 6AP UK

Tel: 01733 343357

Fax: 01733 355710

Email: office@tpsch.co.uk

Website: www.thepeterboroughschool.co.uk

Headmaster: Mr A D Meadows BSc(Hons)

Appointed: September 2007

School type: Coeducational Day

Age range of pupils: 6 weeks–18 years

No. of pupils enrolled as at 01/09/2020: 440

Fees per annum as at 01/09/2020:

Day: £10,467–£15,642

Average class size: 15

The Royal Hospital School

The Royal Hospital School is an independent co-educational boarding and day school for 11-18-year providing an outstanding, full and broad education enriched by a unique naval heritage. Founded in 1712 in Greenwich, London, it moved to its spectacular site set in 200 acres of coastal Suffolk countryside overlooking the River Stour in 1933. The School has continued to develop its inspiring purpose-built site, growing in size and reputation to become one of East Anglia's leading independent schools.

Whilst the school is over 300 years old, discovery, exploration and challenge continue to shape its ethos with a focus on inspiring pupils to pursue their interests and make the most of their talents through learning and a wide range co-curricular activities.

Academic achievement is key to a young person's confidence and ability to succeed in life beyond school. The School works hard to inspire and empower its pupils to realise their full potential, enjoy the experience of learning and develop new skills. By challenging them both inside and outside of the classroom, it achieves effective and stimulating learning and encourages self-discovery. Opportunities exist through its enriched academic curriculum and wealth of co-curricular activities and it provides a safe environment in which young people can step outside of their comfort zone; learn to take risks; foster self-belief and self-awareness; and develop skills such as collaboration, initiative and resilience.

The Royal Hospital School places great importance on developing these skills as well as the traditional values of loyalty and service while providing an excellent education fit for the modern world. Its aim is to give young people the knowledge, skills, confidence and strength of character to go on to lead purposeful and happy lives. Their school days are busy and, at times, challenging but also fun and rewarding.

More recently the School has worked hard at its commitment to the environment which has resulted in it being awarded a Gold Carbon Charter. In 2019, it launched Grow with Us – a way of celebrating every child who joins the school by planting a tree in their name whilst also making a positive contribution to the planet.

Over the next seven years, the School will continue to plant a tree for each new pupil – growing with them throughout their time and maintaining roots to the place as they progress through life.

ROYAL HOSPITAL SCHOOL

(Crown Charity, founded 1712)

Holbrook, Ipswich, Suffolk IP9 2RX UK

Tel: 01473 326200

Email: admissions@royalhospitalschool.org

Website: www.royalhospitalschool.org

Headmaster: Mr Simon Lockyer BSc MEd

Appointed: September 2016

School type: Coeducational Full Boarding and Day

Religious Denomination: Christian

Age range of pupils: 11–18

No. of pupils enrolled as at 01/09/2020: 689

Fees per annum as at 01/09/2020:

Day: £16,440–£18,330

Weekly Boarding: £25,230–£31,335

Full Boarding: £26,490–£34,140

3-Night Boarding: £22,215 – £26,385

Average class size: 15-20

Teacher/pupil ratio: 3.75:1

Tring Park School for the Performing Arts

Tring Park School for the Performing Arts is unique amongst specialist schools in the UK. At Tring Park talented young people from 8–19 specialise in Dance, Acting, Musical Theatre or Commercial Music, while also having the opportunity to study for GCSEs and a choice of up to 23 A Level subjects. Entrance is via audition and scholarships are available for Dance via the Government's Music and Dance Scheme and Dance and Drama Awards (DaDAs) for Sixth Form. School scholarships and bursaries are available for Acting, Musical Theatre and Commercial Music.

Pupils perform regularly both in Tring Park's Markova Theatre as well as in London, throughout the UK and Europe. Our graduating dance students perform in 'Encore Dance', Tring Park's touring company which annually performs a number of shows in England and Wales culminating in a London performance. Tring Park provides ballet dancers annually to perform in the Christmas production of Nutcracker with English National Ballet at the London Coliseum. Six pupils have played the part of Billy in Billy Elliot in the West End and on tour, The Tring Park Chamber Choir "The Sixteen" has won the 2019 BBC Songs of Praise Senior Choir of the Year – the second time in four years and recently came third in the highly competitive International Eisteddfod.

During the Summer Tring Park runs highly sought-after boarding and day courses in Dance, Musical Theatre and Acting.

In September 2019 we opened a new four-storey boarding house and teaching block and during the summer of 2020 we undertook a wide range of internal refurbishments to enhance our day pupil facilities together with further improvements to our sixth form common room. The school continues to look to the future and is currently exploring its next phase of capital developments.

Alumni success
Daisy Ridley – Star Wars
Lily James – Rebecca, Mamma Mia, Cinderella
Joe Griffiths-Brown – Hamilton, Frozen (West End)
Bart Edwards – Singapore Grip(ITV), State of Happiness (BBC)
Drew McOnie – King Kong (Broadway), Jesus Christ Superstar
Paris Fitzpatrick – New Adventures
Natalia Watt – National Moravian-Silesian Theatre
Oliwia Roniarska – Baltic Opera Ballet Poland
Jordan Shaw – Co-writer with Armin Van Buuren
Zachary Wyatt – RSC
Molly Jackson-Shaw – I Hate Suzie (Sky)
Joe Ashman – Free Rein (Netflix)

Testament to Tring Park's academic provision, students have left to read Medicine, Law, Physics and Engineering whilst others have careers in stage management and other performance-related industries.

Please check the website for upcoming Open Days.
To apply online: www.tringpark.com/opendays
Registrar: Adélia Wood-Smith
registrar@tringpark.com
Registered charity No. 1040330

Tring Park
School for the Performing Arts

(Founded 1919)
Tring Park, Tring, Hertfordshire HP23 5LX UK
Tel: 01442 824255
Fax: 01442 891069
Email: info@tringpark.com
Website: www.tringpark.com
Principal: Mr Stefan Anderson MA, ARCM, ARCT
Appointed: September 2002
School type: Co-educational Boarding & Day
Religious Denomination: Non-denominational
Age range of pupils: 8–19
No. of pupils enrolled as at 01/09/2020: 360
Boys: 111 *Girls:* 249 *Sixth Form:* 160
No. of boarders: 220
Fees per annum as at 01/09/2020:
Day: £15,405–£24,510
Full Boarding: £26,190–£37,050

East Midlands

Fairfield Prep School

Fairfield Prep School is a top-performing, independent school for boys and girls aged 3–11. It is part of the Loughborough Schools Foundation which is a charity committed to providing an education to cherish through a Nursery; two complementary Prep Schools and three high achieving Senior Schools: The Grammar School for boys, The High School for girls and The Amherst School, a non-selective co-education school. Uniquely the Schools share a beautiful campus and exceptional resources in many fields including Music, STEM and Sport.

Originally founded in 1929 as part of Loughborough High School, Fairfield Prep became an autonomous school within the Foundation in 1969. It is now a flourishing school of over 500 pupils and is perfectly situated to provide a first-class 21st Century Primary education.

A new chapter for each child
Fairfield Prep School is committed to the development of every pupil; the priority is to ensure that each child enjoys and benefits from their time at the School. That means a friendly and supportive community and endless exciting experiences, all backed by high academic standards.

Every pupil at Fairfield has many opportunities to thrive and to find a passion for things that matter to them. Therefore, success and achievement are both found through the inspiring and lively academic environment, as well as numerous extra-curricular activities which take place outside the classroom.

Fairfield was judged 'Excellent' across all eight categories by the Independent Schools Inspectorate in 2016 and everyone at Fairfield works together to create positive experiences for each and every child. The children continually achieve at the very highest level and thoroughly enjoy everything that the School has to offer and pupils move onto the next stage of their educational journey within

the Foundation as happy, confident and well-rounded individuals, ready to face the wealth of challenges ahead.

Excellent ways of understanding
The pastoral care at Fairfield is excellent and all staff work hard to bring out the best in each and every child. Each child benefits from effective, sensitive and well-coordinated pastoral care that enables academic achievement with individual care and focus, alongside an excellent holistic foundation for future learning.

Excellent experiences and opportunities
From Kindergarten to Year 6, the opportunities are vast and varied. There are over 40 clubs and activities available at lunchtime and after school encompassing Sport, Music, Drama and Art. From Origami to Music Theory, these include a Running Club, Rainbows and Dance. Most importantly, each child is encouraged and given the confidence to participate and enjoy success whatever their interests.

Charity and community work are also part of the School ethos. The School Council decides upon the charity focus for each term and fundraise for a rota of local, national, overseas and animal focused causes.

Excellent spaces and facilities
In 2016, Fairfield opened a new state-of-the-art building which provides new high-tech, light and airy classrooms with access to outdoor space, a large gymnasium and performance hall, specialist Art, Science and Food Technology rooms and a purpose-built Kindergarten. There is also a Forest School in a half-acre of woodland on the campus where children can safely explore the outdoor environment and develop an appreciation of the natural world.

FAIRFIELD
Prep School

(Founded 1969)

Leicester Road, Loughborough, Leicestershire LE11 2AE UK

Tel: 01509 215172

Email: fairfield.admissions@lsf.org

Website: www.lsf.org/fairfield

Headmaster: Mr Andrew Earnshaw

Appointed: January 2013

School type: Coeducational Day

Age range of pupils: 3–11

No. of pupils enrolled as at 01/09/2020: 540

Fees per term as at 01/09/2020:

Kindergarten: £3,660 per term

Prep-Prep (Reception to Year 2): £3,770 per term

Upper Prep (Years 3 to 6): £3,850 per term

Loughborough Amherst School

Loughborough Amherst School is an independent co-educational school for ages 4-18. It is part of the Loughborough Schools Foundation which is a charity committed to providing an education to cherish through a Nursery; two complementary Prep Schools and three high achieving Senior Schools: The Grammar School for boys, The High School for girls and The Amherst School, a non-selective co-education school. Uniquely the Schools share a beautiful campus and exceptional resources in many fields including Music, STEM and Sport.

Loughborough Amherst School became Loughborough's new co-educational independent school in September 2019, however the foundations were laid 170 years ago when the school was founded as a Catholic school for girls.

Ambitious for your child

Staff at Amherst, see their role as not just to help each child realise their academic potential. They also want to help every child in the School find a profound sense of self-belief. Amherst believes that young people with self-belief are not only happier in themselves, but are more able to show compassion to others, and to use their talents to make the world a better place.

Loughborough Amherst School is dedicated to creating an environment where every pupil has the opportunity for long-term spiritual and moral growth, not to mention long-term happiness.

When pupils leave the School, the aim is for them to be confident and successful. But, equally importantly, the staff want them to be caring and empathetic young people; equipped to face the best and worst that life offers. The kind of young person you'll be proud of.

At the heart of the School's ethos is the philosophy of their founder, Blessed Antonio Rosmini, that a 'pupil must be allowed to grow and develop as an integrated human person'.

A new and exciting phase in the history of the School was embarked on when boys were welcomed into the Senior School and Sixth Form in September 2019, making Loughborough Amherst School co-ed from 4 to 18 years. Amherst staff were also excited to welcome their first elite sports Boarders, thanks to their partnership with the Lawn Tennis Association and the Loughborough University National Tennis Academy.

Thanks to the Nursery and Sixth Form, children can develop at Amherst from infancy to adulthood. Together with the small size of the School, it creates a distinctively close school community with a family atmosphere. That's what makes Amherst so warm and welcoming.

With a teacher to pupil ratio of 1:8 enabling exceptionally high levels of individual academic support, each child has every chance of realising their goals. So, whether a child is a high flyer or someone who might benefit from extra educational input, the caring and holistic approach at Amherst will help them grow as a well-rounded individual.

Beyond the Timetable

There is a rich and engaging range of enrichment opportunities at Amherst to encourage the wider development of each child. Activities are offered for every age range during lunchtimes and after school, ranging from dance and football to public speaking, chess and debating. Above all, it is hoped that these opportunities encourage each child to discover life-long passions, interests and skills.

LOUGHBOROUGH
Amherst School

(Founded 1850)

Gray Street, Loughborough, Leicestershire LE11 2DZ UK

Tel: 01509 263901

Email: amherst.admissions@lsf.org

Website: www.lsf.org/amherst

Headmaster: Dr Julian Murphy

Appointed: September 2016

School type: Co-educational Day

Age range of pupils: 4–18

No. of pupils enrolled as at 01/09/2020: 290

Fees per term as at 01/09/2020:

Day Fees (Reception to Year 2): £3,410 per term

Day Fees (Years 3 to 6): £3,490 per term

Day Fees (Years 7 to 9): £4,250 per term

Day Fees (Years 10 to 11): £4,270 per term

Day Fees (Years 12 to 13): £4,310 per term

Loughborough Grammar School

Loughborough Grammar School is a top-performing, independent day and boarding school for boys aged 10-18. It is part of the Loughborough Schools Foundation which is a charity committed to providing an education to cherish through a Nursery; two complementary Prep Schools and three high achieving Senior Schools: The Grammar School for boys, The High School for girls and The Amherst School, a non-selective co-education school. Uniquely the Schools share a beautiful campus and exceptional resources in many fields including Music, STEM and Sport.

Loughborough Grammar School is one of the oldest independent schools in the country, able to trace its origins back to 1495.

A passion for life & learning

Loughborough Grammar School is a school where academic achievement is at the centre of everything. Dedicated staff and outstanding resources enable Loughborough Grammar School boys both to fulfil their potential in examinations and to embark on intellectual adventures beyond the classroom.

However, the boys encounter far more than is required for academic success. Staff at the Grammar School understand that they will only succeed if they feel happy and contented. Considerable focus is therefore placed on the development of a strong moral compass where kindness towards others and a commitment to fairness and equality are valued as key personal attributes.

So that each boy can enjoy his time at Loughborough Grammar School, there is an attentive system of pastoral care that ensures that each boy is supported by pastoral staff who fully know him, his interests and his worries, so that they can both monitor his progress and guide him towards areas in which he will feel challenged and fulfilled.

Each boy is an individual and staff want him to feel totally at ease within himself, whatever his unique interests or pursuits. The Grammar School strongly believes that pupils benefit from a well-rounded education, which is why it is so important that every boy at Loughborough Grammar School has the opportunity to discover passions that he will retain beyond his school days and into adult life.

In the early years, boys are encouraged to try as many experiences as possible, gradually finding their unique niche as they progress through the School. These activities beyond the classroom play a major part in helping boys to develop into resilient young men, who are confident yet sensitive and aware of their responsibilities to others.

The Grammar School provides a myriad of opportunities through an extensive extra-curricular programme which offers Sport, Music and Drama as well as over 100 clubs and societies. Boys are expected to take advantage of the activities and clubs that are on offer and to show pride in representing the School outside its walls.

A Loughborough Grammar School education is therefore a busy one, where each boy thrives through engaging in a broad range of activities that will complement his academic achievement, and help him to develop into a well-rounded and happy young man.

Boarding at the Grammar School

The success of the boarding community has been an enriching part of Loughborough Grammar School for much of its long history. With an active community of some 75 boarders, the boarding is like a concentration of the very best that the School offers, condensed into two wonderfully welcoming Houses within the campus.

Just like the Day pupils, Boarders are supported, individually known, cared for and cared about and encouraged to make the most of all the opportunities such a high achieving School provides.

LOUGHBOROUGH
Grammar School

(Founded 1495)

Buckland House, Burton Walks, Loughborough, Leicestershire LE11 2DU UK

Tel: 01509 233233

Email: grammar.admissions@lsf.org

Website: www.lsf.org/grammar

Headmaster: Mr Duncan Byrne

Appointed: April 2016

School type: Boys' Day & Boarding

Age range of boys: 10–18

No. of pupils enrolled as at 01/01/2020: 900

Fees per term as at 01/09/2020:

Day Fees (Years 6 to 9): £4,460 per term

Day Fees (Years 10 to 11): £4,500 per term

Day Fees (Years 12 to 13): £4,520 per term

Full boarding and tuition fees with EAL:
£11,270 – £11,330 per term

Loughborough High School

Loughborough High School is a top-performing, independent school for girls aged 11–18. It is part of the Loughborough Schools Foundation which is a charity committed to providing an education to cherish through a Nursery; two complementary Prep Schools and three high achieving Senior Schools: The Grammar School for boys, The High School for girls and The Amherst School, a non-selective co-education school. Uniquely the Schools share a beautiful campus and exceptional resources in many fields including Music, STEM and Sport.

Founded in 1850, the High School is one of the country's oldest Grammar Schools for girls. Most of the values that are upheld and the traditions that are celebrated have been established in the ensuing years, always with the goal of creating a wonderfully welcoming community within which every pupil is supported and encouraged to become all that they can be.

Achievement comes from a sense of wellbeing

Everyone is someone at Loughborough High School: whether competing on the sports field, performing with our world-class Music department or volunteering to help others, the individual talents of every student are nurtured in a warm and supportive community that enjoys all the advantages of a single-sex environment within a Foundation of four closely-linked Schools.

The High School takes great pride in their pupils' academic achievements but also believe that education is about so much more than excellent examination results. This is a school with a love of learning at its heart and where there are no limits placed on female aspiration: whether a pupil wants to be an astrophysicist, an actress or an anthropologist, the teachers help and encourage all the girls to achieve success. The aim is to develop adaptable, independent and socially responsible young women, who approach their learning with imagination, energy and a sense of adventure.

At the heart of everything lies the wellbeing of each pupil: diversity and difference are celebrated and the caring, committed staff support each girl in developing the self-awareness, courage and resilience needed to negotiate the challenges of modern life. As part of the Loughborough Schools Foundation, each pupil will be a lifelong member of a vibrant and happy family.

Remarkable Results

Pupils are encouraged to be enthusiastic about learning and the girls are supported by dedicated teachers who will encourage them to be curious, and question and debate in the classroom and beyond to help them develop key learning skills.

The smaller class sizes, superb teaching and well-resourced departments, and an overall environment that's ideal for learning, create the conditions where each girl can do her very best.

Remarkable Choices

The enrichment programme is extensive and constantly evolving – ranging from numerous sporting and musical pursuits to hobbies such as chess and gardening.

Activities are offered for every age range during lunchtimes and after school. This includes opportunities for the Adventure Service Challenge (Years 7 to 9) and the Duke of Edinburgh's Award Scheme (Years 9 to 13) which help girls to push boundaries and acquire new skills. Girls can also join the Combined Cadet Force where cadets not only follow the ethos of the School, but also develop core values of loyalty, integrity, courage, respect for others and selfless commitment. All High School girls are encouraged to express themselves and enjoy as wide a range of school experiences as possible.

LOUGHBOROUGH
High School

(Founded 1850)

Burton Walks, Loughborough, Leicestershire LE11 2DU UK

Tel: 01509 212348

Email: high.admissions@lsf.org

Website: www.lsf.org/high

Head: Dr Fiona Miles

Appointed: April 2019

School type: Girls' Day

Age range of girls: 11–18

No. of pupils enrolled as at 01/09/2020: 550

Fees per term as at 01/09/2020:

Day Fees (Years 7 to 9): £4,460 per term

Day Fees (Years 10 to 11): £4,500 per term

Day Fees (Years 12 to 13): £4,520 per term

Oakham School

Oakham is well known and loved for being a friendly and unpretentious school. Our key strengths lie in the spectacularly wide range of academic and extra-curricular opportunities that we provide and our exceptionally caring and vibrant school community.

Academic excellence lies at the heart of everything we do, yet our focus goes far beyond just encouraging our students to achieve outstanding results in their IB Diploma or A-level examinations. Our genuinely holistic approach to education means that students leave Oakham as effective and independent learners, well equipped with the skills and habits of mind to thrive in tomorrow's world.

Students also benefit from the School's location close to Rutland Water, in the heart of safe, rural England. The beautifully green campus is just a few minutes' walk from Oakham's historic town centre, whilst Oakham's excellent road and rail links mean that London, Birmingham and Cambridge are all within easy reach.

Academic

Oakham's rich curriculum combines innovation with the best of traditional approaches. Our vision is to nurture intellectually ambitious thinkers, giving them the ability to learn effectively and independently at school and beyond, and to build the knowledge, skills and habits of mind everyone needs to succeed and thrive.

We have offered the IB Diploma successfully since 2002 with a quarter of candidates regularly scoring 40 or above points, and 75% of A-level students gaining A*-B.

The majority of students go on to top universities in the UK, Europe and the USA, including Oxbridge and Russell Group universities. Our full-time Head of Careers and Higher Education and her team offer in-depth guidance and information on career options and admissions procedures for UK and non-UK universities.

Pastoral care

Our outstanding pastoral care ensures we nurture all aspects of our pupils' intellectual, physical, mental and spiritual development throughout their Oakham journey.

Each of our 8 Boarding Houses is home to the Housemaster or Housemistress and their families, supported by an experienced team of Resident Tutors and a Matron. Form 7 (Year 13) students are in their own Houses, one for boys and one for girls, where they experience a more university-oriented lifestyle.

House life is vibrant with over 125 activities on offer. Tutors meet with their tutees as a group each week, with one-to-ones and informal catch-ups as needed, and work closely with the wider pastoral team to manage pupils' overall progress and development.

The Barraclough Dining Hall serves an extensive choice of nutritious and freshly prepared food. Our state-of-the-art Medical and Pastoral Centre offers a dedicated space to promote well-being, as well as offering medical support 24 hours a day, 7 days a week.

Co-curricular

We offer over 30 different sports with internationally experienced coaching staff, including a full-time Strength & Conditioning coach. Our facilities include 40 acres of outstanding playing areas, a sports centre with squash courts and fitness suite, an indoor swimming pool, all-weather pitches for hockey and tennis, and access to nearby Rutland Water for sailing.

Hundreds of students take part in the Arts – there are five major drama productions every year; we teach over 500 individual music lessons each week, and around half of all pupils play in musical ensembles, choirs, bands, orchestras, and musical theatre productions.

(Founded 1584)

Chapel Close, Oakham, Rutland LE15 6DT UK

Tel: 01572 758500

Email: admissions@oakham.rutland.sch.uk

Website: www.oakham.rutland.sch.uk

Headmaster: Mr Henry Price MA (Oxon)

Appointed: September 2019

Director of IB: Simone Lorenz-Weir

School type: Coeducational Boarding & Day

Religious Denomination: Church of England

Age range of pupils: 10–18

No. of pupils enrolled as at 01/09/2020:

Boys: 540 **Girls:** 484 **Sixth Form:** 376

No. of boarders: 515

Fees per annum as at 01/09/2020:

Day: £17,685–£21,915

Full Boarding: £27,000–£36,195

Flexi Boarding (2-5 nights): £21,250 – £34,365

Average class size: 18 (10-16); 10 (16-18)

Teacher/pupil ratio: 1:7

Greater London

Bishop Challoner School

A holistic Education is offered at Bishop Challoner Bishop Challoner School is an independent Catholic co-educational establishment situated in Shortlands, Bromley. It is steeped in a rich tradition of history and the school is housed in the oldest building in Shortlands.

The 3 -18 school boasts of an all-through education offering a unique learning experience from nursery through to sixth form. Bishop Challoner is about much more than gaining excellent academic success but about development of the whole individual, offering an educational foundation for life to the full, ensuring that each child develops spiritually, morally, socially, physically and emotionally.

Bishop Challoner attracts children of all faiths and none, parents choose the school because they know that their son or daughter will gain a unique experience in a caring, nurturing and supportive environment that has high expectations and excellent discipline. The school is a place of great ethnic richness, characterised by tolerance, respect, love, fairness, forgiveness, and generosity to others, a genuine spirit of enquiry and search for truth. This is another reason why many parents who are not of the Catholic faith, also choose to send their children to Bishop Challoner.

In February 2020, Bishop Challoner was judged to be an outstanding Catholic school in their Diocesan Denominational Inspection. The report documented that, *'Pastoral care at Bishop Challoner is outstanding. This has resulted in a highly inclusive and welcoming learning community where the pupils feel safe and very well cared for. Consequently, relationships between pupils and their teachers are excellent, as are the peer to peer relationships'.*

The numerous events that the children enjoy from art competitions, drama, music, sporting fixtures and extra-curricular activities, enhances their holistic life at the school and provides for a happy environment.

Bishop Challoner continues to go from strength to strength with a dedicated team of highly qualified staff and supportive parents. Through partnership of family and staff, the school fosters an education of the whole person in preparation for adult life.

Pupils are able to be challenged, take risks and feel comfortable through consistent, well-planned teaching by staff who know them. The school is able to track and monitor their progress and provide on-going support to ensure each pupil reaches their full potential.

The School offers 7+, 11+, 13+ and sixth form scholarships, and has a selected number of bursaries available. The fees are reasonable compared to many other independent schools. The school is a 4-5 minute walk from Shortlands station and has excellent transport links. Pupils travel from a wide catchment area on public transport.

You will be warmly welcomed to the school where every day is 'open day' and where the pupils are the school's best advertisement. Find out more by visiting bishopchallonerschool.com, emailing admissions@ bishopchallonerschool.com or calling 020 8460 3546.

(Founded 1950)

228 Bromley Road, Shortlands, Bromley, Kent BR2 0BS UK

Tel: 020 8460 3546

Email: admissions@bishopchallonerschool.com

Website: www.bishopchallonerschool.com

Headteacher: Mrs Paula Anderson

Appointed: September 2014

School type: Coeducational Day

Religious Denomination: Catholic, welcoming all faiths

Age range of pupils: 3–18

No. of pupils enrolled as at 01/09/2020: 340

Fees per term as at 01/09/2020:

Day: £3,150–£4,500 per term

Nursery: £902 – £2,880 per term

Average class size: 18-20

Kew College

Set in leafy South-West London, Kew College is a gem of a school. In terms of education, it is a centre of excellence providing a rich, relevant and varied curriculum, but it is much more than that.

The minute you walk through the door, the ethos of the school is apparent; it is a friendly and caring environment which is relaxed but purposeful. The relationship between staff and pupils is warm and open and there is a tangible buzz of creativity in the air. The children are respectful, responsible, hard-working, and fun-loving individuals who thrive given opportunities to take risks in their learning and set challenges for themselves.

The results of entrance exams to secondary schools at Year 6 are excellent year on year, with numerous scholarships attained. Set this against the school's non-selective background and it is testimony to the quality of education that it provides. The children display an overwhelming desire to achieve and are inspired by staff who work with boundless energy, dedication and determination. No stone is left unturned as they strive to support and nurture every child to achieve to their full potential.

Education at Kew College is also about helping the pupils to develop their intellectual character. The children have a concrete sense of their own strengths and a confidence that goes hand in hand with that self-belief. This is coupled with a gracious sense of humility and open-mindedness, the realisation that the way forward in tomorrow's world is through co-operation and team work. This strong moral value system is embedded from an early age so that, by the time the pupils leave Kew College, they are able to think independently and critically. They are inquisitive, reflective and well-rounded; true individuals who are prepared for the rigours of secondary school and for the changing world in which they live.

"Both of our boys joined the school in the Nursery and have flourished in the nurturing and caring environment the school provides. The children are all confident, articulate, well-mannered, and thoroughly nice kids who are comfortable in the company of adults. Our boys have thrived at Kew College and always raced enthusiastically into school each day. The teaching and school philosophy is very much focused on helping each child to achieve their best in a happy environment. As parents, we really couldn't ask for more." **The Stewart family**

"We chose Kew College for our four daughters for its warm atmosphere and its happy, friendly, and well-mannered pupils. We feel fortunate to have also found a school which fulfils its promise of educating our children to their highest potential. We have children with differing abilities and personalities but Kew College has provided support and education for all of them. Every child at this school is unique, but one thing that every child here has in common is that they will leave strengthened by their experience." **The Ahmed Family**

Registrar: Mwarburton@kewcollege.com

(Founded 1927)

24-26 Cumberland Road, Kew, Surrey TW9 3HQ UK

Tel: 020 8940 2039

Fax: 020 8332 9945

Email: enquiries@kewcollege.com

Website: www.kewcollege.com

Head:
Mrs Marianne Austin BSc(Hons), MA(Hons), ACA, PGCE

School type: Coeducational Day

Age range of pupils: 3–11

No. of pupils enrolled as at 01/09/2020: 296

Boys: 144 **Girls:** 152

Fees per annum as at 01/09/2020:

Nursery: £7,350

Kindergarten – Year 6: £12,750

Average class size: 20

Laleham Lea School

At Laleham Lea we firmly believe in putting the child at the centre of everything we do. From the warm welcome as you walk through the door in the morning to the playground where all ages play, run and socialise together as one happy family.

Bright, light filled classrooms and enthusiastic, experienced teachers engage young minds' thirst for knowledge, helping each developing individual to reach their full potential and ultimately move on to the school of their choice.

Our pupils become happy, confident, fulfilled young people through both academic and extra-curricular activities. Every child takes part in team sports and every child is involved in school productions and concerts. Our greatest pleasure is to watch a once shy child blossom into the confident soloist, take a leading role in school assembly or simply help a fellow pupil through a challenging moment.

A high standard of teaching and learning is central to our success. Your son or daughter will be taught in well-equipped classrooms and our teachers hold specialist qualifications and have experience in specific areas of the curriculum such as Science, Modern Languages, Computer Studies (ICT), Art, Music and Sports.

As a Catholic school we put our Christian values at the forefront of our daily routine and welcome children of all faiths who are sympathetic to our Catholic ethos. We encourage a high standard of behaviour based on values of love, respect, and a positive work ethic. We regularly celebrate Mass together either in our own Long Room or in the calm serenity of the John Fisher School Chapel.

Recognising that Gospel values are central to the life of the school, we at Laleham Lea aim to create a loving, welcoming environment in which our children may grow intellectually, socially and emotionally; an environment in which their talents are recognised and fostered and their weaknesses treated with compassion; an environment which provides quality teaching and learning within a balanced curriculum framework and which helps every child to reach their true potential.

Together with parents, who are the first educators, we aim to lead our children towards tolerance, understanding and sensitivity to the needs of others so that they may grow up as well balanced individuals with a strong sense of personal identity and an awareness of God's love.

Through our close relationship with other schools in the area, we benefit from the use of the extensive sports field, stage and Chapel of the neighbouring John Fisher School and our children enjoy weekly swimming lessons at Waddon Swimming Pool.

Our outstanding pastoral care provides for a happy, caring community for all and we invite you to come and visit Laleham Lea; we can assure you of a very warm welcome.

Contact Mrs Edwards in the School Office to book your tour and secure your child's place for 2020/21 and beyond. 0208 660 3351. www.lalehamlea.co.uk.

(Founded 1965)

29 Peaks Hill, Purley, Surrey CR8 3JJ UK

Tel: 020 8660 3351

Email: secretary@lalehamlea.co.uk

Website: www.lalehamlea.co.uk

Headteacher: Ms K Barry

School type: Coeducational Day

Age range of pupils: 3–11

No. of pupils enrolled as at 01/09/2020: 112

Fees per annum as at 01/09/2020:

Day: £8,940

Average class size: 14

St Catherine's School

St. Catherine's is a vibrant and caring Catholic school that welcomes girls of all faiths and backgrounds. Our friendly community helps each pupil develop confidence as she explores her gifts and talents, and is inspired to meet challenges creatively. The School proudly combines excellent pastoral care with over 100 years' experience of independent education and a modern curriculum that prepares girls for the 21st century.

Our recent excellent inspection reports from the Independent Schools Inspectorate and the Diocese of Westminster note that *'teaching at St. Catherine's is more than the sum of its classroom parts…pupils have a wraparound experience that leads them to learn exceptionally well'* and that *'pupils flourish because of the secure, caring ethos of the School'*. We see these features in the achievements of our girls and in their readiness to learn.

In the Prep Department, which takes girls from 3 to 11 years of age, an emphasis on curiosity and discovery establishes firm foundations which later allow pupils to excel in the Senior School and Sixth Form. All girls enjoy the wide range of subjects and benefit from teaching staff who are passionate about giving each of them the opportunity to thrive. Teachers and tutors know the girls individually, and so offer support and challenge at all stages, and are in regular contact with parents.

The girls certainly rise to the challenges posed by public examinations. St Catherine's is proud of the value that is added to their achievements as they progress through the School and we enjoy seeing so many young women go on to university courses and careers of their choice, and to bright futures.

Those who visit St. Catherine's often remark on the warm and genuine enthusiasm of our pupils. The school's Christian ethos and emphasis on values helps girls to engage with the world around them, while open discussion, time for reflection, pupil-led committees and a wide range of creative opportunities create a lively environment where they can feel a sense of belonging. Our emphasis on character, and on the deeper values of compassion, integrity and resilience, is also developed through a comprehensive extra-curricular programme.

St Catherine's is committed to developing its facilities and over recent years we have been pleased to see girls enjoying new buildings and refurbishments, like the Science Block and Sixth Form Centre, which are designed to enhance their curriculum and social experiences. We also provide exciting trips, competitions and school events throughout the year; whether it is a trip to Costa Rica, regional athletics finals or a part in the latest school musical, there are plenty of opportunities for girls to develop their skills and their friendships within the school community.

Information about public examination results, extra-curricular opportunities and wrap-around care can all be found on the school website: www.stcatherineschool.co.uk

ST CATHERINE'S SCHOOL
— TWICKENHAM —

(Founded 1914)

Cross Deep, Twickenham, Middlesex TW1 4QJ UK

Tel: 020 8891 2898

Fax: 020 8744 9629

Email: info@stcatherineschool.co.uk

Website: www.stcatherineschool.co.uk

Headmistress: Mrs Johneen McPherson MA

Appointed: September 2018

School type: Girls' Day

Age range of girls: 3–18

No. of pupils enrolled as at 01/09/2020: 449

Fees per annum as at 01/09/2020:

Day: £11,205–£15,585

Average class size: 15-20

Teacher/pupil ratio: 1:11

St Helen's College

Nestled on the edge of Court Park in a quiet corner of Hillingdon, St. Helen's College is a family-run independent school for boys and girls aged 3 to 11, with a separate, thriving Kindergarten for boys and girls aged 2-3.

The school has a real family feel and has been described by inspectors as a 'haven of harmony'. Indeed, the most recent ISI quality inspection judged St. Helen's College outstanding, the quality of teaching excellent, the pupils' personal development outstanding and pupils' achievements, both academic and extra-curricular, excellent.

The report said: 'Pupils achieve high standards in academic work and a wide range of other activities. They are extremely successful in all aspects of learning…this is reflected in their success in entrance examinations both to maintained grammar and independent schools'.

The school's values and ethos set it apart. Led by the Head, Shirley Drummond, staff create a harmonious, loving environment, nurture the individual qualities of every pupil and ensure that children develop a lifelong love of learning, find out where their talents and interests lie, and leave school with traditional values and strength of character, ready to face the challenges of adult life with confidence, resilience and joy!

The children enjoy lessons taught by highly qualified specialist teachers right from the start, allowing them to study at a high level led by teachers with a real passion for their subject. There is also an extremely wide-ranging and quite unique range of 70+ co-curricular activities available, with superb music, drama and sports provision and clubs including cookery, gardening, yoga, taekwondo, ceramics, dance and many, many more.

The school benefits from specialist modern facilities and is strongly rooted in its local community, enjoying links with local churches, Brunel University and local theatres.

The safe, loving, encouraging environment at St. Helen's College fosters excellent academic achievement and well-rounded, confident pupils. Inspectors noted, 'Pupils' personal development is outstanding, well supported by excellent pastoral care. The overall feeling is of a warm, friendly community where everyone knows each other and feels safe and secure'.

St. Helen's College operates a flexible year-round extended care provision, with Breakfast Club from 7.30 a.m. and after school care until 6 p.m. daily during term time, and Holiday Club running during school holidays to assist working parents.

Parents may register children for entry to the school at 2+ (Kindergarten) or 3+ (Nursery). This is an extremely popular school and early registration is advisable. Prospective parents may register online using the online registration form or by contacting the school using the details below.

'School at work' open mornings are held in October and April/May each year, at which current pupils conduct tours of the school and answer questions for prospective parents. The Head, Head of Lower School and Director of Admissions are available to answer questions and take registrations at these events.

Alternatively, prospective parents may book an individual tour one morning during term time by telephoning 01895 234371 or emailing info@sthelenscollege.com.

(Founded 1924)

Parkway, Hillingdon, Uxbridge, Middlesex UB10 9JX UK

Tel: 01895 234371

Email: info@sthelenscollege.com

Website: www.sthelenscollege.com

Head: Mrs. Shirley Drummond BA, PGCert, MLDP, FCCT

Appointed: 2016

School type: Coeducational Day

Age range of pupils: 2–11

No. of pupils enrolled as at 01/09/2020: 373

Boys: 182 *Girls:* 191

Fees per annum as at 01/09/2020:

Day: £9,900–£12,240

Average class size: 22

Teacher/pupil ratio: varies

The John Lyon School

John Lyon is an academically selective independent boys' day school, based in Harrow-on-the-Hill in North West London.

From September 2021 the School will become coeducational, welcoming girls into Year 7 for the first time in our 145-year history.

Academic Excellence

Academic excellence is at the very heart of what the 600 pupils who study here seek to achieve. Pupils' academic standards and personal development were both rated the highest possible 'excellent' in our recent school inspection.

The curriculum sits at the centre of every working day. Pupils gain a good grounding in all the major academic subjects. Dedicated teachers work to develop learning skills, creativity and the ability to apply learning in all areas of life. Building on this platform, pupils perform well from the point they join – whether at age 11, 13 or 16 – and achieve excellent results in public examinations at GCSE and A-Level. Most gain places at leading UK universities and then move on into the workplace in a huge and varied range of valued professions.

A John Lyon pupil also gains from time spent outside the classroom. In particular, there is a strong reputation for Music, Art, Drama and Sport. Add to this an exciting co-curricular timetable focusing on each pupil's sense of community, achievement and wellbeing, a range of more than 70 extra-curricular activities, and pastoral care that is second to none, John Lyon is a school designed to nurture high-achieving and happy children.

Admissions

John Lyon offers a broad education to pupils who aspire to achieve excellence in all they do. As such, the admissions process at John Lyon tests academic ability, as well as containing elements we use to learn about character and potential. We look to offer places to able young pupils who have a great attitude to learning combined with a desire to be the best that they can be.

Entry is based on a combination of examination and interview (for Years 7 and 9) and on GCSE results and interview for Year 12. Our tests do not contain 'trick' questions and we aim to create a level playing field to allow future John Lyon pupils to shine.

We understand that choosing a school can be a difficult process for both parents and pupils. At John Lyon we pride ourselves in our welcoming and helpful approach to admissions.

All open events are now open for both boys and girls.

Bursaries and Scholarships

John Lyon is committed to widening access, enabling the children of those who could not otherwise afford the fees to benefit from our all-round independent school. Each year, the School makes available a number of means-tested bursaries to pupils who demonstrate exceptional talent and potential.

All pupils who take the 11+ or 13+ examination in January will be considered for an Academic Scholarship. Sixth Form Scholarships are awarded dependent on GCSE results. We also award a small number of Scholarships to candidates of outstanding ability and potential in Drama, Music and Sport.

(Founded 1876)

Middle Road, Harrow on the Hill, Middlesex HA2 0HN UK

Tel: 020 8515 9443

Email: admissions@johnlyon.org

Website: www.johnlyon.org

Head: Miss Katherine Haynes BA, MEd, NPQH

Appointed: September 2009

School type: Boys' Day (Coeducational from 2021)

Religious Denomination: Non-denominational

Age range of boys: 11–18

No. of pupils enrolled as at 01/09/2020: 600

Fees per term as at 01/09/2020:

Years 7-11: £6,411 per term (including lunch costs)

Sixth Form: £6,175 per term (excluding lunch costs)

Average class size: 18

Teacher/pupil ratio: 1:10

Whitgift School

Whitgift is one of Britain's finest independent day and boarding schools, offering a friendly, challenging and inclusive environment for 10-18 year old boys. Our core purpose is to educate bright and talented young men to become independent learners and thinkers, to achieve beyond what they believed they could, and to leave the School ready to give back to the society in which they will be leaders.

The School offers a variety of pathways to qualifications, including the A Levels, Pre U and the International Baccalaureate, where it is the top performing boys school in the UK. Alongside exceptional academic standards, the co-curricular activities feature more than 80 clubs & societies, more than 40 sports and an Outdoor Education programme that travels worldwide. A packed Performing Arts programme performs regularly, staging first-class musicals and plays. Orchestras and choirs tour internationally, and play at major venues, including the Royal Albert Hall, Cadogan Hall and Goodwood House.

The School's Boarding House, opened in 2013, is superbly-equipped and offers full, weekly and flexi-boarding to boys aged 13-18. This option allows boys to make the most of their time at Whitgift without distractions or a lengthy commute. Structured homework and free time sessions, as well as organised evening and weekend activities ensure that boarders build a strong balance between their academic studies and their co-curricular interests. For those who live further afield, there are 11 dedicated bus routes covering a wide radius.

Whitgift takes pride in being a diverse student body and global citizenship and digital literacy are key areas of focus for the entire school community. Over 43 languages are spoken by boarders alone. Pastoral support is at the foundation of our provision, with each pupil and his parents guaranteed a friendly face to turn to for advice and guidance. The latest ISI Report states, *"The quality of pastoral care is outstanding...a calm courteous approach pervades the School, indicated by highly civilised and positive relationships between staff and pupils."*

Whitgift offers generous scholarships and bursaries and more information can be found on our website.

Open Events

We encourage you to come and visit us on one of our Open Events to get a true feel for our inspiring school community.

Open Afternoons appointments to visit can be made via our website or by contacting the Admissions Team (see contact information below).

Whitgift 13+ entry and Boarding Pre-Test

Alongside our general entry process, we are pleased to announce that Whitgift will be undertaking a 13+ entry Day and Boarding Pre-Test for boys who will be in Year 6 in the Academic Year 2020/21. The process will open in mid-August and families that are interested can apply/ register for the Pre-Test to Whitgift via the Admissions Section of our website www.whitgift.co.uk, by completing an online Application Form by Friday 9 October 2020.

If you have any questions regarding our admissions process or the 13+ Day and Boarding Pre-Test, please do not hesitate to contact our Admissions Office.

Contact the Whitgift Admissions Team
T: 0208 633 9935
E: admissions@whitgift.co.uk

WHITGIFT

(Founded 1596)

Haling Park, South Croydon, Surrey CR2 6YT UK

Tel: +44 20 8633 9935

Email: admissions@whitgift.co.uk

Website: www.whitgift.co.uk

Headmaster: Mr Christopher Ramsey

Appointed: September 2017

School type: Boys' Day & Boarding

Religious Denomination: Accepting of all faiths

Age range of boys: 10–18

No. of pupils enrolled as at 01/09/2020: 1560

Fees per annum as at 01/09/2020:

Day: £20,640

Weekly Boarding: £33,081

Full Boarding: £40,140

Average class size: 20

Teacher/pupil ratio: 1:7

London

Bassett House School

At Bassett House, we believe that all children deserve to learn to fly and achieve their very best. The school was founded in 1947 by Sylvia Rentoul who recognised children as individuals, and encouraged them to express themselves, helping to grow their achievements and self-confidence. Our teaching techniques and apparatus are continually updated but our ethos remains constant.

Our children's energy, exuberance and curiosity for learning stand out. These have been engendered by our whole school commitment to adopting a growth mindset. Mention you cannot do something at Bassett House and any child will roar back at you "I can't do it YET!"

Focused attention remains our hallmark. We believe tailor-made teaching opens up young minds to endless possibilities, encouraging them to think creatively. We start by ensuring high staff-to-pupil ratios and many specialist teaching staff. Our teachers know every child in their care inside out and use great teaching supported by our excellent equipment (including cutting-edge technology) to bring lessons to life for each child.

Our 'sport for all' ethos encourages all our children to think of themselves as athletes, while allowing our sporting stars to shine. We offer football, netball, tag rugby, hockey, tennis, rounders, athletics, gymnastics and eurhythmics as part of the core curriculum and clubs in swimming, fencing, volleyball, yoga and dance.

We don't stop there. Vibrant music and drama give our children a passion for participation and performance, fostering a sense of achievement and boosting self-confidence. Our children first take to the stage from age 3 and have many opportunities to shine throughout life at Bassett House, whether in whole-school assemblies, stage shows or concerts. We have choirs, musical ensembles and an orchestra and provide individual instrumental music lessons from specialist music teachers.

Our extra-curricular clubs, together with our weekly enrichment hour, expand our children's horizons beyond the core curriculum. Each term children can choose to add a variety of activities to the school day, be it Lego modelling, computer coding, Scottish dancing, origami, chess, geography, cookery, arts and crafts or debating.

Residential trips from year 3 onwards create a sense of adventure and build self-reliance. The glow of a 7-year-old's face recounting a night-time bug-hunting expedition, a 9-year-old's thrill at working with a friend to sail a dinghy, a 10-year-old embracing the challenge of sleeping out under a self-made shelter: we create these memorable moments, knowing that their positive effects will last a lifetime.

All of this makes not only for well-rounded individuals, it translates into excellent academic results. When they leave aged 11, Bassett House children are ready to thrive at London's best senior schools. And they do: our children win places to the cream of London's senior schools. For those who want to board, Bassett House prepares them well for life at leading boarding schools.

Bassett House School is proudly non-selective. True to our belief, children are not tested and judged at the tender age of 3 or 4 years. Our outstanding results repeatedly show all children can fulfil their potential, regardless of early learning ability. We encourage our high-flyers to skyrocket, whilst children who need a little extra help are given the support they need to reach their fullest potential.

Our last full ISI inspection awarded us 'excellent' and 'outstanding' in all areas and we flew through our 2016 compliance inspection.

BASSETT
HOUSE SCHOOL

(Founded 1947)

60 Bassett Road, London, W10 6JP UK

Tel: 020 8969 0313

Email: info@bassetths.org.uk

Website: www.bassetths.org.uk

Headmistress:
Mrs Philippa Cawthorne MA (Soton) PGCE Mont Cert

Appointed: January 2014

School type: Co-educational Day

Age range of pupils: 3–11

No. of pupils enrolled as at 01/09/2020: 190

Fees per annum as at 01/09/2020:

Day: £5,499–£19,200

Average class size: 20

Teacher/pupil ratio: 1:7

City of London School
A rounded education in the Square Mile

There is no such thing as a typical CLS pupil. What characterises the education offered is a true preparation for life.

City of London School is a truly unique independent school, not least because of its unrivalled location on the banks of the Thames, between St. Paul's Cathedral and the Tate Modern. We are at the heart of the capital and our pupils benefit enormously from all that is on offer on our doorstep. Our location allows us to attract the very best outside speakers, offer top-class work shadowing placements and visit the many places of interest in this world-class city. We are a modern and forward-looking institution drawing on clever pupils from all social, economic and ethnic backgrounds and, in so doing, truly reflect the diversity of the capital in the 21st century. Pupils come from a huge number of both state primary and independent preparatory schools and, once here, receive an academic yet liberal education. Our central location allows pupils to travel to City from all over London, encouraging resourcefulness and self-reliance in their journey to school, and in their wider life.

Our examination results are excellent, but, more importantly, pupils leave us ready for life beyond school, with a sense of identity and an independence of thought and action which are rare among leavers from independent schools; it is significant that the vast majority of pupils go on to their first choice of university, with a large number attending Oxford and Cambridge universities, and various medical schools. Facilities are outstanding (the school moved downstream to its new buildings in 1986) and are continually updated. The state-of-the-art Winterflood Theatre and refurbished Science laboratories provide a first-rate environment in which our pupils learn and thrive. We are generously endowed with academic, music and sports scholarships and, in addition, the bursary campaign has raised significant funding for a number of full-fee places to be awarded each year to those who could not otherwise afford even a proportion of fees. In this way, the school seeks to maintain the socio-economic mix which has always been its tradition and strength. Admission at 10+, 11+, 13+ and 16+ is by entrance examinations, followed by interviews for those candidates who complete their examination papers to a satisfactory standard.

For dates and to book onto one of our open days please visit our website.
Tel: 020 3680 6300
Email: admissions@cityoflondonschool.org.uk

City of London School

(Founded 1442)

Queen Victoria Street, London, EC4V 3AL UK

Tel: 020 3680 6300

Email: admissions@cityoflondonschool.org.uk

Website: www.cityoflondonschool.org.uk

Head: Mr A R Bird MSc

Appointed: January 2018

School type: Boys' Day

Age range of boys: 10–18

No. of pupils enrolled as at 01/09/2020: 950

Sixth Form: 250

Fees per annum as at 01/09/2020:

Day: £18,939

Devonshire House Preparatory School

Academic and leisure facilities

The school is situated in fine premises in the heart of Hampstead with its own walled grounds. The aim is to achieve high academic standards whilst developing enthusiasm and initiative throughout a wide range of interests. It is considered essential to encourage pupils to develop their own individual interests and a good sense of personal responsibility.

Curriculum

Early literacy and numeracy are very important and the traditional academic subjects form the core curriculum. The younger children all have a class teacher and classroom assistant and their day consists of a mixture of formal lessons and learning through play. Whilst children of all ages continue to have a form teacher, as they grow older an increasing part of the curriculum is delivered by subject specialists. The combined sciences form an increasingly important part of the timetable as the children mature. The use of computers is introduced from an early stage, both as its own skill and as an integrated part of the pupils' education.

Expression in all forms of communication is encouraged, with classes having lessons in art, music and drama, and French. Physical exercise and games also play a key part of the curriculum. Much encouragement is given to pupils to help widen their horizons and broaden their interests. The school fosters a sense of responsibility amongst the pupils, and individuality and personal attention for each pupil is considered essential to make progress in the modern world.

The principal areas of the National Curriculum are covered, though subjects may be taken at a higher level, or at a quicker pace. For the girls approaching the 11+ senior schools' entry examinations, special emphasis is given to the requirements for these, and in the top two years for the boys, Common Entrance curriculum is taught. The pupils achieve great success in these examinations and a number also sit successfully for senior school scholarships.

The school has its own nursery, The Oak Tree Nursery, which takes children from two-and-a-half years of age.

Entry requirements

The Oak Tree Nursery: For children entering the Oak Tree Nursery, places are offered on the basis on an informal assessment made at the nursery. Children in The Oak Tree Nursery transfer directly to the Junior School.

The Junior School: For children entering the junior school from the ages of three to five, places are offered on the basis of assessment made at the school. From the age of six, places are usually subject to a written test taken at school. At eight, children transfer directly into the upper school. Parents and their children are welcome to visit for interview and to see around the school.

The Upper School: Entry to the upper school is principally from the junior school. For pupils seeking to join the school from elsewhere places are normally subject to a written entrance test.

(Founded 1989)

2 Arkwright Road, Hampstead, London, NW3 6AE UK

Tel: 020 7435 1916

Email: enquiries@dhprep.co.uk

Website: www.devonshirehouseschool.co.uk

Headmistress: Mrs S. Piper BA(Hons)

School type:
Preparatory, Pre-preparatory & Nursery Day School

Religious Denomination: Non-denominational

Age range of boys: 2½–13

Age range of girls: 2½–11

No. of pupils enrolled as at 01/09/2020: 650

Boys: 350 **Girls:** 300

Fees per annum as at 01/09/2020:

Day: £10,545–£19,470

Durston House

Durston House is a leading London prep school. The school began life in 1886 and has, from its earliest years, enjoyed a strong academic reputation and encouraged keen sporting and lively cultural interests. Durston House has a fine record of preparing boys for Senior School. Our pupils leave at 13 heading to top Independent London schools such as St Pauls, Merchant Taylors, Hampton and Harrow.

Durston House places an emphasis on high standards of work and targets that are commensurate with each pupil's personal development. We believe that it is hugely important to create an educational environment that encourages all pupils to be curious and enthusiastic about their opportunities to learn and grow. At Durston House, the manner in which this growth is guided is one of relaxed, quiet integrity of purpose, allowing boys the freedom to develop themselves. This is the essence of our ongoing success.

A boy's education here is shaped by the development of his character, his curiosity to learn and discover more, and his expanding capability. These three concepts – Character, Curiosity and Capability – are the cornerstones of his success at Durston House and his success in life. The curriculum we offer is very broad, deep and rigorous, allowing ample opportunity for boys to question and explore. Independent learning is valued and encouraged by our well-qualified staff, always keen to inspire and engage boys beyond the lesson objective. A particular interest in an idea or a subject is fostered and nurtured by teachers, who themselves are enthusiasts for learning. In essence, here at Durston House, we are all learners, old and young; this positive interaction is supported by small class sizes, where individuality and independence can flourish. Full specialist teaching is introduced at Year 5, with some specialism occurring in specific subjects lower down the school. Boys with specific needs are offered Learning Support.

Lessons are delivered in a range of ways, taking account of different learning styles and preferences, and the certainty that boys should explore and experience practically, not just from a textbook. Workshops, Outings, Trips and outdoor adventures complement the classroom experience across all year groups. Throughout the school there is an Enrichment Programme, offering a wide range of activities from yoga, engineering, debate, chess, cooking and philosophy to name a few. The aim of the Enrichment programme is to enhance the boys' critical thinking and develop life skills.

Extensive use is made of local facilities, especially for drama and swimming. Sport is strong, with both of the school's playing field sites having floodlit, all-weather facilities; fixtures against other schools are common and there has been much sporting success in recent years.

Entry into the Reception year is in order of registration and is non-selective. For all other years, entry assessment procedures are in place. After-School Care is offered for boys whose parents cannot collect them until later in the day. Generous ancillary staffing helps Durston House run smoothly and effectively.

We take pride in the true and visible diversity of our community and embrace pupils and staff from all ethnic, cultural and religious backgrounds. We have built a community in which mutual respect and understanding, fairness and opportunities for all are promoted within the framework of our broadly Christian foundation.

(Founded 1886)

12-14 Castlebar Road, Ealing, London, W5 2DR UK

Tel: 020 8991 6530

Email: info@durstonhouse.org

Website: www.durstonhouse.org

Headmaster: Mr Giles Entwisle

Appointed: September 2020

School type: Boys' Day

Age range of boys: 4–13

No. of pupils enrolled as at 01/09/2020: 380

Fees per term as at 01/09/2020:

Day: £4,160–£5,060 per term

Average class size: 16

Hall School Wimbledon

Situated close to the village, Hall School Wimbledon is the only co-educational, all-through school (5-18) in Wimbledon which thrives on its inclusive and independent nature.

Pastoral care is paramount, with its small class sizes, caring staff and a commitment to co-education coming together to draw a circle of care around each child, where every pupil is known, valued and able to develop his or her own talents. This has been central to the school's ethos since it was founded and was recognised in its recent Ofsted inspection (February 2019), which highlighted *"Outstanding provision in the early years"* and *"Extensive enrichment opportunities for pupils of all ages contribute well to the school's strong provision for their spiritual, moral, social and cultural development."*

Hall School Wimbledon provides a happy and nurturing environment where children study a broad and exciting curriculum. Through this programme of study, enhanced by an extensive range of extra-curricular activities, HSW aims to instil an enthusiasm and joy for learning at every level, as children progress through the school. For example, great emphasis is placed on practical learning and problem solving, encouraging inquisitiveness and an ability to think for oneself.

The school works within a culture of praise and encouragement, rewarding good behaviour, kindness and consideration for others. It believes that cultivating characteristics of resilience, adaptability, confidence, good humour, collaboration and empathy are important to its pupils' long-term success.

Well Being Hub
The school has a Well Being Hub which offers a sanctuary away from life's pressures which anyone can access – children, staff or parents. It recognises that it has a pivotal role in supporting its pupils to make healthy lifestyle choices and to understand the benefits of lifelong health and wellbeing. Simple steps shared with the pupils can promote mental, emotional and physical resilience. The Wellbeing Hub is stocked with up to date guidance and books on a wide range of topics and is open at break times and lunchtimes and is also made available, when needed, throughout the day. The safe and brightly furnished space is visited by Doug the dog, who is a much valued member of staff at Hall School Wimbledon

School's playing fields
In addition to its well-resourced school buildings, HSW is greatly enhanced by its Oberon Fields site which affords nine acres of playing fields and an Edwardian pavilion. Less than a mile away, it has been re-developed to become a hub for curriculum enrichment, with outdoor learning spaces, performing arts and cookery facilities, tennis court, netball courts, nature trail, orchard, garden allotments and a Forest School area.

Sixth Form
In September 2021, HSW will launch its brand new Sixth Form, delivering its vision of becoming Wimbledon's only non-selective, co-educational all through 5-18 school. The Sixth Form will embrace the school's philosophy of small classes and personalised learning, alongside outstanding teaching and pastoral care.

Open Events:
Please contact Head of Admissions, Suzi Abensur on 020 8394 6144 or email admissions@hsw.co.uk

(Founded 1990)

17, The downs, Wimbledon, London, SW20 8HF UK

Tel: 020 8879 9200

Email: enquiries@hsw.co.uk

Website: www.hsw.co.uk

Headmaster: Mr. Robert Bannon

Appointed: 1990

School type: Co-educational Day

Age range of pupils: 5–18

No. of pupils enrolled as at 01/09/2020: 150

Fees per term as at 01/09/2020:

Day: £4,420–£5,950 per term

Average class size: 15-18

Teacher/pupil ratio: 1:9

Heathside School

Welcome to Heathside

Children come first at Heathside. We help each child find their own path to learning so they can fulfil their unique potential. The result is young people who are happy, articulate, independent, confident in their abilities and keen to find their place in the world. This is the time when your child will start to define their interests, open up their horizons and discover the educational pathway that will lead to their future. Our approach is to offer the level of academic challenge that will encourage your child to be the best they can possibly be.

Your child will receive an exceptional degree of support, so they gain confidence and grow – emotionally, socially and academically. Day by day, we will show your child the steps they need to take to get to where they want to be. Every aspect of our teaching builds their confidence, respects their progress, and acknowledges where they are before helping them go further.

English and maths are taught each morning, with additional attention given to children who benefit from a slower pace or thrive on greater challenge. From an early age, your child will learn the traditional skills of handwriting, spelling and times tables. Through art, music, STEM subjects and humanities we delve into topics, exploring them from every avenue, making our curriculum rich and rewarding.

Children thrive in a relaxed environment where they call their teachers by their first name. Working in small groups, teachers know each child extremely well so are able to provide precisely the right amount of support or challenge at precisely the right time.

For many, the right educational pathway means the traditional 11+ route to senior school. In Years 5 and 6, your child will have access to outstanding 11+ tuition, including early morning and holiday preparation classes, as well as specialist interview guidance. Outcomes for Heathside pupils are consistently high, with most Year 6 pupils gaining places at their first choice senior school in London or beyond. For others, the 13+ route is preferred, and this small group of students receive specialist support and tuition in our 'Prometheans' group. Heathside has an excellent record of achieving academic scholarships at both 11+ and 13+ including the prestigious Queens Scholarship at Westminster. Many pupils opt to carry on their senior schooling at Heathside where they continue to flourish in familiar surroundings.

Throughout their time at Heathside, your child will have the chance to take part in a range of sporting and outdoor activities both on Hampstead Heath and in other local facilities. Our long-term relationship with Hampstead Heath enables us to capitalise on the value of outdoor play and Forest School. A recent study from Hasselt University in Belgium found that growing up in a greener urban environment boosts children's intelligence. Add to this an extensive array of lunch time and after school clubs, and your child will have every opportunity to stretch themselves and broaden their interests.

HEATHSIDE SCHOOL
HAMPSTEAD

(Founded 1993)

84a Heath Street, Hampstead, London, NW3 1DN UK

Tel: +44 (0)20 3058 4011

Email: info@heathsideprep.co.uk

Website: www.heathsideprep.co.uk

Headteacher: Katherine Vintiner

Appointed: 2019

School type: Co-educational Day

Age range of pupils: 2–14

No. of pupils enrolled as at 01/09/2020: 230

Fees per annum as at 01/09/2020:

Day: £16,000–£19,200

Kensington Park School

A stone's throw away from Hyde Park, Kensington Park School is a co-educational, independent school for students aged 11-18, with exceptional boarding facilities for students aged 14 and over. KPS boasts some of the country's most dedicated and passionate teachers and offers excellent cultural and sporting opportunities, all in the heart of London.

Outstanding teaching, innovation, and a personalised delivery are the three crucial pillars of a KPS education. Our broad and balanced curriculum is delivered in small class sizes in a modern, dynamic and technology-rich environment. As we prepare students for GCSE and A-Level qualifications, we also enable them to develop the skills that they need to succeed outside the classroom, (at university and beyond).

Our 21st century curriculum has been carefully selected and designed to meet the needs of our students as they grow and develop. From Computer Science to Mandarin, introduced from Year 7, our curriculum prepares our young people for the fast-paced and ever-changing world around us. As important as our formal curriculum, which challenges and develops our students academically, is our wide-ranging programme of co-curricular activities. From high-quality music and drama clubs, to a variety of sports activities with local providers, including netball, football, swimming, tennis, rock climbing, and even ice hockey, our clubs aim to spark enquiring young minds and inspire the development of new skills.

This year our students embraced learning via online platforms, and as our lessons went on virtually uninterrupted, those in Year 11 and Year 13 secured exceptional GCSE and A Level results. While 66% of KPS A-level students achieved an A or A* grade, 65% of our Year 11s achieved grades 9 – 7 at GCSE, far exceeding the national average.

KPS students are courageous, confident, bold and emotionally intelligent. Encouraged to question the world around them, our students grow to be leaders in their subjects and in their passions. We welcome families to visit Kensington Park School at one of our Open Evenings, which are held throughout the academic year.

Kensington Park
S C H O O L

Sixth Form: 59 Queen's Gate, South Kensington, London, SW7 5JP UK

Lower School: 40-44 Bark Place, London, W2 4AT

Tel: +44 (0)20 7225 0577

Email: admissions@kps.co.uk

Website: www.kps.co.uk

Headmaster (Interim): Mr Stephen Mellor MA, MCCT

School type: Co-educational Boarding & Day

Age range of pupils: 11–18

Fees per term as at 01/09/2020:

Day (UK): £8,000 per term

Day (International): £8,167 per term

Boarding (twin rooms): £5,300 – £5,600 per term

Boarding (single rooms): £7,800 – £8,000 per term

Lloyd Williamson Schools

Introduction

The Lloyd Williamson Schools have grown in both size and reputation to become the established schools they are today. The main departments are: three Nurseries, a Transition School for 5-7 year olds, a Senior School for 7-11 year olds and an Upper School for 11-16 year olds. We plan to expand the age range to 18 taking one extra year group per year from 2021.

The names *Lloyd* and *Williamson* are family names that belong to the proprietor. We believe they convey one of the main points of ethos at the school: that we are a *family* – and a strong one at that!

We have built an excellent reputation for strong academic standards and personalised, holistic learning for individual children.

We are based in W10 and W8 in the Borough of Kensington and Chelsea, with small classes to a maximum of 16 in Primary and 18 in Secondary. The schools have extended opening hours, competitive, realistic fees and all-year-round provision, including Holiday Clubs.

Mission Statement and Ethos:

- We celebrate childhood and nurture each child to be the best they can be in a challenging and inspiring environment that ignites a passion for life and learning – we are not a one-size-fits-all school
- Teachers build positive relationships, working with each child to be curious, intellectual and creative – we all like to think outside the box – fear of failure is banished!
- Equality and diversity permeate the fabric of our school – we are a family where everyone belongs, based on empathy and respect
- We encourage partnership and dialogue with parents and children thrive academically without losing their childhood – we cherish each child's self-esteem
- A blend of traditional and forward thinking teaching prepares our children for their next school and for life

Admissions

Parents are invited to meet the Co-Principals for personal and individual tours of the school during school hours in order to gain a real flavour of how the school operates on a daily basis.

The school supports requests for places from families with a diverse range of backgrounds; the binding quality is motivation! We do not compare children with one another; we challenge them against their own goals and next steps. This allows children to feel safe, be creative and curious instead of managing anxiety about 'not keeping up'! Our children are happy, confident students available to learn – they develop a rich and positive sense of who they are and can be.

The school is open from 7:30am-6:00pm (main school hours from 8:30am-3:30pm). This means that working parents can drop off their children and get to work knowing their children are safe and without the additional cost of nannies.

As a small school, everyone knows everyone from the babies up to our oldest member of staff!

We cherish individuality and self-confidence and our aim is that every child will develop an organic and strong positive sense of self. We enable this through the development of positive relationships so that all our children can learn to be strong and independent.

Contact Information

www.lws.org.uk
Admissions: admin@lws.org.uk
Main School and W10 Nursery: 020 8962 0345
W8 Nurseries: 020 7243 3331

LLOYD WILLIAMSON
——— SCHOOLS ———

12 Telford Road, London, W10 5SH UK

Tel: 020 8962 0345

Email: admin@lws.org.uk

Website: www.lloydwilliamson.co.uk

Co-Principals: Ms Lucy Meyer & Mr Aaron Williams

Appointed: December 1999

School type: Coeducational Day

Age range of pupils: 4 months–16 years

Fees per annum as at 01/09/2020:

Day: £16,950

Nursery: £79 – £99.50 per 10.5 hours day

Average class size: 12-16

Teacher/pupil ratio: 1:12

Lyndhurst House Prep School

Lyndhurst House provides a structured but individually responsive education from Reception (4+) to Common Entrance and scholarship at 13, delivered by an experienced, well-qualified staff team. For 68 years Lyndhurst has been sending its 13-year-olds to the many renowned senior schools in London, and some to boarding schools further afield with an excellent record of academic success and achievement, balanced by strong participation in sports, music, art and drama.

Our pupils are lively, enthusiastic and engaged. We focus on providing a full-rounded education, by paying particular attention to the individual needs of every pupil. This is achieved by keeping class sizes small throughout the school. Staff are able to give boys the individual attention they need – whether that means pushing them on towards scholarship work or giving them extra support in areas where they may be struggling.

Reflecting its diverse north west London community, our school is non-denominational and welcomes families of all religions and cultures. Pupils from a wide range of cultural backgrounds work and play together harmoniously and are taught to be tolerant and respectful of the opinions of others. Put simply, they are taught to value the importance of kindness. Ask a Lyndhurst House boy what the most important thing about being at the school is and the most common answer will be to be kind to each other. Our recent ISI inspection report graded both pupils' achievements and personal development as "Excellent" and said: *"Pupils are extremely considerate, caring and respectful of each other and all members of their school community. This is strongly encouraged by positive relationships with staff, firmly underpinned by strong values and well-established routines.*

For the first half of the Summer Term we welcomed children of key workers to school every day as well as providing a full remote learning programme for everyone learning from home. A few creative ideas that have come from remote learning include Year 5's Asian Food Project where students made sushi and fortune cookies and Year 3's Mindfulness lessons to help navigate the new learning environment. After half term, small changes at Lyndhurst enabled each year group to return to school before breaking up for the Summer Holidays. These changes included extra hygiene measures and individually wrapped packed lunches made onsite by our chefs.

(Founded 1952)

24 Lyndhurst Gardens, Hampstead, London, NW3 5NW UK

Tel: 020 7435 4936

Email: office@lyndhursthouse.co.uk

Website: www.lyndhursthouse.co.uk

Head of School: Mr Andrew Reid MA (Oxon)

Appointed: September 2008

School type: Boys' Day

Age range of boys: 4–13

No. of pupils enrolled as at 01/09/2020: 138

Fees per term as at 01/09/2020:

Day: £6,470–£7,245 per term

Average class size: 15

Teacher/pupil ratio: 1:8

Newton Prep

In a London landscape crowded with prep schools, Newton Prep stands out for its unbeatable combination of vibrant size and eclecticism, its extraordinary facilities and outside spaces and its position at the heart of Central London's most burgeoning community: the rapidly growing Battersea Power Station development, where Apple (the holder of the OTHER famous apple logo) will have their Europe HQ from 2021 and the massive regeneration of Nine Elms.

There's an electricity in the air and it's important that we are a part of that buzz. It is also key to our ethos: to ensure that Newton children are well-educated, curious, kind and articulate but, above all, in this modern world (and equipped with the best of British values), to encourage them to think for, and be, themselves, while also being kind to others.

At Newton Prep, we provide a liberal environment in which children are equipped with a sense of self, resilience and hopefulness, beyond the obvious need to excel academically. We encourage children to think beyond the curriculum and they hoover it up. Whether it's piano lessons, judo or Boggle, children need ways of engaging. We aim for our Newton Prep children to enter adolescence feeling that they already have more to contribute than just academic achievements. Yes, we need to get them into the right schools but not at the expense of their well-being and character.

We encourage all our children to reflect on school life, not just power through it. Delegates from throughout the school take part in both Pupil Parliaments, which meet regularly. Through this means, children can express their views and make suggestions about how we might improve the school. Each child is therefore encouraged to embrace the notion of using their voice to influence things for the good of the many.

Despite the excellence of their education, Newton Prep children are notable for their lack of arrogance and entitlement. The kindness and generosity shown by the pupils towards their peers is remarkable and we are particularly proud of the engagement between the older children and the little ones. This spirit of community is also built into the Newton Diploma, our revolutionary humanities curriculum for our Years 7 and 8, now into its second year. This is a cross-curricular, rigorous and exciting programme that scraps the creaky arts syllabi of Common Entrance and allows pupils to exploit links between subjects, extend initiatives for service and leadership and breathe real fire into their intellectual curiosity. Luckily, our extensive resources enable such personal growth, in whichever direction a child wants. With a huge all-weather pitch capable of supporting four fixtures at a time, a state-of-the-art, 120-seat recital hall, a music technology suite, recording studio, 300 seat auditorium, three gymnasiums, bustling art studios, dance studios, a library and collegiate-style science labs, children are encouraged to "do" as well as "learn". We even have an oasis of a garden: where our children perform Shakespeare, hunt for mini-beasts and conduct scientific experiments: like when Year 8 students lit up the London skies with their own explosion.

We are not a blazers-and-boaters kind of school. We don't have to look to the past and can focus all our present energies on ensuring a bright future for our children. Above all, we want Newton Prep children to enjoy their precious childhood years.

Admission to the Nursery is by registration; to the Lower School (Reception to Y2) by registration, with a gentle and informal assessment; to the Upper School (Y3-8) by registration and competitive testing.

(Founded 1991)

149 Battersea Park Road, London, SW8 4BX UK

Tel: 020 7720 4091

Fax: 020 7498 9052

Email: enquiries@newtonprep.co.uk

Website: www.newtonprepschool.co.uk

Headmistress: Mrs Alison Fleming BA, MA Ed, PGCE

Appointed: September 2013

School type:
Coeducational Pre-Preparatory & Preparatory Day

Age range of pupils: 3–13

No. of pupils enrolled as at 01/09/2020: 631

Boys: 311 *Girls:* 320

Fees per annum as at 01/09/2020:

Day: £9,600–£20,340

Average class size: 20 (smaller in Years 7 & 8)

North Bridge House

North Bridge House prides itself on its impressive results and academically non-selective co-education, challenging and inspiring pupils throughout every stage of their school career. With specialist expertise from the Early Years through to A Level, we are on a constant journey of getting to know and understand every learner as a unique individual, helping them to find and realise their true academic and personal potential.

Celebrating results well above the national average, the Nursery and Pre-Prep Schools develop the fundamental skills upon which pupils' future successes are built. The warm and nurturing environment in which children find the confidence to express themselves assertively and creatively offers a rich and forward-thinking curriculum, allowing them to develop a genuine love of learning without the added pressure of entrance exams; NBH provides a stress-free through education up to age 18. With everything from Philosophy for Children and Forest School to a vegetable garden and chicken run, the schools' focus is on promoting children's social and emotional development as much as their academic achievement.

NBH Prep School maintains its outstanding provision through its bespoke senior school preparation: pupils are taught by subject specialists and individually prepared – according to their personal strengths and interests – for entry to some of the country's best schools, with a strong focus on confidence and wellbeing. We advise on and facilitate every path to success, with pupils either leaving the Prep School at the end of Year 6 (taking the 11+, the Consortium exam, or going to one of the NBH Senior Schools), or at the end of Year 8 (taking the Common Pre-Test, the Common Entrance exam, or schools' individual entrance tests) and often gaining highly competitive scholarship places.

Our high-achieving Senior Schools prepare pupils for university life and the world of work with unrivalled UCAS support and careers events, and celebrate top GCSE and A Level results. 2020 saw NBH Senior Schools achieve 67% Grades 7-9 at GCSE and the Sixth Form gain 68% A*/A grades at A Level. The expert teaching teams harness research into teen development and learning patterns to further understand and maximize pupils' potential. For example, using evidence-based research, we have implemented a later (midweek) start time for teens, which reflects the current findings regarding the teenage brain and sleeping patterns, and continue to work with the Institute of Education on developing metacognition in our students.

PE is essential to our schools' offering and our prime north London location sees us benefit from the best facilities for track and field, outdoor adventure, and water sports.

From Bushcraft to the Duke of Edinburgh Award, there is also a busy schedule of enrichment activities, workshops and school trips, all centred around our aim to cultivate character and promote wellbeing. This, together with our outstanding pastoral support, sees our students leave as articulate, confident, determined young people, proud to be themselves.

School locations:
North Bridge House Nursery School
33 Fitzjohn's Avenue, Hampstead, London NW3 5JY
North Bridge House Pre-Prep School
8 Netherhall Gardens, Hampstead, London NW3 5RR
North Bridge House Nursery & Pre-Prep West Hampstead
85-87 Fordwych Road, West Hampstead, London NW2 3TL
North Bridge House Prep School
1 Gloucester Avenue, Regent's Park, London NW1 7AB
North Bridge House Senior Hampstead
65 Rosslyn Hill, Hampstead, London NW3 5UD
North Bridge House Senior & Sixth Form Canonbury
6-9 Canonbury Place, Islington, London N1 2NQ

North Bridge House

(Founded 1939)
65 Rosslyn Hill, London, NW3 5UD UK
Tel: 020 7428 1520
Email: admissionsenquiries@northbridgehouse.com
Website: www.northbridgehouse.com
Head of Nursery & Pre-Prep Schools:
Mrs. Christine McLelland
Head of Prep School: Mr. James Stenning
Head of Senior Schools: Mr. Brendan Pavey
School type: Co-educational Day
Age range of pupils: 2–18 years
No. of pupils enrolled as at 01/09/2020: 1400
Fees per annum as at 01/09/2020:
Day: £7,635–£20,400
Average class size: 20

Orchard House School

At Orchard House School, children are loved first and taught second. Our Pupil Pastoral Plan monitors the well-being of each child and was recently shortlisted for a TES (Times Educational Supplement) national award for educational innovation. This emphasis on a nurturing environment is not, however, at the cost of academic excellence. In fact, our outstanding results show how creating the right environment enables every child to thrive academically and emotionally. We believe learning should be exciting and fun, and the children should positively want to come to Orchard House every day. And they do: we harness the exuberance and energy of every child in our care, and instil within them a lifelong love of learning.

Orchard House's diverse curriculum creates a sense of adventure, developing the children's appetite for risk. This feeds into greater academic and creative achievements. Whether it's a whole-school skipping day, a project with Jaguar to enable our 10- and 11-year-old mathematicians to engineer performance cars or learning archery in Normandy (taught solely in French), Orchard House children embrace novel tasks throughout their time with us. By the time they sit 11+ exams, they are past masters at tackling new challenges with verve: this shows in our stellar results.

Sport at Orchard House encourages a respectful, competitive attitude, teaching children the value of camaraderie and the buzz of going for gold, or goal. We offer football, netball, rugby, hockey, lacrosse, cross country, tennis, athletics, triathlon, cricket, rounders, swimming and gymnastics and arrange regular team-sport fixtures against other schools, often lifting the trophy but always relishing the match.

Similarly, music and drama build confidence and self-esteem, as well as many opportunities for every child to perform. Visiting music teachers offer individual instrumental tuition on a variety of instruments. We have a school orchestra, Pippin choir, chamber choir, senior and junior choir and a parent and staff choir. There are many other instrumental groups including a pupil-led rock band.

Orchard House School is proudly non-selective. True to our belief, children are not tested and judged at the tender age of 3 or 4 years. Our educational success shows all children can fulfil their potential, regardless of early learning ability.

The Independent Schools Inspectorate awarded Orchard House the highest accolades of 'excellent' in all areas and 'exceptional' in achievements and learning in its last full inspection and we flew through our 2018 compliance inspection. The top-notch education we provide leads to our first-class academic results and the scholarships our pupils win to their next schools.

ORCHARD
HOUSE SCHOOL

(Founded 1993)

16 Newton Grove, Bedford Park, London, W4 1LB UK

Tel: 020 8742 8544

Email: info@orchardhs.org.uk

Website: www.orchardhs.org.uk

Headmistress:
Mrs Maria Edwards BEd(Beds) PGCE(Man) Mont Cert

Appointed: September 2015

School type: Co-educational Day

Age range of pupils: 3–11

No. of pupils enrolled as at 01/09/2020: 290

Fees per annum as at 01/09/2020:

Day: £9,210–£19,200

Average class size: 20

Teacher/pupil ratio: 1:7

Prospect House School

At Prospect House School, we focus on making each child feel valued and secure and on making their educational experience both challenging and fun. This allows us to develop every child to their fullest potential, as our outstanding results demonstrate. Our most recent full Independent Schools Inspectorate inspection, in 2013, rated us 'excellent' against all the inspectors' criteria and we flew through our 2017 regulatory compliance inspection.

Prospect House's superb teachers provide a supportive and encouraging academic environment in which children excel. The sound of laughter is never far away, as Prospect House children discover their aptitude for sport, music, art, computing, drama or a whole host of other opportunities both within the curriculum or before or after school. Whether taking up the trombone, building a go-cart or orienteering on Putney Heath, our children relish each new challenge and emerge better able to face the next challenge that comes their way.

Music is an important part of life at Prospect House. We have over 200 individual music lessons taking place each week and a school orchestra, chamber choir and senior and junior choirs, as well as a number of ensembles. All children act in assemblies, school plays, musical productions and concerts throughout the year. Children in Years 1 to 6 enjoy drama lessons and our high-quality staging, lighting, sound and props give every production a professional feel.

Physical activity promotes wellbeing, so we offer a busy sports programme. This includes football, netball, hockey, running, cross country, tennis, athletics, cricket, rounders, swimming, dance and gymnastics. Our approach to fixtures and tournaments successfully balances participation for everyone with letting our sports stars shine.

Residential trips thrill the children with the sense of adventure, encouraging risk-taking and building self-reliance, whether on a history expedition, a bushcraft adventure or a week in Normandy immersed in the French language and culture.

We encourage our children to think for themselves, to be confident and to develop a sense of responsibility for the world in which they live. By the time they leave us aged 11, Prospect House children are ready to thrive at London's best senior schools. This is reflected in our impressive 11+ results. Every year, a notable proportion of our children win scholarships to leading senior schools.

Prospect House School is proudly non-selective. True to our belief, children are not tested and judged at the tender age of 3 or 4 years. Our stellar results repeatedly show all children can fulfil their potential, regardless of early learning ability. We encourage our high-flyers to soar, whilst children who need a little extra help are given the support they need to reach their fullest potential. At Prospect House, every child is helped to achieve a personal best.

PROSPECT
HOUSE SCHOOL

(Founded 1991)

75 Putney Hill, London, SW15 3NT UK

Tel: 020 8246 4897

Email: info@prospecths.org.uk

Website: www.prospecths.org.uk

Headmaster: Mr Michael Hodge BPED(Rhodes) QTS

Appointed: September 2017

School type: Co-educational Day

Age range of pupils: 3–11

No. of pupils enrolled as at 01/09/2020: 316

Fees per annum as at 01/09/2020:

Day: £9,210–£19,200

Average class size: 20

Teacher/pupil ratio: 1:7

Queen's Gate School

Queen's Gate School is an independent day school for girls between the ages of 4 and 18 years. Established in 1891, the school is an Educational Trust situated in five large Victorian Houses within easy walking distance of Kensington Gardens, Hyde Park, and the South Kensington museums.

The School offers an education for life in a challenging environment where sound values and individuality are nurtured within a supportive atmosphere. Our aim is to create a secure, happy, yet stimulating environment in which each girl can realise their academic and personal potential and make full use of individual interests and talents. We encourage the development of self-discipline and create an atmosphere where freedom of thought and ideas can flourish.

The Principal, Mrs Rosalynd Kamaryc, has been in post since 2006 and has built on the existing strengths of the School, whilst enabling girls to enjoy new opportunities in and out of the classroom.

Girls follow as wide a curriculum as possible and generally take GCSEs in ten subjects that must include English, Mathematics, a science and a modern language. A full range of A Level subjects is offered. In the Lower Sixth girls normally take four subjects, reducing to three in the Upper Sixth. The girls are offered excellent careers advice to assist in their UCAS and US applications.

Sport is highly valued at Queen's Gate with two compulsory sessions for all girls each week. We have many sports available at other times during the School day including netball, athletics, basketball, hockey, fencing, swimming, rowing, cross-country, biathlon and dance. Girls achieve much success, with some earning national and international status.

Co-curricular activities at Queen's Gate see girls taking part in Model United Nations meets throughout the year, become part of clubs including horticultural society, STEM club and Cosmetics club and experience trips around the UK and abroad to enhance their learning experience.

Music plays a large role in the School life, with concerts and mini recitals throughout the School year both in school and at local venues, and Drama productions across both schools see girls performing at venues including RADA and the Chelsea Theatre.

The Junior School is situated just a few yards down the road from the Senior School at 125 and 126 Queen's Gate. The beautifully restored buildings boast spacious form rooms, three fully equipped laboratories, a state-of-the-art STEAM (Science, Technology, Engineering, Art and Mathematics) Room and an elegant Assembly Hall. Junior pupils also use Senior School facilities and benefit from specialist subject teaching from Senior School staff. Senior girls often visit the Junior School to assist with activities, thus reinforcing the continuity of education from 4-18 available at the School.

Admission is by test and interview in the Junior School. Entrance to the Senior School is by the London 11+ Consortium entrance examination. Applicants for the Sixth Form must achieve six GCSEs at Grade 7 or above with Grade 8 or 9 (or their equivalent) required in those subjects they wish to pursue at A level.

In addition to the Open Events that are run by the Senior and Junior Schools throughout the year, parents are always welcome to make a private visit to see the schools at work. Appointments can be made by contacting the Registrar on 0207 594 4982 or by email registrar@queensgate.org.uk.

Queen's Gate

133 Queen's Gate, London, SW7 5LE UK

Tel: 020 7589 3587

Fax: 020 7584 7691

Email: registrar@queensgate.org.uk

Website: www.queensgate.org.uk

Principal: Mrs R M Kamaryc BA, MSc, PGCE

Appointed: January 2006

School type: Girls' Day

Age range of girls: 4–18

No. of pupils enrolled as at 01/09/2020: 529

Sixth Form: 94

Junior School: 141

Senior School: 388

Fees per term as at 01/09/2020:

Junior School: £6,500 per term

Senior School & Sixth Form: £7,200 per term (*fees for Spring and Summer 2021 may be subject to change)

Average class size: 23

Teacher/pupil ratio: 1:10

St Paul's Cathedral School

Governed by the Dean and Chapter and seven lay governors, the original residential choir school, which can date its history back to the 12th century, has, since the 1980s, included non-chorister day boys and girls aged 4-13. The number of pupils is currently 260.

In its 2017 inspection, the ISI awarded the School its highest accolade of 'Excellent' in both educational attainment and pupil progress.

A broad curriculum prepares all pupils for 11+ and 13+ examinations including scholarship and Common Entrance examinations. The school has an excellent record in placing pupils in outstanding senior schools, many with scholarships. With its unique and central location, the school is able to make the most of what London can offer culturally and artistically in particular. A wide variety of sports and musical instrument tuition is offered: the school has an exceptional record in preparing pupils for ABRSM exams. Choristers receive an outstanding choral training as members of the renowned St Paul's Cathedral Choir.

The life of the school is based on the following aims and principles:

St Paul's Cathedral School is a Christian, co-educational community which holds to the values of love, justice, tolerance, respect, honesty, service and trust in its life and practice, to promote positive relationships throughout the school community and where the safety, welfare and emotional well-being of each child is of the utmost importance.

The school aims to instil a love of learning through a broad curriculum. It aims to give each pupil the opportunity to develop intellectually, socially, personally, physically, culturally and spiritually. All pupils are encouraged to work to the best of their ability and to achieve standards of excellence in all of their endeavours.

Through the corporate life of the school, and through good pastoral care, the school encourages the independence of the individual as well as mutual responsibility. It aims to make its pupils aware of the wider community, espouses the democratic process and encourages a close working relationship with parents and guardians.

Facilities: the school is situated on one site to the east of St Paul's Cathedral. It has a separate Pre-Prep department, excellent Science lab and ICT room. It has two outside play areas and a hall. There are plans to provide new boarding facilities for the choristers.

Entry is at 4+ and 7+ years. 4+ entry is held in the November preceding the September a child will enter the school and 7+ entry is held in the January preceding the September a child will enter the school. At 7+, pupils are given a short test and spend a day in school. Chorister voice trials are held throughout the year for boys between 6 and 8 years old. Occasional places in other year groups sometimes become available and, at 11+, the school now offers scholarship awards in music, the arts, sport and academics. Further information can be found on the school's website www.spcslondon.com

St Paul's Cathedral School is a registered charity (No. 312718), which exists to provide education for the choristers of St Paul's Cathedral and for children living in the local area.

ST PAUL'S CATHEDRAL SCHOOL

(Founded 12th Century or earlier)

2 New Change, London, EC4M 9AD UK

Tel: 020 7248 5156

Fax: 020 7329 6568

Email: admissions@spcs.london.sch.uk

Website: www.spcslondon.com

Headmaster: Simon Larter-Evans BA (Hons), PGCE, FRSA

Appointed: September 2016

School type: Coeducational Pre-Prep, Day Prep & Boarding Choir School

Religious Denomination:
Church of England, admits pupils of all faiths

Age range of pupils: 4–13

No. of pupils enrolled as at 01/09/2020: 260

Boys: 147 **Girls:** 113

Fees per term as at 01/09/2020:

Day: £4,911–£5,287 per term

Full Boarding: £2,970 per term

Average class size: 15-20

Teacher/pupil ratio: 1:10

The Merlin School

Choosing a school for your child at 4 years old is an important decision and a significant first opportunity to inspire a little learner and prepare them for the next stage. At Merlin School we specialise in these precious early years. The Merlin School, established in 1986, is a creative and nurturing co-educational pre-prep school, which does not assess on entry. You'll find us in the heart of Putney, in a beautiful Victorian house. We offer a warm and homely atmosphere where all staff take time to engage with our children, supporting the development of their independence and confidence. Creative and practical activities enhance learning and stimulate their imagination.

Our school motto is 'have a go' and our main area of focus is to evoke a thirst for learning, encouraging curiosity in the world around us. Whilst Maths and English underpin our syllabus, we very much delight in the breadth and depth of subjects taught here. Pupils relish the challenge of their first formal sports lessons, learning about team work and sportsmanship, alongside their specific sports skills, gearing them up to find their own sporting pathway. Our children bounce in to Science lessons wondering what practical activity awaits, they master thinking in their computing lessons and build confidence with presentations, assemblies and innovative drama productions which are written specifically for them.

We believe that losing sight of the importance of the broad spectrum of subjects and cramming children in one or two areas only, can result in denying pupils crucial and exciting opportunities. It is about the child enjoying their childhood and 'doing!'.

Over half of our timetable is taught by specialist teachers including Science, Drama, Music, Art/DT, Computing, French and PE/Games with both our Deputy and Head being actively involved in the teaching of all year groups. Our Topic work is both vibrant and stimulating; a wander around our classrooms will take you on a journey through various topics from Gods and Monsters to The Seven Wonders of The World.

At the end of their educational journey with us we send our pupils off to their next schools with the confidence to build new relationships, the enthusiasm to learn and a positive attitude to new challenges. Despite being a non-selective school Merlin children make excellent progress, from their individual starting points, and go on to a range of prestigious Prep Schools.

At Merlin School we are immensely proud of our recent Ofsted inspection (November 2017), where we were graded 'Outstanding' in all five areas. Ofsted described our curriculum as being 'planned carefully to captivate pupils' interests'. Merlin children were described as 'resilient and independent learners who set about every activity with enthusiasm... they display excellent communication skills and are confident learners'. Our EYFS provision was reported as Outstanding, highlighting the strong and sustained progress the children make in all areas of learning.

Please do book an appointment to come and see for yourself – we look forward to welcoming you!

(Founded 1986)

4 Carlton Drive, London, SW15 2BZ UK

Tel: 020 8788 2769

Email: admissionenquiries@merlinschool.net

Website: www.merlinschool.net

Principal: Mrs Kate Prest

Appointed: March 2003

School type: Co-educational Pre-Prep

Age range of pupils: 4–8

No. of pupils enrolled as at 01/09/2020: 155

Fees per annum as at 01/09/2020:

Day: £5,041 (Inclusive)

Average class size: 15

The Study Preparatory School

The Study Preparatory School, Wimbledon, is a successful all girls prep school based on two picturesque sites, adjacent to Wimbledon Common, and in the heart of Wimbledon Village. Established in 1893; it is proudly non-selective and is renowned for its nurturing, creative ethos as well as its excellent 11+ results. Girls join the school at Reception through ballot entry when they are 4+, and leave at 11+ to go onto top Day and Boarding Schools. Day schools include Wimbledon, Putney and Surbiton High Schools, St Paul's Girls' School, The Lady Eleanor Holles, Epsom College, Francis Holland, Marymount, Notre Dame and St John's Leatherhead. Boarding schools include Benenden, Downe House, St Mary's Ascot and Wycombe Abbey.

The Study Prep has achieved an outstanding record of scholarships and offers from leading senior schools over the years, which has been surpassed this year, with a total of 40 scholarships offered to the 2020 Year 6 cohort. This brings the total of scholarship offers over the last three years to an impressive 104, across academic, drama, music, art and sport.

Although academic rigour is at the heart of the school, The Study Prep is highly creative, with a reputation for excellence in music and the performing and visual arts, and has had Artsmark Gold status from Arts Council England since 2009. Girls may do the LAMDA drama programme with specialist teachers, and music lessons are offered by the school's fifteen peripatetic music teachers in a vast array of instruments. The school offers weekly class music lessons from Reception and has a number of vibrant choirs, music ensembles and orchestras. Girls learn French from Reception, taught by specialist language teachers, and they also do a taster in Spanish at the beginning of Year 6. The dynamic PE department ensures success at both regional and national level across netball, athletics, hockey, and cross country and the School has a spacious off-site sports ground with multi-use pitches for training and matches. The Study Prep has been ISA National Netball champions in recent years.

New Head, Miss Vicky Ellis, will continue with the School's mission to enable each individual to fulfil her potential in a supportive, kind and happy environment when she joins in September 2020. The girls enjoy a rich diversity of experiences, in and out of the classroom, and an understanding of important issues beyond the school gates. Every year group experience outings, school trips and workshops, and the older girls enjoy residential trips also.

Miss Ellis describes The Study Prep as having, "*The family feel of a village school and the results and facilities of a leading London prep.*" Facilities have been enhanced at both sites over recent years, and 2020 will see the completion of an ambitious development which will add a new library, six new classrooms, and a performing arts space to the School. The school provides regular tours with the Head, and also holds an annual Open Morning in March.

(Founded 1893)

Wilberforce House, Camp Road, Wimbledon Common, London, SW19 4UN UK

Tel: 020 8947 6969

Email: admissions@thestudyprep.co.uk

Website: www.thestudyprep.co.uk

Head of School: Miss Vicky Ellis BSc (Hons), QTS, MA

Appointed: September 2020

School type: Girls' Day

Religious Denomination: Non-denominational

Age range of girls: 4–11

No. of pupils enrolled as at 01/09/2020: 320

Fees per term as at 01/09/2020:

Day: £4,725 per term

Average class size: 20-24

Ursuline Preparatory School

The Ursuline Preparatory school is a Roman Catholic school that welcomes children of all faiths and none. Non-selective by choice, the school offers a values-driven, academic education to girls from 3-11 years of age and to boys in the Nursery class.

Established in 1892 to promote the values of St Angela Merici OSU, the Ursuline Preparatory School places equal value on the education of heart, mind and soul in the certain knowledge that only through the equal development of all three can a child truly excel. The school's mission is to develop a community that lives each day working together (Insieme) and united in harmony, valuing the contributions of all and championing the virtues of love, compassion, kindness and generosity. The children are encouraged to be grateful for the gifts they have been given and to develop these gifts to the full, in generous service to others. The school seeks to pass on the living and faith-filled tradition of Jesus Christ by having unswerving faith in every single one of our pupils and by encouraging them, in turn, to have faith and hope in others. A keen focus is to educate and create future leaders in the spirit of Serviam (I will serve), keeping justice at the centre of their lives.

The core provision of this school is three-fold:

- A strong Ursuline ethos;
- An academic provision, whether in the classroom or online, that prepares children fully for secondary school;
- A strong partnership between pupils, parents and staff.

Our children enjoy a rich diversity of experiences, both inside and outside of the classroom. Our 11+ preparation curriculum, full sporting programme, and developed range of extra-curricular activities, provides an enriching and engaging provision. We are ready and able to replicate this provision by distance learning, ensuring our children are fully prepared for the next step in their educational journey no matter the circumstances, as well as enabling them to look forward to the future with confidence, keen to make a difference in the world.

The girls at the Ursuline Preparatory School follow an academic curriculum and are fully supported, securing places in their senior school of choice. As a result of the Ursuline ethos, and the academic preparation process put in place, the girls here can face the 11+ process with confidence. Last year girls received offers from the following schools: Ursuline High School, Kingston Grammar, Danes Hill School, Emanuel, Marymount, Nonsuch, Notre Dame, Putney High, St John's Leatherhead, Surbiton High, Sutton High, Tiffin Girls, St John's and Wimbledon High.

An Ursuline education seeks to help the young people here grow and flourish in an environment in which every child is loved and valued. On such sure foundations, we help them become the very best that they can be. Please do come and visit; you will be made most welcome.

(Founded 1892)

18 The Downs, Wimbledon, London, SW20 8HR UK

Tel: 020 8947 0859

Email: headteacherea@ursulineprep.org

Website: www.ursulineprep.org

Head Teacher: Mrs Caroline Molina BA

Appointed: July 2020

School type:
Girls' Day School with Co-educational Nursery

Religious Denomination: Roman Catholic

Age range of boys: 3–4

Age range of girls: 3–11

No. of pupils enrolled as at 01/09/2020: 202

Fees per term as at 01/09/2020:

Nursery Mornings: £2,345 per term

Nursery – Year 6 Full Time: £3,800 per term

Average class size: 18

Teacher/pupil ratio: 1:5

North-East

Argyle House School

Nestled in Ashbrooke – the leafy suburb of Sunderland, lies an educational establishment of repute. Argyle House School is the North East's only family owned independent school. The school was established in 1884 by Mr. Hanna M A. In 1968, Mr. Jeff Johnson, a student of the school and later a teacher there, bought the school from Mr. Hanna's family. In 2002, Jeff Johnson handed over the reins of Argyle House School to his two sons, Chris and Neil. After taking over as Headteacher, Mr. Chris Johnson has since developed the school into a place of nurture by providing an environment for children to enjoy learning whilst instilling in them strong family values; the core values upon which the school was built.

The strengths of the school lie on many levels. It is a school where children come willingly to learn. Studying and learning are two different things. The willingness to learn comes from the kind of environment that a school has. When they are happy, they are more receptive to learn. Argyle House School provides such an environment. Also, this is not a school with 1000 children! Class numbers are small and there is merit in this structure. This enables our teachers to focus on a child's strength, his or her interests and then guide them accordingly. When a child is known individually to a teacher, this makes a tremendous difference in their development. Our teachers know each and every one of them. We never look upon a child as a student of the school. They are always looked upon as sons and daughters. When they come to school, they're coming home. A place where they are loved and respected.

We emphasise the importance of values, of honesty, of respect, of kindness, of being responsible citizens, of humanity and above all, the value of hardwork and the importance of being a good human being. What we lay down as a foundation today will enable our children to build their future with confidence. We stress the importance of what we call 'The R-Principle' where we encourage our children to be; resourceful, resilient, respectful, responsible, reflective and to possess the ability to reason. Our teachers take on different roles apart from teaching such as being mentors and guides; a friend who listens and comforts; a father or mother who is stern but loving as well. When a school has such an environment, happiness takes over.

We are of the opinion that education must be enjoyed and it must give the child the chance to develop not just academically, but also physically, socially and emotionally too. Extra-curricular activities are crucial here. In fact, our clubs and activities are far ranging and we have close to 30 clubs for children to utilise. We've attained the highest possible rating by ISI in our most recent inspection.

Our facilities are updated regularly and we've increased our wider partnership links. We've also devised new curriculums with our pupils in mind, which feature extra GCSE subjects. The environment of the school not only creates well-rounded individuals but also academic achievers. Government statistics have once again named Argyle House School as number one for GCSE results in Sunderland. To ensure a healthy body and mind, children are encouraged to participate in Sport, Music, Drama and Arts. From a student accomplishment perspective, we are proud to have a number of children who have excelled in their sporting endeavours. Two brothers claimed gold in European Gymnastics and one child represented Great Britain in Karate.

We consider the happiness of children to be the key factor to both academic and social success. With no airs or graces, our down to earth approach to education and development allows children to achieve to the maximum of their abilities. Outstanding facilities, backed by dedicated teachers, a comfortable environment and deep rooted values make Argyle House School truly exceptional.

ARGYLE HOUSE SCHOOL
SUNDERLAND

(Founded 1884)

19-20 Thornhill Park, Sunderland, Tyne & Wear SR2 7LA UK

Tel: 0191 5100726

Email: info@argylehouseschool.co.uk

Website: www.argylehouseschool.co.uk

Headteacher: Mr. Chris Johnson

School type: Co-educational Day

Age range of pupils: 3–16

No. of pupils enrolled as at 01/09/2020: 233

Fees per annum as at 01/09/2020: Please enquire

Average class size: 17

Teacher/pupil ratio: 1:6

North-West

Chetham's School of Music

Chetham's School of Music is a world-class music school, the largest in the UK and the only one of its kind in the North of England.

Based in the heart of Manchester, Chetham's is housed in a state-of-the-art new school building, with an acoustically designed concert hall offering a flawless venue for student performances and professional concerts.

The thriving creative community at Chetham's involves more than 300 students, aged 8-18, whose common passion is music. This common bond of musical passion makes for a truly inspirational place which transforms the lives of all who are part of it.

For the majority of the 300 students, Chetham's is home as well as school. Whether you are a boarding or day student, the friendly atmosphere and sense of community within the school is a central to the Chetham's experience.

Every student's week is individually timetabled to include individual lessons, ensemble rehearsals, structured practice and academic classes. From day one, life at Chetham's helps every musician to find their own musical pathway, whether as a performer, teacher or creator, whether music becomes a profession or remains a lifelong joy.

Chetham's offers a superb academic education alongside its unparalleled music programme. Although there are no academic criteria for entrance, Chetham's students regularly celebrate outstanding results at GCSE and A-level and progress to leading conservatoires and universities across the world. Students' success is born of small class sizes, a motivated teaching team, and a school community which encourages hard work and high achievement.

Entry to the school is based solely on musical ability or potential, never on background or ability to pay, thanks to generous bursaries through the Government's Music and Dance Scheme.

The school is a national and international resource for music education—welcoming teachers, professional players, composers and conductors, community groups, school children and other young musicians, both experienced and novices, to come together and make music. Our network of partnerships with professional orchestras and organisations extends across the music industry, and our alumni populate orchestras and ensembles across the world.

Chetham's concert venue, The Stoller Hall, delivers a dynamic music programme that connects Chetham's students with the professional musical community, building on the school's already strong position within Manchester's cultural sector. Students regularly perform alongside leading orchestras including Manchester Camerata and Northern Chamber Orchestra, and with contemporary music and comedy artists.

Chetham's long history began in 1421, and students still enjoy opportunities to perform in the 600-year old Baronial Hall attached to Chetham's Library. It opened as a charitable school in 1653, and educated the poor boys of the district for 400 years before becoming a co-educational music school in 1969. For half a century, Chetham's students and alumni have enjoyed success at major competitions, taken up positions across the music profession as performers, leaders and teachers, and established the School as a vital element of music education in the UK.

Chetham's
School of Music

(Founded 1969)

Long Millgate, Manchester,
Greater Manchester M3 1SB UK

Tel: 0161 834 9644

Email: aliceherbert@chethams.com

Website: www.chethams.com

Joint Principals: Nicola Smith & Tom Redmond

Appointed: September 2020

School type: Coeducational Boarding & Day

Age range of pupils: 8–18

No. of pupils enrolled as at 01/09/2020: 300

Fees per annum as at 01/09/2020:

Full Day Student Fee: £25,821

Full Boarding Student Fee: £33,324

Full Chorister Day Student Fee: £9,954

*Entry is based on musical ability or potential, not ability to pay, thanks to generous bursaries through the Government's Music and Dance Scheme.

Lime House School

Finding the right school for your child is one of the most important decisions you will make. A good education can make all the difference to a child's future.

Lime House School – www.limehouseschool.co.uk – just south of Carlisle on the edge of the Lake District National Park, is an independent, co-educational boarding and day school which welcomes pupils, aged seven to 18, from all over the world.

Lime House School offers a rigorous academic and intellectual education which will challenge and engage your child. Supportive and nurturing in approach, the school empowers pupils to establish secure foundations for independent learning from which to launch their futures in tertiary education, and the careers of their choice.

The school has a wide and varied curriculum at both Primary and Secondary levels, with a dynamic range of subjects offered to Sixth Form. Pupils of all abilities are welcome, those with Special Education Needs are supported by a dedicated team of professionals.

Headteacher, Mary Robertson-Barnett, MA (Oxon), PGCE, says: *"It is a privilege to lead a school of such vibrancy. The academic programme is rich and fulfilling, with pupils benefiting from tailored programmes, delivered by subject specialists, who enthuse our learners with their passion. The super-curricular opportunities inform the academic life of the school with a range of cultural, performance, and sporting activities.*

"Pupils are guided in their growth as future global citizens and custodians, by their personal development tutors, and are encouraged to explore their dreams and define their path. Lime House School is a joyous and enriching place for all who are involved in our community."

The school's ethos is that learning should be integrated and fun, extending beyond the classroom and informing all we do.

The activities programme includes: sporting; music; art; photography; debating; environmental and strategic thinking. The school garden – a new initiative to support the school's ecological work – is thriving under the tender care of pupils who engage wholeheartedly with their beautiful surroundings. Weekends are structured, with pupils exploring diverse educational, cultural and fun filled experiences.

Lime House is a school of outstanding potential, its vibrancy and tolerance reflected in each of its pupils. Why not arrange a visit to see what we can offer your child?

(Founded 1899)

Holm Hill, Dalston, Carlisle, Cumbria CA5 7BX UK

Tel: 01228 710225

Fax: 01228 710508

Email: office@limehouseschool.co.uk

Website: www.limehouseschool.co.uk

Headteacher:
Mrs Mary Robertson-Barnett MA(Oxon), PGCE

Appointed: September 2017

School type: Coeducational Day & Boarding

Age range of pupils: 7–18

No. of pupils enrolled as at 01/09/2020: 182

Fees per annum as at 01/09/2020: £10,750

Average class size: 15

Teacher/pupil ratio: 1:20

Rossall School

For many, a childhood by the sea is a dream; at Rossall, that dream becomes a reality. Rossall is an exceptional school, rooted in its heritage yet innately dynamic, brimming with personality and excited about the future.

We are shaped by our coastal location and somehow infused with the sense of anticipation, curiosity and adventure that early explorers must have felt – where can we go? What will we find? How can we get there?

We are shaped by the wonderful architecture which creates a safe haven within its Cambridge-like quads, by the vast dining hall, atmospheric Chapel and beautiful rooms.

We are shaped by our expansive site and make full use of our 160 acres, particularly for outdoor activities and sport, from cross country running and CCF field exercises to golf practice and Ross-hockey on the beach. Our ponds, trees, marsh, grassland and dunes also provide unending scope for outdoor learning and discovery.

But above all, we are shaped by the great people, both staff and students, who live and work at Rossall. There is an indelible Rossall spirit that is cultivated here – warmth, courage, humour, empathy, resilience, curiosity and the ability to talk to anyone are some of its most prominent features! It is a compelling mix.

Our teachers provide a brilliant balance of inspiration, care and deep subject knowledge to fire the imagination and ensure that our students have all the building blocks they need for success, not only at school and not only in the classroom, but also later on in life. We are proud of our students' academic achievements and delighted that they achieve consistently above national and world averages in their examinations.

We deliver a broad and balanced curriculum with the principles of the International Baccalaureate learner profile at its heart. In the Nursery, we follow the Early Years Foundation Stage (EYFS) learning goals. From the age of 0 to 11, we offer a bespoke curriculum. At age 16, students sit GCSE and iGCSE examinations, then students choose between the IB or A Level route in the Sixth Form.

With nearly forty different nationalities living and learning together at Rossall, we truly are a global village.

The combination of UK day students and students from right across the world creates an exciting international dimension and an appreciation of diverse culture, religions and politics.

Whether joining Rossall as a day or boarding pupil, you will be coming to a vibrant and happy community. All the basic needs are catered for, but in a most generous way – food is plentiful and delicious, we have an on-site Medical Centre, our houses are beautifully appointed and our houseparents and tutors are amazing – adept, knowledgeable and attuned to the needs of the young people in their care.

To come and experience the School first hand, you can arrange a private tour to fit in with your commitments.

Scholarships: To enable a wide range of children to join Rossall, we offer a number of scholarships each year. We offer academic, music, drama and sports scholarships to children in Years 7, 9 and 12.

EXPANDING HORIZONS

(Founded 1844)

Broadway, Fleetwood, Lancashire FY7 8JW UK

Tel: +44 (0)1253 774201

Email: admissions@rossall.org.uk

Website: www.rossall.org.uk

Head: Mr Jeremy Quartermain

Appointed: August 2018

School type: Co-educational Boarding & Day

Religious Denomination:
Church of England but accept all religions

Age range of pupils: 0–18

No. of pupils enrolled as at 01/09/2020: 665

Boys: 347 **Girls:** 318 **Sixth Form:** 170

No. of boarders: 245

Fees per annum as at 01/09/2020:

Day: £8,445–£13,740

Full Boarding: £21,645–£39,210

Average class size: 16

Teacher/pupil ratio: 1:11

South-East

Bethany School

Set on a 60 acre rural campus in the beautiful Kent countryside, Bethany School is a flourishing co-educational day, full and weekly boarding School that provides a welcoming and caring environment for pupils between the ages of 11 and 18.

Bethany enjoys an excellent reputation as a particularly friendly and happy community. It is a strong, thriving School with an enviable building programme, including recent and regular upgrading of boarding School facilities; a fantastic six lane 25 metre indoor swimming pool, state-of-the-art fitness suite, a sixth form centre with excellent facilities and an expansive outdoor high ropes course.

Location
Situated in Kent, known as the 'Garden of England', Bethany has an idyllic location with easy accessibility. London is less than an hour by train, Gatwick Airport one hour by taxi and Heathrow an hour and a half. The Eurostar terminal at Ashford International is just 30 minutes away.

The very best academic education
As a mainstream School, Bethany prides itself on nurturing academic excellence while catering for pupils with a broad range of abilities. The School offers a wide variety of subjects in modern classrooms with specialist facilities, including a Science Centre with modern laboratories.

The entire campus is served by a wireless network and all pupils have their own laptop. Much of the curriculum is delivered through ICT and pupils gain important digital skills. Almost all of our sixth formers progress on to university courses, leaving Bethany with a mature, self-confident sense of purpose.

CReSTeD registered since 1994, Bethany's Learning Support department enjoys an international reputation for its success in giving specialist help to dyslexic pupils within the mainstream curriculum. In addition, for those pupils who require it, we offer support for English as an Additional Language.

Boarding life and overseas pupils
Our boarding community brings great diversity to Bethany. We are a small School and yet we have boarders coming from over 20 different countries, enriching our education with a variety of experiences and backgrounds.

We aim to inspire individual excellence in every pupil and this approach underlies everything we do at Bethany. Its success is evidenced by the excellent transition from School to university made by our pupils each year. Sixth form boarders benefit from single bedrooms with en suite bathrooms, all with easy access to kitchens and laundry rooms. This experience, combined with our Body for Life programme, is designed to be a stepping stone to life at university, all within the supportive environment of the School.

Due to Covid-19 we have decided to reduce full boarding fees to reflect weekly boarding fee levels thus enabling more weekly boarders to become full boarders.

Outside the classroom
At Bethany, we believe that pursuits outside the classroom are very important in developing pupils' personalities. Everyone takes part in sport at least three times a week, and chooses from a huge array of extra-curricular activities including horse riding, chef school, golf, fishing, clay pigeon shooting, archery, orchestra and country pursuits. The Duke of Edinburgh's Award is hugely popular and very successful at Bethany.

The Headmaster firmly believes that School should be enjoyed rather than endured and it is the positive and nurturing atmosphere and the level of focus given to each individual pupil, that helps makes Bethany 'refreshingly different'.

Bethany since 1866

(Founded 1866)

Curtisden Green, Goudhurst, Cranbrook, Kent TN17 1LB UK

Tel: 01580 211273

Email: registrar@bethanyschool.org.uk

Website: www.bethanyschool.org.uk

Headmaster: Mr Francie Healy BSc, HDipEd, NPQH

Appointed: 2010

School type: Co-educational Boarding & Day

Age range of pupils: 11–18 years

No. of pupils enrolled as at 01/09/2020: 352

Boys: 248 **Girls:** 104 **Sixth Form:** 86

No. of boarders: 89

Fees per annum as at 01/09/2020:

Day: £17,310–£19,110

Weekly Boarding: £26,865–£29,670

Full Boarding: £26,865–£29,670

Average class size: 15-17

Teacher/pupil ratio: 1:8

Burgess Hill Girls

"The community at Burgess Hill Girls is very special. The way we bond with our teachers is not something you come across every day. I feel very lucky to be a part of this school."

Laura, Year 10, Burgess Hill Girls

A transformative education

Burgess Hill Girls is an Excellent rated independent school in Sussex for girls aged 2 to 18 years of age.

Whatever the stage at which your daughter joins Burgess Hill Girls you can be confident of two things: that she will be known for who she is as an individual and she will be provided with an outstanding, transformative education of the whole person.

I am, I can, I should, I will

Our school motto, 'I am, I can, I should, I will', conveys and underpins our whole approach, identifying and realising the potential of your daughter as she proceeds, giving her the very best possible opportunities to become a successful women of the future.

As parents, success will be having a happy and healthy daughter who loves going to school, loves to learn, loves participating, and is able to make friends for life. For the girls, success may be doing well in lessons and tests, being part of a team, playing a musical instrument and having fun with friends.

At Burgess Hill Girls we pride ourselves on unlocking the academic talent that is found within our girls and strongly believe each individual will thrive in our high-achieving environment. Whilst Burgess Hill Girls aims to provide the very best opportunities for everyone to excel, we believe that success is more than obtaining the highest marks and grades. We recognise just as much all those fantastic qualities that are not materialistic or target driven. Success at our school is when we produce bright, confident and independent young women who have and will continue to achieve great things.

Perfectly located

Burgess Hill Girls stands in 14 acres of beautiful grounds within a conservation area close to Burgess Hill's town centre in the centre of Sussex. All aspects of the school are located on this one campus; Nursery, Pre-Prep & Prep, Senior, Sixth Form and Boarding Houses. The school is only a five minute walk from the railway station (on the London to Brighton line) and close to excellent road networks (10 miles from Brighton and only 20 miles from Gatwick); the school is easily accessible for local and international students. A flexible, daily minibus service is provided for girls across Sussex and beyond.

Visit Burgess Hill Girls

We would be very pleased to meet you, put a name to a face and show you round our school. Please get in touch to arrange a visit.

BURGESS HILL
—— GIRLS ——
Tomorrow's Women

(Founded 1906)

Keymer Road, Burgess Hill, West Sussex RH15 0EG UK

Tel: 01444 241050

Email: admissions@burgesshillgirls.com

Website: burgesshillgirls.com

Head of School: Liz Laybourn

Appointed: 2017

School type: Girls' Day & Boarding

Religious Denomination: Interdenominational

Age range of boys: 2½–4

Age range of girls: 2½–18

No. of pupils enrolled as at 01/09/2020: 505

Boys: 29 **Girls:** 476 **Sixth Form:** 70

No. of boarders: 50

Fees per annum as at 01/09/2020:

Day: £8,100–£20,100

Full Boarding: £31,050–£35,850

Average class size: Max 20

Teacher/pupil ratio: 1:11

Churcher's College

Churcher's College is an Independent day school for boys and girls from 3-18 years of age offering Nursery, Junior, Senior and Sixth Form education. With around 950 pupils in the Senior School and 235 pupils in the Junior School (excluding the Nursery) of approximately equal numbers of boys and girls, Churcher's College enjoys recognition as one of the most accomplished independent, co-educational day schools in the country.

Location

The school is hosted on two campus sites in Hampshire enabling the Junior School and Nursery pupils to flourish in their own beautiful grounds in Liphook, whilst maintaining close links to the Senior School and Sixth Form located in nearby Petersfield. Both sites offer on-site playing fields and unrivalled facilities, providing the comfort and opportunities of an open, green environment.

Limitless Potential

We seek to give the widest range of experiences and the opportunity to excel. The children at Churcher's College thrive in an atmosphere of high expectation but even higher achievement in a happy, well-disciplined and caring environment.

Excellent examination results are clearly important; the achievement of these forms a core element in a child's time here. Equally, the development of self-esteem, moral values and leadership are vitally important parts of a child's education.

By developing the full academic, creative and sporting talents of the girls and boys, within the context of social awareness, our aim is to fully prepare them for all they will face in the dynamic and challenging world in which we live.

The pupils of Churcher's College become confident, responsible, respected and selfless citizens in a world which will require gifted, flexible young people of character, dedication and compassion.

An inclusive school

Churcher's is an inclusive school where parents, children, staff and friends all contribute to the rich and broad education provided.

"My son describes the Junior School as the best time ever, and it gave him such great foundations from which he has sprung and grown." Parent

"We love all the variety, there really is something for everyone. It really is a place for both my son and daughter to find their niche and fly." Parent

"I am given the perfect balance of independence and responsibility paired with the support of the Sixth Form teachers." Student

"Pupils personal development is excellent. The pastoral systems provide a secure base where pupils can feel confident and can flourish." ISI Inspection

"The extra-curricular provision is excellent." ISI Inspection

"Teachers have a strong knowledge which they present enthusiastically to their pupils; this acts as a stimulus for increasingly sophisticated thinking." ISI Inspection

Come and see for yourself

You are warmly invited to come and explore our school to find out more. Open events are held throughout the year, simply visit the website or contact the Admissions Team for more details. We look forward to meeting you soon.

For more information, please contact our Admissions Team on 01730 236825 or admissions@churcherscollege.com.

CHURCHER'S COLLEGE
NURSERY·JUNIOR·SENIOR & SIXTH FORM

(Founded 1722)

Petersfield, Hampshire GU31 4AS UK

Tel: 01730 263033

Email: admissions@churcherscollege.com

Website: www.ChurchersCollege.com

Headmaster: Mr Simon Williams MA, BSc

Appointed: September 2004

School type: Coeducational Independent Day

Age range of pupils: 3–18 years

No. of pupils enrolled as at 01/09/2020:

Senior School: 950

Junior School: 235

Fees per annum as at 01/09/2020:

Day: £10,320–£16,035

Average class size: 22

Teacher/pupil ratio: 1:12

Claremont Fan Court School

The world has changed, and Claremont Fan Court has changed with it. We are growing both in size and reputation – pupil recruitment is up 55% in the last two years to date – despite the pandemic. We continued to deliver excellence during lockdown through a full, live virtual learning experience, and will continue to build on what we've learnt, whatever the future holds.

The pandemic has actually allowed us to demonstrate our core value and motto to 'Be Strong in Understanding'. It's embedded in our culture, a way of teaching and learning that sets us apart from other schools, not just an inherited phrase from our long and varied history.

We believe that when pupils truly understand both themselves and the world around them, they can achieve what perhaps seemed impossible. If a pupil says 'I can't do it', Claremont will add a 'yet' to the end of that statement. This critical positive thinking creates a robust strength of character to take them through into the adult world, and embracing all the challenges that come with it.

So when we took our entire teaching experience online to ensure all of our pupils continued to learn and be supported throughout lockdown, both our staff and pupils dived willingly into the unknown. They knew the experience might be challenging. They just hadn't mastered it. Yet.

That's because at Claremont, there is a space for every kind of individual to find their niche and thrive within it. We invest in pupils' character, so they can unlock potential they didn't even know they had and explore subjects, sports and activities they'd never tried before. Both staff and pupils flourish in an atmosphere of respect, courtesy, love of learning and the value of friendship held dear at our school.

In practice, our teaching philosophy links academic rigour with a character education. Each month we focus on a different character quality, such as confidence, courage or responsibility, and incorporate it into everything from assemblies, discussions, activities and curriculum work. The academic programme then ensures that pupils attain the highest qualifications of which they are capable. The pastoral curriculum includes three weekly assemblies, discussing the importance of contributing positively to school and home life, and weekly PSHE lessons. Behavioural standards are high and pupils develop and value respect for peers, teachers, the school and greater society.

We do all of this within 100 acres of stunning, historic landscaped grounds to offer a wide range of fully co-ed sports, a brand-new science and technology building with outstanding facilities and a broad curriculum of arts, alongside over 60 co-curricular activities with everything from dissection, dragon's den, yoga and Lego clubs.

To see what being strong in understanding could mean for your child, please visit our website to access our virtual tours, or sign up for one of our regular open events.

(Founded 1922)

Claremont Drive, Esher, Surrey KT10 9LY UK

Tel: 01372 473780

Email: admissionsandmarketing@claremont.surrey.sch.uk

Website: www.claremontfancourt.co.uk

Head: Mr William Brierly

Appointed: September 2018

School type: Coeducational Day

Religious Denomination: Non-Denominational

Age range of pupils: 2½–18

No. of pupils enrolled as at 01/09/2020: 890

Fees per term as at 01/09/2020:

Day:
£790 (Pre-Nursery)–£6,125 (Year 9 and above) per term

Average class size: 15

Teacher/pupil ratio: 1:10

Cranleigh School

Cranleigh is Surrey's leading co-educational independent school offering both day and boarding education for children aged 7-18, enabling siblings to be educated together.

Set on adjacent hills, the Preparatory School and the Senior School enjoy a spectacular 280-acre rural setting on the Surrey/West Sussex border, by the Surrey Hills, an Area of Outstanding Natural Beauty; yet they are conveniently situated close to the mainline city of Guildford, roughly equidistant between Gatwick and Heathrow, and only an hour's drive from London, where Cranleigh pupils regularly visit professional exhibitions and performances.

Both the Prep and the Senior Schools are proud of their excellent academic track records, culminating in outstanding performances at Common Entrance, GCSE and A-level. 99% of pupils go on to Higher Education, and Cranleigh also has a consistently strong Oxbridge contingent.

Such academic excellence does not come at the expense of co-curricular success at Cranleigh and the Schools currently boast national and county level representatives in a wide range of sports, including cricket, riding, hockey, rugby and swimming.

Pupil participation in sport, music and drama is actively encouraged at all levels; most Saturdays see every pupil playing sport for the school. More than 10 dramatic productions each academic year provide acting opportunities for all and the hugely popular Technical Theatre encourages the development of backstage skills.

Around 40 per cent of pupils play at least one musical instrument. Many take the opportunity to perform in more than 30 concerts a year, with over 10 musical groups, including symphony orchestra, wind band, chapel choir, big band, strings, trios, quartets and several other choirs.

The Schools offer outstanding facilities alongside new academic blocks. Sports facilities enjoyed by both the Prep and the Senior School include a double-sized indoor sports centre, four artificial playing surfaces, full equestrian centre, two expansive hard court areas for netball and tennis, a generous array of rugby and cricket pitches, a three-par, nine-hole golf course and an indoor pool. Equally outstanding sports staff includes former England players, an England national coach and an Olympic Gold Medallist (Hockey).

The Schools also boast professional-standard theatre facilities, rehearsal rooms, beautiful art studio spaces and a modern design centre fully equipped with 3D printers. The students have the opportunity to showcase their work in professional exhibitions several times a year.

Most importantly, Cranleigh prides itself on providing a happy, nurturing environment, founded upon an extremely supportive pastoral system (every pupil has their own tutor) and a high staff to pupil ratio, underscored by an invariably passionate house spirit. In such an environment, pupils can flourish into the well-rounded, self-motivated and confident individuals Cranleighans are famed for becoming, well prepared for life after school and invariably blessed with a circle of lifelong friends.

Pupils enter Cranleigh following a process of holistic review, at the main entry points of 13 and 16, and in other years where places are available. Regular Welcome Mornings are held and a wide range of academic and non-academic Scholarships are available.

CRANLEIGH
EX CULTU ROBUR

(Founded 1865)

Horseshoe Lane, Cranleigh, Surrey GU6 8QQ UK

Tel: +44 (0) 1483 273666

Fax: +44 (0) 1483 267398

Email: admissions@cranleigh.org

Website: www.cranleigh.org

Headmaster: Mr Martin Reader MA, MPhil, MBA

Appointed: September 2014

School type: Co-educational Boarding & Day

Age range of pupils: 7–18 (including Prep School)

No. of pupils enrolled as at 01/09/2020: 690

Boys: 406 **Girls:** 284 **Sixth Form:** 252

No. of boarders: 491

Fees per annum as at 01/09/2020:

Day: £32,370

Full Boarding: £39,330

Average class size: 20 (9 in Sixth Form)

Teacher/pupil ratio: 1:7

Eagle House School

Eagle House is a coeducational, boarding and day Prep, Pre-Prep and Nursery located in Berkshire and only 50 minutes from London, that celebrated its 200th anniversary in 2020. The school's superb grounds and excellent facilities are the background to an experience where success, confidence and happiness are paramount. The school is proud of its academic record, preparing children for a host of top independent schools and boasting a diverse and robust curriculum.

Younger pupils follow the International Primary Curriculum and our older children have embarked on a new 'Curriculum 200', specially created for Years 5 to 8 that links subjects through topics and themes. Great teaching, new technology and a focus on the basics mean that children make good progress and love to be in the classroom. Independent learning is a focus for all children and our Extended Project programme helps drive inquisitive minds.

We unashamedly offer lots as part of our Golden Eagle activities experience. Children benefit from a huge range of opportunities in sport, music, drama, art, outward bound and community programmes. Busy children are happy and fulfilled children and we like to think that all pupils are Learning for Life.

Learning for Life means that children benefit from the best all-round education. They can feel confident in the classroom, on the games field, on stage, in the concert hall and in the community. Everyone is given the chance to stretch themselves in every area. Challenge is an important part of growing up and at Eagle House we learn that success and failure are both positive experiences.

Bright learning environments, outdoor learning areas and wonderful sporting facilities are important, but it is the community that shapes a young person. Through the excellent pastoral care and tutor system, coupled with a buddy structure, ensuring children have an older pupil to support them, Eagle House seeks to develop wellbeing from the youngest to the oldest.

Recognising how to be a positive influence within a community is also part of the Eagle House journey. Our wonderful Learning for Life programme teaches children about themselves and the wider community. Through community service we aim to make all our pupils responsible and independent as well as able to show empathy and understanding towards others. Time for reflection in chapel and assemblies also improves the way we look at the world and mindfulness sessions help us all take stock.

Boarding is a popular option and allows children to experience a varied evening programme of activities as well as being part of a vibrant and caring community. Boarding encourages independence but it is also great fun and whether full, weekly or flexi, boarders have the most wonderful time.

We often say that Eagle House children have the time of their lives and we firmly believe this. Learning for Life at Eagle House opens the doors to all sorts of opportunities and this results in children who are highly motivated and enthusiastic in all they do.

Eagle House buzzes with achievement and laughter – not a bad way to grow up!

Eagle House is a registered charity (No 309093) for the furtherance of education.

(Founded 1820)

Sandhurst, Berkshire GU47 8PH UK

Tel: 01344 772134

Email: info@eaglehouseschool.com

Website: www.eaglehouseschool.com

Headmaster: Mr A P N Barnard BA(Hons), PGCE

Appointed: September 2006

School type: Coeducational Day & Boarding

Age range of pupils: 3–13

No. of pupils enrolled as at 01/09/2020: 380

Boys: 207 *Girls:* 173

No. of boarders: 50

Fees per annum as at 01/09/2020:

Day: £12,030–£18,810

Full Boarding: £25,275

Average class size: 16

Teacher/pupil ratio: 1:8

Gordon's School

Gordon's – The Most Unique School in England

Built by public subscription over a century ago at the insistence of Queen Victoria, Gordon's School is the national monument to General Charles Gordon of Khartoum and is listed as one of Britain's outstanding schools by Her Majesty's Chief Inspector.

A non-selective, co-educational residential and day boarding school, the School's academic record outstrips many selective schools. The progress made by students over the past three years has put Gordon's in the top one per cent of schools in England and Wales for progress at A Level.

But while Gordon's School embraces modern ideas, General Gordon's legacy of traditional values remains. The School's ethos is that high performance without good character is not true success.

To this end, it's not just in the classrooms where students excel. Successes are achieved in drama and the arts; debating and public speaking; dance and sport. The School also boasts an enviable record in attaining Duke of Edinburgh awards.

While the individual is celebrated, the whole School unites for parades. Since its inception, students have marched and there has always been a Pipes and Drums band. Dressed in their Blues uniform, the students parade around eight times a year and the School is the only one permitted to march along Whitehall – an annual tradition in remembrance of General Gordon.

Set in over 50 acres of beautiful Surrey countryside within easy access of major airports and roads, the School is home to some 900 students and offers Day and Residential (weekly and termly) Boarding.

Each Student is assigned to one of the ten Houses – four residential boarding and six day boarding. Recently opened has been a dedicated Year 7 Residential Boarding House for our youngest students. Inter-House competitions are fiercely contested.

Spiritual guidance and support is given through chapel services and informal worship. And House Parents provide a 'home from home', lending special atmosphere to each Boarding House and ensuring that free time off for students is fun, with numerous activities.

There are three main admission points – at 11 years old; 13 years old and for Sixth Form.

Scholarships are offered for those coming into the Sixth Form. The scholarships enable those awarded to benefit from a programme to enhance their development and give them wider opportunities to progress in their field. Bursaries are also available.

The real judgement of Gordon's is the students. All who visit are struck by the friendliness, discipline and vibrancy throughout the school and by the family atmosphere, exemplified by the special rapport between staff and students. This is borne from a community that strives to live with integrity, to be courteous, enthusiastic and diligent, even in adversity.

Gordon's School is unique. Please book a visit and find out why.

(Founded 1885)

West End, Woking, Surrey GU24 9PT UK

Tel: 01276 858084

Fax: 01276 855335

Email: registrar@gordons.school

Website: www.gordons.school

Head Teacher: Andrew Moss MEd

Appointed: September 2010

School type: Co-educational Day & Boarding

Age range of pupils: 11–18

No. of pupils enrolled as at 01/09/2020: 959

Boys: 503 *Girls:* 389 *Sixth Form:* 350

Fees per annum as at 01/09/2020 (provisional):

Day: £8,209

Weekly Boarding: £17,295

Full Boarding: £18,459

Average class size: 22

Teacher/pupil ratio: 1:12

Hampton Court House

Hampton Court House is an independent, co-educational day school in South West London. The school was founded in 2001 and offers places for children from the age of 3 to 18 years old. The school is situated in its own private parkland and is 35 minutes from Central London.

Hampton Court House pupils are truly made to feel a part of the school. They offer their own ideas and opinions and many school activities are pupil-led.

Pupils as young as 3 years of age have a weekly ballet lesson with a Royal Academy of Dance Ballet teacher as well as Forest School lessons in the grounds or in neighbouring Bushy Park with a qualified Forest School teacher.

The school follows the National Curriculum, the teaching staff are subject specialists who teach year groups across the school. In addition to the many subjects taught at Hampton Court House, languages such as French, Latin, Spanish and Mandarin are highly valued. Pupils have daily French lessons in the early years of the school and in Years 1 to 4 they are taught in a French/English immersion programme. Latin and Mandarin are introduced to pupils from Year 5, Spanish is also introduced in Year 9, giving pupils a breadth of languages to study in GCSE and A level years.

Students are encouraged to take part in co-curricular activities, clubs, and school trips. Many of the pupils are involved in charitable fundraising including a recent sponsored run for a Syrian refugee camp in France. In addition to sports on the timetable for all pupils from Pre-Nursery to Year 11 the pupils can take part in lunchtime and after school clubs and activities. The sports programme at Hampton Court House is tailor-made for its size and location with sports such as rowing, athletics and Olympic lifting offered to all pupils from Year 7 upwards.

Hampton Court House promotes an active engagement in media and current affairs, believing that it is important to have an opinion on the events and decisions which shape our world. A sense of humour and an understanding of the opinions and feelings of others encourages pupils to feel supported and nurtured. Every member of Hampton Court House strives to be honest, considerate, compassionate and generous.

Hampton Court House is a school which places an emphasis on kindness and values but also encourages pupils to strive for academic excellence. The trend of ever improving GCSE results has continued with a higher proportion than ever before getting A grades or equivalent. 78% of the GCSE results were 7, 8 or 9 on the new scale (where 7 is an A) and 46% were 8 or 9 (A*). Nationally, only 20.6% of grades were 7 or better and only 11.4% were 8 or 9.

In recent years Hampton Court House has been recognised by UNESCO for their commitment to transcending cultural boundaries. The school has received two TES Independent School nominations, two Good Schools Guide Awards, and a Computing in Schools: Network of Excellence award.

If you would like to find out more about Hampton Court House contact the school on: 020 8614 0857; alternatively visit www.hamptoncourthouse.co.uk.

HAMPTON COURT HOUSE
FORTITER IN RE SUAVITER IN MODO

(Founded 2000)

Hampton Court Road, East Molesey, Surrey KT8 9BS UK

Tel: 020 8614 0857

Fax: 020 8977 5357

Email: admissions@hchnet.co.uk

Website: www.hamptoncourthouse.co.uk

Headmaster: Mr Guy Holloway

Appointed: 2013

School type: Coeducational Day

Age range of pupils: 3–18

Average class size: Approx 20

Teacher/pupil ratio: 1:10

Kent College, Canterbury

Kent College is an outstanding day and boarding school that celebrates both its 130 years of history and tradition, and its forward-looking, innovative approach to education. It has a reputation as a friendly school, and is most definitely a place where teachers really get to know the pupils, with the time and space to give individual attention, both academically and pastorally. Music, drama and sport all play central roles in the life of the School, and many pupils also enjoy the opportunities provided by the School's Farm and Riding Centre.

Part of the Methodist Schools group, Kent College is deeply rooted in the Methodist tradition that welcomes all pupils of every faith and none. 'Do all the good you can do' is a guiding principle, and one that allows pupils to develop into confident young adults, aware of their responsibilities and their place in the world.

Location

The School's location, on the outskirts of the historic city of Canterbury, provides a safe, healthy and beautiful environment for pupils to grow up. The School sits in 80 acres (32 hectares) of land with extensive sports fields, as well as the Farm and Riding Centre. Yet the centre of Canterbury, with its wide selection of shops, restaurants, theatres, cinemas and world-heritage site, within which sits Canterbury Cathedral, is only a 5-minute journey by car. A high-speed train service links Canterbury to London, and the School is within 100 minutes of Gatwick, Heathrow, Stansted and City of London airports.

Boarding

Kent College has a long history of welcoming boarding pupils from abroad, as well as from British families resident in the UK or working overseas. Boarders make up around one third of pupils, and there are over 40 countries represented in the boarding community. The five friendly and comfortable Senior boarding houses truly become a 'home away from home'. The School also offers weekly and occasional boarding.

Sporting success

Kent College teams make formidable competitors in any sport. Hockey is a particular strength, with national titles won every year. Regular representation by our pupils in county, regional and national squads is encouraged and enhanced by the School's scholarship programme.

Beyond the classroom

The performing arts are a particular strength at Kent College, with an impressive line-up of vocal and instrumental ensembles, and many opportunities to perform for all ages and abilities. An exciting new development is the construction of the Great Hall, a state-of-the-art 600-seat auditorium, due to open in Summer 2019. In sport, the aim is to provide something for every pupil, from recreational sport and promoting fitness to top-level coaching for our elite players. Hockey and cricket are particular strengths, with regular representation by Kent College pupils in county and national squads. There is also a wide-ranging list of activities and clubs, on offer for all pupils, including a full Duke of Edinburgh programme, and the opportunity to work on the School Farm.

KENT COLLEGE
CANTERBURY

(Founded 1885)

Whitstable Road, Canterbury, Kent CT2 9DT UK

Tel: +44 (0)1227 763 231

Email: admissions@kentcollege.co.uk

Website: www.kentcollege.com

Senior School Head: Dr David Lamper

Junior School Head: Mr Simon James

School type: Coeducational Day & Boarding

Religious Denomination: Methodist

Age range of pupils: 0–18 years (Boarding from 8)

No. of pupils enrolled as at 01/09/2020: 770

No. of boarders: 205

Fees per term as at 01/09/2020:

Day: £5,598–£6,288 per term

Full Boarding: £8,748–£11,867 per term

Average class size: 15, max 18

King Edward VI School

King Edward VI School, Southampton, has been at the heart of the city for over 460 years and is one of the UK's leading independent 11-18 co-educational day schools.

With a reputation for academic excellence, the School boasts a thriving Sixth Form that produces consistently excellent A Level examination results ensuring students continue on to a range of competitive institutions, most to one of the UK's top 25 universities and, on average, approximately 10% of students proceed to Oxford or Cambridge. Results at GCSE and IGCSE are equally outstanding.

Outside of the academic, King Edward's also aims to foster a sense of personal worth in every pupil through a wide range of co-curricular activities, particularly with an active engagement in community work, so that every individual emerges as a fully responsible member of society. In the last year alone the student Charities Commission has raised over £27,000 for local and national charitable causes.

Each year students can be found taking part in excursions to worldwide destinations. The most recent co-curricular trips have included a technology trip to Tokyo, a biology field trip to Ecuador and the Galapagos Islands, a cultural exchange with a school in North Carolina, and a trekking expedition in Vietnam. Language students regularly participate in the exchange programmes on offer to Germany, France and Spain as well as in cultural visits to schools in the USA and Prague. Closer to home the School also organises an annual summer camp to Swanage for local young carers, run by our Sixth Formers.

Sport and the arts are an integral part of school life. Students are given the opportunity to represent the School across the major team games as well as individual sports. Overseas tours, regular fixtures, tournaments and school events offer a competitive sporting environment and King Edward's boasts 33 acres of sports ground, a fully equipped gym and multiple all weather pitches. The Creative Arts Faculty offers an amazing array of facilities from recital rooms, a recording studio and music technology suite to a custom-built dance studio. The state-of-the-art Dobson Theatre has a capacity for 400 seats and provides a superb venue for our talented dramatists and musicians. An array of public performances throughout the year allow King Edward's performers to showcase their talents, whatever their ability level.

Students are actively encouraged to become involved in fund-raising and community work and take part in some of the 150 clubs and societies that are available outside of lesson time. King Edward's also runs a well-established Duke of Edinburgh's Award Scheme that makes use of the school's Rural Studies Centre in Dartmoor.

King Edward's strives to ensure that all pupils reach and fulfil their full potential. A happy atmosphere amongst first-class teaching facilities provide exceptional academic stimulus alongside an extraordinary breadth of co-curricular opportunities. Seventeen bus routes extend throughout south Hampshire, allowing students from the New Forest, Salisbury, Winchester and east of Southampton easy and direct access to the School.

Founded 1553

(Founded 1553)

Wilton Road, Southampton, Hampshire SO15 5UQ UK

Tel: 023 8070 4561

Fax: 023 8070 5937

Email: registrar@kes.hants.sch.uk

Website: www.kes.hants.sch.uk

Head Master: Mr N T Parker

Appointed: August 2019

School type: Coeducational Day

Age range of pupils: 11–18

No. of pupils enrolled as at 01/09/2020: 961

Fees per annum as at 01/09/2020:

Day: £17,130

Average class size: 22

Teacher/pupil ratio: 1:10

Maltman's Green School

Our Approach

At Maltman's Green we believe in the pursuit of excellence with a sense of fun. Girls are inspired to do their best inside and outside of the classroom through an exceptional academic curriculum and extensive extra-curricular opportunities. We prepare girls for the modern world through a relevant, adaptable and innovative approach that is supported by a foundation of traditional values. Our girls are given every opportunity to succeed across multiple disciplines, fostering confidence and self-belief, and empowering them for whatever future awaits.

We believe that the emotional, social and physical wellbeing of our girls is paramount. By providing a personalised learning experience in an encouraging and nurturing environment, we ensure our girls feel happy, confident and valued – a perfect foundation from which children can flourish. This ethos has been recognised by the ISI who applauded our "outstanding" pastoral care.

Games and The Arts

Our sports provision is an outstanding feature of the School, with dedicated facilities and daily lessons. All girls enjoy friendly tournaments between houses and within year groups where those with the talent and inclination can progress to squad level to compete locally, regionally or nationally, usually with exceptional results.

Music is a very important part of life at Maltman's Green. Specialist teaching, exceptional facilities and lots of choice give our girls plenty of opportunity to explore and showcase their musical talents. Over 100 girls participate in our various choirs and we have nine different musical instrument lessons available as well as a variety of instrumental ensemble groups to join. Drama too has a big part to play in school life where regular performances and workshops give girls a strong sense of confidence and creative expression. Our dedicated performance space with high-quality staging, lighting, costumes and props give our shows a professional feel.

Achievements

Our girls are encouraged to be independent thinkers, to challenge themselves and to always try their best. Maltman's Green provides a firm foundation, preparing girls to face senior school and beyond with confidence, determination and a lifelong love of learning. This is reflected in our impressive 11+ results and a record number of scholarships awarded to Independent Senior Schools. This, combined with our girls' impressive achievements across sport, music and drama, affirm our position as one of the foremost prep schools in the country.

Outstanding Characteristics

2018 marked our 100th Anniversary and, since the School was founded in 1918, we have seen numerous developments and upgrades to our facilities, including dedicated subject classrooms, a 6-lane, 25-metre indoor swimming pool, an IT suite, a multi-use gymnasium, a state-of-the art theatre space and a dedicated 2-3yr olds day-care centre. We place great importance on outdoor learning and our woodland school, discovery garden and landscaped grounds offer a secluded, peaceful and nurturing environment. This excellent suite of facilities is complemented by our highly committed, well-qualified and experienced body of staff who enable us to provide an outstanding and unique breadth of challenge and opportunity for our girls.

MALTMAN'S GREEN
SCHOOL

(Founded 1918)

Maltmans Lane, Gerrards Cross, Buckinghamshire SL9 8RR UK

Tel: 01753 883022

Email: registrar@maltmansgreen.com

Website: www.maltmansgreen.com

Headmistress: Mrs Jill Walker BSc (Hons), MA Ed, PGCE

Appointed: 2020

School type: Girls' Day

Age range of girls: 2–11

No. of pupils enrolled as at 01/09/2020: 355

Fees per term as at 01/09/2020:

Day: £1,925–£5,275 per term

Manor House School, Bookham

Founded in 1920 and celebrating its' Centenary Year in 2020-2021, Manor House School can be found nestled amidst seventeen acres of gardens, woodland and sports fields in the village of Bookham, Surrey.

Manor House School is a member of the GSA (Girls' Schools Association) and, as a community of approximately 300 girls, offers a smaller, nurturing learning environment producing consistently great academic results in a happy, friendly and caring school environment. An individual approach to teaching and learning enables each pupil at the School to achieve their personal best, both academically and personally. The School aims to develop happy young women who love coming to school and believe in their abilities to learn and succeed.

There is an extensive co-curricular enrichment programme with up to 50 extra-curricular clubs and activities operating across the school each term. Girls are encouraged to seek out new experiences and try something new. Manor House achieves excellent Key Stage 2 and GCSE results. For more information on their latest results, please visit www.manorhouseschool.org/academic-results/gcseresults.

Seven school values form the foundations of school life and the school motto 'To Love is to Live' was chosen in 1921 by the Bishop of Plymouth. Dr. Masterman, who was a close friend of one of the school's original founders.

Manor House girls enjoy high levels of success in all areas of Sport boasting some future world class soccer players, cyclists, triathletes and tennis stars in its midst. There is a popular Senior Scholarships Programme from Year 7 (application in Year 6) offering Major and Minor Academic Scholarships at up to 50% and 40% of the basic annual tuition fee and up to 10% for an Art, Drama or Music award. Additionally, two Year 3 scholarships, including an Academic and a Performing Arts award are available.

Facilities include an award-winning Nursery, Forest School, indoor sports hall which transforms into a seated theatre space for professional productions, outdoor swimming pool, a Tennis Academy, tennis and netball courts and purpose-built science blocks. Girls enjoy many opportunities in the creative and expressive arts, with additional music, singing and drama lessons a popular choice. The School was shortlisted for an Independent Schools Award in 2019.

The School day operates from 7.45am to 6pm to accommodate working and/or busy parents. Fees include a daily hot lunch and there is a local minibus service in the mornings and afternoons and a late bus to Effingham train station which is serviced by good rail connections. The School bus routes service Ashtead, Dorking, Claygate, Cobham, Epsom, Esher, Fetcham, Hinchley Wood, Guildford, Kingswood, Walton-on-Thames, Weybridge, Wimbledon/Kingston, West Byfleet and surrounding areas.

For more information visit www.manorhouseschool.org. There are three main Open Morning events per year in October, February and May. For more information, contact: admissions@manorhouseschool.org.

MANOR HOUSE BOOKHAM EST.1920

(Founded 1920)

Manor House Lane, Little Bookham, Leatherhead, Surrey KT23 4EN UK

Tel: 01372 457077

Email: admin@manorhouseschool.org

Website: www.manorhouseschool.org

Headteacher: Ms Tracey Fantham BA (Hons) MA NPQH

School type:
Girls' Day School with Co-educational Nursery

Age range of boys: 2–4

Age range of girls: 2–16

No. of pupils enrolled as at 01/09/2020: 300

Fees per annum as at 01/09/2020:

Day: £9,555–£17,955

Average class size: 15-20

Northbourne Park School

Northbourne Park School is an independent day and boarding school for children from 2 to 13. Set in over 100 acres of beautiful park and woodland in rural Kent, the school is within easy reach from central London, Eurostar and Gatwick Airport. Northbourne Park School provides children with a first-class education focusing on the individual needs of every child, inspiring them to succeed across a wide range of learning experiences. Our setting offers each child a safe environment with freedom and space and countless opportunities to grow in confidence and succeed.

Academic

Northbourne Park School is an environment where each and every child can flourish. Pupils gain confidence in their learning and through inspirational teaching from dedicated staff and an engaging and stimulating curriculum, their results are phenomenal. We focus on individual needs and consistently achieve academic excellence, with many of our pupils gaining scholarships to top Senior Schools. The school's Language Programme helps every child develop foreign languages in an integrated learning environment. The result is a clear advantage when they move on to Senior Schools.

Sport

We are passionate about sport and through an excellent sports programme the pupils develop key skills and learn the importance of teamwork and leadership. We coach traditional sports as well as more diverse such as archery. The school has excellent facilities including a brand new all-weather sports pitch.

Creative Arts

We nurture a love for all the Arts. Many pupils learn one or more instruments in our purpose-built Music suite. They have the opportunity to take part in the choir, band, orchestra, string and brass groups performing regularly within the school and in the local area. Other opportunities include LAMDA lessons, regular drama productions and Public Speaking that ensure the pupils are articulate and confident in their performances. Artistic talents are encouraged through a range of media including sculpture, costume design, 3D printing and pottery.

Community

Pupils are provided with a first-class level of pastoral care in a safe and nurturing environment with a real family atmosphere. Our welcoming boarding community provides a home-from-home environment and a continuous boarding service at weekends throughout the term. Boarders enjoy regular excursions and activities, and the accompanied services to London and Paris provide opportunities for weekends at home. Northbourne Park School holds Tier 4 Status for non-European pupils requiring visas under the UK Visa and Immigration Service scheme.

Extra Curricular

We provide the pupils with a fun and extensive programme of afternoon clubs that help develop their interests and skills. Love of the outdoors and respect for the environment begins in the Pre-Prep and develops through into the Prep School with fun physical adventures. Whether they are playing in the woods, camping out overnight or following our Outdoor Education Programme, children love Northbourne Park life.

The children are at the heart of everything we do and it is important to us that they learn with confidence and enjoy each and every day at school. All prospective pupils are welcome and we offer a wide range of scholarships.

Every day is an Open Day at Northbourne Park School, come and visit us!

(Founded 1936)

Betteshanger, Deal, Kent CT14 0NW UK

Tel: 01304 611215/218

Fax: 01304 619020

Email: admissions@northbournepark.com

Website: www.northbournepark.com

Headmaster: Mr Sebastian Rees BA(Hons), PGCE, NPQH

Appointed: September 2015

School type: Coeducational Day & Boarding

Age range of pupils: 2–13

No. of pupils enrolled as at 01/09/2020: 185

Boys: 93 **Girls:** 92

No. of boarders: 43

Fees per annum as at 01/09/2020:

Day: £7,632–£17,007

Weekly Boarding: £21,405

Full Boarding: £24,786

Average class size: 15

Teacher/pupil ratio: 1:9

Parkside School

Whilst Parkside's rich history has its roots steeped in tradition, the boys (and girls in Nursery) enjoy a hugely diverse and exciting curriculum which embraces and prepares them for the future. The values and ethos of the School have remained strong and have come into their own in recent times. The outstanding standards of education and support already delivered to Parkside families were never compromised even the threat of a Global Pandemic. Indeed, during these most testing of times, the Spirit of Parkside was never more apparent.

In the summer of 2019, Nicole Janssen (the Head Teacher since January 2019) confirmed; *"It is a wonderful environment where the children's curiosity is awakened. Their journey is one of discovery; where talents and passions are nurtured and developed and our pupils are encouraged to take responsibility for their learning."*

A genuine pride for each and every pupil who attends Parkside is clear, and achievements are celebrated whether they are academic, creative, pastoral, sporting or based around the importance of etiquette, good manners and character building.

The Class of 2019, saw 41% of leavers achieving scholarship status for their senior school, with a 100% pass rate in their Common Entrance exams. This is a direct result of a unique and innovative curriculum delivered through the inspired teaching of a passionate and dedicated staff team; underpinned by the 'make it happen mantra led by the Head.

Being part of the 'Parkside Family' is a privilege, but not one which is taken for granted. The importance of recognising the wider community and world we live in, serves to teach valuable life lessons about appreciation and gratitude rather than entitlement. This, as a result, means that Parkside boys leave as well rounded, exceptional individuals with solid foundations and outstanding moral fibre.

Ms Janssen states *"(the children) develop the courage to rise to each challenge, persevere when the going gets tough and face their fears with confidence. We catch them when they fall and guide them back on their individual journey."*

Indeed, when the Covid 19 pandemic was declared, Parkside tackled remote learning head on and successfully supported their families through unchartered territory. The School delivered a slick, virtual delivery system for its innovative and engaging curriculum through the use of technology and innovation: the boys enjoyed 6 x 45 minute virtual classes a day (the same as they do when physically at school). Food Tech and Forest School ran alongside the core academic subjects. Individual learning packs were printed, collated (by class) and collected weekly by parents at the 'drive thru' collection point in front of the Manor, which offers an opportunity for families to plan and prepare for the week ahead.

The Nursery and Pre Prep children also enthusiastically participated in their reading sessions, music and dance sessions and 'teacher time' via Zoom. Progress and praise for work was established through ILDs (Individual Learning Diaries), which was filled with videos and photos of children enjoying their education, virtually.

The School remained very much open for business as 'unusual' for the whole school community; and it was an honour to provide continuity, humour, reassurance and calm for children living in a world where panic, grief and hardship are felt daily.

Parkside has been shortlisted for the Best Independent Boys' School in the 2020 Independent School of the Year Awards, which pays testament to the School's ethos, culture and dedication to its whole community.

PARKSIDE
SCHOOL

(Founded 1875)

The Manor, Stoke d'Abernon, Cobham, Surrey KT11 3PX UK

Tel: 01932 862749

Email: office@parkside-school.co.uk

Website: www.parkside-school.co.uk

Headteacher: Ms Nicole Janssen

Appointed: January 2019

School type: Boys' Day

Age range of boys: 2–13

Age range of girls: 2–4

No. of pupils enrolled as at 01/09/2020: 270

Fees per annum as at 01/09/2020: Please enquire

Average class size: 12-15

Seaford College

Seaford College is a coeducational independent day and boarding school for pupils aged 6 to 18, situated amid 400 acres of picturesque parkland in West Sussex. The College, with its excellent amenities and outstanding panoramic views, offers an inspirational environment that nurtures academic excellence, sporting success and creative talent.

The college uses its resources to provide and enhance educational, cultural, spiritual and social opportunities so that students leave school as confident, articulate and well-rounded individuals.

Pupils in the Preparatory School at Seaford College share the superb facilities with the Senior School and enjoy a seamless education from 6 to 18. The Prep School prides itself on its friendly atmosphere.

Boarding is offered to students from the age of 10 and many pupils elect to board in order to take full advantage of the social, sporting and extracurricular activities on offer. The College offers full boarding, weekly and flexible boarding in order to meet the needs of pupils and their parents.

A new boys' boarding house, has individual and twin bedrooms opened in 2011. Girls board in the historic Mansion house. Recent developments include a new music suite, which consists of individual teaching and practice rooms, a computer and keyboard room, a sound-proofed band practice room and outdoor concert arena.

A state-of-the-art maths and science block offers the latest technologies and facilities, while the College has long been recognised as a centre of excellence for art and design. A large exhibition gallery is incorporated into the purpose-built arts faculty.

Seaford College offers outstanding sports facilities, including an all-weather water-based Astroturf hockey pitch, golf course and driving range. Students regularly play at county level. A state-of-the-art sports centre was opened in 2017.

Overseas students are expected to study English as a foreign language and study for the International Language Testing System, which is a requirement for UK university entrance.

Seaford opened an impressive Sixth Form centre in September 2019. They have their own social areas, study areas and cafe. Seaford sees its Sixth Form very much as a transitional stage. They have their own social centre, which has facilities for individual study, a lounge area and several classrooms where subjects such as Economics, Business Studies and Media Studies are taught.

Sixth Form boarders have study bedrooms, as well as their own common room. Students are divided into small tutor groups, but most commonly meet on a 1-to-1 basis with their tutors to discuss aspects of their work and progress.

Many of Seaford's Sixth Formers go on to university or higher education – all are equipped with self-confidence, as well as a passion for life and a willingness to succeed.

Entry to the College is by test and Trial Day and, although intake is non-selective, expectations are high. If your child is talented and enthusiastic, the College offers a range of scholarships at 11+, 13+ and Sixth Form, including Academic Studies, Music, Art and Sport.

The college has its own dedicated learning support unit, catering for pupils with dyslexia, dyscalculia and dyspraxia.

Whatever their chosen path, Seaford College seeks to prepare young people for adult life so that they have the personal skills and confidence to make it a success. The school allows its pupils to achieve their potential and beyond, inspiring personal ambition and success so that personal ambitions are achieved inside and outside the classroom.

(Founded 1884)

Lavington Park, Petworth, West Sussex GU28 0NB UK

Tel: 01798 867392

Fax: 01798 867606

Email: headmasterpa@seaford.org

Website: www.seaford.org

Headmaster: J P Green MA BA

School type: Coeducational Boarding & Day

Age range of pupils: 6–18

No. of pupils enrolled as at 01/09/2020: 869

Boys: 527 *Girls:* 342 *Sixth Form:* 219

No. of boarders: 161

Fees per annum as at 01/09/2020:

Day: £10,725–£22,230

Weekly Boarding: £22,350–£30,120

Full Boarding: £34,380

Average class size: 15-20

Teacher/pupil ratio: 1:9

Sherfield School

Sherfield school is a leading co-educational independent day and boarding school for children from 3 months to 18 years. It offers an outstanding, all-round academic, active and creative environment where children of all ages have the opportunity to thrive and flourish as they experience the excitement and enjoyment of learning.

Set in 76 acres of idyllic parkland in Hampshire, the 12th Century manor house is at the heart of Sherfield school and boasts a wealth of history linked to the local community. Sherfield School lies nestled in beautiful countryside between Reading and Basingstoke. With good public transport links and its own minibus service, Sherfield is set in a safe, semi-rural setting, yet within close proximity to London.

Pupils at Sherfield benefit from rich and diverse learning experiences, both within and outside the classroom. There are a range of high quality facilities including indoor sports hall, drama studio, two synthetic all-weather surfaces, fitness suite, recording studio and extensive woodland. The state of the art boarding house offers full, weekly and flexi boarding options, in a vibrant and engaging environment offered to domestic and international pupils.

The co-curricular provision is extensive, with provision from 7.30am to 6pm for day pupils and evening and weekend activities for boarders. A high-quality enrichment programme enables pupils to develop a wide range of skills for the future, leading to an Ad Vitam Paramus diploma, unique to Sherfield. Outdoor learning is embedded in the ethos of the school, providing opportunities for pupils to learn in different contexts and develop a blend of academic and non-academic experiences.

At Sherfield, we strongly believe in a holistic approach to learning, and one that results in continued development, unleashing the true potential of passionate and creative problem solvers that make up this vibrant school. Children are ready to continue their journey long after leaving Sherfield and contribute to an everchanging global society.

An education at Sherfield is unique, as every pupil receives personalised support and guidance, identifying their individual talents and nurturing their potential. The Sherfield experience enables young people to thrive and flourish as they experience the excitement and enjoyment of learning. Pupils at Sherfield are ambitious, enterprising, inventive, thoughtful, inquisitive and supportive of each other. As a close knit community, they develop the confidence and desire to be the best they can possibly be as they take control of their futures. In an ever changing and evolving society, Sherfield pupils are adept at developing the necessary skills, qualities and experiences to meet the challenges of the future.

At Sherfield great academic results are just a by-product of something even bigger, a brilliant, well-rounded education that identifies and celebrates every child's strengths, and teaches them how to become the best version of themselves. As our Latin motto 'Ad Vitam Paramus' suggests, Sherfield prepares children for life.

South Drive, Sherfield-on-Loddon, Hook, Hampshire RG27 0HU UK

Tel: 01256 884800

Email: admissions@sherfieldschool.co.uk

Website: www.sherfieldschool.co.uk

Headmaster: Mr Nick Brain BA(Hons), PGCE, MA, NPQH

Appointed: September 2018

School type: Coeducational Day & Boarding

Age range of pupils: 3 months–18 years

No. of pupils enrolled as at 01/09/2020: 450

Fees per annum as at 01/09/2020:

Day: £10,320–£17,085

Weekly Boarding: £18,960–£26,130

Full Boarding: £22,125–£30,495

Average class size: 14

Sir William Perkins's School

Building Confidence, Integrity and Excellence

Sir William Perkins's School is an independent day school for girls aged 11-18 in Chertsey, Surrey.

Offering a world-class curriculum, enhanced by a wide-ranging and enriching co-curricular programme, the school produces excellent academic results.

Rated 'Excellent in all areas' by the Independent Schools Inspectorate in 2019, Sir William Perkins's School encourages girls to develop confidence, resilience and self-reliance in pursuit of their goals.

The school takes pride in providing students with inspirational teaching, extensive co-curricular opportunities and sector leading pastoral care. Students understand that hard work and curiosity are vital to success, and they accept these challenges with determination and good humour.

The school strives to cultivate ambition, fostering a desire amongst students to broaden horizons and push boundaries, educating the whole person to produce confident and well-rounded young people ready to face the world.

Students are encouraged to take every opportunity to develop their interests and creativity, as well as building strong interpersonal, teamwork and leadership skills.

At Sir William Perkins's School, financial and honorary academic scholarships are offered, and candidates have the opportunity to apply for Art, Drama and Music Scholarships as well as Bursaries; in the Sixth Form there is an additional opportunity to apply for a Scholarship in Sport.

The school has convenient transport links and is easily accessible by train or car, as well as providing coach services to a wide area.

The school sits on twelve acres of Surrey greenbelt land and boasts two all-weather pitches as well as a large secluded sports field.

Offering a wide range of subjects, the School features several purpose-built departments with continuously updated contemporary equipment and technologies to stay at the forefront of education.

Facilities include: a Sports centre with sprung-floored dance studio and specialist strength and conditioning gallery; Design Technology department with Product Design workshops, nutrition kitchen and textiles workshop; Art and Design studios with photography darkroom, print-making facilities and ceramics kiln; Drama department with purpose-built theatre and fully equipped production decks and editing equipment.

Further afield, the SWPS Boat House – sitting on Laleham Reach, five minutes from the school – is home to SWPS Boat Club, the school's elite rowing facility. SWPS Boat Club is used regularly by over a third of students, and successful teams have competed in finals at Henley Royal Regatta as well as racing at Championship standard in The National Schools Regatta.

The School has an established Sixth Form, housed in a 'penthouse' Sixth Form centre complete with wrap-around terrace, silent study rooms and access to a wide range of purpose-built facilities.

Sixth Form students benefit from small class sizes, and their own bespoke programmes of study. Students are provided with university and careers guidance, as well as access to an extensive enrichment programme, Oxbridge Programme, Medicine, Dentistry & Veterinary Science Programme, a range of extended qualifications and much more besides.

We would love to welcome you to Sir William Perkins's School to attend an open event, meet our staff and take a tour of our wonderful school. Dates and bookings are available on the SWPS website at www.swps.org.uk.

(Founded 1725)

Guildford Road, Chertsey, Surrey KT16 9BN UK

Tel: 01932 574900

Fax: 01932 574901

Email: office@swps.org.uk

Website: www.swps.org.uk

Head: Mr C C Muller

Appointed: September 2014

School type: Girls' Day

Age range of girls: 11–18 years

No. of pupils enrolled as at 01/09/2020: 600

Fees per term as at 01/09/2020:

Day: £5,618 per term

Average class size: Senior School: 24, Sixth Form: 10

Teacher/pupil ratio: 1:8

St Catherine's, Bramley

Founded as both a boarding and day school for girls in 1885, we believe that the successful blending of these two aspects of school life into one happily integrated community is part of what makes St Catherine's. Everyone, boarder or day girl, feels part of the whole. Boarding fosters a strong respect and care for others and gives girls the confidence to develop their independence and their own sense of style. We are building a vibrant new boarding house, with generous accommodation and bright bathrooms, and a social space where all Sixth Form girls can relax. The 6 will open in Spring 2021.

Academic results place us comfortably within the most prestigious girls' independent boarding schools in the UK. The curriculum is designed to ensure it has breadth and variety. Our very impressive Destinations of Leavers' data is testament to the excellent outcomes at A Level, enabling our Sixth Formers to go to their chosen universities, in the UK and worldwide, and feel well prepared to take on new challenges.

Bramley village is set in the heart of attractive Surrey countryside with acres of opportunity for outside activities. Being under an hour from Heathrow and Gatwick means no long journeys at the start and end of terms. Regular trains to London from nearby Guildford, make a day in the capital city very easy to organise. On Fridays/Sundays a return bus service into SW London runs for weekly boarders.

St Catherine's weekend boarding programme is carefully thought-out and has been singled out on a number of occasions for particular praise; from cultural excursions to theatres, museums and galleries to theme parks, the seaside, Christmas Markets and culturally interesting cities: Bath, Winchester, Windsor, Portsmouth etc. London's cultural and entertainment attractions are just an hour away, whilst the historic county town of Guildford is on our doorstep which offers theatres, a multiplex cinema and shopping opportunities.

The Anniversary Halls sports and performing arts complex houses a multi-function sports hall and professional dance studio as well as a superb auditorium for concerts and theatrical productions. Girls can choose from around 15 different sports which they can commit to and enjoy at their own level. Numerous choirs, Wind Band, String Orchestra, Symphony Orchestra, Concert Band, Jazz Band, and Brass Ensemble represent some of the musical groups girls enjoy. Musicians benefit from superb acoustics and a full orchestra pit. Girls can master skills in stage design, lighting and sound under the guidance of our Technical Director. They enjoy learning ballet, jazz, tap and modern dance in St Catherine's own professional dance school. Art, Chess, Debating, Sailing, Equestrianism, Young Enterprise, community projects, Charity fund-raising and The Duke of Edinburgh's Award Scheme feature in a long list of extra-curricular activities.

St Catherine's is unequivocally for girls. It is a school where girls grow and develop at their own pace, not one dictated by others. The advantages of girls' schools are legion – not only do girls achieve better examination results, they also have more opportunities for leadership. Girls do particularly well in Science, Technology, Engineering, and Mathematics and are more likely to continue these subjects at A level and into university. We educate girls to see themselves as future leaders in society, movers and shakers, politicians, thinkers, creators and industrialists. The St Catherine's Association, comprising thousands of alumnae, parents, and friends of the School gives the girls access to invaluable careers' advice, global networks and opportunities for work experience/internships and sponsorships.

The St Catherine's experience is unforgettable creating indelible, affectionate memories that girls take onward through life.

(Founded 1885)

Station Road, Bramley, Guildford, Surrey GU5 0DF UK

Tel: 01483 899609

Email: admissions@stcatherines.info

Website: www.stcatherines.info

Headmistress: Alice Phillips

Headmistress of Preparatory School:
Miss Naomi Bartholomew

School type: Girls' Day & Boarding

Religious Denomination: Church of England

Age range of girls: 4–18

No. of pupils enrolled as at 01/09/2020:

Prep School: 255

Senior School: 655

Fees per annum as at 01/01/2021:

Day: £9,240–£18,885

Full Boarding: £31,125

Average class size: 18

Teacher/pupil ratio: 1:8/9

St Lawrence College

Founded in 1879, St Lawrence College is a thriving independent day and boarding school, providing a first class education for boys and girls from 3 to 18 years. Currently, we have approximately 600 pupils – 175 in the Junior School and 425 in the Senior School, of which 175 are boarders (boarding from 7 years of age).

Located in the Kent coastal town of Ramsgate, and within easy walking distance of the sea, the school is set in 45 acres of safe and spacious grounds, housing both beautiful historic architecture and outstanding contemporary facilities.

In the Classroom

Academic standards are high across the school, which offers an extensive choice of GCSEs and A-levels, with an excellent success rate of pupils going on to their first choice of university. We ensure pupils attain their personal best academically, whilst preparing them for life in a rapidly changing global society. Modern facilities combined with traditional values, based on our Christian roots, draw out the talents of each pupil, whilst our policy for keeping class sizes small ensures that our teachers can look after the individual needs of each pupil.

Outside the Classroom

Sporting facilities are exceptional, and expert coaching is provided at all levels in a variety of disciplines, including rugby, netball, hockey and cricket. We were national champions in boys' indoor hockey and girls' outdoor hockey last year. The magnificent sports centre houses a fitness suite, squash courts, climbing wall, dance studio and a large sports hall for activities such as badminton and basketball.

Music and drama flourish, enhanced by the school's 500-seat theatre, and there are many opportunities for pupils to perform. All pupils benefit from an extensive activities programme which in the Senior School includes the CCF (Combined Cadet Force) and a thriving Duke of Edinburgh's Award Scheme, as well as chess, archery, golf, fencing, football, sailing, horse riding, swimming, table tennis, musical theatre and many more activities.

Boarding at St Lawrence

Strong pastoral care, high quality teaching and a great emphasis on extra-curricular activity make this a very special community in which to live and learn. Boarding is central to the school's life and is one of our great strengths. A wide range of evening and weekend activities are provided for boarders, along with additional events and fun day trips. We offer full time and weekly boarding options, and we aim to provide a 'home-from-home' for our boarding pupils, both in terms of comfort and atmosphere. In recent years, a substantial programme of investment has created exceptional boarding facilities, with all rooms en-suite.

Location

The self-contained campus is situated within easy walking distance of the historic seaside town of Ramsgate. It has excellent transport links to the continent, being near to both Dover and the Channel Tunnel. London is only 75 minutes away by high-speed rail link to St Pancras International. Gatwick and Heathrow are under two hours away.

St LAWRENCE
COLLEGE

(Founded 1879)

Ramsgate, Kent CT11 7AE UK

Tel: 01843 572931

Email: admissions@slcuk.com

Website: www.slcuk.com

Head of College: Mr Barney Durrant

School type: Coeducational Boarding & Day

Age range of pupils: 3–18

No. of pupils enrolled as at 01/09/2020: 600

Fees per annum as at 01/09/2020:

Day: £7,845–£16,245

Full Boarding: £27,765–£36,909

Teacher/pupil ratio: 1:8

St Neot's School

St Neot's, founded in 1888 is a co-educational day school for children aged 2–13 years, where the number one priority is to prepare children for successful, happy and purposeful lives. The school is situated on the border of Hampshire and Berkshire and is set in 70 acres of beautiful grounds and woodland.

Staff are inspired to awaken intellectual curiosity and encourage children to challenge themselves in a supportive and happy environment. Each individual is motivated to achieve their full academic potential, to discover their talents and to develop the passion to pursue them. They are given the tools to embrace opportunities, think creatively, develop self-confidence and foster empathy towards others, preparing them both intellectually and emotionally for success in the 21st Century.

We aim to provide the highest standards in teaching and learning within a well rounded educational experience and St Neot's has a very strong record of success in achieving Scholarships and Awards to numerous Senior Schools.

St Neot's is committed to providing a World of Opportunity in every aspect of school life. Stimulating learning environments ensure that engaged pupils work towards the highest academic standards, whilst also enjoying a holistic education, pursuing sport, music, art, drama and dance.

Forest School, Outdoor Learning and Leadership Days encourage the children to venture outside their comfort zones, to take risks and develop the purpose and drive to make the most of their talents in life beyond school. The St Neot's journey culminates in the Years 7 and 8 leadership programme, which draws together a mix of skills developed through the school's commitment to the Pre Senior Baccalaureate (PSB).

Physical Education is a strength of the school and our sports complex, comprising sports hall, 25m indoor swimming pool, all-weather astro, cricket nets, hard tennis and netball courts, significantly supplement our extensive playing fields. There is also an on-site mountain bike track and a traversing wall. Judo, dance, tennis and swimming are taught by specialist coaches and there are many after school clubs and activities covering a wide range of interests. Holiday Clubs run in all school breaks and offer a wealth of opportunities, both sporting and creative.

St Neot's holds a Gold Artsmark award, giving recognition to achievements in art, music, drama and dance. A number of plays, concerts and recitals take place throughout the school year for all age groups, either in the school grounds or the Performing Arts Centre.

Open Mornings take place termly and details of these can be found on the school website – www.stneotsprep.co.uk. We would also be delighted to arrange an individual tour and a meeting with the Head. Please contact Admissions on 0118 9739650 – e-mail – admissions@stneotsprep.co.uk

ST NEOT'S
PREPARATORY SCHOOL

(Founded 1888)

St Neot's Road, Eversley, Hampshire RG27 0PN UK

Tel: 0118 9739650

Email: admissions@stneotsprep.co.uk

Website: www.stneotsprep.co.uk

Head of School: Deborah Henderson

Appointed: September 2015

School type: Co-educational Day, Preparatory

Age range of pupils: 2–13 years

No. of pupils enrolled as at 01/09/2020: 248

Fees per term as at 01/09/2020:

Day: £3,780–£5,408 per term

Average class size: 18

Teacher/pupil ratio: 1:8

St Swithun's School

Compassion, integrity, and a quiet sense of self-confidence
St Swithun's School is a renowned independent day, weekly and full-boarding school for girls set in 45 acres overlooking the Hampshire Downs on the outskirts of Winchester, yet only 50 minutes by train from central London. It offers excellent teaching, sporting and recreational facilities.

The school has a long-standing reputation for academic rigour and success. Girls are prepared for public examinations and higher education in a stimulating environment in which they develop intellectual curiosity, independence of mind and the ability to take responsibility for their own learning. They achieve almost one grade higher at GCSE than their already significant baseline ability would suggest, and approximately half a grade higher at A level. St Swithun's offers a comprehensive careers and higher education support service throughout the school years. Its Oxbridge preparation is part of a whole-school academic enrichment programme providing additional challenge and stimulation.

St Swithun's describes itself as an 'appropriately academic' school, celebrating intellectual curiosity and the life of the mind, but not to the exclusion of all else. They expect their pupils to develop individual passions and through them to acquire a range of skills and characteristics. These characteristics will include a willingness to take risks, to question and to debate, and to persevere in the face of difficulty. In the words of Samuel Beckett: *"Ever tried. Ever failed. No matter. Try again. Fail again. Fail better."*

Whilst achieving academic excellence, girls also have the opportunity to do 'something else'. There is an extensive co-curricular programme of over 100 weekly and 50 weekend activities to choose from.

As well as academic classrooms and science laboratories, there is a magnificent performing arts centre with a 600-seat auditorium, a music school, an art and technology block, a sports hall and a full-size indoor swimming pool. There is an impressive library and ICT facility. The grounds are spacious and encompass sports fields, tennis courts and gardens.

With kindness and tolerance at the heart of its community, St Swithun's provides a civilised and caring environment in which all girls are valued for their individual gifts. By the time a girl leaves she will be courageous, compassionate, committed and self-confident with a love of learning, a moral compass and a sense of humour.

Open days provide an excellent introduction to the school and include a student-led tour, an opportunity to meet the staff and a presentation from the head giving an overview of the unique atmosphere and opportunities at St Swithun's. To book a place on an open day, or to arrange an individual visit at a more convenient time, please contact Kate Cairns on 01962 835703 or email registrar@stswithuns.com. Keep up to date with latest news by visiting www.stswithuns.com, or on Twitter @StSwithunsGirls.

St Swithun's
WINCHESTER

(Founded 1884)

Alresford Road, Winchester, Hampshire SO21 1HA UK

Tel: 01962 835700

Fax: 01962 835779

Email: office@stswithuns.com

Website: www.stswithuns.com

Head of School: Jane Gandee MA(Cantab)

Appointed: 2010

School type: Girls' Boarding & Day

Age range of girls: 11–18

No. of pupils enrolled as at 01/09/2020: 510

Sixth Form: 161

No. of boarders: 212

Fees per annum as at 01/09/2020:

Day: £20,976

Full Boarding: £34,776

CANTABRIAN

St. Andrew's School

St. Andrew's School was founded in 1937 and is a respected and thriving coeducational prep school, of around 300 children. Set in 11 acres of grounds approximately half a mile from Woking town centre, the School seeks to create a nurturing and happy environment of trust and support in which all pupils are encouraged and enabled to develop their skills, talents, interests and potential to the full – intellectually, physically and spiritually.

At St. Andrew's children feel secure and confident and are highly motivated to perform to the best of their ability in all aspects of school life. They are competitive without losing sight of their responsibility to share and they are justifiably proud of their school and their own personal achievements. We also place great emphasis on consideration for others. Courtesy and mutual respect underpins the behaviour policy at St. Andrew's and we aim to teach children about patience, empathy and unselfishness, whilst encouraging them to use their time wisely in an independent and self-reliant manner.

St. Andrew's School prides itself in providing a broad based curriculum that focuses on enabling our children to enjoy a full range of subjects. Educating the whole child is central to our ethos and, whilst academic standards are high, there are also real opportunities to develop their skills in art, music and sport together with a fantastic programme of after school activities. This is supported by specialist teaching facilities for all subjects including science, ICT, music and art. In our latest ISI inspection (Jan 2016) the school was rated 'excellent' in all areas and, with the benefit of individual attention and specialist teachers in all areas of the curriculum, the children are able to reach their full potential in a happy, caring and supportive environment.

When it is time to move on to senior schools at the end of Year 8, the children are prepared for entrance and scholarship exams to a wide range of independent senior schools and the school provides guidance and advice to parents on the senior school choices that best suit each individual child.

St. Andrew's is very proud of its excellent on-site facilities including a brand new theatre, food tech room, classrooms, library and changing rooms together with excellent sports pitches, all weather sports surface, tennis courts, cricket nets and a swimming pool. We are very fortunate to enjoy the benefits of carefully designed school grounds that meet the needs of the children's physical and social development. Main school games are football, hockey, cricket and netball. Other activities include cross-country running, swimming, tennis and athletics.

Children can be supervised at school from 8am and, through our extensive after-school activities programme for Year 3 and above, until 6-6.30pm most evenings during the week. An after-school club is available from 4.15pm to 6pm (chargeable) for Pre-Prep, Year 3 and Year 4 children.

Children are assessed for entry into Year 2 and above. The school has a number of scholarships and bursaries available.

Don't just take our word for it, come and visit the school to see for yourself! We have three open days, one per term, but you are also welcome to visit the school at other times. Please contact the Headmaster's PA (Registrar) for more information and to arrange a visit. We look forward to welcoming you.

ST. ANDREW'S
SCHOOL · WOKING

(Founded 1937)

Church Hill House, Horsell, Woking, Surrey GU21 4QW UK

Tel: 01483 760943

Email: admin@st-andrews.woking.sch.uk

Website: www.st-andrews.woking.sch.uk

Headmaster: Mr D Fitzgerald

Appointed: 2020

School type: Coeducational Day Preparatory

Age range of pupils: 3–13

No. of pupils enrolled as at 01/09/2020: 300

Fees per annum as at 01/09/2020:

Day: £3,933–£15,495

Teacher/pupil ratio: 1:10

Stroud School

Stroud School is an exciting, independent preparatory school where boys and girls aged 3 to 13 years old thrive in its unique family environment. In May 2012, it became the preparatory school for King Edward VI School, Southampton, bringing together two highly successful academic Hampshire independent schools.

Highwood House is a beautiful Victorian building standing in 22 acres of beautiful rural countryside. With only five former Heads since its foundation in 1926, Stroud has always been a school that values the family ethos. It is a school with a strong academic record, fantastic sports facilities and links to strong academic secondary schools. Stroud's curriculum achieves the highest academic standard without compromising the key skills its children need to be successful in the workplace and generally in life.

All pupils learn in a relaxed and fun environment. Inside the classroom, Stroud offers academic excellence with a keen grasp on individualised learning. The breadth of co-curricular activities and after school clubs allows every student to find and feed their passion. The School's values: 'Honesty, Respect, and Happiness' underpins all activities at Stroud and the School sees these values reflected in its pupils' behaviour every day. As a result, Stroud fosters a culture in which the children have a genuine desire to achieve success.

Taking lessons outside of the classroom, with expansive grounds at its disposal, forms an integral part of learning and Stroud has recently been awarded the 'Council for Learning Outside the Classroom' (CLOtC) Silver Award, a national accreditation that has been endorsed by the Department for Education. This award sits perfectly alongside the School's 'Eco Schools Green Flag', which it has maintained for the past six years.

A large body of research shows that outdoor learning improves children's health, increases their enjoyment and engagement with learning and leads to a greater connection with nature. Stroud offers an extended programme of 'Learning Outside the Classroom' for this very reason. From week long overseas trips to day visits to local country parks, to Forest and Beach School. Forest School has been an integrated part of Pre-Prep education at Stroud for many years and the Beach School has been a hugely popular and rewarding addition to the curriculum.

Extra-curricular activities also enhance its core curricular programme. It is the School's responsibility to build the whole child and encourage growth and independence whilst introducing new opportunities, allowing children to explore different roads they wouldn't normally venture down. All clubs at Stroud lead to this; whether it's solving a maths equation in Maths Club, holding a conversation in German Club or perfecting a tackle at rugby practice. Extra clubs help build confidence and the School has seen a huge benefit to pupils' well-being and a greater sense of achievement and resilience.

Stroud regularly uses the pitches at Wellington Sports Ground, the Outward Bound Centre in the Dartmoor National Park, and is looking forward to its pupils performing in the new multi-million pound theatre at King Edward VI School. New development plans allow for new facilities that will keep pace with a 21st Century educational need. What has not changed at Stroud, however, is the opportunities that it provides for its pupils.

To find out more about life at Stroud or to arrange a visit, call 01794 513231 or email registrar@stroud-kes.org.uk. www.stroud-kes.org.uk

Stroud School, Romsey
King Edward VI Preparatory School

(Founded 1926)

Highwood House, Highwood Lane, Romsey, Hampshire SO51 9ZH UK

Tel: 01794 513231

Email: registrar@stroud-kes.org.uk

Website: www.stroud-kes.org.uk

Headmistress: Mrs Rebecca Smith

School type: Coeducational Day

Age range of pupils: 3–13

Average class size: 16-18

Upton House School

Upton House is a progressive and highly regarded Nursery, Pre-Prep and Prep school educating boys and girls from aged 2–11 years. Located in the heart of Windsor, Upton boasts excellent academic standards, high calibre staff and a warm and nurturing environment where children blossom and are prepared with confidence for the very best senior schools. Individual talent is developed, and a progressive curriculum offers a balanced co-education ensuring children are equipped with vital life skills for the future.

"Our children progress to their next schools as confident, successful and independent individuals. We were delighted to be awarded 'Excellent' in all areas in our recent Independent Schools Inspection Report." Rhian Thornton, Headmistress

Although non-selective, 30% of pupils in the past 3 years have achieved one or more scholarships to their chosen senior school. Details of scholarships and next schools can be found on the website.

Little Upton Pre-Nursery and Nursery is a very special environment where children begin their Upton journey from as young as age 2. Little Upton is open a flexible 48 weeks a year should parents require and benefits from being in a beautiful whole school setting. Staff are highly qualified, experienced practitioners and engage the children in stimulating, challenging and exciting activities that enable them to develop their love of learning within the Early Years Foundation Stage. Specialist subjects include French from 2 years old and Mandarin from 3 years old as well as regular PE and music lessons.

Facilities in the Pre-Prep and Prep departments at Upton House include a newly opened arts block housing music rooms, an art and DT studio and a media room with green screen filming facilities. A modern and vibrant computer suite is equipped for a progressive computing curriculum including coding and robotics. All classrooms are furnished with interactive white boards and iPads are used daily by pupils to support learning throughout the school. Facilities also include a kitchen for Food Technology lessons, a drama and dance studio, gymnasium, two libraries and a delightful Nursery music room. Diverse sporting activities include netball, rugby, hockey, cricket and athletics as well as rowing, judo, fencing and ballet. A wide range of individual musical instrument lessons are also available.

Children at Upton House enjoy breakfast club from 7.45am, healthy meals prepared on site and a wide range of after school extra-curricular activities until 6pm. Holiday clubs are run on site outside of term time.

To book for an open morning, or to arrange a personal tour of the school, please register online or contact Miss Harriet Barnes: registrar@uptonhouse.org.uk. We look forward to welcoming you!

We look forward to welcoming you!

(Founded 1936)

115 St Leonard's Road, Windsor, Berkshire SL4 3DF UK

Tel: 01753 862610

Email: registrar@uptonhouse.org.uk

Website: www.uptonhouse.org.uk

Head: Mrs Rhian Thornton BA (Hons) NPQH LLE PGCE

Appointed: September 2016

School type: Co-educational Prep, Pre-prep & Nursery

Age range of pupils: 2–11 years

No. of pupils enrolled as at 01/09/2020: 245

Boys: 60 *Girls:* 185

Fees per term as at 01/09/2020:

Day: £3,143–£5,225 per term

Average class size: 16

Vinehall

Overview

Children come first at Vinehall. We believe that in providing a wide range of opportunities we can allow our children to achieve success, instilling in them a strong sense of purpose and self-confidence. Our staff and parents work together to create a warm and thriving community, where kindness and tolerance towards others are leading values. The School's ethos is encapsulated in our motto, 'to do our best for the benefit of others'.

Idyllic Setting: Within an unrivalled setting of 49 acres in the East Sussex countryside, our children enjoy much freedom to explore our expansive grounds, to benefit from the simply outstanding facilities and to discover life for themselves. Our facilities include a full-size sports hall, a 250-seat theatre, an indoor heated pool, an all-weather astro turf, six tennis courts and a nine-hole golf course.

Outstanding education, academic innovation: At Vinehall, we want to foster a love of learning for its own sake by encouraging our children to ask questions and think for themselves. We want our children to develop the necessary skills to work productively as part of a group and to become resilient, resourceful and reflective learners, unafraid of trying something new or making mistakes.

Alongside the established curriculum subjects, pupils at Vinehall have Life Skills lessons; the content of these lessons is broad, ranging from study skills and financial literacy to global citizenship, mental health and well-being. STEM (Science, Technology, Engineering and Maths) is also taught as a curriculum subject from Year 5, providing pupils with the opportunity to 'think like an engineer' and to develop practical problem-solving skills.

After two years of planning, September 2019 will see the introduction of a bespoke programme of study for pupils in Years 7 and 8, focusing on a thematic approach to learning. As part of a rigorous academic curriculum that we hope will give children a more relevant and stimulating learning experience, our focus will be on ensuring that our children have the skills and dispositions that will mean they leave Vinehall as independent, engaged learners.

"All pupils are successful at gaining entry to senior schools of their choice and many regularly gain academic scholarships and music, performing arts and sports awards." ISI inspection Report January 2018

Full, weekly and flexible boarding: Vinehall has a well-established boarding community of boys and girls. We offer full, weekly or flexible boarding open to all. For full boarders there are regular exeat weekend breaks every two or three weeks. Most boarders describe the weekends at Vinehall as the highlight of their week, with a wide range of trips and activities on offer. Weekly boarding is available for those wishing to spend weekends with their families. Flexible boarding is on offer to provide a helping hand to day pupils. The Vinehall Express offers accompanied train travel to and from Charing Cross.

"Boarders say that the boarding experience increases their independence and personal skills in readiness for full-time boarding in their future senior schools." ISI Inspection report January 2018.

"Pupils at Vinehall have excellent attitudes towards learning, nurtured by high expectations and the mutually supportive, inclusive and enabling culture of the school." Independent Schools Inspectorate Report January 2018

(Founded 1938)

Robertsbridge, East Sussex TN32 5JL UK

Tel: 01580 880413

Fax: 01580 882119

Email: admissions@vinehallschool.com

Website: www.vinehallschool.com

Headmaster: Joff Powis

Appointed: September 2017

School type: Co-educational Day & Boarding

Age range of pupils: 2–13

No. of pupils enrolled as at 01/09/2020: 220

Fees per annum as at 01/09/2020:

Day: £10,350–£19,290

Weekly Boarding: £22,575–£23,100

Full Boarding: £24,525–£25,125

Average class size: 14

Teacher/pupil ratio: 1:6.5

Wellington College

Wellington College is a vibrant and inspiring coeducational boarding and day school set in 400 acres of parkland, 40 minutes from Heathrow. The College, whose educational philosophy is based on values of kindness, courage, respect, integrity and responsibility is celebrated not only for its academic achievements but also for its sporting, artistic and dramatic provision which are second to none. Stellar examination results, outstanding provision across all co-curricular areas, and a raft of national accolades contribute to the College's national and international reputation.

Wellingtonians study GCSEs, followed by the IB Diploma or A Levels and, whichever route they take, results are superb: in 2019, the average A Level outcome was AAA, and the College's incredible IB average of 40.2 yet again made Wellington one of the UK's highest achieving boarding schools to offer the IB Diploma. 62% achieved 40 points or above and nine students achieved the maximum 45 points. On average 9% of the cohort gain places at Oxford or Cambridge every year and, in 2019, 19 students went on to US universities, many to Ivy League institutions.

The College has an outstanding reputation for boys' and girls' sport, with over 30 different activities offered with emphasis placed on both excellence and general participation (every year sees over 2,000 fixtures). In 2019/20 national team success came in Cross Country, Equestrian, Fencing, Golf, Gymnastics, Hockey, Polo, Rackets, Real Tennis, Rugby (where the boys' 1st XV became the first side to defend the RFU Champions Trophy title), Sailing, Skiing, and Shooting. In addition to team success, many individuals gained national or international honours across 11 different sports, with several going on to take up professional contracts, scholarships at US universities and places on UK based performance squads in Rugby and Hockey.

Performing Arts are equally strong. Music and Drama are stunning, with nearly two-thirds of pupils taking music or LAMDA lessons. Recent activities have included a choir tour to Germany, a recording of carols, an orchestral recording, an annual musical (this year Sweeney Todd), contemporary Shakespeare productions and imaginative and inclusive junior plays. Dance enjoys a purpose-designed studio and two spectacular shows each year play to packed houses. The G.W. Annenberg Performing Arts Centre, Wellington's 900-seater performing arts venue, opened in September 2018. It was no surprise that Wellington was awarded Artsmark Gold by the Arts Council.

Leadership and service to others are central: co-curricular activities include its outward-facing Global Citizenship programme in which pupils create and run innovative social action projects, as well as the CCF and Duke of Edinburgh's Award. Over 70 clubs and societies provide unique opportunities, from WTV (Wellington's own television company) to the pupil-run radio station, DukeBox, which broadcasts 24/7, reaching listeners in 41 countries across the globe.

Wellington's family of schools includes its prep school Eagle House, five schools in China and one in Thailand. Wellington was the first HMC school to be accredited as a Teaching School and now partners with a broad range of local state schools. All of this provides pupils and staff with meaningful opportunities for partnership and service within national and international communities.

Further information including details about Visitors Days can be found on the website and the Admissions Office can be contacted on +44 (0)1344 444013.

WELLINGTON COLLEGE

(Founded 1853)

Duke's Ride, Crowthorne, Berkshire RG45 7PU UK

Tel: +44 (0)1344 444000

Email: admissions@wellingtoncollege.org.uk

Website: www.wellingtoncollege.org.uk

Master: Mr James Dahl

Appointed: September 2019

Director of IB: Mr Richard Atherton

School type: Coeducational Boarding & Day

Religious Denomination: Church of England

Age range of pupils: 13–18

No. of pupils enrolled as at 01/09/2020: 1080

Boys: 615 **Girls:** 465 **Sixth Form:** 485

No. of boarders: 860

Fees per annum as at 01/09/2020:

Day: £30,375–£34,890

Full Boarding: £41,580

Average class size:
Lower + Middle = 20 Upper School = 12

Teacher/pupil ratio: 1:7

South-West

Kingsley School

Welcome to Kingsley School

There are many reasons students could fall in love with Kingsley School, an independent co-educational boarding and day school located in Bideford on the banks of the River Torridge in North Devon.

One reason could be location – Kingsley is set in 25 acres of playfields and woodland, surrounded by stunning countryside, and just five minutes from popular surfing beaches. And another reason could be the school's strong academic tradition – at Kingsley every sixth form student typically goes on to university, including top-tier higher education institutes like Oxford and Cambridge.

But ultimately our students rate the opportunity to find their place, the exceptional support they receive and the welcome as the prime reasons they just can't see themselves going anywhere else but Kingsley.

Kingsley students are happily celebrating their exceptional A-Level and BTEC Summer 2020 results. 55% of all grades awarded are A* and A at Kingsley this year, up from 51% in 2019.

Kingsley School is an inclusive day and boarding school where every child is important and is treated with dignity and respect. As a relatively small school of around 400 boys and girls, Kingsley's atmosphere is like that of a large family where everybody knows each other well.

The school's philosophy encourages personal qualities such as courage, generosity, honesty, imagination, tolerance and kindness. In addition, we develop the students' wider interests and skills in sport, music, art, and drama. Kingsley also has a national reputation for its Learning Development Centre which provides additional support for students with moderate learning needs. Overall, a Kingsley education develops the individual character and talents of each and every student both inside and outside the classroom.

Becoming part of the family: The boarding houses at Kingsley help form part of the family atmosphere at the school. Students live in three comfortable and well-equipped houses in the school's grounds; two for boys and one for girls. Each house has 30-40 students who are supervised by two teachers and their families who live in the houses as well.

Sport and Clubs: Sport includes traditional sports plus judo, handball and gymnastics squads competing at a National level. As part of the National Theatre Connections programme, the school drama cast performed at the Theatre Royal, Plymouth and the National Theatre, London this year. Popular extra-curricular clubs include the Duke of Edinburgh's Award Scheme, orchestra, computing, art, film making, choir and surfing.

Transport: we run an accompanied coach service to and from Heathrow Airport and Bristol Airport at the beginning and end of each term. Weekly boarding options with transport to London and the South East.

Headteacher Gill Jackson said: "As a parent, I know that choosing the right school can be daunting, but Kingsley is a place which really does recognise that each child has individual needs, with their own set of skills and talents that deserve to be developed. Smaller, more attentive classes with caring and supportive teachers gives the school a familial feel. I am proud of each and every student, their progress, support of one another and their outstanding personal achievements."

Do follow us on social media

Facebook: Kingsley School Bideford
Instagram: Kingsley School
Twitter: @KSBideford
YouTube: Kingsley School Bideford
www.kingsleyschoolbideford.co.uk

(Founded 1884)

Northdown Road, Bideford, Devon EX39 3LY UK

Tel: 01237 426200

Fax: 01237 425981

Email: admissions@kingsleyschoolbideford.co.uk

Website: www.kingsleyschoolbideford.co.uk

Headteacher: Mrs Gill Jackson

Appointed: January 2020

Head of the Prep School: Mr Andrew Trythall

School type: Coeducational Day & Boarding

Age range of pupils: 0–18

No. of pupils enrolled as at 01/09/2018: 395

No. of boarders: 100

Fees per term as at 01/09/2019:

Day: £2,020 per term

Weekly Boarding: £5,695 per term

Full Boarding: £7,685 per term

Average class size: 14

Teacher/pupil ratio: 1:9

Plymouth College

At Plymouth College, we believe our purpose is to educate, enrich and empower every single one of our pupils in an environment that is intellectually and emotionally stimulating, progressive and adventurous. First and foremost, Plymouth College is a place of learning. Exceptional teaching and support in very small classes help to ensure that every pupil fulfils and often exceeds their academic and intellectual potential. Our pupils achieve great exam results and secure places at Oxbridge and Russell group universities or top-flight apprenticeships.

In summer 2020, our pupils achieved a 99% success rate of grades A* – C at A level. Subjects that our pupils can study at A level include EPQ, STEM subjects and Business and Economics, as well as Languages, Art and Drama and Music. University destinations for our alumni include the University of York, the University of Exeter, Cardiff University and University of the Arts London, to name a few.

Beyond the classroom, the personal development of our children is at the heart of everything we do. Our pastoral care and wellbeing education are second-to-none and, through our wonderfully enriching programme of co-curricular activities, pupils learn to develop qualities such as resilience, humility and compassion, and skills, such as leadership, communication and team-working.

We want our pupils to become both leaders and champions: leaders of sports teams, leaders of the industry, leaders of their communities; and champions of their favourite subject or favourite activity or favourite cause. In doing so, we want them to understand the importance of service and society so that they lead for the benefit of everyone in society, not just themselves.

This holistic education is part of our DNA. Everything we do – every lesson, every form period, every activity – is a truly enriching experience for pupils and enables them to develop intellectually, academically, socially, morally and physically. They emerge from their Plymouth College education with fantastic exam results and as rounded, grounded, happy and confident young men and women.

"Pupils throughout the school are proud of what they achieve and speak with great passion about their experiences both in and out of the classroom." ISI, January 2019

Plymouth College at a Glance

- Pupils are at the heart of all we do and we provide a holistic education that inspires excellence and empowers pupils to believe that everything is possible.
- We welcome students from all over the world looking for a British boarding school education, plus flexible boarding options for families living a little closer.
- We have a unique community of pupils who form lifelong friendships in a safe environment that values their wellbeing, happiness and personal development as much as their academic performance.
- Small class sizes enable our talented teachers to deliver bespoke learning to each and every pupil.
- We maintain the best performance scores in the city and some of the highest in Devon and Cornwall, meaning our pupils exceed their potential and achieve excellent exam results.
- Pupils progress to Oxford, Cambridge and other Russell Group and world-leading universities.
- There is access to over 60 co-curricular activities – everything from Young Enterprise to Photography.
- We have an international reputation for sporting excellence with access to leading coaches and facilities, developing Olympic athletes of the future. We also have partnerships with Plymouth Leander Swimming Club, Plymouth Fencing Club and Plymouth Raiders Basketball Club.

(Founded 1877)

Ford Park, Plymouth, Devon PL4 6RN UK

Tel: 01752 505100

Email: mail@plymouthcollege.com

Website: www.plymouthcollege.com

Headteacher: Mrs Jo Hayward

Appointed: August 2020

School type: Coeducational Day & Boarding

Religious Denomination: Church of England

Age range of pupils: 3–18

No. of pupils enrolled as at 01/09/2020: 569

Boys: 329 *Girls:* 240

Prep School: 146

Senior School: 423

No. of boarders: 104

Fees per term as at 01/09/2020:

Prep: £2,625 – £3,625 per term

Senior (Day): £4,700 – £5,565 per term

Senior (Boarding): £9,735 – £10,745 per term

Average class size: 13

West Midlands

Ellesmere College

Since its founding in 1884, Ellesmere College has retained its focus on individual student success while promoting a nurturing, family atmosphere. An incredibly friendly co-ed boarding school, 550 students from ages 7 to 18, and from all across the globe, are encouraged to explore, engage and evolve to the best of their potential through the College's innovative and dynamic academic and co-curricular opportunities.

At every entry point to the College students are offered a broad choice of academic subjects as well as a vast range of co-curricular activities (DofE, CCF, ESB, EPQ, ILM, Survive & Thrive, expeditions, career conventions, affiliations, etc) that develop essential life skills – leadership, initiative, confidence, teambuilding, and above all a belief in themselves that they can achieve if they try their best – the ethos at the heart of the school – to be 'Life:Ready'.

Academic
At Key Stages 2 & 3 we offer a wide curriculum preparing them for their choice of i/GCSEs as they move up to Middle School at age 13 – providing subjects that appeal to all pupils' interests and academic strengths, while keeping class sizes small. Our award winning Support for Learning department supports those students with diverse academic needs including dyslexia, dyspraxia and dyscalculia.

In Sixth Form, students choose A Levels, BTEC or International Baccalaureate (IB), and our students regularly gain entrance to their first-choice university including Oxford, Cambridge and Russell Group institutions. We are ranked in the top 20 British schools offering the IB with students regularly attaining >30 points and are launching our International Foundation Programme (IFP) in the Autumn.

Pastoral Care
Ellesmere provides a friendly and warm environment with family values at its heart, and all students at the College – whether day pupils or boarders – are assigned to a House, under which they compete in termly House Competitions. Our student accommodation provides a high-quality, comfortable and secure environment for our students from Year 8, with residential staff on site to tend to the pupils' personal and pastoral needs 24 hours a day.

Drama, Music and the Arts
The College was the first independent school to be awarded Artsmark Platinum by the Arts Council of Great Britain for its commitment and delivery of the arts from the traditional to more modern media. Singing is an area of real excellence with four award winning choirs and a wide range of ensembles with opportunities to perform. Participation at every level is encouraged and supported by ESB, LAMDA, ballet & dance classes, and individual tuition.

Sports
We are immensely proud of our sporting tradition at Ellesmere College and physical education is an integral part of the curriculum – playing for ones' house or school, or at national, international and Olympic level. We are an accredited WAoS (World Academy of Sport) Athlete Friendly Education Centre (AFEC), which provides greater flexibility to students so they can balance their studies with demanding training and competition schedules. There are seven distinct Sports Academies – rugby, cricket, tennis, swimming, shooting, football and golf – as well as a High Performance Hockey Programme and many other sports.

We believe very strongly that the foundations for a successful adult life are built at a young age – and at Ellesmere College we empower and enrich our students to become confident, strong and exceptional young adults.

 Ellesmere

(Founded 1884)

Ellesmere, Shropshire SY12 9AB UK

Tel: 01691 622321

Fax: 01691 623286

Email: registrar@ellesmere.com

Website: www.ellesmere.com

Head of School: Mr Brendan Wignall MA, FRSA, MCMI

School type: Coeducational Day & Boarding

Age range of pupils: 7–18

No. of pupils enrolled as at 01/09/2020: 550

Fees per term as at 01/09/2020:

Day: £6,330 per term

Weekly Boarding: £8,217 per term

Full Boarding: £11,511 per term

Teacher/pupil ratio: 1:8

King's Worcester

A 21st Century Education in the heart of historic Worcester

A sense of history permeates every brick of this remarkable school, from the medieval Edgar Tower to the ancient College Hall. Around every corner, however, the stunning, contemporary architecture blends seamlessly with the ancient fabric of the school, and that encapsulates the school's ethos perfectly, respecting the school's proud history, and traditional values, whilst embracing technology and innovative teaching methods.

King's Worcester is a dynamic and supportive community where pupils discover and develop their passions in the classroom and beyond. A community made up not just of pupils but also of dedicated teachers. Pastoral care at King's is not just a complementary practice, it is a caring approach fully integrated and interwoven into the fabric of teaching and learning; the school's organisation and engagement with the world beyond the school gates.

Through the school's focus on the development of each individual, they provide a genuinely caring environment where young people can thrive and develop as curious and engaged members of the King's community and a broader society. The school's ethos emphasises mutual respect, openness, and warmth; it is the quality of relationships within the school that makes the pastoral care at King's so special.

The young people who come to King's do outstandingly well academically (the school is not only one of the highest-ranking school in Worcestershire, but in 2019 was one of the Top 10 in the West Midlands,) because they enjoy what is on offer and throw themselves into the opportunities which school life presents and push themselves to give their best. They develop a passion for learning inside and outside of the classroom, a curiosity about the world and a desire to know more about it which will last long after they leave school.

Discovering new experiences and getting involved in activities that stretch both mind and body are what make the days at King's Worcester special. In addition to music, drama and sporting activities, there are over 100 clubs that are enjoyed by the pupils. From chess and Mandarin to sub-aqua and climbing, there is something for everyone to get involved in. For the adventurous, there is The Duke of Edinburgh Award Scheme for which they have received an exceptional 79 gold awards over the last 3 years, a Cadet Force that has achieved outstanding success in regional and national competitions, and the school's own outdoor activity centre in the beautiful Welsh mountains.

Pupils travel far and wide, enjoying Art workshops in St. Ives, History trips, Geography trips to the Alps, Politics trips to London and Washington, and Sports tours to locations such as New Zealand and Sri Lanka, just a few of the incredible opportunities to explore the world, expand horizons and create memories that last a lifetime which King's provides.

The school enjoys a wonderful location adjacent to the Cathedral with fantastic sporting facilities on site, an amazing boathouse and 43 acres of the most beautiful playing fields in the country across the river.

(Founded 1541)

5 College Green, Worcester, Worcestershire WR1 2LL UK

Tel: 01905 721742

Email: registrar@ksw.org.uk

Website: www.ksw.org.uk

Headteacher: Mr Gareth Doodes

Appointed: 2020

School type: Co-educational Day

Age range of pupils: 11–18

No. of pupils enrolled as at 01/09/2020: 896

Fees per term as at 01/09/2020:

Day: £4,850 per term

Teacher/pupil ratio: 1:9

Lucton School

Lucton is a thriving independent day and boarding school set in Herefordshire's idyllic countryside. We build on our 300-year heritage and traditions to provide a stimulating and forward-looking environment.

Lucton's teachers are dedicated to bringing out the full potential of each student whether in the class, on the sports field, in music, or through the many extra-curricular activities we offer. Small classes, and a family atmosphere helps to create a homely place in which students feel accepted, valued and secure.

The school day at Lucton is particularly balanced, allowing our students to be involved in a wide variety of activities both in and out the classroom. In fact, one our greatest assets is our location; 55 acres of beautiful countryside allows children to explore fields and woodland without ever leaving the campus!

Lucton achieves consistently good results. This year our Year 11 students achieved a fantastic 97% pass rate in their GCSEs with 87% attaining 5 or more passes including English and maths. Again, this year, sciences did very well at Lucton and the separate science subjects were amongst many subjects that achieved a 100% pass rate. A significant number of our A level students achieved top grades of three A*, 40% of results were A* and A grades, and 80% being awarded A* to C.

Lucton has a vibrant performing arts community, with individual music lessons, ensembles, choirs, and our own orchestra. As well as drama lessons, as part of the curriculum, and regular opportunities to perform, we also offer LAMDA lessons within the school day.

Sport is an integral part of Lucton School, and we offer an impressive range of activities for a small school; traditional sports such as hockey, football, tennis, netball, basketball, cricket, and rugby sit alongside triathlon and dance. We have our own indoor swimming pool, and our own Equestrian Centre where we annually host NSA competitions. We can even accommodate students own horses or ponies.

For many students boarding is central to their life at Lucton. Based at the heart of the school, we have two boarding houses; School Cottage for children aged between 7 and 13, and Croft House for our older students, which boasts their own single rooms. On weekends boarders enjoy a fantastic programme of activities including cultural trips, theme parks, visiting major cities and attractions, river rafting, paintballing, and much more.

(Founded 1708)

Lucton, Herefordshire HR7 4RW UK

Tel: 01568 782000

Email: admissions@luctonschool.org

Website: www.luctonschool.org

Acting Heads: Mr. Goode & Mrs. Niblett

Appointed: 2020

School type: Coeducational Day & Boarding

Religious Denomination: Christian

Age range of pupils:
6 months–19 years (Boarding from 7)

No. of pupils enrolled as at 01/09/2020: 360

No. of boarders: 80

Fees per annum as at 01/09/2020:

Day: £7,350–£14,250

Weekly Boarding: £23,400–£27,600

Full Boarding: £27,885–£33,780

Average class size: 12

Mander Portman Woodward – Birmingham

MPW Birmingham was founded in 1980 with the goal of ensuring that students experience an education based on the Oxford and Cambridge tutorial system. This means that lessons are more relaxed and informal than a typical school, but are also academically stimulating and demanding. With fewer than ten students in any class, lessons are intensive but rewarding with plenty of opportunity for individual attention and personalised teaching.

MPW Birmingham guides students in their learning by encouraging them to focus on our model of success: aspiration, attitude, attendance, application and achievement. We help students obtain results that all too often they never thought were possible. With almost 30 subjects to choose from at A level and many at GCSE, MPW Birmingham provides a breadth of study opportunity that is unique for a small college. MPW helps students demystify the examination process and develop both the technical skills and academic knowledge needed to perform well under timed conditions. We offer all of our students the opportunity to sit weekly assessments enabling students to perfect examination technique.

We run a university support programme that values every student in equal measure regardless of aspiration; we treat all students as though they are elite. We prepare students for a range of courses including medicine, dentistry and Oxbridge and ensure that they are well equipped to cope with the demands of university life.

Students benefit from outstanding pastoral care with each student being allocated a Personal Tutor. This builds upon our core values of diligence, respect, tolerance and care. We expect our students to work hard but we also expect to provide more support to our students than they would receive at other schools. Our culture is one based on high expectations but one that is both nurturing and unpretentious. We run a non-compulsory enrichment programme in which many students participate, developing both sporting and cultural interests. There is no glass ceiling in MPW Birmingham and we strive to enable all students to reach their potential and use their talents without inhibition.

Our mission is to be one of the leading colleges of its type within the country, enabling students to develop confidence, maturity, knowledge and skills, turning academic aspirations into reality. MPW helps build the character of students enabling them to develop good self-discipline regarding work, intellectual curiosity and a sense of duty regarding community. Our best ambassadors are our students and we are rightly proud of what they achieve with us and what they go on to achieve afterwards. We change lives for the better and help bring about progress and success. Irrespective of where a student is starting from, MPW helps young people achieve special things.

(Founded 1980)

16-18 Greenfield Crescent, Edgbaston, Birmingham, West Midlands B15 3AU UK

Tel: 0121 454 9637

Fax: 0121 454 6433

Email: birmingham@mpw.ac.uk

Website: www.mpw.ac.uk

Principal: Mr Mark Shingleton

School type: Coeducational Day

Age range of pupils: 14–19

Average class size: 8

Shrewsbury School

Located on a beautiful 110-acre site, perched above the historic town of Shrewsbury and the banks of the River Severn, Shrewsbury School has a world-class reputation for all-round excellence. Fully co-educational, with a seven-day boarding heartbeat and an integral day community, we deliver a dynamic education that develops the abilities and enthusiasms of every individual girl and boy.

School should be serious fun. Learning and enjoyment go hand in hand: in the classroom, through a vibrant co-curricular programme and in the communal life of the School. At Shrewsbury, we aim to provide the most diverse, challenging and supportive environment in which all our children can thrive and exceed their own expectations.

A good education opens doors. This means getting the best possible examination results and qualifications. Academic excellence is achieved through a wide-ranging curriculum that uncovers and encourages a genuine love of learning, alongside inspirational teaching that challenges each pupil to strive for her or his personal best.

In 2020, both A Level and GCSE results have been determined by teachers rather than examination. Although the headline A Level figures make for excellent reading (28% A*, 84.6% A*-B), what has mattered more than ever has been the transition of pupils to their chosen universities and over 90% of Shrewsbury School pupils have been confirmed in their first choice places. At GCSE level, 50% of grades were awarded at 9 or 8 (an A* on the old system) and 72% at 9 to 7. Pupils now have an excellent base from which they can move forward with confidence towards their A Level studies.

However, examination certificates are just one product of education. Many skills, values and aptitudes do not come with a piece of paper, but they are nonetheless vital for happy and purposeful living. A great education nurtures character; and it lasts a lifetime.

We want all our pupils to enjoy their life beyond the classroom and Shrewsbury has a long-standing reputation for musical, dramatic and sporting excellence. We compete internationally in cricket and rowing and, on a national level, we are one of the strongest schools for football, cross-country and fives. Facilities and coaching are first-rate across each of these sports, as well as a host of others, including rugby, hockey, netball, lacrosse, fencing, swimming and tennis.

The breadth and quality of drama and music-making at Shrewsbury is remarkable. Shrewsbury School plays and musicals have regularly drawn praise at the Edinburgh Fringe Festival and each year our pupils have the opportunity to perform at prestigious venues, such as London's Cadogan Hall and Birmingham Town Hall. A number of our pupils win places at top music colleges year-on-year.

The Barnes Theatre opened in 2020, providing a fantastic home for Drama at Shrewsbury. The building houses an intimate 206-seat auditorium, two drama studios, a fully equipped dance studio and a state-of-the-art technical workshop.

Shrewsbury pupils also enjoy an extraordinary variety of clubs, societies and co-curricular activities, many of which take place on a dedicated weekly basis. Surrounded by glorious unspoilt countryside, the School makes the most of its close proximity to the Shropshire hills and Snowdonia.

The Shrewsbury School motto gets to the heart of our vision: *Intus Si Recte Ne Labora* – 'if all is right within, trouble not'. Ours is not a superficial, skin-deep education but one that seeks to develop the whole person. If our values are true, and we live by them with honesty and conviction; if we look beyond the surface of things to question and champion independence of mind; and if we learn deeply in order to lead lives of meaning, generosity and purpose, then we will see the full fruits of a Shrewsbury education.

Shrewsbury School

(Founded 1552)

The Schools, Shrewsbury, Shropshire SY3 7BA UK

Tel: 01743 280552

Fax: 01743 243107

Email: admissions@shrewsbury.org.uk

Website: www.shrewsbury.org.uk

Headmaster: Mr. Leo Winkley

Appointed: 2018

School type: Coeducational Day & Boarding

Religious Denomination: Anglican

Age range of pupils: 13–18

No. of pupils enrolled as at 07/09/2020: 819

Boys: 538 **Girls:** 281

No. of boarders: 619

Fees per annum as at 01/09/2020:

Day: £25,770

Full Boarding: £37,560

Average class size: GCSE: 18; A level: 10

Teacher/pupil ratio: 1:9

Tettenhall College

Tettenhall College prides itself on its heritage foundations. With a history dating back to 1863, the School has played a significant role in educating boys and girls across the West Midlands, further afield and internationally for many years.

The emphasis at Tettenhall College is centred around developing each and every pupil. Enabling each pupil to discover, create and drive their skills and talents in every facet of their education – truly being able to 'release their potential'. The School is built on a core vision and values through the School's overarching mission for everyone to do their best.

A vision to provide outstanding personalised education. A mission to nurture the pupils to achieve their potential and discover their unique talents, to thrive for excellence and to foster self-belief. Creativity to have the freedom to adapt and evolve for the pupil's future. The School community – to foster a safe and secure family environment. To cultivate emotional intelligence.

Tettenhall College is known to all of the School community as the 'TC Family'. Staff provide support and guidance to every pupil, creating a warm, friendly and caring environment. The School believes in a single, inclusive community in which everyone is valued equally. Teachers know their pupils extremely well and are able to respond to their individual needs, whether academic, practical or emotional.

Boarding life is a 'home from home', with international senior and junior boarders, flexi, weekly and day boarders, forging life-long friendships together and with the local day pupils. Boarders have their dedicated well-equipped single sex boarding houses. Dedicated weekend trips and activities are planned and a well-balanced nutritious varied menu is served each day for all of the pupils.

In the Preparatory School, the unique enrichment programme aims to deepen and widen the experience of pupils with subjects ranging from Latin to Mandarin and a dedicated Forest School that is deeply in bedded into the core curriculum, right from the beginning.

In the Senior School, the dedicated Head of Sixth Form and Head of Careers, work closely with every pupil, understanding and supporting the pupil to make the right choices for their next important stage in their education. The School's 'Pathways' Programme introduces a wide variety of unique opportunities, to aid each pupil to obtain an in depth, first-hand experience and knowledge regarding industry sectors, to enable them to make that vital 'career path'.

Pupils are taught in small class sizes for each individual to reach their true potential across the curriculum. Academic success is a major focus across the whole School, with consistently high GCSE and A Level grades above national averages. In 2019, 25% of pupils achieved A*, A or B in all of their subjects, with the majority of pupils gaining places at their first choice of university, including some of the top institutions in the country. BTEC in Performing Arts will be offered from September 2020. Scholarship programmes are offered from Y7 to Sixth Form across: Academic, Art, Music, Sport and Drama.

An extensive Sports programme is offered for all ages through the School. From swimming to squash, seasonal sports to fencing. Regular sporting fixtures to interschool matches. The Performing Arts (Music and Drama) and Art departments attract and nurture incredible talent – winning numerous accolades and entrances into future specialist academies and universities.

The 30 acre estate boasts an original heritage Victorian theatre and indoor swimming pool, state of the art squash courts, playing fields, MUGA court, an extensive Music department, Art studios and Science labs. A truly outstanding heritage educational site with modern facilities for day and boarding boys and girls.

Tettenhall College
AN INDEPENDENT SCHOOL FOR AGES 2 TO 18

(Founded 1863)

Wood Road, Tettenhall, Wolverhampton, West Midlands WV6 8QX UK

Tel: 01902 751119

Email: admissions@tettcoll.co.uk

Website: www.tettenhallcollege.co.uk

Headteacher: Mr Christopher McAllister

Appointed: January 2020

School type: Coeducational Day & Boarding

Age range of pupils: 2–18

No. of pupils enrolled as at 01/09/2020: 410

Fees per term as at 01/09/2020:

Day Fees: £2,552 – £4,858 per term

Flexi Boarding Fees: £4,078 – £5,362 per term

Weekly Boarding Fees: £6,103 – £8,791 per term

Full Boarding Fees: £7,709 – £11,060 per term

Average class size: 16

Teacher/pupil ratio: 1:10

The Royal School Wolverhampton

The building works continue! After opening as a Free school/ State Boarding School in 2016, and following the ambitious and successful growth programme in pupil numbers over the past four years, The Royal School's exciting building programme is now well under way to develop first class teaching facilities for pupils from five to 19. Phase one of the school's development plan saw a new Sixth Form Centre and refurbished classrooms. Phase two starts in the summer with new labs and more classrooms coming on line.

At the centre of all that we do is our inclusive community where students study, play and live together harmoniously. The Royal is a small, cohesive community with a friendly atmosphere for both day pupils and boarders alike. Our strong academic tradition is based upon individual attention and encouragement, as well as excellent pastoral care founded on respect, tolerance and understanding of others. Students achieve their full academic potential, whilst a wide range of extended-day activities is available to develop character and leadership. We prepare pupils for Oxbridge and other top universities while also catering to pupils of all abilities. The School regularly achieves high standards in both A-Level and GCSE results, particularly in STEM subjects of mathematics and the sciences. The Royal combines traditional values with a modern outlook and a 'real-world' attitude. At The Royal, education is about developing the whole individual.

Developing the 'whole person' in sport, drama, music and adventurous activity, young people at The Royal are also better placed to make the best of their opportunities to become well-rounded individuals with confidence and empathy for those around them.

The Royal School
Wolverhampton

Penn Road, Wolverhampton, West Midlands WV3 0EG UK

Tel: +44 (0)1902 341230

Email: info@theroyal.school

Website: www.theroyalschool.co.uk

Head of School: Mark Heywood

School type: Co-educational Day & Boarding

Age range of pupils: 4–19

Boarding: 11–19

No. of pupils enrolled as at 01/09/2020: 1432

Fees per annum as at 01/09/2020:

Full Boarding: £12,900

Average class size: 25

West House School

Situated in the leafy oasis of the Calthorpe Estate, West House School has occupied the same site since its foundation in 1895. Since that time, the school has evolved significantly to become an independent preparatory school for boys aged 4-11 years, with a co-educational Early Years Department offering care and education for children aged from 12 months. West House is a member of The Independent Association of Preparatory Schools and, as such, upholds the requirement to provide a 'world class education'.

Set within five acres of beautiful grounds, less than two miles from Birmingham city centre, the school lies at the heart of a thriving community. Pupils of all ages benefit from two all-weather playing surfaces, a nature reserve and the multi-functional Duce Hall, providing indoor sporting and theatrical facilities. The school is also surrounded by many outstanding cultural and recreational amenities which enrich the lives of all pupils and allow them to explore and extend their talents in numerous curricular and extra-curricular pursuits.

West House is a non-denominational school, guided by Christian principles. It is divided into three departments – Prep (Years 3-6), Pre-Prep (Years 1 & 2) and the Early Years Foundation Stage (Nursery – Reception). From their earliest years, children are encouraged to adopt the core values of the school which are actively promoted throughout the working day and frequently form the focus of assemblies and PSHE lessons.

The school continues to boast a unique family atmosphere of which founding Headmaster, Arthur Perrott Cary Field, would have been proud. In the spirit of combining the best of its traditions with an education that prepares pupils for life in the middle part of the twenty first century, it remains determined to be at the forefront of innovation. This is reflected in the delivery of an ambitious curriculum which complements academic rigour with significant opportunities for pupils to explore personal interests in sport, art, music and drama.

Employing 45 full-time and part-time academic staff, many of whom are subject specialists, West House has grown considerably during the last five years to accommodate approximately 330 pupils, with 130 attending the EYFS Department.

Pupils are prepared for a wide range of senior schools, and standards at 11+ are consistently high, with most Year 6 boys transferring to local grammar schools, King Edward's School, Birmingham and Solihull School. A number of pupils are awarded academic and sporting scholarships and the school also enjoys outstanding success in academic challenges, quizzes and competitions at regional and national level.

Further details about the school can be found at www.westhouseprep.com

(Founded 1895)

24 St James's Road, Edgbaston, Birmingham, West Midlands B15 2NX UK

Tel: 0121 440 4097

Fax: 0121 440 5839

Email: secretary@westhouseprep.com

Website: www.westhouseprep.com

Headmaster:
Mr Alistair M J Lyttle BA(Hons), PGCE, NPQH

School type: Boys' Day

Age range of boys: 1–11

Age range of girls: 1–4

No. of pupils enrolled as at 01/09/2020: 350

Fees per term as at 01/09/2020:

Day: £1,466–£4,083 per term

Average class size: 17 (two form entry)

Teacher/pupil ratio: 1:12

Yorkshire & Humberside

Pocklington School

Pocklington is an inclusive, family focussed and academic school that offers incredible experiences inside and outside the classroom. We believe in encouraging pupils to seize opportunities from the broad range of activities on offer. Along with our approach to teaching and learning, these help to form the bedrock of our young Pocklingtonians' character and grow the qualities that support our values. Our sense of community, care for each other and pride in the school is tangible. This is no more evident than in our outstanding boarding provision. At the heart of this ethos lie our Values and Virtues. They drive all that we do at Pocklington and mean our pupils leave with a deep sense of social responsibility and the ability to shape their own future.

Pocklington School lies 12 miles east of York in a safe, rural setting on the edge of a small, friendly market town, on a 50-acre campus with good public transport links and its own minibus pick-up service. The School was founded in 1514 and has retained its strong tradition of encouraging pupils to have the courage to take chances with learning and always remain true to themselves.

Numerous co-curricular activities for day and boarding pupils take place every day until 5pm, and each pupil is encouraged to pursue their own interests to help develop the depth of character and self-awareness to tackle life's challenges on their own terms. Extensive facilities include a 300-seat theatre, an indoor sports hall, conditioning room and swimming pool, plus 21 acres of grass sports pitches and two full-sized synthetic pitches. Full, flexible and casual boarding options are available, in boarding houses which create a home from home for both domestic and international students.

Right through from Prep School, with its emphasis on nurturing children's natural curiosity, imagination and enthusiasm for learning, to the Sixth Form where independent thought is prized, our pupils are encouraged to be resilient, resourceful learners. Lessons are planned around giving pupils the opportunity to develop their independence and character, rather than simply acquiring and retaining facts. We employ the best educational tools and appropriate new technology facilities to ensure youngsters are enthused and inspired by the world of knowledge available to them. Flexible learning platforms and an individual approach allows each pupil to progress at his or her pace, boosting their confidence and self-esteem so they often exceed their expectations.

Our £3m Art and Design Technology Centre, which opened in Autumn 2017, has every facility to encourage the pursuit of traditional arts and crafts, as well as provide cutting-edge equipment for digital and computer design, and manufacturing technology. The innovation and cross fertilisation of ideas the Centre promotes are increasingly valued in society today.

Sixth Form facilities include spacious communal areas, a study centre, and comprehensive library. Students are encouraged to work both collaboratively and independently as they begin to make the transition to university study and/or workplace success.

Recent former pupils who retain links with the school include Davis Cup winner Kyle Edmund, England rugby star Rob Webber and world-renowned concert pianist Alexandra Dariescu.

We aim to instil the Pocklington Values and Virtues into all our pupils, to engage with our families and support them in raising the Pocklingtonians of tomorrow and to be open to innovation, conscious of tradition and so secure our Foundation's future.

POCKLINGTON SCHOOL

Ages 3 to 18

(Founded 1514)

West Green, Pocklington, York, North Yorkshire YO42 2NJ UK

Tel: 01759 321200

Fax: 01759 306366

Email: admissions@pocklingtonschool.com

Website: www.pocklingtonschool.com

Headmaster: Mr Toby Seth MA (Cantab)

Appointed: January 2019

School type: Coeducational Day & Boarding

Religious Denomination:
Christian ethos welcoming all faiths and none

Age range of pupils: 3–18

No. of pupils enrolled as at 01/09/2020: 705

Boys: 371 **Girls:** 334 **Sixth Form:** 135

No. of boarders: 70

Fees per annum as at 01/09/2020:

Day: £15,057

Weekly Boarding: £26,991

Full Boarding: £29,346

Queen Ethelburga's Collegiate Foundation

Students and staff at Queen Ethelburga's College and Faculty are celebrating another successful year, following the publishing of the 2020 A level and BTEC examination results. University destinations include: Oxford, Cambridge, Bristol, Imperial College London, UCL (University College London), University of Sheffield and London School of Economics. We congratulate them as they reap the rewards of their hard work over many years.

QE also places great emphasis on our students growing into resilient, caring, compassionate and confident adults, who develop independence and initiative, and who can take responsibility for their own learning and futures. We provide opportunities for students to take part in a range of wider enrichment and extra-curricular activities to help them to gain skills in leadership, teamwork and collaboration, and decision making.

Students at QE have access to an impressive 150 sports and activities each week, including popular sports such as rugby, hockey, football, netball, cricket, swimming, basketball, rounders, tennis, dance, gymnastics, trampolining, climbing, athletics, badminton, and volleyball. Our team of sports staff cater for all abilities and encourage each student to make the most of all the fantastic opportunities on offer during their time here. We have a well-honed mix of physical education teachers and specialist sports coaches, many of whom are ex-professional sportspeople themselves. This means there really is no limit to the level our students can train to. Health and fitness is so central to school life for students that many continue with sport and exercise, either recreationally or as a route of study, that it continues to be a key part of their lives long after they have left us for the next step in their education or career.

What enables us to deliver all of this sporting activity so successfully of course is the outstanding range of high quality facilities on campus. We're pretty unique in that we have a dedicated Sports Village, completed in 2016, to which all students have access to inside and outside of formal school hours. The Village is home to a 25-metre swimming pool, triple court sports hall, 100 station fitness suite and free weights centre. Outside we have a four-lane synthetic cushioned running track and over 30 acres of both grass and artificial 3G pitches. We also have a number of specialist studios used for; martial arts, wrestling, dance, gymnastics, table tennis, cycling, archery, fencing and boxing.

In addition to all this, the students can make use of an eight-metre climbing wall at the campus activity centre, which also houses an assault course, BMX track and additional tennis courts.

There really is something for everyone and for all abilities.

All of Queen Ethelburga's students follow a sports programme with the values of fair play, honesty and determination at its heart. Our motto of 'be the best that I can, with the gifts that I have' is never more evident than through the work we do as TEAM QE.

(Founded 1912)

Thorpe Underwood Hall, Ouseburn, York, North Yorkshire YO26 9SS UK

Tel: 01423 33 33 33

Email: info@qe.org

Website: www.qe.org

Principal: Jeff Smith

Appointed: August 2020

School type: Coeducational Day & Boarding

Religious Denomination: Multi-Denominational

Age range of pupils: 3–19

No. of pupils enrolled as at 01/09/2020: 1248

Average class size: 18

Teacher/pupil ratio: 1:10

The Froebelian School

The Froebelian School in Horsforth is a thriving and dynamic independent prep school, which places children at the very heart of all it strives to achieve. From the age of three, we seek to equip our boys and girls with a lifelong thirst for and love of learning and the school continually achieves impressive levels of academic success; preparing our children for the next stage in their educational journey.

The children and staff work harmoniously together creating a special place, with a uniquely happy atmosphere.

Our aim is to provide a first class all-round education and committed pastoral care in which the unique needs, abilities, interests and aspirations of our bright, inquisitive children are met and their talents can flourish in a caring, structured and secure environment. This enables us to develop the whole child and we work hard to build solid foundations, which balance both the co-curricular and academic spheres of school life and honour our school motto – 'Giving a flying start to the citizens of tomorrow.' As a result, our children regularly secure a place at their first choice senior school and we enjoy an excellent scholarship success rate.

We are delighted that Froebelian children are happy and want to come to school every day and are passionate that all children enjoy a positive experience. Throughout the year extensive learning opportunities are balanced by a wide range of co-curricular activities in sport, music, art and technology and events. We foster our children's curiosity and imagination at every stage of school life and the children are nurtured and supported by an excellent staff:pupil ratio of 1:10.

Welcoming over 170 pupils between the ages of 3 and 11, we set the highest standards and expectations and The Froebelian School is acknowledged as one of the North's leading Independent prep schools.

The latest Independent Schools Inspectorate report judged The Froebelian School as 'excellent' for the quality of the pupils' achievements and the quality of pupils' personal development – this is the highest judgement available from the Independent Schools Inspectorate.

"The pupils' attitudes to learning are exceptional" **ISI Inspectorate 2017**

Awarded 'Outstanding' by Ofsted, our private day nursery, First-Steps at Froebelian, follows the school's ethos closely and offers younger children the opportunity to start realising their full potential at an earlier age.

"The leadership and management are inspirational" **Ofsted**

Situated in Horsforth, a pleasant and vibrant suburb of Leeds near to the ring road, the school is easily accessible from most areas of Leeds, Bradford and Harrogate. Our site is very secure with a wooded area offering delightful views over the Aire valley.

The school is an educational charity where ultimate responsibility rests with a School Council (governors). The day-to-day running of the school is delegated to the Headteacher, supported by a Senior Leadership Team.

Our children adore their school and are justly proud of all they do. They love learning and there is a true sense of fun. We would love you to experience the warmth and politeness of our children for yourselves – please do come and meet them!

Visit www.froebelian.com to find out more.

THE FROEBELIAN SCHOOL
GIVING A FLYING START TO THE CITIZENS OF TOMORROW

(Founded 1913)

Clarence Road, Horsforth, Leeds, West Yorkshire LS18 4LB UK

Tel: 0113 2583047

Fax: 0113 2580173

Email: office@froebelian.co.uk

Website: www.froebelian.com

Head Teacher: Mrs Catherine Dodds BEd (Hons), PGCE

Appointed: 2015

School type: Coeducational Day

Age range of pupils: 3–11

No. of pupils enrolled as at 01/09/2020: 172

Boys: 86 **Girls:** 86

Fees per annum as at 01/09/2020:

Day: £5,430–£8,100

Teacher/pupil ratio: 1:10

Scotland

Strathallan School

Our mission is to provide an outstanding education that gives opportunities for all pupils to perform to the very best of their abilities. Each individual, no matter their passion or interest, is supported and inspired to shine during their time at school. Our pupils excel academically, compete in sports at national and international levels, succeed in scholastic championships and play as part of nationwide orchestras and ensembles. In the 2018-19 academic year, 60 of our pupils played as part of a national sporting team and we became British and Scottish Champions across six sports.

Our aim is to send pupils out into the world with close friends and the ability to make new ones, with the knowledge and skills to succeed at university and beyond. We will be delighted to welcome you and discuss how your child or children might join the Strathallan family and benefit from the opportunities on offer for them here.

Academic excellence

Academically, we strive for excellence and our ambition is to inspire a lifelong enjoyment of learning for learning's sake. Our flexible curriculum and innovative teaching means we can support every pupil, whatever their ambitions and style of learning. In 2019, Strathallan students achieved their best A Level results in almost a decade, with a quarter of all A Level students awarded straight A* or A grades. Our leavers go on to Oxbridge and Russell Group universities, international study, work placements, the Armed Forces and professional sporting careers.

Global community

Strathallan is a friendly, welcoming place with a strong sense of community. In 2019 The Care Inspectorate rated Strathallan a Grade 6 (Sector Leading) Excellent for the Quality of care and support. It's an outstanding environment in which to learn and each pupil is encouraged to explore their talents and to realise their potential academically, in the arts, in sport and in a host of interests and activities. We make the most of our self-contained, rural location every day, but at our core, we are a truly international community with pupils and alumni around the globe. This diversity of community and experience means Strathallians leave our school with the maturity and cultural intelligence to succeed, wherever they go.

Opportunities for all to excel

Our pupils find confidence in themselves at Strathallan. They have the freedom and space to develop their own skills in an idyllic environment with the support of a close, caring community. We believe that learning outside the classroom bolsters success inside the classroom, and it's this holistic approach to education that leads to a rich diversity of pupil experience and consistently exceptional achievements. We ensure there is something for every one of our pupils, and any parent choosing Strathallan will quickly realise that their child will be known here – for who they are, for their individual abilities and for their potential. Young people leave Strathallan with the skills and knowledge to succeed in their chosen career, and the confidence to make their mark on the world.

"I look back at my time at Strathallan with fondness. The quality of education in the classroom, in the creative arts and on the sports field was of the highest possible level. With Strathallan on my CV there are no doors that are not open to me."
Former pupil

STRATHALLAN SCHOOL

Opportunities for all to excel

(Founded 1913)

Forgandenny, Perth, Perth & Kinross PH2 9EG UK

Tel: 01738 812546

Fax: 01738 812549

Email: admissions@strathallan.co.uk

Website: www.strathallan.co.uk

Headmaster: Mr Mark Lauder MA Hons

Appointed: 2017

School type: Coeducational Boarding & Day

Age range of pupils: 8–18

No. of pupils enrolled as at 01/09/2020: 520

Fees per annum as at 01/09/2020:

Day: £15,435–£23,532

Full Boarding: £24,174–£34,650

Average class size: 14

Teacher/pupil ratio: 1:7

Wales

Westbourne School

1st in the UK League Tables for 5 consecutive years and awarded The Sunday Times Schools Guide, IB School of the Year 2019, Westbourne School is one of the UK's leading academic schools. Established in 1896, Westbourne develops well-rounded students, equipped with the skills, knowledge, confidence and character to become leaders of the future in their chosen field.

Nationally recognised excellence
- 1st in the UK League Tables for the past 5 years (Daily Telegraph/Best-Schools; smaller schools)
- IB School of the Year 2019 (Sunday Times Schools Guide)
- 1st IB Sixth Form (Sunday Times Schools Guide)
- 3rd Overall in the UK (Sunday Times Schools Guide)
- Awarded 'excellent' in all 5 inspection categories (Estyn National Inspectorate 2018)

"Its sixth form results last summer were beaten by just two schools in England, Wales and Northern Ireland. Students achieved A*-B equivalent A-level grades of 97.9% in their Higher Level IB papers, the best results of any school offering only the IB in the sixth form." Alistair McCall, Editor, The Sunday Times Schools Guide

Gold standard programmes
IB Diploma: Internationally recognized and widely respected for its breadth of programme. 2/3rd of Westbourne Higher Level grades are consistently 7s and 6s (A*/A equivalent). 2/3rd of students received a Bilingual Diploma.

GCSE/IGCSE: Full course and 1 year GCSE/IGCSE programmes: 40% of GCSE grades are A* equivalent; (20% Grade 9 | 20% Grade 8s), 5 times the UK national average.

Pre-IB: One year, Pre-Diploma foundation course for international students, specifically designed for 15-16 year.

Certainty of university entry
90% Russell Group University average. Westbourne graduates progress to study highly competitive courses including Medicine, Engineering, Economics, Computer Science, Business and Law.

Outstanding teachers and unparalleled support
Offering individualised academic excellence, Westbourne has a warm and highly supportive culture. Small class sizes, an 8:1 pupil-to-teacher ratio and a tutorial style ensures every student excels.

More than 50% of teachers at Westbourne have a PhD or Masters and more than 50% have taught internationally, so can quickly relate with local and international students alike.

Boarding environment
Located in the safe seaside town of Penarth, ranked as one of the Top 10 best places to live in the UK, also just minutes from the vibrant capital city of Cardiff, Westbourne is a resoundingly British school. A student body of 72% British students, complemented by 16% European, 12% Asian students drawn from 24 different countries; no one nationality dominates.

Boarding students live within 2 minutes-walk of the main school building, in a modern fully-equipped boarding house, supported by live in, caring and professional House Parents.

Co-curricular activities and world-class facilities
Westbourne runs an expansive co-curricular programme, enriched with opportunities for students to test themselves through competitions, Olympiads and Duke of Edinburgh Awards.

WESTBOURNE SCHOOL

(Founded 1896)

Hickman Road, Penarth, Glamorgan CF64 2AJ UK

Tel: 029 2070 5705

Email: enquiries@westbourneschool.com

Website: www.westbourneschool.com

Headteacher: Dr GW Griffiths BSc, PhD, ARCS, PGCE

School type: Co-educational Day & Boarding

Age range of pupils: 2–18

No. of pupils enrolled as at 01/09/2020: 300

Fees per annum as at 01/09/2020:

Day: £8,100–£14,010

Full Boarding: £32,750–£35,850

Average class size: 16

Teacher/pupil ratio: 1:8

Overseas

École Jeannine Manuel – Lille

École Jeannine Manuel Lille is a non-profit pre-K-12 coeducational school founded in 1992. As the sister school of École Jeannine Manuel Paris, they have the same educational project and the same mission: promote international understanding through bilingual (French/ English) education. An associated UNESCO school, École Jeannine Manuel Lille is the only non-denominational independent school in Nord-Pas-de-Calais, with over 900 pupils representing 50 nationalities and every major cultural tradition. The school's academic excellence matches its diversity: École Jeannine Manuel Lille achieves excellent performances, both at the French Baccalaureate and the International Baccalaureate. The school is accredited by the French Ministry of Education, the International Baccalaureate Organization (IBO), the Council of International Schools (CIS) and the New England Association of Schools and Colleges (NEASC).

The campus of school extends over 3.5 hectares and includes a boarding house, a restaurant, two football fields, a multi-sport room, and high standard sports facilities and equipment. The boarding house welcomes this year 120 pupils from 6th to 12th grades.

Each year, École Jeannine Manuel Lille welcomes non-French speaking students. Over the years École Jeannine Manuel has developed a program to suit the needs of these students, for whom the emotional challenge of relocation is often as great than its academic challenge. Thanks to their French teachers and their methods, the students will be fluent in French in a few months.

The lower and middle school follow the French national curriculum with several exceptions: English is taught every day and, in middle school, experimental sciences, history and geography are taught in English. The curriculum is enriched at all levels, not only with a more advanced English language and literature curriculum, but also, for example, with Chinese language instruction (compulsory in grades 3-4-5), an integrated science programme in lower school, and independent research projects in middle school.

In upper school, 10th graders follow the French national curriculum, albeit taught 50% in French and 50% in English. In 11th grade, pupils choose between the French track (international option of the French baccalaureate (OIB)) and the International Baccalaureate Diploma Programme (IBDP). Approximately 25% of our pupils opt for the IBDP. (Please note that, since the IBDP does not receive any government subsidies, its tuition is three times the French track tuition.)

Admission

Although admission is competitive, every effort is made to reserve space for international applicants, including children of families who expect to remain in France for a limited period of time and wish to combine a cultural immersion in French education with the ability to re-enter their own school systems and excel.

ÉCOLE Jeannine Manuel

International understanding through a bilingual education

(Founded 1992)

418 bis rue Albert Bailly, Marcq-en-Baroeul, 59700 France

Tel: +33 3 20 65 90 50

Fax: +33 3 20 98 06 41

Email: admissions-lille@ejm.net

Website: www.ecolejeanninemanuel.org

Head of School: Constance Devaux

School type: Coeducational Day & Boarding

Age range of pupils: 3–18 years

No. of pupils enrolled as at 01/09/2020: 975

Fees per annum as at 01/09/2020:

Day: €5,637

Full Boarding: €14,835–€21,465

IB Classes: €20,685

Average class size: 25 (15 in IBDP)

École Jeannine Manuel – Paris

École Jeannine Manuel is a non-profit pre-K-12 coeducational school founded in 1954 with the mission to promote international understanding through bilingual (French/English) education. An associated UNESCO school, École Jeannine Manuel welcomes pupils representing 80 nationalities and every major cultural tradition. The school's academic excellence matches its diversity: École Jeannine Manuel is regularly ranked among the top French high schools (state and independent) for its overall academic performance (ranked first for eight consecutive years). The school is accredited by the French Ministry of Education, the International Baccalaureate Organization (IBO), the Council of International Schools (CIS) and the New England Association of Schools and Colleges (NEASC).

Each year, the school welcomes more than 100 new non-French speaking pupils. These students, key to the cultural diversity of the school, are enrolled in an adaptation programme where they receive intensive and immersive French tuition tailored to their individual level.

The lower and middle school follow the French national curriculum with several exceptions: English is taught every day and, in middle school, experimental sciences, history and geography are taught in English. The curriculum is enriched at all levels, not only with a more advanced English language and literature curriculum, but also, for example, with Chinese language instruction (compulsory in grades 3-4-5), an integrated science programme in lower school, and independent research projects in middle school.

In upper school, 10th graders follow the French national curriculum, albeit taught 50% in French and 50% in English. In 11th grade, pupils choose between the French track (international option of the French baccalaureate (OIB)) and the International Baccalaureate Diploma Programme (IBDP). Approximately 25% of our pupils opt for the IBDP. (Please note that, since the IBDP does not receive any government subsidies, its tuition is three times the French track tuition.)

Over the past three years, approximately 20% of our graduating class have gone to US colleges or universities, 48% chose the UK or Canada, 37% entered the French higher education system, and the balance pursued their education all over the world.

Admission

Although admission is competitive and applications typically exceed available spaces by a ratio of 7:1, every effort is made to reserve space for international applicants, including children of families who expect to remain in France for a limited period of time and wish to combine a cultural immersion in French education with the ability to re-enter their own school systems and excel.

ÉCOLE Jeannine Manuel

International understanding through a bilingual education

(Founded 1954)

70 rue du Théâtre, Paris, 75015 France

Tel: +33 1 44 37 00 80

Fax: +33 1 45 79 06 66

Email: admissions@ejm.net

Website: www.ecolejeanninemanuel.org

Principal: Jérôme Giovendo

School type: Coeducational Day

Age range of pupils: 4–18 years

No. of pupils enrolled as at 01/09/2020: 2400

Fees per annum as at 01/09/2020:

Day: €6,417–€6,765

IB Classes: €21,390

Average class size: 25

Geographical directory of schools

KEY TO SYMBOLS

(♂) *Boys' school*

(♀) *Girls' school*

(🌐) *International school*

(16) *Tutorial or sixth form college*

(A) *A levels*

(🏫) *Boarding accommodation*

(£) *Bursaries*

(IB) *International Baccalaureate*

(✎) *Learning support*

(16) *Entrance at 16+*

(🎓) *Vocational qualifications*

(IAPS) *Independent Association of Preparatory Schools*

(HMC) *The Headmasters' & Headmistresses' Conference*

(ISA) *Independent Schools Association*

(GSA) *Girls' School Association*

(BSA) *Boarding Schools' Association*

(S) *Society of Heads*

Unless otherwise indicated, all schools are coeducational day schools.
Single-sex and boarding schools will be indicated by the relevant icon.

D272

Channel Islands

Guernsey D274
Jersey D274

KEY TO SYMBOLS
- ⓕ *Boys' school*
- ⓐ *Girls' school*
- ⓒ *International school*
- ⓰ *Tutorial or sixth form college*
- ⓐ *A levels*
- ⓑ *Boarding accommodation*
- ⓔ *Bursaries*
- ⓘ *International Baccalaureate*
- ⓛ *Learning support*
- ⓰ *Entrance at 16+*
- ⓥ *Vocational qualifications*
- (IAPS) *Independent Association of Preparatory Schools*
- (HMC) *The Headmasters' & Headmistresses' Conference*
- (ISA) *Independent Schools Association*
- (GSA) *Girls' School Association*
- (BSA) *Boarding Schools' Association*
- ⓢ *Society of Heads*

Unless otherwise indicated, all schools are coeducational day schools.
Single-sex and boarding schools will be indicated by the relevant icon.

Guernsey

Elizabeth College Junior School
Beechwood, Queen's Road, St
Peter Port, Guernsey GY1 1PU
Tel: 01481 722123
Headteacher: Richard Fyfe
Age range: 2 1/2–11
No. of pupils: 270
Fees: Day £10,350–£11,370

The Ladies' College
Les Graves, St Peter Port,
Guernsey GY1 1RW
Tel: 01481 721602
Principal: Ashley Clancy
Age range: G2 1/2–18
No. of pupils: 600 VIth100
Fees: Day £10,560–£11,175

Jersey

Beaulieu Convent School
Wellington Road, St Helier,
Jersey JE2 4RJ
Tel: 01534 731280
Headmaster: Mr C Beirne
Age range: B16–19 G3–19
No. of pupils: 829 VIth99
Fees: Day £6,780

De La Salle College
Wellington Road, St Saviour,
Jersey JE2 7TH
Tel: 01534 754100
Head of College: Mr Jason Turner
Age range: 3–18
No. of pupils: 762
Fees: Day £5,805

FCJ Primary School
Deloraine Road, St Saviour,
Jersey JE2 7XB
Tel: 01534 723063
Headmistress: Ms Donna Lenzi
Age range: 4–11
No. of pupils: 290
Fees: Day £4,440

Helvetia House School
14 Elizabeth Place, St
Helier, Jersey JE2 3PN
Tel: 01534 724928
Headmistress: Mrs Lindsey
Woodward BA, DipEd
Age range: G4–11
No. of pupils: 82
Fees: Day £4,725

Jersey College For Girls
Le Mont Millais, St Saviour,
Jersey JE2 7YB
Tel: 01534 516200
Principal: Carl Howarth
Age range: G11–18

St George's Preparatory School
La Hague Manor, Rue de la
Hague, St Peter, Jersey JE3 7DB
Tel: 01534 481593
Headmaster: Mr Cormac Timothy
Age range: 2–11
No. of pupils: 244
Fees: Day £5,796–£15,495

**ST MICHAEL'S PREPARATORY
SCHOOL**
For further details see p.44
La Rue de la Houguette, St
Saviour, Jersey JE2 7UG
Tel: 01534 856904
Email: office@stmichaels.je
Website: www.stmichaels.je
Age range: 3–14
No. of pupils: 315
Fees: Day £10,230–£16,080

Victoria College
Le Mont Millais, St Helier, Jersey JE1 4HT
Tel: 01534 638200
Headmaster: Mr Alun Watkins
Age range: B11–18
No. of pupils: 720 VIth200
Fees: Day £5,310

**Victoria College
Preparatory School**
Pleasant Street, St Helier, Jersey JE2 4RR
Tel: 01534 723468
Headmaster: Dan Pateman BA (Hons)
Age range: B7–11
No. of pupils: 300
Fees: Day £5,268

Central & West

KEY TO SYMBOLS
- ⚲ Boys' school
- ⚲ Girls' school
- 🌐 International school
- 16⁺ Tutorial or sixth form college
- Ⓐ A levels
- 🏛 Boarding accommodation
- £ Bursaries
- IB International Baccalaureate
- ✎ Learning support
- 16⁺ Entrance at 16+
- 🎓 Vocational qualifications
- IAPS Independent Association of Preparatory Schools
- HMC The Headmasters' & Headmistresses' Conference
- ISA Independent Schools Association
- GSA Girls' School Association
- BSA Boarding Schools' Association
- S Society of Heads

Unless otherwise indicated, all schools are coeducational day schools. Single-sex and boarding schools will be indicated by the relevant icon.

Buckinghamshire

Akeley Wood School
Akeley Wood, Buckingham,
Buckinghamshire MK18 5AE
Tel: 01280 814110
Headmaster: Dr Jerry Grundy BA, PhD
Age range: 12 months–18 years
No. of pupils: 833 VIth119
Fees: Day £7,185–£10,575
Ⓐ Ⓔ ✎ 16+

Ashfold School
Dorton House, Dorton, Aylesbury,
Buckinghamshire HP18 9NG
Tel: 01844 238237
Headmaster: Mr Michael Chitty BSc
Age range: 3–13
No. of pupils: 280 VIth28
Fees: Day £9,525–£16,845 WB £20,190
Ⓑ Ⓔ ✎

Broughton Manor Preparatory School
Newport Road, Broughton, Milton
Keynes, Buckinghamshire MK10 9AA
Tel: 01908 665234
Headmaster: Mr J Smith
and Mrs R Smith
Age range: 2 months–11 years
No. of pupils: 250
Fees: Day £13,980
Ⓔ

Caldicott
Crown Lane, Farnham Royal,
Buckinghamshire SL2 3SL
Tel: 01753 649301
Headmaster: Mr Jeremy
Banks BA (Hons) QTS, MEd
Age range: B7–13
No. of pupils: 250
Fees: Day £16,833–£18,780 WB
£24,918–£27,687 FB £24,918–£27,687
🏃 Ⓑ Ⓔ ✎

Chesham Preparatory School
Two Dells Lane, Chesham,
Buckinghamshire HP5 3QF
Tel: 01494 782619
Headmaster: Mr Jonathan Beale
Age range: 3–13
No. of pupils: 392
Fees: Day £9,270–£14,400
✎

Child First Aylesbury Nursery
Green End, Aylesbury,
Buckinghamshire HP20 2SA
Tel: 01296 392516
Nursery Manager: Lela White

Child First Aylesbury Pre-School
35 Rickfords Hill, Aylesbury,
Buckinghamshire HP20 2RT
Tel: 01296 433224
Pre-School Manager: Sara Foster

Crown House Preparatory School
Bassetsbury Manor, Bassetsbury
Lane, High Wycombe,
Buckinghamshire HP11 1QX
Tel: 01494 529927
Headmaster: Mr David Ward
Age range: 3–11
No. of pupils: 120
Fees: Day £9,005–£10,185
✎

Dair House School
Bishops Blake, Beaconsfield
Road, Farnham Royal,
Buckinghamshire SL2 3BY
Tel: 01753 643964
Headmaster: Mr Terry Wintle BEd(Hons)
Age range: 3–11
No. of pupils: 125
Fees: Day £3,425–£4,345
Ⓔ ✎

Davenies School
Station Road, Beaconsfield,
Buckinghamshire HP9 1AA
Tel: 01494 685400
Headmaster: Mr Carl
Rycroft BEd (Hons)
Age range: B4–13
No. of pupils: 339
Fees: Day £11,985–£17,985
🏃 Ⓔ ✎

Filgrave School
Filgrave Village, Newport
Pagnell, Milton Keynes,
Buckinghamshire MK16 9ET
Tel: 01234 711534
Headteacher: Mrs H Schofield
BA(Hons), MA, PGCE
Age range: 2–7
No. of pupils: 27
Fees: Day £5,160
Ⓔ ✎

Focus School – Stoke Poges Campus
School Lane, Stoke Poges,
Buckinghamshire SL2 4QA
Tel: 01753 662167

Gateway School
1 High Street, Great Missenden,
Buckinghamshire HP16 9AA
Tel: 01494 862407
Headteacher: Mrs Sue
LaFarge BA(Hons), PGCE
Age range: 2–11
No. of pupils: 355
Fees: Day £2,235–£11,175
✎

Godstowe Preparatory School
Shrubbery Road, High Wycombe,
Buckinghamshire HP13 6PR
Tel: 01494 529273
Headmistress: Sophie Green
Age range: B3–7 G3–13
No. of pupils: 409
Fees: Day £10,800–£16,620 FB £24,645
Ⓑ Ⓔ ✎

Griffin House Preparatory School
Little Kimble, Aylesbury,
Buckinghamshire HP17 0XP
Tel: 01844 346154
Headmaster: Mr Tim Walford
Age range: 3–11
No. of pupils: 100
Fees: Day £8,238–£8,580
✎

Heatherton House School
Copperkins Lane, Chesham Bois,
Amersham, Buckinghamshire HP6 5QB
Tel: 01494 726433
Headteacher: Mrs Debbie Isaachsen
Age range: B3–4 G3–11
Fees: Day £1,140–£13,335
🏃 ✎

High March
23 Ledborough Lane, Beaconsfield,
Buckinghamshire HP9 2PZ
Tel: 01494 675186
Head of School: Mrs Kate Gater
Age range: B3–4 G3–11
No. of pupils: 293
Fees: Day £5,850–£15,480
🏃 Ⓔ ✎

Milton Keynes Preparatory School
Tattenhoe Lane, Milton Keynes,
Buckinghamshire MK3 7EG
Tel: 01908 642111
Heads of School: Mr C
Bates & Mr S Driver
Age range: 2 months–11 years
No. of pupils: 500
Fees: Day £4,560–£15,120
Ⓔ

Pipers Corner School
Pipers Lane, Great Kingshill, High
Wycombe, Buckinghamshire HP15 6LP
Tel: 01494 718 255
Headmistress: Mrs H J Ness-
Gifford BA(Hons), PGCE
Age range: G4–18
No. of pupils: VIth72
Fees: Day £8,880–£18,390
🏃 Ⓐ Ⓔ ✎ 16+ ♣

St Teresa's Catholic School & Nursery
Aylesbury Road, Princes Risborough,
Buckinghamshire HP27 0JW
Tel: 01844 345005
Joint Head Teachers: Mrs Jane
Draper & Mrs Yasmin Roberts
Age range: 3–11
No. of pupils: 110
Fees: Day £8,610–£9,360

Stowe School
Buckingham, Buckinghamshire
MK18 5EH
Tel: 01280 818000
Headmaster: Dr Anthony Wallersteiner
Age range: 13–18
No. of pupils: 769 VIth318
Fees: Day £26,355 FB £36,660
🏃 Ⓐ Ⓔ ✎ 16+

Swanbourne House School
Swanbourne, Milton Keynes,
Buckinghamshire MK17 0HZ
Tel: 01296 720264
Head of School: Mrs Jane Thorpe
Age range: 3–13
No. of pupils: 323
Fees: Day £1,410–£18,360 FB £23,520
Ⓑ Ⓔ ✎

The Beacon School
Chesham Bois, Amersham,
Buckinghamshire HP6 5PF
Tel: 01494 433654
Headmaster: William Phelps
Age range: B3–13
No. of pupils: 470
Fees: Day £11,850–£17,250
🏃 Ⓔ ✎

The Chalfonts Independent Grammar School
19 London Road, High Wycombe,
Buckinghamshire HP11 1BJ
Tel: +44 (0)1494 875502
Principal: Mr David Shandley
Age range: 11–18
🏃 IB

The Grove Independent School
Redland Drive, Loughton, Milton
Keynes, Buckinghamshire MK5 8HD
Tel: 01908 690590
Principal: Mrs Deborah Berkin
Age range: 3 months–13 years
No. of pupils: 210

The Webber Independent School
Soskin Drive, Stantonbury Fields, Milton
Keynes, Buckinghamshire MK14 6DP
Tel: 01908 574740
Principal: Mrs Hilary Marsden
Age range: 3–18
No. of pupils: 300 VIth15
Fees: Day £9,030–£12,705
Ⓐ Ⓔ ✏ ⓰

THORNTON COLLEGE
For further details see p.58
College Lane, Thornton,
Buckinghamshire MK17 0HJ
Tel: 01280 812610
Email:
admissions@thorntoncollege.com
Website: www.thorntoncollege.com
Headteacher: Mrs Val Holmes
Age range: B2–4 G2–18
No. of pupils: 414
Fees: Day £10,035–£16,005
WB £17,310–£21,900 FB £21,525–£26,700

♟ ⓰ Ⓐ ✏ ⓰

**Walton Pre-Preparatory
School & Nursery**
The Old Rectory, Walton Drive, Milton
Keynes, Buckinghamshire MK7 6BB
Tel: 01908 678403
Headmistress: Mrs Chantelle
McLaughlan
Age range: 2 months–5 years
No. of pupils: 120
Fees: Day £7,200–£14,280

WYCOMBE ABBEY
For further details see p.60
High Wycombe,
Buckinghamshire HP11 1PE
Tel: +44 (0)1494 897008
Email:
registrar@wycombeabbey.com
Website: www.wycombeabbey.com
Headmistress: Mrs Jo Duncan MA
(St Andrews), PGCE (Cantab)
Age range: G11–18
No. of pupils: 649
Fees: Day £30,270 FB £40,350
♟ ⓰ Ⓐ ⓫ ✏ ⓰

Gloucestershire

Airthrie School
29 Christchurch Road, Cheltenham,
Gloucestershire GL50 2NY
Tel: 01242 512837
Headteacher: Mrs Sara Jackson
Age range: 3–11
No. of pupils: 168
Fees: Day £6,770–£9,930
✏

**Al-Ashraf Secondary
School for Girls**
Sinope Street, off Widden Street,
Gloucester, Gloucestershire GL1 4AW
Tel: 01452 300465
Head: Mufti Abdullah Patel
Age range: G11–16
No. of pupils: 67
Fees: Day £1,325–£2,000
♟

Beaudesert Park School
Minchinhampton, Stroud,
Gloucestershire GL6 9AF
Tel: 01453 832072
Headmaster: Mr J P R
Womersley BA, PGCE
Age range: 3–13
No. of pupils: 450
Fees: Day £5,745–£17,661 FB £22,677
⓫ ✏

Berkhampstead School
Pittville Circus Road, Cheltenham,
Gloucestershire GL52 2QA
Tel: 01242 523263
Head: R P Cross BSc(Hons)
Age range: 3–11
No. of pupils: 215
Fees: Day £2,397–£10,380
Ⓔ ✏

Bredon School
Pull Court, Bushley, Tewkesbury,
Gloucestershire GL20 6AH
Tel: 01684 293156
Headteacher: Mr N Oldham
Age range: 7–18
No. of pupils: 220
⓰ Ⓐ ⓫ Ⓔ ✏ ⓰ ✿

Cheltenham College
Bath Road, Cheltenham,
Gloucestershire GL53 7LD
Tel: 01242 265600
Headmaster: Nicola Huggett
Age range: 13–18
No. of pupils: 650 VIth270
Fees: Day £27,585–£28,575
FB £36,780–£37,770
⓰ Ⓐ ⓫ Ⓔ ✏ ⓰

**Cheltenham College
Preparatory School**
Thirlestaine Road, Cheltenham,
Gloucestershire GL53 7AB
Tel: 01242 522697
Headmaster: Mr Tom O'Sullivan
Age range: 7–13
No. of pupils: 420
Fees: Day £11,985–£18,315
FB £18,255–£23,790
⓫ Ⓔ ✏

Cheltenham Ladies' College
Bayshill Road, Cheltenham,
Gloucestershire GL50 3EP
Tel: +44 (0)1242 520691
Principal: Eve Jardine-Young MA
Age range: G11–18
No. of pupils: 840 VIth305
Fees: Day £25,740–£29,280
FB £38,340–£43,170
♟ ⓰ Ⓐ ⓫ Ⓔ ⒾⒷ ✏ ⓰

**Dean Close Pre-Preparatory
& Preparatory School**
Lansdown Road, Cheltenham,
Gloucestershire GL51 6QS
Tel: +44 (0)1242 512217
**Headmaster Preparatory
School:** Mr Paddy Moss
Age range: 2+–13
⓫

Dean Close School
Shelburne Road, Cheltenham,
Gloucestershire GL51 6HE
Tel: +44 (0)1242 258000
Headmaster: Mr Bradley
Salisbury MEd, PGCE
Age range: 13–18
⓰ Ⓐ ⓫ Ⓔ ✏ ⓰

Focus School – Bristol Campus
Station Road, Wanswell, Berkeley,
Gloucestershire GL13 9RS
Tel: 01453 511282

Hatherop Castle School
Hatherop, Cirencester,
Gloucestershire GL7 3NB
Tel: 01285 750206
Headmaster: Mr Nigel Reed
M.Ed, B.Sc (Hons), PGCE
Age range: 2–13
No. of pupils: 210
Fees: Day £6,285–£10,455
FB £15,270–£16,110
⓫ Ⓔ ✏

Hopelands Preparatory School
38 Regent Street, Stonehouse,
Gloucestershire GL10 2AD
Tel: 01453 822164
Headmistress: Mrs S Bradburn
Age range: 3–11
No. of pupils: 59
Fees: Day £6,288–£9,123
✏

Kitebrook Preparatory School
Kitebrook House, Moreton-in-
Marsh, Gloucestershire GL56 0RP
Tel: 01608 674350
Headmistress: Mrs Susan McLean
Age range: 3–13
No. of pupils: 200
⓫ Ⓔ ✏

Rendcomb College
Rendcomb, Cirencester,
Gloucestershire GL7 7HA
Tel: 01285 831213
Headmaster: Mr R Jones BA(Hons), MEd
Age range: 3–18
No. of pupils: 350 VIth72
Fees: Day £2,070–£7,775 WB
£8,140–£9,785 FB £8,925–£11,995
⓰ Ⓐ ⓫ Ⓔ ✏ ⓰

St Edward's Preparatory School
London Road, Charlton
Kings, Cheltenham,
Gloucestershire GL52 6NR
Tel: 01242 538900
Headmaster: Mr Stephen
McKernan BA(Hons) MEd NPQH
Age range: 1–11
No. of pupils: 295
Fees: Day £7,770–£12,975
🏊

St Edward's School
Cirencester Road, Cheltenham,
Gloucestershire GL53 8EY
Tel: 01242 538600
Head: Mrs P Clayfield BSc
Age range: 11–18
No. of pupils: 344 VIth105
Fees: Day £14,550–£17,760
(A)(£)(🏊)(16)

The Acorn School
Church Street, Nailsworth,
Gloucestershire GL6 0BP
Tel: 01453 836508
Headmaster: Mr Graeme E B Whiting
Age range: 7–18
No. of pupils: VIth30
Fees: Day £6,675–£12,045
(16)

The King's School
Gloucester, Gloucestershire GL1 2BG
Tel: 01452 337337
Headmaster: David Morton
Age range: 3–18
No. of pupils: VIth80
Fees: Day £7,350–£19,185
(A)(£)(🏊)(16)

The Richard Pate School
Southern Road, Cheltenham,
Gloucestershire GL53 9RP
Tel: 01242 522086
Headmaster: Mr Robert MacDonald
Age range: 3–11 years
No. of pupils: 300
Fees: Day £3,330–£10,410
🏊

Westonbirt Prep School
Westonbirt, Tetbury,
Gloucestershire GL8 8QG
Tel: 01666 881400
Headmaster: Mr Sean Price
Age range: 3–11
Fees: Day £2,680–£3,865
(£)(🏊)

Westonbirt School
Westonbirt, Tetbury,
Gloucestershire GL8 8QG
Tel: 01666 881333
Headmistress: Mrs Natasha
Dangerfield
Age range: 2–18
No. of pupils: 435
Fees: Day £8,335–£15,585 FB £30,450
(👤)(🏊)(A)(🏛)(£)(🏊)(16)

Wotton House International School
Wotton House, Horton Road,
Gloucester, Gloucestershire GL1 3PR
Tel: +44 (0)1452 764248
Principal: Dr Daniel Sturdy
Age range: 11–16
No. of pupils: 25
(🌐)(IB)

Wycliffe Preparatory
& Senior School
Bath Road, Stonehouse,
Gloucestershire GL10 2JQ
Tel: 01453 822432
Senior School Head: Mr
Nick Gregory BA, MEd
Age range: 2–18
No. of pupils: VIth178
Fees: Day £9,675–£20,985
FB £20,625–£38,115
(🌐)(A)(🏛)(£)(🏊)(16)

Wynstones School
Whaddon Green, Gloucester,
Gloucestershire GL4 0UF
Tel: 01452 429220
**Chair of the College of
Teachers:** Marianna Law-Lindberg
Age range: 3–18
No. of pupils: VIth9
Fees: Day £2,820–£9,540 FB £8,160
(🌐)(A)(🏊)(16)

Hampshire

Thorngrove School
The Mount, Highclere, Newbury,
Hampshire RG20 9PS
Tel: 01635 253172
Headmaster: Mr Adam King
Age range: 2–13
Fees: Day £14,070–£17,595
(£)(🏊)

Oxfordshire

Abingdon Preparatory School
Josca's House, Kingston Road,
Frilford, Oxfordshire OX13 5NX
Tel: 01865 391570
Headmaster: Mr Craig Williams
Age range: B4–13
(👤)(£)(🏊)

Abingdon School
Park Road, Abingdon,
Oxfordshire OX14 1DE
Tel: 01235 521563
Head: Michael Windsor
Age range: B11–18
No. of pupils: 1000
Fees: Day £19,950 WB £33,210 FB £39,750
(👤)(🌐)(A)(🏛)(£)(16)

Bloxham School
Bloxham, Banbury,
Oxfordshire OX15 4PE
Tel: 01295 720222 or 724301
Headmaster: Mr Paul Sanderson
Age range: 11–18
No. of pupils: 431
Fees: Day £17,985–£25,785 WB
£25,785 FB £33,675–£35,175
(🌐)(A)(🏛)(£)(🏊)(16)

Burford School
Cheltenham Road, Burford,
Oxfordshire OX18 4PL
Tel: 01993 823303/823283
Headteacher: Mrs K Haig BA, MEd
Age range: 11–18
No. of pupils: 1156 VIth200
Fees: FB £9,900
(A)(🏛)(£)(🏊)(16)

Carfax College
25 Beaumont Street, Oxford,
Oxfordshire OX1 2NP
Tel: +44 1865 200 676
Principal: Dr Victoria Jefferson
(🌐)(A)(🏛)

Carrdus School
Overthorpe Hall, Banbury,
Oxfordshire OX17 2BS
Tel: 01295 263733
Head: Mr Edward Way
Age range: B3–8 G3–11
No. of pupils: 122
Fees: Day £735–£11,625
(£)(🏊)

Chandlings
Bagley Wood, Kennington,
Oxford, Oxfordshire OX1 5ND
Tel: 01865 730771
Head: Christine Cook
Age range: 2–11
Fees: Day £10,110–£15,870
🏊

Cherwell College
Cantay House, Park End Street,
Oxford, Oxfordshire OX1 1JD
Tel: 01865 242670
Principal: Stephen Clarke
Age range: 15+
No. of pupils: 100
Fees: Day £26,520 FB £13,600
(16)(A)(🏛)(£)(🏊)

Child First Banbury Nursery
The Old Museum, 8 Horsefair,
Banbury, Oxfordshire OX16 0AA
Tel: 01295 273743
Nursery Manager: Amy Ames

Child First Bicester Nursery
32 Launton Road, Bicester,
Oxfordshire OX26 6PZ
Tel: 01869 323730
Nursery Manager: Andrea Leonard

Christ Church Cathedral School
3 Brewer Street, Oxford,
Oxfordshire OX1 1QW
Tel: 01865 242561
Headmaster: Richard Murray
Age range: B3–13 G3–4
No. of pupils: 159
Fees: Day £5,667–£16,569 FB £7,560
(👤)(🏊)

Cokethorpe School
Witney, Oxfordshire OX29 7PU
Tel: 01993 703921
Headmaster: Mr D Ettinger
BA, MA, PGCE
Age range: 4–18
No. of pupils: 666 VIth133
Fees: Day £12,600–£19,200

Cothill House
Abingdon, Oxfordshire OX13 6JL
Tel: 01865 390800
Headmaster: Mr D M Bailey
Age range: B8–13
No. of pupils: 250
Fees: FB £27,660

Cranford House School
Moulsford, Wallingford,
Oxfordshire OX10 9HT
Tel: 01491 651218
Age range: B3–11 G3–16
No. of pupils: 380
Fees: Day £10,500–£16,530

d'Overbroeck's
333 Banbury Road, Oxford,
Oxfordshire OX2 7PL
Tel: 01865 310000
Acting Principal: Mr Jonathan Cuff
Age range: 11–18
No. of pupils: 595 VIth325
Fees: Day £18,150–£24,300
FB £34,800–£41,550

Dragon School
Bardwell Road, Oxford,
Oxfordshire OX2 6SS
Tel: 01865 315405
Head: Mr Crispin Hyde-Dunn
Age range: 4–13
No. of pupils: 785
Fees: Day £7,256 FB £10,562

EF Academy Oxford
Pullens Lane, Headington,
Oxfordshire OX3 0DT
Tel: +41 (0) 43 430 4095
Head of School: Dr. Paul Ellis
Age range: 16–19
No. of pupils: 188

Emmanuel Christian School
Sandford Road, Littlemore,
Oxford, Oxfordshire OX4 4PU
Tel: 01865 395236
Principal: Mrs Elizabeth Nesbitt
Age range: 3–11
No. of pupils: 43
Fees: Day £5,550

Greene's Tutorial College
45 Pembroke Street, Oxford,
Oxfordshire OX1 1BP
Tel: 01865 664400
Principal: Zoë Spilberg
No. of pupils: VIth49

Headington Preparatory School
26 London Road, Oxford,
Oxfordshire OX3 7PB
Tel: +44 (0)1865 759116
Head: Mrs Jane Crouch BA (Hons), MA
Age range: G3–11
No. of pupils: 280

HEADINGTON SCHOOL OXFORD
For further details see p.50
London Road, Oxford,
Oxfordshire OX3 7TD
Tel: +44 (0)1865 759100
Email: admissions@headington.org
Website: www.headington.org
Headmistress: Mrs Caroline
Jordan MA(Oxon)
Age range: G11–18
Fees: Day £6,090–£6,635
FB £8,282–£13,395

Kingham Hill School
Kingham, Chipping Norton,
Oxfordshire OX7 6TH
Tel: 01608 658999
Age range: 11–18
No. of pupils: 352
Fees: Day £17,895–£20,385 WB
£25,350–£31,305 FB £26,160–£34,350

Magdalen College School
Cowley Place, Oxford,
Oxfordshire OX4 1DZ
Tel: 01865 242191
Master: Helen Pike
Age range: B7–18
No. of pupils: 669 VIth161
Fees: Day £17,799–£18,477

Moulsford Preparatory School
Moulsford-on-Thames,
Oxfordshire OX10 9HR
Tel: 01491 651438
Headmaster: Mr B Beardmore-Gray
Age range: B4–13
No. of pupils: 361
Fees: FB £7,395

New College School
2 Savile Road, Oxford,
Oxfordshire OX1 3UA
Tel: 01865 285 560
Headmaster: Mr N R Gullifer MA, FRSA
Age range: B4–13
No. of pupils: 160
Fees: Day £9,870–£15,951

Our Lady's Abingdon School
Radley Road, Abingdon-on-
Thames, Oxfordshire OX14 3PS
Tel: 01235 524658
Principal: Mr Stephen Oliver
Age range: 7–18
No. of pupils: 374 VIth61
Fees: Day £11,280–£16,815

Oxford High School GDST
Belbroughton Road, Oxford,
Oxfordshire OX2 6XA
Tel: 01865 559888
Head: Dr Helen Stringer
Age range: G4–18
No. of pupils: 900
Fees: Day £9,000–£15,546

Oxford Montessori School
Forest Farm, Elsfield, Oxford,
Oxfordshire OX3 9UW
Tel: 01865 352062
Age range: 5–10
No. of pupils: 169

Oxford Sixth Form College
12-13 King Edward Street,
Oxford, Oxfordshire OX1 4HT
Tel: +44 (0)1865 793233
Principal: Mr Mark Love
Age range: 15–19
No. of pupils: 197

Radley College
Radley, Abingdon,
Oxfordshire OX14 2HR
Tel: 01235 543000
The Warden: Mr J S Moule
Age range: B13–18
No. of pupils: 690
Fees: FB £38,325

Rupert House School
90 Bell Street, Henley-on-Thames,
Oxfordshire RG9 2BN
Tel: 01491 574263
Headmistress: Mrs C Lynas
Age range: B4–7 G4–11
No. of pupils: 214
Fees: Day £5,640–£13,785

Rye St Antony
Pullens Lane, Oxford,
Oxfordshire OX3 0BY
Tel: 01865 762802
Headmistress: Miss A M Jones BA, PGCE
Age range: B3–11 G3–18
No. of pupils: 400 VIth70
Fees: Day £9,870–£15,330 WB
£21,000–£24,690 FB £22,230–£25,935

SHIPLAKE COLLEGE
For further details see p.52
Henley-on-Thames,
Oxfordshire RG9 4BW
Tel: +44 (0)1189 402455
Email: registrar@shiplake.org.uk
Website: www.shiplake.org.uk
Headmaster: Mr T G
Howe MA, MSt, MBA
Age range: B11–18 G16–18
No. of pupils: 478 VIth192
Fees: Day £18,985–£23,850 WB
£26,615–£33,280 FB £35,470

Sibford School
Sibford Ferris, Banbury,
Oxfordshire OX15 5QL
Tel: 01295 781200
Head of School: Toby Spence
No. of pupils: VIth840
Fees: Day £9,180–£14,739 WB
£26,154–£26,670 FB £28,077–£28,644

St Clare's, Oxford
139 Banbury Road, Oxford,
Oxfordshire OX2 7AL
Tel: +44 (0)1865 552031
Principal: Mr Andrew Rattue
Age range: 14–18
No. of pupils: 271
Fees: Day £20,276 FB £42,203

St Edward's, Oxford
Woodstock Road, Oxford,
Oxfordshire OX2 7NN
Tel: +44 (0)1865 319200
Warden: Stephen Jones
Age range: 13–18
No. of pupils: 700
Fees: Day £10,530 FB £13,160

St Helen and St Katharine
Faringdon Road, Abingdon,
Oxfordshire OX14 1BE
Tel: 01235 520173
Headmistress: Mrs Rebecca
Dougall BA MA
Age range: G9–18
No. of pupils: 730
Fees: Day £5,665

St Hugh's School
Carswell Manor, Faringdon,
Oxfordshire SN7 8PT
Tel: 01367 870700
Headmaster: Mr Andrew
Nott BA (Wales), PGCE
Age range: 3–13
Fees: Day £11,655–£20,085
WB £21,600–£23,100

St John's Priory School
St John's Road, Banbury,
Oxfordshire OX16 5HX
Tel: 01295 259607
Headmistress: Tracey Wilson
Age range: 3–11
Fees: Day £6,715–£9,450

St Mary's Preparatory School
13 St Andrew's Road, Henley-on-
Thames, Oxfordshire RG9 1HS
Tel: 01491 573118
Headmaster: Mr Rob Harmer (BA)Hons
Age range: 2–11
No. of pupils: 129
Fees: Day £4,010

Summer Fields
Mayfield Road, Oxford,
Oxfordshire OX2 7EN
Tel: 01865 454433
Headmaster: Mr David
Faber MA(Oxon)
Age range: B4–13
No. of pupils: 256
Fees: Day £12,000–£21,159 FB £30,360

The King's School, Witney
New Yatt Road, Witney,
Oxfordshire OX29 6TA
Tel: 01993 778463
Principal: Mr Steve Beegoo
Age range: 3–16
No. of pupils: 200
Fees: Day £5,244

THE MANOR PREPARATORY SCHOOL
For further details see p.56
Faringdon Road, Abingdon,
Oxfordshire OX13 6LN
Tel: 01235 858458
Email: admissions@manorprep.org
Website: www.manorprep.org
Headmaster: Mr Alastair Thomas
Age range: 2–11 years
No. of pupils: 370

The Unicorn School
20 Marcham Road, Abingdon,
Oxfordshire OX14 1AA
Tel: 01235 530222
Headteacher: Mr. Andrew Day BEd
(Hons)University of Wales (Cardiff)
Age range: 6–16 years

Tudor Hall School
Wykham Park, Banbury,
Oxfordshire OX16 9UR
Tel: 01295 263434
Headmistress: Miss Wendy Griffiths BSc
Age range: G11–18
No. of pupils: 325
Fees: Day £7,365 FB £11,870

Windrush Valley School
The Green, London Lane,
Ascott-under-Wychwood,
Oxfordshire OX7 6AN
Tel: 01993 831793
Headteacher: Amanda Douglas
Age range: 3–11
No. of pupils: 120
Fees: Day £7,005–£7,341

Wychwood School
74 Banbury Road, Oxford,
Oxfordshire OX2 6JR
Tel: 01865 557976
Headmistress: Mrs A K
Johnson BSc (Dunelm)
Age range: G11–18
No. of pupils: 120 VIth40
Fees: Day £15,900 WB
£24,300 FB £27,900

West Berkshire

Brockhurst & Marlston House Schools
Hermitage, Newbury, West
Berkshire RG18 9UL
Tel: 01635 200293
Head of School: Mr David Fleming
Age range: 2 1/2–13
No. of pupils: 275
Fees: Day £10,650–£17,850
FB £23,925–£25,800

Cheam School
Headley, Newbury, West
Berkshire RG19 8LD
Tel: +44 (0)1635 268242
Headmaster: Mr Martin Harris
Age range: 3–13
No. of pupils: 407
Fees: Day £11,940–£21,285
FB £26,055–£27,630

DOWNE HOUSE SCHOOL
For further details see p.48
Downe House, Cold Ash, Thatcham,
West Berkshire RG18 9JJ
Tel: +44 (0)1635 200286
Email: registrar@downehouse.net
Website: www.downehouse.net
Headmistress: Mrs Emma
McKendrick BA(Liverpool)
Age range: G11–18
No. of pupils: 593
Fees: Day £9,705 FB £13,050

Horris Hill
Newtown, Newbury, West
Berkshire RG20 9DJ
Tel: 01635 40594
Headmaster: Mr G F Tollit B.A.(Hons)
Age range: B4–13
No. of pupils: 130
Fees: Day £5,600 FB £9,550

Marlston House Preparatory School
Hermitage, Newbury, West
Berkshire RG18 9UL
Tel: 01635 200293
Headmistress: Mrs Caroline
Riley MA, BEd
Age range: G3–13
No. of pupils: 110
Fees: Day £10,650–£17,850 FB £23,925

Newbury Hall
Enborne Road, (corner of
Rockingham Road), Newbury,
West Berkshire RG14 6AD
Tel: +44 (0)1635 36879

St Gabriel's
Sandleford Priory, Newbury,
West Berkshire RG20 9BD
Tel: 01635 555680
Principal: Mr Richard Smith
MA (Hons), MEd, PGCE
Age range: B6 months–11
G6 months–18
No. of pupils: 469 VIth40
Fees: Day £10,668–£17,418

St Michael's School
Harts Lane, Burghclere, Newbury,
West Berkshire RG20 9JW
Tel: 01635 278137
Headmaster: Rev. Fr. John Brucciani
Age range: B5–18 G5–11

The Cedars School
Church Road, Aldermaston,
West Berkshire RG7 4LR
Tel: 0118 971 4251
Headteacher: Mrs Jane O'Halloran
Age range: 4–11
No. of pupils: 50
Fees: Day £8,910

Wiltshire

Avondale School
High Street, Bulford, Salisbury,
Wiltshire SP4 9DR
Tel: 01980 632387
Head of School: Mr Ben Coombes
Age range: 2–11
Fees: Day £8,097
⚲

Bishopstrow College
Bishopstrow, Warminster,
Wiltshire BA12 9HU
Tel: +44 (0)1985 219210
Principal: Ms Lorraine Atkins
Age range: 7–17 years
🏫

Chafyn Grove School
33 Bourne Avenue, Salisbury,
Wiltshire SP1 1LR
Tel: 01722 333423
Headmaster: Mr Simon Head
Age range: 3–13
No. of pupils: 265
🏫 £ ⚲

Dauntsey's School
High Street, West Lavington,
Devizes, Wiltshire SN10 4HE
Tel: 01380 814500
Head Master: Mr Mark Lascelles
Age range: 11–18
No. of pupils: 820 VIth270
Fees: Day £19,650 FB £32,550
🌐 A 🏫 £ ⚲ 16+

Emmaus School
School Lane, Staverton,
Trowbridge, Wiltshire BA14 6NZ
Tel: 01225 782684
Head: Mrs M Wiltshire
Age range: 5–16
No. of pupils: 75
Fees: Day £3,500–£4,400

Focus School – Salisbury Campus
The Hollows, Wilton, Salisbury,
Wiltshire SP2 0JE
Tel: 01722 741910

Godolphin Preparatory School
Laverstock Road, Salisbury,
Wiltshire SP1 2RB
Tel: 01722 430 652
Headmistress: Emma Hattersley
Age range: G3–11
No. of pupils: 100
Fees: Day £7,125–£13,935
WB £21,540 FB £25,230
👦 £

Godolphin School
Milford Hill, Salisbury, Wiltshire SP1 2RA
Tel: 01722 430509
Headmistress: Mrs Emma Hattersley
BA (Dunelm) Postgrad RAM
Age range: G11–18
No. of pupils: 380 VIth100
👦 🌐 A 🏫 £ 16+

Heywood Prep
The Priory, Corsham, Wiltshire SN13 0AP
Tel: 01249 713379
Headmistress: Rebecca Mitchell
Age range: 2–11
No. of pupils: 140
Fees: Day £5,760–£8,985
£ ⚲

Leehurst Swan School
Campbell Road, Salisbury,
Wiltshire SP1 3BQ
Tel: 01722 333094
Headmaster: Mr Terence Ayres
Age range: Reception–16 years
Fees: Day £8,985–£15,300
£ ⚲

Maranatha Christian School
Queenlaines Farm, Sevenhampton,
Swindon, Wiltshire SN6 7SQ
Tel: 01793 762075

Marlborough College
Bath Road, Marlborough,
Wiltshire SN8 1PA
Tel: 01672 892300
Master: Louise Moelwyn-Hughes
Age range: 13–18
No. of pupils: 960
Fees: FB £37,815
🌐 A 🏫 £ ⚲ 16+

**Meadowpark Nursery
& Pre-Preparatory**
Calcutt Street, Cricklade,
Wiltshire SN6 6BA
Tel: 01793 752600
Headteacher: Mrs R Kular
Age range: 0–11
Fees: Day £6,585–£8,550
⚲

Pinewood School
Bourton, Swindon, Wiltshire SN6 8HZ
Tel: 01793 782205
Headmaster: Mr P J Hoyland
Age range: 3–13
No. of pupils: 313
Fees: Day £8,790–£17,895 WB £22,260
🏫 £ ⚲

Prior Park Preparatory School
Calcutt Street, Cricklade,
Wiltshire SN6 6BB
Tel: 01793 750275
Headteacher: Guy Barrett
Age range: 2–13
No. of pupils: 240
Fees: Day £6,900–£14,460
🏫 £ ⚲

Salisbury Cathedral School
The Old Palace, 1 The Close,
Salisbury, Wiltshire SP1 2EQ
Tel: 01722 555300
Head Master: Mr Clive Marriott BEd MA
Age range: 3–13
🏫 £ ⚲

Sandroyd School
Rushmore, Tollard Royal,
Salisbury, Wiltshire SP5 5QD
Tel: 01725 516264
Headmaster: Mr Alastair Speers
Age range: 5–13
No. of pupils: 225
Fees: Day £8,760–£25,410
FB £20,100–£25,410
🏫 £ ⚲

St Francis School
Marlborough Road, Pewsey,
Wiltshire SN9 5NT
Tel: 01672 563228
Headmaster: Mr David Sibson
Age range: 0–13
Fees: Day £4,821–£12,571
£ ⚲

St Margaret's Preparatory School
Curzon Street, Calne, Wiltshire SN11 0DF
Tel: 01249 857220
Headmistress: Mrs Karen Cordon
GLCM LLCM (TD) ALCM
Age range: 3–11
No. of pupils: 200
Fees: Day £9,900–£13,500
£ ⚲

ST MARY'S CALNE
For further details see p.54
Curzon Street, Calne,
Wiltshire SN11 0DF
Tel: 01249 857200
Email: office@stmaryscalne.org
Website: www.stmaryscalne.org
Headmistress: Dr Felicia Kirk
BA(University of MD), MA,
PhD (Brown University)
Age range: G11–18
No. of pupils: 360 VIth120
Fees: Day £30,045 FB £40,275
👦 🌐 A 🏫 £ ⚲ 16+

Warminster School
Church Street, Warminster,
Wiltshire BA12 8PJ
Tel: +44 (0)1985 210100
Headmaster: Mr Mark
Mortimer MBA BA
Age range: 3–18
No. of pupils: 530
Fees: Day £5,110 FB £10,880
🌐 A 🏫 £ IB ⚲ 16+

Stonar School
Cottles Park, Atworth, Melksham,
Wiltshire SN12 8NT
Tel: 01225 701740
Head of School: Dr Sally Divall
Age range: 2–18
No. of pupils: 330
Fees: Day £8,496–£16,500
FB £21,954–£33,195
🌐 A 🏫 £ ⚲ 16+

East

*See also Greater London (D299)
for schools in Essex and Hertfordshire

KEY TO SYMBOLS
- ⓐ *Boys' school*
- ⓐ *Girls' school*
- ⓖ *International school*
- ⑯ *Tutorial or sixth form college*
- Ⓐ *A levels*
- 🏛 *Boarding accommodation*
- £ *Bursaries*
- ⓘⓑ *International Baccalaureate*
- ⌀ *Learning support*
- ⑯ *Entrance at 16+*
- 🎓 *Vocational qualifications*
- (IAPS) *Independent Association of Preparatory Schools*
- (HMC) *The Headmasters' & Headmistresses' Conference*
- (ISA) *Independent Schools Association*
- (GSA) *Girls' School Association*
- (BSA) *Boarding Schools' Association*
- Ⓢ *Society of Heads*

*Unless otherwise indicated, all schools are coeducational day schools.
Single-sex and boarding schools will be indicated by the relevant icon.*

Bedfordshire

Bedford Girls' School
Cardington Road, Bedford,
Bedfordshire MK42 0BX
Tel: 01234 361900
Headmistress: Miss Jo
MacKenzie BSc, MSc
Age range: G7–18
No. of pupils: 903

Bedford Modern School
Manton Lane, Bedford,
Bedfordshire MK41 7NT
Tel: 01234 332500
Headmaster: Mr Alex Tate
Age range: 7–18
No. of pupils: 1236
Fees: Day £10,074–£13,821

Bedford Preparatory School
De Parys Avenue, Bedford,
Bedfordshire MK40 2TU
Tel: 01234 362271/362274
Headmaster: Ian Silk
Age range: B7–13
No. of pupils: 438
Fees: Day £12,333–£16,161 WB
£20,919–£25,038 FB £21,948–£26,067

Bedford School
De Parys Avenue, Bedford,
Bedfordshire MK40 2TU
Tel: +44 (0)1234 362216
Head Master: Mr James Hodgson BA
Age range: B7–18 years
No. of pupils: 1121
Fees: Day £12,333–£19,032 WB
£20,919–£31,125 FB £21,948–£32,190

Focus School –
Biggleswade Campus
The Oaks, Potton Road, Biggleswade,
Bedfordshire SG18 0EP
Tel: 01767 602800

Focus School – Dunstable Campus
Ridgeway Avenue, Dunstable,
Bedfordshire LU5 4QL
Tel: 01582 665676

Luton Pentecostal Church
Christian Academy
15 Church Street, Luton,
Bedfordshire LU1 3JE
Tel: 01582 412276
Principal: Rev. Chris Oakey
Age range: 3–13

Orchard School & Nursery
High Gobion Road, Barton-le-Clay,
Bedford, Bedfordshire MK45 4RB
Tel: 01582 882054
Headmistress: Mrs Anne Burton
Age range: 0–6

Pilgrims Pre-Preparatory School
Brickhill Drive, Bedford,
Bedfordshire MK41 7QZ
Tel: 01234 369555
Head: Mrs J Webster BEd(Hons), EYPS
Age range: 3 months–7 years
No. of pupils: 385
Fees: Day £9,771–£13,980

Polam School
45 Lansdowne Road, Bedford,
Bedfordshire MK40 2BU
Tel: 01234 261864
Head: Darren O'Neil
Age range: 1–9
No. of pupils: 110
Fees: Day £9,465

Rabia Girls' & Boys' School
12-16 Portland Road, Luton,
Bedfordshire LU4 8AX
Tel: 01582 493239
Headteacher: Hafsa Bilquees
Age range: 5–16
No. of pupils: 41

Rushmoor School
58-60 Shakespeare Road, Bedford,
Bedfordshire MK40 2DL
Tel: 01234 352031
Headteacher: Ian Daniel BA, NPQH
Age range: B3–16 G3–11
Fees: Day £6,429–£11,022

St Andrew's School
78 Kimbolton Road, Bedford,
Bedfordshire MK40 2PA
Tel: 01234 267272
Headmaster: Mr Ian Daniel
Age range: B3–9 G3–16
No. of pupils: 385
Fees: Day £5,598–£11,022

St George's School
28 Priory Road, Dunstable,
Bedfordshire LU5 4HR
Tel: 01582 661471
Head Teacher: Ms Ellie Graham
Age range: 3–11
No. of pupils: 120
Fees: Day £6,852–£7,119

Cambridgeshire

Abbey College Cambridge
Homerton Gardens, Purbeck Road,
Cambridge, Cambridgeshire CB2 8EB
Tel: 01223 578280
Principal: Dr Julian Davies
Age range: 13–21
No. of pupils: VIth370
Fees: Day £22,000 FB £39,000–£43,000

Bellerbys College Cambridge
Queens Campus, Bateman Street,
Cambridge, Cambridgeshire CB2 1LU
Tel: +44 (0)1223 652 800
Principal: Mr Nicholas Waite
Age range: 14–25

Cambridge International School
The Temple, Bourn Bridge Road, Little
Abington, Cambridgeshire CB21 6AN
Tel: 01223 832719
Principal: Mr Joel Dixon
Age range: 11–16 years

Cambridge Seminars
Tutorial College
Logic House, 143-147 Newmarket Road,
Cambridge, Cambridgeshire CB5 8HA
Tel: 01223 313464
Principal: M R Minhas BSc, CEng
Age range: 16–20
Fees: Day £1,800–£24,000

Cambridge Steiner School
Hinton Road, Fulbourn, Cambridge,
Cambridgeshire CB21 5DZ
Tel: 01223 882727
Age range: 2–14
No. of pupils: 125
Fees: Day £7,665

CATS College Cambridge
1 High Street, Chesterton, Cambridge,
Cambridgeshire CB4 1NQ
Tel: 01223 314431
Principal: Dr Craig Wilson
Age range: 14–19+

Kimbolton School
Kimbolton, Huntingdon,
Cambridgeshire PE28 0EA
Tel: 01480 860505
Headmaster: Jonathan Belbin BA
Age range: 4–18
No. of pupils: VIth170
Fees: Day £9,870–£15,795 FB £26,280

King's Acremont, King's
Ely Nursery & Pre-Prep
30 Egremont Street, Ely,
Cambridgeshire CB6 1AE
Tel: 01353 660702
Head: Sue Freestone
Age range: 3–7
Fees: Day £10,077

King's College School
West Road, Cambridge,
Cambridgeshire CB3 9DN
Tel: 01223 365814
Head: Mrs Yvette Day
BMus, MMus, GDL
Age range: 4–13
No. of pupils: 420
Fees: Day £12,870–£16,350 FB £25,320

KING'S ELY
For further details see p.70
Ely, Cambridgeshire CB7 4EW
Tel: 01353 660707
Email: admissions@kingsely.org
Website: www.kingsely.org
Principal: Mr John
Attwater MA (Oxon)
Age range: 2–18
No. of pupils: 1016
Fees: Day £10,470–£31,005
FB £23,580–£40,980

King's Ely Junior
Ely, Cambridgeshire CB7 4DB
Tel: 01353 660707
Head: Mr Richard Whymark
Age range: 7–13
No. of pupils: 356
Fees: Day £14,790–£16,140
FB £23,580–£24,900

Landmark International School
The Old Rectory, 9 Church
Lane, Fulbourn, Cambridge,
Cambridgeshire CB21 5EP
Tel: 01223 755100
Headteacher: Gareth Turnbull-Jones
Age range: 4–16
No. of pupils: 94

**Magdalene House
Preparatory School**
North Brink, Wisbech,
Cambridgeshire PE13 1JX
Tel: 01945 586 780
Head: Mr Chris Staley
Age range: 3–11
No. of pupils: 180
Fees: Day £9,297–£9,597

**MANDER PORTMAN
WOODWARD – CAMBRIDGE**
For further details see p.72
3-4 Brookside, Cambridge,
Cambridgeshire CB2 1JE
Tel: 01223 350158
Email: cambridge@mpw.ac.uk
Website: www.mpw.ac.uk
Principal: Mr Tom Caston
Age range: 15–19

Oaks International School
Cherry Hinton Road, Cambridge,
Cambridgeshire CB1 8DW
Tel: +44 (0) 1223 416938
Headteacher: Amanda Gibbard
Age range: 2–11

Sancton Wood School
2 St Paul's Road, Cambridge,
Cambridgeshire CB1 2EZ
Tel: +44 (0)1223 471703
Head of School: Mr Richard Settle
Age range: 1–16
Fees: Day £10,740–£14,070

St Andrew's Cambridge
2A Free School Lane, Cambridge,
Cambridgeshire CB2 3QA
Tel: 01223 360040
Principal: Wayne Marshall
Age range: 14–20
No. of pupils: VIth130
Fees: FB £15,000–£17,000

ST FAITH'S
For further details see p.80
Trumpington Road, Cambridge,
Cambridgeshire CB2 8AG
Tel: 01223 352073
Email: admissions@stfaiths.co.uk
Website: www.stfaiths.co.uk
Headmaster: Mr N L Helliwell
Age range: 4–13
No. of pupils: 540
Fees: Day £13,170–£16,590

St John's College School
73 Grange Road, Cambridge,
Cambridgeshire CB3 9AB
Tel: 01223 353532
Headmaster: Mr N. Chippington
MA(Cantab), FRCO
Age range: 4–13
No. of pupils: 453
Fees: Day £12,210–£15,330 FB £24,210

St Mary's School
Bateman Street, Cambridge,
Cambridgeshire CB2 1LY
Tel: 01223 353253
Headmistress: Ms Charlotte Avery
Age range: G4–18
No. of pupils: 619 VIth90
Fees: Day £9,909–£15,861 WB
£26,286–£28,032 FB £30,819–£32,562

**Stephen Perse Nursery
– Madingley**
Cambridge Road,
Madingley, Cambridge,
Cambridgeshire CB23 8AH
Tel: 01223 454700 (Ext:5000)
Head of Pre-prep: Mrs Sarah Holyoake
Age range: 3–7
No. of pupils: 60
Fees: Day £12,000

Stephen Perse Rosedale House
St Eligius Street, Cambridge,
Cambridgeshire CB2 1HX
Tel: 01223 454700 (Ext:2000)
Head of School: Mr D Hewlett
Age range: 5–11
No. of pupils: 135
Fees: Day £15,750

Stephen Perse Senior School
Union Road, Cambridge,
Cambridgeshire CB2 1HF
Tel: 01223 454700 (Ext:1000)
Principal: Dr A Kemp
Age range: 11–16 years
No. of pupils: VIth150
Fees: Day £18,240

THE LEYS SCHOOL
For further details see p.84
Trumpington Road, Cambridge,
Cambridgeshire CB2 7AD
Tel: 01223 508900
Email: admissions@theleys.net
Website: www.theleys.net
Headmaster: Mr Martin Priestley
Age range: 11–18
No. of pupils: 572
Fees: Day £16,545–£22,920
FB £24,960–£34,245

**The Perse Pelican Nursery and
Pre-Preparatory School**
Northwold House, 92 Glebe Road,
Cambridge, Cambridgeshire CB1 7TD
Tel: 01223 403940
Headmistress: Mrs S C Waddington MA
Age range: 3–7
No. of pupils: 154
Fees: Day £13,530

The Perse Preparatory School
Trumpington Road, Cambridge,
Cambridgeshire CB2 8EX
Tel: 01223 403920
Head: Mr James Piper
Age range: 7–11
No. of pupils: 283
Fees: Day £15,705

The Perse School
Hills Road, Cambridge,
Cambridgeshire CB2 8QF
Tel: 01223 403800
Head: Mr Ed Elliott
Age range: 11–18
No. of pupils: 851 VIth250
Fees: Day £17,322

THE PETERBOROUGH SCHOOL
For further details see p.86
Thorpe Road, Peterborough,
Cambridgeshire PE3 6AP
Tel: 01733 343357
Email: office@tpsch.co.uk
Website:
www.thepeterboroughschool.co.uk
Headmaster: Mr A D
Meadows BSc(Hons)
Age range: 6 weeks–18 years
No. of pupils: 440
Fees: Day £10,467–£15,642

Whitehall School
117 High Street, Somersham,
Cambridgeshire PE28 3EH
Tel: 01487 840966
Principal: Rebecca Hutley
Age range: 3–11
No. of pupils: 109
Fees: Day £6,975–£7,980

Wisbech Grammar School
North Brink, Wisbech,
Cambridgeshire PE13 1JX
Tel: 01945 583 631
Head: Mr Chris Staley BA, MBA
Age range: 11–18
No. of pupils: 410
Fees: Day £13,347

Essex

Alleyn Court Preparatory School
Wakering Road, Southend-on-Sea, Essex SS3 0PW
Tel: 01702 582553
Headmaster: Mr Rupert Snow
Age range: 2–11
Fees: Day £3,258–£12,729
£ ✎

Brentwood Preparatory School
Middleton Hall, Brentwood, Essex CM15 8EQ
Tel: +44 (0)1277 243333
Headmaster: Mr Jason Whiskerd
Age range: 3–11
No. of pupils: 423
✎

BRENTWOOD SCHOOL
For further details see p.66
Middleton Hall Lane, Brentwood, Essex CM15 8EE
Tel: 01277 243243
Email: headmaster@brentwood.essex.sch.uk
Website: www.brentwoodschool.co.uk
Headmaster: Mr Michael Bond
Age range: 3–18
No. of pupils: 1800
Fees: Day £20,097 FB £39,381
🏴 Ⓐ ⓔ £ ⒾⒷ ✎ ⑯

Colchester High School
Wellesley Road, Colchester, Essex CO3 3HD
Tel: 01206 573389
Headteacher: Ms Karen Gracie-Langrick
Age range: 2–16
No. of pupils: 320
Fees: Day £9,465–£13,620
£ ✎

Coopersale Hall School
Flux's Lane, off Stewards Green Road, Epping, Essex CM16 7PE
Tel: 01992 577133
Headmistress: Miss Kaye Lovejoy
Age range: 2–11
No. of pupils: 275
Fees: Day £10,350–£10,575

Dame Bradbury's School
Ashdon Road, Saffron Walden, Essex CB10 2AL
Tel: 01223 454700 (Ext:4000)
Head of School: Mrs Louise Graham
Age range: 1–11
No. of pupils: 258
Fees: Day £9,150–£14,400
£ ✎

Elm Green Preparatory School
Parsonage Lane, Little Baddow, Chelmsford, Essex CM3 4SU
Tel: 01245 225230
Principal: Ms Ann Milner
Age range: 4–11
No. of pupils: 220
Fees: Day £8,844

Felsted Preparatory School
Felsted, Great Dunmow, Essex CM6 3JL
Tel: 01371 822610
Headmaster: Mr Simon James
Age range: 4–13
No. of pupils: 460
Fees: Day £9,285–£17,820 FB £23,250–£24,465
⓪ £ ✎

Felsted School
Felsted, Great Dunmow, Essex CM6 3LL
Tel: 01371 822605
Headmaster: Mr Chris Townsend
Age range: 13–18
No. of pupils: 556 VIth249
Fees: Day £24,495 WB £34,725 FB £37,485
🏴 Ⓐ ⓪ £ ⒾⒷ ✎ ⑯

Gosfield School
Cut Hedge Park, Halstead Road, Gosfield, Halstead, Essex CO9 1PF
Tel: 01787 474040
Headteacher: Mr Guy Martyn
Age range: 4–18
No. of pupils: VIth21
Fees: Day £6,690–£15,525
🏴 Ⓐ £ ✎ ⑯

Heathcote School
Eves Corner, Danbury, Chelmsford, Essex CM3 4QB
Tel: 01245 223131
Headmistress: Caroline Forgeron
Age range: 2–11
Fees: Day £4,830–£7,245
£ ✎

Herington House School
1 Mount Avenue, Hutton, Brentwood, Essex CM13 2NS
Tel: 01277 211595
Principal: Mr R. Dudley-Cooke
Age range: 3–11
No. of pupils: 130
Fees: Day £1,955–£3,865
£ ✎

Holmwood House Preparatory School
Chitts Hill, Lexden, Colchester, Essex CO3 9ST
Tel: 01206 574305
Headmaster: Alexander Mitchell
Age range: 4–13
No. of pupils: 302
Fees: Day £10,140–£17,895 FB £35
⓪ £ ✎

Littlegarth School
Horkesley Park, Nayland, Colchester, Essex CO6 4JR
Tel: 01206 262332
Headmaster: Mr Peter H Jones
Age range: 2–11 years
No. of pupils: 318
Fees: Day £3,205–£3,723
£ ✎

Maldon Court Preparatory School
Silver Street, Maldon, Essex CM9 4QE
Tel: 01621 853529
Headteacher: Elaine Mason
Age range: 3–11
Fees: Day £8,236
✎

New Hall School
The Avenue, Boreham, Chelmsford, Essex CM3 3HS
Tel: 01245 467588
Principal: Mrs Katherine Jeffrey MA, BA, PGCE, MA(Ed Mg), NPQH
Age range: Coed 3-11, Single 11-16, Coed 16–18
No. of pupils: 1180 VIth217
Fees: Day £9,801–£19,878 WB £19,761–£28,569 FB £21,531–£30,681
🏴 Ⓐ ⓔ £ ✎ ⑯

Oxford House School
2-4 Lexden Road, Colchester, Essex CO3 3NE
Tel: 01206 576686
Head Teacher: Mrs Sarah Leyshon
Age range: 2–11
No. of pupils: 158

Saint Nicholas School
Hillingdon House, Hobbs Cross Road, Harlow, Essex CM17 0NJ
Tel: 01279 429910
Headmaster: Mr D Bown
Age range: 4–16
No. of pupils: 400
Fees: Day £9,960–£12,660
£

Saint Pierre School
16 Leigh Road, Leigh-on-Sea, Southend-on-Sea, Essex SS9 1LE
Tel: 01702 474164
Headmaster: Mr Chris Perkins
Age range: 2–11+
Fees: Day £7,218–£8,181
£

ST CEDD'S SCHOOL
For further details see p.76
178a New London Road, Chelmsford, Essex CM2 0AR
Tel: 01245 392810
Email: info@stcedds.org.uk
Website: www.stcedds.org.uk
Head: Mr Matthew Clarke
Age range: 3–11
No. of pupils: 400
Fees: Day £8,550–£10,935
✎

St John's School
Stock Road, Billericay, Essex CM12 0AR
Tel: 01277 623070
Head Teacher: Mrs F Armour BEd(Hons)
Age range: 2–16 years
No. of pupils: 392
Fees: Day £5,328–£13,500
✎

St Margaret's Preparatory School
Hall Drive, Gosfield, Halstead, Essex CO9 1SE
Tel: 01787 472134
Headteacher: Mrs Carolyn Moss
Age range: 2–11
Fees: Day £3,240–£4,055
£ ✎

St Mary's School
Lexden Road, Colchester, Essex CO3 3RB
Tel: 01206 572544 Admissions: 01206 216420
Principal: Mrs H K Vipond MEd, BSc(Hons), NPQH
Age range: B3–4 G3–16
No. of pupils: 430
Fees: Day £6,855–£14,985
⓪ £ ✎

St Michael's Church Of England Preparatory School
198 Hadleigh Road, Leigh-on-Sea, Southend-on-Sea, Essex SS9 2LP
Tel: 01702 478719
Head: Steve Tompkins BSc(Hons), PGCE, MA, NPQH
Age range: 3–11
No. of pupils: 271
Fees: Day £4,104–£9,600

St Philomena's Catholic School
Hadleigh Road, Frinton-on-Sea, Essex CO13 9HQ
Tel: 01255 674492
Headmistress: Mrs B McKeown DipEd
Age range: 4–11
Fees: Day £6,240–£7,500

St. Anne's Preparatory School
New London Road, Chelmsford, Essex CM2 0AW
Tel: 01245 353488
Head of School: FValerie Eveleigh
Age range: 3–11
No. of pupils: 160
Fees: Day £3,450–£8,100

The Christian School (Takeley)
Dunmow Road, Brewers End, Takeley, Bishop's Stortford, Essex CM22 6QH
Tel: 01279 871182
Headmaster: M E Humphries
Age range: 3–16
Fees: Day £6,012–£8,436

Thorpe Hall School
Wakering Road, Southend-on-Sea, Essex SS1 3RD
Tel: 01702 582340
Headmaster: Mr Andrew Hampton
Age range: 2–16 years
No. of pupils: 359
Fees: Day £9,000–£12,600

Ursuline Preparatory School
Old Great Ropers, Great Ropers Lane, Warley, Brentwood, Essex CM13 3HR
Tel: 01277 227152
Headmistress: Mrs Pauline Wilson MSc
Age range: 3–11
Fees: Day £6,450–£12,015

Widford Lodge School
Widford Road, Chelmsford, Essex CM2 9AN
Tel: 01245 352581
Headteacher: Miss Michelle Cole A.C.I.B. – P.G.C.E.
Age range: 2–11
No. of pupils: 230
Fees: Day £7,800–£9,657

Woodlands School, Great Warley
Warley Street, Great Warley, Brentwood, Essex CM13 3LA
Tel: 01277 233288
Head: Mr David Bell
Age range: 3 months–11 years

Woodlands School, Hutton Manor
428 Rayleigh Road, Hutton, Brentwood, Essex CM13 1SD
Tel: 01277 245585
Head: Paula Hobbs
Age range: 3 months–11 years

Hertfordshire

ABBOT'S HILL SCHOOL
For further details see p.64
Bunkers Lane, Hemel Hempstead, Hertfordshire HP3 8RP
Tel: 01442 240333
Email: registrar@abbotshill.herts.sch.uk
Website: www.abbotshill.herts.sch.uk
Headmistress: Mrs K Gorman BA, MEd (Cantab)
Age range: G4–16
No. of pupils: 502

Aldenham School
Elstree, Hertfordshire WD6 3AJ
Tel: 01923 858122
Headmaster: Mr James C Fowler MA
Age range: 3–18
No. of pupils: 700
Fees: Day £16,491–£22,614 FB £22,791–£33,234

Aldwickbury School
Wheathampstead Road, Harpenden, Hertfordshire AL5 1AD
Tel: 01582 713022
Headmaster: Mr V W Hales
Age range: B4–13
No. of pupils: 330
Fees: Day £13,110–£16,215

Beechwood Park School
Markyate, St Albans, Hertfordshire AL3 8AW
Tel: 01582 840333
Headmaster: Mr E Balfour BA (Hons), PGCE
Age range: 3–13
No. of pupils: 547
Fees: Day £11,700–£17,355 WB £21,480

Berkhamsted School
Overton House, 131 High Street, Berkhamsted, Hertfordshire HP4 2DJ
Tel: 01442 358001
Principal: Mr Richard Backhouse MA(Cantab)
Age range: 3–18
No. of pupils: 2006 VIth379
Fees: Day £10,620–£21,420 WB £28,770 FB £34,275

Bhaktivedanta Manor School
Hilfield Lane, Aldenham, Watford, Hertfordshire WD25 8EZ
Tel: 01923 851000 Ext:241
Headteacher: Guru Carana Padma dasi
Age range: 4–12
No. of pupils: 45
Fees: Day £1,860

Bishop's Stortford College
10 Maze Green Road, Bishop's Stortford, Hertfordshire CM23 2PJ
Tel: 01279 838575
Headmaster: Mr Jeremy Gladwin
Age range: 13–18
No. of pupils: VIth249
Fees: Day £20,349–£20,532 WB £31,569–£31,917 FB £33,402–£33,930

Bishop's Stortford College Prep School
Maze Green Road, Bishop's Stortford, Hertfordshire CM23 2PH
Tel: 01279 838607
Head of the Prep School: Mr Bill Toleman
Age range: 4–13
No. of pupils: 590
Fees: Day £9,408–£16,281 WB £22,359–£24,273 FB £23,610–£25,536

Charlotte House Preparatory School
88 The Drive, Rickmansworth, Hertfordshire WD3 4DU
Tel: 01923 772101
Head: Miss P Woodcock
Age range: G3–11
No. of pupils: 140
Fees: Day £3,432–£12,102

Duncombe School
4 Warren Park Road, Bengeo, Hertford, Hertfordshire SG14 3JA
Tel: 01992 414100
Headmaster: Mr Jeremy Phelan M.A. (Ed)
Age range: 2–11
No. of pupils: 301
Fees: Day £10,380–£14,565

Edge Grove School
Aldenham Village, Hertfordshire WD25 8NL
Tel: 01923 855724
Headmaster: Mr Ben Evans BA (Hons), PGCE
Age range: 3–13
No. of pupils: 494
Fees: Day £6,930–£16,935 WB £20,756–£23,150

Egerton Rothesay School
Durrants Lane, Berkhamsted, Hertfordshire HP4 3UJ
Tel: 01442 865275
Headteacher: Mr Colin Parker BSc(Hons), Dip.Ed (Oxon), PGCE, C.Math MIMA
Age range: 6–19

Haberdashers' Aske's School for Girls
Aldenham Road, Elstree,
Borehamwood, Hertfordshire WD6 3BT
Tel: 020 8266 2300
Head of School: Ms Rose Hardy
Age range: G4–18
No. of pupils: 1190
Fees: Day £17,826–£19,311
🏃 Ⓐ Ⓔ 16·

HAILEYBURY
For further details see p.68
Haileybury, Hertford,
Hertfordshire SG13 7NU
Tel: +44 (0)1992 706353
Email:
uk.admissions@haileybury.com
Website: www.haileybury.com
The Master: Mr Martin
Collier MA BA PGCE
Age range: 11–18
No. of pupils: 880 VIth319
Fees: Day £17,712–£26,646
FB £22,929–£36,141
Ⓒ Ⓐ Ⓔ ⒾⒷ 16·

Heath Mount School
Woodhall Park, Watton-at-Stone,
Hertford, Hertfordshire SG14 3NG
Tel: 01920 830230
Headmaster: Mr Chris Gillam BEd(Hons)
Age range: 3–13
No. of pupils: 478
Fees: Day £11,955–£18,435
🏫 Ⓔ

High Elms Manor School
High Elms Lane, Watford,
Hertfordshire WD25 0JX
Tel: 01923 681 103
Headmistress: Ms Liadain
O'Neill BA (Hons), AMI 0-3, AMI
3-6, Early Years FdA Dist.+
Age range: 2–12
No. of pupils: 100
Fees: Day £10,500–£12,675

Hockerill Anglo-European College
Dunmow Road, Bishops Stortford,
Hertfordshire CM23 5HX
Tel: 01279 658451
Principal: David Woods
Age range: 11–18
No. of pupils: 850
Fees: FB £13,200–£17,862
Ⓒ ⒾⒷ 16·

Howe Green House School
Great Hallingbury, Bishop's
Stortford, Hertfordshire CM22 7UF
Tel: 01279 657706
Headmistress: Ms Deborah
Mills BA (Hons) Q.T.S
Age range: 2–11
Ⓔ

Immanuel College
87/91 Elstree Road, Bushey,
Hertfordshire WD23 4EB
Tel: 020 8950 0604
Headmaster: Mr Gary Griffin
Age range: 4–18
No. of pupils: 520 VIth127
Fees: Day £10,995
Ⓐ 16·

Kingshott
Stevenage Road, St Ippolyts,
Hitchin, Hertfordshire SG4 7JX
Tel: 01462 432009
Headmaster: Mr David Weston
Age range: 3–13 years
No. of pupils: 410
Fees: Day £6,390–£13,770
Ⓔ

Little Acorns Montessori School
Lincolnsfield Centre, Bushey Hall Drive,
Bushey, Hertfordshire WD23 2ER
Tel: 01923 230705
Age range: 12 months–6
No. of pupils: 28
Fees: Day £2,120

Lochinver House School
Heath Road, Little Heath, Potters
Bar, Hertfordshire EN6 1LW
Tel: 01707 653064
Headmaster: Ben Walker
BA(Hons), PGCE, CELTA
Age range: B4–13
No. of pupils: 349
Fees: Day £11,175–£14,685

Lockers Park
Lockers Park Lane, Hemel
Hempstead, Hertfordshire HP1 1TL
Tel: 01442 251712
Headmaster: Mr C R Wilson
Age range: B4–13 G4–7
No. of pupils: 171
Fees: Day £11,175–£17,730
WB £16,035–£23,670
Ⓒ Ⓔ

Longwood School
Bushey Hall Drive, Bushey,
Hertfordshire WD23 2QG
Tel: 01923 253715
Head Teacher: Claire May
Age range: 3 months–11
Fees: Day £3,705–£7,800

Manor Lodge School
Rectory Lane, Ridge Hill, Shenley,
Hertfordshire WD7 9BG
Tel: 01707 642424
Head of School: Mrs A Lobo BEd(Hons)
Age range: 3–11
No. of pupils: 427
Fees: Day £11,100–£12,300
Ⓔ

Merchant Taylors' Prep
Moor Farm, Sandy Lodge Road,
Rickmansworth, Hertfordshire WD3 1LW
Tel: 01923 825648
Headmaster: Dr Karen McNerney
BSc (Hons), PGCE, MSc, EdD
Age range: B4–13
No. of pupils: 300
Fees: Day £5,148–£16,000
Ⓒ Ⓔ

Princess Helena College
School Lane, Preston, Hitchin,
Hertfordshire SG4 7RT
Tel: +44 (0)1462 432100
Headmistress: Mrs Sarah Davis
MA Hons (Edinburgh) PGCE
Age range: G11–18
No. of pupils: 194 VIth35
Fees: Day £16,125–£19,635
FB £22,965–£28,545
Ⓒ 🏃 Ⓐ 🏫 Ⓔ 16·

Queenswood
Shepherd's Way, Brookmans Park,
Hatfield, Hertfordshire AL9 6NS
Tel: 01707 602500
Principal: Mrs Jo Cameron
Age range: G11–18
No. of pupils: 400 VIth120
Fees: Day £20,925–£24,825 WB
£23,355–£31,035 FB £23,985–£33,750
Ⓒ 🏃 Ⓐ Ⓔ 16·

Radlett Preparatory School
Kendal Hall, Watling Street,
Radlett, Hertfordshire WD7 7LY
Tel: 01923 856812
Principal: Mr G White BEd (Hons)
Age range: 4–11
Fees: Day £9,735

Sherrardswood School
Lockleys, Welwyn, Hertfordshire AL6 0BJ
Tel: 01438 714282
Headmistress: Mrs Anna Wright
Age range: 2–18
No. of pupils: 357
Fees: Day £10,383–£16,113
Ⓐ Ⓔ 16·

St Albans High School for Girls
Townsend Avenue, St Albans,
Hertfordshire AL1 3SJ
Tel: 01727 853800
Headmistress: Amber Waite
Age range: G4–18
No. of pupils: 940 VIth170
Ⓒ Ⓐ Ⓔ 16·

St Albans Independent College
69 London Road, St Albans,
Hertfordshire AL1 1LN
Tel: 01727 842348
Principals: Mr. A N Jemal
& Mr Elvis Cotena
Age range: 15+
Fees: Day £2,700–£5,900
16· Ⓐ

St Albans School
Abbey Gateway, St Albans,
Hertfordshire AL3 4HB
Tel: 01727 855521
Headmaster: Mr JWJ Gillespie
MA(Cantab), FRSA
Age range: B11–18 G16–18
No. of pupils: 870
Fees: Day £18,600
Ⓒ Ⓐ Ⓔ 16·

St Christopher School
Barrington Road, Letchworth,
Hertfordshire SG6 3JZ
Tel: 01462 650 850
Head: Richard Palmer
Age range: 3–18
No. of pupils: 511 VIth78
Fees: Day £4,590–£18,075 WB
£19,950–£24,675 FB £31,650
Ⓒ Ⓐ Ⓔ 16· ⓦ

ST COLUMBA'S COLLEGE
For further details see p.78
King Harry Lane, St Albans,
Hertfordshire AL3 4AW
Tel: 01727 892040
Email:
admissions@stcolumbascollege.org
Website:
www.stcolumbascollege.org
Head: Mr David Buxton
Age range: B4–18
No. of pupils: 760
Ⓒ Ⓐ Ⓔ 16·

St Edmund's College & Prep School
Old Hall Green, Nr Ware,
Hertfordshire SG11 1DS
Tel: 01920 824247
Headmaster: Mr Matthew
Mostyn BA (Hons) MA (Ed)
Age range: 3–18
No. of pupils: 852
Fees: Day £9,882–£18,345 WB
£24,165–£27,630 FB £28,302–£32,460
(ⓖ) (A) (⌂) (£) (✎) (16·)

St Edmund's Prep
Old Hall Green, Ware,
Hertfordshire SG11 1DS
Tel: 01920 824239
Head: Mr Steven Cartwright
BSc (Surrey)
Age range: 3–11
No. of pupils: 185
Fees: Day £10,650–£13,365
(✎)

St Francis' College
Broadway, Letchworth Garden
City, Hertfordshire SG6 3PJ
Tel: 01462 670511
Headmistress: Mrs B Goulding
Age range: G3–18
No. of pupils: 460 VIth75
Fees: Day £9,990–£16,980 WB
£22,350–£26,475 FB £27,990–£31,995
(♣) (A) (⌂) (£) (16·)

St Hilda's
High Street, Bushey,
Hertfordshire WD23 3DA
Tel: 020 8950 1751
Headmistress: Miss Sarah-
Jane Styles MA
Age range: B2–4 G2–11
Fees: Day £12,012–£12,843
(♣) (✎)

St Hilda's School
28 Douglas Road, Harpenden,
Hertfordshire AL5 2ES
Tel: 01582 712307
Headmaster: Mr Dan Sayers
Age range: G3–11 years
No. of pupils: 144
Fees: Day £6,615–£11,535
(♣) (✎)

St Joseph's In The Park
St Mary's Lane, Hertingfordbury,
Hertford, Hertfordshire SG14 2LX
Tel: 01992 513810
Age range: 3–11
No. of pupils: 150
Fees: Day £5,718–£16,899
(£) (✎)

ST MARGARET'S SCHOOL, BUSHEY
For further details see p.82
Merry Hill Road, Bushey,
Hertfordshire WD23 1DT
Tel: +44 (0)20 8416 4400
Email: admissions@smbushey.com
Website:
www.stmargaretsbushey.co.uk
Headteacher: Lara Péchard
Age range: 3–18 years
No. of pupils: 445

(ⓖ) (A) (⌂) (£) (✎) (16·)

St. John's Prep. School
The Ridgeway, Potters Bar,
Hertfordshire EN6 5QT
Tel: +44 (0)1707 657294
Head Teacher: Mrs C Tardios
Age range: 4–11
(✎)

Stanborough School
Stanborough Park, Garston,
Watford, Hertfordshire WD25 9JT
Tel: 01923 673268
Acting Head Teacher: Ms Eileen Hussey
Age range: 3–17
No. of pupils: 300
Fees: Day £6,630–£10,224
WB £10,350–£13,995
(ⓖ) (⌂) (16·)

Stormont
The Causeway, Potters Bar,
Hertfordshire EN6 5HA
Tel: 01707 654037
Head Teacher: Miss Louise Martin
Age range: G4–11
Fees: Day £12,300–£13,050
(♣) (£) (✎)

The Haberdashers' Aske's Boys' School
Butterfly Lane, Elstree, Borehamwood,
Hertfordshire WD6 3AF
Tel: 020 8266 1700
Headmaster: Gus Lock MA (Oxon)
Age range: B5–18 years
No. of pupils: 1428
Fees: Day £15,339–£20,346
(♣) (A) (£) (16·)

The King's School
Elmfield, Ambrose Lane, Harpenden,
Hertfordshire AL5 4DU
Tel: 01582 767566
Principal: Mr Clive John Case BA, HDE
Age range: 4–16
Fees: Day £7,680
(£) (✎)

The Purcell School, London
Aldenham Road, Bushey,
Hertfordshire WD23 2TS
Tel: 01923 331100
Headteacher: Dr Bernard Trafford
Age range: 10–18
No. of pupils: 180
Fees: Day £25,707 FB £32,826
(ⓖ) (A) (⌂) (£) (✎) (16·)

TRING PARK SCHOOL FOR THE PERFORMING ARTS
For further details see p.90
Tring Park, Tring,
Hertfordshire HP23 5LX
Tel: 01442 824255
Email: info@tringpark.com
Website: www.tringpark.com
Principal: Mr Stefan Anderson
MA, ARCM, ARCT
Age range: 8–19
No. of pupils: 354 VIth150
Fees: Day £15,405–£24,510
FB £26,190–£37,050
(ⓖ) (A) (⌂) (£) (✎) (16·) (❀)

Westbrook Hay Prep School
London Road, Hemel Hempstead,
Hertfordshire HP1 2RF
Tel: 01442 256143
Headmaster: Mark Brain
Age range: 3–13
No. of pupils: 340
Fees: Day £10,905–£15,690
(£) (✎)

York House School
Redheath, Sarratt Road,
Croxley Green, Rickmansworth,
Hertfordshire WD3 4LW
Tel: 01923 772395
Headmaster: Jon Gray BA(Ed)
Age range: 3–13
No. of pupils: 240
Fees: Day £10,440–£13,905
(£) (✎)

Norfolk

All Saints School
School Road, Lessingham,
Norwich, Norfolk NR12 0DJ
Tel: 01692 582083
Head teacher: P Wright
Age range: 7–16
Fees: Day £3,600–£5,400
(✎) (❀)

Aurora Eccles School
Quidenham, Norwich,
Norfolk NR16 2NZ
Tel: 01953 887217
Interim Headteacher: Chris MacKinnon
Age range: 7–19
(ⓖ) (⌂)

Beeston Hall School
Beeston Regis, West Runton,
Cromer, Norfolk NR27 9NQ
Tel: 01263 837324
Headmaster: Mr Fred de
Falbe BA(Hons) PGCE
Age range: 4–13
Fees: Day £8,550–£17,730
FB £18,360–£23,820
(⌂) (£) (✎)

Downham Preparatory School & Montessori Nursery
The Old Rectory, Stow Bardolph,
Kings Lynn, Norfolk PE34 3HT
Tel: 01366 388066
Headmistress: Mrs E Laffeaty-
Sharpe MontDip
Age range: 3 months–11
No. of pupils: 170
Fees: Day £6,426–£8,721
(✎)

Focus School – Swaffham Campus
Turbine Way, Swaffham,
Norfolk PE37 7XD
Tel: 01760 336939

Glebe House School
2 Cromer Road, Hunstanton,
Norfolk PE36 6HW
Tel: 01485 532809
Headmaster: Mr Crofts
Age range: 0–13
No. of pupils: 110
Fees: Day £8,316–£13,290
🌐 £ ✎

**Gresham's Nursery and
Pre-Prep School**
Market Place, Holt, Norfolk NR25 6BB
Tel: 01263 714575
Headmistress: Mrs Sarah Hollingsworth
Age range: 2–7
No. of pupils: 90
Fees: Day £10,350–£11,100
🌐 ✎

Gresham's Prep School
Cromer Road, Holt, Norfolk NR25 6EY
Tel: 01263 714600
Head: Mrs Cathy Braithwaite
Age range: 7–13
No. of pupils: 240
Fees: Day £15,120–£18,630 FB £26,100
🌐 ♘ £ ✎

Gresham's Senior School
Cromer Road, Holt, Norfolk NR25 6EA
Tel: 01263 714 614
Headmaster: Mr Douglas
Robb MA, MEd
Age range: 13–18
No. of pupils: 500
Fees: Day £24,140 FB £36,030
🌐 Ⓐ ♘ £ ⒤ᴮ ✎ 16·

**Langley Preparatory School
at Taverham Hall**
Taverham, Norwich, Norfolk NR8 6HU
Tel: 01603 868206
Headmaster: Mr Mike A
Crossley NPQH, BEd(Hons)
Age range: 2–13
Fees: Day £10,275–£14,175 WB £18,315
♘ £ ✎

Langley School
Langley Park, Loddon,
Norwich, Norfolk NR14 6BJ
Tel: 01508 520210
Headmaster: Mr Dominic Findlay
Age range: 10–18
No. of pupils: 515
Fees: Day £15,720 WB £26,649 FB £31,941
🌐 Ⓐ ♘ £ ✎ 16·

Norwich High School for Girls GDST
95 Newmarket Road, Norwich,
Norfolk NR2 2HU
Tel: 01603 453265
Headmistress: Mrs Kirsty von Malaise
Age range: G3–18
No. of pupils: VIth120
Fees: Day £9,198–£14,562
♘ Ⓐ £ ✎ 16·

Norwich School
70 The Close, Norwich, Norfolk NR1 4DD
Tel: 01603 728430
Head Master: Steffan D A Griffiths
Age range: 4–18
No. of pupils: 1065
Fees: Day £10,998–£16,212
Ⓐ £ 16·

Norwich Steiner School
Hospital Lane, Norwich,
Norfolk NR1 2HW
Tel: 01603 611175
Headteacher: Mr Andrew Vestrini
Age range: 3–18
No. of pupils: 91
Fees: Day £3,830–£7,010
✎

Notre Dame Preparatory School
147 Dereham Road, Norwich,
Norfolk NR2 3TA
Tel: 01603 625593
Headmaster: Mr Rob Thornton MA
Age range: 2–11
£ ✎

**Riddlesworth Hall
Preparatory School**
Hall Lane, Diss, Norfolk IP22 2TA
Tel: 01953 681 246
Acting Headmaster: Mr A Bentley
Age range: 2–13
No. of pupils: 137
Fees: Day £6,435–£8,970
FB £18,000–£20,100
♘ £ ✎

Thetford Grammar School
Bridge Street, Thetford, Norfolk IP24 3AF
Tel: 01842 752840
Headmaster: Mr Michael Brewer
Age range: 3–18
No. of pupils: 200
Fees: Day £8,250–£13,665
Ⓐ £ ✎ 16·

**Town Close House
Preparatory School**
14 Ipswich Road, Norwich,
Norfolk NR2 2LR
Tel: 01603 620180
Headmaster: Mr Nicholas Bevington
Age range: 3–13
No. of pupils: 455
Fees: Day £8,670–£13,152
£ ✎

Suffolk

**Barnardiston Hall
Preparatory School**
Barnardiston, Nr Haverhill,
Suffolk CB9 7TG
Tel: 01440 786316
Headmaster:
Lt Col K A Boulter MA(Cantab)
Age range: 6 months–13 years
No. of pupils: 220
Fees: Day £8,235–£13,725
WB £18,975 FB £20,580
♘ £ ✎

Brookes Cambridge
Flempton Road, Risby, Bury St
Edmunds, Suffolk IP28 6QJ
Tel: 01284 760531
Director: Mr D Rose
Age range: 2–16
No. of pupils: 100
Fees: Day £9,150–£14,280
FB £19,590–£28,170
♘

Culford Preparatory School
Culford, Bury St Edmunds,
Suffolk IP28 6TX
Tel: 01284 385383
Headmaster: Mr Mike Schofield
Age range: 7–13
No. of pupils: 214
Fees: Day £11,625–£15,225
FB £22,485–£23,985
♘

Culford Pre-Preparatory School
Fieldgate House, Bury St
Edmunds, Suffolk IP28 6TX
Tel: 01284 385412
Headmistress: Mrs Sarah Preston BA
Age range: 1–7
Fees: Day £8,940–£9,645

Culford School
Culford, Bury St Edmunds,
Suffolk IP28 6TX
Tel: 01284 728615
Headmaster:
Mr J F Johnson-Munday MA, MBA
Age range: 1–18
No. of pupils: 650 VIth150
Fees: Day £8,940–£19,500
FB £22,485–£29,985
🌐 Ⓐ ♘ £ ✎ 16·

Fairstead House School
Fordham Road, Newmarket,
Suffolk CB8 7AA
Tel: 01638 662318
Head: Lynda Brereton
Age range: 9 months–11 years
No. of pupils: 118
Fees: Day £9,747–£10,611
£ ✎

Felixstowe International College
Maybush House, Maybush Lane,
Felixstowe, Suffolk IP11 7NA
Tel: +44 (0)1394 282388
Principal: Rebecca Mainprice
Age range: 10–17
♘ 16·

Finborough School
The Hall, Great Finborough,
Stowmarket, Suffolk IP14 3EF
Tel: 01449 773600
Principal: Mr Steven Clark
Age range: 2–18
No. of pupils: 226 VIth20
Fees: Day £8,775–£13,590 WB
£16,455–£22,020 FB £20,475–£27,450
🌐 Ⓐ ♘ £ ✎ 16· ❀

Framlingham College
College Road, Framlingham,
Suffolk IP13 9EY
Tel: 01728 723789
Headmistress: Mrs Louise North
Age range: 2–18
No. of pupils: 700
Fees: Day £8,409–£19,176 FB £29,823
🌐 Ⓐ ♘ £ ✎ 16·

Ipswich High School
Woolverstone, Ipswich, Suffolk IP9 1AZ
Tel: 01473 780201
Head of School: Ms Oona Carlin
Age range: 3–18
No. of pupils: 500 VIth40
Fees: Day £8,769–£14,322
Ⓐ ⓔ ⓢ ⑯

Ipswich Preparatory School
3 Ivry Street, Ipswich, Suffolk IP1 3QW
Tel: 01473 282800
Age range: 2–11
ⓢ

Ipswich School
Henley Road, Ipswich, Suffolk IP1 3SG
Tel: 01473 408300
Headmaster: Mr Nicholas Weaver MA
Age range: 2–18
No. of pupils: 739 VIth218
Fees: Day £11,850–£15,579
WB £24,402–£27,381 FB £26,376–£30,171
ⓖ Ⓐ ⓑ ⓔ ⓢ ⑯

Old Buckenham Hall School
Old Buckenham Hall, Brettenham
Park, Ipswich, Suffolk IP7 7PH
Tel: 01449 740252
Headmaster: Mr David Griffiths
Age range: 3–13 years
No. of pupils: 202
Fees: Day £6,424 FB £8,370
ⓑ ⓔ ⓢ

ORWELL PARK SCHOOL
For further details see p.74
Nacton, Ipswich, Suffolk IP10 0ER
Tel: 01473 659225
Email: admissions@orwellpark.org
Website: www.orwellpark.co.uk
Headmaster:
Mr Adrian Brown MA(Cantab)
Age range: 2–13
No. of pupils: 248
ⓑ ⓔ ⓢ

Queen's House School
Bredfield Street, Woodbridge,
Suffolk IP12 4NH
Tel: 01394 615070
Headteacher: Nicola Mitchell
Age range: 4–7

Saint Felix School
Halesworth Road, Southwold,
Suffolk IP18 6SD
Tel: 01502 722175
Headmaster: Mr. James Harrison
Age range: 2–18
No. of pupils: 312 VIth65
Fees: Day £7,485–£16,185
WB £17,670–£22,470 FB £23,370–£28,170
ⓖ Ⓐ ⓑ ⓔ ⓢ ⑯

South Lee Preparatory School
Nowton Road, Bury St
Edmunds, Suffolk IP33 2BT
Tel: 01284 754654
Headmaster:
Mr Mervyn Watch BEd (Hons)
Age range: 2–13
Fees: Day £9,645–£11,820
ⓢ

St Joseph's College
Birkfield, Belstead Road,
Ipswich, Suffolk IP2 9DR
Tel: 01473 690281
Principal: Mrs Danielle Clarke
Age range: 3–18
No. of pupils: 564
Fees: Day £6,045–£15,150
WB £24,990–£27,315 FB £26,145–£33,795
ⓖ Ⓐ ⓑ ⓔ ⓢ ⑯

Stoke College
Stoke-by-Clare, Sudbury,
Suffolk CO10 8JE
Tel: 01787 278141
Head: Mr Frank Thompson
Age range: 3–18
Fees: Day £6,132–£14,979
WB £20,829–£24,231 FB £27,096–£31,518
ⓖ ⓑ ⓔ ⓢ

Summerhill School
Leiston, Suffolk IP16 4HY
Tel: 01728 830540
Principal: Mrs Zoe Readhead
Age range: 5–17
No. of pupils: 69
Fees: Day £5,475–£11,205
FB £12,069–£19,041
ⓑ ⓢ

The Meadows Montessori School
32 Larchcroft Road, Ipswich,
Suffolk IP1 6AR
Tel: 01473 233782
Headteacher: Ms Samantha Sims
Age range: 4–11
No. of pupils: 54

The Old School Henstead
Toad Row, Beccles, Suffolk NR34 7LG
Tel: 01502 741150
Head: Mr W J McKinney
Age range: 2–11
No. of pupils: 123
Fees: Day £6,990–£10,077

THE ROYAL HOSPITAL SCHOOL
For further details see p.88
Holbrook, Ipswich, Suffolk IP9 2RX
Tel: 01473 326200
Email:
admissions@royalhospitalschool.org
Website:
www.royalhospitalschool.org
Headmaster:
Mr Simon Lockyer BSc MEd
Age range: 11–18
No. of pupils: 689
Fees: Day £16,440–£18,330 WB
£25,230–£31,335 FB £26,490–£34,140
ⓖ Ⓐ ⓑ ⓔ ⓢ ⑯

Woodbridge School
Burkitt Road, Woodbridge,
Suffolk IP12 4JH
Tel: +44 (0)1394 615000
Acting Head: Miss Shona Norman
Age range: 4–18
No. of pupils: 901
Fees: Day £9,741–£16,505 FB £30,885
ⓖ Ⓐ ⓑ ⓔ ⓢ ⑯

Woodbridge School Prep
Church Street, Woodbridge,
Suffolk IP12 1DS
Tel: +44 (0)1394 382673
Head of School: Mrs N Mitchell
Age range: 4–11

D292

East Midlands

KEY TO SYMBOLS

- (♂) *Boys' school*
- (♀) *Girls' school*
- (🌐) *International school*
- (16) *Tutorial or sixth form college*
- (A) *A levels*
- (🏫) *Boarding accommodation*
- (£) *Bursaries*
- (IB) *International Baccalaureate*
- (✎) *Learning support*
- (16) *Entrance at 16+*
- (💼) *Vocational qualifications*
- (IAPS) *Independent Association of Preparatory Schools*
- (HMC) *The Headmasters' & Headmistresses' Conference*
- (ISA) *Independent Schools Association*
- (GSA) *Girls' School Association*
- (BSA) *Boarding Schools' Association*
- (S) *Society of Heads*

Unless otherwise indicated, all schools are coeducational day schools.
Single-sex and boarding schools will be indicated by the relevant icon.

Derbyshire

Barlborough Hall School
Park Street, Barlborough,
Chesterfield, Derbyshire S43 4ES
Tel: 01246 810511
Headteacher: Mrs Karen Keeton
Age range: 3–11

Dame Catherine Harpur's School
Rose Lane, Ticknall, Derby,
Derbyshire DE73 7JW
Tel: 01332 862792
Head: Ms Whyte
Age range: 3–11
No. of pupils: 28
Fees: Day £4,794

Derby Grammar School
Rykneld Hall, Rykneld Road, Littleover,
Derby, Derbyshire DE23 4BX
Tel: 01332 523027
Head: Dr Ruth Norris
Age range: B7–18 G16–18
No. of pupils: 255
Fees: Day £8,823–£13,449

Derby High School
Hillsway, Littleover, Derby,
Derbyshire DE23 3DT
Tel: 01332 514267
Headteacher: Mrs Denise Gould
Age range: B3–11 G3–18
No. of pupils: 576 VIth74
Fees: Day £8,820–£12,870

Emmanuel School
Juniper Lodge, 43 Kedleston Road,
Derby, Derbyshire DE22 1FP
Tel: 01332 340505
Headteacher: Mr Ben Snowdon
Age range: 3–16

Foremarke Hall
Milton, Derby, Derbyshire DE65 6EJ
Tel: 01283 707100
Headmaster: Mr R Merriman
MA, BSc(Hons), FCollP
Age range: 3–13

Mount St Mary's College
College Road, Spinkhill,
Derbyshire S21 3YL
Tel: 01246 433388
Headmaster: Dr Nicholas Cuddihy
Age range: 11–18
No. of pupils: 360
Fees: Day £11,669–£13,406 WB
£18,202–£23,431 FB £22,128–£29,046

Normanton House School
Normanton House, Village Street,
Derby, Derbyshire DE23 8DF
Tel: 01332 769333
Head of School: Mrs Nazia Iqbal
Age range: 5–16

Ockbrook School
The Settlement, Ockbrook,
Derby, Derbyshire DE72 3RJ
Tel: 01332 673532
Head: Mr Tom Brooksby
Age range: 2–18
No. of pupils: 409 VIth55
Fees: Day £8,955–£13,170

Old Vicarage School
11 Church Lane, Darley Abbey,
Derby, Derbyshire DE22 1EW
Tel: 01332 557130
Headmaster: Mr M J Adshead
Age range: 3–13
No. of pupils: 95
Fees: Day £7,650–£8,124

Repton School
The Hall, Repton, Derbyshire DE65 6FH
Tel: 01283 559222
Head of School: M J
Semmence MA, MBA
Age range: 13–18
No. of pupils: 653 VIth299
Fees: Day £26,493 FB £35,712

S. Anselm's School
Stanedge Road, Bakewell,
Derbyshire DE45 1DP
Tel: 01629 812734
Headmaster: Peter Phillips BA
(Hons), MA, PGCE (SPLD), NPQH
Age range: 3–13
No. of pupils: 215
Fees: Day £10,950–£20,700 FB £26,100

St Peter & St Paul School
Brambling House, Hady Hill,
Chesterfield, Derbyshire S41 0EF
Tel: 01246 278522
Headteacher: Mrs Jill Phinn
Age range: 3 months–11 years
No. of pupils: 120
Fees: Day £8,658–£9,159

St Wystan's School
High Street, Repton,
Derbyshire DE65 6GE
Tel: 01283 703258
Head Teacher: Karan Hopkinson
Age range: 3–11
Fees: Day £4,500–£8,655

Leicestershire

Al-Aqsa Schools Trust
The Wayne Way, Leicester,
Leicestershire LE5 4PP
Tel: 0116 2760953
Headteacher: Mrs Amina Patel
Age range: 5–16
No. of pupils: 231

Ashby School
School House, Leicester Road, Ashby-
de-la-Zouch, Leicestershire LE65 1DH
Tel: +44 (0) 1530 413748
Headteacher: Mr Geoff Staniforth
Age range: B11–19
No. of pupils: 1643

Brooke House College
Leicester Road, Market Harborough,
Leicestershire LE16 7AU
Tel: 01858 462452
Principal: Mr Mike Oliver
Age range: 14–20
No. of pupils: VIth73
Fees: Day £19,650–£21,525
FB £33,000–£36,000

Brooke House Day School
Croft Road, Cosby, Leicester,
Leicestershire LE9 1SE
Tel: 0116 286 7372
Head: Mrs Joy Parker
Age range: 3–14

Darul Uloom Leicester
119 Loughborough Road,
Leicester, Leicestershire LE4 5LN
Tel: 0116 2668922
Headteacher: Moulana Ishaq Boodi
Age range: B11–25
Fees: Day £1,800 FB £2,700

FAIRFIELD PREP SCHOOL
For further details see p.94
Leicester Road, Loughborough,
Leicestershire LE11 2AE
Tel: 01509 215172
Email: fairfield.admissions@lsf.org
Website: www.lsf.org/fairfield
Headmaster: Mr Andrew Earnshaw
Age range: 3–11
No. of pupils: 540

Jameah Girls Academy
49 Rolleston Street, Leicester,
Leicestershire LE5 3SD
Tel: 0116 262 7745
Headteacher: Ms Erfana Bora
Age range: G6–16
No. of pupils: 142

Leicester Grammar Junior School
London Road, Great Glen,
Leicester, Leicestershire LE8 9FL
Tel: 0116 259 1950
Age range: 3–11
No. of pupils: 391

Leicester Grammar School
London Road, Great Glen,
Leicester, Leicestershire LE8 9FL
Tel: 0116 259 1900
Headmaster: Mr John Watson
Age range: 10–18
No. of pupils: 830
Fees: Day £13,485

Leicester High School for Girls
454 London Road, Leicester,
Leicestershire LE2 2PP
Tel: 0116 2705338
Headmaster: Mr Alan Whelpdale
Age range: G3–18
No. of pupils: 435 VIth60
Fees: Day £2,995–£4,065

Leicester Islamic Academy
320 London Road, Leicester,
Leicestershire LE2 2PJ
Tel: 01162 705343
Headteacher: Mrs S Khan
Age range: 3–11

Leicester Prep School
2 Albert Road, Leicester,
Leicestershire LE2 2AA
Tel: 0116 2707414
Headmaster: Paul Hitchcock
Age range: 3–11
No. of pupils: 130
Fees: Day £7,800

LOUGHBOROUGH AMHERST SCHOOL
For further details see p.96
Gray Street, Loughborough,
Leicestershire LE11 2DZ
Tel: 01509 263901
Email: amherst.admissions@lsf.org
Website: www.lsf.org/amherst
Headmaster: Dr Julian Murphy
Age range: 4–18
No. of pupils: 290

LOUGHBOROUGH GRAMMAR SCHOOL
For further details see p.98
Buckland House, Burton
Walks, Loughborough,
Leicestershire LE11 2DU
Tel: 01509 233233
Email: grammar.admissions@lsf.org
Website: www.lsf.org/grammar
Headmaster: Mr Duncan Byrne
Age range: B10–18
No. of pupils: 900

LOUGHBOROUGH HIGH SCHOOL
For further details see p.100
Burton Walks, Loughborough,
Leicestershire LE11 2DU
Tel: 01509 212348
Email: high.admissions@lsf.org
Website: www.lsf.org/high
Head: Dr Fiona Miles
Age range: G11–18
No. of pupils: 550

Ratcliffe College
Fosse Way, Ratcliffe on the Wreake,
Leicester, Leicestershire LE7 4SG
Tel: +44 (0)1509 817000
Headmaster: Mr J Reddin
BSc, MSc, NPQH
Age range: 3–18

St Crispin's School
6 St Mary's Road, Stoneygate,
Leicester, Leicestershire LE2 1XA
Tel: 0116 2707648
Head Master: Andrew Atkin
Age range: 2–16

Stoneygate School
6 London Road, Great Glen,
Leicester, Leicestershire LE8 9DJ
Tel: 0116 259 2282
Headmaster: Mr J F Dobson
Age range: 4–16
No. of pupils: 180
Fees: Day £11,469–£14,379

The Dixie Grammar School
Station Road, Market Bosworth,
Leicestershire CV13 0LE
Tel: 01455 292244
Headmaster: Richard Lynn MA
Age range: 3–18
No. of pupils: 474 VIth71
Fees: Day £8,835–£12,015

Lincolnshire

Ayscoughfee Hall School
Welland Hall, London Road,
Spalding, Lincolnshire PE11 2TE
Tel: 01775 724733
Headmistress: Mrs Clare
Ogden BA(Hons), PGCE
Age range: 3–11
No. of pupils: 146
Fees: Day £4,560–£6,720

Bicker Preparatory School & Early Years
School Lane, Bicker, Boston,
Lincolnshire PE20 3DW
Tel: 01775 821786
Head Teacher: Mrs J Miles BA.PGCE
Age range: 3–11
No. of pupils: 74

Copthill Independent Day School
Barnack Road, Uffington,
Stamford, Lincolnshire PE9 3AD
Tel: 01780 757506
Headmaster: Mr J A Teesdale
BA(Hons), PGCE
Age range: 2–11
No. of pupils: 300
Fees: Day £9,255–£10,350

Dudley House School
1 Dudley Road, Grantham,
Lincolnshire NG31 9AA
Tel: 01476 400184
Headmistress: Mrs Jenny Johnson
Age range: 3–11
No. of pupils: 50
Fees: Day £5,220

Grantham Preparatory International School
Gorse Lane, Grantham,
Lincolnshire NG31 7UF
Tel: +44 (0)1476 593293
Headmistress: Mrs K A Korcz
Age range: 3–11
No. of pupils: 140
Fees: Day £9,786

Greenwich House School
106 High Holme Road, Louth,
Lincolnshire LN11 0HE
Tel: 01507 609252
Headmistress: Mrs J Brindle
Age range: 9 months–11 years

Handel House Preparatory School
The Northolme, Gainsborough,
Lincolnshire DN21 2JB
Tel: 01427 612426
Headmistress: Mrs Victoria Haigh
Age range: 2–11

Kirkstone House School
Main Street, Baston, Peterborough,
Lincolnshire PE6 9PA
Tel: 01778 560350
Head: Mrs C Jones BSocSc
Age range: 3–18
No. of pupils: 234
Fees: Day £9,498–£11,640

Lincoln Minster School
Upper Lindum Street, Lincoln,
Lincolnshire LN2 5RW
Tel: 01522 551300
Headmaster: Mr J M Wallace
Age range: 2–18
No. of pupils: 840 VIth144
Fees: Day £9,276–£13,632 WB
£23,013–£26,715 FB £20,901–£24,186

St Hugh's School
Cromwell Avenue, Woodhall
Spa, Lincolnshire LN10 6TQ
Tel: 01526 352169
Head: C Ward BEd(Hons)
Age range: 2–13
No. of pupils: 195
Fees: Day £8,880–£14,928 FB £18,750

Stamford Endowed Schools
Brazenose House, St Paul's Street,
Stamford, Lincolnshire PE9 2BE
Tel: 01780 668 000
Principal: Mrs Vicky Buckman
Age range: 2–18
No. of pupils: 1634 VIth400
Fees: Day £9,414–£15,318 WB
£19,821–£24,801 FB £21,864–£28,446

Stamford High School
St Martin's, Stamford,
Lincolnshire PE9 2LL
Tel: 01780 428200
Principal: Mrs Vicky Buckman
Age range: G11–18
No. of pupils: 633 VIth201
Fees: Day £15,318 WB £21,552–
£24,801 FB £28,446

Stamford Junior School
Kettering Road, Stamford,
Lincolnshire PE9 2LR
Tel: 01780 484400
Headteacher: Mrs Emma Maria Smith
Age range: 2–11
No. of pupils: 344
Fees: Day £9,414–£12,102 WB
£17,415–£19,821 FB £21,864

Viking School
140 Church Road North, Skegness,
Lincolnshire PE25 2QJ
Tel: 01754 765749
Principal: Mrs S J Barker
Age range: 3–11
No. of pupils: 100
Fees: Day £4,050–£4,350

Witham Hall Preparatory School
Witham-on-the-Hill, Bourne,
Lincolnshire PE10 0JJ
Tel: +44(0)1778 590222
Headmaster: Mr Charles
Welch B.Ed (Hons)
Age range: 4–13
No. of pupils: 250
Fees: Day £9,555–£16,080 FB £21,690

Northamptonshire

Beachborough School
Westbury, Brackley,
Northamptonshire NN13 5LB
Tel: 01280 700071
Interim Head: Elizabeth Hill
Age range: 2–13
No. of pupils: 260
Fees: Day £10,728–£16,845

Bosworth Independent College
Nazareth House, Barrack
Road, Northampton,
Northamptonshire NN2 6AF
Tel: 01604 235090
Principal: Fiona Pocock MA PGCE
Age range: 13–University
No. of pupils: VIth250
Fees: Day £12,600 WB £20,030–
£21,230 FB £21,900–£23,100

Child First Moulton Nursery
Moulton Lodge, Moulton Way North,
Moulton, Northamptonshire NN3 7RW
Tel: 01604 790440
Nursery Manager: Angela Green

Laxton Junior School
East Road, Oundle,
Northamptonshire PE8 4BX
Tel: 01832 277159
Head of School: Mr Sam Robertson
Age range: 4–11
No. of pupils: 260
Fees: Day £9,720–£14,115

Maidwell Hall
Maidwell, Northampton,
Northamptonshire NN6 9JG
Tel: 01604 686234
Headmaster: Mr R A
Lankester MA, PGCE
Age range: 7–13
Fees: WB £27,150 FB £27,150

Northampton High School GDST
Newport Pagnell Road,
Hardingstone, Northampton,
Northamptonshire NN4 6UU
Tel: 01604 765765
Headmistress: Dr Helen
Stringer DPhil, MA, PGCE
Age range: G2–18
No. of pupils: 649 VIth128
Fees: Day £9,750–£14,331

Oundle School
The Great Hall, New Street, Oundle,
Northamptonshire PE8 4GH
Tel: 01832 277 122
Head of School: Mrs Sarah Kerr-Dineen
Age range: 11–18
No. of pupils: 1115
Fees: Day £18,465–£24,270
FB £28,880–£37,890

Overstone Park School
Overstone Park,
Overstone, Northampton,
Northamptonshire NN6 0DT
Tel: 01604 643787
Principal: Mrs M F Brown
BA(Hons), PGCE
Age range: 0–18
No. of pupils: 85

Pitsford School
Pitsford Hall, Pitsford, Northampton,
Northamptonshire NN6 9AX
Tel: 01604 880306
Head of School: Dr C Walker
Age range: 4–18
No. of pupils: VIth49
Fees: Day £8,223–£14,277

Quinton House School
Upton Hall, Upton, Northampton,
Northamptonshire NN5 4UX
Tel: 01604 752050
Headteacher: Mr Tim Hoyle
Age range: 2–18
No. of pupils: 390
Fees: Day £8,040–£11,985

Spratton Hall
Smith Street, Spratton,
Northamptonshire NN6 8HP
Tel: 01604 847292
Head Master: Mr Simon Clarke
Age range: 4–13
No. of pupils: 365
Fees: Day £10,350–£15,660

St Peter's Independent School
Lingswood Park,
Blackthorn, Northampton,
Northamptonshire NN3 8TA
Tel: 01604 411745
Acting Head: Julie Fenlon
Age range: 4–18
No. of pupils: 130
Fees: Day £6,825–£9,150

St Peter's School
52 Headlands, Kettering,
Northamptonshire NN15 6DJ
Tel: 01536 512066
Head of School: Mark Thomas
Age range: 2–11
No. of pupils: 161

Wellingborough School
Wellingborough,
Northamptonshire NN8 2BX
Tel: 01933 222427
Headmaster: Mr A N Holman
Age range: 3–18
No. of pupils: VIth145
Fees: Day £9,420–£15,990

Winchester House School
High Street, Brackley,
Northamptonshire NN13 7AZ
Tel: 01280 702483
Head: Mrs Emma Goldsmith
Age range: 3–13
No. of pupils: 307
Fees: Day £10,905–£19,230 WB £24,330

Nottinghamshire

**Colston Bassett
Preparatory School**
School Lane, Colston
bassett, Nottingham,
Nottinghamshire NG12 3FD
Tel: 01949 81118
Headteacher: Mrs Ruth O'Dell
Age range: 4–11
Fees: Day £7,098

**Coteswood House Pre-
school & Day Nursery**
19 Thackeray's Lane, Woodthorpe,
Nottingham, Nottinghamshire NG5 4HT
Tel: 0115 9676551
Age range: 3–11

Fig Tree Primary School
30 Bentinck Road, Nottingham,
Nottinghamshire NG7 4AF
Tel: 0115 978 8152
Head of School: Mrs Nabeela Hussain
Age range: 5–11

Highfields School
London Road, Newark,
Nottinghamshire NG24 3AL
Tel: 01636 704103
Headmaster: Mr R C R Thomson
BEd (Hons) NPQH
Age range: 2–11
No. of pupils: 140
Fees: Day £9,195

Hollygirt School
Elm Avenue, Nottingham,
Nottinghamshire NG3 4GF
Tel: 0115 958 0596
Headmistress: Mrs Pam Hutley
BA(Hons), PGCE, MSc
Age range: 3–16
No. of pupils: 200
Fees: Day £9,300–£12,234

Iona School
310 Sneinton Dale, Nottingham,
Nottinghamshire NG3 7DN
Tel: 01159 415295
Chair of College: Richard Moore
Age range: 3–11
Fees: Day £6,724

Jamia Al-Hudaa Residential College
Forest House, Berkeley Avenue,
Mapperley Park, Nottingham,
Nottinghamshire NG3 5TT
Tel: 0115 9690800
Principal: Raza ul-Haq Siakhvy
Age range: 11–19
No. of pupils: 224

Lammas School
Lammas Road, Sutton-in-Ashfield,
Nottinghamshire NG17 2AD
Tel: 0208 424 8475
Head: Mrs Sara Baldry
Age range: 4–19
No. of pupils: 57
Fees: Day £6,544–£8,489

Nottingham Girls' High School GDST
9 Arboretum Street, Nottingham,
Nottinghamshire NG1 4JB
Tel: 0115 9417663
Head: Miss Julie Keller
Age range: G4–18
No. of pupils: 786 VIth155
Fees: Day £9,873–£13,581

Nottingham High Infant and Junior School
Waverley Mount, Nottingham,
Nottinghamshire NG7 4ED
Tel: 0115 845 2214
Headteacher: Mrs Clare Bruce
Age range: 4–11
No. of pupils: 180
Fees: Day £3,393–£4,955

Nottingham High School
Waverley Mount, Nottingham,
Nottinghamshire NG7 4ED
Tel: 0115 9786056
Headmaster: Mr Kevin Fear BA
Age range: 4–18
No. of pupils: 1053
Fees: Day £10,179–£14,865

Plumtree School
Church Hill, Plumtree, Nottingham,
Nottinghamshire NG12 5ND
Tel: 0115 937 5859
Head Teacher: Phil Simpson
Age range: 3–11
Fees: Day £6,540

Salterford House School
Salterford Lane, Calverton,
Nottingham, Nottinghamshire
NG14 6NZ
Tel: 0115 9652127
Head: Ms Kimberley Venables
Age range: 3–11
No. of pupils: 124
Fees: Day £7,800–£7,890

Saville House School
11 Church Street, Mansfield
Woodhouse, Mansfield,
Nottinghamshire NG19 8AH
Tel: 01623 625068
Joint Head: Mrs See & Mrs Hill
Age range: 3–11
No. of pupils: 89
Fees: Day £5,475

St Joseph's School
33 Derby Road, Nottingham,
Nottinghamshire NG1 5AW
Tel: 0115 9418356
Head Teacher: Mr Ashley Crawshaw
Age range: 1–11
Fees: Day £7,728

The Orchard School
South Leverton, Retford,
Nottinghamshire DN22 0DJ
Tel: 01427 880395
Principal: Mrs S M Fox BA, PGCE
Age range: 5–16
No. of pupils: 150
Fees: Day £4,770–£7,575

Trent College and The Elms
Derby Road, Long Eaton, Nottingham,
Nottinghamshire NG10 4AD
Tel: 0115 8494949
Head: Mr Bill Penty
Age range: 0–18
No. of pupils: 1135
Fees: Day £3,420–£5,994

Wellow House School
Wellow, Newark,
Nottinghamshire NG22 0EA
Tel: 01623 861054
Principal: Kirsty Lamb
Age range: 3–13
No. of pupils: 152
Fees: Day £7,485–£11,985

Worksop College
Worksop, Nottinghamshire S80 3AP
Tel: 01909 537100
Headmaster: G W Horgan MA (Oxon)
Age range: 3–18
No. of pupils: 614 VIth141
Fees: Day £8,385–£17,985
FB £19,485–£29,085

Worksop College Preparatory School, Ranby House
Retford, Nottinghamshire DN22 8HX
Tel: 01777 714387 (Admissions)
Headmaster: C S J Pritchard
MA, BA(Hons), QTS
Age range: 3–11 years
No. of pupils: 190
Fees: Day £8,385–£13,485
FB £19,485–£20,085

Rutland

Brooke Priory School
Station Approach, Oakham,
Rutland LE15 6QW
Tel: 01572 724778
Headmaster: Mr R Outwin-
Flinders BEd (Hons)
Age range: 2–11
No. of pupils: 193
Fees: Day £7,395–£9,195

OAKHAM SCHOOL
For further details see p.102
Chapel Close, Oakham,
Rutland LE15 6DT
Tel: 01572 758500
Email: admissions@
oakham.rutland.sch.uk
Website:
www.oakham.rutland.sch.uk
Headmaster: Mr Henry
Price MA (Oxon)
Age range: 10–18
No. of pupils: VIth376
Fees: Day £17,685–£21,915
FB £27,000–£36,195

Uppingham School
Uppingham, Rutland LE15 9QE
Tel: 01572 822216 Admissions:
01572 820611
Headmaster: Dr Richard Maloney
Age range: 13–18
No. of pupils: 798 VIth344
Fees: Day £7,990 FB £12,906

D298

Greater London

Essex D300
Hertfordshire D301
Kent D301
Middlesex D302
Surrey D303

*See also East (D283) for schools in Essex and Hertfordshire; South-East (D331) for schools in Kent and Surrey

KEY TO SYMBOLS

- Boys' school
- Girls' school
- International school
- Tutorial or sixth form college
- A levels
- Boarding accommodation
- Bursaries
- International Baccalaureate
- Learning support
- Entrance at 16+
- Vocational qualifications
- Independent Association of Preparatory Schools
- The Headmasters' & Headmistresses' Conference
- Independent Schools Association
- Girls' School Association
- Boarding Schools' Association
- Society of Heads

Unless otherwise indicated, all schools are coeducational day schools. Single-sex and boarding schools will be indicated by the relevant icon.

D299

Essex

Al-Noor Primary School
Newton Industrial Estate, Eastern Avenue, Chadwell Heath, Romford, Essex RM6 5SD
Tel: 020 8597 7576
Head: Mrs Someera Butt
Age range: 4–10
No. of pupils: 175
Fees: Day £3,600

Avon House Preparatory School
490 High Road, Woodford Green, Essex IG8 0PN
Tel: 020 8504 1749
Headteacher: Mrs Amanda Campbell
Age range: 3–11
No. of pupils: 242
Fees: Day £9,750–£10,740

Bancroft's School
High Road, Woodford Green, Essex IG8 0RF
Tel: 020 8505 4821
Head: Mr Simon Marshall MA, PGCE (Cantab), MA, MPhil (Oxon)
Age range: 7–18
No. of pupils: 1120 VIth247

Beehive Preparatory School
233 Beehive Lane, Redbridge, Ilford, Essex IG4 5ED
Tel: 020 8550 3224
Headteacher: Miss Richards
Age range: 4–11

Braeside School for Girls
130 High Road, Buckhurst Hill, Essex IG9 5SD
Tel: 020 8504 1133
Headmistress: Claire Osborn
Age range: G3–16
No. of pupils: 199
Fees: Day £8,700–£12,750

Chigwell School
High Road, Chigwell, Essex IG7 6QF
Tel: 020 8501 5700
Headmaster: Mr M E Punt MA, MSc
Age range: 4–18
No. of pupils: 915 VIth185
Fees: Day £11,985–£17,985 FB £30,885

Daiglen School
68 Palmerston Road, Buckhurst Hill, Essex IG9 5LG
Tel: 020 8504 7108
Headteacher: Mrs P Dear
Age range: 3–11
No. of pupils: 130
Fees: Day £10,125–£10,275

Eastcourt Independent School
1 Eastwood Road, Goodmayes, Ilford, Essex IG3 8UW
Tel: 020 8590 5472
Headmistress: Mrs Christine Redgrave BSc(Hons), DipEd, MEd
Age range: 3–11
Fees: Day £7,200

Gidea Park College
2 Balgores Lane, Gidea Park, Romford, Essex RM2 5JR
Tel: 01708 740381
Headmistress: Mrs Katherine Whiskerd
Age range: 3–11
No. of pupils: 177
Fees: Day £9,675

Guru Gobind Singh Khalsa College
Roding Lane, Chigwell, Essex IG7 6BQ
Tel: 020 8559 9160
Principal: Mr Amarjit Singh Toor BSc(Hons), BSc, BT
Age range: 3–19
Fees: Day £5,892–£6,720

Immanuel School
Havering Grange, Havering Road, Romford, Essex RM1 4HR
Tel: 01708 764449
Head of School: Mr Simon Reeves
Age range: 3–16

Loyola Preparatory School
103 Palmerston Road, Buckhurst Hill, Essex IG9 5NH
Tel: 020 8504 7372
Headteacher: Mrs Kirsty Anthony
Age range: B3–11
No. of pupils: 200
Fees: Day £10,485

Maytime Montessori Nursery – Cranbrook Road
341 Cranbrook Road, Ilford, Essex IG1 4UF
Tel: 020 8554 3079

Maytime Montessori Nursery – Eastwood Road
2 Eastwood Road, Goodmayes, Essex IG3 8XB
Tel: 020 8599 3744

Maytime Montessori Nursery – Wanstead Road
293 Wanstead Park Rd, Ilford, Essex IG1 3TR
Tel: 020 8554 6344
Age range: 0–6

Oakfields Montessori School
Harwood Hall, Harwood Hall Lane, Upminster, Essex RM14 2YG
Tel: 01708 220117
Headmistress: Katrina Carroll
Age range: 2 –11
No. of pupils: 202
Fees: Day £10,296–£11,121

Oaklands School
8 Albion Hill, Loughton, Essex IG10 4RA
Tel: 020 8508 3517
Group Managing Principal: Mr M Hagger
Age range: 2–16
No. of pupils: 243
Fees: Day £10,350–£10,575

Park School for Girls
20-22 Park Avenue, Ilford, Essex IG1 4RS
Tel: 020 8554 2466
Head Teacher: Mrs Androulla Nicholas BSc Hons (Econ) PGCE
Age range: G4–16
No. of pupils: 160
Fees: Day £2,375–£3,580

Raphael Independent School
Park Lane, Hornchurch, Essex RM11 1XY
Tel: 01708 744735
Head of School: Mrs C Salmon
Age range: 4–16
No. of pupils: 135
Fees: Day £6,285–£9,045

St Aubyn's School
Bunces Lane, Woodford Green, Essex IG8 9DU
Tel: 020 8504 1577
Headmaster: Mr Leonard Blom BEd(Hons) BA NPQH
Age range: 3–13
No. of pupils: 525
Fees: Day £5,370–£12,195

St Mary's Hare Park School & Nursery
South Drive, Gidea Park, Romford, Essex RM2 6HH
Tel: 01708 761220
Head Teacher: Mrs K Karwacinski
Age range: 2 –11
No. of pupils: 180
Fees: Day £8,775

The Ursuline Preparatory School Ilford
2-8 Coventry Road, Ilford, Essex IG1 4QR
Tel: 020 8518 4050
Headteacher: Mrs Victoria McNaughton
Age range: G3–11
No. of pupils: 159
Fees: Day £7,320–£9,828

Woodford Green Preparatory School
Glengall Road, Woodford Green, Essex IG8 0BZ
Tel: 020 8504 5045
Headmaster: Mr J P Wadge
Age range: 3–11
No. of pupils: 384
Fees: Day £3,585

Hertfordshire

Lyonsdown School
3 Richmond Road, New Barnet,
Barnet, Hertfordshire EN5 1SA
Tel: 020 8449 0225
Head: Mr C Hammond BA (Hons) PGCE
Age range: B3–7 G3–11
No. of pupils: 185
Fees: Day £4,080–£10,200

Mount House School
Camlet Way, Hadley Wood,
Barnet, Hertfordshire EN4 0NJ
Tel: 020 8449 6889
Principal: Mr Toby Mullins
Age range: 11–18
No. of pupils: 190
Fees: Day £16,560

Susi Earnshaw Theatre School
68 High Street, Barnet,
Hertfordshire EN5 5SJ
Tel: 020 8441 5010
Age range: 9–16
No. of pupils: 60
Fees: Day £9,000–£12,000

The Royal Masonic School for Girls
Rickmansworth Park, Rickmansworth,
Hertfordshire WD3 4HF
Tel: 01923 773168
Headmaster: Mr Kevin Carson
M.Phil (Cambridge)
Age range: G4–18
No. of pupils: 930 VIth165
Fees: Day £11,475–£17,475 WB
£20,115–£27,495 FB £21,225–£29,835

Kent

Ashgrove School
116 Widmore Road,
Bromley, Kent BR1 3BE
Tel: 020 8460 4143
Principal: Patricia Ash CertEd,
BSc(Hons), PhD, CMath, FIMA
Age range: 4–11
No. of pupils: 106
Fees: Day £8,730

Babington House School
Grange Drive, Chislehurst, Kent BR7 5ES
Tel: 020 8467 5537
Headmaster: Mr Tim Lello
MA, FRSA, NPQH
Age range: 3–18
No. of pupils: 419

Benedict House Preparatory School
1-5 Victoria Road, Sidcup,
Kent DA15 7HD
Tel: 020 8300 7206
Headteacher: Mr Malcolm Gough
Age range: 3–11
Fees: Day £3,807–£7,929

Bickley Park School
24 Page Heath Lane, Bickley,
Bromley, Kent BR1 2DS
Tel: 020 8467 2195
Headmaster: Mr Patrick Wenham
Age range: B3–13 G3–4
No. of pupils: 370
Fees: Day £6,990–£14,940

BISHOP CHALLONER SCHOOL
For further details see p.106
228 Bromley Road, Shortlands,
Bromley, Kent BR2 0BS
Tel: 020 8460 3546
Email: admissions@
bishopchallonerschool.com
Website:
www.bishopchallonerschool.com
Headteacher: Mrs Paula Anderson
Age range: 3–18
No. of pupils: 340
Fees: Day £3,150–£4,500

Breaside Preparatory School
41-43 Orchard Road,
Bromley, Kent BR1 2PR
Tel: 020 8460 0916
Executive Principal: Mrs Karen A
Nicholson B.Ed, NPQH, Dip EYs
Age range: 2 1/2–11
No. of pupils: 376
Fees: Day £11,580–£13,494

Bromley High School GDST
Blackbrook Lane, Bickley,
Bromley, Kent BR1 2TW
Tel: 020 8781 7000/1
Head: Mrs A M Drew
BA(Hons), MBA (Dunelm)
Age range: G4–18
No. of pupils: 892
Fees: Day £14,265–£17,691

Darul Uloom London
Foxbury Avenue, Perry Street,
Chislehurst, Kent BR7 6SD
Tel: 020 8295 0637
Principal: Mufti Mustafa
Age range: B11–18
No. of pupils: 160
Fees: FB £2,400

Farringtons School
Perry Street, Chislehurst, Kent BR7 6LR
Tel: 020 8467 0256
Head: Mr David Jackson
Age range: 3–18
No. of pupils: 700 VIth100
Fees: Day £15,690 WB £30,960 FB 32,880

Merton Court Preparatory School
38 Knoll Road, Sidcup, Kent DA14 4QU
Tel: 020 8300 2112
Headmaster: Mr Dominic
Price BEd, MBA
Age range: 3–11
Fees: Day £8,670–£12,765

St Christopher's The Hall School
49 Bromley Road, Beckenham,
Kent BR3 5PA
Tel: 020 8650 2200
Headmaster: Mr A Velasco
MEd, BH(Hons), PGCE
Age range: 3–11
No. of pupils: 305
Fees: Day £3,750–£9,165

St. David's Prep
Justin Hall,, Beckenham Road,
West Wickham, Kent BR4 0QS
Tel: 020 8777 5852
Principal: Mrs J Foulger
Age range: 4–11
No. of pupils: 155
Fees: Day £5,850–£8,550

West Lodge School
36 Station Road, Sidcup, Kent DA15 7DU
Tel: 020 8300 2489
Head Teacher: Mr Robert Francis
Age range: 3–11
No. of pupils: 163
Fees: Day £5,475–£9,150

Wickham Court School
Schiller International, Layhams Road,
West Wickham, Kent BR4 9HW
Tel: 020 8777 2942
Head: Mrs Lisa Harries
Age range: 2–16
No. of pupils: 121
Fees: Day £6,983.40–£12,344.55

Middlesex

Acorn House College
39-47 High Street, Southall,
Middlesex UB1 3HF
Tel: 020 8571 9900
Principal: Dr Francis Choi
Age range: 13–19
No. of pupils: 121 VIth85
Fees: Day £4,100–£15,525
16ͦ Ⓐ

ACS Hillingdon
International School
Hillingdon Court, 108 Vine
Lane, Hillingdon, Uxbridge,
Middlesex UB10 0BE
Tel: +44 (0) 1895 259 771
Head: Martin Hall
Age range: 4–18
No. of pupils: 520
Fees: Day £10,640–£24,400
🌐 £ ⒤B ✎ 16ͦ

Alpha Preparatory School
21 Hindes Road, Harrow,
Middlesex HA1 1SH
Tel: 020 8427 1471
Head: Mr P Fahy
Age range: 3–11
No. of pupils: 154
Fees: Day £3,400–£3,750

Ashton House School
50-52 Eversley Crescent,
Isleworth, Middlesex TW7 4LW
Tel: 020 8560 3902
Headteacher: Mrs Angela Stewart
Age range: 3–11
Fees: Day £7,986–£11,586
✎

Buckingham Preparatory School
458 Rayners Lane, Pinner,
Harrow, Middlesex HA5 5DT
Tel: 020 8866 2737
Head of School: Mrs Sarah Hollis
Age range: B3–11 G3–4
Fees: Day £9,600–£12,300
⚥ £ ✎

Buxlow Preparatory School
5/6 Castleton Gardens, Wembley,
Middlesex HA9 7QJ
Tel: 020 8904 3615
Headteacher: Mr Ralf Furse
Age range: 2–11
Fees: Day £8,970–£9,330

Edgware Jewish Girls
– Beis Chinuch
296 Hale Lane, Edgware,
Middlesex HA8 8NP
Tel: 020 8905 4376
Headteacher: Mr M Cohen
Age range: G3–11
⚥

Halliford School
Russell Road, Shepperton,
Middlesex TW17 9HX
Tel: 01932 223593
Head: Mr James Davies BMus (Hons)
LGSM FASC ACertCM PGCE
Age range: B11–18 G16–18
No. of pupils: 435
Fees: Day £16,590
⚥ Ⓐ £ ✎ 16ͦ

Hampton Prep and
Pre-Prep School
Gloucester Road, Hampton,
Middlesex TW12 2UQ
Tel: 020 8979 1844
Headmaster: Mr Tim Smith
Age range: 3–11
Fees: Day £6,030–£13,935
✎

Hampton School
Hanworth Road, Hampton,
Middlesex TW12 3HD
Tel: 020 8979 9273
Headmaster: Mr Kevin
Knibbs MA (Oxon)
Age range: B11–18
No. of pupils: 1200
Fees: Day £6,390
⚥ Ⓐ £ ✎ 16ͦ

Harrow School
5 High Street, Harrow on the
Hill, Middlesex HA1 3HT
Tel: 020 8872 8000
Head Master: Mr Alastair Land
Age range: B13–18
No. of pupils: 830 VIth320
Fees: FB £40,050
⚥ Ⓐ ⌂ £ ✎ 16ͦ

Holland House School
1 Broadhurst Avenue, Edgware,
Middlesex HA8 8TP
Tel: 020 8958 6979
Headmistress: Mrs H Stanton-
Tonner BEd(Hons) PGCE
Age range: 4–11
No. of pupils: 150
Fees: Day £8,100
£

Jack and Jill School
30 Nightingale Road, Hampton,
Middlesex TW12 3HX
Tel: 020 8979 3195
Principal: Miss K Papirnik BEd(Hons)
Age range: B2–5 G2–7
No. of pupils: 155
Fees: Day £4,608–£13,143
⚥

Kew House School
Kew House, 6 Capital Interchange
Way, London, Middlesex TW8 0EX
Tel: 0208 742 2038
Headmaster: Mr Mark Hudson
Age range: 11–18
No. of pupils: 550
Fees: Day £7,129
Ⓐ ✎ 16ͦ

Lady Eleanor Holles
Hanworth Road, Hampton,
Middlesex TW12 3HF
Tel: 020 8979 1601
Head of School: Mrs Heather Hanbury
Age range: G7–18
No. of pupils: 930
Fees: Day £20,802
⚥ Ⓐ £ ✎ 16ͦ

Lady Nafisa Independent
Secondary School for Girls
83A Sunbury Road, Feltham,
Middlesex TW13 4PH
Tel: 020 8751 5610
Headteacher: Ms Fouzia Butt
Age range: G11–16
⚥

Menorah Grammar School
Abbots Road, Edgware,
Middlesex HA8 0QS
Tel: 020 8906 9756
Head of School: Mr David Vincent
Age range: B11–21

Merchant Taylors' School
Sandy Lodge, Northwood,
Middlesex HA6 2HT
Tel: 01923 820644
Head: Mr S J Everson MA (Cantab)
Age range: B11–18
No. of pupils: 865 VIth282
Fees: Day £19,998
⚥ Ⓐ £ ✎ 16ͦ

Newland House School
Waldegrave Park, Twickenham,
Middlesex TW1 4TQ
Tel: 020 8865 1234
Headmaster: Mr D A Alexander
Age range: B3–13 G3–11
No. of pupils: 425
Fees: Day £3,848–£4,306
£

North London Collegiate School
Canons, Canons Drive, Edgware,
Middlesex HA8 7RJ
Tel: +44 (0)20 8952 0912
Headmistress: Mrs Sarah Clark
Age range: G4–18
No. of pupils: 1080
Fees: Day £5,641–£6,676
⚥ 🌐 Ⓐ £ ⒤B 16ͦ

Northwood College for Girls GDST
Maxwell Road, Northwood,
Middlesex HA6 2YE
Tel: 01923 825446
Head: Ms Zara Hubble
Age range: G3–18
⚥ Ⓐ £ ✎ 16ͦ

Oak Heights
3 Red Lion Court, Alexandra Road,
Hounslow, Middlesex TW3 1JS
Tel: 020 8577 1827
Head: Mr S Dhillon
Age range: 11–16
No. of pupils: 48
Fees: Day £6,000

Orley Farm School
South Hill Avenue, Harrow,
Middlesex HA1 3NU
Tel: 020 8869 7600
Headmaster: Mr Tim Calvey
Age range: 4–13
No. of pupils: 497
Fees: Day £14,160–£16,335
£ ✎

Quainton Hall School & Nursery
91 Hindes Road, Harrow,
Middlesex HA1 1RX
Tel: 020 8861 8861
Headmaster: S Ford BEd
(Hons), UWE Bristol
Age range: B2–13 G2–11
Fees: Day £11,850–£13,050
£

Radnor House
Pope's Villa, Cross Deep,
Twickenham, Middlesex TW1 4QG
Tel: 020 8891 6264
Age range: 9–18
No. of pupils: 417
🌐 16ͦ Ⓐ

Reddiford School
36-38 Cecil Park, Pinner,
Middlesex HA5 5HH
Tel: 020 8866 0660
Headteacher: Mrs J Batt CertEd, NPQH
Age range: 3–11
No. of pupils: 320
Fees: Day £4,860–£11,565
£

Regent College
Sai House, 167 Imperial Drive,
Harrow, Middlesex HA2 7HD
Tel: 020 8966 9900
Principal: Mrs Tharshiny Pankaj
Age range: 11–19
No. of pupils: 167
Fees: Day £4,100–£15,525
16+ A 16+

Roxeth Mead School
Buckholt House, 25 Middle Road,
Harrow, Middlesex HA2 0HW
Tel: 020 8422 2092
Headmistress: Mrs A Isaacs
Age range: 3–7
No. of pupils: 54
Fees: Day £4,800–£10,665

St Catherine's Prep
Cross Deep, Twickenham,
Middlesex TW1 4QJ
Tel: 020 8891 2898
Headmistress: Mrs Johneen
McPherson MA
Age range: G3–11
No. of pupils: 101
Fees: Day £11,205–£12,954

ST CATHERINE'S SCHOOL
For further details see p.112
Cross Deep, Twickenham,
Middlesex TW1 4QJ
Tel: 020 8891 2898
Email: info@stcatherineschool.co.uk
Website:
www.stcatherineschool.co.uk
Headmistress: Mrs Johneen
McPherson MA
Age range: G3–18
No. of pupils: 449
Fees: Day £11,205–£15,585

St Christopher's School
71 Wembley Park Drive,
Wembley, Middlesex HA9 8HE
Tel: 020 8902 5069
Headteacher: Mr G. P. Musetti
Age range: 4–11
Fees: Day £9,006–£9,906

ST HELEN'S COLLEGE
For further details see p.114
Parkway, Hillingdon, Uxbridge,
Middlesex UB10 9JX
Tel: 01895 234371
Email: info@sthelenscollege.com
Website: www.sthelenscollege.com
Head: Mrs. Shirley Drummond
BA, PGCert, MLDP, FCCT
Age range: 2–11
No. of pupils: 373
Fees: Day £9,900–£12,240

St Helen's School
Eastbury Road, Northwood,
Middlesex HA6 3AS
Tel: +44 (0)1923 843210
Headmistress: Dr Mary Short BA, PhD
Age range: G3–18
No. of pupils: VIth165

St John's School
Potter Street Hill, Northwood,
Middlesex HA6 3QY
Tel: 020 8866 0067
Headmaster: Mr M S Robinson BSc
Age range: B3–13 years
No. of pupils: 350
Fees: Day £10,420–£15,110

St Martin's School
40 Moor Park Road, Northwood,
Middlesex HA6 2DJ
Tel: 01923 825740
Headmaster: Mr D T
Tidmarsh BSc(Wales)
Age range: B3–13
No. of pupils: 400
Fees: Day £5,775–£15,135

St. John's Senior School
North Lodge, The Ridgeway,
Enfield, Middlesex EN2 8BE
Tel: +44 (0)20 8366 0035
Head Teacher: Mr A Tardios
Age range: 11–18 years

Tashbar of Edgware
Mowbray Road, Edgware,
Middlesex HA8 8JL
Age range: B3–11

**The Hall Pre-Preparatory
School & Nursery**
The Grange Country House,
Rickmansworth Road, Northwood,
Middlesex HA6 2RB
Tel: 01923 822807
Headmistress: Mrs S M Goodwin
Age range: 1–7
No. of pupils: 273
Fees: Day £4,650–£9,900

THE JOHN LYON SCHOOL
For further details see p.116
Middle Road, Harrow on the
Hill, Middlesex HA2 0HN
Tel: 020 8515 9443
Email: admissions@johnlyon.org
Website: www.johnlyon.org
Head: Miss Katherine
Haynes BA, MEd, NPQH
Age range: B11–18
No. of pupils: 600

The Mall School
185 Hampton Road, Twickenham,
Middlesex TW2 5NQ
Tel: 0208 977 2523
Headmaster: Mr D C Price BSc, MA
Age range: B4–13
No. of pupils: 320
Fees: Day £12,240–£13,767

The St Michael Steiner School
Park Road, Hanworth Park,
London, Middlesex TW13 6PN
Tel: 0208 893 1299
Age range: 3–16 (17 from Jul 2014)
No. of pupils: 101
Fees: Day £3,850–£9,500

Twickenham Preparatory School
Beveree, 43 High Street, Hampton,
Middlesex TW12 2SA
Tel: 020 8979 6216
Head: Mr David Malam BA(Hons)
(Southampton), PGCE(Winchester)
Age range: B4–13 G4–11
No. of pupils: 273
Fees: Day £10,470–£11,340

Surrey

Al-Khair School
109-117 Cherry Orchard Road,
Croydon, Surrey CR0 6BE
Tel: 020 8662 8664
Headteacher: Mr Mohammad
R Chaudhry
Age range: 5–16
No. of pupils: 126

Broomfield House School
Broomfield Road, Kew Gardens,
Richmond, Surrey TW9 3HS
Tel: 020 8940 3884
Head Teacher: Mr N O York
BA(Hons), MA, MPhil, FRSA
Age range: 3–11
No. of pupils: 160
Fees: Day £4,389–£15,054

Cambridge Tutors College
Water Tower Hill, Croydon,
Surrey CR0 5SX
Tel: 020 8688 5284/7363
Principal: Dr Chris Drew
Age range: 15–19
No. of pupils: 215 VIth200
Fees: Day £10,400–£22,995
16+ A 16+

Canbury School
Kingston Hill, Kingston upon
Thames, Surrey KT2 7LN
Tel: 020 8549 8622
Headmistress: Ms Louise Clancy
Age range: 11–18
No. of pupils: 58
Fees: Day £16,401

Collingwood School
3 Springfield Road, Wallington,
Surrey SM6 0BD
Tel: 020 8647 4607
Headmaster: Mr Leigh Hardie
Age range: 3–11
No. of pupils: 120
Fees: Day £4,980–£8,925

Croydon High School GDST
Old Farleigh Road, Selsdon, South
Croydon, Surrey CR2 8YB
Tel: 020 8260 7500
Headmistress: Mrs Emma Pattison
Age range: G3–18
No. of pupils: 580 VIth75

Cumnor House Nursery
91 Pampisford Road, South
Croydon, Surrey CR2 6DH
Tel: +44 (0)20 8660 3445
Headmaster: Mr Daniel Cummings
Age range: 2–4
No. of pupils: 200
Fees: Day £4,980–£10,635

Cumnor House School for Boys
168 Pampisford Road, South
Croydon, Surrey CR2 6DA
Tel: 020 8645 2614
Headmaster: Mr Daniel Cummings
Age range: B2–13
No. of pupils: 423
Fees: Day £3,880–£4,655

Cumnor House School for Girls
1 Woodcote Lane, Purley,
Surrey CR8 3HB
Tel: 020 8645 2614
Headmistress: Mrs Amanda McShane
Age range: G2–11
No. of pupils: 138
Fees: Day £3,880–£4,655

Date Valley School Trust
Mitcham Court, Cricket Green,
Mitcham, Surrey CR4 4LB
Tel: +44 (0)20 8648 4647
Headteacher: Neena Lone
Age range: 3–11

Educare Small School
12 Cowleaze Road, Kingston
upon Thames, Surrey KT2 6DZ
Tel: 020 8547 0144
Head Teacher: Mrs E Steinthal
Age range: 3–11
No. of pupils: 46
Fees: Day £6,240

Elmhurst School
44-48 South Park Hill Rd, South
Croydon, Surrey CR2 7DW
Tel: 020 8688 0661
Headmaster: Mr Tony Padfield
Age range: B3–11
No. of pupils: 207
Fees: Day £6,129–£11,403

Holy Cross Preparatory School
George Road, Kingston upon
Thames, Surrey KT2 7NU
Tel: 020 8942 0729
Headteacher: Mrs S Hair BEd(Hons)
Age range: G4–11
No. of pupils: 285
Fees: Day £12,996

Homefield Preparatory School
Western Road, Sutton, Surrey SM1 2TE
Tel: 0208 642 0965
Headmaster: Mr John Towers
Age range: B4–13
No. of pupils: 350
Fees: Day £6,345–£13,650

KEW COLLEGE
For further details see p.108
24-26 Cumberland Road,
Kew, Surrey TW9 3HQ
Tel: 020 8940 2039
Email: enquiries@kewcollege.com
Website: www.kewcollege.com
Head: Mrs Marianne Austin
BSc(Hons), MA(Hons), ACA, PGCE
Age range: 3–11
No. of pupils: 296

Kew Green Preparatory School
Layton House, Ferry Lane, Kew
Green, Richmond, Surrey TW9 3AF
Tel: 020 8948 5999
Headmaster: Mr J Peck
Age range: 4–11
No. of pupils: 280
Fees: Day £6,120

King's House School
68 King's Road, Richmond,
Surrey TW10 6ES
Tel: 020 8940 1878
Head: Mr Mark Turner BA, PGCE, NPQH
Age range: B3–13 G3–4
No. of pupils: 460
Fees: Day £2,370–£5,560

Kingston Grammar School
70 London Rd, Kingston upon
Thames, Surrey KT2 6PY
Tel: 020 8546 5875
Head: Mr Stephen Lehec
Age range: 11–18
No. of pupils: 829
Fees: Day £6,225

LALEHAM LEA SCHOOL
For further details see p.110
29 Peaks Hill, Purley, Surrey CR8 3JJ
Tel: 020 8660 3351
Email: secretary@lalehamlea.co.uk
Website: www.lalehamlea.co.uk
Headteacher: Ms K Barry
Age range: 3–11
No. of pupils: 112
Fees: Day £8,940

Marymount London
George Road, Kingston upon
Thames, Surrey KT2 7PE
Tel: +44 (0)20 8949 0571
Headmistress: Mrs Margaret Frazier
Age range: G11–18
No. of pupils: 275
Fees: Day £25,985 WB
£42,135 FB £44,000

Oakwood Independent School
Godstone Road, Purley,
Surrey CR8 2AN
Tel: 020 8668 8080
Headmaster: Mr Ciro Candia
BA(Hons), PGCE
Age range: 3–11
No. of pupils: 176
Fees: Day £9,030–£9,840

Old Palace of John Whitgift School
Old Palace Road, Croydon,
Surrey CR0 1AX
Tel: 020 8686 7347
Head: Mrs. C Jewell
Age range: B3 months–4 years
G3 months–19 years
No. of pupils: 740 VIth120
Fees: Day £11,316–£15,366

Old Vicarage School
48 Richmond Hill, Richmond,
Surrey TW10 6QX
Tel: 020 8940 0922
Headmistress: Mrs G D Linthwaite
Age range: G4–11
No. of pupils: 200
Fees: Day £4,740

Park Hill School
8 Queens Road, Kingston upon
Thames, Surrey KT2 7SH
Tel: 020 8546 5496
Headmaster: Mr Alistair Bond
Age range: 2–11
No. of pupils: 100
Fees: Day £10,440

Rokeby School
George Road, Kingston upon
Thames, Surrey KT2 7PB
Tel: 020 8942 2247
Head: Mr J R Peck
Age range: B4–13
No. of pupils: 386
Fees: Day £14,607–£18,189

Royal Russell Junior School
Coombe Lane, Croydon,
Surrey CR9 5BX
Tel: 020 8651 5884
Junior School Headmaster: Mr
James C Thompson
Age range: 3–11
No. of pupils: 300
Fees: Day £11,160–£14,220

Royal Russell School
Coombe Lane, Croydon,
Surrey CR9 5BX
Tel: 020 8657 3669
Headmaster: Christopher Hutchinson
Age range: 11–18
No. of pupils: 590 VIth180
Fees: Day £18,480 FB £36,525

Seaton House School
67 Banstead Road South,
Sutton, Surrey SM2 5LH
Tel: 020 8642 2332
Headmistress: Mrs Debbie Morrison
Higher Diploma in Education (RSA)
Age range: B3–5 G3–11
No. of pupils: 164
Fees: Day £10,188

Shrewsbury House School
107 Ditton Road, Surbiton,
Surrey KT6 6RL
Tel: 020 8399 3066
Headmaster: Mr K Doble
BA, PDM, PGCE
Age range: B7–13
No. of pupils: 320
Fees: Day £18,060

St David's School
23/25 Woodcote Valley Road,
Purley, Surrey CR8 3AL
Tel: 020 8660 0723
Headmistress: Cressida Mardell
Age range: 3–11
No. of pupils: 167
Fees: Day £6,375–£10,650
(£)(✎)

St James Senior Boys School
Church Road, Ashford, Surrey TW15 3DZ
Tel: 01784 266930
Headmaster: Mr David Brazier
Age range: B11–18
No. of pupils: 403 VIth65
Fees: Day £18,930
(✦)(✿)(A)(£)(✎)(16·)

Staines Preparatory School
3 Gresham Road, Staines-upon-
Thames, Surrey TW18 2BT
Tel: 01784 450909
Head of School: Ms Samantha
Sawyer B.Ed (Hons), M.Ed, NPQH
Age range: 3–11
No. of pupils: 339
Fees: Day £10,080–£12,060
(£)(✎)

Surbiton High School
13-15 Surbiton Crescent, Kingston
upon Thames, Surrey KT1 2JT
Tel: 020 8546 5245
Principal: Mrs Rebecca Glover
Age range: B4–11 G4–18
No. of pupils: 1210 VIth186
Fees: Day £10,857–£17,142
(✦)(A)(£)(✎)(16·)

Sutton High School GDST
55 Cheam Road, Sutton,
Surrey SM1 2AX
Tel: 020 8642 0594
Headmistress: Mrs Katharine Crouch
Age range: G3–18
No. of pupils: 600 VIth60
Fees: Day £10,095–£17,043
(✦)(A)(£)(✎)(16·)

The Cedars School
Coombe Road, Lloyd Park,
Croydon, Surrey CR0 5RD
Tel: 020 8185 7770
Headmaster: Robert Teague Bsc (Hons)
Age range: B11–18
(✦)

**The Falcons Preparatory
School for Boys**
41 Kew Foot Road, Richmond,
Surrey TW9 2SS
Tel: 020 8948 9490
Headmistress: Miss O Buchanan
Age range: B7–13
(✦)(✎)

The Royal Ballet School
White Lodge, Richmond,
Surrey TW10 5HR
Tel: 020 7836 8899
Artistic Director: Christopher Powney
Age range: 11–19
No. of pupils: VIth80
Fees: Day £18,939–£24,885
FB £29,328–£33,567
(A)(✿)(£)(✎)(16·)

The Study School
57 Thetford Road, New
Malden, Surrey KT3 5DP
Tel: 020 8942 0754
Head of School: Mrs Donna
Brackstone-Drake
Age range: 3–11
No. of pupils: 134
Fees: Day £4,860–£11,388

Trinity School
Shirley Park, Croydon, Surrey CR9 7AT
Tel: 020 8656 9541
Head: Alasdair Kennedy MA (Cantab)
Age range: B10–18 G16–18
No. of pupils: 1007
Fees: Day £16,656
(✦)(A)(£)(✎)(16·)

Unicorn School
238 Kew Road, Richmond,
Surrey TW9 3JX
Tel: 020 8948 3926
Headmaster: Mr Kit Thompson
Age range: 3–11
Fees: Day £7,170–£13,170
(£)(✎)

Westbury House
80 Westbury Road, New
Malden, Surrey KT3 5AS
Tel: 020 8942 5885
Age range: 3–11
Fees: Day £4,860–£11,115

WHITGIFT SCHOOL
For further details see p.118
Haling Park, South Croydon,
Surrey CR2 6YT
Tel: +44 20 8633 9935
Email: admissions@whitgift.co.uk
Website: www.whitgift.co.uk
Headmaster: Mr Christopher Ramsey
Age range: B10–18
No. of pupils: 1560
Fees: Day £20,640 WB
£33,081 FB £40,140
(✦)(✿)(A)(✿)(£)(IB)(✎)(16·)

London

KEY TO SYMBOLS

- ⚥ *Boys' school*
- ⚥ *Girls' school*
- 🌐 *International school*
- 16⁺ *Tutorial or sixth form college*
- Ⓐ *A levels*
- 🏛 *Boarding accommodation*
- £ *Bursaries*
- Ⓘ *International Baccalaureate*
- ✎ *Learning support*
- 16⁺ *Entrance at 16+*
- ✦ *Vocational qualifications*
- (IAPS) *Independent Association of Preparatory Schools*
- (HMC) *The Headmasters' & Headmistresses' Conference*
- (ISA) *Independent Schools Association*
- (GSA) *Girls' School Association*
- (BSA) *Boarding Schools' Association*
- Ⓢ *Society of Heads*

Unless otherwise indicated, all schools are coeducational day schools.
Single-sex and boarding schools will be indicated by the relevant icon.

Central London

CATS London
43-45 Bloomsbury Square,
London WC1A 2RA
Tel: 02078 411580
Principal: Mario Di Clemente
Age range: 15–24

Charterhouse Square School
40 Charterhouse Square,
London EC1M 6EA
Tel: 020 7600 3805
Age range: 3–11
No. of pupils: 196
Fees: Day £5,680

CITY OF LONDON SCHOOL
For further details see p.124
Queen Victoria Street,
London EC4V 3AL
Tel: 020 3680 6300
Email:
admissions@cityoflondonschool.org.uk
Website:
www.cityoflondonschool.org.uk
Head: Mr A R Bird MSc
Age range: B10–18
No. of pupils: 950 VIth250
Fees: Day £18,939

City of London School for Girls
St Giles' Terrace, Barbican,
London EC2Y 8BB
Tel: 020 7847 5500
Headmistress: Mrs E Harrop
Age range: G7–18
No. of pupils: 725

Dallington School
8 Dallington Street, Islington,
London EC1V 0BW
Tel: 020 7251 2284
Headteacher: Maria Blake
Age range: 3–11
No. of pupils: 131
Fees: Day £10,950–£13,800

École Jeannine Manuel – London
43-45 Bedford Square,
London WC1B 3DN
Tel: 020 3829 5970
Head of School: Pauline Prévot
Age range: 3–18 years
No. of pupils: 496
Fees: Day £18,948–£21,558

Italia Conti Academy of Theatre Arts
Italia Conti House, 23 Goswell
Road, London EC1M 7AJ
Tel: 020 7608 0047
Director: Chris White
Age range: 10–21

ST PAUL'S CATHEDRAL SCHOOL
For further details see p.150
2 New Change, London EC4M 9AD
Tel: 020 7248 5156
Email:
admissions@spcs.london.sch.uk
Website: www.spcslondon.com
Headmaster: Simon Larter-
Evans BA (Hons), PGCE, FRSA
Age range: 4–13
No. of pupils: 260
Fees: Day £4,911–£5,287 FB £2,970

The College of Central London
Tower Bridge Business Centre, 46-48
East Smithfield, London E1W 1AW
Tel: +44 (0) 20 3667 7607
Principal: Nicolas Kailides
Fees: Day £3,850

The Lyceum School
65 Worship Street, London EC2A 2DU
Tel: +44 (0)20 7247 1588
Head of School: Ms Hilary
Wyatt NPQH, MA, PGCE
Age range: 3–11
Fees: Day £16,185

Urdang Academy
The Old Finsbury Town Hall, Rosebery
Avenue, London EC1R 4RP
Tel: +44 (0)20 7713 7710
Age range: 16+

East London

Al-Falah Primary School
48 Kenninghall Road,
Hackney, London E5 8BY
Tel: 020 8985 1059
Headteacher: Mr M A Hussain
Age range: 5–11

Al-Mizan School
46 Whitechapel Road, London E1 1JX
Tel: 020 7650 3070
Head: Mr Askor Ali
Age range: B7–11

Azhar Academy
235A Romford Road, Forest
Gate, London E7 9HL
Tel: 020 8534 5959
Headteacher: Mrs R Rehman
Age range: G11–16
No. of pupils: 189

Beis Trana Girls' School
186 Upper Clapton Road,
London E5 9DH
Tel: 020 8815 8000
Head of School: Mrs M Shmaya
Age range: G3–16

Chingford House School
22 Marlborough Road, Waltham
Forest, London E4 9AL
Tel: 020 8527 2902; 07749 899 498
Head teacher: Helen McNulty
Age range: 0–5

Faraday School
Old Gate House, 7 Trinity Buoy
Wharf, London E14 0JW
Tel: 020 8965 7374
Head Teacher: Claire Murdoch
Age range: 4–11
No. of pupils: 95
Fees: Day £3,686

Forest School
College Place, Snaresbrook,
London E17 3PY
Tel: 020 8520 1744
Warden: Mr Cliff Hodges
Age range: 4–18
No. of pupils: 1355 VIth260
Fees: Day £13,095–£18,681

Gatehouse School
Sewardstone Road, Victoria
Park, London E2 9JG
Tel: 020 8980 2978
Acting Headmistress: Sevda Corby
Age range: 3–11
No. of pupils: 320
Fees: Day £11,610–£12,225

Grangewood Independent School
Chester Road, Forest
Gate, London E7 8QT
Tel: 020 8472 3552
Headteacher: Mrs B A Roberts
B.Ed (Hons); PG Cert (SEN)
Age range: 2–11
No. of pupils: 71
Fees: Day £5,157–£6,751

Hyland House School
Holcombe Road, Tottenham,
, London N17 9AD
Tel: 0208 520 4186
Head Teacher: Mrs Gina Abbequaye
Age range: 3–11
Fees: Day £2,520

London East Academy
46 Whitechapel Road, London E1 1JX
Tel: 020 7650 3070
Headteacher: Askor Ali
Age range: B11–18

Lubavitch House School (Junior Boys)
135 Clapton Common, London E5 9AE
Tel: 020 8800 1044
Head: Mr R Leach
Age range: B5–11
No. of pupils: 101

Madani Girls School
Myrdle Street, London E1 1HL
Tel: 020 7377 1992
Headteacher: Muhammad S. Rahman
Age range: G11–18
No. of pupils: 248 VIth11
Fees: Day £2,400

Normanhurst School
68-74 Station Road, Chingford,
London E4 7BA
Tel: 020 8529 4307
Headmistress: Mrs Claire Osborn
Age range: 2–16
No. of pupils: 250
Fees: Day £10,350–£13,050

Pillar Box Montessori Nursery & Pre-Prep School
107 Bow Road, London E3 2AN
Tel: 020 8980 0700
Director: Lorraine Redknapp
Age range: 0–5
Fees: Day £12,000

PromisedLand Academy
St Cedds Hall, Webb Gardens,
Plaistow, London E13 8SR
Tel: 07572 614 770
Head: Mrs M S Coote
Age range: 4–16

Quwwat-ul Islam Girls School
16 Chaucer Road, Forest
Gate, London E7 9NB
Tel: 020 8548 4736
Head of School: Shazia Member
Age range: G4–11
No. of pupils: 150

River House Montessori School
3-4 Shadwell Pierhead, Glamis
Road, London E1W 3TD
Tel: 020 7538 9886
Headmistress: Miss S Greenwood
Age range: 3–16
Fees: Day £3,410–£3,625

Snaresbrook Preparatory School
75 Woodford Road, South
Woodford, London E18 2EA
Tel: 020 8989 2394
Head of School: Mr Ralph Dalton
Age range: 3–11
Fees: Day £8,922–£11,934

**Talmud Torah Machzikei
Hadass School**
1 Belz Terrace, Clapton, London E5 9SN
Tel: 020 8800 6599
Headteacher: Rabbi C Silbiger
Age range: B3–16

Winston House Preparatory School
140 High Road, London E18 2QS
Tel: 020 8505 6565
Head Teacher: Mrs Marian Kemp
Age range: 3–11

North London

Annemount School
18 Holne Chase, Hampstead
Garden Suburb, London N2 0QN
Tel: 020 8455 2132
Principal: Mrs G Maidment
BA(Hons), MontDip
Age range: 2–7
No. of pupils: 100
Fees: Day £3,275–£6,000

Avenue Pre-Prep & Nursery School
2 Highgate Avenue, Highgate,
London N6 5RX
Tel: 020 8348 6815
Principal: Mrs. Mary Fysh
Age range: 2–8

Beis Chinuch Lebonos Girls School
Woodberry Down Centre,
Woodberry Down, London N4 2SH
Tel: 020 88097 737
Head of School: Mrs Leah Klein
Age range: G2–16

Beis Malka Girls School
93 Alkham Road, London N16 6XD
Tel: 020 8806 2070
Head of School: Mrs G Wind
Age range: G2–16

Beis Rochel D'Satmar Girls School
51-57 Amhurst Park, London N16 5DL
Tel: 020 8800 9060
Headmistress: Mrs E Katz
Age range: G2–18

Bnois Jerusalem School
79-81 Amhurst Park, London N16 5DL
Tel: 020 8211 7136
Age range: G3–16

Bobov Primary School
87 Egerton Road, London N16 6UE
Tel: 020 8809 1025
Headmaster: Mr Chaim Weissman
Age range: B3–13

Channing School
The Bank, Highgate, London N6 5HF
Tel: 020 8340 2328
Head: Mrs B M Elliott
Age range: G4–18
No. of pupils: 746 VIth108
Fees: Day £17,610–£19,410

Dwight School London
6 Friern Barnet Lane, London N11 3LX
Tel: +44 (0)20 8920 0637
Head: Mrs Alison Cobbin
BA, Dip Ed, MBA
Age range: 3–18

Finchley & Acton Yochien School
6 Hendon Avenue, Finchley,
London N3 1UE
Tel: 020 8343 2191
Headteacher: J Tanabe
Age range: 2–6
No. of pupils: 145

Grange Park Preparatory School
13 The Chine, Grange Park,
Winchmore Hill, London N21 2EA
Tel: 020 8360 1469
Headteacher: Miss F Rizzo
Age range: G4–11
No. of pupils: 90
Fees: Day £10,300–£10,378

**Greek Secondary
School of London**
22 Trinity Road, London N22 8LB
Tel: +44 (0)20 8881 9320
Headteacher: Nikos Kazantzakis
Age range: 13–18

Highgate
North Road, Highgate, London N6 4AY
Tel: 020 8340 1524
Head Master: Mr A S Pettitt MA
Age range: 3–18
No. of pupils: 1541 VIth312
Fees: Day £18,165–£20,970

Highgate Junior School
Cholmeley House, 3 Bishopswood
Road, London N6 4PL
Tel: 020 8340 9193
Principal: Mr S M James BA
Age range: 7–11
Fees: Day £19,230

Highgate Pre-Preparatory School
7 Bishopswood Road, London N6 4PH
Tel: 020 8340 9196
Principal: Mrs Diane Hecht
Age range: 3–7
No. of pupils: 150
Fees: Day £18,165

Keble Prep
Wades Hill, Winchmore
Hill, London N21 1BG
Tel: 020 8360 3359
Headmaster: Mr M J Mitchell
Age range: B4–13
No. of pupils: 228
Fees: Day £3,850–£4,930

Kerem School
Norrice Lea, London N2 0RE
Tel: 020 8455 0909
Head Teacher: Miss Alyson Burns
Age range: 3–11
Fees: Day £9,435

**Lubavitch House School
(Senior Girls)**
107-115 Stamford Hill, Hackney,
London N16 5RP
Tel: 020 8800 0022
Headmaster: Rabbi Shmuel Lew FRSA
Age range: G11–18
No. of pupils: 102
Fees: Day £3,900

Norfolk House School
10 Muswell Avenue, Muswell
Hill, London N10 2EG
Tel: 020 8883 4584
Head Teacher: Mr Paul Jowett
Age range: 4–11
No. of pupils: 130
Fees: Day £12,066

North London Grammar School
110 Colindeep Lane, Hendon,
London NW9 6HB
Tel: 0208 205 0052
Head Teacher: Mr Fatih Adak
Age range: 6–18
No. of pupils: 150
Fees: Day £10,800–£13,500
FB £18,900–£21,600

**North London Rudolf
Steiner School**
1-3 The Campsbourne, London N8 7PN
Tel: 020 8341 3770
Age range: 0–7
No. of pupils: 40

Palmers Green High School
Hoppers Road, Winchmore
Hill, London N21 3LJ
Tel: 020 8886 1135
Headmistress: Mrs Wendy Kempster
Age range: G3–16
No. of pupils: 300
Fees: Day £5,880–£15,930

Pardes House Grammar School
Hendon Lane, Finchley, London N3 1SA
Tel: 020 8349 4222
Headteacher: Rabbi Yitzchok Lev
Age range: B10–16
No. of pupils: 222

Phoenix Academy
85 Bounces Road, Edmonton,
London N9 8LD
Tel: 020 8887 6888
Headteacher: Mr Paul Kelly
Age range: 5–18
No. of pupils: 19

**Rosemary Works
Independent School**
1 Branch Place, London N1 5PH
Tel: 020 7739 3950
Head: Rob Dell
Age range: 3–11
No. of pupils: 104
Fees: Day £14,097

Salcombe Preparatory School
224-226 Chase Side, Southgate,
London N14 4PL
Tel: 020 8441 5356
Headmistress: Mrs Sarah-Jane
Davies BA(Hons) QTS MEd
Age range: 3–11
No. of pupils: 250
Fees: Day £11,673

St Paul's Steiner School
1 St Paul's Road, Islington,
London N1 2QH
Tel: 020 7226 4454
College of Teachers: College
of Teachers
Age range: 2–14
No. of pupils: 136

Sunrise Nursery, Stoke Newington
1 Cazenove Road, Stoke Newington,
Hackney, London N16 6PA
Tel: 020 8806 6279
Principal: Didi Ananda Manika

Sunrise Primary School
55 Coniston Road, Tottenham,
London N17 0EX
Tel: 020 8806 6279 (Office);
020 8885 3354 (School)
Head: Mrs Mary-Anne
Lovage MontDipEd, BA
Age range: 2–11
No. of pupils: 30
Fees: Day £5,550

**Talmud Torah Chaim
Meirim School**
26 Lampard Grove, London N16 6XB
Tel: 020 8806 0898
Principal: Rabbi S Hoffman
Age range: B4–13

Talmud Torah Yetev Lev School
111-115 Cazenove Road,
London N16 6AX
Tel: 020 8806 3834
Age range: B2–11

Tawhid Boys School
21 Cazenove Road, London N16 6PA
Tel: 020 8806 2999
Headteacher: Mr Usman Mapara
Age range: B10–15
No. of pupils: 115

Tayyibah Girls School
88 Filey Avenue, Stamford
Hill, London N16 6JJ
Tel: 020 8880 0085
Headmistress: Mrs N B Qureishi MSc
Age range: G5–18
No. of pupils: 270

The Children's House Upper School
King Henry's Walk, London N1 4PB
Tel: 020 7249 6273
Headteacher: Kate Orange
Age range: 4–7
No. of pupils: 60
Fees: Day £14,730

**The Gower School
Montessori Nursery**
18 North Road, Islington, London N7 9EY
Tel: 020 7700 2445
Principal: Miss Emma Gowers
Age range: 3 months–5 years
No. of pupils: 237

**The Gower School
Montessori Primary**
10 Cynthia Street, Barnsbury,
London N1 9JF
Tel: 020 7278 2020
Principal: Miss Emma Gowers
Age range: 4–11
No. of pupils: 237
Fees: Day £15,576

TTTYY School
14 Heathland Road, London N16 5NH
Tel: 020 8802 1348
Head of School: Rabbi A Friesel
Age range: B2–13

Vita et Pax School
Priory Close, Southgate,
London N14 4AT
Tel: 020 8449 8336
Headteacher: Miss Gillian Chumbley
Age range: 3–11
Fees: Day £9,360

Yesodey Hatorah School
Egerton Road, London N16 6UB
Tel: 020 8826 5500
Headteacher: Rabbi Pinter
Age range: 3–16
No. of pupils: 920

North-West London

Abercorn School
38 Portland Place, London NW8 9XP
Tel: 020 7286 4785
High Mistress: Mrs Andrea
Greystoke BA(Hons)
Age range: 2–13
No. of pupils: 360
Fees: Day £10,020–£20,055

Al-Sadiq & Al-Zahra Schools
134 Salusbury Road, London NW6 6PF
Tel: 020 7372 7706
Headteacher: Dr M Movahedi
Age range: 4–16

Arnold House School
1 Loudoun Road, St John's
Wood, London NW8 0LH
Tel: 020 7266 4840
Headmaster: Mr Vivian Thomas
Age range: B5–13
No. of pupils: 270
Fees: Day £6,100

Barnet Hill Academy
10A Montagu Road, Hendon,
London NW4 3ES
Tel: 02034112660
Headteacher: Mr Shakil Ahmed
Age range: 3–11 G11–16
Fees: Day £3,000

Beis Soroh Schneirer
Arbiter House, Wilberforce
Road, London NW9 6AX
Tel: 020 8201 7771
Head of School: Mrs Sonia Mossberg
Age range: G2–11

**Belmont, Mill Hill
Preparatory School**
The Ridgeway, London NW7 4ED
Tel: 020 8906 7270
Headmaster: Mr Leon Roberts MA
Age range: 7–13
No. of pupils: 540
Fees: Day £18,099

**Beth Jacob Grammar
School for Girls**
Stratford Road, Hendon,
London NW4 2AT
Tel: 020 8203 4322
Headteacher: Mrs M Gluck
Age range: G11–17

Brampton College
Lodge House, Lodge Road,
Hendon, London NW4 4DQ
Tel: 020 8203 5025
Principal: B Canetti BA(Hons), MSc
Age range: 15–20
Fees: Day £19,935

Brondesbury College for Boys
8 Brondesbury Park, London NW6 7BT
Tel: 020 8830 4522
Headteacher: Mr Amzad Ali
Age range: B11–16
No. of pupils: 93

**Collège Français
Bilingue de Londres**
87 Holmes Road, Kentish
Town, , London NW5 3AX
Tel: 020 7993 7400
Head of School: Mr Denis Bittmann
Age range: 3–15
No. of pupils: 700
Fees: Day £11,115–£11,980

Fine Arts College
Centre Studios, 41-43 England's
Lane, London NW3 4YD
Tel: +44 (0)207 586 0312
Principal: Ms Candida Cave
Age range: 13–18
Fees: Day £22,560

**Francis Holland School,
Regent's Park, NW1**
Clarence Gate, Ivor Place,
Regent's Park, London NW1 6XR
Tel: 020 7723 0176
Head: Mr C B Fillingham MA
(King's College London)
Age range: G11–18
No. of pupils: 495 VIth120
Fees: Day £19,260

Golders Hill School
666 Finchley Road, London NW11 7NT
Tel: 020 8455 2589
Headmistress: Mrs A T Eglash BA(Hons)
Age range: 2–7
No. of pupils: 180
Fees: Day £1,575–£13,827

Goodwyn School
Hammers Lane, Mill Hill,
London NW7 4DB
Tel: 020 8959 3756
Principal: Struan Robertson
Age range: 3–11
No. of pupils: 193
Fees: Day £5,436–£11,943

**Grimsdell, Mill Hill Pre-
Preparatory School**
Winterstoke House, Wills Grove,
Mill Hill, London NW7 1QR
Tel: 020 8959 6884
Head: Mrs Kate Simon BA, PGCE
Age range: 3–7
No. of pupils: 191
Fees: Day £14,895

**Hampstead Hill Pre-Prep
& Nursery School**
St Stephen's Hall, Pond Street,
Hampstead, London NW3 2PP
Tel: 020 7435 6262
Principal: Mrs Andrea Taylor
Age range: B2–7+ G2–7+
Fees: Day £10,175–£16,830

HEATHSIDE SCHOOL
For further details see p.132
84a Heath Street, Hampstead,
London NW3 1DN
Tel: +44 (0)20 3058 4011
Email: info@heathsideprep.co.uk
Website: www.heathsideprep.co.uk
Headteacher: Katherine Vintiner
Age range: 2–14
No. of pupils: 230
Fees: Day £16,000–£19,200

Hendon Prep School
20 Tenterden Grove, Hendon,
London NW4 1TD
Tel: 020 8203 7727
Age range: 2–13 years
No. of pupils: 165
Fees: Day £6,345–£14,175

Hereward House School
14 Strathray Gardens, London NW3 4NY
Tel: 020 7794 4820
Headmaster: Mr P Evans
Age range: B4–13
No. of pupils: 170
Fees: Day £15,615–£16,065

ICS London
7B Wyndham Place, London W1H 1PN
Tel: +44 (0) 20 7298 8817
Head of School: Mr. Rod Jackson
Age range: 3–18 years
No. of pupils: 205

Islamia Girls' High School
129 Salusbury Road, London NW6 6PE
Tel: 020 7372 3472
Headteacher: Mrs Fawziah Islam
Age range: G11–16 years
Fees: Day £6,900

LYNDHURST HOUSE PREP SCHOOL
For further details see p.138
24 Lyndhurst Gardens,
Hampstead, London NW3 5NW
Tel: 020 7435 4936
Email: office@lyndhursthouse.co.uk
Website: www.lyndhursthouse.co.uk
Head of School: Mr Andrew
Reid MA (Oxon)
Age range: B4–13
No. of pupils: 138
Fees: Day £6,470–£7,245

Maple Walk School
62A Crownhill Road, London NW10 4EB
Tel: 020 8963 3890
Head Teacher: Mrs S Gillam
Age range: 4–11
No. of pupils: 200
Fees: Day £3,580

Maria Montessori Institute
26 Lyndhurst Gardens, Hampstead,
London NW3 5NW
Tel: 020 7435 3646
Director of Training & School: Mrs Lynne
Lawrence BA, Mont Int Dip(AMI)
Age range: 2–12
No. of pupils: 50
Fees: Day £5,580–£13,560

**Maria Montessori School
– Hampstead**
26 Lyndhurst Gardens, Hampstead,
London NW3 5NW
Tel: +44 (0)20 7435 3646
Director of School: Miss L Kingston
Age range: 2–12
No. of pupils: 100
Fees: Day £6,270–£13,560

Mill Hill School
The Ridgeway, Mill Hill Village,
London NW7 1QS
Tel: 020 8959 1176
Head: Mrs Jane Sanchez
BSc (Hons) PGCE
Age range: 13–18
No. of pupils: 689 VIth259
Fees: Day £21,141 WB £28,524 FB £33,717

Naima Jewish Preparatory School
21 Andover Place, London NW6 5ED
Tel: 020 7328 2802
Headteacher: Mr Bill Pratt
Age range: 3–11
Fees: Day £7,605–£12,705

Nancy Reuben Primary School
Finchley Lane, Hendon,
London NW4 1DJ
Tel: 020 82025646
Head: Anthony Wolfson
Age range: 3–11
No. of pupils: 207

**NORTH BRIDGE HOUSE NURSERY
AND PRE-PREP HAMPSTEAD**
For further details see p.142
8 Netherhall Gardens,
London NW3 5RR
Tel: 020 7428 1520
Head of School: Mrs
Christine McLelland
Age range: 2–7 years
No. of pupils: 190

**NORTH BRIDGE HOUSE NURSERY
AND PRE-PREP WEST HAMPSTEAD**
For further details see p.142
85-87 Fordwych Rd, London NW2 3TL
Tel: 020 7428 1520
Head of School: Mrs
Christine McLelland
Age range: 2–7 years

**NORTH BRIDGE HOUSE PREP
SCHOOL REGENT'S PARK**
For further details see p.142
1 Gloucester Avenue,
London NW1 7AB
Tel: 020 7428 1520
Head of School: Mr James Stenning
Age range: 7–13 years
No. of pupils: 460
Fees: Day £19,275

**NORTH BRIDGE HOUSE
SENIOR CANONBURY**
For further details see p.142
6-9 Canonbury Place,
Islington, London N1 2NQ
Tel: 020 7428 1520
Head of School: Mr Brendan Pavey
Age range: 11–18 years
No. of pupils: 220
Fees: Day £19,230–£20,400

**NORTH BRIDGE HOUSE
SENIOR HAMPSTEAD**
For further details see p.142
65 Rosslyn Hill, London NW3 5UD
Tel: 020 7428 1520
Email: admissionsenquiries@
northbridgehouse.com
Website:
www.northbridgehouse.com
Head of School: Mr Brendan Pavey
Age range: 11–16 years
No. of pupils: 430
Fees: Day £19,230

Rainbow Montessori School
13 Woodchurch Road,
Hampstead, London NW6 3PL
Tel: 020 7328 8986
Head Mistress: Maggy Miller MontDip
Age range: 2–5
Fees: Day £12,240–£12,417

Saint Christina's School
25 St Edmunds Terrace, Regent's
Park, London NW8 7PY
Tel: 020 7722 8784
Headteacher: Miss J Finlayson
Age range: 3–11
No. of pupils: 224
Fees: Day £13,500

Sarum Hall
15 Eton Avenue, London NW3 3EL
Tel: 020 7794 2261
Headmistress: Mrs Christine Smith
Age range: G3–11
No. of pupils: 170
Fees: Day £14,025–£15,180

**South Hampstead
High School GDST**
3 Maresfield Gardens, London NW3 5SS
Tel: 020 7435 2899
Head of School: Mrs V Bingham
Age range: G4–18
No. of pupils: 900
Fees: Day £15,327–£18,654

**Southbank International
School – Hampstead**
16 Netherhall Gardens,
London NW3 5TH
Tel: 020 7243 3803
Principal: Shirley Harwood
Age range: 3–11
No. of pupils: 210

St Anthony's School for Boys
90 Fitzjohn's Avenue, Hampstead,
London NW3 6NP
Tel: 020 7431 1066
Headmaster: Mr Paul Keyte
Age range: B4–13
No. of pupils: 310

St Christopher's School
32 Belsize Lane, Hampstead,
London NW3 5AE
Tel: 020 7435 1521
Head: Emma Crawford-Nash
Age range: G4–11
No. of pupils: 235
Fees: Day £14,700

**St John's Wood Pre-
Preparatory School**
St Johns Hall, Lords Roundabout,
London NW8 7NE
Tel: 020 7722 7149
Principal: Adrian Ellis
Age range: 3–7

St Margaret's School
18 Kidderpore Gardens,
Hampstead, London NW3 7SR
Tel: 020 7435 2439
Principal: Mr M Webster BSc, PGCE
Age range: G4–16
No. of pupils: 156
Fees: Day £12,591–£14,589

St Martin's School
22 Goodwyn Avenue, Mill
Hill, London NW7 3RG
Tel: 020 8959 1965
Head Teacher: Mrs Samantha Mbah
Age range: 3–11
No. of pupils: 90
Fees: Day £7,800

St Mary's School Hampstead
47 Fitzjohn's Avenue, Hampstead,
London NW3 6PG
Tel: 020 7435 1868
Head Teacher: Mrs Harriet Connor-Earl
Age range: G2 years 9 months–11 years
No. of pupils: 300
Fees: Day £8,370–£15,480

St Nicholas School
22 Salmon Street, London NW9 8PN
Tel: 020 8205 7153
Headmaster: Mr Matt Donaldson
BA (Hons), PGCE, PGDip (Surv)
Age range: 3 months–11
No. of pupils: 80
Fees: Day £8,550–£8,850

The Academy School
3 Pilgrims Place, Rosslyn Hill,
Hampstead, London NW3 1NG
Tel: 020 7435 6621
Headteacher: Mr Garth Evans
Age range: 6–14

The American School in London
One Waverley Place, London NW8 0NP
Tel: 020 7449 1221
Head: Robin Appleby
Age range: 4–18
No. of pupils: 1350
Fees: Day £27,050–£31,200

The Cavendish School
31 Inverness Street, Camden
Town, London NW1 7HB
Tel: 020 7485 1958
Headmistress: Miss Jane Rogers
Age range: G3–11
No. of pupils: 260
Fees: Day £15,300

The Hall School
23 Crossfield Road, Hampstead,
London NW3 4NU
Tel: 020 7722 1700
Headmaster: Mr Chris Godwin
Age range: B4–13
No. of pupils: 440
Fees: Day £17,940–£18,486

The King Alfred School
Manor Wood, North End
Road, London NW11 7HY
Tel: 020 8457 5200
Head: Robert Lobatto MA (Oxon)
Age range: 4–18
No. of pupils: 650 VIth100
Fees: Day £15,531–£18,723

The Mount, Mill Hill International
Milespit Hill, London NW7 2RX
Tel: +44 (0)20 3826 33
Head of School: Ms Sarah Bellotti
Age range: 13–17
No. of pupils: 68
Fees: Day £24,990 WB
£34,461 FB £40,539

The Mulberry House School
7 Minster Road, West Hampstead,
London NW2 3SD
Tel: 020 8452 7340
Headteacher: Ms Victoria
Playford BA Hons, QTS
Age range: 2–7 years
No. of pupils: 190

**The School of the Islamic
Republic of Iran**
100 Carlton Vale, London NW6 5HE
Tel: 020 7372 8051
Headteacher: Mr Seyed Abbas Hosseini
Age range: 6–16

The Village School
2 Parkhill Road, Belsize Park,
London NW3 2YN
Tel: 020 7485 4673
Headmistress: Miss C E F
Gay BSc(Hons), PGCE
Age range: G3–11
No. of pupils: 106
Fees: Day £15,525

Torah Vodaas
Brent Park Road, West Hendon
Broadway, London NW9 7AJ
Tel: 020 3670 4670
Head of School: Rabbi Y Feldman
Age range: B2–11

Trevor-Roberts School
55-57 Eton Avenue, London NW3 3ET
Tel: 020 7586 1444
Headmaster: Simon Trevor-Roberts BA
Age range: 5–13
Fees: Day £14,700–£16,200

**University College School
Hampstead (UCS)**
Frognal, Hampstead, London NW3 6XH
Tel: 020 7435 2215
Headteacher: Mr Mark J Beard
Age range: B11–18 G16–18

**University College School
Hampstead (UCS) Junior**
11 Holly Hill, London NW3 6QN
Tel: 020 7435 3068
Headmaster: Mr Lewis Hayward
MA (Oxon Lit. Hum), MA (OU,
ED. Management), PGCE
Age range: B7–11

University College School Hampstead (UCS) Pre-Prep
36 College Crescent, Hampstead,
London NW3 5LF
Tel: 020 7722 4433
Headmistress: Dr Zoe Dunn
Age range: B4–7
⊕

Wentworth College
6-10 Brentmead Place,
London NW11 9LH
Tel: 020 8458 8524/5
Principal: Manuel Guimaraes
Age range: 14–19
No. of pupils: 115
16+ Ⓐ 16+

South-East London

Alleyn's School
Townley Road, Dulwich,
London SE22 8SU
Tel: 020 8557 1500
Headmaster: Dr G Savage
MA, PhD, FRSA
Age range: 4–18
No. of pupils: 1200
Fees: Day £18,363–£20,850
Ⓐ £ ✐ 16+

Bellerbys College London
Bounty House, Greenwich,
London SE8 3DE
Tel: +44 (0)208 694 7000
Principal: Ms Alison Baines
Age range: 15–19
⊕ 16+ Ⓐ ⊞

Blackheath High School GDST
Vanbrugh Park, Blackheath,
London SE3 7AG
Tel: 020 8853 2929
Head: Mrs Carol Chandler-Thompson
BA (Hons) Exeter, PGCE Exeter
Age range: G3–18
No. of pupils: 780
⚥ Ⓐ £ ✐ 16+

Blackheath Preparatory School
4 St Germans Place, Blackheath,
London SE3 0NJ
Tel: 020 8858 0692
Acting Head: Mrs C Dawe
Age range: 3–11
No. of pupils: 377
Fees: Day £8,190–£13,680
£ ✐

Colfe's Junior School
Horn Park Lane, Lee, London SE12 8AW
Tel: 020 8463 8240
Head: Ms C Macleod
Age range: 3–11
No. of pupils: 355
Fees: Day £13,230–£13,995
✐

Colfe's School
Horn Park Lane, Lee, London SE12 8AW
Tel: 020 8852 2283
Head: Mr R F Russell MA(Cantab)
Age range: 3–18
No. of pupils: 1120
Ⓐ £ ✐ 16+

DLD College London
199 Westminster Bridge
Road, London SE1 7FX
Tel: +44 (0)20 7935 8411
Principal: Irfan H Latif BSc
(Hons) PGCE FRSA FRSC
No. of pupils: 426
Fees: Day £23,500–£29,950
FB £18,000–£28,000
⊕ 16+ Ⓐ ⊞ £ ✐

Dulwich College
Dulwich Common, , London SE21 7LD
Tel: 020 8693 3601
Master: Dr J A F Spence
Age range: B0–18
No. of pupils: 1589 VIth470
Fees: Day £20,448 WB
£40,017 FB £42,681
⚥ ⊕ Ⓐ ⊞ £ ✐ 16+

Dulwich College Kindergarten & Infants School
Eller Bank, 87 College Road,
London SE21 7HH
Tel: 020 8693 1538
Head: Mrs Nicky Black
Age range: 3 months–7 years
No. of pupils: 251

Dulwich Prep London
42 Alleyn Park, Dulwich,
London SE21 7AA
Tel: 020 8766 5500
Headmaster: Mr M W
Roulston MBE, MEd
Age range: B3–13 G3–5
No. of pupils: 817
Fees: Day £13,074–£19,314
⊕ ⊞ ✐ 16+

Eltham College
Grove Park Road, Mottingham,
London SE9 4QF
Tel: 0208 857 1455
Headmaster: Guy Sanderson
Age range: 7–18
No. of pupils: 911 VIth199
Ⓐ £ ✐ 16+

Greenwich Steiner School
Woodlands, 90 Mycenae Road,
Blackheath, London SE3 7SE
Tel: 020 8858 4404
Age range: 3–14
No. of pupils: 180
Fees: Day £7,310–£8,100
£

Heath House Preparatory School
37 Wemyss Road, Blackheath,
London SE3 0TG
Tel: 020 8297 1900
Head Teacher: Mrs Sophia
Laslett CertEd PGDE
Age range: 3–11
No. of pupils: 125
Fees: Day £13,485–£14,985
£ ✐

Herne Hill School
The Old Vicarage, 127 Herne
Hill, London SE24 9LY
Tel: 020 7274 6336
Headteacher: Mrs Ngaire Telford
Age range: 2–7
No. of pupils: 296
Fees: Day £6,225–£14,955

James Allen's Girls' School
144 East Dulwich Grove,
Dulwich, London SE22 8TE
Tel: 020 8693 1181
Head of School: Mrs Sally-
Anne Huang MA, MSc
Age range: G4–18
No. of pupils: 1075
⚥ Ⓐ £ ✐ 16+

Kings Kids Christian School
100 Woodpecker Road,
Newcross, London SE14 6EU
Tel: 020 8691 5813
Headteacher: Mrs M Okenwa
Age range: 5–11

London Christian School
40 Tabard Street, London SE1 4JU
Tel: 020 3130 6430
Headmistress: Miss N Collett-White
Age range: 3–11
No. of pupils: 105
Fees: Day £9,390
£

Marathon Science School
1-9 Evelyn Street, Surrey
Quays, London SE8 5RQ
Tel: +44 (0)20 7231 3232
Headteacher: Mr Uzeyir Onur
Age range: B11–16
No. of pupils: 67
⊕ ⊞

Oakfield Preparatory School
125-128 Thurlow Park Road, West
Dulwich, London SE21 8HP
Tel: 020 8670 4206
Age range: 2–11 years
No. of pupils: 420
Fees: Day £10,785

Octavia House School, Kennington
214b Kennington Road,
London SE11 6AU
Tel: 020 3651 4396 (option 3)
Executive Headteacher: Mr P Foster

Octavia House School, Vauxhall
Vauxhall Primary School, Vauxhall
Street, London SE11 5LG
Tel: 020 3651 4396 (option 1)
Executive Headteacher: Mr P Foster
Age range: 5–14

Octavia House School, Walworth
Larcom House, Larcom
Street, , London SE17 1RT
Tel: 020 3651 4396 (option 2)
Executive Headteacher: Mr P Foster

Riverston School
63-69 Eltham Road, Lee
Green, London SE12 8UF
Tel: 020 8318 4327
Principal: Michael Lewis
Age range: 9 months–19 years
£ ✐ 16+ ♿

Rosemead Preparatory School & Nursery, Dulwich
70 Thurlow Park Road, London SE21 8HZ
Tel: 020 8670 5865
Headmaster: Mr Phil Soutar
Age range: 2–11
No. of pupils: 366
Fees: Day £10,272–£11,286
£ ✐

St Dunstan's College
Stanstead Road, London SE6 4TY
Tel: 020 8516 7200
Headmaster: Mr Nicholas Hewlett
Age range: 3–18
No. of pupils: 870
⚥ Ⓐ £ ✐ 16+

St Olave's Preparatory School
106 Southwood Road, New
Eltham, London SE9 3QS
Tel: 020 8294 8930
Headteacher: Miss Claire
Holloway BEd, QTS
Age range: 3–11
No. of pupils: 220
Fees: Day £10,848–£12,300

Sydenham High School GDST
15 & 19 Westwood Hill, London SE26 6BL
Tel: 020 8557 7004
Headmistress: Mrs
Katharine Woodcock
Age range: G4–18
No. of pupils: 665

The Pointer School
19 Stratheden Road, Blackheath,
London SE3 7TH
Tel: 020 8293 1331
Headmaster: Mr R J S Higgins
MA, BEd, CertEd, FCollP
Age range: 3–11
No. of pupils: 370
Fees: Day £11,415–£13,449

The Villa School & Nursery
54 Lyndhurst Grove, Peckham,
London SE15 5AH
Tel: 020 7703 6216
Head Teacher: Maughan Louise
Age range: 2–7

South-West London

Al-Risalah Secondary School
145 Upper Tooting Road,
London SW17 7TJ
Tel: 020 8767 6057
Headteacher: Suhayl Lee
Age range: 3–16
No. of pupils: 250

Beechwood Nursery School
55 Leigham Court Road,
Streatham, London SW16 2NJ
Tel: 020 8677 8778
Age range: 0–5

Bertrum House Nursery
290 Balham High Road,
London SW17 7AL
Tel: 020 8767 4051
Headteacher: Miss Vicky
Age range: 2–5
No. of pupils: 94
Fees: Day £1,775–£2,140

Broomwood Hall Lower School
50 Nightingale Lane, London SW12 8TE
Tel: 020 8682 8820
Headmistress: Mrs Carole Jenkinson
Age range: 4–8
No. of pupils: 320
Fees: Day £5,610

Broomwood Hall Upper School
68-74 Nightingale Lane,
London SW12 8NR
Tel: 020 8682 8810
Headmistress: Mrs Carole Jenkinson
Age range: G8–13
No. of pupils: 240
Fees: Day £6,880

Cameron House
4 The Vale, Chelsea, London SW3 6AH
Tel: 020 7352 4040
Headmistress: Mrs Dina Mallett
Age range: 4–11
Fees: Day £19,305

Centre Academy London
92 St John's Hill, Battersea,
London SW11 1SH
Tel: 020 7738 2344
Headteacher: Rachel Maddison
Age range: 9–19

Chelsea Independent College
517-523 Fulham Road, London SW6 1HD
Tel: +44 (0) 20 7610 1114
Principal: Dr Martin Meenagh
Age range: 14–19
No. of pupils: 164

Collingham
23 Collingham Gardens,
London SW5 0HL
Tel: 020 7244 7414
Principal: Sally Powell
Age range: 14–19
No. of pupils: VIth200
Fees: Day £4,260–£22,560

Dolphin School
106 Northcote Road,
London SW11 6QW
Tel: 020 7924 3472
Principal: Mrs. N. Baldwin
Age range: 2–11
No. of pupils: 292
Fees: Day £12,270–£13,485

Donhead
33 Edge Hill, London SW19 4NP
Tel: 020 8946 7000
Headmaster: Mr P J J Barr
Age range: B4–11
No. of pupils: 280
Fees: Day £11,175–£11,622

Eaton House Belgravia
3-5 Eaton Gate, London SW1W 9BA
Tel: 020 7924 6000
Head of School: Mr Huw May
Age range: B3–11
Fees: Day £17,850–£20,700

Eaton House The Manor
58 Clapham Common
Northside, London SW4 9RU
Tel: 020 7924 6000
Head: Mr Oliver Snowball
Age range: G4–11
Fees: Day £16,143

**Eaton House The Manor
Pre Prep and Nursery**
58 Clapham Common
Northside, London SW4 9RU
Tel: 020 7924 6000
Nursery Head of School: Miss Roosha
Age range: B31/2–8
Fees: Day £16,143

**Eaton House The Manor
Prep School**
58 Clapham Common
Northside, London SW4 9RU
Tel: 020 7924 6000
Head: Mrs Sarah Segrave
Age range: B8–13
Fees: Day £19,743

Eaton Square School Belgravia
79 Eccleston Square, London SW1V 1PP
Tel: +44 (0)20 7931 9469
Principal: Mr Sebastian Hepher
Age range: 4–11

Eaton Square School Kensington
24 Elvaston Place, London SW7 5NL
Tel: +44 (0)20 7225 3131
Headmistress: Mrs Trish Watt
Age range: 4–11

Ecole Charles De Gaulle – Wix
Clapham Common North
Side, London SW4 0AJ
Tel: +44 20 7738 0287
Headteacher: Mr Blanchard
Age range: 5–11
No. of pupils: 100

École Primaire Marie D'Orliac
60 Clancarty Road, London SW6 3AA
Tel: +44 (0)20 7736 5863
Director: Mr Blaise Fenart
Age range: 4–11

Emanuel School
Battersea Rise, London SW11 1HS
Tel: 020 8870 4171
Headmaster: Mr Robert Milne
Age range: 10–18
No. of pupils: 930
Fees: Day £18,372

Eveline Day & Nursery Schools
14 Trinity Crescent, Upper
Tooting, London SW17 7AE
Tel: 020 8672 4673
Headmistress: Ms Eveline Drut
Age range: 3 months–11 years
No. of pupils: 80
Fees: Day £13,859

Falkner House
19 Brechin Place, South
Kensington, London SW7 4QB
Tel: 020 7373 4501
Headteacher: Mrs Anita
Griggs BA(Hons), PGCE
Age range: B3–11 G3–11

Finton House School
171 Trinity Road, London SW17 7HL
Tel: 020 8682 0921
Head of School: Mr Ben Freeman
Age range: 4–11
No. of pupils: 300
Fees: Day £15,378–£15,588

**Francis Holland School,
Sloane Square, SW1**
39 Graham Terrace, London SW1W 8JF
Tel: 020 7730 2971
Head: Mrs Lucy Elphinstone
MA(Cantab)
Age range: G4–18
No. of pupils: 520 VIth70
Fees: Day £17,760–£20,085

Garden House School
Boys' School & Girls' School,
Turk's Row, London SW3 4TW
Tel: 020 7730 1652
Boys' Head: Mr Christian
Warland BA(Hons), LLB.
Age range: 3–11
No. of pupils: 490
Fees: Day £17,700–£22,800

Glendower School
86/87 Queen's Gate, London SW7 5JX
Tel: 020 7370 1927
Headmistress: Mrs Sarah
Knollys BA, PGCE
Age range: G4–11+
No. of pupils: 206
Fees: Day £19,200

HALL SCHOOL WIMBLEDON
For further details see p.130
17, The downs, Wimbledon,
London SW20 8HF
Tel: 020 8879 9200
Email: enquiries@hsw.co.uk
Website: www.hsw.co.uk
Headmaster: Mr. Robert Bannon
Age range: 5–18
No. of pupils: 150
Fees: Day £4,420–£5,950

Hall School Wimbledon Junior School
Beavers Holt, Stroud Crescent,
Putney Vale, London SW15 3EQ
Tel: 020 8788 2370
Headmaster: Timothy J Hobbs MA
Age range: 4–16
No. of pupils: 520
Fees: Day £13,126–£17,336

Harrodian School
Lonsdale Road, London SW13 9QN
Tel: 020 8748 6117
Headmaster: James R Hooke
Age range: 4–18
No. of pupils: 890 VIth95
Fees: Day £15,000–£23,040

Hill House International Junior School
17 Hans Place, Chelsea,
London SW1X 0EP
Tel: 020 7584 1331
Proprietors: Richard, Janet,
William & Edmund Townend
Age range: 4–13
No. of pupils: 680
Fees: Day £14,700–£18,800

Hornsby House School
Hearnville Road, Balham,
London SW12 8RS
Tel: 020 8673 7573
Headmaster: Mr Edward Rees
Age range: 4–11
Fees: Day £14,280–£15,345

Hurlingham Nursery School
The Old Methodist Hall, Gwendolen
Avenue, London SW15 6EH
Tel: 020 8103 0807
Headmaster: Mr Simon Gould
Age range: 2–4 years

Hurlingham School
122 Putney Bridge Road,
Putney, London SW15 2NQ
Tel: 020 8103 1083
Headmaster: Mr Simon Gould
Age range: 4–11

Ibstock Place School
Clarence Lane, London SW15 5PY
Tel: 020 8876 9991
Head: Mrs Anna Sylvester-
Johnson BA(Hons), PGCE
Age range: 4–18
No. of pupils: 970
Fees: Day £16,290–£20,880

KENSINGTON PARK SCHOOL
For further details see p.134
59 Queen's Gate, South
Kensington, London SW7 5JP
Tel: +44 (0)20 7225 0577
Email: admissions@kps.co.uk
Website: www.kps.co.uk
Headmaster (Interim): Mr
Stephen Mellor MA, MCCT
Age range: 11–18

Kensington Prep School
596 Fulham Road, London SW6 5PA
Tel: 0207 731 9300
Head of School: Mrs Caroline
Hulme-McKibbin
Age range: G4–11
No. of pupils: 289
Fees: Day £17,193

King's College School
Southside, Wimbledon
Common, London SW19 4TT
Tel: 020 8255 5300
Head Master: Mr A D Halls OBE
Age range: B7–18 G16–18
No. of pupils: 1439

Knightsbridge School
67 Pont Street, Knightsbridge,
London SW1X 0BD
Tel: +44 (0)20 7590 9000
Head of School: Shona Colaço
Age range: 3–13
Fees: Day £18,756–£19,965

L'Ecole de Battersea
Trott Street, Battersea, London SW11 3DS
Tel: 020 7371 8350
Principal: Mrs F Brisset
Age range: 3–11
No. of pupils: 265
Fees: Day £13,500–£13,740

L'Ecole des Petits
2 Hazlebury Road, Fulham,
London SW6 2NB
Tel: 020 7371 8350
Principal: Mrs F Brisset
Age range: 3–6
No. of pupils: 130
Fees: Day £13,200–£13,365

London Steiner School
9 Weir Road, Balham, London SW12 0LT
Tel: 0208 772 3504
Age range: 3–14

Lycée Français Charles de Gaulle
35 Cromwell Road, London SW7 2DG
Tel: 020 7584 6322
Head of School: Mr Olivier Rauch
Age range: 5–19
No. of pupils: 4000

Mander Portman Woodward – London
90-92 Queen's Gate, London SW7 5AB
Tel: 020 7835 1355
Principal: Mr John Southworth BSc MSc
Age range: 14–19
No. of pupils: 618
Fees: Day £9,905

More House School
22-24 Pont Street, Knightsbridge,
London SW1X 0AA
Tel: 020 7235 2855
Co-Heads: Mrs. Amanda Leach
& Mr. Michael Keeley
Age range: G11–18
No. of pupils: 205
Fees: Day £6,950

NEWTON PREP
For further details see p.140
149 Battersea Park Road,
London SW8 4BX
Tel: 020 7720 4091
Email: enquiries@newtonprep.co.uk
Website:
www.newtonprepschool.co.uk
Headmistress: Mrs Alison
Fleming BA, MA Ed, PGCE
Age range: 3–13
No. of pupils: 631
Fees: Day £9,600–£20,340

Northcote Lodge
26 Bolingbroke Grove, London SW11 6EL
Tel: 020 8682 8888
Headmaster: Clive Smith-Langridge
Age range: B8–13
No. of pupils: 260
Fees: Day £6,880

NorthWood Senior
3 Garrad's Road, London SW16 1JZ
Tel: 020 8682 8821
Head: Mrs Susan Brooks
Age range: 11–16
Fees: Day £6,800

Oliver House Preparatory School
7 Nightingale Lane, London SW4 9AH
Tel: 020 8772 1911
Headteacher: Mr Rob Farrell
Age range: 3–11
No. of pupils: 144
Fees: Day £6,600–£15,090

Parkgate House School
80 Clapham Common North
Side, London SW4 9SD
Tel: +44 (0)20 7350 2461
Principal: Miss Catherine Shanley
Age range: 2½–11 years
No. of pupils: 220
Fees: Day £5,940–£15,600

Parsons Green Prep School
1 Fulham Park Road, Fulham,
London SW6 4LJ
Tel: 020 7371 9009
Headmaster: Tim Cannell
Age range: 4–11
No. of pupils: 200
Fees: Day £16,857–£18,201

Prince's Gardens Preparatory School
10–13 Prince's Gardens,
London SW7 1ND
Tel: 0207 591 4622
Headmistress: Mrs Alison Melrose
Age range: 3–11

PROSPECT HOUSE SCHOOL
For further details see p.146
75 Putney Hill, London SW15 3NT
Tel: 020 8246 4897
Email: info@prospecths.org.uk
Website: www.prospecths.org.uk
Headmaster: Mr Michael
Hodge BPED(Rhodes) QTS
Age range: 3–11
No. of pupils: 316
Fees: Day £9,210–£19,200

Putney High School GDST
35 Putney Hill, London SW15 6BH
Tel: 020 8788 4886
Headmistress: Mrs Suzie
Longstaff BA, MA, PGCE
Age range: G4–18
No. of pupils: 976 VIth150

QUEEN'S GATE SCHOOL
For further details see p.148
133 Queen's Gate, London SW7 5LE
Tel: 020 7589 3587
Email: registrar@queensgate.org.uk
Website: www.queensgate.org.uk
Principal: Mrs R M Kamaryc
BA, MSc, PGCE
Age range: G4–18
No. of pupils: 529 VIth94

Redcliffe School Trust Ltd
47 Redcliffe Gardens, Chelsea,
London SW10 9JH
Tel: 020 7352 9247
Head: Sarah Lemmon
Age range: 3–11
Fees: Day £6,660–£17,730

Sinclair House Preparatory School
59 Fulham High Street,
Fulham, London SW6 3JJ
Tel: 0207 736 9182
Principal: Mrs Carlotta T M O'Sullivan
Age range: 2–11
No. of pupils: 120
Fees: Day £5,280–£17,025

St Mary's Summerstown Montessori
46 Wimbledon Road, Tooting,
London SW17 0UQ
Tel: 020 8947 7359
Head: Liz Maitland NNEB, RSH, MontDip
Age range: 18 months–5 years
No. of pupils: 30
Fees: Day £1,300

St Paul's Juniors
St Paul's School, Lonsdale
Road, London SW13 9JT
Tel: 020 8748 3461
Age range: B7–13
No. of pupils: 436
Fees: Day £20,010

St Paul's School
Lonsdale Road, Barnes,
London SW13 9JT
Tel: 020 8748 9162
High Master: Prof Mark Bailey
Age range: B13–18
No. of pupils: 897
Fees: Day £25,032 FB £37,611

St Philip's School
6 Wetherby Place, London SW7 4NE
Tel: 020 7373 3944
Headmaster: Mr Wulffen-Thomas
Age range: B7–13
No. of pupils: 110
Fees: Day £16,200

Streatham & Clapham High School GDST
42 Abbotswood Road,
London SW16 1AW
Tel: 020 8677 8400
Headmaster: Dr Millan Sachania
Age range: G3–18
No. of pupils: 603 VIth70
Fees: Day £10,431–£19,743

Sussex House School
68 Cadogan Square, London SW1X 0EA
Tel: 020 7584 1741
Headmaster: Mr N P Kaye
MA(Cantab), ACP, FRSA, FRGS
Age range: B8–13
No. of pupils: 182
Fees: Day £19,770

Swedish School
82 Lonsdale Road, London SW13 9JS
Tel: 020 8741 1751
Head of School: Ms. Annika
Simonsson Bergqvist
Age range: 3–18
No. of pupils: 300 VIth145
Fees: Day £8,600–£9,100

Thames Christian College
Wye Street, Battersea,
London SW11 2HB
Tel: 020 7228 3933
Executive Head: Stephen
Holsgrove PhD
Age range: 11–16
No. of pupils: 120
Fees: Day £15,780

The Falcons School for Girls
11 Woodborough Road,
Putney, London SW15 6PY
Tel: 020 8992 5189
Head of School: Mrs Sophia
Ashworth Jones
Age range: G3–11
No. of pupils: 102
Fees: Day £8,580–£15,705

The Hampshire School, Chelsea
15 Manresa Road, Chelsea,
London SW3 6NB
Tel: 020 7352 7077
Principal: Mr Donal Brennan
Age range: 3–13
No. of pupils: 300
Fees: Day £16,965–£17,955

The Laurels School
126 Atkins Road, Clapham,
London SW12 0AN
Tel: 020 8674 7229
Headmistress: Linda Sanders BA
Hons (Bristol), MA (Madrid)
Age range: G11–18

THE MERLIN SCHOOL
For further details see p.152
4 Carlton Drive, London SW15 2BZ
Tel: 020 8788 2769
Email: admissionenquiries@
merlinschool.net
Website: www.merlinschool.net
Principal: Mrs Kate Prest
Age range: 4–8
No. of pupils: 155
Fees: Day £5,041

The Moat School
Bishops Avenue, Fulham,
London SW6 6EG
Tel: 020 7610 9018
Headteacher: Mr K Claeys
Age range: 9–18
No. of pupils: 110

The Montessori Pavilion – The Kindergarten School
Vine Road, Barnes, London SW13 0NE
Tel: 07554 277 746
Headmistress: Ms Georgina Dashwood
Age range: 3–8
No. of pupils: 50

The Norwegian School
28 Arterberry Road, Wimbledon,
London SW20 8AH
Tel: 020 8947 6617
Head: Mr Ivar Chavannes
Age range: 3–16

The Roche School
11 Frogmore, London SW18 1HW
Tel: 020 8877 0823
Headmistress: Mrs Vania Adams
BA(Hons), PGCE, MA
Age range: 2–11 years
No. of pupils: 302
Fees: Day £14,970–£15,690

The Rowans School
19 Drax Avenue, Wimbledon,
London SW20 0EG
Tel: 020 8946 8220
Head Teacher: Mrs. Joanna Hubbard
MA BA (Hons) PGCE QTS PGDipSEN
Age range: 3–8
Fees: Day £7,905–£13,170

**THE STUDY PREPARATORY
SCHOOL**
For further details see p.154
Wilberforce House, Camp
Road, Wimbledon Common,
London SW19 4UN
Tel: 020 8947 6969
Email: admissions@
thestudyprep.co.uk
Website: www.thestudyprep.co.uk
Head of School: Miss Vicky
Ellis BSc (Hons), QTS, MA
Age range: G4–11
No. of pupils: 320
Fees: Day £4,725

**The White House Preparatory
School & Woodentops
Kindergarten**
24 Thornton Road, London SW12 0LF
Tel: 020 8674 9514
Principal: Mrs. Mary McCahery
Age range: 2–11
Fees: Day £4,436–£4,740

**Thomas's Preparatory
School – Battersea**
28-40 Battersea High Street,
London SW11 3JB
Tel: 020 7978 0900
Head: Simon O'Malley
Age range: 4–13
No. of pupils: 547
Fees: Day £18,747–£20,868

**Thomas's Preparatory
School – Clapham**
Broomwood Road, London SW11 6JZ
Tel: 020 7326 9300
Headmaster: Mr Philip Ward BEd(Hons)
Age range: 4–13
No. of pupils: 647
Fees: Day £17,262–£19,518

**Thomas's Preparatory
School – Fulham**
Hugon Road, London SW6 3ES
Tel: 020 7751 8200
Head: Miss Annette Dobson
BEd(Hons), PGCertDys
Age range: 4–11
Fees: Day £17,880–£20,016

Tower House School
188 Sheen Lane, London SW14 8LF
Tel: 020 8876 3323
Head: Mr Gregory Evans
Age range: B4–13

URSULINE PREPARATORY SCHOOL
For further details see p.156
18 The Downs, Wimbledon,
London SW20 8HR
Tel: 020 8947 0859
Email: headteacherea@
ursulineprep.org
Website: www.ursulineprep.org
Head Teacher: Mrs
Caroline Molina BA
Age range: B3–4 G3–11
No. of pupils: 202

Wandsworth Preparatory School
The Old Library, 2 Allfarthing
Lane, London SW18 2PQ
Tel: 0208 870 4133
Head of School: Miss Bridget
Saul BA (Hons), PGCE, MA
Age range: 4–11
No. of pupils: 115
Fees: Day £4,570

Westminster Abbey Choir School
Dean's Yard, London SW1P 3NY
Tel: 0207 654 4918
Headmaster: Mr Peter Roberts
Age range: B8–13
No. of pupils: 35
Fees: FB £8,571

**Westminster Cathedral
Choir School**
Ambrosden Avenue, London SW1P 1QH
Tel: 020 7798 9081
Headmaster: Mr Neil McLaughlan
Age range: B4–13
No. of pupils: 150
Fees: Day £16,350–£19,233 FB £10,086

Westminster School
Little Dean's Yard, Westminster,
London SW1P 3PF
Tel: 020 7963 1003
Headmaster: Mr Patrick Derham
Age range: B13–18 G16–18
No. of pupils: 744
Fees: Day £26,130–£28,566 FB £37,740

Westminster Tutors
86 Old Brompton Road, South
Kensington, London SW7 3LQ
Tel: 020 7584 1288
Principal: Virginia Maguire
BA, MA, MLitt
Age range: 14–mature
No. of pupils: VIth40
Fees: Day £4,000–£25,000

Westminster Under School
Adrian House, 27 Vincent
Square, London SW1P 2NN
Tel: 020 7821 5788
Headteacher: Mr Mark O'Donnell
Age range: B7–13
No. of pupils: 265
Fees: Day £19,344

Willington Prep
Worcester Road, Wimbledon,
London SW19 7QQ
Tel: 020 8944 7020
Acting Headmaster: Mr
Marcus Tattersal
Age range: B4–13
No. of pupils: 250
Fees: Day £12,150–£14,640

Wimbledon Common Preparatory
113 Ridgway, Wimbledon,
London SW19 4TA
Tel: 020 8946 1001
Head Teacher: Mrs Tracey Buck
Age range: B4–8
No. of pupils: 160
Fees: Day £13,185

Wimbledon High School GDST
Mansel Road, Wimbledon,
London SW19 4AB
Tel: 020 8971 0900
Headmistress: Mrs Jane Lunnon
Age range: G4–18
No. of pupils: 900 VIth155
Fees: Day £14,622–£18,810

West London

Albemarle Independent College
18 Dunraven Street, London W1K 7FE
Tel: 020 7409 7273
Co-Principals: Beverley
Mellon & James Eytle
Age range: 16–19
No. of pupils: 160
Fees: Day £7,000–£24,000

**Arts Educational Schools
London Sixth Form**
Cone Ripman House, 14 Bath
Road, Chiswick, London W4 1LY
Tel: 020 8987 6666
Head Teacher: Mr Adrian Blake
Age range: 16–18
No. of pupils: 85
Fees: Day £16,830–£16,990

**Arts Educational Schools
London Years 7-11**
Cone Ripman House, 14 Bath
Road, Chiswick, London W4 1LY
Tel: 020 8987 6666
Head Teacher: Mr Adrian Blake
Age range: 11–16
No. of pupils: 141
Fees: Day £15,390–£15,540

**Ashbourne Independent
Sixth Form College**
17 Old Court Place, Kensington,
London W8 4PL
Tel: 020 7937 3858
Principal: M J Kirby MSc, BApSc
Age range: 16–19
No. of pupils: 170
Fees: Day £24,750–£26,250

Ashbourne Middle School
17 Old Court Place, Kensington,
London W8 4PL
Tel: 020 7937 3858
Principal: M J Kirby MSc, BApSc
Age range: 13–16
No. of pupils: VIth150
Fees: Day £24,750–£26,250

Avenue House School
70 The Avenue, Ealing, London W13 8LS
Tel: 020 8998 9981
Headteacher: Mr J Sheppard
Age range: 3–11
No. of pupils: 135
Fees: Day £11,250

Bales College
742 Harrow Road, Kensal
Town, London W10 4AA
Tel: 020 8960 5899
Principal: William Moore
Age range: 11–19
No. of pupils: 90
Fees: Day £11,550–£12,750

Barbara Speake Stage School
East Acton Lane, East Acton,
London W3 7EG
Tel: 020 8743 1306
Headteacher: Mr David
Speake BA (Hons)
Age range: 3–16
Fees: Day £7,500–£9,000

BASSETT HOUSE SCHOOL
For further details see p.122
60 Bassett Road, London W10 6JP
Tel: 020 8969 0313
Email: info@bassetths.org.uk
Website: www.bassetths.org.uk
Headmistress: Mrs Philippa
Cawthorne MA (Soton)
PGCE Mont Cert
Age range: 3–11
No. of pupils: 190
Fees: Day £5,499–£19,200

Bute House Preparatory School for Girls
Bute House, Luxemburg
Gardens, London W6 7EA
Tel: 020 7603 7381
Head: Mrs Helen Lowe
Age range: G4–11
No. of pupils: 306
Fees: Day £16,458

Chepstow House School
108a Lancaster Road, London W11 1QS
Tel: 0207 243 0243
Headteacher: Angela Barr
Age range: 2½–12 years

Chiswick & Bedford Park Prep School
Priory House, Priory Avenue,
London W4 1TX
Tel: 020 8994 1804
Headmistress: Mrs S Daniell
Age range: B4–7+ G4–11
No. of pupils: 180
Fees: Day £13,275

Clifton Lodge
8 Mattock Lane, Ealing,
London W5 5BG
Tel: 020 8579 3662
Executive Head: Mr. Floyd Steadman
Age range: 3–13
No. of pupils: 140
Fees: Day £12,240–£14,010

Connaught House School
47 Connaught Square, London W2 2HL
Tel: 020 7262 8830
Principal: Mrs V Hampton
Age range: 4–11
No. of pupils: 75
Fees: Day £16,650–£18,300

David Game College
31 Jewry Street, London EC3N 2ET
Tel: 020 7221 6665
Principal: D T P Game MA, MPhil
Age range: 14–19
No. of pupils: 200 VIth150
Fees: Day £3,680–£30,630

DURSTON HOUSE
For further details see p.128
12-14 Castlebar Road,
Ealing, London W5 2DR
Tel: 020 8991 6530
Email: info@durstonhouse.org
Website: www.durstonhouse.org
Headmaster: Mr Giles Entwisle
Age range: B4–13
No. of pupils: 380
Fees: Day £4,160–£5,060

Ealing Independent College
83 New Broadway, Ealing,
London W5 5AL
Tel: 020 8579 6668
Principal: Dr Ian Moores
Age range: 13–19
No. of pupils: 100 VIth70
Fees: Day £2,910–£18,120

Eaton Square School Mayfair
106 Piccadilly, Mayfair, London W1J 7NL
Tel: +44 (0)20 7491 7393
Co-Heads: Caroline Townshend
(Lower) & John Wilson (Upper)
Age range: 11–18

Ecole Francaise Jacques Prevert
59 Brook Green, London W6 7BE
Tel: 020 7602 6871
Headteacher: Delphine Gentil
Age range: 4–11

Fulham Prep School
200 Greyhound Road, London W14 9SD
Tel: 020 7386 2444
Headmaster: Mr Will le Fleming
Age range: 4–18
No. of pupils: 647
Fees: Day £16,869–£19,749

Great Beginnings Montessori Nursery
39 Brendon Street, London W1H 5JE
Tel: 020 7258 1066
Head: Mrs Wendy Innes
Age range: 2–6

Greek Primary School of London
3 Pierrepoint Road, Acton,
London W3 9JR
Tel: 020 899 26156
Primary School Head Teacher: Mrs
Despoina Kyriakidou BA, MA, QTS
Age range: 1–11

Halcyon London International School
33 Seymour Place, , London W1H 5AU
Tel: +44 (0)20 7258 1169
Headteacher: Mr Barry Mansfield
Age range: 11–18
No. of pupils: 195

Harvington School
20 Castlebar Road, Ealing,
London W5 2DS
Tel: 020 8997 1583
Headmistress: Mrs Anna Evans
Age range: B3–4 G3–11
No. of pupils: 140
Fees: Day £6,525–£12,615

Hawkesdown House School Kensington
27 Edge Street, Kensington,
London W8 7PN
Tel: 020 7727 9090
Headmistress: Mrs. J. A. K.
Mackay B.Ed (Hons)
Age range: 2–11
No. of pupils: 100
Fees: Day £17,085–£20,100

Heathfield House School
Heathfield Gardens, Chiswick,
London W4 4JU
Tel: 020 8994 3385
Headteacher: Mrs Goodsman
Age range: 4–11
No. of pupils: 197
Fees: Day £2,471–£3,676

Holland Park Pre Prep School and Day Nursery
5, Holland Road, Kensington,
London W14 8HJ
Tel: 020 7602 9066/020 7602 9266
Head Mistress: Mrs Kitty Mason
Age range: 3 months–8 years
No. of pupils: 39
Fees: Day £9,180–£18,120

Instituto Español Vicente Cañada Blanch
317 Portobello Road, London W10 5SZ
Tel: +44 (0) 20 8969 2664
Principal: Carmen Pinilla Padilla
Age range: 4–19
No. of pupils: 405

International School of London (ISL)
139 Gunnersbury Avenue,
London W3 8LG
Tel: +44 (0)20 8992 5823
Principal: Mr Richard Parker
Age range: 3–18 years
No. of pupils: 500
Fees: Day £19,000–£26,300

King Fahad Academy
Bromyard Avenue, Acton,
London W3 7HD
Tel: 020 8743 0131
Director General: Dr
Abdulghani Alharbi
Age range: 3–19
No. of pupils: 500
Fees: Day £3,300–£4,300

La Petite Ecole Francaise
73 Saint Charles Square,
London W10 6EJ
Tel: +44 208 960 1278
Principal: Mme Marjorie Lacassagne
Age range: 3–11

Latymer Prep School
36 Upper Mall, Hammersmith,
London W6 9TA
Tel: 020 7993 0061
Principal: Ms Andrea
Rutterford B.Ed (Hons)
Age range: 7–11
No. of pupils: 165
Fees: Day £18,330

Latymer Upper School
King Street, Hammersmith,
London W6 9LR
Tel: 020862 92024
Head: Mr D Goodhew MA(Oxon)
Age range: 11–18
No. of pupils: 1200
Fees: Day £20,130
Ⓐ Ⓔ ⚹16⃠

Le Herisson
River Court Methodist
Church, Rover Court Road,
Hammersmith, London W6 9JT
Tel: 020 8563 7664
Director: Maria Frost
Age range: 2–6
Fees: Day £8,730–£8,970
⚲

L'Ecole Bilingue
St David's Welsh Church, St Mary's
Terrace, London W2 1SJ
Tel: 020 7224 8427
Headteacher: Ms Veronique Ferreira
Age range: 3–11
No. of pupils: 68
Fees: Day £9,960–£10,770

Leiths School of Food & Wine
16-20 Wendell Road, Shepherd's
Bush, London W12 9RT
Tel: 020 8749 6400
Managing Director: Camilla
Schneideman
Age range: 17–99
No. of pupils: 96
16⃠ ⚲

LLOYD WILLIAMSON SCHOOLS
For further details see p.136
12 Telford Road, London W10 5SH
Tel: 020 8962 0345
Email: admin@lws.org.uk
Website: www.lloydwilliamson.co.uk
Co-Principals: Ms Lucy Meyer
& Mr Aaron Williams
Age range: 4 months–16 years
Fees: Day £16,950
⚲

London Welsh School Ysgol Gymraeg Llundain
Hanwell Community Centre,
Westcott Crescent, London W7 1PD
Tel: 020 8575 0237
Lead Teacher: Mrs Rachel King
Age range: 3–11

Maida Vale School
18 Saltram Crescent, London W9 3HR
Tel: 020 3196 1860
Headmaster: Steven Winter
Age range: 11–18
No. of pupils: 600

Norland Place School
162-166 Holland Park Avenue,
London W11 4UH
Tel: 020 7603 9103
Headmaster: Mr Patrick Mattar MA
Age range: B4–8 years G4–11 years
Fees: Day £16,107–£18,072
⚲

Notting Hill & Ealing High School GDST
2 Cleveland Road, West
Ealing, London W13 8AX
Tel: (020) 8799 8400
Headmaster: Mr Matthew Shoults
Age range: G4–18
No. of pupils: 903 VIth150
Fees: Day £14,313–£18,561
⚹ Ⓐ Ⓔ 16⃠

Notting Hill Preparatory School
95 Lancaster Road, London W11 1QQ
Tel: 020 7221 0727
Headmistress: Mrs Jane Cameron
Age range: 4–13
No. of pupils: 325
Fees: Day £6,355
Ⓔ ⚲

One World Montessori Nursery
56 Minford Gardens, London W14 0AW
Tel: 020 7603 6065
Headteacher: Ms N Greer
Age range: 2–8

ORCHARD HOUSE SCHOOL
For further details see p.144
16 Newton Grove, Bedford
Park, London W4 1LB
Tel: 020 8742 8544
Email: info@orchardhs.org.uk
Website: www.orchardhs.org.uk
Headmistress: Mrs Maria Edwards
BEd(Beds) PGCE(Man) Mont Cert
Age range: 3–11
No. of pupils: 290
Fees: Day £9,210–£19,200
Ⓔ ⚲

Pembridge Hall
18 Pembridge Square, London W2 4EH
Tel: 020 7229 0121
Headteacher: Mr Henry Keighley-Elstub
Age range: G4–11
No. of pupils: 413
⚹

Portland Place School
56-58 Portland Place, London W1B 1NJ
Tel: 0207 307 8700
Headmaster: Mr David Bradbury
Age range: 9–18
No. of pupils: 300 VIth50
Fees: Day £21,030
Ⓐ Ⓔ ⚹16⃠

Queen's College
43-49 Harley Street, London W1G 8BT
Tel: 020 7291 7000
Principal: Mr Richard Tillet
Age range: G11–18
No. of pupils: 360 VIth90
⚹ Ⓐ Ⓔ 16⃠

Queen's College Preparatory School
61 Portland Place, , London W1B 1QP
Tel: 020 7291 0660
Headmistress: Mrs Emma Webb
Age range: G4–11
⚹

Ravenscourt Park Preparatory School
16 Ravenscourt Avenue, London W6 0SL
Tel: 020 8846 9153
Headmaster: Mr Carl Howes
MA (Cantab), PGCE (Exeter)
Age range: 4–11
No. of pupils: 419
Fees: Day £5,857
⚲

Ray Cochrane Beauty School
118 Baker Street, London W1U 6TT
Tel: 02033224738
Principal: Miss Baljeet Suri
Age range: 16–50
No. of pupils: 30
Fees: Day £650–£8,495
16⃠ 16⃠ ⚹

Southbank International School – Kensington
36-38 Kensington Park
Road, London W11 3BU
Tel: +44 (0)20 7243 3803
Principal: Siobhan McGrath
Age range: 3–18
⚹ IB ⚲

Southbank International School – Westminster
63-65 Portland Place, London W1B 1QR
Tel: 020 7243 3803
Principal: Dr Paul Wood
Age range: 11–19
⚹ IB ⚲ 16⃠

St Augustine's Priory
Hillcrest Road, Ealing, London W5 2JL
Tel: 020 8997 2022
Headteacher: Mrs Sarah
Raffray M.A., N.P.Q.H
Age range: B3–4 G3–18
No. of pupils: 485
Fees: Day £11,529–£16,398
⚹ Ⓐ 16⃠

St Benedict's School
54 Eaton Rise, Ealing, London W5 2ES
Tel: 020 8862 2000
Headmaster: Mr A Johnson BA
Age range: 3–18
No. of pupils: 1073 VIth203
Fees: Day £13,485–£17,655
Ⓐ Ⓔ 16⃠

St James Preparatory School
Earsby Street, London W14 8SH
Tel: 020 7348 1777
Headmistress: Mrs Catherine
Thomlinson BA(Hons)
Age range: 3–11
Fees: Day £16,425–£17,910
Ⓔ

St James Senior Girls' School
Earsby Street, London W14 8SH
Tel: 020 7348 1777
Headmistress: Mrs Sarah Labram BA
Age range: G11–18
No. of pupils: 295 VIth67
Fees: Day £20,100
⚹ Ⓐ Ⓔ 16⃠

St Paul's Girls' School
Brook Green, London W6 7BS
Tel: 020 7603 2288
High Mistress: Mrs Sarah Fletcher
Age range: G11–18 years
No. of pupils: 750 VIth200
Fees: Day £24,891–£26,760
⚹ Ⓐ Ⓔ 16⃠

Sylvia Young Theatre School
1 Nutford Place, London W1H 5YZ
Tel: 020 7258 2330
Headteacher: Mrs Frances Chave
Age range: 10–16
16⃠ Ⓔ ⚲

Tabernacle School
32 St Anns Villas, Holland
Park, London W11 4RS
Tel: 020 7602 6232
Headteacher: Mrs P Wilson
Age range: 3–16
Fees: Day £6,500–£9,500

The Falcons School for Boys
2 Burnaby Gardens, Chiswick,
London W4 3DT
Tel: 020 8747 8393
**Head of Pre-Preparatory
School:** Mr Andrew Forbes
Age range: B3–13
No. of pupils: 225
Fees: Day £8,475–£17,475
(symbols)

**The Godolphin and
Latymer School**
Iffley Road, Hammersmith,
London W6 0PG
Tel: +44 (0)20 8741 1936
Head Mistress: Dr Frances Ramsey
Age range: G11–18
No. of pupils: 800
Fees: Day £23,085
(symbols)

The Japanese School
87 Creffield Road, Acton,
London W3 9PU
Tel: 020 8993 7145
Age range: 6–16

**Thomas's Preparatory
School – Kensington**
17-19 Cottesmore Gardens,
London W8 5PR
Tel: 020 7361 6500
Headmistress: Miss Joanna Ebner
MA, BEd(Hons)(Cantab), NPQH
Age range: 4–11
Fees: Day £20,526–£21,789
(symbols)

Wetherby Preparatory School
48 Bryanston Square, London W1H 2EA
Tel: 020 7535 3520
Headteacher: Mr Nick Baker
Age range: B8–13
No. of pupils: 192
Fees: Day £21,660
(symbols)

Wetherby Pre-Preparatory School
11 Pembridge Square, London W2 4ED
Tel: 020 7727 9581
Headmaster: Mr Mark Snell
Age range: B2 1/2–8
No. of pupils: 350
Fees: Day £21,600
(symbols)

Wetherby Senior School
100 Marylebone Lane,
London W1U 2QU
Tel: 020 7535 3530
Headmaster: Mr Seth Bolderow
Age range: B11–18
Fees: Day £22,995
(symbols)

Young Dancers Academy
25 Bulwer Street, London W12 8AR
Tel: 020 8743 3856
Head: Mrs K Williams
Age range: 11–16
Fees: Day £12,237–£12,690

North-East

KEY TO SYMBOLS

- ⚥ *Boys' school*
- ⚥ *Girls' school*
- 🌐 *International school*
- 16 *Tutorial or sixth form college*
- Ⓐ *A levels*
- 🏫 *Boarding accommodation*
- £ *Bursaries*
- IB *International Baccalaureate*
- ✎ *Learning support*
- 16+ *Entrance at 16+*
- ✺ *Vocational qualifications*
- IAPS *Independent Association of Preparatory Schools*
- HMC *The Headmasters' & Headmistresses' Conference*
- ISA *Independent Schools Association*
- GSA *Girls' School Association*
- BSA *Boarding Schools' Association*
- S *Society of Heads*

Unless otherwise indicated, all schools are coeducational day schools. Single-sex and boarding schools will be indicated by the relevant icon.

Durham

Barnard Castle Preparatory School
Westwick Road, Barnard
Castle, Durham DL12 8UW
Tel: 01833 696032
Headmistress: Mrs Laura Turner
Age range: 4–11
No. of pupils: 180
Fees: Day £6,240–£9,450 FB £18,300
🏫 ✎

Barnard Castle Senior School
Barnard Castle, Durham DL12 8UN
Tel: 01833 690222
Headmaster: Mr Anthony
C Jackson BA (Hons)
Age range: 11–18
No. of pupils: 570 VIth160
Fees: Day £13,500 FB £24,300
🌐 Ⓐ 🏫 £ ✎ 16+

Bow, Durham School
South Road, Durham DH1 3LS
Tel: 0191 384 8233
Headmistress: Mrs Sally Harrod
Age range: 3–11
No. of pupils: 155
Fees: Day £5,676–£11,043
£ ✎

Durham High School for Girls
Farewell Hall, Durham DH1 3TB
Tel: 0191 384 3226
Headmistress: Mrs Lynne Renwick
Age range: G3–18
No. of pupils: 421
🚶 Ⓐ £ ✎ 16+

Durham School
Durham City, Durham DH1 4SZ
Tel: +44 (0)191 386 4783
Headmaster: Mr K McLaughlin
Age range: 3–18
No. of pupils: 560 VIth156
Fees: Day £2,756–£5,331 WB
£7,347–£8,786 FB £8,460–£9,846
🌐 🚶 Ⓐ 🏫 £ ✎ 16+

The Chorister School
The College, Durham DH1 3EL
Tel: 0191 384 2935
Headmaster: Mr Ian Wicks
Age range: 3–13 years
No. of pupils: 214
Fees: Day £9,420–£12,825
FB £11,520–£21,960
🏫 £ ✎

**The Independent Grammar
School: Durham**
Claypath, Durham DH1 1RH
Principal: Mr Chris Gray
Fees: Day £2,995

Northumberland

Longridge Towers School
Longridge Towers, Berwick-upon-
Tweed, Northumberland TD15 2XH
Tel: 01289 307584
Headmaster: Mr Jonathan Lee
Age range: 3–18
No. of pupils: VIth46
Fees: Day £9,300–£13,650 WB
£20,100–£21,600 FB £26,340–£29,400
🌐 Ⓐ 🏫 £ ✎ 16+

Mowden Hall School
Newton, Stocksfield,
Northumberland NE43 7TP
Tel: 01661 842147
Headmaster: Mr Neil Bailey
Age range: 3–13
Fees: Day £9,000–£17,160 FB £23,700
🏫 £ ✎

Stockton-on-Tees

Red House School
36 The Green, Norton,
Stockton-on-Tees TS20 1DX
Tel: 01642 553370
Headmaster: Mr Ken James LLB
Age range: 3–16
No. of pupils: 363
Fees: Day £4,710–£10,620
£ ✎

Teesside High School
The Avenue, Eaglescliffe,
Stockton-on-Tees TS16 9AT
Tel: 01642 782095
Head of School: Mrs K Mackenzie
Age range: 3–18
No. of pupils: 350 VIth70
🚶 Ⓐ £ ✎ 16+

Yarm Preparatory School
Grammar School Lane, Yarm,
Stockton-on-Tees TS15 9ES
Tel: 01642 781447
Headteacher: Mr William Sawyer
Age range: 3–11
No. of pupils: 360
Fees: Day £5,232–£10,755
✎

Yarm School
The Friarage, Yarm, Stockton-
on-Tees TS15 9EJ
Tel: 01642 786023
Headmaster: Mr D M Dunn BA
Age range: 3–18
No. of pupils: VIth200
Fees: Day £5,232–£12,888
Ⓐ £ 16+

Tyne & Wear

ARGYLE HOUSE SCHOOL
For further details see p.160
19-20 Thornhill Park, Sunderland,
Tyne & Wear SR2 7LA
Tel: 0191 5100726
Email: info@
argylehouseschool.co.uk
Website:
www.argylehouseschool.co.uk
Headteacher: Mr. Chris Johnson
Age range: 3–16
No. of pupils: 233
✎

Dame Allan Junior School
Hunters Road, Spital Tongues,
Newcastle upon Tyne, Tyne
& Wear NE2 4NG
Tel: 0191 275 0608
Head: Mr A J Edge
Age range: 3–11
No. of pupils: 140
Fees: Day £7,266–£10,419

Dame Allan's Boys' School
Fowberry Crescent, Fenham,
Newcastle upon Tyne,
Tyne & Wear NE4 9YJ
Tel: 0191 275 0608
Head: Mr P Wildsmith
Age range: B11–16
No. of pupils: 304
Fees: Day £12,936–£13,236
🚶 Ⓐ £ ✎ 16+

Dame Allan's Girls' School
Fowberry Crescent, Fenham,
Newcastle upon Tyne,
Tyne & Wear NE4 9YJ
Tel: 0191 275 0708
Head: Mrs E Fiddaman
Age range: G11–16
No. of pupils: 225
Fees: Day £12,936–£13,236
🚶 Ⓐ £ ✎ 16+

Dame Allan's Sixth Form
Fowberry Crescent, Fenham,
Newcastle upon Tyne,
Tyne & Wear NE4 9YJ
Tel: 0191 275 0608
Head: Mr D Henry
Age range: 16–18
No. of pupils: 200
Fees: Day £12,936–£13,236
(16) (A) (£) (16)

**Gateshead Jewish
Boarding School**
10 Rydal Street, Gateshead,
Tyne & Wear NE8 1HG
Tel: 0191 477 1431
Age range: B10–16
(♦)

Gateshead Jewish Primary School
18-22 Gladstone Terrace,
Gateshead, Tyne & Wear NE8 4EA
Tel: 0191 477 2154
Age range: 5–11
(✎)

**Newcastle High School
for Girls GDST**
Tankerville Terrace, Jesmond,
Newcastle upon Tyne,
Tyne & Wear NE2 3BA
Tel: 0191 281 1768
Acting Head: Mr Michael Tippett
Age range: G3–18
No. of pupils: G850 VIth200
Fees: Day £8,409–£13,023
(♦) (A) (£) (✎) (16)

Newcastle Preparatory School
6 Eslington Road, Jesmond, Newcastle
upon Tyne, Tyne & Wear NE2 4RH
Tel: 0191 281 1769
Head of School: Ms Fiona Coleman
Age range: 3–11
No. of pupils: 270
Fees: Day £8,742–£11,307
(£) (✎)

Newcastle School for Boys
30 West Avenue, Gosforth, Newcastle
upon Tyne, Tyne & Wear NE3 4ES
Tel: 0191 255 9300
Headmaster: Mr David Tickner
Age range: B3–18
(♦) (A) (£) (✎) (16)

Royal Grammar School
Eskdale Terrace, Newcastle upon
Tyne, Tyne & Wear NE2 4DX
Tel: 0191 281 5711
Headmaster: Mr John Fern
Age range: 7–18
No. of pupils: 1325 VIth341
Fees: Day £10,662–£12,657
(A) (£) (✎) (16)

Westfield School
Oakfield Road, Gosforth, Newcastle
upon Tyne, Tyne & Wear NE3 4HS
Tel: 0191 255 3980
Headmaster: Mr Neil Walker
Age range: G3–18
No. of pupils: 315 VIth50
Fees: Day £7,755–£13,590
(♦) (🌐) (A) (16)

D324

North-West

KEY TO SYMBOLS

- ⚦ *Boys' school*
- ⚧ *Girls' school*
- 🌐 *International school*
- 16⁺ *Tutorial or sixth form college*
- Ⓐ *A levels*
- 🏛 *Boarding accommodation*
- £ *Bursaries*
- ⒤ᵇ *International Baccalaureate*
- ✎ *Learning support*
- 16⁺ *Entrance at 16+*
- 🎓 *Vocational qualifications*
- ⒤ᵃᵖˢ *Independent Association of Preparatory Schools*
- ⒣ᵐᶜ *The Headmasters' & Headmistresses' Conference*
- ⒤ˢᵃ *Independent Schools Association*
- ⒢ˢᵃ *Girls' School Association*
- Ⓑˢᵃ *Boarding Schools' Association*
- Ⓢ *Society of Heads*

Unless otherwise indicated, all schools are coeducational day schools. Single-sex and boarding schools will be indicated by the relevant icon.

Cheshire

Abbey Gate College
Saighton Grange, Saighton,
Chester, Cheshire CH3 6EN
Tel: 01244 332077
Head: Mrs Tracy Pollard
Age range: 4–18
No. of pupils: 468 VIth71
Fees: Day £8,955–£12,840
(A)(£)(✎)(16)

Alderley Edge School for Girls
Wilmslow Road, Alderley
Edge, Cheshire SK9 7QE
Tel: 01625 583028
Head of School: Mrs Helen Jeys
Age range: G2–18
(♟)(A)(£)(IB)(✎)(16)

Beech Hall School
Beech Hall Drive, Tytherington,
Macclesfield, Cheshire SK10 2EG
Tel: 01625 422192
Headmaster: Mr James Allen
Age range: 6 months–16 years
No. of pupils: 230
Fees: Day £9,720–£13,020
(£)(✎)

Bowdon Preparatory
School for Girls
Ashley Road, Altrincham,
Cheshire WA14 2LT
Tel: 0161 928 0678
Headmistress: Mrs Helen Gee
Age range: G3–11
No. of pupils: 200
(♟)

Brabyns Preparatory School
34-36 Arkwright Road, Marple,
Stockport, Cheshire SK6 7DB
Tel: 0161 427 2395
Headteacher: Mr Lee Sanders
Age range: 2–11
No. of pupils: 134
Fees: Day £1,900–£2,640
(£)(✎)

Cransley School
Belmont Hall, Great Budworth,
Northwich, Cheshire CW9 6HN
Tel: 01606 891747
Head of School: Mr Richard Pollock
LL.B, PGCE, PG Dip (RNCM)
Age range: 4–16
No. of pupils: 150
Fees: Day £7,923–£11,172
(£)(✎)

Greater Grace Christian School
Church Lane, Backford,
Chester, Cheshire CH2 4BE
Tel: 01244 851797
Head Teacher: Mrs A Mulligan
Age range: 5–18

Green Meadow Independent
Primary School
Robson Way, Lowton, Warrington,
Cheshire WA3 2RD
Tel: 01942 671138
Head: Mrs S Green
Age range: 4–11

Hale Preparatory School
Broomfield Lane, Hale,
Cheshire WA15 9AS
Tel: 0161 928 2386
Headmaster: Mr J F Connor
Age range: 4–11
No. of pupils: 202
Fees: Day £7,650

Lady Barn House School
Schools Hill, Cheadle, Cheshire SK7 1JE
Tel: 0161 428 2912
Age range: 3–11
No. of pupils: 483
Fees: Day £8,640
(£)(✎)

Pownall Hall School
Carrwood Road, Pownall Park,
Wilmslow, Cheshire SK9 5DW
Tel: 01625 523141
Headmaster: Mr David Goulbourn
Age range: 2–11
Fees: Day £8,475–£9,975
(✎)

Terra Nova School
Jodrell Bank, Holmes Chapel,
Crewe, Cheshire CW4 8BT
Tel: 01477 571251
Headmaster: Mr Philip Stewart
Age range: 3–13
No. of pupils: 295
Fees: Day £5,940–£14,697
(♟)(£)(✎)

The Firs School
Newton Lane, Upton, Chester,
Cheshire CH2 2HJ
Tel: 01244 322443
Head Teacher: Mrs L Davies
BA (Hons) Durham, PGCE
(Exeter), PGCDL (York), NP+
Age range: 3–11
No. of pupils: 172
Fees: Day £9,147
(£)(✎)

The Grange School
Bradburns Lane, Hartford,
Northwich, Cheshire CW8 1LU
Tel: 01606 74007 or 77447
Headmistress: Mrs Deborah Leonard
Age range: 4–18
No. of pupils: 1185 VIth193
Fees: Day £8,340–£11,160
(A)(£)(✎)(16)

The Hammond School
Mannings Lane, Chester,
Cheshire CH2 4ES
Tel: 01244 305350
Principal: Ms Maggie Evans BA
(Hons) MA, PGCE, NPQH, FRSA
Age range: 6–19
No. of pupils: 280
Fees: Day £8,370–£18,750
FB £20,400–£27,600
(♫)(♟)(A)(£)(✎)(16)

The King's School Chester
Wrexham Road, Chester,
Cheshire CH4 7QL
Tel: 01244 689500
Headmaster: G J Hartley MA, MSc
Age range: 4–18
No. of pupils: 1080 VIth218
Fees: Day £9,150–£13,515
(A)(£)(✎)(16)

The King's School in Macclesfield
Alderley Road, Prestbury,
Cheshire SK10 4SP
Tel: 01625 260000
Headmaster: Dr Simon Hyde
Age range: 3–18
No. of pupils: 1200 VIth250
Fees: Day £8,235–£12,990
(A)(£)(✎)(16)

The Queen's School
City Walls Road, Chester,
Cheshire CH1 2NN
Tel: 01244 312078
Headmistress: Mrs Sue
Wallace-Woodroffe
Age range: G4–18
No. of pupils: 610 VIth100
Fees: Day £9,351–£13,341
(♟)(A)(£)(16)

The Ryleys School
Ryleys Lane, Alderley Edge,
Cheshire SK9 7UY
Tel: 01625 583241
Headteacher: Mrs Julia Langford
Age range: 2–11
No. of pupils: 251
Fees: Day £10,260–£11,538
(£)(✎)

Wilmslow Preparatory School
Grove Avenue, Wilmslow,
Cheshire SK9 5EG
Tel: 01625 524246
Headteacher: Mrs Helen Rigby
Age range: 3–11
No. of pupils: 117
Fees: Day £4,635–£10,365
(£)(✎)

Yorston Lodge School
18 St John's Road, Knutsford,
Cheshire WA16 0DP
Tel: 01565 633177
Headmistress: Mrs J
Dallimore BEd(Hons)
Age range: 3–11
Fees: Day £8,250–£8,310

Cumbria

Austin Friars School
Etterby Scaur, Carlisle,
Cumbria CA3 9PB
Tel: 01228 528042
Headmaster: Mr Matt Harris
Age range: 3–18
No. of pupils: 507 VIth70
Fees: Day £7,653–£14,952
(A)(£)(✎)(16)

Casterton, Sedbergh
Preparatory School
Casterton, Carnforth, Cumbria LA6 2SG
Tel: 01524 279200
Headmaster: Mr Will Newman
BA(Ed) Hons MA
Age range: 3–13
No. of pupils: 210
(♟)(£)(✎)

Hunter Hall School
Frenchfield, Penrith, Cumbria CA11 8UA
Tel: 01768 891291
Head Teacher: Mrs Donna Vinsome
Age range: 3–11
No. of pupils: 101
Fees: Day £7,749–£8,979
(£)(✎)

Sedbergh School
Sedbergh, Cumbria LA10 5HG
Tel: 015396 20535
Headmaster: Mr A Fleck MA
Age range: 3–18
No. of pupils: 500 VIth200
Fees: Day £24,915 FB £33,840
🛌 Ⓐ ⓐ ⓔ 🖊 ⑯

Windermere School
Patterdale Road, Windermere,
Cumbria LA23 1NW
Tel: 015394 46164
Age range: 3–18
No. of pupils: 350
Fees: Day £18,300 WB
£31,050 FB £32,280
🛌 ⓐ ⓔ ⒾⒷ ⑯

**Windermere School,
Elleray Campus**
Ambleside Road, Windermere,
Cumbria LA23 1AP
Tel: +44 (0) 15394 43308
Head: Mrs Julie King
Age range: 3–11
No. of pupils: 75
ⓐ ⓔ 🖊

Greater Manchester

Abbey College Manchester
5-7 Cheapside, King Street,
Manchester, Greater
Manchester M2 4WG
Tel: 0161 817 2700
Principal: Ms Liz Elam
Age range: 15–19
No. of pupils: 220 VIth175
Fees: Day £12,750
⑯ Ⓐ ⓔ 🖊 ⑯

Abbotsford Preparatory School
211 Flixton Road, Urmston, Manchester,
Greater Manchester M41 5PR
Tel: 0161 748 3261
Head Teacher: Catherine Howard
Age range: 3–11
No. of pupils: 106
Fees: Day £7,029–£7,704
ⓔ

**Al Jamiatul Islamiyah –
Bolton Darul Uloom**
Mount St Joseph's Convent,
Willows Lane, Bolton, Greater
Manchester BL3 4HF
Tel: 01204 62622
Head of School: Dr A G Shaikh
Age range: B11–25
Ⓐ Ⓐ ⑯ 🛌

Altrincham Preparatory School
Marlborough Road, Bowdon,
Altrincham, Greater
Manchester WA14 2RR
Tel: 0161 928 3366
Headmaster: Mr Andrew C Potts
Age range: B2–11
No. of pupils: 310
Fees: Day £6,300–£8,340
Ⓐ 🖊

Beech House School
184 Manchester Road, Rochdale,
Greater Manchester OL11 4JQ
Tel: 01706 646309
Principal: Mr A Sartain BSc(Hons),
PGCE, DipSp, CBiol, FIBiol
Age range: 2–16
Fees: Day £5,376–£6,546
🖊

Beis Ruchel Girls School
1-7 Seymour Road, Crumpsall,
Manchester, Greater
Manchester M8 5BQ
Tel: 01617 951830
Headmistress: Mrs E Krausz
Age range: G3–11
ⓐ

Bnos Yisroel School
Foigel Esther Shine House,
Leicester Road, Manchester,
Greater Manchester M7 4DA
Tel: 0161 792 3896
Headmaster: Rabbi R Spitzer
Age range: G2–16
No. of pupils: 489
ⓐ

Bolton School (Boys' Division)
Chorley New Road, Bolton,
Greater Manchester BL1 4PA
Tel: 01204 840201
Headmaster: Philip J Britton MBE
Age range: B7–18
No. of pupils: VIth210
Fees: Day £9,771–£12,216
Ⓐ Ⓐ ⓔ 🖊 ⑯

Bolton School (Girls' Division)
Chorley New Road, Bolton,
Greater Manchester BL1 4PB
Tel: 01204 840201
Headmistress: Miss Sue
Hincks MA(Oxon)
Age range: B0–7 G0–18
No. of pupils: VIth210
Fees: Day £9,771–£12,216
Ⓐ 🖊

Branwood Preparatory School
Stafford Road, Monton,
Eccles, Manchester, Greater
Manchester M30 9HN
Tel: 0161 789 1054
Head of School: Mr Andrew Whittell
Age range: 3–11
No. of pupils: 156
Fees: Day £6,597
🖊

Bridgewater School
Drywood Hall, Worsley Road,
Worsley, Manchester, Greater
Manchester M28 2WQ
Tel: 0161 794 1463
Head Teacher: Mrs JAT Nairn
CertEd(Distinction)
Age range: 3–18
No. of pupils: 484
Ⓐ ⓔ ⑯

Bury Catholic Preparatory School
Arden House, Manchester Road,
Bury, Greater Manchester BL9 9BH
Tel: 0161 764 2346
Acting Headteacher: Mrs C Baumber
Age range: 3–11
Fees: Day £3,800–£6,486
ⓔ 🖊

Bury Grammar School Boys
Tenterden Street, Bury, Greater
Manchester BL9 0HN
Tel: 0161 797 2700
Headmaster: Mr D Cassidy
Age range: B7–18
No. of pupils: 602 VIth92
Fees: Day £7,992–£10,755
Ⓐ Ⓐ ⓔ 🖊 ⑯

Bury Grammar School for Girls
Bridge Road, Bury, Greater
Manchester BL9 0HH
Tel: 0161 696 8600
Headmistress: Mrs J Anderson
Age range: B4–7 G4–18
No. of pupils: VIth120
Fees: Day £7,836–£10,755
ⓐ Ⓐ ⓔ 🖊 ⑯

Cheadle Hulme School
Claremont Road, Cheadle Hulme,
Cheadle, Greater Manchester SK8 6EF
Tel: 0161 488 3345
Head: Mr Neil Smith
Age range: 4–18
No. of pupils: 1396 VIth254
Fees: Day £8,950–£11,880
Ⓐ ⓔ 🖊 ⑯

CHETHAM'S SCHOOL OF MUSIC
For further details see p.164
Long Millgate, Manchester,
Greater Manchester M3 1SB
Tel: 0161 834 9644
Email: aliceherbert@chethams.com
Website: www.chethams.com
Joint Principals: Nicola
Smith & Tom Redmond
Age range: 8–18
No. of pupils: 300
🛌 Ⓐ ⓐ 🖊 ⑯

Clarendon Cottage School
Ivy Bank House, Half Edge Lane,
Eccles, Manchester, Greater
Manchester M30 9BJ
Tel: 0161 950 7868
Headteacher: Mrs A Hartley
Age range: 3–11
No. of pupils: 81
Fees: Day £4,590–£4,740
🖊

Clevelands Preparatory School
425 Chorley New Road, Bolton,
Greater Manchester BL1 5DH
Tel: 01204 843898
Headteacher: Mrs Lesley Parlane
Age range: 2–11
No. of pupils: 141
Fees: Day £7,485
ⓔ

Covenant Christian School
The Hawthorns, 48 Heaton
Moor Road, Stockport, Greater
Manchester SK4 4NX
Tel: 0161 432 3782
Head: Dr Roger Slack
Age range: 5–16
No. of pupils: 32

**Darul Uloom Al Arabiya
Al Islamiya**
Holcombe Hall, Holcombe, Bury,
Greater Manchester BL8 4NG
Tel: 01706 826106
Head: Mr Mohammed Mulla
Age range: B11–23

**Farrowdale House
Preparatory School**
Farrow Street, Shaw, Oldham,
Greater Manchester OL2 7AD
Tel: 01706 844533
Headteacher: Miss Z. N.
Campbell BA (Hons) PGCE
Age range: 3–11
No. of pupils: 90
Fees: Day £5,790–£6,270

Forest Park School
Lauriston House, 27 Oakfield, Sale,
Greater Manchester M33 6NB
Tel: 0161 973 4835
Headteacher: Mr Tucker
Age range: 3–11
No. of pupils: 145
Fees: Day £6,690–£7,269

Forest Preparatory School
Moss Lane, Timperley, Altrincham,
Greater Manchester WA15 6LJ
Tel: 0161 980 4075
Headmaster: Rick Hyde
Age range: 2–11
No. of pupils: 197
Fees: Day £6,549–£7,395

Grafton House Preparatory School
1 Warrington Street, Ashton-under-
Lyne, Greater Manchester OL6 6XB
Tel: 0161 343 3015
Head: Mrs Pamela Oaks
Age range: 2–11
No. of pupils: 110

Greenbank Preparatory School
Heathbank Road, Cheadle Hulme,
Cheadle, Greater Manchester SK8 6HU
Tel: 0161 485 3724
Headmistress: Mrs J L Lowe
Age range: 3–11
Fees: Day £8,400

Hulme Hall Grammar School
Beech Avenue, Stockport,
Greater Manchester SK3 8HA
Tel: 0161 485 3524
Headmaster: Mr Dean Grierson
Age range: 2–16
No. of pupils: 200
Fees: Day £2,840–£3,300

**Kassim Darwish Grammar
School for Boys**
Hartley Hall, Alexandra Road
South, Manchester, Greater
Manchester M16 8NH
Tel: 0161 8607676
Headteacher: Mr Akhmed Hussain
Age range: B11–16

King of Kings School
142 Dantzic Street, Manchester,
Greater Manchester M4 4DN
Tel: 0161 834 4214
Head Teacher: Mrs B Lewis
Age range: 3–18
No. of pupils: 29

Lord's Independent School
53 Manchester Road, Bolton,
Greater Manchester BL2 1ES
Tel: 01204 523731
Headteacher: Mrs Anne Ainsworth
Age range: 11–16
No. of pupils: 83

Loreto Preparatory School
Dunham Road, Altrincham,
Greater Manchester WA14 4GZ
Tel: 0161 928 8310
Headteacher: Mrs Anne Roberts
Age range: G3–11

**Madrasatul Imam
Muhammad Zakariya**
Keswick Street, Bolton, Greater
Manchester BL1 8LX
Tel: 01204 384434
Headteacher: Mrs Amena Sader
Age range: G11–19

Manchester High School for Girls
Grangethorpe Road, Manchester,
Greater Manchester M14 6HS
Tel: 0161 224 0447
Head Mistress: Mrs A C Hewitt
Age range: G4–18
No. of pupils: 936 VIth182
Fees: Day £8,712–£11,874

**Manchester Islamic
High School for Girls**
55 High Lane, Chorlton, Manchester,
Greater Manchester M21 9FA
Tel: 0161 881 2127
Headmistress: Mrs Mona Mohamed
Age range: G11–16

Manchester Junior Girls School
64 Upper Park Road, Salford,
Greater Manchester M7 4JA
Tel: 0161 740 0566
Head of School: Ms Esther Lieberman
Age range: G3–11

**Manchester Muslim
Preparatory School**
551 Wilmslow Road, Withington,
Manchester, Greater
Manchester M20 4BA
Tel: 0161 445 5452
Head Teacher: Mrs Doris
Ghafori-Kanno
Age range: 3–11
No. of pupils: 186
Fees: Day £5,225–£5,500

Mechinoh School
13 Upper Park Road, Salford,
Greater Manchester M7 4HY
Tel: 0161 7959275
Head of School: Rabbi N Baddiel
Age range: B11–16

Monton Village Nursery School
The School House, Francis Street,
Monton, Manchester, Greater
Manchester M30 9PR
Tel: 0161 789 0472
Age range: 1–7

Moor Allerton Preparatory School
131 Barlow Moor Road, West
Didsbury, Manchester, Greater
Manchester M20 2PW
Tel: 0161 445 4521
Headmistress: Mrs Adriana Ewart-Jones
Age range: 3–11
Fees: Day £8,310–£8,550

Oldham Hulme Grammar School
Chamber Road, Oldham,
Greater Manchester OL8 4BX
Tel: 0161 624 4497
Principal: Mr CJD Mairs
Age range: 2–18
No. of pupils: 766
Fees: Day £8,220–£11,235

OYY Lubavitch Girls School
Beis Menachem, Park Lane, Salford,
Greater Manchester M7 4JD
Tel: 0161 795 0002
Headmistress: Mrs J Hanson
Age range: 2–16
No. of pupils: 82

Prestwich Preparatory School
St Margaret's Building, 400 Bury
Old Road, Prestwich, Manchester,
Greater Manchester M25 1PZ
Tel: 0161 773 1223
Headmistress: Miss P Shiels
Age range: 2–11
No. of pupils: 122
Fees: Day £6,300

Rochdale Islamic Academy
Greenbank Road, Rochdale,
Greater Manchester OL12 0HZ
Tel: 01706 710184
Headteacher: Mrs Aishah Akhtar
Age range: G11–16
No. of pupils: 165
Fees: Day £1,600

St Ambrose Preparatory School
Hale Barns, Altrincham, Greater
Manchester WA15 0HF
Tel: 0161 903 9193
Headmaster: F J Driscoll
Age range: B3–11 G3–4

St Bede's College
Alexandra Park Road, Manchester,
Greater Manchester M16 8HX
Tel: 0161 226 3323
Headmaster: Dr Richard Robson
Age range: 3–18
Fees: Day £8,076–£11,325

Stella Maris Junior School
St Johns Road, Heaton Mersey,
Stockport, Greater Manchester SK4 3BR
Tel: 0161 432 0532
Headteacher: Mrs N Johnson
Age range: 3–11
No. of pupils: 68
Fees: Day £7,713

Stockport Grammar School
Buxton Road, Stockport, Greater
Manchester SK2 7AF
Tel: 0161 456 9000
Headmaster: Dr Paul Owen
Age range: 3–18
No. of pupils: 1439 VIth193
Fees: Day £8,766–£11,700
Ⓐ ⓔ ⌗ ⑯

Tashbar of Manchester
20 Upper Park Road, Salford,
Greater Manchester M7 4HL
Tel: 01617 208254
Head of School: Rabbi
David Hammond
Age range: B3–12
⚘

**The Chadderton Preparatory
Grammar School**
Broadway, Chadderton, Oldham,
Greater Manchester OL9 0AD
Tel: 0161 6206570
Headteacher: Mrs Caroline
Greenwood
Age range: 2–11
Fees: Day £6,270
ⓔ ⌗

The Manchester Grammar School
Old Hall Lane, Fallowfield, Manchester,
Greater Manchester M13 0XT
Tel: 0161 224 7201
High Master: Dr Martin Boulton
Age range: B7–18
Fees: Day £12,570
⚘ ⚘ Ⓐ ⓔ ⌗ ⑯

Trinity Christian School
Birbeck Street, Stalybridge,
Greater Manchester SK15 1SH
Tel: 0161 303 0674
Head: Mr Michael Stewart
Age range: 3–16
Fees: Day £4,038–£5,874
⌗

Withington Girls' School
Wellington Road, Fallowfield,
Manchester, Greater
Manchester M14 6BL
Tel: 0161 224 1077
Headmistress: Mrs S J Haslam BA
Age range: G7–18
No. of pupils: 660 VIth150
Fees: Day £9,195–£12,252
⚘ Ⓐ ⓔ ⌗ ⑯

Yeshivah Ohr Torah School
28 Broom Lane, Salford, Greater
Manchester M7 4FX
Tel: 01617 921230
Headteacher: Rabbi Y Wind
Age range: B11–16
⚘

Isle of Man

King William's College
Castletown, Isle of Man IM9 1TP
Tel: +44 (0)1624 820110
Principal: Mr Joss Buchanan
Age range: 11–18
No. of pupils: 370
Fees: Day £18,250–£23,250
FB £29,250–£34,250
⊕ ⚘ ⓔ ⒤Ⓑ ⌗ ⑯

The Buchan School
Westhill, Arbory Road, Castletown,
Isle of Man IM9 1RD
Tel: +44 (0)1624 820481
Head of School: G R Shaw-Twilley

Lancashire

Abrar Academy
34-36 Garstang Road, Preston,
Lancashire PR1 1NA
Tel: 01772 82 87 32
Head of School: Mr A Chowdhury
Age range: 11–21
⚘ ⚘

AKS Lytham
Clifton Drive South, Lytham St
Annes, Lancashire FY8 1DT
Tel: 01253 784100
Headmaster: Mr. Mike Walton
BA, MA (Ed), PGCE, NPQH
Age range: 2–18
No. of pupils: 800 VIth165
Fees: Day £8,895–£11,787
Ⓐ ⓔ ⌗ ⑯

Al Islah Girls High School
108 Audley Range, Blackburn,
Lancashire BB1 1TF
Tel: 01254 261573
Headteacher: Ms Nikhat Pardesi
Age range: G11–16
⚘

Ashbridge Independent School
Lindle Lane, Hutton, Preston,
Lancashire PR4 4AQ
Tel: 01772 619900
Headteacher: Karen Mehta
Age range: 0–11
No. of pupils: 315
Fees: Day £7,800
⌗

Ghausia Girls' High School
1-3 Cross Street, Nelson,
Lancashire BB9 7EN
Tel: 01282 699214
Headteacher: Miss B Ghafoor
Age range: G11–16
⚘

Heathland School
Broad Oak, Sandy Lane,
Accrington, Lancashire BB5 2AN
Tel: 01254 234284
Principal: Mrs J Harrison
BA(Hons), CertEd, FRSA
Age range: 4–16

Highfield Priory School
Fulwood Row, Fulwood, Preston,
Lancashire PR2 5RW
Tel: 01772 709624
Headteacher: Mrs Sarah H Lyons
Age range: 18 months–11 years
No. of pupils: 273
Fees: Day £7,850
ⓔ

Islamiyah School
Willow Street, Blackburn,
Lancashire BB1 5RQ
Tel: 01254 661 259
Headteacher: Mr Yusuf Seedat
Age range: G11–16
No. of pupils: 178
⚘

Jamea Al Kauthar
Ashton Road, Lancaster,
Lancashire LA1 5AJ
Tel: +44 (0)1524 389898
Age range: G11–16
⚘ ⚘

Jamiatul-Ilm Wal-Huda UK School
15 Moss Street, Blackburn,
Lancashire BB1 5HW
Tel: 01254 673105
Headteacher: Mr A Ahmed
Age range: B11–16
No. of pupils: 348
⚘

Kirkham Grammar School
Ribby Road, Kirkham, Preston,
Lancashire PR4 2BH
Tel: 01772 684264
Headmaster: Mr Daniel Berry
Age range: 3–18 years
No. of pupils: 850 VIth180
⚘ Ⓐ ⚘ ⓔ ⌗ ⑯

Lancaster Steiner School
Lune Road, Lancaster,
Lancashire LA1 5QU
Tel: 01524 381876
Age range: 0–11

Markazul Uloom
Park Lee Road, Blackburn,
Lancashire BB2 3NY
Tel: 01254 581569
Head of School: Mr S Bargit
Age range: G11–19

Moorland School
Ribblesdale Avenue, Clitheroe,
Lancashire BB7 2JA
Tel: 01200 423833
Principal: Mr Jonathan Harrison
Age range: 3 months–16 years
Fees: Day £6,996–£9,996 WB
£18,000–£22,800 FB £19,800–£24,900
🏫 £

Oakhill School and Nursery
Wiswell Lane, Whalley, Clitheroe,
Lancashire BB7 9AF
Tel: 01254 823546
Head of School: Mrs Jane Buttery
Age range: 2–16
No. of pupils: 330
Fees: Day £7,440–£11,574
£ 🖊

ROSSALL SCHOOL
For further details see p.168
Broadway, Fleetwood,
Lancashire FY7 8JW
Tel: +44 (0)1253 774201
Email: admissions@rossall.org.uk
Website: www.rossall.org.uk
Head: Mr Jeremy Quartermain
Age range: 0–18
No. of pupils: 665 VIth170
Fees: Day £8,445–£13,740
FB £21,645–£39,210
🏫 Ⓐ 🏫 £ Ⓘ🅑 🖊 16 🏴

Scarisbrick Hall School
Southport Road, Scarisbrisk,
Ormskirk, Lancashire L40 9RQ
Tel: 01704 841151
Headmaster: Mr J Shaw
Age range: 0–18
Fees: Day £7,185–£11,160
Ⓐ £ 🖊

**St Anne's College
Grammar School**
293 Clifton Drive South, Lytham
St Annes, Lancashire FY8 1HN
Tel: +44 (0)1253 725815
Principal: Mr S R Welsby
Age range: 2–18
No. of pupils: VIth16
Fees: Day £5,370–£7,320
Ⓐ 🏫 £ 🖊 16

St Joseph's School, Park Hill
Park Hill, Padiham Road,
Burnley, Lancashire BB12 6TG
Tel: 01282 455622
Headmistress: Mrs Annette Robinson
Age range: 3–11
Fees: Day £6,195

St Pius X Preparatory School
Oak House, 200 Garstang Road,
Fulwood, Preston, Lancashire PR2 8RD
Tel: 01772 719937
Acting Head Teacher: Mrs H Porter
Age range: 2–11
No. of pupils: 260
Fees: Day £7,800
£ 🖊

Stonyhurst College
Stonyhurst, Clitheroe,
Lancashire BB7 9PZ
Tel: 01254 827073
Headmaster: Mr John
Browne BA LLB MBA
Age range: 13–18
No. of pupils: 756
Fees: Day £20,550 WB
£30,750 FB £35,850
🏫 Ⓐ 🏫 £ Ⓘ🅑 🖊 16

Stonyhurst St Mary's Hall
Stonyhurst, Lancashire BB7 9PU
Tel: 01254 827073
Headmaster: Mr Ian Murphy
BA (Hons), PGCE Durham
Age range: 3–13
No. of pupils: 272
Fees: Day £8,370–£15,960
WB £21,330 FB £24,570
Ⓐ 🏫 £ Ⓘ🅑 🖊

The Alternative School
The Old Library, Fern Lea Avenue,
Barnoldswick, Lancashire BB18 5DW
Tel: 01282 851800
**Founder and Executive
Head:** Ms Kirsty-Anne Pugh
Age range: 8–18

Westholme School
Meins Road, Blackburn,
Lancashire BB2 6QU
Tel: 01254 506070
Principal: Mrs Lynne Horner
Age range: 2–18
No. of pupils: 792 VIth72
Fees: Day £7,890–£10,875
Ⓐ £ 🖊 16

Merseyside

Auckland College
65-67 Parkfield Road, Wavertree,
Liverpool, Merseyside L17 4LE
Tel: 0151 727 0083
Headteacher: Miss Stephanie Boyd
Age range: 0–18
No. of pupils: 172 VIth15
Fees: Day £5,000–£7,500
Ⓐ 🖊

Avalon Preparatory School
Caldy Road, West Kirby, Wirral,
Merseyside CH48 2HE
Tel: 0151 625 6993
Age range: 2–11
No. of pupils: 178
Fees: Day £4,539–£8,469
🖊

Belvedere Preparatory School
23 Belvidere Road, Princes Park,
Aigburth, Liverpool, Merseyside L8 3TF
Tel: 0151 471 1137
Age range: 3–11
No. of pupils: 180

Birkenhead School
The Lodge, 58 Beresford Road,
Birkenhead, Merseyside CH43 2JD
Tel: 0151 652 4014
Headmaster: Mr Paul Vicars
Age range: 3 months–18 years
No. of pupils: VIth103
Fees: Day £8,010–£11,994
Ⓐ £ 🖊 16

**Carleton House
Preparatory School**
145 Menlove Avenue, Liverpool,
Merseyside L18 3EE
Tel: 0151 722 0756
Head of School: Mrs Sandy Coleman
Age range: 3–11
No. of pupils: 179
Fees: Day £7,771
🖊

Christian Fellowship School
Overbury Street, Edge Hill,
Liverpool, Merseyside L7 3HL
Tel: 0151 709 1642
Headteacher: Mr Richard Worsley
Age range: 4–16
No. of pupils: 136
Fees: Day £2,628–£5,220
£ 🖊

Merchant Taylors' Boys' School
186 Liverpool Road, Crosby,
Liverpool, Merseyside L23 0QP
Tel: 0151 928 3308
Headmaster: Mr Deiniol Williams
Age range: B7–18
No. of pupils: 727
Fees: Day £8,517–£11,394
🏫 Ⓐ £ 🖊 16

Merchant Taylors' Girls' School
Liverpool Road, Crosby,
Liverpool, Merseyside L23 5SP
Tel: 0151 924 3140
Headmistress: Mrs Claire Tao
Age range: B4–7 G4–18
No. of pupils: 801
Fees: Day £8,517–£11,394
🏫 Ⓐ £ 🖊 16

Prenton Preparatory School
Mount Pleasant, Oxton, Wirral,
Merseyside CH43 5SY
Tel: 0151 652 3182
Headteacher: Mr M Jones BSC Hons, PGCE
Age range: 2–11
Fees: Day £800–£8,586
£ 🖊

St Mary's College
Everest Road, Crosby, Liverpool,
Merseyside L23 5TW
Tel: 0151 924 3926
Principal: Mr Michael Kennedy Bsc, MA
No. of pupils: 880 VIth132
Fees: Day £7,573–£11,161
Ⓐ £ 🖊 16

Tower College
Mill Lane, Rainhill, Prescot,
Merseyside L35 6NE
Tel: 0151 426 4333
Principal: Miss R J Oxley NNEB, RSH
Age range: 3–16
🖊

South-East

*See also Greater London (D299)
for schools in Kent and Surrey

KEY TO SYMBOLS
- (♂) *Boys' school*
- (♀) *Girls' school*
- (🌐) *International school*
- (16) *Tutorial or sixth form college*
- (Ⓐ) *A levels*
- (🏛) *Boarding accommodation*
- (£) *Bursaries*
- (IB) *International Baccalaureate*
- (✐) *Learning support*
- (16) *Entrance at 16+*
- (💼) *Vocational qualifications*
- (IAPS) *Independent Association of Preparatory Schools*
- (HMC) *The Headmasters' & Headmistresses' Conference*
- (ISA) *Independent Schools Association*
- (GSA) *Girls' School Association*
- (BSA) *Boarding Schools' Association*
- (S) *Society of Heads*

*Unless otherwise indicated, all schools are coeducational day schools.
Single-sex and boarding schools will be indicated by the relevant icon.*

Berkshire

Alder Bridge School
Bridge House, Mill Lane, Padworth,
Reading, Berkshire RG7 4JU
Tel: 0118 971 4471
Age range: 0–14 years
No. of pupils: 65
Fees: Day £6,015–£8,880

Bradfield College
Bradfield, Berkshire RG7 6AU
Tel: 0118 964 4516
Headmaster: Dr Christopher Stevens
Age range: 13–18
No. of pupils: 815
Fees: Day £31,080 FB £38,850

Caversham School
16 Peppard Road, Caversham,
Reading, Berkshire RG4 8JZ
Tel: 01189 478 684
Head: Mr Chris Neal
Age range: 4–11
No. of pupils: 60
Fees: Day £9,900

Claires Court Junior Boys
Maidenhead Thicket,
Maidenhead, Berkshire SL6 3QE
Tel: 01628 327700
Head: J M E Spanswick
Age range: B4–11
No. of pupils: 248
Fees: Day £9,270–£15,930

Claires Court Nursery, Girls and Sixth Form
1 College Avenue, Maidenhead,
Berkshire SL6 6AW
Tel: 01628 327700
Head of School: Mrs M Heywood
Age range: B16–18 G3–18
No. of pupils: 495 VIth111
Fees: Day £9,270–£16,740

Claires Court Senior Boys
Ray Mill Road East, Maidenhead,
Berkshire SL6 8TE
Tel: 01628 327700
Headmaster: Mr J M Rayer BSc, PGCE
Age range: B11–16
No. of pupils: 335 VIth112
Fees: Day £15,930–£16,740

Crosfields School
Shinfield, Reading, Berkshire RG2 9BL
Tel: 0118 987 1810
Headmaster: Mr Craig Watson
Age range: 3–13
No. of pupils: 510
Fees: Day £10,314–£15,159

Deenway Montessori School & Unicity College
3-5 Sidmouth Street, Reading,
Berkshire RG1 4QX
Tel: 0118 9574737
Headmaster: Mr Munawar Karim
LL.B (Hons), M.A, Mont. Dip.
Age range: 3–11

Dolphin School
Waltham Road, Hurst, Reading,
Berkshire RG10 0FR
Tel: 0118 934 1277
Head: Mr Adam Hurst
Age range: 3–13
Fees: Day £10,170–£14,070

EAGLE HOUSE SCHOOL
For further details see p.182
Sandhurst, Berkshire GU47 8PH
Tel: 01344 772134
Email: info@eaglehouseschool.com
Website:
www.eaglehouseschool.com
Headmaster: Mr A P N
Barnard BA(Hons), PGCE
Age range: 3–13
No. of pupils: 380
Fees: Day £12,030–£18,810 FB £25,275

Elstree School
Woolhampton, Reading,
Berkshire RG7 5TD
Tel: 0118 971 3302
Headmaster: Mr S Inglis
Age range: B3–13 G3–8
No. of pupils: 248
Fees: Day £11,550–£21,000 WB
£26,250–£26,850 FB £26,700–£27,300

Eton College
Windsor, Berkshire SL4 6DW
Tel: 01753 671249
Head Master: Simon Henderson MA
Age range: B13–18
No. of pupils: 1300 VIth520
Fees: FB £40,668

Eton End PNEU School
35 Eton Road, Datchet,
Slough, Berkshire SL3 9AX
Tel: 01753 541075
Headmistress: Sarah Stokes
BA(Hons), PGCE
Age range: B3–7 G3–11
No. of pupils: 245
Fees: Day £9,375–£11,985

Heathfield School
London Road, Ascot, Berkshire SL5 8BQ
Tel: 01344 898342
Head of School: Mrs Marina
Gardiner Legge
Age range: G11–18
No. of pupils: 200

Hemdean House School
Hemdean Road, Caversham,
Reading, Berkshire RG4 7SD
Tel: 0118 947 2590
Head Teacher: Mrs H Chalmers BSc
Age range: B4–11 G4–11
Fees: Day £8,490–£9,300

Herries Preparatory School
Dean Lane, Cookham
Dean, Berkshire SL6 9BD
Tel: 01628 483350
Headmistress: Fiona Long
Age range: 3–11 years

Highfield Preparatory School
2 West Road, Maidenhead,
Berkshire SL6 1PD
Tel: 01628 624918
Headteacher: Mrs Joanna Leach
Age range: B3–5 G3–11
No. of pupils: 107
Fees: Day £1,119–£12,675

Holme Grange School
Heathlands Road, Wokingham,
Berkshire RG40 3AL
Tel: 0118 978 1566
Headteacher: Mrs Claire Robinson
BA (Open) PGCE NPQH
Age range: 3–16 years
No. of pupils: 509
Fees: Day £11,160–£15,525

Lambrook School
Winkfield Row, Nr Ascot,
Berkshire RG42 6LU
Tel: 01344 882717
Headmaster: Mr Jonathan Perry
Age range: 3–13
No. of pupils: 570
Fees: Day £12,669–£20,310
WB £22,740–£24,354

Leighton Park School
Shinfield Road, Reading,
Berkshire RG2 7ED
Tel: 0118 987 9600
Head: Mr Matthew L S Judd BA, PGCE
Age range: 11–18
No. of pupils: 491

Long Close School
Upton Court Road, Upton,
Slough, Berkshire SL3 7LU
Tel: 01753 520095
Headteacher: Miss K Nijjar
BA (Hons), Med, MA
Age range: 2–16
No. of pupils: 329

Luckley House School
Luckley Road, Wokingham,
Berkshire RG40 3EU
Tel: 0118 978 4175
Head: Mrs Jane Tudor
Age range: 11–18
No. of pupils: 300
Fees: Day £5,662 WB £9,183 FB £9,907

Ludgrove
Wokingham, Berkshire RG40 3AB
Tel: 0118 978 9881
Head of School: Mr Simon Barber
Age range: B8–13
No. of pupils: 190

LVS Ascot
London Road, Ascot, Berkshire SL5 8DR
Tel: 01344 882770
Headmistress: Mrs Christine
Cunniffe BA (Hons), MMus, MBA
Age range: 4–18
No. of pupils: 830
Fees: Day £10,380–£18,606
FB £26,562–£32,691

Meadowbrook Montessori School
Malt Hill Road, Warfield,
Bracknell, Berkshire RG42 6JQ
Tel: 01344 890869
Director of Education: Mrs S Gunn
Age range: 3–11
No. of pupils: 78
Fees: Day £10,044–£11,385

Newbold School
Popeswood Road, Binfield,
Bracknell, Berkshire RG42 4AH
Tel: 01344 421088
Headteacher: Mrs Jaki Crissey
MA, BA, PGCE Primary
Age range: 3–11
Fees: Day £4,500

Our Lady's Preparatory School
The Avenue, Crowthorne,
Wokingham, Berkshire RG45 6PB
Tel: 01344 773394
Headmistress: Mrs Helene Robinson
Age range: 3 months–11 years
No. of pupils: 100
Fees: Day £7,080

Padworth College
Padworth, Reading, Berkshire RG7 4NR
Tel: 0118 983 2644
Acting Principal: Mr Chris Randell
Age range: 13–19
No. of pupils: 116 VIth50
Fees: Day £14,400 FB £29,400

Pangbourne College
Pangbourne, Reading,
Berkshire RG8 8LA
Tel: 0118 984 2101
Headmaster: Thomas J C Garnier
Age range: 11–18
No. of pupils: 450 VIth134
Fees: Day £18,000–£25,380
FB £25,860–£36,660

Papplewick School
Windsor Road, Ascot, Berkshire SL5 7LH
Tel: 01344 621488
Head: Mr Tom Bunbury
Age range: B6–13
No. of pupils: 195

Queen Anne's School
6 Henley Road, Caversham,
Reading, Berkshire RG4 6DX
Tel: 0118 918 7300
Headmistress: Mrs Julia Harrington
BA(Hons), PGCE, NPQH
Age range: G11–18

Reading Blue Coat School
Holme Park, Sonning Lane, Sonning,
Reading, Berkshire RG4 6SU
Tel: 0118 944 1005
Headmaster: Mr Jesse Elzinga
Age range: B11–18 G16–18
No. of pupils: 710 VIth230
Fees: Day £16,695

Reddam House Berkshire
Bearwood Road, Sindlesham,
Wokingham, Berkshire RG41 5BG
Tel: 0118 974 8300
Principal: Mrs Tammy Howard
Age range: 3 months–18 years
No. of pupils: 570
Fees: Day £11,100–£17,970 WB
£27,165–£31,305 FB £28,665–£32,805

**Redroofs School for the Performing
Arts (Redroofs Theatre School)**
26 Bath Road, Maidenhead,
Berkshire SL6 4JT
Tel: 01628 674092
Principal: June Rose
Age range: 8–18
No. of pupils: 100
Fees: Day £4,882–£5,527

St Andrew's School
Buckhold, Pangbourne,
Reading, Berkshire RG8 8QA
Tel: 0118 974 4276
Headmaster: Mr Jonathan
Bartlett BSc QTS
Age range: 3–13
Fees: Day £5,430–£18,150 WB £3,360

St Bernard's Preparatory School
Hawtrey Close, Slough, Berkshire SL1 1TB
Tel: 01753 521821
Head Teacher: Mr N Cheesman
Age range: 2–11
Fees: Day £8,850–£10,545

St Edward's Prep
64 Tilehurst Road, Reading,
Berkshire RG30 2JH
Tel: 0118 957 4342
Headmaster: Derek Suttie
Age range: B4–11
No. of pupils: 170
Fees: Day £6,585–£11,025

St George's Ascot
Wells Lane, Ascot, Berkshire SL5 7DZ
Tel: 01344 629920
Headmistress: Mrs Liz Hewer
MA (Hons) (Cantab) PGCE
Age range: G11–18
No. of pupils: 270 VIth70
Fees: Day £22,800 WB
£34,050–£34,680 FB £35,460

St George's School Windsor Castle
Windsor Castle, Windsor,
Berkshire SL4 1QF
Tel: 01753 865553
Head Master: Mr W Goldsmith
BA (Hons), FRSA, FCCT
Age range: 3–13

**St John's Beaumont
Preparatory School**
Priest Hill, Old Windsor, Berkshire SL4 2JN
Tel: 01784 432428
Headmaster: Mr G E F Delaney
BA(Hons), PGCE, MSc
Age range: B3–13
No. of pupils: 270
Fees: Day £3,410–£6,525
FB £7,647–£10,005

St Joseph's College
Upper Redlands Road,
Reading, Berkshire RG1 5JT
Tel: 0118 966 1000
Headmaster: Mr Andrew Colpus
Age range: 3–18
No. of pupils: VIth65
Fees: Day £6,672–£11,406

St Mary's School Ascot
St Mary's Road, Ascot, Berkshire SL5 9JF
Tel: 01344 296614
Headmistress: Mrs Danuta Staunton
Age range: G11–18
No. of pupils: 386 VIth120
Fees: Day £27,630 FB £38,790

St Piran's Preparatory School
Gringer Hill, Maidenhead,
Berkshire SL6 7LZ
Tel: 01628 594302
Headmaster: Mr J A Carroll
BA(Hons), BPhilEd, PGCE, NPQH
Age range: 3–11
Fees: Day £10,857–£16,566

Sunningdale School
Dry Arch Road, Sunningdale,
Berkshire SL5 9PY
Tel: 01344 620159
Headmaster: Tom Dawson MA, PGCE
Age range: B7–13
No. of pupils: 90

Teikyo School UK
Framewood Road, Wexham,
Slough, Berkshire SL2 4QS
Tel: 01753 663711
Headmaster: Tadashi Nakayama
Age range: 16–18

The Abbey School
Kendrick Road, Reading,
Berkshire RG1 5DZ
Tel: 0118 987 2256
Head: Mr Will Le Fleming
Age range: G3–18
No. of pupils: 1059
Fees: Day £17,640

The Marist Preparatory School
King's Road, Sunninghill,
Ascot, Berkshire SL5 7PS
Tel: 01344 626137
Vice Principal: Jane Gow
Age range: G2–11
No. of pupils: 225
Fees: Day £9,780–£11,940

The Marist School
King's Road, Sunninghill,
Ascot, Berkshire SL5 7PS
Tel: 01344 624291
Principal: Mr Karl McCloskey
Age range: G3–18

The Oratory Preparatory School
Great Oaks, Goring Heath,
Reading, Berkshire RG8 7SF
Tel: 0118 984 4511
Headmaster: Mr Rob Stewart
Age range: 2–13
No. of pupils: 400
Fees: Day £10,266–£16,443
WB £21,153 FB £24,522

The Oratory School
Woodcote, Reading, Berkshire RG8 0PJ
Tel: 01491 683500
Head Master: Mr J J Smith
BA(Hons), MEd, PGCE
Age range: B11–18
No. of pupils: 380 VIth120
Fees: Day £24,966 FB £34,299

The Vine Christian School
SORCF Christian Centre,
Basingstoke Road, Three Mile Cross,
Reading, Berkshire RG7 1AT
Tel: 0118 988 6464
Head of School: Mrs Eve Strike
Age range: 5–13
No. of pupils: 9

UPTON HOUSE SCHOOL
For further details see p.218
115 St Leonard's Road,
Windsor, Berkshire SL4 3DF
Tel: 01753 862610
Email: registrar@uptonhouse.org.uk
Website: www.uptonhouse.org.uk
Head: Mrs Rhian Thornton BA
(Hons) NPQH LLE PGCE
Age range: 2–11 years
No. of pupils: 245
Fees: Day £3,143–£5,225

Waverley School
Waverley Way, Finchampstead,
Wokingham, Berkshire RG40 4YD
Tel: 0118 973 1121
Principal: Mr Guy Shore
Age range: 3–11
Fees: Day £8,589–£11,982

WELLINGTON COLLEGE
For further details see p.222
Duke's Ride, Crowthorne,
Berkshire RG45 7PU
Tel: +44 (0)1344 444000
Email: admissions@
wellingtoncollege.org.uk
Website:
www.wellingtoncollege.org.uk
Master: Mr James Dahl
Age range: 13–18
No. of pupils: 1080 VIth485
Fees: Day £30,375–
£34,890 FB £41,580

Buckinghamshire

Gayhurst School
Bull Lane, Gerrards Cross,
Buckinghamshire SL9 8RJ
Tel: 01753 882690
Headmaster: Gareth R A Davies
Age range: 3–11
Fees: Day £12,159–£15,438

MALTMAN'S GREEN SCHOOL
For further details see p.192
Maltmans Lane, Gerrards Cross,
Buckinghamshire SL9 8RR
Tel: 01753 883022
Email: registrar@
maltmansgreen.com
Website: www.maltmansgreen.com
Headmistress: Mrs Jill Walker
BSc (Hons), MA Ed, PGCE
Age range: G2–11
No. of pupils: 355
Fees: Day £1,925–£5,275

St Mary's School
94 Packhorse Road, Gerrards
Cross, Buckinghamshire SL9 8JQ
Tel: 01753 883370
Head of School: Mrs P Adams
Age range: G3–18
No. of pupils: 350 VIth50
Fees: Day £5,670–£16,980

Thorpe House School
Oval Way, Gerrards Cross,
Buckinghamshire SL9 8QA
Tel: 01753 882474
Headmaster: Mr Terence Ayres
Age range: B3–16
Fees: Day £10,950–£16,962

East Sussex

Ashdown House School
Forest Row, East Sussex RH18 5JY
Tel: 01342 822574
Headmaster: Mike Davies
Age range: 4–13
No. of pupils: 141
Fees: Day £8,970–£20,100 FB £27,450

Bartholomews Tutorial College
22-23 Prince Albert Street,
Brighton, East Sussex BN1 1HF
Tel: 01273 205965/205141
Director of Studies: Mike Balmer BEd
Age range: 16+
No. of pupils: 40 VIth25
Fees: Day £25,000 WB
£30,000 FB £30,000

Battle Abbey School
Battle, East Sussex TN33 0AD
Tel: 01424 772385
Headmaster: Mr D Clark BA(Hons)
Age range: 2–18
No. of pupils: 286 VIth48
Fees: Day £6,939–£16,914
FB £26,649–£31,932

Bede's School
The Dicker, Upper Dicker,
Hailsham, East Sussex BN27 3QH
Tel: +44 (0)1323843252
Head: Mr Peter Goodyer
Age range: 3 months–18
No. of pupils: 800 VIth295
Fees: Day £10,230–£17,400
FB £22,290–£25,650

Bellerbys College Brighton
1 Billinton Way, Brighton,
East Sussex BN1 4LF
Tel: +44 (0)1273 339333
Principal: Mr Simon Mower
Age range: 13–18

Brighton & Hove Montessori School
67 Stanford Avenue, Brighton,
East Sussex BN1 6FB
Tel: 01273 702485
Headteacher: Mrs Daisy
Cockburn AMI, MontDip
Age range: 2–11

Brighton College
Eastern Road, Brighton,
East Sussex BN2 0AL
Tel: 01273 704200
Head Master: Richard Cairns MA
Age range: 3–18
No. of pupils: 950
Fees: Day £10,050–£24,540 WB
£33,390–£34,410 FB £37,470–£45,210

Brighton Girls GDST
Montpelier Road, Brighton,
East Sussex BN1 3AT
Tel: 01273 280280
Head: Jennifer Smith
Age range: G3–18
No. of pupils: 680 VIth70
Fees: Day £7,191–£14,421

Brighton Steiner School
John Howard House, Roedean Road,
Brighton, East Sussex BN2 5RA
Tel: 01273 386300
**Chair of the College of
Teachers:** Carrie Rawle
Age range: 3–16
Fees: Day £7,800–£8,100

Buckswood School
Broomham Hall, Rye Road, Guestling,
Hastings, East Sussex TN35 4LT
Tel: 01424 813 813
School Director: Mr Giles Sutton
Age range: 10–19
No. of pupils: 420

Charters Ancaster
Woodsgate Place, Gunters Lane,
Bexhill-on-Sea, East Sussex TN39 4EB
Tel: 01424 216670
Nursery Manager: Susannah Crump
Age range: 6 months–5
No. of pupils: 125

**Claremont Preparatory
& Nursery School**
Ebdens Hill, Baldslow, St Leonards-
on-Sea, East Sussex TN37 7PW
Tel: 01424 751555
Headmistress: Abra Stoakley
Age range: 1–13
Fees: Day £6,900–£12,600

**Claremont Senior &
Sixth Form School**
Bodiam, Nr Robertsbridge,
East Sussex TN32 5UJ
Tel: 01580 830396
Headmaster: Mr. Giles Perrin
Age range: 14–18
Fees: Day £17,400

Darvell School
Darvell, Brightling Road,
Robertsbridge, East Sussex TN32 5DR
Tel: 01580 883300
Head of School: Mr Timothy Maas
Age range: 4–16

Deepdene School
195 New Church Road, Hove,
East Sussex BN3 4ED
Tel: 01273 418984
Heads: Mrs Nicola Gane &
Miss Elizabeth Brown
Age range: 6 months–11 years
Fees: Day £8,349

Dharma School
The White House, Ladies Mile Road,
Patcham, Brighton, East Sussex BN1 8TB
Tel: 01273 502055
Headteacher: Clare Eddison
Age range: 3–11
Fees: Day £8,208
£ ✎

Didac School
16 Trinity Trees, Eastbourne,
East Sussex BN21 3LE
Tel: +44 1323 417276
Age range: 16–18
✎

Eastbourne College
Old Wish Road, Eastbourne,
East Sussex BN21 4JX
Tel: 01323 452323 (Admissions)
Headmaster: Mr Tom
Lawson MA (Oxon)
Age range: 13–18
No. of pupils: 650 VIth312
Fees: Day £23,895–£24,375
FB £36,420–£36,975
✎ A ♠ £ 16

Greenfields Independent Day & Boarding School
Priory Road, Forest Row,
East Sussex RH18 5JD
Tel: +44 (0)1342 822189
Executive Head: Mr. Jeff Smith
Age range: 2–19
✎ A ♠ ✎ 16

Lancing College Preparatory School at Hove
The Droveway, Hove,
East Sussex BN3 6LU
Tel: 01273 503452
Headmistress: Mrs Kirsty Keep BEd
Age range: 3–13
No. of pupils: 181
Fees: Day £3,960–£15,975
£ ✎

Lewes Old Grammar School
High Street, Lewes, East Sussex BN7 1XS
Tel: 01273 472634
Headmaster: Mr Robert Blewitt
Age range: 3–18
No. of pupils: 463 VIth50
Fees: Day £8,760–£14,625
A £ ✎ 16

Mayfield School
The Old Palace, Mayfield,
East Sussex TN20 6PH
Tel: +44 (0)1435 874600
Head: Ms Antonia Beary MA,
Mphil (Cantab), PGCE
Age range: G11–18
No. of pupils: 365 VIth100
Fees: Day £21,000 FB £33,900
✎ ♠ A ♠ £ ✎ 16

Michael Hall School
Kidbrooke Park, Priory Road, Forest
Row, East Sussex RH18 5JA
Tel: 01342 822275
Age range: 0 years–18 years
No. of pupils: VIth102
Fees: Day £9,245–£12,670
✎ A ♠ ✎ 16

Roedean Moira House
Upper Carlisle Road, Eastbourne,
East Sussex BN20 7TE
Tel: 01323 644144
Headmaster: Mr Andrew Wood
Age range: G0–18
No. of pupils: 289
✎ ✎ A ♠ £ ✎ 16

Roedean School
Roedean Way, Brighton,
East Sussex BN2 5RQ
Tel: 01273 667500
Headmaster: Mr. Oliver Bond
BA(Essex), PGCE, NPQH
Age range: G11–18
No. of pupils: 630 VIth155
Fees: Day £5,607–£7,415 WB
£10,030–£11,185 FB £10,990–£13,305
✎ ✎ A ♠ £ ✎ 16

Sacred Heart School
Mayfield Lane, Durgates,
Wadhurst, East Sussex TN5 6DQ
Tel: 01892 783414
Headteacher: Mrs H Blake
BA(Hons), PGCE
Age range: 2–11
No. of pupils: 121
Fees: Day £8,355
£ ✎

Skippers Hill Manor Prep School
Five Ashes, Mayfield, East
Sussex TN20 6HR
Tel: 01825 830234
Headmaster: Mr M Hammond
MA, BA, PGCE
Age range: 2–13
No. of pupils: 174
Fees: Day £8,400–£13,440
£ ✎

St Andrew's Prep
Meads Street, Eastbourne,
East Sussex BN20 7RP
Tel: 01323 733203
Headmaster: Gareth Jones
MEd, BA(Hons), PGCE
Age range: 9 months–13 years
No. of pupils: 352
♠ £ ✎

St Bede's Preparatory School
Duke's Drive, Eastbourne,
East Sussex BN20 7XL
Tel: +44 (0)1323 734222
Age range: 3 months–13 years
♠ £ ✎

St Christopher's School
33 New Church Road, Hove,
East Sussex BN3 4AD
Tel: 01273 735404
Headmaster: Mr Julian Withers
Age range: 4–13
Fees: Day £8,370–£12,720
£ ✎

St George's Business & Language College
28-29 Grand Parade, Hastings,
East Sussex TN37 6DN
Tel: 01424 813696
Principal: Mr Richard Lawless

The Drive Prep School
101 The Drive, Hove, East
Sussex BN3 6GE
Tel: 01273 738444
Head Teacher: Mrs S Parkinson
CertEd, CertPerfArts
Age range: 7–16

Torah Montessori Nursery
29 New Church Road, Hove,
East Sussex BN3 4AD
Tel: 01273 328675
Head Teacher: Ms Penina Efune
Age range: 1–4
✎

Windlesham School
190 Dyke Road, Brighton,
East Sussex BN1 5AA
Tel: 01273 553645
Headmaster: Mr John Ingrassia
Age range: 3–11
No. of pupils: 195
Fees: Day £6,015–£8,955
£ ✎

Hampshire

Alton School
Anstey Lane, Alton,
Hampshire GU34 2NG
Tel: 01420 82070
Head: Karl Guest
Age range: 0–18
No. of pupils: 420
A £ 16

Ballard School
Fernhill Lane, New Milton,
Hampshire BH25 5SU
Tel: 01425 626900
Headmaster: Mr Andrew McCleave
Age range: 2–16 years
No. of pupils: 447
Fees: Day £2,875–£5,285
£ ✎

Bedales Prep School, Dunhurst
Petersfield, Hampshire GU32 2DP
Tel: 01730 300200
Head of School: Colin Baty
Age range: 8–13
No. of pupils: 200
Fees: Day £16,920–£18,765
FB £22,215–£24,930
A ♠ £ ✎

Bedales School
Church Road, Steep, Petersfield,
Hampshire GU32 2DG
Tel: 01730 711733
Head of School: Magnus Bashaarat
Age range: 13–18
No. of pupils: 463
Fees: Day £28,515 FB £36,285
✎ A ♠ £ ✎ 16

Boundary Oak School
Roche Court, Fareham,
Hampshire PO17 5BL
Tel: 01329 280955/820373
Head: Mr James Polansky
Age range: 2–16
No. of pupils: 120
Fees: Day £8,949–£14,487 WB
£15,723–£20,514 FB £17,658–£22,449
♠ £ ✎

Brockwood Park & Inwoods School
Brockwood Park, Bramdean,
Hampshire SO24 0LQ
Tel: +44 (0)1962 771744
Principal: Mr Antonio Autor
Age range: 14–19
No. of pupils: 112 VIth39
Fees: Day £5,630–£6,400 FB £21,400

CHURCHER'S COLLEGE
For further details see p.176
Petersfield, Hampshire GU31 4AS
Tel: 01730 263033
Email: admissions@
churcherscollege.com
Website:
www.ChurchersCollege.com
Headmaster:
Mr Simon Williams MA, BSc
Age range: 3–18 years
Fees: Day £10,320–£16,035

Daneshill School
Stratfield Turgis, Basingstoke,
Hampshire RG27 0AR
Tel: 01256 882707
Headmaster: Mr David Griffiths
Age range: 3–13
Fees: Day £10,650–£14,000

Ditcham Park School
Ditcham Park, Petersfield,
Hampshire GU31 5RN
Tel: 01730 825659
Headmaster: Mr Graham
Spawforth MA, MEd
Age range: 21/2–16
No. of pupils: 379
Fees: Day £2,835–£4,753

Durlston Court
Becton Lane, Barton-on-Sea, New
Milton, Hampshire BH25 7AQ
Tel: 01425 610010
Age range: 2–13
No. of pupils: 296
Fees: Day £3,540–£15,390

Embley
Embley Park, Romsey,
Hampshire SO51 6ZE
Tel: 01794 512206
Headteacher: Mr Cliff Canning
Age range: 2–18
No. of pupils: 500
Fees: Day £8,754–£31,338

Farleigh School
Red Rice, Andover,
Hampshire SP11 7PW
Tel: 01264 710766
Headmaster: Father Simon Everson
Age range: 3–13
Fees: Day £5,385–£19,590
FB £21,675–£25,485

Farnborough Hill
Farnborough Road, Farnborough,
Hampshire GU14 8AT
Tel: 01252 545197
Head: Mrs A Neil BA, MEd, PGCE
Age range: G11–18
No. of pupils: 550 VIth90
Fees: Day £14,796

Forres Sandle Manor
Fordingbridge, Hampshire SP6 1NS
Tel: 01425 653181
Headmaster: Mr M N Hartley BSc(Hons)
Age range: 3–13
No. of pupils: 264

Glenhurst School
16 Beechworth Road, Havant,
Hampshire PO9 1AX
Tel: 023 9248 4054
Principal: Mrs E M Haines
Age range: 3 months–5 years

**Grantham Farm Montessori
School & The Children's House**
Grantham Farm, Baughurst,
Tadley, Hampshire RG26 5JS
Tel: 0118 981 5821
Head Teacher: Ms Emma Wetherley
Age range: 3–8

Highfield and Brookham Schools
Highfield Lane, Liphook,
Hampshire GU30 7LQ
Tel: 01428 728000
Headteachers: Mr Phillip Evitt MA
(Hons), PGCE & Mrs Sophie Baber
BA (Hons), PGCE, PG Cert
Age range: 2–13
No. of pupils: 427

KING EDWARD VI SCHOOL
For further details see p.190
Wilton Road, Southampton,
Hampshire SO15 5UQ
Tel: 023 8070 4561
Email: registrar@kes.hants.sch.uk
Website: www.kes.hants.sch.uk
Head Master: Mr N T Parker
Age range: 11–18
No. of pupils: 961
Fees: Day £17,130

Kingscourt School
182 Five Heads Road, Catherington,
Hampshire PO8 9NJ
Tel: 023 9259 3251
Head of School: Mr Jamie Lewis
Age range: 3–11
No. of pupils: 158
Fees: Day £2,856

Lord Wandsworth College
Long Sutton, Hook, Hampshire RG29 1TB
Tel: 01256 862201
Head of School: Mr Adam Williams
Age range: 11–18 years
No. of pupils: 615
Fees: Day £21,240–£24,390 WB
£29,400–£33,000 FB £30,345–£34,650

Mayville High School
35/37 St Simon's Road, Southsea,
Portsmouth, Hampshire PO5 2PE
Tel: 023 9273 4847
Headteacher: Mrs Rebecca Parkyn
Age range: 6 months–16 years
No. of pupils: 479
Fees: Day £7,635–£11,235

Meoncross School
Burnt House Lane, Stubbington,
Fareham, Hampshire PO14 2EF
Tel: 01329 662182
Headmaster: Mr Mark Cripps
Age range: 2–16
No. of pupils: 405
Fees: Day £8,736–£12,576

Moyles Court School
Moyles Court, Ringwood,
Hampshire BH24 3NF
Tel: 01425 472856
Headmaster: Mr Richard Milner-Smith
Age range: 3–16
No. of pupils: 195
Fees: Day £6,885–£14,655
FB £21,246–£26,805

New Forest Small School
1 Southampton Road, Lyndhurst,
Hampshire SO43 7BU
Tel: 02380 284415
Headteacher: Mr Nicholas Alp
Age range: 3–16

Norman Court
West Tytherley, Stockbridge,
Hampshire SP5 1NH
Tel: 01980 322 322

Portsmouth High School GDST
Kent Road, Southsea, Portsmouth,
Hampshire PO5 3EQ
Tel: 023 9282 6714
Headmistress: Mrs Jane
Prescott BSc NPQH
Age range: G3–18
No. of pupils: 500
Fees: Day £2,574–£4,800

Prince's Mead School
Worthy Park House, Kings Worthy,
Winchester, Hampshire SO21 1AN
Tel: 01962 888000
Headmaster: Peter Thacker
Age range: 4–11

Ringwood Waldorf School
Folly Farm Lane, Ashley, Ringwood,
Hampshire BH24 2NN
Tel: 01425 472664
Age range: 3–18
No. of pupils: 235
Fees: Day £6,240–£9,000

Rookwood School
Weyhill Road, Andover,
Hampshire SP10 3AL
Tel: 01264 325900
Headmaster: Mr A Kirk-Burgess
BSc, PGCE, MSc (Oxon)
Age range: 2–16
Fees: Day £9,360–£15,600
FB £23,250–£27,465

Salesian College
Reading Road, Farnborough,
Hampshire GU14 6PA
Tel: 01252 893000
Headmaster: Mr Gerard Owens
Age range: B11–18 G16–18
No. of pupils: 650 VIth140
Fees: Day £11,961

Sherborne House School
Lakewood Road, Chandlers Ford,
Eastleigh, Hampshire SO53 1EU
Tel: 023 8025 2440
Head Teacher: Mrs Heather Hopson-Hill
Age range: 3–11
No. of pupils: 293
Fees: Day £8,295–£9,675
£ ✎

SHERFIELD SCHOOL
For further details see p.202
South Drive, Sherfield-on-Loddon,
Hook, Hampshire RG27 0HU
Tel: 01256 884800
Email: admissions@
sherfieldschool.co.uk
Website: www.sherfieldschool.co.uk
Headmaster: Mr Nick Brain
BA(Hons), PGCE, MA, NPQH
Age range: 3 months–18 years
No. of pupils: 450
Fees: Day £10,320–£17,085 WB
£18,960–£26,130 FB £22,125–£30,495
🌐 Ⓐ 🏠 £ ✎ 16 👪

St John's College
Grove Road South, Southsea,
Portsmouth, Hampshire PO5 3QW
Tel: 023 9281 5118
Headmaster: Mr Timothy Bayley
BSc (Hons), MA, PGCE
Age range: 2–18
No. of pupils: 560 VIth86
Fees: Day £9,225–£12,090
FB £25,200–£28,740
🌐 Ⓐ 🏠 £ ✎ 16 👪

ST NEOT'S SCHOOL
For further details see p.210
St Neot's Road, Eversley,
Hampshire RG27 0PN
Tel: 0118 9739650
Email: admissions@
stneotsprep.co.uk
Website: www.stneotsprep.co.uk
Head of School: Deborah
Henderson
Age range: 2–13 years
No. of pupils: 248
Fees: Day £3,780–£5,408
£ ✎

St Nicholas' School
Redfields House, Redfields
Lane, Church Crookham,
Fleet, Hampshire GU52 0RF
Tel: 01252 850121
Headmistress: Dr O Wright
PhD, MA, BA Hons, PGCE
Age range: B3–7 G3–16
No. of pupils: 325
🏠 £

St Swithun's Prep
Alresford Road, Winchester,
Hampshire SO21 1HA
Tel: 01962 835750
Head of School: Mrs
Rebecca Lyons-Smith
Age range: B3–4 G3–11
No. of pupils: 200
🏠 ✎

ST SWITHUN'S SCHOOL
For further details see p.212
Alresford Road, Winchester,
Hampshire SO21 1HA
Tel: 01962 835700
Email: office@stswithuns.com
Website: www.stswithuns.com
Head of School: Jane
Gandee MA(Cantab)
Age range: G11–18
No. of pupils: 510 VIth161
Fees: Day £20,976 FB £34,776
🏠 🌐 Ⓐ 🏠 £ ✎ 16

Stockton House School
Stockton Avenue, Fleet,
Hampshire GU51 4NS
Tel: 01252 616323
Early Years Manager: Mrs
Jenny Bounds BA EYPS
Age range: 2–5
£ ✎

STROUD SCHOOL
For further details see p.216
Highwood House, Highwood Lane,
Romsey, Hampshire SO51 9ZH
Tel: 01794 513231
Email: registrar@stroud-kes.org.uk
Website: www.stroud-kes.org.uk
Headmistress: Mrs Rebecca Smith
Age range: 3–13
✎

The Gregg Prep School
17-19 Winn Road, Southampton,
Hampshire SO17 1EJ
Tel: 023 8055 7352
Head Teacher: Mrs J Caddy
Age range: 3–11
Fees: Day £8,295
£ ✎

The Gregg School
Townhill Park House, Cutbush Lane,
Southampton, Hampshire SO18 2GF
Tel: 023 8047 2133
Headteacher: Mrs S Sellers PGDip,
MSc, BSc(Hons), NPQH, PGCE
Age range: 11–16
No. of pupils: 300
Fees: Day £12,825
£ ✎

The King's School
Lakesmere House, Allington Lane,
Fair Oak, Eastleigh, Southampton,
Hampshire SO50 7DB
Tel: 023 8060 0986
Age range: 3–16
No. of pupils: 256
Fees: Day £4,560–£7,680
✎

The Pilgrims' School
3 The Close, Winchester,
Hampshire SO23 9LT
Tel: 01962 854189
Head: Dr Sarah Essex
Age range: B4–13
No. of pupils: 250
Fees: Day £18,150–£19,245 FB £24,330
🏃 🏠 £ ✎

The Portsmouth Grammar School
High Street, Portsmouth,
Hampshire PO1 2LN
Tel: +44 (0)23 9236 0036
Headmistress: Dr Anne Cotton
Age range: 2–18
No. of pupils: 1556 VIth336
Fees: Day £10,233–£15,951
🌐 Ⓐ £ IB ✎ 16

The Westgate School
Cheriton Road, Winchester,
Hampshire SO22 5AZ
Tel: 01962 854757
Headteacher: Mrs Dean
Age range: 4–16
🏠 ✎ 👪

Twyford School
Twyford, Winchester,
Hampshire SO21 1NW
Tel: 01962 712269
Headmaster: Dr S J Bailey
BEd, PhD, FRSA
Age range: 3–13
Fees: Day £10,953–£19,509 WB £24,552
🏠 £ ✎

Walhampton
Walhampton, Lymington,
Hampshire SO41 5ZG
Tel: 01590 613 300
Headmaster: Mr Titus Mills
Age range: 2–13
No. of pupils: 353
Fees: Day £9,000–£17,625
FB £20,250–£24,750
🏠 £ ✎

West Hill Park Preparatory School
Titchfield, Fareham,
Hampshire PO14 4BS
Tel: 01329 842356
Headmaster: A P Ramsay
BEd(Hons), MSc
Age range: 2–13
No. of pupils: 288
Fees: Day £10,800–£18,300
FB £19,500–£22,650
🏠 £ ✎

Winchester College
College Street, Winchester,
Hampshire SO23 9NA
Tel: 01962 621247
Headmaster: Dr. T R Hands
Age range: B13–18
No. of pupils: 690 VIth280
Fees: FB £39,912
🏃 🏠 £ ✎ 16

Yateley Manor School
51 Reading Road, Yateley,
Hampshire GU46 7UQ
Tel: 01252 405500
Headmaster: Mr Robert Upton
Age range: 3–13
No. of pupils: 453
Fees: Day £11,160–£15,300
£ ✎

Isle of Wight

Priory School
Beatrice Avenue, Whippingham,
Isle of Wight PO32 6LP
Tel: 01983 861222
Principal: Mr E J Matyjaszek
Age range: 4–18
Fees: Day £5,840–£9,900
Ⓐ Ⓔ 🖊 16

Ryde School with Upper Chine
Queen's Road, Ryde, Isle
of Wight PO33 3BE
Tel: 01983 562229
Headmaster: Mr M. A.
Waldron MA (Cantab)
Age range: 2–18
No. of pupils: 750
Fees: Day £7,935–£13,740
WB £27,030 FB £30,300
Ⓐ Ⓐ 🏛 Ⓔ IB 🖊 16

Kent

Ashford School
East Hill, Ashford, Kent TN24 8PB
Tel: 01233 739030
Head: Mr Michael Hall
Age range: 3 months–18 years
No. of pupils: 835 VIth170
Fees: Day £10,500–£16,800
WB £24,000 FB £36,000
Ⓐ Ⓐ 🏛 Ⓔ 🖊 16

Beech Grove School
Forest Drive, Nonington,
Dover, Kent CT15 4FB
Tel: 01304 842980
Head of School: Mr Timothy Maas
Age range: 4–19

Beechwood Sacred Heart
12 Pembury Road, Tunbridge
Wells, Kent TN2 3QD
Tel: 01892 532747
Acting Head: Mrs Helen Rowe
Age range: 3–18
No. of pupils: 400 VIth70
Fees: Day £8,685–£17,385
WB £26,850 FB £29,850
Ⓐ 🏛 Ⓔ 🖊 16

Benenden School
Cranbrook, Kent TN17 4AA
Tel: 01580 240592
Headmistress: Mrs S Price
Age range: G11–18
No. of pupils: 550
Fees: FB £12,650
Ⓐ Ⓐ Ⓐ 🏛 Ⓔ 🖊 16

BETHANY SCHOOL
For further details see p.172
Curtisden Green, Goudhurst,
Cranbrook, Kent TN17 1LB
Tel: 01580 211273
Email: registrar@
bethanyschool.org.uk
Website: www.bethanyschool.org.uk
Headmaster: Mr Francie
Healy BSc, HDipEd, NPQH
Age range: 11–18 years
No. of pupils: 352 VIth86
Fees: Day £17,310–£19,110 WB
£26,865–£29,670 FB £26,865–£29,670
Ⓐ Ⓐ 🏛 Ⓔ 🖊 16

Bronte School
Mayfield, 7 Pelham Road,
Gravesend, Kent DA11 0HN
Tel: 01474 533805
Headmistress: Ms Emma Wood
Age range: 3–11
No. of pupils: 120
Fees: Day £9,330
🖊

Bryony School
Marshall Road, Rainham,
Gillingham, Kent ME8 0AJ
Tel: 01634 231511
Joint Head: Mr D Edmunds
Age range: 2–11
No. of pupils: 168
Fees: Day £5,978–£6,511
🖊

CATS Canterbury
68 New Dover Road,
Canterbury, Kent CT1 3LQ
Tel: +44 (0)1227866540
Principal: Dr Sarah Lockyer
Age range: 14–18
No. of pupils: 400
Ⓐ 16 Ⓐ 🏛 IB 16

Chartfield School
45 Minster Road, Westgate
on Sea, Kent CT8 8DA
Tel: 01843 831716
Head & Proprietor: Miss L P Shipley
Age range: 4–11
🖊

Cobham Hall School
Cobham, Kent DA12 3BL
Tel: 01474 823371
Headmistress: Ms Maggie Roberts
Age range: G11–18
No. of pupils: 180
Ⓐ Ⓐ 🏛 Ⓔ 🖊 16

Cranbrook School
Waterloo Road, Cranbrook,
Kent TN17 3JD
Tel: 01580 711800
Head Teacher: Mr John Weeds
Age range: 13–18
No. of pupils: 757 VIth307
Fees: FB £13,362–£16,032
Ⓐ 🏛 🖊

Derwent Lodge School for Girls
Somerhill, Tonbridge, Kent TN11 0NJ
Tel: 01732 352124
Head of School: Mrs Helen Hoffmann
Age range: G7–11
No. of pupils: 134
Fees: Day £15,465
Ⓐ Ⓔ 🖊

Dover College
Effingham Crescent,
Dover, Kent CT17 9RH
Tel: 01304 205969
Headmaster: Mr Gareth
Doodes MA (Hons)
Age range: 3–18
No. of pupils: 301
Fees: Day £7,725–£16,050 WB
£21,000–£25,500 FB £24,750–£31,500
Ⓐ Ⓐ 🏛 Ⓔ 🖊 16

Dulwich Prep Cranbrook
Coursehorn, Cranbrook, Kent TN17 3NP
Tel: 01580 712179
Headmaster: Mr Paul David BEd(Hons)
Age range: 3–13
No. of pupils: 535
Fees: Day £5,970–£18,390
Ⓔ 🖊

Elliott Park School
18-20 Marina Drive, Minster,
Sheerness, Kent ME12 2DP
Tel: 01795 873372
Head: Ms Colleen Hiller
Age range: 3–11
🖊

Fosse Bank School
Mountains, Noble Tree
Road, Hildenborough,
Tonbridge, Kent TN11 8ND
Tel: 01732 834212
Headmistress: Miss Alison Cordingley
Age range: 2–11
No. of pupils: 124
Fees: Day £10,605–£13,185
Ⓔ

Gad's Hill School
Higham, Rochester,
Medway, Kent ME3 7PA
Tel: 01474 822366
Headmaster: Mr Paul Savage
Age range: 3–16
No. of pupils: 370
Fees: Day £8,988–£12,504
Ⓔ

Haddon Dene School
57 Gladstone Road,
Broadstairs, Kent CT10 2HY
Tel: 01843 861176
Head: Miss Alison Hatch
Age range: 3–11
No. of pupils: 200
Fees: Day £5,700–£7,230
🖊

Hilden Grange School
62 Dry Hill Park Road,
Tonbridge, Kent TN10 3BX
Tel: 01732 352706
Headmaster: Mr J Withers BA(Hons)
Age range: 3–13
No. of pupils: 311

Hilden Oaks School & Nursery
38 Dry Hill Park Road,
Tonbridge, Kent TN10 3BU
Tel: 01732 353941
Head of School: Mrs. K Joiner
Age range: 3 months–11 years
No. of pupils: 184
Fees: Day £9,975–£13,290

Holmewood House School
Barrow Lane, Langton Green,
Tunbridge Wells, Kent TN3 0EB
Tel: 01892 860000
Headmaster: Mr Scott Carnochan
Age range: 3–13
No. of pupils: 450

Kent College Junior School
Harbledown, Canterbury,
Kent CT2 9AQ
Tel: 01227 762436
Headmaster: Mr Andrew Carter
Age range: 0–11
No. of pupils: 219
Fees: Day £10,191–£16,332 FB £26,224

Kent College Pembury
Old Church Road, Pembury,
Tunbridge Wells, Kent TN2 4AX
Tel: +44 (0)1892 822006
Headmistress: Ms J Lodrick
Age range: G3–18
No. of pupils: 650 VIth102
Fees: Day £9,459–£20,571 WB
£25,710 FB £25,710–£32,778

KENT COLLEGE, CANTERBURY
For further details see p.188
Whitstable Road, Canterbury,
Kent CT2 9DT
Tel: +44 (0)1227 763 231
Email: admissions@
kentcollege.co.uk
Website: www.kentcollege.com
Senior School Head: Dr
David Lamper
Age range: 0–18 years
(Boarding from 8)
No. of pupils: 770
Fees: Day £5,598–£6,288
FB £8,748–£11,867

**King's Preparatory
School, Rochester**
King Edward Road, Rochester,
Medway, Kent ME1 1UB
Tel: 01634 888577
Headmaster: Mr Tom Morgan
Age range: 8–13
No. of pupils: 220
Fees: Day £13,185–£14,955

**King's Pre-Preparatory
School, Rochester**
Chadlington House, Lockington
Grove, Rochester, Kent ME1 1RH
Tel: 01634 888566
Headmistress: Mrs C Openshaw
Age range: 3–8
No. of pupils: 149
Fees: Day £10,155–£11,010

King's Rochester
Satis House, Boley Hill,
Rochester, Kent ME1 1TE
Tel: 01634 888555
Principal: Mr B Charles
Age range: 13–18
No. of pupils: 600 VIth95
Fees: Day £7,440–£20,190
FB £22,950–£33,015

Lorenden Preparatory School
Painter's Forstal, Faversham,
Kent ME13 0EN
Tel: 01795 590030
Headmistress: Mrs K Uttley
Age range: 3–11
No. of pupils: 120
Fees: Day £8,640–£12,540

Marlborough House School
High Street, Hawkhurst, Kent TN18 4PY
Tel: 01580 753555
Head: Mr Eddy Newton
Age range: 3–13
No. of pupils: 250
Fees: Day £9,165–£18,690

NORTHBOURNE PARK SCHOOL
For further details see p.196
Betteshanger, Deal, Kent CT14 0NW
Tel: 01304 611215/218
Email: admissions@
northbournepark.com
Website:
www.northbournepark.com
Headmaster: Mr Sebastian
Rees BA(Hons), PGCE, NPQH
Age range: 2–13
No. of pupils: 185
Fees: Day £7,632–£17,007
WB £21,405 FB £24,786

**OneSchool Global UK
Maidstone Campus**
Heath Road, Maidstone ME17 4HT
Tel: 01622 740820
Age range: 7–18

Radnor House, Sevenoaks
Combe Bank Drive,
Sevenoaks, Kent TN14 6AE
Tel: 01959 563720
Head: Mr David Paton
BComm (Hons) PGCE MA
Age range: 21/2–18
No. of pupils: 250

Rochester Independent College
254 St Margaret's Banks,
Rochester, Kent ME1 1HY
Tel: +44 (0)163 482 8115
Head of School: Mr Alistair Brownlow
Age range: 11–18
Fees: Day £13,000–£18,600
WB £12,400 FB £14,100

Rose Hill School
Coniston Avenue, Tunbridge
Wells, Kent TN4 9SY
Tel: 01892 525591
Head: Emma Neville
Age range: 3–13
Fees: Day £11,325–£15,225

Russell House School
Station Road, Otford,
Sevenoaks, Kent TN14 5QU
Tel: 01959 522352
Headmaster: Mr Craig McCarthy
Age range: 2–11

Sackville School
Tonbridge Rd, Hildenborough,
Tonbridge, Kent TN11 9HN
Tel: 01732 838888
Headmaster: Mr Justin Foster-
Gandey BSc (hons)
Age range: 11–18
No. of pupils: 160 VIth29
Fees: Day £15,750

Saint Ronan's School
Water Lane, Hawkhurst, Kent TN18 5DJ
Tel: 01580 752271
Headmaster: William Trelawny-
Vernon BSc(Hons)
Age range: 3–13
No. of pupils: 300
Fees: Day £10,869–£18,624 FB £22,497

Sevenoaks Preparatory School
Godden Green, Sevenoaks,
Kent TN15 0JU
Tel: 01732 762336
Headmaster: Mr Luke Harrison
Age range: 2–13
No. of pupils: 388
Fees: Day £10,755–£14,865

Sevenoaks School
High Street, Sevenoaks, Kent TN13 1HU
Tel: +44 (0)1732 455133
Acting Head (to August 2020): Miss
Theresa Homewood BSc MA
Age range: 11–18
No. of pupils: 1165
Fees: Day £24,291–£27,585
FB £38,790–£42,084

Shernold School
Hill Place, Queens Avenue,
Maidstone, Kent ME16 0ER
Tel: 01622 752868
Head Teacher: Ms. Sandra
Dinsmore BA Hons. PGCE
Age range: 3–11
No. of pupils: 142
Fees: Day £7,245–£8,190

Solefield School
Solefield Road, Sevenoaks,
Kent TN13 1PH
Tel: 01732 452142
Headmaster: Mr D A Philps BSc(Hons)
Age range: B4–13
No. of pupils: 180
Fees: Day £12,600–£15,345

Somerhill Pre-Prep
Somerhill, Five Oak Green Road,
Tonbridge, Kent TN11 0NJ
Tel: 01732 352124
**Principal of The Schools at
Somerhill:** Duncan Sinclair
Age range: 3–7
No. of pupils: 245
Fees: Day £10,050–£11,685

Spring Grove School
Harville Road, Wye, Kent TN25 5EZ
Tel: 01233 812337
Headmaster: Mr Bill Jones
Age range: 2–11 years
No. of pupils: 212
Fees: Day £9,000–£12,900
£ ✎

St Andrew's School
24-28 Watts Avenue, Rochester,
Medway, Kent ME1 1SA
Tel: 01634 843479
Principal: Mrs E Steinmann-Gilbert
Age range: 2–11
No. of pupils: 367
Fees: Day £7,725–£8,178
✎

St Edmund's Junior School
St Thomas Hill, Canterbury,
Kent CT2 8HU
Tel: 01227 475600
Head: Edward O'Connor
Age range: 3–13
No. of pupils: 230
Fees: Day £9,696–£16,101
WB £25,455 FB £27,933
🏫 ✎

St Edmund's School
St Thomas Hill, Canterbury,
Kent CT2 8HU
Tel: 01227 475601
Head: Mr Edward O'Connor MA
(Cantab), MPhil (Oxon), MEd (Cantab)
Age range: 3–18
No. of pupils: 552
🏫 Ⓐ 🏫 £ ✎ 16

St Faith's at Ash School
5 The Street, Ash, Canterbury,
Kent CT3 2HH
Tel: 01304 813409
Headmaster: Mr Lawrence Groves
Age range: 2–11
No. of pupils: 225
Fees: Day £5,415–£9,885
£ ✎

St Joseph's Convent Prep School
46 Old Road East, Gravesend,
Kent DA12 1NR
Tel: 01474 533012
Head Teacher: Miss D Buckley
Age range: 3–11
No. of pupils: 146
Fees: Day £8,580
✎

ST LAWRENCE COLLEGE
For further details see p.208
Ramsgate, Kent CT11 7AE
Tel: 01843 572931
Email: admissions@slcuk.com
Website: www.slcuk.com
Head of College: Mr Barney Durrant
Age range: 3–18
No. of pupils: 600
Fees: Day £7,845–£16,245
FB £27,765–£36,909
🏫 Ⓐ 🏫 £ ✎ 16

St Michael's Preparatory School
Otford Court, Otford,
Sevenoaks, Kent TN14 5SA
Tel: 01959 522137
Headteacher: Mrs Jill Aisher
Age range: 2–13
No. of pupils: 472
Fees: Day £12,210–£14,835
£ ✎

Steephill School
Off Castle Hill, Fawkham,
Longfield, Kent DA3 7BG
Tel: 01474 702107
Head: Mrs Caroline Birtwell
BSc, MBA, PGCE
Age range: 3–11
No. of pupils: 131
Fees: Day £9,750
£ ✎

**Sutton Valence
Preparatory School**
Chart Sutton, Maidstone, Kent ME17 3RF
Tel: 01622 842117
Head: Miss C Corkran
Age range: 3–11
No. of pupils: 320
Fees: Day £3,000–£4,610
✎

Sutton Valence School
North Street, Sutton Valence,
Kent ME17 3HL
Tel: 01622 845200
Headmaster: Bruce Grindlay MA
Cantab, MusB, FRCO, CHM
Age range: 11–18
No. of pupils: 570
🏫 Ⓐ 🏫 £ ✎ 16

The Granville School
2 Bradbourne Park Road,
Sevenoaks, Kent TN13 3LJ
Tel: 01732 453039
Headmistress: Mrs Louise
Lawrance B. Prim. Ed. (Hons)
Age range: B3–4 G3–11
🏫 ♿ £ ✎

**The Junior King's School,
Canterbury**
Milner Court, Sturry,
Canterbury, Kent CT2 0AY
Tel: 01227 714000
Head: Emma Károlyi
Age range: 3–13
Fees: Day £11,475–£19,290 FB £26,475
🏫 ✎

The King's School, Canterbury
The Precincts, Canterbury, Kent CT1 2ES
Tel: 01227 595501
Head: Mr Peter Roberts
Age range: 13–18
No. of pupils: 858 VIth385
Fees: Day £27,495 FB £38,955
🏫 Ⓐ 🏫 £ ✎ 16

The Mead School
16 Frant Road, Tunbridge
Wells, Kent TN2 5SN
Tel: 01892 525837
Headmaster: Mr Andrew Webster
Age range: 3–11
No. of pupils: 188
Fees: Day £4,536–£11,625
✎

The New Beacon School
Brittains Lane, Sevenoaks,
Kent TN13 2PB
Tel: 01732 452131
Headmaster: Mr M Piercy BA(Hons)
Age range: B4–13
No. of pupils: 400
Fees: Day £11,400–£16,350
♿ £ ✎

Tonbridge School
High Street, Tonbridge, Kent TN9 1JP
Tel: 01732 304297
Headmaster: Mr James
Priory MA (Oxon)
Age range: B13–18
No. of pupils: 786
Fees: Day £31,587 FB £42,105
♿ 🏫 Ⓐ 🏫 £ ✎ 16

**Walthamstow Hall Pre-
Prep and Junior School**
Sevenoaks, Kent TN13 3LD
Tel: 01732 451334
Headmistress: Miss S Ferro
Age range: G2 –11
No. of pupils: 218
Fees: Day £12,135–£15,300
♿ ✎

Walthamstow Hall School
Sevenoaks, Kent TN13 3UL
Tel: 01732 451334
Headmistress: Miss S Ferro
Age range: G2 –18
No. of pupils: 500 VIth80
🏫 Ⓐ 🏫 £ ✎ 16

Wellesley House
114 Ramsgate Road,
Broadstairs, Kent CT10 2DG
Tel: 01843 862991
Headmaster: Mr G D Franklin
Age range: 7–13
No. of pupils: 133
Fees: Day £12,231–£19,917 FB £26,331
🏫 £ ✎

Yardley Court
Somerhill, Five Oak Green Road,
Tonbridge, Kent TN11 0NJ
Tel: 01732 352124
Headmaster: Duncan Sinclair
Age range: B7–13
No. of pupils: 260
Fees: Day £15,465
♿ £ ✎

Surrey

Aberdour School
Brighton Road, Burgh Heath,
Tadworth, Surrey KT20 6AJ
Tel: 01737 354119
Headmaster: Mr S. D. Collins
Age range: 2–13 years
No. of pupils: 357
Fees: Day £1,500–£5,175
£ ✎

ACS Cobham International School
Heywood, Portsmouth Road,
Cobham, Surrey KT11 1BL
Tel: +44 (0) 1932 867251
Head of School: Mr Barnaby Sandow
Age range: 2–18
No. of pupils: 1460
Fees: Day £11,480–£27,650 WB
£39,590–£42,400 FB £45,060–£47,870
🌐 ✈ £ IB ✎ 16

ACS Egham International School
Woodlee, London Road,
Egham, Surrey TW20 0HS
Tel: +44 (0) 1784 430 800
Head of School: Jeremy Lewis
Age range: 4–18
Fees: Day £11,090–£25,870
🌐 £ IB ✎ 16

Aldro School
Shackleford, Godalming,
Surrey GU8 6AS
Tel: 01483 810266
Head: Mr and Mrs C P & L B Rose
Age range: B7–13
No. of pupils: 220
Fees: Day £17,544–£19,479
FB £23,346–£25,281
♟ ✈ £ ✎

Amesbury
Hazel Grove, Hindhead,
Surrey GU26 6BL
Tel: 01428 604322
Head of School: Miss Sheina Wright
Age range: 2–13
No. of pupils: 360
✈ £ ✎

Banstead Preparatory School
Sutton Lane, Banstead, Surrey SM7 3RA
Tel: 01737 363601
Headteacher: Miss Vicky Ellis
Age range: 2–11
No. of pupils: 225

Barfield School
Guildford Road, Runfold,
Farnham, Surrey GU10 1PB
Tel: 01252 782271
Headmaster: Mr Andy Boyle
Age range: 2–13 years
No. of pupils: 170
Fees: Day £3,456–£14,895
£ ✎

Barrow Hills School
Roke Lane, Witley, Godalming,
Surrey GU8 5NY
Tel: +44 (0)1428 683639
Headmaster: Mr Philip Oldroyd
Age range: 2–13
No. of pupils: 200
Fees: Day £15,975
£ ✎

Belmont School
Feldemore, Holmbury St Mary,
Dorking, Surrey RH5 6LQ
Tel: 01306 730852
Headmistress: Mrs Helen Skrine
BA, PGCE, NPQH, FRSA
Age range: 2–16 years
Fees: Day £9,660–£16,740
WB £20,430–£21,300
✈ £ ✎

Bishopsgate School
Bishopsgate Road, Englefield
Green, Egham, Surrey TW20 0YJ
Tel: 01784 432109
Headmaster: Mr R Williams
Age range: 3–13
Fees: Day £5,580–£15,840
£ ✎

Box Hill School
London Road, Mickleham,
Dorking, Surrey RH5 6EA
Tel: 01372 373382
Headmaster: Cory Lowde
Age range: 11–18
No. of pupils: 425
Fees: Day £17,985 WB
£28,350 FB £34,950
🌐 ✈ £ IB ✎ 16

Caterham School
Harestone Valley, Caterham,
Surrey CR3 6YA
Tel: 01883 343028
Head: Mr C. W. Jones MA(Cantab)
Age range: 11–18
No. of pupils: VIth321
Fees: Day £18,735–£19,620 WB
£30,936–£33,270 FB £36,795–£38,760
🌐 A ✈ £ ✎ 16

Charterhouse
Godalming, Surrey GU7 2DX
Tel: +44 (0)1483 291501
Headmaster: Dr Alex Peterken
Age range: B13–18 G16–18
No. of pupils: 820
🌐 A ✈ £ IB ✎ 16

Chinthurst School
Tadworth Street, Tadworth,
Surrey KT20 5QZ
Tel: 01737 812011
Head: Miss Catherine Trundle
Age range: B3–11
No. of pupils: 170
Fees: Day £11,010–£14,850
£ ✎

City of London Freemen's School
Ashtead Park, Ashtead, Surrey KT21 1ET
Tel: 01372 277933
Headmaster: Mr R Martin
Age range: 7–18
No. of pupils: 877 VIth213
Fees: Day £14,067–£19,194 WB
£29,784–£29,841 FB £30,780–£30,816
🌐 A ✈ £ ✎ 16

CLAREMONT FAN COURT SCHOOL
For further details see p.178
Claremont Drive, Esher,
Surrey KT10 9LY
Tel: 01372 473780
Email: admissionsandmarketing@
claremont.surrey.sch.uk
Website:
www.claremontfancourt.co.uk
Head: Mr William Brierly
Age range: 2 1/2–18
No. of pupils: 890
Fees: Day £790–£6,125
A £ ✎ 16

Coworth Flexlands School
Valley End, Chobham, Surrey GU24 8TE
Tel: 01276 855707
Head of School: Miss Nicola Cowell
Age range: B21/2–7 G21/2–11
No. of pupils: 135
✎

Cranleigh Preparatory School
Horseshoe Lane, Cranleigh,
Surrey GU6 8QH
Tel: 01483 274199
Headmaster: Mr Neil R Brooks BSc
Age range: 7–13
No. of pupils: 290
Fees: Day £16,062–£20,838 FB £25,164
✈

CRANLEIGH SCHOOL
For further details see p.180
Horseshoe Lane, Cranleigh,
Surrey GU6 8QQ
Tel: +44 (0) 1483 273666
Email: admissions@cranleigh.org
Website: www.cranleigh.org
Headmaster: Mr Martin
Reader MA, MPhil, MBA
Age range: 7–18 (including
Prep School)
No. of pupils: 690 VIth252
Fees: Day £32,370 FB £39,330
🌐 A ✈ £ ✎ 16

Cranmore School
Epsom Road, West Horsley,
Surrey KT24 6AT
Tel: 01483 280340
Headmaster: Mr Michael
Connolly BSc, BA, MA, MEd
Age range: 2–13
No. of pupils: 420
Fees: Day £12,825–£15,300
£ ✎

Danes Hill School
Leatherhead Road, Oxshott,
Surrey KT22 0JG
Tel: 01372 842509
Headmaster: Mr W Murdock BA
Age range: 3–13
No. of pupils: 872
Fees: Day £14,421–£20,340
£ ✎

Danesfield Manor School
Rydens Avenue, Walton-on-
Thames, Surrey KT12 3JB
Tel: 01932 220930
Principal: Mrs Jo Smith
Age range: 2–11
No. of pupils: 170
Fees: Day £9,456–£10,098
✎

Downsend School
1 Leatherhead Road,
Leatherhead, Surrey KT22 8TJ
Tel: 01372 372197
Headmaster: Mr Ian Thorpe
Age range: 2–13
No. of pupils: 670
Fees: Day £11,970–£17,985
✎

Downsend School
(Ashtead Pre-Prep)
Ashtead Lodge, 22 Oakfield
Road, Ashtead, Surrey KT21 2RE
Tel: 01372 385439
Head Teacher: Tessa Roberts
Age range: 2–6
No. of pupils: 66
Fees: Day £11,535

Downsend School (Epsom Pre-Prep)
Epsom Lodge, 6 Norman Avenue, Epsom, Surrey KT17 3AB
Tel: 01372 385438
Head Teacher: Vanessa Conlan
Age range: 2–6
No. of pupils: 110
Fees: Day £11,535

Downsend School (Leatherhead Pre-Prep)
Leatherhead Lodge, Epsom Road, Leatherhead, Surrey KT22 8ST
Tel: 01372 385437
Headteacher: Mrs Gill Brooks
Age range: 2–6
No. of pupils: 106
Fees: Day £11,535

Drayton House Pre-School and Nursery
35 Austen Road, Guildford, Surrey GU1 3NP
Tel: 01483 504707
Headmistress: Mrs J Tyson-Jones Froebel Cert.Ed. London University
Age range: 6 months–5 years
No. of pupils: 65
Fees: Day £4,420–£12,500

Duke of Kent School
Peaslake Road, Ewhurst, Surrey GU6 7NS
Tel: 01483 277313
Head: Mrs Sue Knox
Age range: 3–16
No. of pupils: 234
Fees: Day £7,245–£19,050

Dunottar School
High Trees Road, Reigate, Surrey RH2 7EL
Tel: 01737 761945
Head of School: Mr Mark Tottman
Age range: 11–18
No. of pupils: 365
Fees: Day £17,055

Edgeborough
Frensham, Farnham, Surrey GU10 3AH
Tel: 01252 792495
Headmaster: Mr Dan Thornburn
Age range: 2–13
No. of pupils: 335
Fees: Day £11,070–£17,970

Emberhurst School
94 Ember Lane, Esher, Surrey KT10 8EN
Tel: 020 8398 2933
Headmistress: Mrs P Chadwick BEd
Age range: 2–7
No. of pupils: 70

Epsom College
Epsom, Surrey KT17 4JQ
Tel: 01372 821000
Headmaster: Mr Jay A Piggot MA
Age range: 11–18
No. of pupils: 884
Fees: Day £19,611–£26,151 WB £35,034 FB £38,568

Essendene Lodge School
Essendene Road, Caterham, Surrey CR3 5PB
Tel: 01883 348349
Head Teacher: Mrs K Ali
Age range: 2–11
No. of pupils: 153
Fees: Day £3,315–£7,305

Ewell Castle School
Church Street, Ewell, Epsom, Surrey KT17 2AW
Tel: 020 8393 1413
Principal: Mr Silas Edmonds
Age range: 3–18
No. of pupils: 557
Fees: Day £5,175–£17,442

Feltonfleet School
Cobham, Surrey KT11 1DR
Tel: 01932 862264
Head of School: Mrs S Lance
Age range: 3–13
No. of pupils: 435
Fees: Day £12,315–£18,090 WB £18,090

Focus School – Hindhead Campus
Tilford Road, Hindhead, Surrey GU26 6SJ
Tel: 01428 601800

Frensham Heights
Rowledge, Farnham, Surrey GU10 4EA
Tel: 01252 792561
Head: Mr Rick Clarke
Age range: 3–18
No. of pupils: 497 VIth105
Fees: Day £7,110–£21,060 FB £27,450–£32,070

Glenesk School
Ockham Road North, East Horsley, Surrey KT24 6NS
Tel: 01483 282329
Headmistress: Mrs Sarah Bradley
Age range: 2–7
No. of pupils: 100
Fees: Day £11,658–£13,176

GORDON'S SCHOOL
For further details see p.184
West End, Woking, Surrey GU24 9PT
Tel: 01276 858084
Email: registrar@gordons.school
Website: www.gordons.school
Head Teacher: Andrew Moss MEd
Age range: 11–18
No. of pupils: 959 VIth350
Fees: Day £8,209 WB £17,295 FB £18,459

Greenfield School
Old Woking Road, Woking, Surrey GU22 8HY
Tel: 01483 772525
Headmistress: Mrs Tania Botting BEd
Age range: 3–11
No. of pupils: 179
Fees: Day £5,976–£14,079

Guildford High School
London Road, Guildford, Surrey GU1 1SJ
Tel: 01483 561440
Headmistress: Mrs F J Boulton BSc, MA
Age range: G4–18
No. of pupils: 1000
Fees: Day £11,052–£17,733

Hall Grove School
London Road, Bagshot, Surrey GU19 5HZ
Tel: 01276 473059
Headmaster: Mr Alastair Graham
Age range: 3–13
No. of pupils: 430
Fees: Day £11,250–£15,450

Halstead Preparatory School
Woodham Rise, Woking, Surrey GU21 4EE
Tel: 01483 772682
Headmistress: Mrs P Austin
Age range: G3–11
No. of pupils: 220
Fees: Day £10,800–£15,210

HAMPTON COURT HOUSE
For further details see p.186
Hampton Court Road, East Molesey, Surrey KT8 9BS
Tel: 020 8614 0857
Email: admissions@hchnet.co.uk
Website: www.hamptoncourthouse.co.uk
Headmaster: Mr Guy Holloway
Age range: 3–18

HawleyHurst School
Fernhill Road, Blackwater, Camberley, Surrey GU17 9HU
Tel: 01276 587190
Head Teacher: Miss V S Smit
Age range: 2–19

Hazelwood School
Wolf's Hill, Limpsfield, Oxted, Surrey RH8 0QU
Tel: 01883 712194
Head: Mrs Lindie Louw
Age range: 2–13
No. of pupils: 399
Fees: Day £10,275–£16,380

Hoe Bridge School
Hoe Place, Old Woking Road, Woking, Surrey GU22 8JE
Tel: 01483 760018 & 01483 772194
Headmaster: Mr C Webster MA BSc (Hons) PGCE
Age range: 3–13
No. of pupils: 460
Fees: Day £5,940–£15,885

Hurtwood House
Holmbury St Mary, Dorking, Surrey RH5 6NU
Tel: 01483 279000
Principal: Mr Cosmo Jackson
Age range: 16–18
No. of pupils: 360
Fees: Day £29,748 FB £44,622

King Edward's Witley
Godalming, Surrey GU8 5SG
Tel: +44 (0)1428 686700
Head: Mrs Joanna Wright
Age range: 11–18
No. of pupils: 400
Fees: Day £15,975–£21,285 WB £31,125–£32,325 FB £32,775–£34,050

Kingswood House School
56 West Hill, Epsom, Surrey KT19 8LG
Tel: 01372 723590
Headmaster: Mr Duncan Murphy BA (Hons), MEd, FRSA
Age range: B4–16
No. of pupils: 210

Lanesborough
Maori Road, Guildford, Surrey GU1 2EL
Tel: 01483 880650
Head: Mrs Clare Turnbull BA(Hons) MEd
Age range: B3–13
No. of pupils: 350
Fees: Day £10,890–£15,270
Ⓐ ⓔ ✎

Lingfield College
Racecourse Road, Lingfield,
Surrey RH7 6PH
Tel: 01342 832407
Headmaster: Mr R Bool B.A. Hons, MBA
Age range: 2–18
No. of pupils: 935
Fees: Day £11,250–£21,801
Ⓐ ⓔ ✎ 16+

Longacre School
Hullbrook Lane, Shamley Green,
Guildford, Surrey GU5 0NQ
Tel: 01483 893225
Head of School: Mr Matthew Bryan
MA(Cantab.), MA(Oxon.), MSc, FRSA
Age range: 2–11
No. of pupils: 267
Fees: Day £10,290–£15,300
ⓔ ✎

Lyndhurst School
36 The Avenue, Camberley,
Surrey GU15 3NE
Tel: 01276 22895
Head: Mr A Rudkin BEd(Hons)
Age range: 3–11
No. of pupils: 126
ⓔ ✎

MANOR HOUSE SCHOOL, BOOKHAM
For further details see p.194
Manor House Lane, Little Bookham,
Leatherhead, Surrey KT23 4EN
Tel: 01372 457077
Email: admin@
manorhouseschool.org
Website:
www.manorhouseschool.org
Headteacher: Ms Tracey
Fantham BA (Hons) MA NPQH
Age range: B2–4 G2–16
No. of pupils: 300
Fees: Day £9,555–£17,955
Ⓐ ⓔ ✎

Micklefield School
10/12 Somers Road, Reigate,
Surrey RH2 9DU
Tel: 01737 224212
Head: Mr R Ardé
Age range: 3–11
No. of pupils: 272
Fees: Day £3,465–£13,125
✎

Milbourne Lodge School
Arbrook Lane, Esher, Surrey KT10 9EG
Tel: 01372 462737
Head: Mrs Judy Waite
Age range: 4–13
No. of pupils: 283
Fees: Day £12,855–£16,155
ⓔ

Notre Dame School
Cobham, Surrey KT11 1HA
Tel: 01932 869990
Head of Seniors: Mrs Anna King
MEd, MA (Cantab), PGCE
Age range: 2–18
No. of pupils: 600
Ⓐ Ⓐ ⓔ ✎ 16+

Oakhyrst Grange School
160 Stanstead Road,
Caterham, Surrey CR3 6AF
Tel: 01883 343344
Headmaster: Mr Alex Gear
Age range: 4–11 years
No. of pupils: 155

PARKSIDE SCHOOL
For further details see p.198
The Manor, Stoke d'Abernon,
Cobham, Surrey KT11 3PX
Tel: 01932 862749
Email: office@parkside-school.co.uk
Website:
www.parkside-school.co.uk
Headteacher: Ms Nicole Janssen
Age range: B2–13 G2–4
No. of pupils: 270
Ⓐ

Prior's Field
Priorsfield Road, Godalming,
Surrey GU7 2RH
Tel: 01483 810551
Age range: G11–18
No. of pupils: 450
Fees: Day £18,900 FB £30,825
Ⓐ Ⓐ Ⓐ ⓔ ✎ 16+

Reed's School
Sandy Lane, Cobham, Surrey KT11 2ES
Tel: 01932 869001
Headmaster: Mr Mark
Hoskins BA MA MSc
Age range: B11–18 G16–18
No. of pupils: 650 VIth230
Fees: Day £20,430–£25,530
FB £27,225–£32,910
Ⓐ Ⓐ Ⓐ ⓔ ✎ 16+

Reigate Grammar School
Reigate Road, Reigate, Surrey RH2 0QS
Tel: 01737 222231
Headmaster: Mr Shaun Fenton
MA (Oxon) MEd (Oxon)
Age range: 11–18
No. of pupils: 969 VIth262
Fees: Day £19,140–£19,350
Ⓐ ⓔ ✎ 16+

Reigate St Mary's Prep & Choir School
Chart Lane, Reigate, Surrey RH2 7RN
Tel: 01737 244880
Headmaster: Mr Marcus Culverwell MA
Age range: 3–11
No. of pupils: 350
Fees: Day £12,360–£15,300
ⓔ ✎

Ripley Court School
Rose Lane, Ripley, Surrey GU23 6NE
Tel: 01483 225217
Headmistress: Ms Aislinn Clarke
Age range: 3–13
ⓔ ✎

Rowan Preparatory School
6 Fitzalan Road, Claygate,
Surrey KT10 0LX
Tel: 01372 462627
Headmistress: Mrs Susan
Clarke BEd, NPQH
Age range: G2–11
No. of pupils: 317
Fees: Day £11,526–£15,294
Ⓐ ⓔ ✎

Royal Alexandra and Albert School
Gatton Park, Reigate, Surrey RH2 0TD
Tel: 01737 649 000
Headmaster: Mr Mark Dixon
Age range: 7–18 years
No. of pupils: 1000 VIth200
Fees: FB £15,750
Ⓐ Ⓐ ⓔ ✎ 16+

Royal Grammar School, Guildford
High Street, Guildford, Surrey GU1 3BB
Tel: 01483 880600
Headmaster: Dr J M Cox BSc, PhD
Age range: B11–18
No. of pupils: 940
Fees: Day £19,035
Ⓐ Ⓐ ⓔ ✎ 16+

Rydes Hill Preparatory School
Rydes Hill House, Aldershot Road,
Guildford, Surrey GU2 8BP
Tel: 01483 563160
Headmistress: Mrs Sarah Norville
Age range: B3–7 G3–11
No. of pupils: 180
ⓔ ✎

Shrewsbury House Pre-Preparatory School
22 Milbourne Lane, Esher,
Surrey KT10 9EA
Tel: 01372 462781
Head: Mr Jon Akhurst BA (Hons) PGCE
Age range: 3–7
Fees: Day £6,225–£13,740

SIR WILLIAM PERKINS'S SCHOOL
For further details see p.204
Guildford Road, Chertsey,
Surrey KT16 9BN
Tel: 01932 574900
Email: office@swps.org.uk
Website: www.swps.org.uk
Head: Mr C C Muller
Age range: G11–18 years
No. of pupils: 600
Fees: Day £5,618
Ⓐ Ⓐ ⓔ Ⓑ 16+

ST CATHERINE'S, BRAMLEY
For further details see p.206
Station Road, Bramley,
Guildford, Surrey GU5 0DF
Tel: 01483 899609
Email: admissions@stcatherines.info
Website: www.stcatherines.info
Headmistress: Alice Phillips
Age range: G4–18
Fees: Day £9,240–£18,885 FB £31,125
Ⓐ Ⓐ Ⓐ Ⓐ ⓔ ✎ 16+

St Christopher's School
6 Downs Road, Epsom, Surrey KT18 5HE
Tel: 01372 721807
Headteacher: Mrs A C
Thackray MA, BA(Hons)
Age range: 3–7
No. of pupils: 137
Fees: Day £10,485
£ ✐

St Edmund's School
Portsmouth Road, Hindhead,
Surrey GU26 6BH
Tel: 01428 604808
Headmaster: Mr A J Walliker
MA(Cantab), MBA, PGCE
Age range: 2–16
No. of pupils: 410
Fees: Day £9,585–£16,746
⛫ £ ✐

St George's College
Weybridge Road, Addlestone,
Weybridge, Surrey KT15 2QS
Tel: 01932 839300
Headmistress: Mrs Rachel Owens
Age range: 11–18
No. of pupils: 909 VIth250
Fees: Day £17,655–£20,100
Ⓐ ✐ 16·

St George's Junior School
Thames Street, Weybridge,
Surrey KT13 8NL
Tel: 01932 839400
Head Master: Mr Antony Hudson
MA (CANTAB), PGCE, NPQH
Age range: 3–11 years
No. of pupils: 644
Fees: Day £5,640–£14,640
£ ✐

St Hilary's School
Holloway Hill, Godalming,
Surrey GU7 1RZ
Tel: 01483 416551
Headmistress: Mrs Jane Whittingham
BEdCert, ProfPracSpLD
Age range: B2–11 G2–11
No. of pupils: 250
Fees: Day £10,092–£14,850
£ ✐

St Ives School
Three Gates Lane, Haslemere,
Surrey GU27 2ES
Tel: 01428 643734
Headteacher: Kay Goldsworthy
Age range: 2–11
No. of pupils: 149
Fees: Day £9,900–£13,950
£ ✐

St John's School
Epsom Road, Leatherhead,
Surrey KT22 8SP
Tel: 01372 373000
Head of School: Mrs Rowena Cole
Age range: 11–18
No. of pupils: 761
Fees: Day £19,590–£24,555
WB £24,780–£31,035
⛫ Ⓐ ⛫ ✐

**St Teresa's Effingham
(Preparatory School)**
Effingham, Surrey RH5 6ST
Tel: 01372 453456
Headmaster: Mr. Mike Farmer
Age range: B2–4 G2–11
No. of pupils: 100
Fees: Day £1,185–£14,685
WB £25,515 FB £28,665
⛫ ⛫ ✐

**St Teresa's Effingham
(Senior School)**
Beech Avenue, Effingham,
Surrey RH5 6ST
Tel: 01372 452037
Executive Director: Mr Mike Farmer
Age range: G11–18
No. of pupils: 640 VIth90
Fees: Day £17,865–£18,465 WB
£28,875–£29,175 FB £30,795–£31,455
⛫ ⛫ Ⓐ ⛫ £ ✐ 16·

ST. ANDREW'S SCHOOL
For further details see p.214
Church Hill House, Horsell,
Woking, Surrey GU21 4QW
Tel: 01483 760943
Email: admin@st-andrews.
woking.sch.uk
Website:
www.st-andrews.woking.sch.uk
Headmaster: Mr D Fitzgerald
Age range: 3–13
No. of pupils: 300
Fees: Day £3,933–£15,495
£ ✐

Surbiton Preparatory School
3 Avenue Elmers, Surbiton,
Surrey KT6 4SP
Tel: 020 8390 6640
Principal: Mrs Rebecca Glover
Age range: B4–11 G4–11
No. of pupils: 135
Fees: Day £10,857–£13,974
⛫ ✐

**TASIS The American
School in England**
Coldharbour Lane, Thorpe,
Surrey TW20 8TE
Tel: +44 (0)1932 582316
Head of School: Mr Bryan Nixon
Age range: 3–18
No. of pupils: 620
Fees: Day £11,920–£25,605 FB £47,565
⛫ ⛫ ⒾⒷ 16·

The Hawthorns School
Pendell Court, Bletchingley,
Redhill, Surrey RH1 4QJ
Tel: 01883 743048
Head of School: Mr Adrian Floyd
Age range: 2–13
No. of pupils: 520
Fees: Day £10,680–£15,780
£ ✐

The Royal Junior School
Portsmouth Road, Hindhead,
Surrey GU26 6BW
Tel: 01428 607977
Principal: Mrs Anne J P Lynch
Age range: 6 weeks–11 years
Fees: Day £10,200–£11,955
🌐

The Royal School
Farnham Lane, Haslemere,
Surrey GU27 1HQ
Tel: 01428 605805
Head: Mrs Pippa Smithson
Age range: 11–18 years
Fees: Day £10,506–£18,507
WB £27,747 FB £31,557
🌐 Ⓐ ⛫ £ ✐ 16·

Tormead School
27 Cranley Road, Guildford,
Surrey GU1 2JD
Tel: 01483 575101
Headmistress: Mrs Christina Foord
Age range: G4–18
No. of pupils: 760 VIth120
Fees: Day £8,385–£15,915
⛫ Ⓐ £ ✐ 16·

Warlingham Park School
Chelsham Common,
Warlingham, Surrey CR6 9PB
Tel: 01883 626844
Headmaster: Mrs S S Buist
Age range: 2–11
No. of pupils: 96
Fees: Day £4,230–£8,565
✐

Weston Green School
Weston Green Road, Thames
Ditton, Surrey KT7 0JN
Tel: 020 8398 2778
Head: Mrs Sarah Evans
Age range: 4–11
Fees: Day £10,164–£11,427
✐

Westward School
47 Hersham Road, Walton-on-
Thames, Surrey KT12 1LE
Tel: 01932 220911
Headmistress: Mrs Shelley Stevenson
Age range: 3–12
No. of pupils: 140
Fees: Day £7,380–£8,235
£ ✐

Woldingham School
Marden Park, Woldingham,
Surrey CR3 7YA
Tel: 01883 349431
Head of School: Dr James Whitehead
Age range: G11–18
No. of pupils: 590
Fees: Day £21,945–£23,910
FB £36,135–£39,330
⛫ 🌐 Ⓐ ⛫ £ ✐ 16·

Woodcote House School
Snows Ride, Windlesham,
Surrey GU20 6PF
Tel: 01276 472115
Headmaster: Mr D.M.K. Paterson
Age range: B7–13
No. of pupils: 100
Fees: Day £18,300 FB £24,600
⛫ ⛫ £ ✐

Yehudi Menuhin School
Stoke Road, Stoke d'Abernon,
Cobham, Surrey KT11 3QQ
Tel: 01932 864739
Interim Head: Richard Tanner
Age range: 7–19
No. of pupils: 80 VIth36
Fees: FB £34,299
🌐 Ⓐ ⛫ £ ✐ 16·

West Sussex

Ardingly College
College Road, Ardingly, Haywards Heath, West Sussex RH17 6SQ
Tel: +44 (0)1444 893320
Headmaster: Mr Ben Figgis
Age range: 13–18
No. of pupils: 559
Fees:–£23,985 FB £35,865–£29,250

Ardingly College Preparatory School
Haywards Heath, West Sussex RH17 6SQ
Tel: 01444 893200
Headmaster: Mr Harry Hastings
Age range: 2 –13
Fees: Day £9,195–£15,750

Ashton Park School
Brinsbury Campus East, Stane Street, North Heath, Pulborough, West Sussex RH20 1DJ
Tel: 01798 875836
Head: Mr G Holding
Age range: 11–16
No. of pupils: 66

Brambletye
Brambletye, East Grinstead, West Sussex RH19 3PD
Tel: 01342 321004
Headmaster: Will Brooks
Age range: 2–13
No. of pupils: 280
Fees: Day £10,050–£21,660 FB £25,815–£26,415

BURGESS HILL GIRLS
For further details see p.174
Keymer Road, Burgess Hill, West Sussex RH15 0EG
Tel: 01444 241050
Email: admissions@burgesshillgirls.com
Website: burgesshillgirls.com
Head of School: Liz Laybourn
Age range: B21/2–4 G21/2–18
No. of pupils: 505 Vlth70
Fees: Day £8,100–£20,100 FB £31,050–£35,850

Christ's Hospital
Horsham, West Sussex RH13 0LJ
Tel: 01403 211293
Head Teacher: Mr Simon Reid
Age range: 11–18
No. of pupils: 900
Fees: Day £18,510–£23,310 FB £35,850

Conifers School
Egmont Road, Midhurst, West Sussex GU29 9BG
Tel: 01730 813243
Headmistress: Mrs Emma Smyth
Age range: 2–13
No. of pupils: 104
Fees: Day £7,350–£9,750

Copthorne Prep School
Effingham Lane, Copthorne, West Sussex RH10 3HR
Tel: 01342 712311
Headmaster: Mr Chris Jones
Age range: 2–13
No. of pupils: 340
Fees: Day £9,750–£16,740 WB £20,400 FB £25,500

Cottesmore School
Buchan Hill, Pease Pottage, West Sussex RH11 9AU
Tel: 01293 520648
Head: T F Rogerson
Age range: 4–13
No. of pupils: 170
Fees: Day £3,199–£4,267 FB £9,095

Cumnor House Sussex
London Road, Danehill, Haywards Heath, West Sussex RH17 7HT
Tel: 01825 792 006
Headmaster: Fergus Llewellyn
Age range: 2–13
No. of pupils: 385
Fees: Day £8,985–£19,530 WB £22,635 FB £23,250

Dorset House School
The Manor, Church Lane, Bury, Pulborough, West Sussex RH20 1PB
Tel: 01798 831456
Headmaster: Matt Thomas
Age range: 3–13
No. of pupils: 135
Fees: Day £8,550–£17,850

Farlington School
Strood Park, Horsham, West Sussex RH12 3PN
Tel: 01403 282573
Headmistress: Ms Louise Higson BSc, PGCE
Age range: 3–18
No. of pupils: 300
Fees: Day £5,400–£17,670 WB £23,205–£28,515 FB £24,540–£29,850

Great Ballard School
Eartham House, Eartham, Nr Chichester, West Sussex PO18 0LR
Tel: 01243 814236
Head: Mr Richard Evans
Age range: 2–13
No. of pupils: 136
Fees: Day £8,580–£15,930 WB £17,010

Great Walstead School
East Mascalls Lane, Lindfield, Haywards Heath, West Sussex RH16 2QL
Tel: 01444 483528
Headmaster: Mr Chris Calvey
Age range: 21/2–13
No. of pupils: 465
Fees: Day £11,055–£15,510

Handcross Park School
Handcross, Haywards Heath, West Sussex RH17 6HF
Tel: 01444 400526
Headmaster: Mr Richard Brown
Age range: 2–13
No. of pupils: 339
Fees: Day £3,230–£6,360 WB £5,370–£7,480 FB £6,030–£8,130

Hurstpierpoint College
College Lane, Hurstpierpoint, West Sussex BN6 9JS
Tel: 01273 833636
Headmaster: Mr. T J Manly BA, MSc
Age range: 4–18
No. of pupils: 1156
Fees: Day £8,790–£22,860 WB £28,800

Hurstpierpoint College Prep School
Hurstpierpoint, West Sussex BN6 9JS
Tel: 01273 834975
Head: Mr I D Pattison BSc
Age range: 4–13
No. of pupils: 360

Lancing College
Lancing, West Sussex BN15 0RW
Tel: 01273 465805
Head Master: Mr Dominic T Oliver MPhil
Age range: 13–18
No. of pupils: 550 Vlth255
Fees: Day £8,190 FB £11,995

Lancing College Preparatory School at Worthing
Broadwater Road, Worthing, West Sussex BN14 8HU
Tel: 01903 201123
Head: Mrs Heather Beeby
Age range: 2–13
No. of pupils: 165
Fees: Day £8,115–£11,460

Oakwood Preparatory School
Chichester, West Sussex PO18 9AN
Tel: 01243 575209
Headteacher: Mrs Clare Bradbury
Age range: 21/2–11
No. of pupils: 260
Fees: Day £1,715–£5,010

Our Lady of Sion School
Gratwicke Road, Worthing, West Sussex BN11 4BL
Tel: 01903 204063
Headmaster: Dr Simon Orchard
Age range: 3–18
No. of pupils: 410
Fees: Day £8,640–£13,575

Pennthorpe School
Church Street, Horsham, West Sussex RH12 3HJ
Tel: 01403 822391
Headmistress: Alexia Bolton
Age range: 2–13
No. of pupils: 362
Fees: Day £2,070–£16,605

Rikkyo School in England
Guildford Road, Rudgwick, Horsham, West Sussex RH12 3BE
Tel: 01403 822107
Headmaster: Mr Roger Munechika
Age range: 10–18
No. of pupils: 116
Fees: FB £15,000–£21,600

SEAFORD COLLEGE
For further details see p.200
Lavington Park, Petworth,
West Sussex GU28 0NB
Tel: 01798 867392
Email: headmasterpa@seaford.org
Website: www.seaford.org
Headmaster: J P Green MA BA
Age range: 6–18
No. of pupils: 869 VIth219
Fees: Day £10,725–£22,230 WB
£22,350–£30,120 FB £34,380

(icons)

Shoreham College
St Julians Lane, Shoreham-by-
Sea, West Sussex BN43 6YW
Tel: 01273 592681
Headmaster: Mr R Taylor-West
Age range: 3–16 years
No. of pupils: 375
Fees: Day £9,750–£15,150

(icons)

Slindon College
Slindon House, Slindon, Arundel,
West Sussex BN18 0RH
Tel: 01243 814320
Head Teacher: Mr Mark Birkbeck
Age range: B8–18 years

(icons)

Sompting Abbotts Preparatory School for Boys and Girls
Church Lane, Sompting,
West Sussex BN15 0AZ
Tel: 01903 235960
Principal: Mrs P M Sinclair
Age range: 2–13
No. of pupils: 185
Fees: Day £9,195–£11,805

(icons)

Steyning Grammar School
Shooting Field, Steyning,
West Sussex BN44 3RX
Tel: +44 (0)1903 814555
Headteacher: Mr Nick Wergan
Age range: 11–18
No. of pupils: 1975
Fees: WB £9,100 FB £11,100

(icons)

The Prebendal School
52-55 West Street, Chichester,
West Sussex PO19 1RT
Tel: 01243 772220
Headteacher: Mrs L Salmond Smith
Age range: 3–13
No. of pupils: 181
Fees: Day £8,160–£15,495 WB
£18,975–£20,100 FB £22,290

(icons)

Westbourne House School
Shopwyke, Chichester,
West Sussex PO20 2BH
Tel: 01243 782739
Headmaster: Mr Martin Barker
Age range: 21/2–13 years
No. of pupils: 420
Fees: Day £10,440–£17,985
FB £21,465–£24,105

(icons)

Willow Tree Montessori Kindergarten
Charlwood House, Charlwood
Road, Lowfield Heath, Crawley,
West Sussex RH11 0QA
Tel: 01293 820721
Headmistress: Mrs G Kerfante MontDip
Age range: 1–8
Fees: Day £2,310–£2,700

(icons)

Windlesham House School
London Road, Washington,
Pulborough, West Sussex RH20 4AY
Tel: 01903 874701
Head of School: Richard Foster (to Sept
2020) & Ben Evans (from Sept 2020)
Age range: 4–13
No. of pupils: 320

(icons)

Worth School
Paddockhurst Road, Turners Hill,
Crawley, West Sussex RH10 4SD
Tel: +44 (0)1342 710200
Head Master: Stuart McPherson
Age range: 11–18
No. of pupils: 580 VIth222
Fees: Day £15,960–£23,730
FB £21,210–£33,690

(icons)

South-West

KEY TO SYMBOLS

- ⊕ *Boys' school*
- ⊛ *Girls' school*
- ⊕ *International school*
- (16) *Tutorial or sixth form college*
- Ⓐ *A levels*
- ⊕ *Boarding accommodation*
- (£) *Bursaries*
- (IB) *International Baccalaureate*
- ⊘ *Learning support*
- (16+) *Entrance at 16+*
- ⊕ *Vocational qualifications*
- (IAPS) *Independent Association of Preparatory Schools*
- (HMC) *The Headmasters' & Headmistresses' Conference*
- (ISA) *Independent Schools Association*
- (GSA) *Girls' School Association*
- (BSA) *Boarding Schools' Association*
- (S) *Society of Heads*

Unless otherwise indicated, all schools are coeducational day schools.
Single-sex and boarding schools will be indicated by the relevant icon.

Bath & North-East Somerset

Bath Academy
27 Queen Square, Bath, Bath & North-East Somerset BA1 2HX
Tel: 01225 334577
Principal: Tim Naylor BA(Hons), MSc, PGCE
Age range: 14–19+
No. of pupils: 120
Fees: Day £23,700 FB £35,000
🎓 16· Ⓐ 🏛 16·

Downside School
Stratton-on-the-Fosse, Radstock, Bath, Bath & North-East Somerset BA3 4RJ
Tel: 01761 235103
Head Master: Andrew Hobbs
Age range: 11–18
No. of pupils: 350 VIth135
Fees: Day £16,242–£19,251 FB £25,236–£33,861
🎓 Ⓐ 🏛 £ ✏ 16·

King Edward's Junior School
North Road, Bath, Bath & North-East Somerset BA2 6JA
Tel: 01225 464218
Head: Mr Greg Taylor
Age range: 7–11
No. of pupils: 182
Fees: Day £11,250
✏

King Edward's Pre-Prep & Nursery School
Weston Lane, Bath, Bath & North-East Somerset BA1 4AQ
Tel: 01225 421681
Head: Ms. Jayne Gilbert
Age range: 3–7
No. of pupils: 107
Fees: Day £8,370–£10,155

King Edward's Senior School
North Road, Bath, Bath & North-East Somerset BA2 6HU
Tel: 01225 464313
Head: Mr MJ Boden MA
Age range: 11–18
No. of pupils: 1085
Ⓐ £ ✏ 16·

Kingswood Preparatory School
College Road, Lansdown, Bath, Bath & North-East Somerset BA1 5SD
Tel: 01225 734460
Headmaster: Mr Mark Breary
Age range: 9 months–11
No. of pupils: 335
Fees: Day £10,002–£11,973 WB £19,809 FB £23,583–£24,720
🏛 £ ✏

Kingswood School
Lansdown Road, Bath, Bath & North-East Somerset BA1 5RG
Tel: 01225 734200
Headmaster: Mr Andrew Gordon-Brown
Age range: 9 months–18 years
No. of pupils: 772 VIth189
Fees: Day £10,463–£15,884 WB £20,723–£30,932 FB £24,671–£34,235
🎓 Ⓐ 🏛 £ ✏ 16·

Monkton Prep School
Church Road, Combe Down, Bath, Bath & North-East Somerset BA2 7ET
Tel: +44 (0)1225 837912
Headmaster: Mr M Davis
Age range: 7–13 (boarding from 8)
No. of pupils: 220
🏛 £ ✏

Monkton Senior School
Monkton Combe, Bath, Bath & North-East Somerset BA2 7HG
Tel: 01225 721133
Principal: Mr Chris Wheeler
Age range: 13–18
No. of pupils: 377
🎓 Ⓐ 🏛 £ ✏ 16·

Prior Park College
Ralph Allen Drive, Bath, Bath & North-East Somerset BA2 5AH
Tel: +44 (0)1225 835353
Headmaster: Mr Ben Horan
Age range: 11–18
🎓 Ⓐ 🏛 £ ✏ 16·

The Paragon School
Lyncombe House, Lyncombe Vale, Bath, Bath & North-East Somerset BA2 4LT
Tel: 01225 310837
Headmaster: Mr Andrew Harvey
Age range: 3–11
No. of pupils: 252
Fees: Day £8,745–£10,245
£ ✏

The Royal High School, Bath GDST
Lansdown Road, Bath, Bath & North-East Somerset BA1 5SZ
Tel: +44 (0)1225 313877
Head: Mrs Kate Reynolds
Age range: G3–18
No. of pupils: 640
Fees: Day £3,432–£4,865 WB £7,961–£9,674 FB £8,906–£10,762
♀ 🎓 Ⓐ 🏛 £ IB ✏ 16·

Bristol

Badminton Junior School
Westbury-on-Trym, Bristol BS9 3BA
Tel: 0117 905 5200
Head of the Junior School: Mrs E Davies
Age range: G3–11
No. of pupils: 130
Fees: Day £9,750–£11,235 FB £21,840–£24,945
♀ Ⓐ 🏛 £ ✏

Badminton School
Westbury-on-Trym, Bristol BS9 3BA
Tel: 0117 905 5271
Headmistress: Mrs Rebecca Tear BSc, MA, PGCE
Age range: G3–18
No. of pupils: 450
Fees: Day £9,750–£16,425 FB £21,840–£37,575
♀ 🎓 Ⓐ 🏛 £ ✏ 16·

Bristol Grammar School
University Road, Bristol BS8 1SR
Tel: 0117 973 6006
Headmaster: Mr Jaideep Barot
Age range: 4–18
🎓 Ⓐ £ IB ✏ 16·

Bristol Waldorf School
Redland Hill House, Redland, Bristol BS6 6UX
Tel: 0117 933 9990
Age range: 3–11
No. of pupils: 213
Fees: Day £7,977

Carmel Christian School
817A Bath Road, Brislington, Bristol BS4 5NL
Tel: 0117 977 5533
Headteacher: Jaap Van Wyk
Age range: 3–16
No. of pupils: 28
Fees: Day £1,440–£2,580

Cleve House School
254 Wells Road, Knowle, Bristol BS4 2PN
Tel: 0117 9777218
Headmaster: Mr Craig Wardle
Age range: 2–11
No. of pupils: 90
Fees: Day £6,525
✏

Clifton College
32 College Road, Clifton, Bristol BS8 3JH
Tel: 0117 315 7000
Headmaster: Dr Tim Greene
Age range: 3–18
No. of pupils: 1330 VIth280
Fees: Day £10,020–£25,590 WB £16,305–£34,200 FB £24,180–£39,405
🎓 Ⓐ 🏛 £ ✏ 16·

Clifton College Preparatory School
The Avenue, Clifton, Bristol BS8 3HE
Tel: +44 (0)117 405 8396
Head of Preparatory School: Mr Jim Walton
Age range: 2–13
No. of pupils: 495
Fees: Day £10,020–£17,460 WB £16,305–£20,565 FB £24,180–£28,650
🏛 £ ✏

Clifton High School
College Road, Clifton, Bristol BS8 3JD
Tel: 0117 973 0201
Head: Dr Alison M Neill BSc, PhD, PGCE
Age range: 3–18
No. of pupils: 527
Fees: Day £8,895–£14,985 FB £19,605
Ⓐ 🏛 £ ✏ 16·

Clifton Tutors Limited
31 Pembroke Road, Clifton, Bristol BS8 3BE
Tel: 0117 973 8376
Director of Studies: Sue Morgan
Age range: 7–19
16· Ⓐ

Colston's School
Stapleton, Bristol BS16 1BJ
Tel: 0117 965 5207
Headmaster: Jeremy McCullough
Age range: 3–18
No. of pupils: 581 VIth138
Fees: Day £7,680–£13,950
🎓 Ⓐ 🏛 £ ✏ 16·

Ecole Française de Bristol
Stanton Road, Southmead,
, Bristol BS10 5SJ
Tel: +44 (0)117 9692410
Headmistress: Mathilde Monnet
Age range: 2–11

Fairfield School
Fairfield Way, Backwell, Bristol BS48 3PD
Tel: 01275 462743
Headmistress: Mrs Lesley Barton
Age range: 2–11
No. of pupils: 136
Fees: Day £7,650–8,445

Gracefield Preparatory School
266 Overndale Road,
Fishponds, Bristol BS16 2RG
Tel: 0117 956 7977
Headmistress: Mrs E Morgan
Age range: 4–11
No. of pupils: 90
Fees: Day £5,382

Queen Elizabeth's Hospital
Berkeley Place, Clifton, Bristol BS8 1JX
Tel: 0117 930 3040
Head: Mr Stephen Holliday
MA (Cantab)
Age range: B7–18 G16–18
No. of pupils: 688
Fees: Day £9,654–£14,406

Silverhill School
Swan Lane, Winterbourne,
Bristol BS36 1RL
Tel: 01454 772156
Principal: Mr Julian Capper
Age range: 2–11
No. of pupils: 185
Fees: Day £5,130–£9,150

The Downs School
Wraxall, Bristol BS48 1PF
Tel: 01275 852008
Head: M A Gunn MA(Ed), BA, PGCE
Age range: 4–13
No. of pupils: 262

The Red Maids' Junior School
Grange Court Road, Westbury-
on-Trym, Bristol BS9 4DP
Tel: 0117 962 9451
Headteacher: Mrs Lisa
Brown BSc (Hons)
Age range: B3–7 G3–11
Fees: Day £3,135

The Red Maids' Senior School
Westbury Road, Westbury-
on-Trym, Bristol BS9 3AW
Tel: +44 (0)117 962 2641
Headmistress: Mrs Isabel
Tobias BA (Hons)
Age range: G11–18

Tockington Manor School
Washingpool Hill Road,
Tockington, Bristol BS32 4NY
Tel: 01454 613229
Headmaster: Mr Stephen Symonds
Age range: 2–14
No. of pupils: 250
Fees: Day £9,333–£14,553 FB £21,045

Torwood House School
8, 27-29 Durdham Park,
Redland, Bristol BS6 6XE
Tel: 0117 9735620
Headmistress: Mrs D Seagrove
Age range: 0–11
No. of pupils: 70
Fees: Day £7,500–£7,800

Cornwall

Polwhele House School
Truro, Cornwall TR4 9AE
Tel: 01872 273011
Headmaster: Mr Alex McCullough
Age range: 3–13
No. of pupils: 100
Fees: Day £8,820–£13,620

St Joseph's School
15 St Stephen's Hill, Launceston,
Cornwall PL15 8HN
Tel: 01566 772580
Head Teacher: Mr Oliver Scott
Age range: 4–16
No. of pupils: 215
Fees: Day £5,490–£13,875

St Petroc's School
Ocean View Road, Bude,
Cornwall EX23 8NJ
Tel: 01288 352876
Headmaster: Mr Hilton
Age range: 0–11
Fees: Day £5,850–£8,850

St. Piran's School
14 Trelissick Road, Hayle,
Cornwall TR27 4HY
Tel: 01736 752612
Headteacher: Mrs Carol de
Labat BEd(Hons), CertEd
Age range: 4–16
Fees: Day £2,775–£7,080

The Valley Nursery
Trevowah Road, Crantock,
Newquay, Cornwall TR8 5RU
Tel: 01637 830680
Principal: Kerry Wilson
Age range: 3 months–5 years

Truro High School for Girls
Falmouth Road, Truro, Cornwall TR1 2HU
Tel: 01872 272830
Headmaster: Glenn Moodie
Age range: B3–5 G3–18
No. of pupils: 432 VIth60
Fees: Day £8,001–£13,896 WB
£25,185–£26,040 FB £27,261–£28,182

Truro School
Trennick Lane, Truro, Cornwall TR1 1TH
Tel: 01872 272763
Headmaster: Mr A S Gordon-
Brown BCom, MSc, CA (SA)
Age range: 3–18
No. of pupils: 780 VIth210

Devon

Abbey School
Hampton Court, St Marychurch,
Torquay, Devon TQ1 4PR
Tel: 01803 327868
Principal: Mrs Sylvia Greinig
Age range: 0–11 years
No. of pupils: 78

Blundell's Preparatory School
Milestones House, Blundell's Road,
Tiverton, Devon EX16 4NA
Tel: 01884 252393
Head Master: Mr Andrew
Southgate BA Ed (Hons)
Age range: 2–11
No. of pupils: 220
Fees: Day £5,880–£12,195

Blundell's School
Tiverton, Devon EX16 4DN
Tel: 01884 252543
Head: Mr Bart Wielenga BComm,
Natal & Johannesburg, BEd
Age range: 11–18
No. of pupils: 604 VIth198
Fees: Day £14,130–£22,410 WB
£21,570–£30,660 FB £24,060–£35,205

EF Academy Torbay
Castle Road, Torquay, Devon TQ1 3BG
Tel: +41 (0) 43 430 4095
Head of School: Mr. Mark Howe
Age range: 14–19
No. of pupils: 300

Exeter Cathedral School
The Chantry, Palace Gate,
Exeter, Devon EX1 1HX
Tel: 01392 255298
Headmaster: James Featherstone
Age range: 2½–13
No. of pupils: 250
Fees: Day £7,338–£12,234
FB £18,768–£19,866

Exeter School
Victoria Park Road, Exeter,
Devon EX2 4NS
Tel: 01392 273679
Headmaster: Mr Bob Griffin
Age range: 7–18
No. of pupils: 924
Fees: Day £12,525–£14,025
(A) (£) ✏ (16·)

Exeter Tutorial College
44/46 Magdalen Road,
Exeter, Devon EX2 4TE
Tel: 01392 278101
Principal: K D Jack BA, DipEd
Age range: 16+
(16·) (A)

Fletewood School
88 North Road East, Plymouth,
Devon PL4 6AN
Tel: 01752 663782
Headteacher: Mrs R Gray
Age range: 3–11
No. of pupils: 70
Fees: Day £4,425

King's School
Hartley Road, Mannamead,
Plymouth, Devon PL3 5LW
Tel: 01752 771789
Headteacher: Mrs Jane Lee
Age range: 3–11
No. of pupils: 142
Fees: Day £5,895–£7,440
✏

KINGSLEY SCHOOL
For further details see p.226
Northdown Road, Bideford,
Devon EX39 3LY
Tel: 01237 426200
Email: admissions@
kingsleyschoolbideford.co.uk
Website:
www.kingsleyschoolbideford.co.uk
Headteacher: Mrs Gill Jackson
Age range: 0–18
No. of pupils: 395
Fees: Day £2,020 WB £5,695 FB £7,685
(🌐) (A) (🏊) (£) ✏ (16·) (🏑)

Magdalen Court School
Mulberry House, Victoria Park
Road, Exeter, Devon EX2 4NU
Tel: 01392 494919
Head: Mrs Sarah Wrightson
Age range: 0–18+
No. of pupils: 150 VIth20
Fees: Day £5,670–£10,200
(A) (£) ✏ (16·) (🏑)

Mount Kelly
Parkwood Road, Tavistock,
Devon PL19 0HZ
Tel: +44 (0)1822 813100
Head of School: Mr. Guy Ayling
Age range: 3–18
No. of pupils: 600
Fees: Day £7,410–£18,000 WB
£17,641–£29,280 FB £19,500–£32,490
(🏊) (A) (🏊) (£) ✏ (16·)

Park School
Park Road, Dartington,
Totnes, Devon TQ9 6EQ
Tel: 01803 864588
Teacher-in-charge: Amanda Bellamy
Age range: 3–12
Fees: Day £6,147–£9,654
(£) ✏

PLYMOUTH COLLEGE
For further details see p.228
Ford Park, Plymouth, Devon PL4 6RN
Tel: 01752 505100
Email: mail@plymouthcollege.com
Website:
www.plymouthcollege.com
Headteacher: Mrs Jo Hayward
Age range: 3–18
No. of pupils: 569
(🌐) (A) (🏊) ✏ (16·)

Plymouth College Preparatory School
St Dunstan's Abbey, The Millfields,
Plymouth, Devon PL1 3JL
Tel: 01752 201352
Headmaster: Chris Gatherer
Age range: 3–11
No. of pupils: 310
Fees: Day £7,680–£10,605
✏

Sands School
Greylands, 48 East Street,
Ashburton, Devon TQ13 7AX
Tel: 01364 653666
Administrator: Sean Bellamy
MA(Cantab), PGCE
Age range: 11–16
Fees: Day £10,710

Shebbear College
Shebbear, Beaworthy, Devon EX21 5HJ
Tel: 01409 282000
Headmaster: Mr S. D. Weale MA (Oxon)
Age range: 3–18
No. of pupils: 350 VIth78
Fees: Day £5,235–£12,975 WB
£14,250–£14,985 FB £18,750–£26,325
(🌐) (A) (🏊) (£) ✏ (16·)

South Devon Steiner School
Hood Manor, Buckfastleigh Road,
Dartington, Totnes, Devon TQ9 6AB
Tel: 01803 897 377
Education Manager: Jeff van Zyl
Age range: 3–19
No. of pupils: 307
(£) ✏

St Christopher's Preparatory School
Mount Barton, Staverton,
Devon TQ9 6PF
Tel: 01803 762202
Headmistress: Alexandra Cottell
Age range: 3–11
No. of pupils: 100
Fees: Day £7,350–£9,900
(£) ✏

St John's International School
Broadway, Sidmouth, Devon EX10 8RG
Tel: 01395 513984
Headmistress: Mrs Caroline Ward
Age range: 2–16
No. of pupils: 200
Fees: Day £6,906–£11,403
FB £19,422–£21,291
(🌐) (A) (🏊) (£) (IB) ✏

St Peter's School
Harefield, Lympstone,
Exmouth, Devon EX8 5AU
Tel: 01395 272148
Headmistress: Mrs Charlotte Johnston
Age range: 3–13
No. of pupils: 275
Fees: Day £7,650–£13,065 WB £19,935
(🏊) (£) ✏

St Wilfrid's School
25-29 St David's Hill, Exeter,
Devon EX4 4DA
Tel: 01392 276171
Headmistress: Mrs Alexandra E
M MacDonald-Dent DPhyEd
Age range: 5–16
(£)

Stover School
Stover, Newton Abbot,
Devon TQ12 6QG
Tel: +44 (0)1626 354505
Headmaster: Mr R W D Notman
Age range: 3–18
(🌐) (A) (🏊) (£) ✏ (16·)

The Maynard School
Denmark Road, Exeter, Devon EX1 1SJ
Tel: 01392 273417
Headmistress: Miss Sarah Dunn
BSc (Hons) PGCE and NPQH
Age range: G4–18
No. of pupils: VIth80
Fees: Day £6,285–£13,248
(🏊) (A) (£) ✏ (16·)

The New School
The Avenue, Exminster,
Exeter, Devon EX6 8AT
Tel: 01392 496122
Headmistress: Miss M Taylor
BA(Hons), PGCE
Age range: 3–7
No. of pupils: 61
Fees: Day £7,497
✏

Trinity School
Buckeridge Road, Teignmouth,
Devon TQ14 8LY
Tel: 01626 774138
Headmaster: Mr Lawrence Coen
Age range: 3–18
No. of pupils: 110
Fees: Day £7,755–£12,300 WB
£18,945–£25,590 FB £20,550–£27,750
(🌐) (A) (🏊) (£) ✏ (16·) (🏑)

West Buckland School
Barnstaple, Devon EX32 0SX
Tel: 01598 760281
Headmaster: Mr Phillip Stapleton
Age range: 3–18
No. of pupils: VIth135
Fees: Day £8,070–£15,060
FB £24,345–£30,720
(🌐) (A) (🏊) (£) ✏ (16·)

Dorset

Bournemouth Collegiate School
St Osmunds Road, Parkstone,
Poole, Dorset BH14 9JY
Tel: 01202 436 550
Headmaster: Mr Russell Slatford
Age range: 2–18
No. of pupils: 301
Fees: Day £7,800–£14,430
WB £27,180 FB £29,670
£

Bryanston School
Blandford Forum, Dorset DT11 0PX
Tel: 01258 484633
Headmaster: Mr M Mortimer
Age range: 13–18
No. of pupils: 687
Fees: Day £32,547 FB £39,693
A £ IB 16

Canford School
Canford Magna, Wimborne,
Dorset BH21 3AD
Tel: 01202 841254
Headmaster: B A M Vessey MA, MBA
Age range: 13–18
No. of pupils: 655
Fees: Day £9,241 FB £12,140
A £ 16

Castle Court School
Knoll Lane, Corfe Mullen,
Wimborne, Dorset BH21 3RF
Tel: 01202 694438
Headmaster: Mr Luke Gollings
Age range: 2–13
No. of pupils: 307
Fees: Day £8,790–£15,825
£

Clayesmore Preparatory School
Iwerne Minster, Blandford
Forum, Dorset DT11 8PH
Tel: 01747 813155
Head of School: Mr William Dunlop
Age range: 3–13
No. of pupils: 230
Fees: Day £13,230–£18,750
FB £17,670–£25,110
£

Clayesmore School
Iwerne Minster, Blandford
Forum, Dorset DT11 8LL
Tel: 01747 812122
Head of School: Mrs Jo Thomson
Age range: 13–18
No. of pupils: VIth161
Fees: Day £26,745 FB £36,444
A £ 16

Dumpton School
Deans Grove House, Deans Grove,
Wimborne, Dorset BH21 7AF
Tel: 01202 883818
Headmaster: Mr Christian Saenger
Age range: 2–13
No. of pupils: 328
Fees: Day £9,198–£16,482
£

Hanford School
Child Okeford, Blandford,
Dorset DT11 8HN
Tel: 01258 860219
Headmaster: Mr Rory Johnston
Age range: G7–13
No. of pupils: 100
Fees: Day £6,250 FB £7,500
£

Knighton House School and The Orchard Pre-prep
Durweston, Blandford
Forum, Dorset DT11 0PY
Tel: 01258 452065
Headmaster: Mr Robin Gainher
Age range: B3–7 G3–13
No. of pupils: 90
Fees: Day £2,325–£4,950
FB £5,800–£7,600
£

Leweston School – Prep School
Sherborne, Dorset DT9 6EN
Tel: 01963 210790
Head: Mrs Kate Reynolds
Age range: 0–11
Fees: Day £5,925–£11,520
WB £17,265 FB £20,700
£

Leweston School – Senior School
Sherborne, Dorset DT9 6EN
Tel: 01963 210691
Head: Mr John Paget-Tomlinson
Age range: G11–18
No. of pupils: 204
Fees: Day £16,137 WB
£22,556 FB £25,923
A £ 16

Milton Abbey School
Blandford Forum, Dorset DT11 0BZ
Tel: 01258 880484
Head: Judith Fremont-Barnes
Age range: 13–18
No. of pupils: 220
Fees: Day £21,630 FB £41,175
A £ 16

Park School
45-49 Queens Park, South Drive,
Bournemouth, Dorset BH8 9BJ
Tel: 01202 396640
Head of School: Mrs Melanie Dowler
Age range: 2–11
No. of pupils: 387
Fees: Day £7,275–£8,805
£

Port Regis
Motcombe Park, Shaftesbury,
Dorset SP7 9QA
Tel: 01747 857800
Head of School: S L Ilett
Age range: 2–13
No. of pupils: 324
£

Sherborne Girls
Bradford Road, Sherborne,
Dorset DT9 3QN
Tel: +44 (0)1935 818224
Headmistress: Dr Ruth Sullivan
BSc, PGCE, MSc, PhD
Age range: G11–18
No. of pupils: 485
Fees: Day £21,285 FB £28,920–£35,880
A £ 16

Sherborne International
Newell Grange, Newell,
Sherborne, Dorset DT9 4EZ
Tel: 01935 814743
Principal: Mr Tim Waters MA
(Oxon), MSc (Oxon)
Age range: 8–17
No. of pupils: 147
£

Sherborne Preparatory School
Acreman Street, Sherborne,
Dorset DT9 3NY
Tel: 01935 812097
Headmaster: Mr Nick Folland
Bsc (Hons), MIAPS, MISI
Age range: 2–13
No. of pupils: 258
Fees: Day £9,060–£17,130 WB
£23,445–£24,540 FB £23,445–£24,540
£

Sherborne School
Abbey Road, Sherborne,
Dorset DT9 3AP
Tel: +44 (0)1935 812249
Headmaster: Dr Dominic
Luckett BA, DPhil, FRSA,FHA
Age range: B13–18
No. of pupils: 596 VIth210
Fees: Day £30,375 FB £37,500
A £ 16

St Martin's School
15 Stokewood Road,
Bournemouth, Dorset BH3 7NA
Tel: 01202 292011
Headteacher: Laura Richards
Age range: 4–11 years
No. of pupils: 100
Fees: Day £5,835–£7,533

Sunninghill Preparatory School
South Court, South Walks,
Dorchester, Dorset DT1 1EB
Tel: 01305 262306
Headmaster: Mr John Thorpe
BSc (Hons), PGCE
Age range: 3–13
No. of pupils: 184
Fees: Day £8,850–£15,450
£

Talbot Heath
Rothesay Road, Bournemouth,
Dorset BH4 9NJ
Tel: 01202 761881
Head: Mrs A Holloway MA, PGCE
Age range: G3–18
No. of pupils: 582
Fees: Day £2,201–£4,801
WB £3,305 FB £3,704
A £ 16

Talbot House Preparatory School
8 Firs Glen Road, Bournemouth,
Dorset BH9 2LR
Tel: 01202 510348
Headteacher: Mrs Emma Haworth
Age range: 3–11
Fees: Day £4,320–£8,097

Yarrells Preparatory School
Yarrells House, Upton, Poole,
Dorset BH16 5EU
Tel: 01202 622229
Headteacher: Mrs Sally Weber-
Spokes BA (Hons), PGCE, IAPS, ISI
Age range: 2–13
No. of pupils: 253
Fees: Day £2,395–£4,250
£

Somerset

All Hallows Preparatory School
Cranmore Hall, Shepton
Mallet, Somerset BA4 4SF
Tel: 01749 881600
Head of School: Dr Trevor Richards
Age range: 3–13
No. of pupils: 265

**Ashbrooke House School
& Pre-School**
9 Ellenborough Park North, Weston-
Super-Mare, Somerset BS23 1XH
Tel: 01934 629515
Headteacher & Director: Miss
Karen Wallington
Age range: 3–11

Bruton School for Girls
Sunny Hill, Bruton, Somerset BA10 0NT
Tel: 01749 814400
Headmistress: Mrs Nicola Botterill
Age range: G2–18
No. of pupils: 250
Fees: Day £8,505-£17,805 FB £30,330

Chard School
Fore Street, Chard, Somerset TA20 1QA
Tel: 01460 63234
Head of School: Katie Hill
Age range: 0–11
No. of pupils: 100
Fees: Day £6,450–£7,650

Hazlegrove Prep School
Hazlegrove House, Sparkford,
Somerset BA22 7JA
Tel: +44 (0)1963 442606
Headmaster: Mr Mark White MA (Hons)
Age range: 2½–13 years
No. of pupils: 364
Fees: Day £3,016–£6,115
FB £7,093–£9,051

King's Bruton
The Plox, Bruton, Somerset BA10 0ED
Tel: 01749 814200
Headmaster: Mr I S Wilmshurst MA
Age range: 13–18
No. of pupils: 350

King's College
Taunton, Somerset TA1 3LA
Tel: 01823 328204
Headmaster: Richard Biggs
Age range: 13–18
No. of pupils: 440 VIth180
Fees: Day £22,380 FB £33,165

King's Hall School
Kingston Road, Taunton,
Somerset TA2 8AA
Tel: 01823 285920
Headmaster: Mr Justin Chippendale
Age range: 2–13
Fees: Day £7,725–£16,500
FB £18,450–£23,985

Millfield Preparatory School
Edgarley Hall, Glastonbury,
Somerset BA6 8LD
Tel: 01458 832446
Headteacher: Shirley Shayler
Age range: 2–13
No. of pupils: 444

Millfield School
Street, Somerset BA16 0YD
Tel: 01458 442291
Headmaster: Gavin Horgan
Age range: 13–18
No. of pupils: 1241
Fees: Day £25,605 FB £38,610

Perrott Hill
North Perrott, Crewkerne,
Somerset TA18 7SL
Tel: 01460 72051
Joint Acting Headteachers: Mr
Bryan Kane & Mr Will Silk
Age range: 3–13
No. of pupils: 183
Fees: Day £6,450–£15,750
WB £19,200 FB £22,740

Queen's College
Trull Road, Taunton, Somerset TA1 4QS
Tel: 01823 272559
Headmistress: Dr Lorraine Earps
Age range: 3–18
No. of pupils: 784 VIth150
Fees: Day £6,450–£18,450
FB £14,655–£31,980

Sidcot School
Oakridge Lane, Winscombe,
Somerset BS25 1PD
Tel: 01934 843102
Headmaster: Iain Kilpatrick
BA MEd FRSA
Age range: 3–18
No. of pupils: 609
Fees: Day £2,720–£6,080
FB £9,180–£11,230

**Springmead Preparatory
School & Nursery**
13 Castle Corner, Beckington,
Frome, Somerset BA11 6TA
Tel: 01373 831555
Principal: Ms Madeleine Taylor
Age range: 2–11

Sunny Hill Prep School
Sunny Hill, Bruton, Somerset BA10 0NT
Tel: 01749 814 427
Head: Mrs Helen Snow BEd
Age range: B2–7 G2–11
No. of pupils: 68
Fees: Day £8,505–£13,116 WB
£21,300–£21,651 FB £23,529–£23,880

Taunton Preparatory School
Staplegrove Road, Taunton,
Somerset TA2 6AE
Tel: 01823 703305
Headmaster: Andrew Edwards
Age range: 0–13
No. of pupils: 418
Fees: Day £7,350–£15,375
FB £14,685–£25,500

Taunton School
Staplegrove Road, Taunton,
Somerset TA2 6AD
Tel: +44 (0)1823 703703
Headmaster: Mr. Lee Glaser
Age range: 0–18
No. of pupils: 520 VIth240
Fees: Day £7,350–£19,395
FB £14,685–£36,225

Wellington Prep School
South Street, Wellington,
Somerset TA21 8NT
Tel: 01823 668700
Headmaster: Adam Gibson
Age range: 3–11
Fees: Day £6,330–£11,520

Wellington School
South Street, Wellington,
Somerset TA21 8NT
Tel: 01823 668800
Headmaster: Henry Price MA (Oxon)
Age range: 3–18
No. of pupils: VIth165
Fees: Day £6,330–£15,225 WB
£23,130–£24,105 FB £28,890–£30,810

Wells Cathedral Junior School
8 New Street, Wells, Somerset BA5 2LQ
Tel: 01749 834400
Headteacher: Julie Barrow
Age range: 3–11
No. of pupils: 150
Fees: Day £7,641–£15,375 WB
£20,322–£22,900 FB £23,458–£26,036

Wells Cathedral School
The Liberty, Wells, Somerset BA5 2ST
Tel: 01749 834200
Head: Mr Alastair Tighe
Age range: 3–18
No. of pupils: 750 VIth194
Fees: Day £7,641–£18,801 WB
£20,322–£27,843 FB £23,458–£31,464

West Midlands

KEY TO SYMBOLS
- Boys' school
- Girls' school
- International school
- Tutorial or sixth form college
- A levels
- Boarding accommodation
- £ Bursaries
- International Baccalaureate
- Learning support
- Entrance at 16+
- Vocational qualifications
- Independent Association of Preparatory Schools
- The Headmasters' & Headmistresses' Conference
- Independent Schools Association
- Girls' School Association
- Boarding Schools' Association
- Society of Heads

Unless otherwise indicated, all schools are coeducational day schools.
Single-sex and boarding schools will be indicated by the relevant icon.

Herefordshire

Hereford Cathedral Junior School
28 Castle Street, Hereford,
Herefordshire HR1 2NW
Tel: 01432 363511
Headmaster: Mr Chris Wright
Age range: 3–11
Fees: Day £8,028–£10,320
£ ✐

Hereford Cathedral School
The Old Deanery, The Cathedral Close,
Hereford, Herefordshire HR1 2NG
Tel: 01432 363522
Headmaster: Mr Paul Smith
Age range: 3–18
No. of pupils: 535 VIth130
Ⓐ £ ✐ 16+

LUCTON SCHOOL
For further details see p.236
Lucton, Herefordshire HR7 4RW
Tel: 01568 782000
Email: admissions@luctonschool.org
Website: www.luctonschool.org
Acting Heads: Mr. Goode
& Mrs. Niblett
Age range: 6 months–19
years (Boarding from 7)
No. of pupils: 360
Fees: Day £7,350–£14,250 WB
£23,400–£27,600 FB £27,885–£33,780
Ⓐ Ⓐ 🏠 £ ✐ 16+

Shropshire

Adcote School for Girls
Little Ness, Shrewsbury,
Shropshire SY4 2JY
Tel: 01939 260202
Headmistress: Mrs Diane Browne
Age range: G7–18
No. of pupils: 220
Fees: Day £9,141–£14,838 WB
£17,263–£24,754 FB £19,618–£27,097
♀ Ⓐ Ⓐ 🏠 £ ✐ 16+

Bedstone College
Bedstone, Bucknell, Shropshire SY7 0BG
Tel: 01547 530303
Headmaster: Mr David Gajadharsingh
Age range: 4–18
No. of pupils: 230
Fees: Day £5,025–£14,655
FB £17,475–£26,520
Ⓐ Ⓐ 🏠 £ ✐ 16+

Birchfield School
Albrighton, Wolverhampton,
Shropshire WV7 3AF
Tel: 01902 372534
Headmistress: Sarah Morris
Age range: 4–13
No. of pupils: 145
Fees: Day £6,750–£14,640
£ ✐

Castle House School
Chetwynd End, Newport,
Shropshire TF10 7JE
Tel: 01952 567600
Headmaster: Mr Ian Sterling
Age range: 2–11
No. of pupils: 87
Fees: Day £7,500–£8,850
£ ✐

Concord College
Acton Burnell Hall, Acton Burnell,
Shrewsbury, Shropshire SY5 7PF
Tel: 01694 731631
Principal: N G Hawkins
MA(Cantab), PGCE
Age range: 13–19
No. of pupils: 521 VIth343
Fees: Day £14,280 FB £39,900
Ⓐ Ⓐ £ ✐ 16+

ELLESMERE COLLEGE
For further details see p.232
Ellesmere, Shropshire SY12 9AB
Tel: 01691 622321
Email: registrar@ellesmere.com
Website: www.ellesmere.com
Head of School: Mr Brendan
Wignall MA, FRSA, MCMI
Age range: 7–18
No. of pupils: 550
Fees: Day £6,330 WB £8,217 FB £11,511
Ⓐ Ⓐ 🏠 £ IB ✐ 16+

Moor Park
Richards Castle, Ludlow,
Shropshire SY8 4DZ
Tel: 01584 876 061
Headmaster: Mr Charles
G O'B Minogue
Age range: 3–13 years
No. of pupils: 201
Fees: Day £2,140–£5,975
FB £7,405–£8,870
🏠 £ ✐

Moreton First
Weston Rhyn, Oswestry,
Shropshire SY11 3EW
Tel: 01691 776028
Head: Mrs Catherine Ford M.A., B.Sc.
Age range: 6 months–11 years
No. of pupils: 180
Fees: Day £10,230–£14,550 FB £23,610
Ⓐ Ⓐ £ ✐ 16+

Moreton Hall
Weston Rhyn, Oswestry,
Shropshire SY11 3EW
Tel: 01691 773671
Headteacher: George Budd
Age range: 11–18
Fees: Day £26,550–£28,725
FB £33,015–£34,875
🏠

Oswestry School
Upper Brook Street, Oswestry,
Shropshire SY11 2TL
Tel: 01691 655711
Headmaster: Mr Julian Noad BEng
Age range: 4–18
No. of pupils: 212
Fees: Day £8,700–£15,690 WB
£23,610 FB £26,850–£31,200
Ⓐ Ⓐ 🏠 £ ✐ 16+

Packwood Haugh School
Ruyton XI Towns, Shrewsbury,
Shropshire SY4 1HX
Tel: 01939 260217
Headmaster: Clive Smith-
Langridge BA(Hons), PGCE
Age range: 4–13
No. of pupils: 212
Fees: Day £8,805–£18,330
FB £23,430–£26,430
🏠 £ ✐

Prestfelde Preparatory School
London Road, Shrewsbury,
Shropshire SY2 6NZ
Tel: 01743 245400
Head of School: Mrs F Orchard
Age range: 3–13
No. of pupils: 300
Fees: Day £9,570–£16,140
🏠 £ ✐

Shrewsbury High School GDST
32 Town Walls, Shrewsbury,
Shropshire SY1 1TN
Tel: 01743 494000
Head: Ms J Sharrock
Age range: B3–13 G3–18
No. of pupils: VIth120
Fees: Day £7,686–£14,481
♀ Ⓐ Ⓐ £ ✐ 16+

SHREWSBURY SCHOOL
For further details see p.240
The Schools, Shrewsbury,
Shropshire SY3 7BA
Tel: 01743 280552
Email: admissions@
shrewsbury.org.uk
Website: www.shrewsbury.org.uk
Headmaster: Mr. Leo Winkley
Age range: 13–18
No. of pupils: 819
Fees: Day £25,770 FB £37,560
Ⓐ Ⓐ 🏠 £ ✐ 16+

St Winefride's Convent School
Belmont, Shrewsbury, Shropshire SY1 1TE
Tel: 01743 369883
Headmistress: Sister M Felicity
CertEd, BA(Hons)
Age range: 3–11
No. of pupils: 179
Fees: Day £4,355–£4,380
✐

The Old Hall School
Stanley Road, Wellington,
Shropshire TF1 3LB
Tel: 01952 223117
Headmaster: Martin Stott
Age range: 4–11
No. of pupils: 239
Fees: Day £8,310–£13,065
£ ✐

White House School
Heath Road, Whitchurch,
Shropshire SY13 2AA
Tel: 01948 662730
Headmistress: Mrs H M Clarke
Age range: 3–11
Fees: Day £4,950
✐

Wrekin College
Wellington, Shropshire TF1 3BH
Tel: 01952 265600
Headmaster: Mr Tim Firth
Age range: 11–18
No. of pupils: 415 VIth140
Fees: Day £14,820–£17,925 WB
£21,360–£25,320 FB £27,360–£32,040

Staffordshire

Abbotsholme School
Rocester, Uttoxeter,
Staffordshire ST14 5BS
Tel: 01889 590217
Headmaster: Mr Bob Barnes
Age range: 2–18
No. of pupils: 310 VIth55
Fees: Day £8,985–£22,485 WB
£17,985–£26,775 FB £23,985–£32,985

Chase Grammar School
Lyncroft House, St John's Road,
Cannock, Staffordshire WS11 0UR
Tel: 01543 501800
Principal: Dr Paul Silverwood
MA(Cantab), MSc, PhD, QTS, CChem
Age range: 2–19
No. of pupils: 300 VIth100
Fees: Day £5,985–£11,685 FB £21,500

**Chase Grammar School
International Study Centre**
Lyncroft House, St John's Road,
Cannock, Staffordshire WS11 0UR
Tel: 01543 501800
Principal: Dr Paul Silverwood
Age range: 2–18
No. of pupils: 102
Fees: Day £5,985–£11,685
FB £21,500–£31,200

Denstone College
Uttoxeter, Staffordshire ST14 5HN
Tel: 01889 590484
Headmaster: Mr Miles Norris MA (Oxon)
Age range: 11–18
No. of pupils: 614 VIth198
Fees: Day £13,596–£16,434 WB
£19,698–£22,152 FB £19,698–£28,617

**Denstone College
Preparatory School**
Smallwood Manor, Uttoxeter,
Staffordshire ST14 8NS
Tel: 01889 562083
Headmaster: Mr Jerry Gear
Age range: 2–11
No. of pupils: 153
Fees: Day £10,185–£12,900

Edenhurst Preparatory School
Westlands Avenue, Newcastle-
under-Lyme, Staffordshire ST5 2PU
Tel: 01782 619348
Headmaster: Mr Michael Hibbert
Age range: 3 months–11 years
Fees: Day £8,880–£10,749

Lichfield Cathedral School
The Palace, The Close, Lichfield,
Staffordshire WS13 7LH
Tel: 01543 306170
Head: Mrs Susan E Hannam
BA (Hons) MA PGCE
Age range: 3–18 years
No. of pupils: 426
Fees: Day £8,805–£13,815

Maple Hayes Hall School
Abnalls Lane, Lichfield,
Staffordshire WS13 8BL
Tel: 01543 264387
Principal: Dr N E Brown MSc, BA, MINS,
MSCMe, AFBPsS, CPsychol, FRSA, CSci
Age range: 7–17

Newcastle-under-Lyme School
Mount Pleasant, Newcastle-under-
Lyme, Staffordshire ST5 1DB
Tel: 01782 631197
Headmaster: Mr Nick Vernon
Age range: 3–18
No. of pupils: 879 VIth152
Fees: Day £8,550–£11,745

St Dominic's Priory School Stone
21 Station Road, Stone,
Staffordshire ST15 8EN
Tel: +44 (0)1785 814181
Head of School: Mrs Rebecca Harrison
Age range: 3–16
No. of pupils: 163
Fees: Day £7,560–£11,508

St Joseph's Preparatory School
London Road, Trent Vale, Stoke-
on-Trent, Staffordshire ST4 5NT
Tel: 01782 417533
Head: Mrs S D Hutchinson
Age range: 3–11
Fees: Day £7,605–£8,040

St. Dominic's Grammar School
32 Bargate Street, Brewood,
Staffordshire ST19 9BA
Tel: 01902 850248
Headteacher: Mr Peter
McNabb BSc Hons, PGCE
Age range: 2–18 years
No. of pupils: 198 VIth31
Fees: Day £6,834–£13,212

Stafford Grammar School
Burton Manor, Stafford,
Staffordshire ST18 9AT
Tel: 01785 249752
Headmaster: Mr M R Darley BA
Age range: 11–18
No. of pupils: 330 VIth96
Fees: Day £12,414

Yarlet School
Yarlet, Stafford, Staffordshire ST18 9SU
Tel: 01785 286568
Headmaster: Mr I Raybould BEd(Hons)
Age range: 2–13
No. of pupils: 169
Fees: Day £7,380–£12,270

Warwickshire

Arnold Lodge School
15-17 Kenilworth Road, Leamington
Spa, Warwickshire CV32 5TW
Tel: 01926 778050
Headmaster: David Preston
Age range: 4–18
No. of pupils: 250
Fees: Day £10,800–£13,116

Bilton Grange
Dunchurch, Rugby,
Warwickshire CV22 6QU
Tel: 01788 810217
Headmaster: Mr Alex
Osiatynski MA Oxon PGCE
Age range: 3–13
No. of pupils: 300

Crackley Hall School
St Joseph's Park, Kenilworth,
Warwickshire CV8 2FT
Tel: 01926 514444
Headmaster: Mr R Duigan
Age range: 2–11
No. of pupils: 233
Fees: Day £9,288–£9,888

Hijaz College
Watling Street, Nuneaton,
Warwickshire CV11 6BE
Tel: 02476 325 859
Headteacher: Mr Tauqir Ishaq
Age range: B11–21
No. of pupils: 61
Fees: FB £4,550–£5,400

King's High School for Girls
Banbury Rd, Warwick,
Warwickshire CV34 6YE
Tel: 01926 494485
Head of School: Mrs Caroline Renton
Age range: G11–18 years
No. of pupils: 780
Fees: Day £4,563

Princethorpe College
Leamington Road, Princethorpe,
Rugby, Warwickshire CV23 9PX
Tel: 01926 634200
Headmaster: Mr Ed Hester
Age range: 11–18
No. of pupils: 817 VIth184
Fees: Day £12,693
Ⓐ Ⓔ ✎ 16+

Rugby School
Rugby, Warwickshire CV22 5EH
Tel: +44 (0)1788 556274
Headmaster: Peter R.A. Green
Age range: 11–18
Fees: Day £22,437 FB £35,760
Ⓐ Ⓑ Ⓔ ⒤Ⓑ ✎ 16+

Stratford Preparatory School
Church House, Old Town, Stratford-
upon-Avon, Warwickshire CV37 6BG
Tel: 01789 297993
Headmaster: Mr N Musk
MA, BA(Jt Hons), PGCE
Age range: 2–11
Fees: Day £9,600–£11,280
✎

The Crescent School
Bawnmore Road, Bilton, Rugby,
Warwickshire CV22 7QH
Tel: 01788 521595
Headmaster: Mr J.P. Thackway
B.A.Hons, P.G.C.E.
Age range: 4–11
No. of pupils: 137
Fees: Day £8,094–£9,714
Ⓔ ✎

The Croft Preparatory School
Alveston Hill, Loxley Road, Stratford-
upon-Avon, Warwickshire CV37 7RL
Tel: 01789 293795
Headmaster: Mr Marcus Cook
Age range: 2–11
No. of pupils: 425
Fees: Day £7,962–£12,213

The Kingsley School
Beauchamp Avenue, Leamington
Spa, Warwickshire CV32 5RD
Tel: 01926 425127
Headteacher: Ms Heather Owens
Age range: B3–11 G3–18
No. of pupils: 333 VIth61
Fees: Day £10,599–£13,254
Ⓑ Ⓐ Ⓔ ✎ 16+

Twycross House Pre-Preparatory School
The Hollies, The Green, Atherstone,
Warwickshire CV9 3PQ
Tel: 01827 880725
Joint Heads: Mr S D Assinder
& Mrs R T Assinder
Age range: 4–8
Fees: Day £8,610

Twycross House School
Main Road, Twycross, Atherstone,
Warwickshire CV9 3QA
Tel: 01827 880651
Headmaster: Mr S D Assinder
Age range: 8–18
Fees: Day £9,270–£10,485
Ⓐ 16+

Warwick Preparatory School
Bridge Field, Banbury Road,
Warwick, Warwickshire CV34 6PL
Tel: 01926 491545
Headmistress: Hellen Dodsworth
Age range: B3–7 G3–11
No. of pupils: 438
Fees: Day £7,767–£12,666
✎

Warwick School
Myton Road, Warwick,
Warwickshire CV34 6PP
Tel: 01926 776400
Head Master: Dr D Smith
Age range: B7–18
No. of pupils: 1214 VIth249
Fees: Day £11,181–£13,194
WB £26,883 FB £28,758
Ⓑ Ⓓ Ⓐ Ⓑ Ⓔ ✎ 16+

West Midlands

Abu Bakr Girls School
Shelly Campus, Scarborough Road,
Walsall, West Midlands WS2 9TY
Tel: 01922 612361
Headteacher: Moulana M Ramzan
Age range: G11–16
Ⓖ

Al Huda Girls School
74-76 Washwood Heath Road, Saltley,
Birmingham, West Midlands B8 1RD
Tel: 0121 328 8999
Headmistress: Mrs Y Jawaid
Age range: G11–17
No. of pupils: 87
Ⓖ

Al-Ameen Primary School
Stanfield House, 447 Warwick Way,
Birmingham, West Midlands B11 2JR
Tel: 0121 706 3322
Head: Maulana Mohammed
Aminur Rahman
Age range: 3–11
No. of pupils: 22

Al-Burhan Grammar School
28A George Street, Balsall Heath,
Birmingham, West Midlands B12 9RG
Tel: 0121 4405454
Head: Dr Mohammad Nasrullah
Age range: G11–16
No. of pupils: 80
Fees: Day £11,700
Ⓖ

Al-Furqan Primary School
Reddings Lane, Tyseley, Birmingham,
West Midlands B11 3EY
Tel: 0121 777 2222
Executive Head Teacher: Ms
Susan Barratt
Age range: 4–11

Archway Academy
86 Watery Lane Middleway, Bordesley,
Birmingham, West Midlands B9 4HN
Tel: 0121 772 7772
Executive Managing Director: Jim Ryan
Age range: 14–19

Bablake Junior School
Coundon Road, Coventry,
West Midlands CV1 4AU
Tel: 024 7627 1260
Headmaster: Mr N Price
Age range: 7–11
Fees: Day £9,411

Bablake PrePrep
The Grange, Brownshill Green Road,
Coventry, West Midlands CV6 3EG
Tel: 024 7622 1677
Head of Pre Prep: Mrs T Horton
Age range: 3–7
Fees: Day £8,097

Bablake School
Coundon Road, Coventry,
West Midlands CV1 4AU
Tel: 024 7627 1200
Headmaster: Mr A M Wright
Age range: 11–18
Fees: Day £12,162
Ⓐ Ⓔ ✎ 16+

Birchfield Independent Girls' School
30 Beacon Hill, Aston, Birmingham,
West Midlands B6 6JU
Tel: 0121 327 7707
Head Teacher: Rehana Mogra
Age range: G11–17
Ⓖ

Copsewood School
168-170 Roland Avenue, Holbrooks,
Coventry, West Midlands CV6 4LX
Tel: 024 7668 0680
Headteacher: Mr A R G Shedden
Age range: 11–16
No. of pupils: 77

Darul Uloom Islamic High School
521 Coventry Road, Small Heath,
Birmingham, West Midlands B10 0LL
Tel: 0121 772 6408
Principal: Dr Asm Abdul Rahim
Age range: B11–16
No. of pupils: 70
Ⓑ Ⓐ 16+

Edgbaston High School for Girls
Westbourne Road, Edgbaston,
Birmingham, West Midlands B15 3TS
Tel: 0121 454 5831
Headmistress: Dr Ruth A
Weeks BSc, PhD
Age range: G2–18
No. of pupils: 920 VIth112
Fees: Day £8,592–£12,774
Ⓖ Ⓐ Ⓑ Ⓔ ✎ 16+

Elmfield Rudolf Steiner School
14 Love Lane, Stourbridge,
West Midlands DY8 2EA
Tel: 01384 394633
College of Teachers: Education Admin
Age range: 3–17
No. of pupils: VIth100
Fees: Day £5,220–£8,034
Ⓔ ✎

Elmhurst Ballet School
249 Bristol Road, Edgbaston,
Birmingham, West Midlands B5 7UH
Tel: 0121 472 6655
Principal: Jessica Wheeler
BA(Hons), NPQH
Age range: 11–19
No. of pupils: VIth69
Fees: Day £18,564–£19,239
FB £23,793–£25,650
Ⓑ Ⓐ Ⓑ Ⓔ ✎ 16+

Emmanuel School (Walsall)
36 Wolverhampton Road, Walsall,
West Midlands WS2 8PR
Tel: 01922 635810
Head Teacher: Mr Jonathan
Swain BA PGCE
Age range: 3–16
No. of pupils: 82
Fees: Day £4,044

Eversfield Preparatory School
Warwick Road, Solihull,
West Midlands B91 1AT
Tel: 0121 705 0354
Headmaster: Mr R A Yates
BA, PGCE, LPSH
Age range: 2–11
Fees: Day £9,583–£10,971
Ⓔ ✎

Green Heath School
43-51 Whitmore Road, Small Heath,
Birmingham, West Midlands B10 0NR
Tel: 0121 213 1171
Age range: 11–19

Greenfields Primary School
472 Coventry Road, Birmingham,
West Midlands B10 0UG
Tel: 0121 7724567
Headteacher: P. Sa'eed Alam
Age range: 5–11

Hallfield School
Church Road, Edgbaston,
Birmingham, West Midlands B15 3SJ
Tel: 0121 454 1496
Headmaster: Mr Keith Morrow
Age range: 3 months–13

Hamd House Preparatory School
730 Bordesley Green, Birmingham,
West Midlands B9 5PQ
Tel: +44 (0) 121 771 3030
Headteacher: Mr S Ali
Age range: 3–11
No. of pupils: 206

Highclare School
10 Sutton Road, Erdington,
Birmingham, West Midlands B23 6QL
Tel: 0121 373 7400
Head: Dr Richard Luker
Age range: B1–12 G1–18
No. of pupils: 638 VIth28
Fees: Day £5,420–£12,645

Hydesville Tower School
25 Broadway North, Walsall,
West Midlands WS1 2QG
Tel: 01922 624374
Headmaster: Mr Warren Honey
BSc (Hons), PGCE Durham
University, MEd Open Univ+
Age range: 3–16
No. of pupils: 289
Fees: Day £9,738–£13,758

Jamia Islamia Birmingham Islamic College
Fallows Road, Sparkbrook,
Birmingham, West Midlands B11 1PL
Tel: 0121 7726400
Headteacher: Mohammed Govalia
Age range: 11–16
No. of pupils: 111

King Edward VI High School for Girls
Edgbaston Park Road, Birmingham,
West Midlands B15 2UB
Tel: 0121 472 1834
Principal: Ms Ann Clark
Age range: G11–18
No. of pupils: 591
Fees: Day £12,888

King Edward's School
Edgbaston Park Road, Birmingham,
West Midlands B15 2UA
Tel: 0121 472 1672
Chief Master: Dr Katy Ricks M.A, DPhil
Age range: B11–18
No. of pupils: 885 VIth221
Fees: Day £13,692

King Henry VIII Preparatory School
Kenilworth Road, Coventry,
West Midlands CV3 6PT
Tel: 024 7627 1307
Head of School: Caroline Soan
Age range: 3–11
Fees: Day £8,652–£8,991

King Henry VIII School
Warwick Road, Coventry,
West Midlands CV3 6AQ
Tel: 024 7627 1111
Headmaster: Mr J Slack MA Ed
Age range: 11–18
No. of pupils: 724 VIth210
Fees: Day £11,694

Kingswood School
St James Place, Shirley, Solihull,
West Midlands B90 2BA
Tel: 0121 744 7883
Headmaster: Mr Rob Luckham
BSc(Hons), PGCE
Age range: 3–11
No. of pupils: 89

Lambs Christian School
113 Soho Hill, Hockley, Birmingham,
West Midlands B19 1AY
Tel: 0121 5543790
Headteacher: Mrs Patricia Ekhuenelo
Age range: 3–11
No. of pupils: 43

Lote Tree Primary
643 Foleshill Road, Coventry,
West Midlands CV6 5JQ
Tel: 024 7626 1803
Head: Mrs Ashique
Age range: 2–11
No. of pupils: 97

MANDER PORTMAN WOODWARD – BIRMINGHAM
For further details see p.238
16-18 Greenfield Crescent,
Edgbaston, Birmingham,
West Midlands B15 3AU
Tel: 0121 454 9637
Email: birmingham@mpw.ac.uk
Website: www.mpw.ac.uk
Principal: Mr Mark Shingleton
Age range: 14–19

Mayfield Preparatory School
Sutton Road, Walsall, West
Midlands WS1 2PD
Tel: 01922 624107
Headmaster: Mr Matthew Draper
Age range: 2–11
No. of pupils: 212
Fees: Day £5,220–£8,700

Newbridge Preparatory School
51 Newbridge Crescent,
Tettenhall, Wolverhampton,
West Midlands WV6 0LH
Tel: 01902 751088
Headmistress: Mrs Sarah Fisher
Age range: B3–4 G3–11
No. of pupils: 148

Norfolk House School
4 Norfolk Road, Edgbaston,
Birmingham, West Midlands B15 3PS
Tel: 0121 454 7021
Headmistress: Mrs Sarah
Morris BA (Hons), PGCE
Age range: 3–11
No. of pupils: 146
Fees: Day £7,176–£10,380

Pattison College
86-90 Binley Road, Coventry,
West Midlands CV3 1FQ
Tel: 024 7645 5031
Principal: Mrs E.A.P.
McConnell B.Ed. (Hons)
Age range: 3–16
No. of pupils: 110 VIth16
Fees: Day £6,585–£8,895

Priory School
39 Sir Harry's Road, Edgbaston,
Birmingham, West Midlands B15 2UR
Tel: 0121 440 4103
Headmaster: Mr J Cramb
Age range: 6 months–18 years

Rosslyn School
1597 Stratford Road, Hall Green,
Birmingham, West Midlands B28 9JB
Tel: 0121 744 2743
Principal: Mr Khan
Age range: 2–11
Fees: Day £3,588–£6,252

Ruckleigh School
17 Lode Lane, Solihull, West
Midlands B91 2AB
Tel: 0121 705 2773
Headmistress: Mrs Barbara Forster
Age range: 3–11
Fees: Day £8,640–£9,120

Saint Martin's School
Malvern Hall, Brueton Avenue,
Solihull, West Midlands B91 3EN
Tel: 0121 705 1265
Headmistress: Mrs Nicola Smillie
BA (Hons), PGCE, NPQH
Age range: G3–18
No. of pupils: 430 VIth40
Fees: Day £9,900–£12,750

Solihull School
Warwick Road, Solihull,
West Midlands B91 3DJ
Tel: 0121 705 0958
Headmaster: Mr David E J J Lloyd
Age range: 7–18
No. of pupils: 1013 VIth279
Fees: Day £10,491–£12,897

St George's School, Edgbaston
31 Calthorpe Road, Birmingham,
West Midlands B15 1RX
Tel: 0121 625 0398
Head of School: Mr Gary
Neal BEd (Hons)
Age range: 3–18
No. of pupils: 368 VIth48
Fees: Day £6,060–£9,765

TETTENHALL COLLEGE
For further details see p.242
Wood Road, Tettenhall,
Wolverhampton, West
Midlands WV6 8QX
Tel: 01902 751119
Email: admissions@tettcoll.co.uk
Website:
www.tettenhallcollege.co.uk
Headteacher: Mr
Christopher McAllister
Age range: 2–18
No. of pupils: 410

The Birmingham Theatre School
The Old Fire Station, 285-287
Moseley Road, Birmingham,
West Midlands B12 0DX
Tel: +44(0) 121 440 1665
Principal: Chris Rozanski
Age range: 5–65

The Blue Coat School
Somerset Road, Edgbaston,
Birmingham, West Midlands B17 0HR
Tel: 0121 410 6800
Headmaster: Mr N G Neeson
Age range: 2–11
Fees: Day £4,059–£12,714

**THE ROYAL SCHOOL
WOLVERHAMPTON**
For further details see p.244
Penn Road, Wolverhampton,
West Midlands WV3 0EG
Tel: +44 (0)1902 341230
Email: info@theroyal.school
Website: www.theroyalschool.co.uk
Age range: 4–19
No. of pupils: 1432
Fees: FB £12,900

The Shrubbery School
Walmley Ash Road, Walmley, Sutton
Coldfield, West Midlands B76 1HY
Tel: 0121 351 1582
Head Teacher: Hilary Atkins
Age range: 3–11
Fees: Day £3,765–£8,808

WEST HOUSE SCHOOL
For further details see p.246
24 St James's Road, Edgbaston,
Birmingham, West Midlands B15 2NX
Tel: 0121 440 4097
Email: secretary@
westhouseprep.com
Website: www.westhouseprep.com
Headmaster: Mr Alistair M J
Lyttle BA(Hons), PGCE, NPQH
Age range: B1–11 G1–4
No. of pupils: 350
Fees: Day £1,466–£4,083

Wolverhampton Grammar School
Compton Road, Wolverhampton,
West Midlands WV3 9RB
Tel: 01902 421326
Head: Kathy Crewe-Read BSc
Age range: 7–18
No. of pupils: 738 VIth156
Fees: Day £3,457–£4,554

Woodstock Girls' School
11-15 Woodstock Road, Moseley,
Birmingham, West Midlands B13 9BB
Tel: 0121 4496690
Headteacher: Mrs
Na'zihah Ahmed-Atif
Age range: G11–16
No. of pupils: 123

Worcestershire

Abberley Hall
Abberley Hall, Worcester,
Worcestershire WR6 6DD
Tel: 01299 896275
Headmaster: Mr Will Lockett
Age range: 2–13
No. of pupils: 202

Bowbrook House School
Peopleton, Pershore,
Worcestershire WR10 2EE
Tel: 01905 841242
Headteacher: Mr C D Allen BSc(Hons)
Age range: 3–16
Fees: Day £5,775–£11,388

Bromsgrove Preparatory School
Old Station Road, Bromsgrove,
Worcestershire B60 2BU
Tel: 01527 579600
Headmistress: Jacqui Deval-Reed
Age range: 7–13
Fees: Day £11,640–£15,105 WB
£17,685–£21,390 FB £24,240–£29,895

**Bromsgrove Pre-preparatory
& Nursery School**
Avoncroft House, Hanbury Road,
Bromsgrove, Worcestershire B60 4JS
Tel: 01527 873007
Headmistress: Jacqui Deval-Reed
Age range: 2–7
Fees: Day £5,625–£8,790

Bromsgrove School
Worcester Road, Bromsgrove,
Worcestershire B61 7DU
Tel: +44 (0)1527 579679
Headmaster: Peter Clague
Age range: 13–18
No. of pupils: 1300
Fees: Day £17,085 WB
£25,335 FB £38,220

Cambian New Elizabethan School
Quarry Bank, Hartlebury,
Kidderminster, Worcestershire DY11 7TE
Tel: 01299 250258
Headteacher: Mr Craig Moreton
Age range: 7–19
No. of pupils: 45

Heathfield Knoll School
Wolverley Road, Wolverley, Nr.
Kidderminster, Worcestershire DY10 3QE
Tel: 01562 850204
Head of School: Mr. L. G. Collins
B.Sc.(Hons), M.A.,P.G.C.E.
Age range: 3 months–16 years
No. of pupils: 251
Fees: Day £7,800–£12,465

King's Hawford
Hawford Lock Lane, Claines,
Worcester, Worcestershire WR3 7SE
Tel: 01905 451292
Headmaster: Mr J Turner
Age range: 2–11
No. of pupils: 330
Fees: Day £7,344–£13,221

King's St Alban's School
Mill Street, Worcester,
Worcestershire WR1 2NJ
Tel: 01905 354906
Headmaster: Mr R Chapman
Age range: 4–11
No. of pupils: 216
Fees: Day £7,008–£12,678

KING'S WORCESTER
For further details see p.234
5 College Green, Worcester,
Worcestershire WR1 2LL
Tel: 01905 721742
Email: registrar@ksw.org.uk
Website: www.ksw.org.uk
Headteacher: Mr Gareth Doodes
Age range: 11–18
No. of pupils: 896
Fees: Day £4,850

Madinatul Uloom Islamic College
Butts Lane, Stone, Kidderminster,
Worcestershire DY10 4BH
Tel: 01562 66894
The Head: Head
Age range: B11–24
No. of pupils: 200

Madresfield Early Years Centre
Hayswood Farm, Madresfield,
Malvern, Worcestershire WR13 5AA
Tel: 01684 574378
Head: Mrs A Bennett M.B.E.
Age range: 1–5
No. of pupils: 216
Fees: Day £5,800–£6,500

Malvern College
College Road, Malvern,
Worcestershire WR14 3DF
Tel: +44 (0)1684 581613
Headmaster: Keith Metcalfe
MA (Cantab)
Age range: 13–18
No. of pupils: 640
Fees: Day £8,807 FB £13,185–£13,646

Malvern St James Girls' School
15 Avenue Road, Great Malvern,
Worcestershire WR14 3BA
Tel: 01684 892288
Headteacher: Mrs Olivera
Raraty BA PGCE
Age range: G4–18
No. of pupils: 410
Fees: Day £7,170–£19,875 WB
£20,520–£34,620 FB £22,905–£38,190

RGS Dodderhill
Crutch Lane, Droitwich,
Worcestershire WR9 0BE
Tel: 01905 778290
Headmistress: Mrs Sarah Atkinson
Age range: G4–16
No. of pupils: 190
Fees: Day £6,870–£11,700

RGS Springfield
Springfield, Britannia Square,
Worcester, Worcestershire WR1 3DL
Tel: 01905 24999
Headmistress: Mrs Laura Brown
Age range: 2–11
No. of pupils: 140
Fees: Day £8,160–£12,546
(£)

RGS The Grange
Grange Lane, Claines, Worcester,
Worcestershire WR3 7RR
Tel: 01905 451205
Headmaster: Mr Gareth Hughes
Age range: 2–11
No. of pupils: 350
Fees: Day £8,160–£12,546
(✎)

River School
Oakfield House, Droitwich Road,
Worcester, Worcestershire WR3 7ST
Tel: 01905 457047
Principal: Mr Adrian Parsonage
Age range: 2–16

The Downs Malvern
Colwall, Malvern,
Worcestershire WR13 6EY
Tel: 01684 544100
Headmaster: Mr Alastair Cook
Age range: 3–13
Fees: Day £7,107–£17,076 WB
£12,882–£19,890 FB £14,640–£22,602
(⚑)(£)(✎)

The Elms
Colwall, Malvern,
Worcestershire WR13 6EF
Tel: 01684 540344
Headmaster: Mr Chris Hattam
Age range: 3–13
No. of pupils: 200
Fees: Day £8,085–£19,500
FB £24,000–£24,480
(⚑)(£)(✎)

**The Royal Grammar
School Worcester**
Upper Tything, Worcester,
Worcestershire WR1 1HP
Tel: 01905 613391
Headmaster: Mr John Pitt
Age range: 11–18
No. of pupils: 764
Fees: Day £13,080
(A)(£)(✎)(16+)

Winterfold House
Chaddesley Corbett, Kidderminster,
Worcestershire DY10 4PW
Tel: 01562 777234
Headmistress: Mrs Denise Toms
Age range: 6 weeks–13 years
(£)(✎)

D360

Yorkshire & Humberside

KEY TO SYMBOLS

- 👤 *Boys' school*
- 👤 *Girls' school*
- 🌐 *International school*
- 16 *Tutorial or sixth form college*
- Ⓐ *A levels*
- 🏛 *Boarding accommodation*
- £ *Bursaries*
- IB *International Baccalaureate*
- ✎ *Learning support*
- 16+ *Entrance at 16+*
- 🎓 *Vocational qualifications*
- IAPS *Independent Association of Preparatory Schools*
- HMC *The Headmasters' & Headmistresses' Conference*
- ISA *Independent Schools Association*
- GSA *Girls' School Association*
- BSA *Boarding Schools' Association*
- Ⓢ *Society of Heads*

Unless otherwise indicated, all schools are coeducational day schools. Single-sex and boarding schools will be indicated by the relevant icon.

East Riding of Yorkshire

Focus School – Cottingham Campus
Old Victorian School, Hallgate, Cottingham, East Riding of Yorkshire HU16 0DD
Tel: 01482 840722

Froebel House School
5 Marlborough Avenue, Kingston upon Hull, East Riding of Yorkshire HU5 3JP
Tel: 01482 342272
Headmaster: Mr A Roberts M.Ed BA Hons PGCE
Age range: 4–11
No. of pupils: 131
Fees: Day £4,398–£4,623
ⓘ

Hessle Mount School
Jenny Brough Lane, Hessle, East Riding of Yorkshire HU13 0JZ
Tel: 01482 643371
Headmistress: Miss Sarah Cutting
Age range: 3–8
No. of pupils: 155
Fees: Day £6,000–£6,300

Hull Collegiate School
Tranby Croft, Anlaby, Kingston upon Hull, East Riding of Yorkshire HU10 7EH
Tel: 01482 657016
Headteacher: Mrs Alex Wilson
Age range: 3–18
No. of pupils: 650
Fees: Day £5,013–£11,796
Ⓐ Ⓔ ⓘ ⑯

Hymers College
Hymers Avenue, Kingston upon Hull, East Riding of Yorkshire HU3 1LW
Tel: 01482 343555
Headmaster: Mr D Elstone
Age range: 8–18
No. of pupils: 977 VIth215
Fees: Day £9,459–£11,358
Ⓐ Ⓔ ⑯

North Yorkshire

Ampleforth College
York, North Yorkshire YO62 4ER
Tel: 01439 766000
Acting Head: Miss Deirdre Rowe
Age range: 11–18
No. of pupils: VIth255
Fees: Day £24,636 FB £35,424
Ⓕ Ⓐ Ⓜ Ⓔ ⓘ ⑯

Ashville College
Green Lane, Harrogate, North Yorkshire HG2 9JP
Tel: 01423 566358
Headmaster: Mr Richard Marshall
Age range: 3–18
No. of pupils: 870
Fees: Day £8,430–£14,640 FB £18,390–£27,780
Ⓕ Ⓐ Ⓜ Ⓔ ⓘ ⑯

Aysgarth School
Newton le Willows, Bedale, North Yorkshire DL8 1TF
Tel: 01677 450240
No. of pupils: 211
Fees: Day £2,820–£6,630 WB £995–£1,325 FB £8,630
Ⓣ Ⓜ Ⓔ ⓘ

Belmont Grosvenor School
Swarcliffe Hall, Birstwith, Harrogate, North Yorkshire HG3 2JG
Tel: 01423 771029
Headmistress: Mrs Sophia Ashworth Jones
Age range: 3 months–11 years
No. of pupils: 153
Fees: Day £9,600–£11,370

Bootham Junior School
Rawcliffe Lane, York, North Yorkshire YO30 6NP
Tel: 01904 655021
Head: Mrs Helen Todd
Age range: 3–11
Fees: Day £6,930–£10,365
ⓘ

Bootham School
York, North Yorkshire YO30 7BU
Tel: 01904 623261
Headmaster: Chris Jeffery BA, FRSA
Age range: 11–18
No. of pupils: 480 VIth172
Fees: Day £16,200–£17,865 WB £18,885–£27,765 FB £18,885–£30,465
Ⓕ Ⓐ Ⓜ Ⓔ ⓘ ⑯

Brackenfield School
128 Duchy Road, Harrogate, North Yorkshire HG1 2HE
Tel: 01423 508558
Headteacher: Ms Patricia Sowa
Age range: 2–11
No. of pupils: 179
Fees: Day £8,235–£8,850
ⓘ

Chapter House Preparatory School
Thorpe Underwood Hall, Ouseburn, York, North Yorkshire YO26 9SZ
Tel: 01423 333330
Head Teacher: Mrs Karen Kilkenny BSc
Age range: 3–10
Ⓜ Ⓔ ⓘ

Clifton School and Nursery
York, North Yorkshire YO30 6AB
Tel: 01904 527361
Head: Philip Hardy BA (Hons) PGCE
Age range: 3–8
No. of pupils: 199
Fees: Day £7,980–£9,240

Cundall Manor School
Helperby, York, North Yorkshire YO61 2RW
Tel: 01423 360200
Joint Heads: Mrs Amanda Kirby BA (Hons) PGCE, NPQH & Mr John Sample BSc (Hons) PGCE
Age range: 2–16
No. of pupils: 350
Fees: Day £9,738–£15,612 WB £20,313–£20,529
Ⓜ Ⓔ ⓘ

Fyling Hall School
Robin Hood's Bay, Whitby, North Yorkshire YO22 4QD
Tel: 01947 880353
Headmaster: Mr. Steven Allen
Age range: 4–18
No. of pupils: VIth54
Fees: Day £6,684–£9,177 WB £9,207–£11,778 FB £16,230–£19,995
Ⓕ Ⓐ Ⓜ Ⓔ ⓘ ⑯

Giggleswick Junior School
Mill Lane, Giggleswick, Settle, North Yorkshire BD24 0DG
Tel: 01729 893100
Headmaster: Mr. James Mundell
Age range: 3–11 (boarding from 9)
No. of pupils: 75
Fees: Day £7,965–£12,765 FB £21,240
Ⓜ Ⓔ ⓘ

Giggleswick School
Giggleswick, Settle, North Yorkshire BD24 0DE
Tel: 01729 893000
Head: Mr Mark Turnbull
Age range: 11–18
No. of pupils: 320 VIth145
Fees: Day £15,585–£20,985 FB £23,550–£33,750
Ⓕ Ⓐ Ⓜ Ⓔ ⓘ ⑯

Harrogate Ladies' College
Clarence Drive, Harrogate, North Yorkshire HG1 2QG
Tel: 01423 504543
Principal: Mrs Sylvia Brett
Age range: G11–18
No. of pupils: 300
Fees: Day £16,035 FB £29,115–£36,510
Ⓣ Ⓕ Ⓐ Ⓜ Ⓔ ⓘ ⑯

Highfield Prep School
Clarence Drive, Harrogate, North Yorkshire HG1 2QG
Tel: 01423 504 543
Head: James Savile
Age range: 4–11
No. of pupils: 216
Fees: Day £9,420–£10,740 FB £23,820

Pocklington Prep School
West Green, Pocklington, York, North Yorkshire YO42 2NH
Tel: 01759 321228
Headmaster: Mr I D Wright BSc(Hons), PGCE, NPQH
Age range: 3–11
No. of pupils: 225
Fees: Day £7,812–£12,255 WB £18,366–£21,393 FB £20,202–£23,046
Ⓜ Ⓔ ⓘ

POCKLINGTON SCHOOL
For further details see p.250
West Green, Pocklington, York, North Yorkshire YO42 2NJ
Tel: 01759 321200
Email: admissions@pocklingtonschool.com
Website: www.pocklingtonschool.com
Headmaster: Mr Toby Seth MA (Cantab)
Age range: 3–18
No. of pupils: 705 VIth135
Fees: Day £15,057 WB £26,991 FB £29,346
Ⓕ Ⓐ Ⓜ Ⓔ ⓘ ⑯

QUEEN ETHELBURGA'S COLLEGIATE FOUNDATION
For further details see p.252
Thorpe Underwood Hall, Ouseburn, York, North Yorkshire YO26 9SS
Tel: 01423 33 33 33
Email: info@qe.org
Website: www.qe.org
Principal: Jeff Smith
Age range: 3–19
No. of pupils: 1248
Ⓕ Ⓐ Ⓜ Ⓔ ⓘ ⑯ Ⓝ

Queen Margaret's School
Escrick Park, York, North
Yorkshire YO19 6EU
Tel: 01904 727600
Head of School: Mrs Jessica Miles
Age range: G11–18
No. of pupils: 302 VIth120
Fees: Day £21,270 FB £30,400

Queen Mary's School
Baldersby Park, Topcliffe, Thirsk,
North Yorkshire YO7 3BZ
Tel: 01845 575000
Head: Carole Cameron
Age range: B3–8 G3–16
No. of pupils: 235
Fees: Day £8,265–£18,420
FB £20,475–£24,165

Scarborough College
Filey Road, Scarborough,
North Yorkshire YO11 3BA
Tel: +44 (0)1723 360620
Headmaster: Mr Charles Ellison
Age range: 3–18
No. of pupils: 418 VIth84
Fees: Day £7,488–£14,694 WB
£17,217–£19,440 FB £22,041–£28,458

St Martins Ampleforth
Gilling Castle, Gilling East, York,
North Yorkshire YO62 4HP
Tel: 01439 766600
Headmaster: Dr D Moses
Age range: 11–13 years
No. of pupils: 155
Fees: Day £16,401 FB £25,251

St Olave's School
Clifton, York, North Yorkshire YO30 6AB
Tel: 01904 527416
The Master: Mr A Falconer
Age range: 8–13
No. of pupils: 355
Fees: Day £12,345–£14,955
FB £23,160–£25,560

St Peter's School
Clifton, York, North Yorkshire YO30 6AB
Tel: 01904 527300
Head Master: Mr L Winkley
MA(Oxon), MEd(OU)
Age range: 13–18
No. of pupils: 375 VIth231
Fees: Day £18,075 FB £30,030

Terrington Hall
Terrington, York, North
Yorkshire YO60 6PR
Tel: 01653 648227
Headmaster: Mr. Simon Kibler
Age range: 3–13
No. of pupils: 150

The Mount Junior School
Dalton Terrace, York, North
Yorkshire YO24 4DD
Tel: 01904 667513
Head: Mr Martyn Andrews
BSc(Hons), PGCE
Age range: 3–11
Fees: Day £1,710–£2,280

The Mount School York
Dalton Terrace, York, North
Yorkshire YO24 4DD
Tel: 01904 667500
Principal: Miss Adrienne Richmond
BSc (Hons), PGCE, MA, NPQH
Age range: B2–11 G2–18
No. of pupils: 260 VIth47
Fees: Day £5,850–£16,950 WB
£18,060–£26,253 FB £20,391–£29,691

The Read School
Drax, Selby, North Yorkshire YO8 8NL
Tel: 01757 618248
Acting Head: M A Voisey
Age range: 3–18
No. of pupils: VIth36
Fees: Day £8,457–£11,970 WB
£21,279–£24,429 FB £22,743–£26,019

Wharfedale Montessori School
Bolton Abbey, Skipton, North
Yorkshire BD23 6AN
Tel: 01756 710452
Headmistress/Principal: Mrs Jane Lord
Age range: 2–12
Fees: Day £7,350

York Steiner School
Danesmead, Fulford Cross, York,
North Yorkshire YO10 4PB
Tel: 01904 654983
Administrator: Maurice Dobie
Age range: 3–14
No. of pupils: 197
Fees: Day £6,750

North-East Lincolnshire

Montessori School
Station Road, Stallingborough,
North-East Lincolnshire DN41 8AJ
Tel: 01472 886000
Headteacher: Ms Theresa Ellerby
Age range: 4–11
No. of pupils: 21

St James' School
22 Bargate, Grimsby, North-
East Lincolnshire DN34 4SY
Tel: 01472 503260
Headteacher: Dr J Price
Age range: 2–18
No. of pupils: 238 VIth25

St Martin's Preparatory School
63 Bargate, Grimsby, North-
East Lincolnshire DN34 5AA
Tel: 01472 878907
Headmaster: Mr S Thompson BEd
Age range: 2–11
Fees: Day £5,580–£6,780

South Yorkshire

Al-Mahad-Al-Islam School
1 Industry Road, Sheffield,
South Yorkshire S9 5FP
Tel: 0114 242 3138
Headteacher: Mrs Juwairiah Khan
Age range: G11–17
No. of pupils: 70

Bethany School
Finlay Street, Sheffield,
South Yorkshire S3 7PS
Tel: 0114 272 6994
Headteacher: Mrs Judith Baxter
Age range: 4–16
No. of pupils: 76

Birkdale School
Oakholme Road, Sheffield,
South Yorkshire S10 3DH
Tel: 0114 2668409
Acting Head: Mr Nicholas Pietrek
Age range: B4–18 G16–18
No. of pupils: VIth200
Fees: Day £8,445–£12,630

Hill House School
6th Avenue, Auckley, Doncaster,
South Yorkshire DN9 3GG
Tel: +44 (0)1302 776300
Principal: David Holland
Age range: 3–18
Fees: Day £8,700–£13,200

Mylnhurst Preparatory School & Nursery
Button Hill, Woodholm Road, Ecclesall,
Sheffield, South Yorkshire S11 9HJ
Tel: 0114 2361411
Headmaster: Christopher
Emmott BSc(Hons), PGCE
Age range: 3–11
No. of pupils: 185
Fees: Day £9,333

Sheffield High School GDST
10 Rutland Park, Sheffield,
South Yorkshire S10 2PE
Tel: 0114 266 0324
Headmistress: Nina Gunson
Age range: G4–18
No. of pupils: 1020
Fees: Day £9,216–£12,975
♿ Ⓐ £ ✎ 16

Sycamore Hall Preparatory School
1 Hall Flat Lane, Balby, Doncaster,
South Yorkshire DN4 8PT
Tel: 01302 856800
Headmistress: Miss J Spencer
Age range: 3–11
Fees: Day £4,890

Westbourne School
Westbourne Road, Sheffield,
South Yorkshire S10 2QT
Tel: 0114 2660374
Headmaster: Mr John B Hicks MEd
Age range: 3–16
No. of pupils: 338
Fees: Day £8,925–£12,750
£ ✎

West Yorkshire

Ackworth School
Pontefract Road, Ackworth,
Pontefract, West Yorkshire WF7 7LT
Tel: 01977 233 600
Headteacher: Mr. Anton
Maree BA Rhodes (HDE)
Age range: 2½–18 years
No. of pupils: 530
Fees: Day £2,830–£3,108
FB £8,016–£10,237
♿ Ⓐ ⚥ £ ✎ 16

Al Mu'min Primary School
Clifton St, Bradford, West
Yorkshire BD8 7DA
Tel: 01274 488593
Headteacher: Mr M M Azam
Age range: 4–11
No. of pupils: 102

Al-Furqaan Preparatory School
Drill Hall House, Bath Street,
Dewsbury, West Yorkshire WF13 2JR
Tel: 01924 453 661
Head of School: Ms
Shaheda Ughratdar
Age range: 2–11

Bradford Christian School
Livingstone Road, Bolton Woods,
Bradford, West Yorkshire BD2 1BT
Tel: 01274 532649
Headmaster: P J Moon BEd(Hons)
Age range: 4–16
Fees: Day £2,460–£4,440
✎

Bradford Grammar School
Keighley Road, Bradford,
West Yorkshire BD9 4JP
Tel: 01274 542492
Headmaster: Dr Simon Hinchliffe
Age range: 6–18
No. of pupils: Vlth266
Ⓐ £ ✎ 16

Bronte House School
Apperley Bridge, Bradford,
West Yorkshire BD10 0NR
Tel: 0113 2502811
Headmaster: Simon W Dunn
Age range: 2–11
No. of pupils: 340
Fees: Day £9,000–£13,575 WB
£26,160–£26,625 FB £27,900–£28,020
⚥ £ ✎

Crystal Gardens
38-40 Greaves Street, Bradford,
West Yorkshire BD5 7PE
Tel: 01274 575400
Headteacher: Rashta Bibi
Age range: 4–11
No. of pupils: 20

**Dale House Independent
School & Nursery**
Ruby Street, Carlinghow, Batley,
West Yorkshire WF17 8HL
Tel: 01924 422215
Headmistress: Mrs S M G
Fletcher BA, CertEd
Age range: 2–11

Darul Uloom Dawatul Imaan
Harry Street, Off Wakefield Road,
Bradford, West Yorkshire BD4 9PH
Tel: 01274 402233
Principal: Mr Mohamed Bilal Lorgat
Age range: B11–13
No. of pupils: 112
♂

Eternal Light Secondary School
Christopher Street, Off Little Horton
Lane, Bradford, West Yorkshire BD5 9DH
Tel: 01274 501597
Headteacher: Mr Yusuf Collector
Age range: B11–15
No. of pupils: 91
♂

Focus School – York Campus
Bishopthorpe Road, York,
West Yorkshire YO23 2GA
Tel: 01904 663300

Fulneck School
Fulneck, Pudsey, Leeds,
West Yorkshire LS28 8DS
Tel: 0113 257 0235
Principal: Mr Paul Taylor
Age range: 3–18
No. of pupils: 350
Fees: Day £7,545–£13,650
WB £24,405 FB £26,985
♿ Ⓐ ⚥ £ ✎ 16

Gateways School
Harewood, Leeds, West
Yorkshire LS17 9LE
Tel: 0113 2886345
Headmistress: Dr Tracy Johnson
Age range: B2–11 G2–18
No. of pupils: 394 Vlth48
Fees: Day £8,445–£13,614
♿ Ⓐ £ ✎ 16

Ghyll Royd School and Pre-School
Greystone Manor, Ilkley Road, Burley in
Wharfedale, West Yorkshire LS29 7HW
Tel: 01943 865575
Headteacher: Mr David
Martin BA MA PGCE
Age range: 2–11
No. of pupils: 110
Fees: Day £2,900–£2,990
£ ✎

Hipperholme Grammar School
Bramley Lane, Hipperholme,
Halifax, West Yorkshire HX3 8JE
Tel: 01422 202256
Head: Mrs Jackie Griffiths
Age range: 3–18
No. of pupils: Vlth30
Fees: Day £8,799–£10,995
Ⓐ £ ✎ 16

Huddersfield Grammar School
Royds Mount, Luck Lane, Marsh,
Huddersfield, West Yorkshire HD1 4QX
Tel: 01484 424549
Headmaster: Mr Mike Seaton
Age range: 3–16
No. of pupils: 510
Fees: Day £8,598–£10,602
£ ✎

Institute of Islamic Education
South Street, Savile Town, Dewsbury,
West Yorkshire WF12 9NG
Tel: 01924 485712/01924 455762
Principal: Mr Mohamed Aswat
Age range: B11–25
No. of pupils: 184
♂ ⚥

**Islamic Tarbiyah
Preparatory School**
Ambler Street, Bradford,
West Yorkshire BD8 8AW
Tel: 01274 490462
Headteacher: Mr S A Nawaz
Age range: 5–10
No. of pupils: 123

**Jaamiatul Imaam Muhammad
Zakaria School**
Thornton View Road, Clayton,
Bradford, West Yorkshire BD14 6JX
Tel: 01274 882007
Headteacher: Mrs Z Hajee
Age range: G11–16
No. of pupils: 416
♀

Lady Lane Park School
Lady Lane, Bingley, West
Yorkshire BD16 4AP
Tel: 01274 551168
Headmaster: Mr Nigel Saunders
Age range: 2–11
No. of pupils: 150
Fees: Day £8,016
✎

Leeds Menorah School
393 Street Lane, Leeds, West
Yorkshire LS17 6HQ
Tel: 0113 268 3390
Headteacher: Rabbi J Refson
Age range: 5–16
No. of pupils: 55

M A Institute
Lumb Lane, Bradford, West
Yorkshire BD8 7RZ
Tel: 01274 395454
Age range: B11–16
No. of pupils: 68
♂

Madni Muslim Girls High School
Thornie Bank, Off Scarborough St, Savile Town, Dewsbury, West Yorkshire WF12 9AX
Tel: 01924 520720
Headmistress: Mrs S A Mirza
Age range: G3–18
No. of pupils: 250

Mill Cottage Montessori School
Wakefield Road, Brighouse, West Yorkshire HD6 4HA
Tel: 01484 400500
Principal: Ailsa Nevile
Age range: 0–11

Moorfield School
Wharfedale Lodge, 11 Ben Rhydding Road, Ilkley, West Yorkshire LS29 8RL
Tel: 01943 607285
Headmistress: Mrs Jessica Crossley
Age range: 2–11
Fees: Day £9,600

Moorlands School
Foxhill, Weetwood Lane, Leeds, West Yorkshire LS16 5PF
Tel: 0113 2785286
Headteacher: Miss J Atkinson
Age range: 2–11
No. of pupils: 149
Fees: Day £8,985–£10,566

Netherleigh & Rossefield School
Parsons Road, Heaton, Bradford, West Yorkshire BD9 4AY
Tel: 01274 543162
Headteacher: Miss A Leary
Age range: 2–11
No. of pupils: 141
Fees: Day £6,735

New Horizon Community School
Newton Hill House, Newton Hill Road, Leeds, West Yorkshire LS7 4JE
Tel: 0113 262 4001
Acting Head: Qudisia Butt
Age range: G11–16
No. of pupils: 87
Fees: Day £1,800

Olive Secondary School
Byron Street, Bradford, West Yorkshire BD3 0AD
Tel: +44+ (0)1274 725005 / +44 (0)1274 725013
Headteacher: Mr Amjad Mohammed
Age range: 11–18
No. of pupils: 115
Fees: Day £2,075

Paradise Primary School
1 Bretton Street, Dewsbury, West Yorkshire WF12 9BB
Tel: 01924 439803
Headteacher: Mrs Hafsa Patel
Age range: 2–11
No. of pupils: 217

Queen Elizabeth Grammar School (Junior School)
158 Northgate, Wakefield, West Yorkshire WF1 3QY
Tel: 01924 373821
Head: Mrs L A Gray
Age range: B4–11
No. of pupils: 261
Fees: Day £9,153–£9,987

Queen Elizabeth Grammar School (Senior School)
154 Northgate, Wakefield, West Yorkshire WF1 3QY
Tel: 01924 373943
Headmaster: David Craig
Age range: B11–18
No. of pupils: 677
Fees: Day £12,636

Queenswood School
Queen Street, Morley, Leeds, West Yorkshire LS27 9EB
Tel: 0113 2534033
Headteacher: Mrs J A Tanner MMus, BA, FTCL, ARCO
Age range: 4–11
Fees: Day £6,000–£6,447

Richmond House School
170 Otley Road, Leeds, West Yorkshire LS16 5LG
Tel: 0113 2752670
Headteacher: Mrs Helen Stiles
Age range: 3–11
No. of pupils: 219
Fees: Day £5,850–£9,150

Rishworth School
Rishworth, Halifax, West Yorkshire HX6 4QA
Tel: 01422 822217
Head: Dr Paul Silverwood
Age range: 3–18
No. of pupils: 600 VIth90
Fees: Day £6,465–£12,660 WB £24,975–£27,300 FB £27,510–£29,985

Silcoates School
Wrenthorpe, Wakefield, West Yorkshire WF2 0PD
Tel: 01924 291614
Headmaster: Philip Rowe
Age range: 4–18
No. of pupils: 768
Fees: Day £7,530–£13,785

The Branch Christian School
Dewsbury Revival Centre, West Park Street, Dewsbury, West Yorkshire WF13 4LA
Tel: +44 (0)1924 452511
Head of School: Jo Holt
Age range: 3–16
No. of pupils: 26

THE FROEBELIAN SCHOOL
For further details see p.254
Clarence Road, Horsforth, Leeds, West Yorkshire LS18 4LB
Tel: 0113 2583047
Email: office@froebelian.co.uk
Website: www.froebelian.com
Head Teacher: Mrs Catherine Dodds BEd (Hons), PGCE
Age range: 3–11
No. of pupils: 172
Fees: Day £5,430–£8,100

The Gleddings School
Birdcage Lane, Savile Park, Halifax, West Yorkshire HX3 0JB
Tel: 01422 354605
School Director: Mrs Jill Wilson CBE
Age range: 3–11
No. of pupils: 191
Fees: Day £3,555–£5,910

The Grammar School at Leeds
Alwoodley Gates, Harrogate Road, Leeds, West Yorkshire LS17 8GS
Tel: 0113 2291552
Principal: Mrs Sue Woodroofe
Age range: 3–18
No. of pupils: 2120 VIth418
Fees: Day £9,441–£13,788

The Mount School
3 Binham Road, Edgerton, Huddersfield, West Yorkshire HD2 2AP
Tel: 01484 426432
Head of School: Mr Euan Burton-Smith
Age range: 3–11
No. of pupils: 115
Fees: Day £8,070

Wakefield Girls' High School (Junior School)
2 St John's Square, Wakefield, West Yorkshire WF1 2QX
Tel: 01924 374577
Headmistress: Mrs Rachel Edwards BEd
Age range: G4–11
No. of pupils: 493
Fees: Day £9,153–£9,987

Wakefield Girls' High School (Senior School)
Wentworth Street, Wakefield, West Yorkshire WF1 2QS
Tel: 01924 372490
Headmistress: Ms Heidi-Jayne Boyes BSc
Age range: G11–18
No. of pupils: 715
Fees: Day £12,636

Wakefield Independent School
The Nostell Centre, Doncaster Road, Nostell, Wakefield, West Yorkshire WF4 1QG
Tel: 01924 865757
Headmistress: Mrs K E Caryl
Age range: 21/2–16
No. of pupils: 190
Fees: Day £5,100–£7,050

West Cliffe Montessori School & Nursery
33, Barlow Road, access Belgrave Road, Keighley, West Yorkshire BD21 2TA
Tel: 01535 609797
Principal: Mrs T Bisby
Age range: 0–8
No. of pupils: 42

Westville House School
Carter's Lane, Middleton, Ilkley,
West Yorkshire LS29 0DQ
Tel: 01943 608053
Headteacher: Mrs Nikki
Hammond BA(Hons) PGCE
Age range: 3–11

Woodhouse Grove School
Apperley Bridge, Bradford,
West Yorkshire BD10 0NR
Tel: 0113 250 2477
Headmaster: Mr James Lockwood MA
Age range: 2–18
No. of pupils: 1090
Fees: Day £9,000–£13,575
FB £27,900–£28,020

Northern Ireland

KEY TO SYMBOLS

- Boys' school
- Girls' school
- International school
- Tutorial or sixth form college
- A levels
- Boarding accommodation
- £ Bursaries
- IB International Baccalaureate
- Learning support
- Entrance at 16+
- Vocational qualifications
- IAPS Independent Association of Preparatory Schools
- HMC The Headmasters' & Headmistresses' Conference
- ISA Independent Schools Association
- GSA Girls' School Association
- BSA Boarding Schools' Association
- S Society of Heads

Unless otherwise indicated, all schools are coeducational day schools. Single-sex and boarding schools will be indicated by the relevant icon.

County Antrim

Belfast Royal Academy
7 Cliftonville Road, Belfast,
County Antrim BT14 6JL
Tel: 028 9074 0423
Principal: Mrs Hilary Woods
Age range: 11–18
No. of pupils: VIth382
Fees: Day £140
Ⓐ 16⁺

Campbell College
Belfast, County Antrim BT4 2ND
Tel: 028 9076 3076
Headmaster: Mr Robert Robinson
Age range: B11–18
No. of pupils: 896 VIth200
Fees: Day £2,708–£8,363
FB £14,095–£19,750
Ⓐ 🌐 Ⓐ 🏛 ✎ 16⁺ 🐾

Campbell College Junior School
Belmont Road, Belfast,
County Antrim BT4 2ND
Tel: 028 9076 3076
Head: Miss Andrea Brown
Age range: B3–11 G3–4
Fees: Day £4,145–£4,449
👤 ✎

Hunterhouse College
Finaghy, Belfast, County
Antrim BT10 0LE
Tel: 028 9061 2293
Principal: Mr A Gibson MA, DipEd, PQH
Age range: G11–18
No. of pupils: 710 VIth180
Fees: Day £320
👤 Ⓐ ✎ 16⁺

Inchmarlo
Cranmore Park, Belfast,
County Antrim BT9 6JR
Tel: 028 9038 1454
👤

Methodist College
1 Malone Road, Belfast,
County Antrim BT9 6BY
Tel: 028 9020 5205
Principal: Mr J Scott W Naismith
Age range: 4–19
No. of pupils: 2307 VIth548
🌐 Ⓐ ✎ 16⁺

Royal Belfast Academical Institution
College Square East, Belfast,
County Antrim BT1 6DL
Tel: 028 9024 0461
Principal: Miss J A Williamson
MA(Oxon), NPQH
Age range: B4–18
No. of pupils: 1290 VIth275
Fees: Day £940–£4,140
👤 Ⓐ £ ✎ 16⁺

St Mary's Christian Brothers Grammar School
Glen Road, Belfast, County
Antrim BT11 8NR
Tel: 028 9029 4000
Head of School: Mrs Siobhan Kelly
Age range: B12–18
No. of pupils: 112
👤 Ⓐ 16⁺

Victoria College Belfast
Cranmore Park, Belfast,
County Antrim BT9 6JA
Tel: 028 9066 1506
Principal: Ms Patricia Slevin
Age range: G2–18
No. of pupils: 1070 VIth224
Fees: Day £4,825–£7,550
FB £11,100–£18,650
👤 Ⓐ 🏛 ✎ 16⁺

County Armagh

The Royal School
College Hill, Armagh, County
Armagh BT61 9DH
Tel: 02837 522807
Headmaster: Mr Graham Montgomery
Age range: 11–18
No. of pupils: 654 VIth157
Fees: Day £3,700–£4,415
WB £7,275 FB £10,925
Ⓐ 🏛 16⁺ 🐾

County Down

Bangor Grammar School
Gransha Road, Bangor,
County Down BT19 7QU
Tel: 028 91 473734
Principal: Mrs E P Huddleson
B.Ed., M.SSc., PQH(NI)
Age range: B3–18
No. of pupils: 900 VIth220
Fees: Day £140–£395
👤 Ⓐ ✎ 16⁺

Holywood Steiner School
34 Croft Road, Holywood,
County Down BT18 0PR
Tel: 028 9042 8029
**Chairperson of the School
Management Team:** Julie Higgins
Age range: 3–17 years
No. of pupils: 110
Fees: Day £4,008–£4,512
£

Rockport School
Craigavad, Holywood,
County Down BT18 0DD
Tel: 028 9042 8372
Headmaster: Mr George Vance
Age range: 3–18
No. of pupils: 200
Fees: Day £6,540–£15,810 WB
£17,970–£22,770 FB £21,450–£26,160
🌐 Ⓐ 🏛 £ ✎

County Tyrone

The Royal School Dungannon
2 Ranfurly Road, Dungannon,
County Tyrone BT71 6EG
Tel: 028 8772 2710
Headmaster: Dr David Burnett
Age range: 11–18
No. of pupils: 652 VIth156
Fees: Day £70–£150 WB £7,950
FB £10,650–£19,050
🌐 Ⓐ 🏛 ✎ 16⁺

Scotland

KEY TO SYMBOLS

ⓧ *Boys' school*

ⓧ *Girls' school*

ⓧ *International school*

⑯ *Tutorial or sixth form college*

Ⓐ *A levels*

ⓧ *Boarding accommodation*

£ *Bursaries*

ⒾⒷ *International Baccalaureate*

⌀ *Learning support*

⑯ *Entrance at 16+*

ⓧ *Vocational qualifications*

⒤ⒶⓅⓈ *Independent Association of Preparatory Schools*

ⒽⓂⒸ *The Headmasters' & Headmistresses' Conference*

ⒾⓈⒶ *Independent Schools Association*

ⒼⓈⒶ *Girls' School Association*

ⒷⓈⒶ *Boarding Schools' Association*

Ⓢ *Society of Heads*

*Unless otherwise indicated, all schools are coeducational day schools.
Single-sex and boarding schools will be indicated by the relevant icon.*

Aberdeen

Albyn School
17-23 Queen's Road,
Aberdeen AB15 4PB
Tel: 01224 322408
Headmaster: Ian E Long
AKC, PhD, FRGS, FRSA
Age range: 2–18
No. of pupils: 675 VIth57
Fees: Day £8,637–£13,636
WB £27,811 FB £29,948
£ ✎ 16

Robert Gordon's College
Schoolhill, Aberdeen AB10 1FE
Tel: 01224 646346
Head of College: Mr Simon Mills
Age range: 4–18
No. of pupils: 1573 VIth350
Fees: Day £8,435–£13,130
£ ✎ 16

St Margaret's School for Girls
17 Albyn Place, Aberdeen AB10 1RU
Tel: 01224 584466
Headmistress: Miss A Tomlinson
MTheol (Hons), PGCE
Age range: B3–5 years G3–18 years
No. of pupils: 380 VIth34
Fees: Day £7,954–£12,600
♦ £ ✎ 16

**The International School
of Aberdeen**
Pitfodels House, North Deeside Road,
Pitfodels, Cults, Aberdeen AB15 9PN
Tel: 01224 730300
Head of School: Ms Sarah Bruce
Age range: 3–18
No. of pupils: 409 VIth39
Fees: Day £12,830–£14,100
♦ £ IB ✎ 16

Angus

Lathallan School
Brotherton Castle, Johnshaven,
Montrose, Angus DD10 0HN
Tel: 01561 362220
Headmaster: Mr R Toley
No. of pupils: 220
Fees: Day £5,031–£6,067
FB £7,281–£8,317
♦ £ ✎ 16

Argyll & Bute

Lomond School
10 Stafford Street, Helensburgh,
Argyll & Bute G84 9JX
Tel: +44 (0)1436 672476
Principal: Mrs Johanna Urquhart
Age range: 3–18
No. of pupils: 360
Fees: Day £8,640–£11,970 FB £27,750
♦ ♦ £ ✎ 16

Borders

St Mary's Prep School
Abbey Park, Melrose, Borders TD6 9LN
Tel: 01896 822517
Headmaster: Mr Liam Harvey
Age range: 2–13
Fees: Day £13,200–£16,050 WB £17,982
♦ £ ✎

Clackmannanshire

Dollar Academy
Dollar, Clackmannanshire FK14 7DU
Tel: 01259 742511
Head of School: Mr Ian Munro
Age range: 5–18
No. of pupils: 1295
Fees: Day £10,476–£14,013 WB
£27,108–£30,645 FB £28,890–£32,427
♦ ♦ £ ✎ 16

Dundee

High School of Dundee
Euclid Crescent, Dundee DD1 1HU
Tel: 01382 202921
Rector: Dr John Halliday
Age range: 3–18
No. of pupils: 1067 VIth102
Fees: Day £9,159–£12,999
£ ✎ 16

East Lothian

Belhaven Hill
Dunbar, East Lothian EH42 1NN
Tel: 01368 862785
Headmaster: Mr. Olly Langton
Age range: 8–13
No. of pupils: 122
Fees: Day £11,520–£16,875 FB £23,760
♦ £ ✎

Loretto Junior School
North Esk Lodge, 1 North High Street,
Musselburgh, East Lothian EH21 6JA
Tel: 0131 653 4570
Headmaster: Mr Andrew Dickenson
Age range: 3–12
No. of pupils: 200
Fees: Day £9,180–£15,900 FB £22,335
♦ £ ✎

Loretto School
Pinkie House, Linkfield Road,
Musselburgh, East Lothian EH21 7AF
Tel: +44 (0)131 653 4455
Head of School: Dr.
Graham R. W. Hawley
Age range: 0 years–18 years
No. of pupils: 550
Fees: Day £2,833–£8,100
FB £7,750–£11,900
♦ A ♦ £ ✎ 16

The Compass School
West Road, Haddington,
East Lothian EH41 3RD
Tel: 01620 822642
Headmaster: Mr Mark Becher
MA(Hons), PGCE
Age range: 4–12
No. of pupils: 125
Fees: Day £6,450–£9,735
£ ✎

Edinburgh

Basil Paterson Tutorial College
66 Queen Street, Edinburgh EH2 4NA
Tel: 0131 225 3802
Head of School: Claire Samuel
Age range: 14+
No. of pupils: 40
Fees: Day £3,990–£12,000
16 A ✎

Cargilfield School
45 Gamekeeper's Road,
Edinburgh EH4 6HU
Tel: 0131 336 2207
Headmaster: Mr. Robert Taylor
Age range: 3–13
No. of pupils: 325
Fees: Day £6,051–£15,843 WB £19,443
♦ £ ✎

Clifton Hall
Newbridge, Edinburgh EH28 8LQ
Tel: 0131 333 1359
Headmaster: Mr R Grant
Age range: 3–18
No. of pupils: 385
Fees: Day £5,100–£12,270
£ ✎ 16

Edinburgh Steiner School
60-64 Spylaw Road,
Edinburgh EH10 5BR
Tel: 0131 337 3410
Age range: 31/2–18
No. of pupils: 300
£ ✎ 16

Fettes College
Carrington Road, Edinburgh EH4 1QX
Tel: +44 (0)131 332 2281
Head of School: Mrs Helen Harrison
Age range: 7–18
No. of pupils: 764 VIth249
Fees: Day £16,500–£28,200
FB £24,210–£34,800
♦ A ♦ £ IB ✎ 16

Fettes College Preparatory School
East Fettes Avenue, Edinburgh EH4 1QZ
Tel: 0131 332 2976
Headmaster: Mr A A Edwards
Age range: 7–13
No. of pupils: 169
Fees: Day £16,500 FB £24,210
Ⓐ Ⓐ ⓔ 🏫 ✏️

George Heriot's School
Lauriston Place, Edinburgh EH3 9EQ
Tel: 0131 229 7263
Principal: Mrs Lesley Franklin
Age range: 3–18
No. of pupils: 1641 VIth352
Fees: Day £8,349–£12,522
ⓔ ✏️ 16 🐾

George Watson's College
69-71 Colinton Road,
Edinburgh EH10 5EG
Tel: 0131 446 6000
Principal: Mr Melvyn Roffe
Age range: 3–18
No. of pupils: 2400
🌐 Ⓐ ⓔ ✏️ 16 🐾

Merchiston Castle School
294 Colinton Road, Edinburgh EH13 0PU
Tel: 0131 312 2201
Headmaster: Mr Jonathan Anderson
Age range: B7–18
No. of pupils: 440
Fees: Day £15,030–£25,530
FB £21,660–£35,190
🧍 🌐 Ⓐ 🏫 ⓔ 16

St George's School for Girls
Garscube Terrace, Edinburgh EH12 6BG
Tel: 0131 311 8000
Head: Mrs Alex Hems BA(Hons) Oxon
Age range: B2–5 years G2–18 years
No. of pupils: 815 VIth170
Fees: Day £8,550–£13,875
FB £26,175–£29,010
🧍 🌐 Ⓐ 🏫 ⓔ 16 🐾

St Mary's Music School
Coates Hall, 25 Grosvenor
Crescent, Edinburgh EH12 5EL
Tel: 0131 538 7766
Headteacher: Dr Kenneth Taylor
BSc Hons, PhD, PGCE, PG Dip
Age range: 9–19
No. of pupils: VIth13
🌐 Ⓐ 🏫 16

Stewart's Melville College
Queensferry Road, Edinburgh EH4 3EZ
Tel: 0131 311 1000
Principal: Mrs Linda Moule
Age range: B12–18 G16–18
No. of pupils: 864
Fees: Day £11,637 FB £23,349
🧍 🌐 🏫 ⓔ ✏️ 16

The Edinburgh Academy
42 Henderson Row, Edinburgh EH3 5BL
Tel: 0131 556 4603
Rector: Barry Welsh
Age range: 2–18
No. of pupils: 992 VIth93
Fees: Day £8,433–£14,121
Ⓐ ⓔ ✏️ 16

The Mary Erskine & Stewart's Melville Junior School
Queensferry Road, Edinburgh EH4 3EZ
Tel: 0131 311 1111
Headmaster: Mr Bryan Lewis
Age range: 3–11
No. of pupils: 1218
Fees: Day £8,142–£9,123 WB
£20,250 FB £20,835
ⓔ ✏️

The Mary Erskine School
Ravelston, Edinburgh EH4 3NT
Tel: 0131 347 5700
Headmaster: Mrs Linda Moule
Age range: B16–18 G12–18
Fees: Day £11,637 FB £23,349
🧍 🌐 🏫 ⓔ 16

Wallace College
12 George IV Bridge, Edinburgh EH1 1EE
Tel: 0131 220 3634
Age range: 8–18
Fees: Day £1,410–£6,900
FB £4,070–£9,590
16 Ⓐ 🏫

Fife

St Leonards School
St Andrews, Fife KY16 9QJ
Tel: 01334 472126
Head of School: Dr Michael Carslaw
Age range: 5–18
No. of pupils: 540
Fees: Day £9,552–£15,474
FB £24,651–£37,452
🌐 🏫 ⓔ IB ✏️ 16

Glasgow

Belmont House School
Sandringham Avenue, Newton
Mearns, Glasgow G77 5DU
Tel: 0141 639 2922
Principal: Mr Melvyn D Shanks
BSc, DipEd, MInstP, CPhys, SQH
Age range: 3–18
No. of pupils: 300
Fees: Day £5,841–£13,263
ⓔ ✏️ 16 🐾

Fernhill School
Fernbrae Avenue, Burnside,
Rutherglen, Glasgow G73 4SG
Tel: 0141 634 2674
Headteacher: Dr Laura Murphy
Age range: B4–11 G4–18
No. of pupils: 300 VIth16
Fees: Day £7,580–£11,090
🧍 ⓔ ✏️ 16

Hutchesons' Grammar School
21 Beaton Road, Glasgow G41 4NW
Tel: 0141 423 2933
Rector: Mr Colin Gambles
BSc (Hons) PGCE
Age range: 5–18
No. of pupils: 1242 VIth139
Fees: Day £7,320–£12,168
Ⓐ ⓔ ✏️ 16

Kelvinside Academy
33 Kirklee Road, Glasgow G12 0SW
Tel: 0141 357 3376
Rector: Mr Ian Munro BSc,
PGCE, MEd(Cantab), FRSB
Age range: 3–18
No. of pupils: 640 VIth73
Fees: Day £7,995–£12,660
Ⓐ ⓔ ✏️ 16

St Aloysius' College
45 Hill Street, Glasgow G3 6RJ
Tel: 0141 332 3190
Head Master: Mr Matthew Bartlett
MA (Cantab), PGCE, NLE, NPQH
Age range: 3–18
No. of pupils: 925 VIth110
Fees: Day £7,263–£12,825
ⓔ ✏️ 16

The Glasgow Academy
Colebrooke Street, Kelvinbridge,
Glasgow G12 8HE
Tel: 0141 334 8558
Rector: Mr Peter Brodie MA, MA(Ed)
Age range: 3–18
No. of pupils: 1148 VIth221
Fees: Day £5,220–£11,623
ⓔ ✏️ 16 🐾

The Glasgow Academy Dairsie
54 Newlands Road, Newlands,
Glasgow G43 2JG
Tel: 0141 632 0736
Rector: Mr Peter Brodie
Age range: 3–8
No. of pupils: 74
Fees: Day £4,770–£12,029

The Glasgow Academy, Milngavie
Mugdock Road, Milngavie,
Glasgow G62 8NP
Tel: +44 (0)1419 563758
Rector: Mr Peter Brodie
Age range: 3–8
Fees: Day £4,680–£9,861

The High School of Glasgow
637 Crow Road, Glasgow G13 1PL
Tel: 0141 954 9628
Rector: John O'Neill
Age range: 3–18
ⓔ ✏️ 16

Moray

Drumduan School
Clovenside Road, Forres,
Moray IV36 2RD
Tel: + 44 (0)1309 676300
Principal Teacher: Krzysztof
Zajaczkowski
Age range: 3–18

Gordonstoun
Elgin, Moray IV30 5RF
Tel: 01343 837829
Principal: Ms Lisa Kerr BA
Age range: 41/2–18
No. of pupils: 542 VIth189
Fees: Day £5,350–£9,950 WB
£8,650 FB £8,650–£13,750

Perth & Kinross

Ardvreck School
Crieff, Perth & Kinross PH7 4EX
Tel: 01764 653112
Headmistress: Mrs Ali Kinge
Age range: 3–13
No. of pupils: 110

Craigclowan Preparatory School
Edinburgh Road, Perth,
Perth & Kinross PH2 8PS
Tel: 01738 626310
Head of School: John Gilmour
Age range: 3–13
No. of pupils: 242
Fees: Day £4,620

Glenalmond College, Perth
Glenalmond, Perth, Perth
& Kinross PH1 3RY
Tel: 01738 842000
Warden: Mr Hugh Ouston
Age range: 12–18
No. of pupils: 400 VIth175
Fees: Day £16,881–£22,503
FB £25,851–£36,510

Kilgraston School
Bridge of Earn, Perth, Perth
& Kinross PH2 9BQ
Tel: 01738 812257
Head: Mrs Dorothy MacGinty
Age range: G5–18
No. of pupils: 260
Fees: Day £10,890–£17,640
FB £23,025–£30,135

Morrison's Academy
Crieff, Perth & Kinross PH7 3AN
Tel: 01764 653885
Principal: Mr Gareth Warren BSc (Hons)
Age range: 3–18
No. of pupils: VIth50
Fees: Day £8,625–£12,996

STRATHALLAN SCHOOL
For further details see p.258
Forgandenny, Perth, Perth
& Kinross PH2 9EG
Tel: 01738 812546
Email: admissions@strathallan.co.uk
Website: www.strathallan.co.uk
Headmaster: Mr Mark
Lauder MA Hons
Age range: 8–18
No. of pupils: 520
Fees: Day £15,435–£23,532
FB £24,174–£34,650

Perthshire

Queen Victoria School
Dunblane, Perthshire FK15 0JY
Tel: 01786 822 288
Head: Donald Shaw BSc(Hons) PGCE
Age range: 11–18
No. of pupils: 267 VIth30
Fees: FB £1,403

Renfrewshire

Cedars School of Excellence
31 Ardgowan Square, Greenock,
Renfrewshire PA16 8NJ
Tel: 01475 723905
Headteacher: Mrs Alison Speirs
Age range: 5–18
No. of pupils: 95
Fees: Day £5,200–£7,180

St Columba's School
Duchal Road, Kilmacolm,
Renfrewshire PA13 4AU
Tel: 01505 872238
Head of School: Mrs
Andrea Y Angus BSc
Age range: 3–18
No. of pupils: 701 VIth125
Fees: Day £3,080–£12,095

South Ayrshire

Wellington School
Carleton Turrets, Ayr, South
Ayrshire KA7 2XH
Tel: 01292 269321
Head: Mr S Johnson MA
(Cantab) PGCE
Age range: 3–18
No. of pupils: VIth45
Fees: Day £6,900–£12,900

South Lanarkshire

Hamilton College
Bothwell Road, Hamilton,
South Lanarkshire ML3 0AY
Tel: 01698 282700
Principal: Mr Tom McPhail
Age range: 3–18
No. of pupils: VIth49
Fees: Day £7,635–£10,800

Wales

KEY TO SYMBOLS

(♂) *Boys' school*

(♀) *Girls' school*

(🌐) *International school*

(16) *Tutorial or sixth form college*

(A) *A levels*

(🏫) *Boarding accommodation*

(£) *Bursaries*

(IB) *International Baccalaureate*

(✐) *Learning support*

(16) *Entrance at 16+*

(💼) *Vocational qualifications*

(IAPS) *Independent Association of Preparatory Schools*

(HMC) *The Headmasters' & Headmistresses' Conference*

(ISA) *Independent Schools Association*

(GSA) *Girls' School Association*

(BSA) *Boarding Schools' Association*

(S) *Society of Heads*

*Unless otherwise indicated, all schools are coeducational day schools.
Single-sex and boarding schools will be indicated by the relevant icon.*

Cardiff

Cardiff Sixth Form College
1-3 Trinity Court, 21-27 Newport
Road, , Cardiff CF24 0AA
Tel: +44 (0)29 2049 3121
Principal: Mr Gareth Collier
Age range: 15–18
Fees: Day £17,700 FB £42,700–£46,450

Carmarthenshire

Llandovery College
Queensway, Llandovery,
Carmarthenshire SA20 0EE
Tel: +44 (0)1550 723005
Warden: Dominic Findlay
Age range: 4–18 years
No. of pupils: 250
Fees: Day £6,165–£18,225
FB £18,450–£27,525

St Michael's School
Bryn, Llanelli, Carmarthenshire SA14 9TU
Tel: 01554 820325
Age range: 3–18
No. of pupils: 420 VIth80
Fees: Day £5,064–£12,369
FB £19,722–£22,269

Clwyd

Rydal Penrhos Preparatory School
Pwllycrochan Avenue, Colwyn
Bay, Clwyd LL29 7BP
Tel: 01492 530381
Age range: 2–11
No. of pupils: 180
Fees: Day £7,452–£9,930

St David's College
Gloddaeth Hall, Llandudno,
Clwyd LL30 1RD
Tel: 01492 875974
Headmaster: Mr Andrew Russell
Age range: 9–19
No. of pupils: 254
Fees: Day £3,930–£6,230
FB £8,120–£11,630

Conwy

Rydal Penrhos School
Pwllycrochan Avenue, Colwyn
Bay, Conwy LL29 7BT
Tel: +44 (0)1492 530155
Head of School: Mrs Alison Hind
Age range: 2–18
No. of pupils: 530
Fees: Day £7,452–£16,785 WB
£20,901–£23,385 FB £27,159–£33,450

Denbighshire

Fairholme School
The Mount, Mount Road, St
Asaph, Denbighshire LL17 0DH
Tel: 01745 583505
Principal: Mrs E Perkins MA(Oxon)
Age range: 3–11
No. of pupils: 110
Fees: Day £6,300–£8,400

Myddelton College
Peakes Lane, Denbigh,
Denbighshire LL16 3EN
Tel: +44 174 547 2201
Age range: 4–18

Ruthin School
Ruthin, Denbighshire LL15 1EE
Tel: 01824 702543
Headmaster: Mr Ian Welsby
BSc, MBiol, PGCE, DipEd
Age range: 3–18
No. of pupils: 240 VIth41
Fees: Day £11,000–£14,000 FB £34,500

Glamorgan

Cardiff Academy
40-41 The Parade, Cardiff,
Glamorgan CF24 3AB
Tel: 029 2040 9630
Principal: Dr S R Wilson
Age range: 14–18
No. of pupils: 51 VIth44
Fees: Day £12,000–£15,000

Ffynone House School
36 St James's Crescent, Swansea,
Glamorgan SA1 6DR
Tel: 01792 464967
Headteacher: Mr Michael Boulding
Age range: 11–18
No. of pupils: VIth25
Fees: Day £10,845–£11,010

Howell's School, Llandaff GDST
Cardiff Road, Llandaff, Cardiff,
Glamorgan CF5 2YD
Tel: 029 2056 2019
Principal: Mrs Sally Davis BSc
Age range: B16–18 G3–18
No. of pupils: 750
Fees: Day £8,670–£14,529

Kings Monkton School
6 West Grove, Cardiff,
Glamorgan CF24 3XL
Tel: 02920 482854
Principal: Mr Paul Norton
Age range: 3–18
No. of pupils: 250
Fees: Day £2,700–£4,068

Oakleigh House School
38 Penlan Crescent, Uplands,
Swansea, Glamorgan SA2 0RL
Tel: 01792 298537
Headmistress: Mrs Rhian
Ferriman BA(Hons)Ed, MEd
Age range: 2½–11
No. of pupils: 200
Fees: Day £6,510–£8,580

St Clare's School
Newton, Porthcawl,
Glamorgan CF36 5NR
Tel: 01656 782509
Head of School: Helen Hier
Age range: 3–18
No. of pupils: 298 VIth45
Fees: Day £6,753–£11,799

St John's College, Cardiff
College Green, Old St Mellons,
Cardiff, Glamorgan CF3 5YX
Tel: 029 2077 8936
Headteacher: Mr Shaun
Moody BA (Hons) PGCE
Age range: 3–18
No. of pupils: 548
Fees: Day £7,443–£14,400

The Cathedral School, Llandaff
Llandaff, Cardiff, Glamorgan CF5 2YH
Tel: 029 2056 3179
Head: Clare Sherwood
Age range: 3–18
Fees: Day £7,785–£12,714

Gwynedd

St Gerard's School
Ffriddoedd Road, Bangor,
Gwynedd LL57 2EL
Tel: 01248 351656
Head Teacher: Mr Campbell Harrison
Age range: 4–18
No. of pupils: 170
Fees: Day £7,260–£10,980
Ⓐ £ 16+

Monmouthshire

Monmouth School for Boys
Almshouse Street, Monmouth,
Monmouthshire NP25 3XP
Tel: 01600 713143
Acting Headmaster: Mr Simon Dorman
Age range: B7–18 years
No. of pupils: 645
Fees: Day £11,415–£16,275
FB £20,868–£33,498
Ⓐ £ 16+

Monmouth School for Girls
Hereford Road, Monmouth,
Monmouthshire NP25 5XT
Tel: 01600 711100
Head: Mrs Jessica Miles
MA (Oxon), PGCE
Age range: G7–18 years
No. of pupils: 600
Fees: Day £11,415–£16,275
FB £20,868–£33,498
Ⓐ £ 16+

Monmouth Schools Pre-Prep & Nursery
Dixton Lane, Monmouth,
Monmouthshire NP25 3SY
Tel: 01600 713970
Head of School: Mrs Jennie Phillips
Age range: 3–7 years
No. of pupils: 80
Fees: Day £4,518–£7,572

Rougemont School
Llantarnam Hall, Malpas Road,
Newport, Monmouthshire NP20 6QB
Tel: 01633 820800
Headmaster: Mr Robert Carnevale
Age range: 3–18
No. of pupils: 700 VIth111
Fees: Day £7,245–£13,536
Ⓐ £ 16+

St John's-on-the-Hill
Tutshill, Chepstow,
Monmouthshire NP16 7LE
Tel: 01291 622045
Head: Mrs Ruth Frett
Age range: 3 months–13 years
No. of pupils: 362
Fees: Day £8,280–£13,632 FB £19,362
£

Pembrokeshire

Nant-y-Cwm Steiner School
Llanycefn, Clunderwen,
Pembrokeshire SA66 7QJ
Tel: 01437 563 640
Age range: 0–14

Redhill Preparatory School
The Garth, St David's
Road, Haverfordwest,
Pembrokeshire SA61 2UR
Tel: 01437 762472
Principal: Mrs Lovegrove
Age range: 0–11
Fees: Day £7,650–£7,800
£

Powys

Christ College
Brecon, Powys LD3 8AF
Tel: 01874 615440
Head: Mr Gareth Pearson
Age range: 7–18
No. of pupils: 350
Fees: Day £9,486–£19,389
FB £18,159–£32,166
Ⓐ £ 16+

Vale of Glamorgan

UWC Atlantic
St Donat's Castle, St Donat's, Llantwit
Major, Vale of Glamorgan CF61 1WF
Tel: +44 (0)1446 799000
Head of College: Mr Peter T. Howe
Age range: 16–19
No. of pupils: 350
£ IB 16+

D376

Examinations and qualifications

Common Entrance

What is Common Entrance?

The Common Entrance examinations are used in UK independent schools (and some independent schools overseas) for transfer from junior to senior schools at the ages of 11+ and 13+. They were first introduced in 1904 and are internationally recognised as being a rigorous form of assessment following a thorough course of study. The examinations are produced by the Independent Schools Examinations Board and backed by HMC (Headmasters' and Headmistresses' Conference), GSA (Girls' Schools Association), and IAPS (Independent Association of Prep Schools) which together represent the leading independent schools in the UK, and many overseas.

Common Entrance is not a public examination as, for example, GCSE, and candidates may normally be entered only in one of the following circumstances:

a) they have been offered a place at a senior school subject to their passing the examination, or

b) they are entered as a 'trial run', in which case the papers are marked by the junior school concerned

Candidates normally take the examination in their own junior or preparatory schools, either in the UK or overseas.

How does Common Entrance fit into the progression to GCSEs?

Rapid changes in education nationally and internationally have resulted in regular reviews of the syllabuses for all the Common Entrance examinations. Reviews of the National Curriculum, in particular, have brought about a number of changes, with the Board wishing to ensure that it continues to set high standards. It is also a guiding principle that Common Entrance should be part of the natural progression from 11-16, and not a diversion from it.

Common Entrance at 11+

At 11+, the examination consists of papers in English, mathematics and science. It is designed so that it can be taken by candidates either from independent preparatory schools or by candidates from schools in the maintained sector or overseas who have had no special preparation. The examination is normally taken in January for entrance to senior schools in the following September.

Common Entrance at 13+

At 13+, most candidates come from independent preparatory schools. The compulsory subjects are English, mathematics and science. Papers in French, geography, German, Classical Greek, history, Latin, religious studies and Spanish are also available and candidates usually offer as many subjects as they can. In most subjects, papers are available at more than one level to cater for candidates of different abilities. There are three examination sessions each year, with the majority of candidates sitting in the summer prior to entry to their senior schools in September.

Marking and grading

The papers are set centrally but the answers are marked by the senior school for which a candidate is entered. Mark schemes are provided by the Board but senior schools are free to set their own grade boundaries. Results are available within two weeks of the examinations taking place.

Pre-Testing and the ISEB Common Pre-Tests

A number of senior independent schools 'pre-test' pupils for entry, prior to them taking their main entrance examinations at a later date. Usually, these pre-tests take place when a pupil is in Year 6 or Year 7 of his or her junior school and will then be going on to sit Common Entrance in Year 8. The tests are designed to assess a pupil's academic potential and suitability for a particular senior school so that the child, the parents and the school know well in advance whether he/she is going to be offered a place at the school, subject to a satisfactory performance in the entrance examinations. The tests enable senior schools to manage their lists and help to ensure that pupils are not entered for examinations in which they are unlikely to be successful. In short, it reduces uncertainty for all concerned.

Pre-tests may be written specifically for the senior school for which the candidate is entered but a growing number of schools are choosing to use the Common Pre-Tests provided by the Independent Schools Examinations Board. These online tests are usually taken in the candidate's own junior school and one of their main advantages is that a pupil need sit the tests only once, with the results then made available to any senior school which wishes to use them. The multiple-choice tests cover verbal reasoning, non-verbal reasoning, English and mathematics, with the results standardised according to the pupil's age when they are taken. Further information is available on the ISEB website at www.iseb.co.uk.

Parents are advised to check the entrance requirements for senior schools to see if their child will be required to sit a pre-test.

Further information

Details of the Common Entrance examinations and how to register candidates are available on the ISEB website www.iseb.co.uk. Copies of past papers and a wide range of textbooks and other resources can be purchased from Galore Park Publishing Ltd at www.galorepark.co.uk. Support materials are also available from Hodder Education and other publishers; see the Resources section of the ISEB website for details.

Independent Schools Examinations Board
Endeavour House, Crow Arch Lane,
Ringwood, Hampshire BH24 1HP

Telephone: 01425 470555
Email: enquiries@iseb.co.uk
Web: www.iseb.co.uk

7+ Entrance Exams

What is the 7+?

The 7+ is the descriptive name given to the entrance exams set by an increasing number of independent schools for pupils wishing to gain admission into their Year 3.

7+ entrance exams may be simply for admission into a selective preparatory school, which will then prepare the child for Common Entrance exams to gain a place at senior school. Alternatively, the 7+ can be a route into a school with both prep and senior departments, therefore often effectively bypassing the 11+ or 13+ Common Entrance exams.

The Independent Schools Examinations Board provides Common Entrance examinations and assessments for pupils seeking entry to independent senior schools at 11+ and 13+, but there is as yet no equivalent for the 7+. The testing is largely undertaken by the individual schools, although some schools might commission the test from external agencies. Many schools in the incredibly competitive London area offer entrance exams at 7+ and some share specimen papers on their website to clarify what 7+ children will face.

Who sits the 7+?

The 7+ is sat by Year 2 children, who may be moving from a state primary school or a stand-alone pre-prep school to an independent prep school (although many prep schools now have their own pre-prep department, with a cohort of children poised to pass into Year 3 there).

Registration for 7+ entrance exams usually closes in the November of Year 2, with the exams then sat in January or February, for entry that September.

How is the 7+ assessed?

Written exam content will be primarily English and maths based, whilst spelling, dictation, mental arithmetic and more creative skills may be assessed verbally on a one-to-one basis. Group exercises are also sometimes used to look at a child's initiative and their ability to work with others.

Schools will not only be looking for academic potential, but also good citizens and a mixture of personalities to produce a well-rounded year group. For this reason, children are often asked to attend an interview. Some schools interview all candidates, whilst others may call back a limited number with good test results. They will be looking for a child's ability to look an adult in the eye and think on their feet, but also simply to show some spark and personality.

After the assessments, children will be told if they have been successful in gaining a firm place, or a place on a waiting list.

Further Information

As the 7+ is not centrally regulated, it is best for parents to seek accurate admissions and testing information direct from the schools in which they are interested. In addition to a school's facilities and ethos, choosing a school for admission at 7+ will probably also involve whether the school has a senior department and if not, the prep school's record in gaining its students places at target senior schools.

Experienced educational consultants may be able to help parents decide which independent prep school is best suited for their child, based on their personality, senior school ambitions and academic potential. Many parents enlist the help of tutors to prepare children for the 7+, if only to reduce the fear of the unknown in these very young children. This is achieved by teaching them the required curriculum, what to expect on their test and interview days, and giving them the opportunity to practice tackling the type of assessments they will face.

PSB

The Pre-Senior Baccalaureate (PSB) is a framework of study for children in junior and preparatory schools that was introduced in 2012, and focuses on the active development and assessment of 6 core skills: Communication, Collaboration, Leadership, Independence, Reviewing and Improving and Thinking and Learning. Member schools promote the core skills across all areas of school life, and provide guidance for pupils in progressing these skills, which are seen as essential for developing capable and balanced adults able to make the most of the opportunities of a fast-changing world. A strong but appropriate knowledge base compliments this, with the use of focused tutoring, pastoral care and Well Being programmes.

Schools do not work to a prescribed curriculum and the emphasis is upon promoting an independent approach which works for each individual school. There are subject INSET days for PSB school staff annually and these are supported by senior school colleagues, to ensure that work done in PSB schools compliments the demands of education at higher levels.

The PSB is a whole school initiative from Early Years to either Year 6 or Year 8, at which point the certificate is awarded at the time of matriculation to senior schools. An additional PSB Year 9 framework is being developed together with international membership.

The development of skills is now recognised as essential by the Independent Schools Inspectorate (ISI), and recent ISI reports on PSB schools highlight the excellent contribution the PSB has in schools achieving excellence.

Assessment

The PSB has a 10 point scale for all subjects studied with a compulsory spine covering: English, Maths, Science, Modern Languages, The Humanities, Art, Design Technology, Music, Sport and PE with each pupil additionally completing a cross curricular project. Optional subjects are agreed with schools but these must be supported by a scheme of work clearly identifying appropriate core skills which are assessed on a 5 point scale. There are distinction levels on both scales and the 10 point scale cross references both ISEB and National Curriculum assessment levels.

Pupils moving on to senior school do so via individual senior school pre-testing arrangements, the award of the PSB certificate, core ISEB papers or a combination of the above.

Membership categories

Partner membership is available to schools developing the PSB with support given from existing schools and the Communications director.

Full membership entitles schools to use the PSB matriculation certificate and join the PSB committee as voting members.

Affiliated membership is for schools that have developed their own skills based approach, in line with PSB principles; staff can participate in all training opportunities and the Heads of Affiliated Schools join committee meetings as non-voting guests.

Membership of the above categories is dependent upon strong ISI reports, the development of a skills based curriculum, with skills clearly identified in schemes of work and excellent teaching.

Associate membership is for senior schools that actively support the PSB in providing staff for subject meetings, hosting meetings, conferences and committee meetings and offer a valuable perspective on the demands of GCSE, A Level and the International Baccalaureate.

Further details

The PSB is an entirely independent charity overseen by a Board of Trustees who have expertise in both primary and secondary education. Details of the PSB can be found on the website – psbacc.org – and you can contact the PSB Administrator at rebecca.morris@psbacc.org and she will answer any questions you may have.

General Certificate of Secondary Education (GCSE)

What are the GCSE qualifications?

GCSE qualifications were first introduced in 1986 and are the principal means of assessment at Key Stage 4 across a range of academic subject areas. They command respect and have status not only in the UK but worldwide.

Main features of the GCSE

There are four unitary awarding organisations for GCSEs in England (see 'Awarding organisations and examination dates' section, p435). WJEC and CCEA also offer GCSE qualifications in Wales and Northern Ireland. Each examining group designs its own specifications but they are required to conform to set criteria. For some aspects of the qualification system, the exam boards adopt common ways of working. When the exam boards work together in this way they generally do so through the Joint Council of Qualifications (JCQ). The award of a grade is intended to indicate that a candidate has met the required level of skills, knowledge and understanding.

In 2015 GCSEs began a series of reform starting with English Language, English literature, and mathematics. New GCSEs in ancient languages (classical Greek, Latin), art and design, biology, chemistry, citizenship studies, combined science (double award), computer science, dance, drama, food preparation and nutrition, geography, history, modern foreign languages (French, German, Spanish), music, physics, physical education and religious studies were first taught in September 2016, with first results in summer 2018. Assessment in these reformed GCSEs consists primarily of formal examinations taken at the end of the student's two-year course. Other types of assessment, non-exam assessment (NEA), is used where there are skills and knowledge which cannot be assessed through exams. Ofqual have set the percentage of the total marks that will come from NEA.

The reformed GCSEs feature new and more demanding content, as required by the government and developed by the exam boards. Courses are designed for two years of study (linear assessment) and no longer divided into different modules.

Exams can only be split into 'foundation tier' and 'higher tier' if one exam paper does not give all students the opportunity to show their knowledge and their abilities. Such tiering is only available in maths, science and modern foreign languages; other subjects do not have tiers. Resit opportunities will only be available each November in English language and maths, and then only for students who have turned 16 by the 31st of August in the year of the November assessment.

New GCSEs taught from September 2017: ancient history, astronomy, business, classical civilisation, design and technology, economics, electronics, engineering, film studies, geology, media studies, psychology, sociology, statistics, other (minority) foreign languages e.g. Italian, Polish.

New GCSEs taught from September 2018: ancient languages (biblical Hebrew) and modern foreign languages (Gujarati, Persian, Portuguese, Turkish).

Grading

The basic principle that exam boards follow when setting grade boundaries is that if the group of students (the cohort) taking a qualification in one year is of similar ability to the cohort in the previous year then the overall results (outcomes) should be comparable.

The reformed exams taken in summer 2017 were the first to show a new grading system, with the A* to G grades being phased out.

The new grading system is 9 to 1, with 9 being the top grade. Ofqual says this allows greater differentiation between students. It expects that broadly the same proportion of students will achieve a grade 4 and above as currently achieve a grade C and above, that broadly the same proportion of students will achieve a grade 7 and above as currently achieve a grade A and above. There are three anchor points between the new grading system and the old one: the bottom of the new 1 grade is the same as the bottom of the old G grade, the bottom of the new 4 grade is the bottom of the old C grade, and the bottom of the 7 grade is the same as the bottom of the old A grade. Grade 9 will be set using the tailored approach formula in the first award.

Grades 2, 3, 5 and 6 will be awarded arithmetically so that the grade boundaries are equally spaced in terms of marks from neighbouring grades.

The government's definition of a 'strong pass' will be set at grade 5 for reformed GCSEs. A grade 4 – or 'standard pass' – will continue to be a level 2 achievement. The DfE does not expect employers, colleges or universities to raise the bar to a grade 5 if a grade 4 would meet their requirements.

Can anyone take GCSE qualifications?

GCSEs are intended mainly for 16-year-old pupils, but are open to anyone of any age, whether studying full-time or part-time at a school, college or privately. There are no formal entry requirements.

Students normally study up to ten subjects over a two-year period. Short course GCSEs are available in some subjects (including PE and religious studies) – these include half the content of a full GCSE, so two short course GCSEs are equivalent to one full GCSE.

The English Baccalaureate

The English Baccalaureate (EBacc) is a school performance measure. It allows people to see how many pupils get a grade C or above (current grading) in the core academic subjects at Key Stage 4 in any government-funded school. The DfE introduced the EBacc measure in 2010.

Progress 8 and Attainment 8

Progress 8 aims to capture the progress a pupil makes from the end of primary school to the end of secondary school. It is a type of value added measure, which means that pupils' results are compared to the actual achievements of other pupils with the same prior attainment.

The new performance measures are designed to encourage schools to offer a broad and balanced curriculum with a focus on an academic core at Key Stage 4, and reward schools for the teaching of all their pupils, measuring performance across 8 qualifications. Every increase in every grade a pupil achieves will attract additional points in the performance tables.

Progress 8 will be calculated for individual pupils solely in order to calculate a school's Progress 8 score, and there will be no need for schools to share individual Progress 8 scores with their pupils. Schools should continue to focus on which qualifications are most suitable for individual pupils, as the grades pupils achieve will help them reach their goals for the next stage of their education or training.

Attainment 8 will measure the achievement of a pupil across 8 qualifications including mathematics (double weighted) and English (double weighted), 3 further qualifications that count in the English Baccalaureate (EBacc) measure and 3 further qualifications that can be GCSE qualifications (including EBacc subjects) or any other non-GCSE qualification on the DfE approved list.

General Certificate of Education (GCE) Advanced level (A level)

Typically, A level qualifications are studied over a two-year period. There are no lower or upper age limits. Schools and colleges usually expect students aged 16-18 to have obtained grades A*-C (grade 5 in the new criteria) in five subjects at GCSE level before taking an advanced level course. This requirement may vary between centres and according to which specific subjects are to be studied. Mature students may be assessed on different criteria as to their suitability to embark on the course.

GCE Qualifications

Over the past few years, AS level and A level qualifications have been in a process of reform. New subjects have been introduced gradually, with the first wave taught from September 2015. Subjects that have not been reformed are no longer be available for teaching.

GCE qualifications are available at two levels: the Advanced Subsidiary (AS), which is generally delivered over one year and is seen as half an A level; and the A level (GCE). Nearly 70 titles are available, covering a wide range of subject areas, including humanities, sciences, language, business, arts, mathematics and technology.

One of the major reforms is that AS level results no longer count towards an A level (they previously counted for 50%). The two qualifications are linear, with AS assessments typically taking place after one year and A levels after two.

New-style AS and A levels were first taught from September 2015 for: art and design, biology, business studies, chemistry, computer studies, economics, English language, English language and literature, English literature, history, physics, psychology, and sociology.

Subjects first taught from September 2016 include: ancient languages such as Latin or Greek, dance, drama (theatre studies), geography, modern languages such as Spanish or French, music, physical education, religious studies.

Those introduced for first teaching from September 2017: accounting, design and technology, music technology, history of art, environmental science, philosophy, maths, further maths, archaeology, accounting, electronics, ancient history, law, classical civilisation, film studies, media studies, politics, geology, statistics, Chinese, Italian, Russian. In 2018 Biblical Hebrew, Modern Hebrew & languages such as Bengali, Polish and Urdu were available for first teaching.

Some GCE AS and A levels, particularly the practical ones, contain a proportion of coursework. All GCE A levels that contain one or more types of assessment will have an element of synoptic assessment that tests students' understanding of the whole specification. GCE AS are graded A-E and A levels are graded A*-E.

Overall the amount of coursework at A level has been reduced in the reforms. In some subjects, such as the sciences, practical work will not contribute to the final A level but will be reported separately in a certificate of endorsement. In the sciences, students will do at least 12 practical activities, covering apparatus and techniques. Exam questions about practical work will make up at least 15% of the total marks for the qualification and students will be assessed on their knowledge, skills and understanding of practical work.

Cambridge International AS & A Level

Cambridge International AS & A Level is an internationally benchmarked qualification, taught in over 130 countries worldwide. It is typically for learners aged 16 to 19 years who need advanced study to prepare for university. It was created specifically for an international audience and the content has been devised to suit the wide variety of schools worldwide and avoid any cultural bias.

Cambridge International A Level is typically a two-year course, and Cambridge International AS Level is typically one year. Some subjects can be started as a Cambridge International AS Level and extended to a Cambridge International A Level. Students can either follow a broad course of study, or specialise in one particular subject area.

Learners use Cambridge International AS and A Levels to gain places at leading universities worldwide, including the UK, Ireland, USA, Canada, Australia, New Zealand, India, Singapore, Egypt, Jordan, South Africa, the Netherlands, Germany and Spain. In places such as the US and Canada, good grades in carefully chosen Cambridge International A Level subjects can result in up to one year of university course credit.

Assessment options:

Cambridge International AS & A Levels have a linear structure with exams at the end of the course. Students can choose from a range of assessment options:

Option 1: take Cambridge International AS Levels only. The Cambridge International syllabus content is half a Cambridge International A Level.

Option 2: staged assessment, which means taking the Cambridge International AS Level in one exam session and the Cambridge International A Level at a later session. However, this route is not possible in all subjects.

Option 3: take all Cambridge International A Level papers in the same examination session, usually at the end of the course.

Grades and subjects

Cambridge International A Levels are graded from A*-E. Cambridge International AS Levels are graded from A-E.

Subjects available: Afrikaans, Afrikaans – Language (AS only), Arabic, Arabic – Language (AS only), Art & Design, Biology, Business, Chemistry, Chinese – Language (AS only), Chinese (A Level only), Classical Studies, Computer Science, Design & Technology, Design & Textiles, Digital Media & Design, Divinity, Divinity (AS only), Drama, Economics, English – Language, English – Language and Literature (AS only), English – Literature, English General Paper (AS only), Environmental Management (AS only), Food Studies, French – Language (AS only), French – Literature (AS only), French (A Level only), General Paper (AS only), General Paper (AS only), Geography, German – Language (AS only), German (A Level only), Global Perspectives and Research, Hindi – Language (AS only), Hindi – Literature (AS only), Hindi (A Level only), Hinduism, Hinduism (AS only), History, Information Technology, Islamic Studies, Islamic Studies (AS only), Japanese Language (AS only), Law, Marathi – Language (AS only), Marathi (A Level only), Marine Science, Mathematics, Mathematics – Further, Media Studies, Music, Music (AS only), Nepal Studies (AS only), Physical Education, Physics, Portuguese – Language (AS only), Portuguese – Literature (AS only), Portuguese (A Level only), Psychology, Sociology, Spanish – First Language (AS only), Spanish – Language (AS only), Spanish – Literature (AS only), Spanish (A Level only), Tamil, Tamil – Language (AS only), Thinking Skills, Travel & Tourism, Urdu – Language (AS only), Urdu – Pakistan only (A Level only), Urdu (A Level only). Website: www.cambridgeinternational.org/alevel

Cambridge IGCSE

Cambridge IGCSE is the world's most popular international qualification for 14 to 16 year olds. It develops skills in creative thinking, enquiry and problem solving, in preparation for the next stage in a student's education. Cambridge IGCSE is taken in over 150 countries, and is widely recognised by employers and higher education institutions worldwide.

Cambridge IGCSE is graded from A*-G. In the UK, Cambridge IGCSE is accepted as equivalent to the GCSE. It can be used as preparation for Cambridge International A & AS Levels, UK A and AS levels, IB or AP and in some instances entry into university. Cambridge IGCSE First Language English and Cambridge IGCSE English Language qualifications are recognised by a significant number of UK universities as evidence of competence in the language for university entrance.

Subjects available: Accounting, Accounting (9-1), Afrikaans – First Language, Afrikaans – Second Language, Agriculture, Arabic – First Language, Arabic – First Language (9-1), Arabic – Foreign Language, Art & Design, Art & Design (9-1), Bahasa Indonesia, Bangladesh Studies, Biology, Biology (9-1), Business Studies, Business Studies (9-1), Chemistry, Chemistry (9-1), Child Development, Chinese - First Language, Chinese – Second Language, Computer Science, Computer Science (9-1), Czech – First Language, Design & Technology, Design & Technology (9-1), Development Studies, Drama, Drama (9-1), Dutch

– First Language, Dutch – Foreign Language, Economics, Economics (9-1), English – First Language, English – First Language (9–1), English – First Language (9–1) (UK only), English – First Language (US), English – Literature (9-1) (UK only), English – Literature (English), English – Literature (US), English – Literature in English, English – Literature in English (9-1), English as a Second Language (Count-in speaking), English as a Second Language (Count-in Speaking) (9-1), English as a Second Language (Speaking endorsement), English Second Language (Speaking Endorsement) (9-1), Enterprise, Environmental Management, Food & Nutrition, French – First Language, French – Foreign Language, French (9-1), Geography, Geography (9-1), German – First Language, German – Foreign Language, German (9-1), Global Perspectives, Greek – Foreign Language, Hindi as a Second Language, History, History – American (US), History (9-1), India Studies, Indonesian – Foreign Language, Information & Communication Technology, Information & Communication Technology (9-1), IsiZulu as a Second Language, Islamiyat, Italian – Foreign Language, Italian (9-1), Japanese – Foreign Language, Kazakh as a Second Language, Korean (First Language), Latin, Malay – First Language, Malay – Foreign Language, Mandarin Chinese – Foreign Language, Marine Science (Maldives only), Mathematics, Mathematics – Additional, Mathematics – Additional (US), Mathematics – International, Mathematics (9-1), Mathematics (9-1) (UK only), Mathematics (US), Music – 0410, Music (9-1), Pakistan Studies, Physical Education, Physical Education (9-1, Physical Science, Physics, Physics (9-1), Portuguese – First Language, Portuguese – Foreign Language, Religious Studies, Russian – First Language, Sanskrit, Science – Combined, Sciences – Co-ordinated (9-1), Sciences – Co-ordinated (Double), Sociology, Spanish – First Language, Spanish – Foreign Language, Spanish – Literature, Spanish (9-1), Swahili, Thai – First Language, Travel & Tourism, Turkish – First Language, Urdu as a Second Language, World Literature.
Website: www.cambridgeinternational.org/igcse

Cambridge Pre-U

Cambridge Pre-U is a post-16 qualification that equips students with the skills they need to succeed at university, developed with universities.

Cambridge Pre-U is a linear course, with exams taken at the end of two years. It encourages the development of well-informed, open and independent-minded individuals; promotes deep understanding through subject specialisation, with a depth and rigour appropriate to progression to higher education; and develops skills in independent research valued by universities.

Assessment

Cambridge Pre-U Principal Subjects are examined at the end of two years. Cambridge Pre-U Short Courses are available in some subjects and are typically examined at the end of one year. Students can study a combination of A Levels and Principal Subjects.

In order to gain the Cambridge Pre-U Diploma, students must study at least three Cambridge Pre-U Principal Subjects (up to two A Levels can be substituted for Principal Subjects) and Cambridge Pre-U Global Perspectives & Research (GPR). Cambridge Pre-U GPR includes an extended project in the second year, developing skills in research and critical thinking.

Grades and subjects

Cambridge Pre-U reports achievement on a scale of nine grades, with Distinction 1 being the highest grade and Pass 3 the lowest grade.

Subjects available: Art & Design, Art History, Biology, Business & Management, Chemistry, Classical Greek, Economics, English, French, Further Mathematics, Geography, German, Global Perspectives & Independent Research (UK only), Global Perspectives (Short Course) (UK only), History, Italian, Latin, Mandarin Chinese, Mathematics, Music, Philosophy & Theology, Physics, Psychology, Russian, Spanish
Website: www.cambridgeinternational.org/cambridgepreu

Edexcel International GCSEs

Pearson's Edexcel International GCSEs are academic qualifications aimed at learners aged 14 to 16. They're equivalent to a UK General Certificate of Secondary Education (GCSE), and are the main requirement for Level 3 studies, including progression to GCE AS or A levels, BTECs or employment. International GCSEs are linear qualifications, meaning that students take all of the exams at the end of the course. They are available at Level 1 (grades 3-1) and Level 2 (grades 9-4). There are currently more than 100,000 learners studying Edexcel International GCSEs, in countries throughout Asia, Africa, Europe, the Middle East and Latin America. Developed by subject specialists and reviewed regularly, many of Pearson's Edexcel International GCSEs include specific international content to make them relevant to students worldwide.

Pearson's Edexcel International GCSEs were initially developed for international schools. They have since become popular among independent schools in the UK, but are not approved for use in UK state schools.

Free Standing Maths Qualifications (FSMQ)

Aimed at those students wishing to acquire further qualifications in maths, specifically additional mathematics and foundations of advanced mathematics (MEI). Further UCAS points can be earned upon completion of the advanced FSMQ in additional mathematics.

AQA Certificate in Mathematical Studies (Core Maths)

This Level 3 qualification has been available since September 2015. It is designed for students who achieved a Grade 4 or above at GCSE and want to continue studying Maths. The qualification carries UCAS points equivalent to an AS level qualification.

AQA Certificate in Further Maths

This level 2 qualification has been designed to provide stretch and challenge to the most able mathematicians. This will be best suited to students who either already have, or are expected to achieve the top grades in GCSE Mathematics and are likely to progress to A level Mathematics and Further Mathematics.

Scottish qualifications

Information supplied by the Scottish Qualifications Authority

In Scotland, qualifications are awarded by the Scottish Qualifications Authority (SQA), the national accreditation and awarding body. A variety of qualifications are offered in schools, including:

- National Qualifications (National Units, National Courses, Skills for Work Courses and Scottish Baccalaureates)

- National Qualification Group Awards (National Certificates and National Progression Awards)

- Awards

National Qualifications cover subjects to suit everyone's interests and skills – from Chemistry to Construction, History to Hospitality, and Computing to Care.

Qualifications in the Scottish qualifications system sit at various levels on the Scottish Credit and Qualifications Framework (SCQF). There are 12 levels on the SCQF and each level represents the difficulty of learning involved. Qualifications in schools span SCQF levels 1 to 7.

National Qualifications (NQ)

National Qualifications are designed to support Curriculum for Excellence (CfE) — the national curriculum in Scotland for young people aged 3 to 18.

National Qualifications are taught in the senior phase of secondary school and they are also offered in colleges, and by some training providers.

The National Qualifications are National 1, National 2, National 3, National 4, National 5, Higher and Advanced Higher. They range from SCQF level 1 (National 1) to SCQF level 7 (Advanced Higher).

National Qualifications help young people to demonstrate the skills, knowledge and understanding they

have developed at school or college and enable them to prepare for further learning, training and employment.

National Units

National Units are the building blocks of National 2 to National 4 Courses and National Qualification Group Awards. They are also qualifications in their own right and can be done on an individual basis — such as National 1 qualifications, which are standalone units. Units are normally designed to take 40 hours of teaching to complete and each one is assessed by completing a unit assessment. Over 3500 National Units are available, including National Literacy and Numeracy Units, which assess students' literacy and numeracy skills.

Between 2016 and 2019, units and unit assessments were removed from National 5, Higher and Advanced Higher courses. These units are now available as freestanding units at SCQF levels 5, 6 and 7 and can be taken on an individual basis.

National Courses

National Courses are skills-based qualifications, which are available at National 2, National 3, National 4, National 5, Higher and Advanced Higher levels (SCQF levels 2 to 7). There are more than 60 subjects available, at various levels.

National 2, National 3 and National 4 courses consist of units and unit assessments, which are internally assessed by teachers and lecturers, and quality assured by SQA. Students complete the unit assessments during class time. National 4 courses also include an Added Value Unit assessment that assesses students' performance across the whole course. National 2 to National 4 courses are not graded but are assessed as pass or fail.

National 5, Higher and Advanced Higher courses are graded A to D or 'no award' and involve a course assessment that takes place at the end of the course. For most subjects, the course assessment is a combination of one or more formal exams and one or more coursework assessments (such as an assignment, performance, project or practical activity). SQA marks all exams and the majority of coursework. In some subjects, coursework is internally assessed by the teacher or lecturer and quality assured by SQA, while performances and practical activities may be subject to visiting assessment by an SQA examiner.

The assessment of National 5, Higher and Advanced Higher courses has recently undergone change. Previously, students completed internally-assessed unit assessments throughout the course, before completing the course assessment at the end. Between 2016 and 2019, units and unit assessments were removed from National 5 to Advanced Higher courses and so the course assessments were strengthened to ensure that students continue to be assessed on the full content of the course.

Skills for Work Courses

Skills for Work courses are designed to introduce students to the demands and expectations of the world of work. They are available in a variety of areas such as construction, hairdressing and hospitality. The courses involve a strong element of learning through involvement in practical and vocational activities, and develop knowledge, skills and experience that are related to employment. They consist of units and unit assessments, which are internally assessed by teachers and lecturers, and quality assured by SQA. Skills for Work courses are not graded but are assessed as pass or fail. They are available at National 4, National 5 and Higher levels (SCQF levels 4 to 6) and are often delivered in partnership between schools and colleges.

Scottish Baccalaureates

Scottish Baccalaureates consist of a coherent group of Higher and Advanced Higher qualifications, with the addition of an interdisciplinary project. They are available in four subject areas: Expressive Arts, Languages, Science and Social Sciences. The interdisciplinary project is marked and awarded at Advanced Higher level (SCQF level 7). It provides students with a platform to apply their knowledge in a realistic context, and to demonstrate initiative, responsibility and independent

working. Aimed at high-achieving sixth year students, the Scottish Baccalaureate encourages personalised, in-depth study and interdisciplinary learning in their final year of secondary school.

National Qualification Group Awards

National Certificates (NCs) and National Progression Awards (NPAs) are referred to as National Qualification Group Awards. These qualifications provide students preparing for work with opportunities to develop skills that are sought after by employers. They are available at SCQF levels 2 to 6.

National Certificates (NCs)

NCs prepare students for employment, career development or progression to more advanced study at HNC/HND level. They are available in a range of subjects, including: Sound Production, Technical Theatre, and Child, Health and Social Care.

National Progression Awards (NPAs)

NPAs develop specific skills and knowledge in specialist vocational areas, including Journalism, Architecture and Interior Design, and Legal Services. They link to National Occupational Standards, which are the basis of Scottish Vocational Qualifications (SVQs) and are taught in partnership between schools, colleges, employers and training providers.

Awards

SQA Awards provide students with opportunities to acquire skills, recognise achievement and promote confidence through independent thinking and positive attitudes, while motivating them to be successful and participate positively in the wider community.

A variety of different awards are offered at a number of SCQF levels and cover subjects including leadership, employability and enterprise. These awards are designed to recognise the life, learning and work skills that students gain from taking part in activities both in and out of school, such as sports, volunteering and fundraising.

For more information on SQA and its portfolio of qualifications, visit www.sqa.org.uk

Additional and Alternative

Cambridge Primary

Cambridge Primary is typically for learners aged 5 to 11 years. It develops learner skills and understanding in 10 subjects: English as a first or second language, mathematics, science, art & design, digital literacy, music, physical education, Cambridge Global Perspectives and ICT. The flexible curriculum frameworks include optional assessment tools to help schools monitor learners' progress and give detailed feedback to parents. At the end of Cambridge Primary, schools can enter students for Cambridge Primary Checkpoint tests which are marked in Cambridge.
Website: www.cambridgeinternational.org/primary

Cambridge ICT Starters introduces learners, typically aged 5 to 14 years, to the key ICT applications they need to achieve computer literacy and to understand the impact of technology on our daily lives. It can be taught and assessed in English or Spanish.

Cambridge Lower Secondary

Cambridge Lower Secondary is typically for learners aged 11 to 14 years. It develops learner skills and understanding in 10 subjects: English, English as a second language, mathematics, science, art & design, digital literacy, music, physical education, Cambridge Global Perspectives and ICT, and includes assessment tools. At the end of Cambridge Lower Secondary, schools can enter students for Cambridge Lower Secondary Checkpoint tests which are marked in Cambridge and provide an external international benchmark for student performance.
Website:
www.cambridgeinternational.org/lowersecondary

European Baccalaureate (EB)

Not to be confused with the International Baccalaureate (IB) or the French Baccalaureate, this certificate is available in European schools and recognised in all EU countries.

To obtain the baccalaureate, a student must obtain a minimum score of 60%, which is made up from: coursework, oral participation in class and tests (40%); five written examinations (36%) – mother-tongue, first foreign language and maths are compulsory for all candidates; four oral examinations (24%) – mother tongue and first foreign language are compulsory (history or geography may also be compulsory here, dependant on whether the candidate has taken a written examination in these subjects).

Throughout the EU the syllabus and examinations necessary to achieve the EB are identical. The only exception to this rule is the syllabus for the mother tongue language. The EB has been specifically designed to meet, at the very least, the minimum qualification requirements of each member state.

Study for the EB begins at nursery stage (age four) and progresses through primary (age six) and on into secondary school (age 12).

Syllabus
Languages: Bulgarian, Czech, Danish, Dutch, English, Estonian, Finnish, Finnish as a second national language, French, German, Greek, Hungarian, Irish, Italian, Latvian, Lithuanian, Maltese, Polish, Portuguese, Romanian, Slovak, Slovenian, Spanish, Swedish, Swedish for Finnish pupils.

Literary: art education, non-confessional ethics, geography, ancient Greek, history, human sciences, Latin, music, philosophy, physical education.

Sciences: biology, chemistry, economics, ICT, integrated science, mathematics, physics.

For more information, contact:
Office of the Secretary-General of the European Schools, rue de la Science 23 – 2nd floor, B-1040 Bruxelles, Belgique
Tel: +32 (0)2 895 26 11
Website: www.eursc.eu

The International Baccalaureate (IB)

The International Baccalaureate (IB) offers four challenging and high quality educational programmes for a worldwide community of schools, aiming to develop internationally minded people who, recognizing their common humanity and shared guardianship of the planet, help to create a better, more peaceful world.

The IB works with schools around the world (both state and privately funded) that share the commitment to international education to deliver these programmes.

Schools that have achieved the high standards required for authorization to offer one or more of the IB programmes are known as IB World Schools. There are over half a million students attending almost 5000 IB World Schools in over 150 countries and this number is growing annually.

The Primary Years, Middle Years and Diploma Programmes share a common philosophy and common characteristics. They develop the whole student, helping students to grow intellectually, socially, aesthetically and culturally. They provide a broad and balanced education that includes science and the humanities, languages and mathematics, technology and the arts. The programmes teach students to think critically, and encourage them to draw connections between areas of knowledge and to use problem-solving techniques and concepts from many disciplines. They instil in students a sense of responsibility towards others and towards the environment. Lastly, and perhaps most importantly, the programmes give students an awareness and understanding of their own culture and of other cultures, values and ways of life.

A fourth programme called the IB Career-related Programme (CP) became available to IB World Schools from September 2012. All IB programmes include:
- A written curriculum or curriculum framework
- Student assessment appropriate to the age range
- Professional development and networking opportunities for teachers
- Support, authorization and programme evaluation for the school

The IB Primary Years Programme

The IB Primary Years Programme (PYP), for students aged three to 12, focuses on the development of the whole child as an inquirer, both in the classroom and in the world outside. It is a framework consisting of five essential elements (concepts, knowledge, skills, attitude, action) and guided by six trans-disciplinary themes of global significance, explored using knowledge and skills derived from six subject areas (language, social studies, mathematics, science and technology, arts, and personal, social and physical education) with a powerful emphasis on inquiry-based learning.

The most significant and distinctive feature of the PYP is the six trans-disciplinary themes. These themes are about issues that have meaning for, and are important to, all of us. The programme offers a balance between learning about or through the subject areas, and learning beyond them. The six themes of global significance create a trans-disciplinary framework that allows students to 'step up' beyond the confines of learning within subject areas:
- Who we are
- Where we are in place and time
- How we express ourselves
- How the world works
- How we organize ourselves
- Sharing the planet

The PYP exhibition is the culminating activity of the programme. It requires students to analyse and propose solutions to real-world issues, drawing on what they have learned through the programme. Evidence of student development and records of PYP exhibitions are reviewed by the IB as part of the programme evaluation process.

Assessment is an important part of each unit of inquiry as it both enhances learning and provides opportunities for students to reflect on what they know, understand and can do. The teacher's feedback to the students provides the guidance, the tools and the incentive for them to become more competent, more skilful and better at understanding how to learn.

The IB Middle Years Programme (MYP)

The Middle Years Programme (MYP), for students aged 11 to 16, comprises eight subject groups:
- Language acquisition
- Language and literature
- Individuals and societies
- Sciences
- Mathematics
- Arts
- Physical and health education
- Design

The MYP requires at least 50 hours of teaching time for each subject group in each year of the programme. In years 4 and 5, students have the option to take courses from six of the eight subject groups within certain limits, to provide greater flexibility in meeting local requirements and individual student learning needs.

Each year, students in the MYP also engage in at least one collaboratively planned interdisciplinary unit that involves at least two subject groups.

MYP students also complete a long-term project, where they decide what they want to learn about, identify what they already know, discovering what they will need to know to complete the project, and create a proposal or criteria for completing it

The MYP aims to help students develop their personal understanding, their emerging sense of self and their responsibility in their community.

The MYP allows schools to continue to meet state, provincial or national legal requirements for students with access needs. Schools must develop an inclusion/special educational needs (SEN) policy that explains assessment access arrangements, classroom accommodations and curriculum modification that meet individual student learning needs.

The IB Diploma Programme (IBDP)

The IB Diploma Programme, for students aged 16 to 19, is an academically challenging and motivating curriculum of international education that prepares students for success at university and in life beyond studies.

DP students choose at least one course from six subject groups, thus ensuring depth and breadth of knowledge and experience in languages, social studies, the experimental sciences, mathematics, and the arts. With more than 35 courses to choose from, students have the flexibility to further explore and learn subjects that meet their interest. Out of the six courses required, at least three and not more than four must be taken at higher level (240 teaching hours), the others at standard level (150 teaching hours). Students can take examinations in English, French or Spanish.

In addition, three unique components of the programme – the DP core – aim to broaden students' educational experience and challenge them to apply their knowledge and skills. The DP core – the extended essay (EE), theory of knowledge (TOK) and creativity, activity, service (CAS) – are compulsory and central to the philosophy of the programme.

The IB uses both external and internal assessment to measure student performance in the DP. Student results are determined by performance against set standards, not by each student's position in the overall rank order. DP assessment is unique in the way that it measures the extent to which students have mastered advanced academic skills not what they have memorized. DP assessment also encourages an international outlook and intercultural skills, wherever appropriate.

The IB diploma is awarded to students who gain at least 24 points out of a possible 45 points, subject to certain minimum levels of performance across the whole programme and to satisfactory participation in the creativity, activity, and service requirement.

Recognized and respected by leading universities globally, the DP encourages students to be knowledgeable, inquiring, caring and compassionate, and to develop intercultural understanding, open-mindedness and the attitudes necessary to respect and evaluate a range of viewpoints.

The IB Career Related Programme (IBCP)

The IB Career-related Programme, for students aged 16 to 19, offers an innovative educational framework that combines academic studies with career-related learning. Through the CP, students develop the competencies they need to succeed in the 21st century. More importantly, they have the opportunity to engage with a rigorous study programme that genuinely interests them while gaining transferable and lifelong skills that prepares them to pursue higher education, apprenticeships or direct employment.

CP students complete four core components – language development, personal and professional skills, service learning and a reflective project – in order to receive the International Baccalaureate Career-related Programme Certificate. Designed to enhance critical thinking and intercultural understanding, the CP core helps students develop the communication and personal skills, as well as intellectual habits required for lifelong learning.

Schools that choose to offer the CP can create their own distinctive version of the programme and select career pathways that suit their students and local community needs. The IB works with a variety of CRS providers around the world and schools seeking to develop career pathways with professional communities can benefit from our existing collaborations. All CRS providers undergo a rigorous curriculum evaluation to ensure that their courses align with the CP pedagogy and meet IB quality standards. The flexibility to meet the needs, backgrounds and contexts of learners allows CP schools to offer an education that is relevant and meaningful to their students.

Launched in 2012, there are 250 CP schools. Many schools with the IB Diploma Programme (DP) and the Middle Years Programme (MYP) have chosen the CP as an alternative IB pathway to offer students. CP schools often report that the programme has helped them raise student aspiration, increase student engagement and retention and encouraged learners to take responsibility for their own actions, helping them foster high levels of self-esteem through meaningful achievements.

For more information on IB programmes, visit: www.ibo.org
Africa, Europe, Middle East IB Global Centre,
Churchillplein 6, The Hague, 2517JW, The Netherlands
Tel: +31 (0)70 352 6000
Email: support@ibo.org

Pearson Edexcel Mathematics Awards

Pearson's Edexcel Mathematics Awards are small, stand-alone qualifications designed to help students to develop and demonstrate proficiency in different areas of mathematics. These Awards enable students to focus on understanding key concepts and techniques, and are available across three subjects, including: Number and Measure (Levels 1 and 2), Algebra (Levels 2 and 3) and Statistical Methods (Levels 1, 2 and 3).

Designed to build students' confidence and fluency; the Awards can fit into the existing programme of delivery for mathematics in schools and colleges, prepare students for GCSE and/or GCE Mathematics, and to support further study in other subjects, training or the workplace. They offer a choice of levels to match students' abilities, with clear progression between the levels. These small, 60-70 guided learning hour qualifications are assessed through one written paper per level. Each qualification is funded and approved for pre-16 and 16-18 year old students in England and in schools and colleges in Wales.

Projects

Extended Project Qualification (EPQ)

AQA, OCR, Pearson and WJEC offer the Extended Project Qualification, which is a qualification aimed at developing a student's research and independent learning skills. The EPQ can be taken as a stand-alone qualification, and it is equivalent to half an A level in UCAS points (but only a third of performance points).

Students complete a research based written report and may produce an artefact or a practical science experiment as part of their project.

Cambridge International Project Qualification (IPQ)

Cambridge International is offering a new standalone project-based qualification, which can be taken alongside Cambridge International AS & A levels. Students complete a 5000-word research project on a topic of their choice. The qualification is assessed by Cambridge International.

For more information, go to www.cambridgeinternational.org/advanced

Entry level and basic skills

Entry Level Qualifications

If you want to take GCSE or NVQ Level 1 but have not yet reached the standard required, then entry level qualifications are for you as they are designed to get you started on the qualifications ladder.

Entry level qualifications are available in a wide range of areas. You can take an entry level certificate in most subjects where a similar GCSE exists. There are also vocational entry level qualifications – some in specific areas like retail or catering and others where you can take units in different work-related subjects to get a taster of a number of career areas. Also available are entry level certificates in life skills and the basic skills of literacy and numeracy.

Anyone can take an entry level qualification – your school or college will help you decide which qualification is right for you.

Entry level qualifications are flexible programmes so the time it takes to complete will vary according to where you study and how long you need to take the qualification.

Subjects available include: Art and Design, Computer Science, English, Geography, History, Latin, Mathematics, Physical Education and Science.

Functional Skills

Functional Skills are qualifications in English and maths that equip learners with the basic practical skills required in everyday life, education and the workplace. They are available at Entry Level, Level 1 and Level 2. Functional Skills are identified as funded 'stepping stone' qualifications to English and maths GCSE for post-16 learners who haven't previously achieved a grade D in these subjects. There are part of apprenticeship completion requirements.

Vocational qualifications

Applied Generals/Level 3 Certificates

Applied General qualifications are available in Business and Science and are a practical introduction to these subjects, they are a real alternative to A level support progression to further study or employment aimed at students aged 16-18.

Developed together with teachers, schools, colleges and higher education institutions, they help learners to develop knowledge and skills.

A mixture of assessment types means learners can apply their knowledge in a practical way. An integrated approach creates a realistic and relevant qualification for learners.

AQA Technical Award

AQA's Technical Award is a practical, vocational Level 1/2 qualification for 14- to 16-year-olds to take alongside GCSEs.

The Technical Award in Performing Arts provides an introduction to life and work, equipping learners with the practical, transferable skills and core knowledge needed to progress to further general or vocational study, including Level 3 qualifications, employment or apprenticeships.

Learners are assessed on doing rather than knowing through the project-based internal assessments, where they can apply their knowledge to practical tasks. There are two internally assessed units worth 30% each, and an externally assessed exam worth 40%.

AQA Tech-levels

Level 3 technical qualifications have been designed in collaboration with employers and professional bodies. They're aimed at learners aged over 16 wanting to progress into a specific sector through apprenticeships, further study or employment. There are 16 individual qualifications within IT, Engineering, Business and Entertainment Technology. These vary in size of qualification.

Transferable skills have been contextualised explicitly within each qualification and are a mandatory part of the qualification outcome.

Learners are assessed through a combination of examinations, internally and externally assessed assignments.

The last time schools could enter Tech-level Business: Marketing was summer 2020.

June 2021 will be the final internally assessed unit certification opportunity, and January 2022 will be the last external exam resit and certification opportunity

BTECs

BTEC Level 2 First qualifications
ie BTEC Level 2 Diplomas, BTEC Level 2 Extended Certificates, BTEC Level 2 Certificates and BTEC Level 2 Award.

BTEC Firsts are Level 2 introductory work-related programmes covering a wide range of vocational areas including business, engineering, information technology, health and social care, media, travel and tourism, and public services.

Programmes may be taken full or part-time. They are practical programmes that provide a foundation for the knowledge and skills you will need in work. Alternatively, you can progress onto a BTEC National qualification, Applied GCE A level or equivalent.

There are no formal entry requirements and they can be studied alongside GCSEs. Subjects available include: Agriculture, Animal Care, Applied Science, Art and Design, Business, Children's Care, Learning and Development, Construction, Countryside and the Environment, Engineering, Fish Husbandry, Floristry, Health and Social care, Horse Care, Horticulture, Hospitality, IT, Land-based Technology, Business, Creative Media Production, Music, Performing Arts, Public Services, Sport, Travel and Tourism, and Vehicle Technology.

BTEC Foundation Diploma in Art and Design (QCF)
For those students preparing to go on to higher education within the field of art and design. This diploma is recognised as one of the best courses of its type in the UK, and is used in preparation for degree programmes. Units offered include researching, recording and responding in art and design, media experimentation, personal experimental studies, and a final major project.

BTEC Nationals

ie BTEC Level 3 Extended Diplomas (QCF), BTEC Level 3 Diplomas (QCF), BTEC Level 3 Subsidiary Diplomas (QCF), BTEC Level 3 Certificates (QCF)

BTEC National programmes are long-established vocational programmes. They are practical programmes that are highly valued by employers. They enable you to gain the knowledge and skills that you will need in work, or give you the choice to progress on to a BTEC Higher National, a Foundation Degree or a degree programme.

BTEC Nationals, which hold UCAS points cover a range of vocationally specialist sectors including child care, children's play, learning and development, construction, art and design, aeronautical engineering, electrical/electronic engineering, IT, business, creative and media production, performing arts, public services, sport, sport and exercise sciences and applied science. The programmes may be taken full- or part-time, and can be taken in conjunction with NVQs and/or functional skills units at an appropriate level.

There are no formal entry requirements, but if you have any of the following you are likely to be at the right level to study a BTEC national qualification.

- a BTEC Level 2 First qualification
- GCSEs – at grades A*-C in several subjects
- Relevant work experience

There are also very specialist BTEC Nationals, such as Pharmaceutical Science and Blacksmithing and Metalworking.

BTEC Higher Nationals

Known as HNDs and HNCs – ie BTEC Level 5 HND Diplomas (QCF) and BTEC Level 4 HNC Diplomas (QCF)

BTEC HNDs and HNCs are further and higher education qualifications that offer a balance of education and vocational training. They are available in over 40 work-related subjects such as Graphic Design, Business, Health and Social Care, Computing and Systems Development, Manufacturing Engineering, Hospitality Management, and Public Services.

BTEC higher national courses combine study with hands-on work experience during your course. Once completed, you can use the skills you learn to begin your career, or continue on to a related degree course.

HNDs are often taken as a full-time course over two years but can also be followed part-time in some cases.

HNCs are often for people who are working and take two years to complete on a part-time study basis by day release, evenings, or a combination of the two. Some HNC courses are done on a full-time basis.

There are no formal entry requirements, but if you have any of the following you are likely to be at the right academic level:

- at least one A level
- a BTEC Level 3 National qualification
- level 3 NVQ

BTEC specialist and professional qualifications

These qualifications are designed to prepare students for specific and specialist work activities. These are split into two distinct groups:

- Specialist qualifications (entry to Level 3)
- Professional qualifications (Levels 4-7)

Cambridge Nationals

Cambridge Nationals are vocationally-related qualifications that take an engaging, practical and inspiring approach to learning and assessment.

They are industry-relevant, geared to key sector requirements and very popular with schools and colleges because they suit such a broad range of learning styles and abilities.

Cambridge Nationals are available in: Child Development, Creative iMedia, Engineering Design, Engineering Manufacture, Enterprise and Marketing, Health and Social Care, ICT, Information Technologies, Principles in Engineering and Engineering Business, Sport Science, Sport Studies, Systems Control in Engineering. They are joint Level 1 and 2 qualifications aimed at students aged 14-16 in full-time study.

Cambridge Technicals

OCR's Cambridge Technicals are practical and flexible vocationally-related qualifications, offering students in-depth study in a wide range of subjects, including business, health and social care, IT, sport, art and design, digital media, science, performing arts and engineering.

Cambridge Technicals are aimed at young people aged 16-19 who have completed Key Stage 4 of their education and want to study in a more practical, work-related way.

Cambridge Technicals are available at Level 2 and Level 3, and carry UCAS points at Level 3.

NVQs

NVQs reward those who demonstrate skills gained at work. They relate to particular jobs and are usefully taken while you are working. Within reason, NVQs do not have to be completed in a specified amount of time. They can be taken by full-time employees or by school and college students with a work placement or part-time job that enables them to develop the appropriate skills. There are no age limits and no special entry requirements.

NVQs are organised into levels, based on the competencies required. Levels 1-3 are the levels most applicable to learners within the 14-19 phase. Achievement of Level 4 within this age group will be rare. See the OCR website for further information.

Occupational Studies (Northern Ireland)

Targeted at learners working towards and at Level 1 and 2 in Key Stage 4 within the Northern Ireland curriculum. For further information see the CCEA website.

OCR Vocational Qualifications

These are available at different levels and different sizes. Levels 1-3 are the levels most applicable to learners within the 14-19 phase. The different sizes are indicated with the use of Award, Certificate and Diploma in the qualification title and indicate the number of hours it typically takes to complete the qualification.

Vocational qualifications are assessed according to each individual specification, but may include practical assessments and/or marked assessments. They are designed to provide evidence of a student's relevant skills and knowledge in their chosen subject. These qualifications can be used for employment or as a path towards further education. See the OCR website for further details.

SVQs (Scotland)

Scottish Vocational Qualifications (SVQs) are based on national standards, which are drawn up by people from industry, commerce and education. They are studied in the workplace, in college or with training providers. Some schools offer them in partnership with colleges and employers. SVQs are available in many subject areas, from forestry to IT, management to catering, and journalism to construction.

Each unit of an SVQ defines one aspect of a job or work role and what it is to be competent in that aspect of the job.

SVQs are available at SCQF Levels 4-11 and Levels 4-7 are most applicable to learners aged 16-18.

Awarding organisations and examination dates

Awarding organisations and examination dates

In England there are four awarding organisations, each offering GCSEs, AS and A levels (Eduqas offers only reformed qualifications in England, whereas WJEC offers in England, Wales, Northern Ireland and independent regions). There are separate awarding organisations in Wales (WJEC) and Northern Ireland (CCEA). The awarding organisation in Scotland (SQA) offers equivalent qualifications.

This information was supplied by the awarding bodies and was accurate at the time of going to press. It is intended as a general guide only for candidates in the United Kingdom. Dates are subject to variation and should be confirmed with the awarding organisation concerned.

AQA

Qualifications offered:
GCSE
AS and A level
Technical levels
Foundation Certificate of Secondary Education (FCSE)
Entry Level Certificate (ELC)
Foundation and Higher Projects
Extended Project Qualification (EPQ)
Applied Generals/AQA Level 3 Certificates and Extended Certificates
Functional Skills
AQA Certificate
Technical Award

Other assessment schemes:
Unit Award Scheme (UAS)

Examination dates for summer 2021: 14 May – 28 June (provisional)

Contact:
Email: eos@aqa.org.uk
Website: www.aqa.org.uk
Tel: 0800 197 7162 (8am–5pm Monday to Friday)
+44 161 696 5995 (Outside the UK)

Devas Street, Manchester M15 6EX
Stag Hill House, Guildford, Surrey GU2 7XJ
Windsor House, Cornwall Road, Harrogate, HG1 2PW
2nd Floor, Lynton House, 7–12 Tavistock Square, London, WC1H 9LT

CCEA – Council for the Curriculum, Examinations and Assessment

Qualifications offered:
GCSE
GCE AS/A level
Key Skills (Levels 1-4)
Entry Level Qualifications
Occupational Studies (Levels 1 & 2)
QCF Qualifications
Applied GCSE and GCE

Contact:
Email: info@ccea.org.uk
Website: www.ccea.org.uk

29 Clarendon Road, Clarendon Dock, Belfast, BT1 3BG
Tel: (028) 9026 1200

Eduqas

Eduqas, part of WJEC, offers Ofqual reformed GCSEs, AS and A levels to secondary schools and colleges. Our qualifications are available in England, Channel Islands, Isle of Man, Northern Ireland and to the independent sector in Wales (restrictions may apply).

Qualifications offered:
GCSE (9-1)
AS
A level
Level 3

Contact:
Email: info@wjec.co.uk
Website: www.eduqas.co.uk

Eduqas (WJEC CBAC Ltd),
245 Western Avenue, Cardiff, CF5 2YX
Telephone: 029 2026 5000

IB – International Baccalaureate

Qualification offered:
IB Diploma
IB Career-related Certificate

Contact:
Email: support@ibo.org
Website: www.ibo.org

IB Global Centre, The Hague, Churchillplein 6, 2517 JW, The Hague, The Netherlands
Tel: +31 70 352 60 00

IB Global Centre, Washington DC, 7501 Wisconsin Avenue, Suite 200 West Bethesda, Maryland 20814, USA
Tel: +1 301 202 3000

IB Global Centre, Singapore, 600 North Bridge Road, #21-01 Parkview Square, Singapore 188778
Tel: +65 6 579 5000

IB Global Centre, Cardiff, Peterson House, Malthouse Avenue, Cardiff Gate, Cardiff, Wales, CF23 8GL, UK
Email: reception@ibo.org
Tel: +44 29 2054 7777

International Baccalaureate Foundation Office, Route des Morillons 15, Grand-Saconnex, Genève, CH-1218, Switzerland
Tel: +41 22 309 2540

OCR – Oxford Cambridge and RSA Examinations – and Cambridge International

Qualifications offered by OCR or sister awarding organisation Cambridge Assessment International Education (Cambridge International) include:
GCSE
GCE AS/A level
IGCSE
International AS/A level
Extended Project
Cambridge International Project Qualification
Cambridge Pre-U
Cambridge Nationals
Cambridge Technicals
Functional Skills
FSMQ – Free Standing Maths Qualification
NVQ

Contact:
OCR
OCR Head Office, The Triangle Building, Shaftesbury Road, Cambridge, CB2 8EA
Website: www.ocr.org.uk
Tel: +44 1223 553998

Cambridge International
Website: www.cambridgeinternational.org
Email: info@cambridgeinternational.org
Tel: +44 1223 553554

Pearson

Qualifications offered:

Pearson's qualifications are offered in the UK but are also available through their international centres across the world. They include:

DiDA, CiDA
GCE A levels
GCSEs
Functional Skills
International GCSEs and Edexcel Certificates
ESOL (Skills for Life)
BTEC Enterprise qualifications
BTEC Entry Level, Level 1 and Level 1 Introductory
BTEC Firsts
BTEC Foundation Diploma in Art and Design
BTEC Industry Skills
BTEC International Level 3
BTEC Level 2 Technicals
BTEC Level 3 Technical Levels in Hospitality
BTEC Nationals
BTEC Specialist and Professional qualifications
BTEC Tech Awards
Higher Nationals
T Levels

Contact:
190 High Holborn, London WC1V 7BH

See website for specific contact details:
qualifications.pearson.com

SQA – Scottish Qualifications Authority

Qualifications offered:

National Qualifications (NQs): National 1 to National 5;
Higher; Advanced Higher
Skills for Work; Scottish Baccalaureates
National Certificates (NCs)
National Progression Awards (NPAs)
Awards
Core Skills
Scottish Vocational Qualifications (SVQs)
Higher National Certificates and Higher National Diplomas (HNCs/HNDs)*

*SQA offers HNCs and HNDs to centres in Scotland. Outside of Scotland, the equivalent qualifications are the SQA Advanced Certificate and SQA Advanced Diploma.

*Examination dates for summer 2021: 26 April – 3 June***

**The 2021 exam timetable is currently planned for these dates, however SQA is reviewing its contingency arrangements in the event of any further Covid-19 disruption to teaching during session 2020-21.

Contact:
Email: customer@sqa.org.uk Tel: 0345 279 1000
Website: www.sqa.org.uk
Glasgow – The Optima Building, 58 Robertson Street, Glasgow, G2 8DQ
Dalkeith – Lowden, 24 Wester Shawfair, Dalkeith, Midlothian, EH22 1FD

WJEC

With over 65 years' experience in delivering qualifications, WJEC is the largest provider in Wales and a leading provider in England and Northern Ireland.

Qualifications offered:

GCSE
GCE A/AS
Functional Skills
Entry Level
Welsh Baccalaureate Qualifications
Essential Skills Wales
Wider Key Skills
Project Qualifications Principal Learning
Other general qualifications such as Level 1 and Level 2 Awards and Certificates including English Language, English Literature, Latin Language, Latin Language & Roman Civilisation and Latin Literature
QCF Qualifications

Contact:
Email: info@wjec.co.uk
Website: www.wjec.co.uk

245 Western Avenue, Cardiff, CF5 2YX
Tel: 029 2026 5000

Educational organisations

Educational organisations

Artsmark

Arts Council England's Artsmark was set up in 2001, and rounds are held annually.

All schools in England can apply for an Artsmark – primary, middle, secondary, special and pupil referral units, maintained and independent – on a voluntary basis. An Artsmark award is made to schools showing commitment to the full range of arts – music, dance, drama and art and design.

Tel: 0161 934 4317
Email: artsmark@artscouncil.org.uk
Website: www.artsmark.org.uk

Association for the Education and Guardianship of International Students (AEGIS)

AEGIS brings together schools and guardianship organisations to ensure and promote the welfare of international students. AEGIS provides accreditation for all reputable guardianship organisations.

AEGIS, The Wheelhouse, Bond's Mill Estate, Bristol Road, Stonehouse, Gloucestershire GL10 3RF.
Tel: 01453 821293
Email: info@aegisuk.net
Website: www.aegisuk.net

The Association of American Study Abroad Programmes (AASAP)

Established in 1991 to represent American study abroad programmes in the UK.
Contact: Kalyn Franke, AASAP/UK,
University of Maryland in London, Connaught Hall,
36-45 Tavistock Square, London WC1H 9EX
Email: info@aasapuk.org
Website: www.aasapuk.org

The Association of British Riding Schools (ABRS)

An independent body of proprietors and principals of riding establishments, aiming to look after their interests and those of the riding public and to raise standards of management, instruction and animal welfare.
The Association of British Riding Schools, Unit 8, Bramble Hill Farm, Five Oaks Road, Slinfold, Horsham,
West Sussex RH13 0RL. Tel: 01403 790294
Email: office@abrs-info.org
Website: www.abrs-info.org

Association of Colleges (AOC)

Created in 1996 to promote the interest of further education colleges in England and Wales.
2-5 Stedham Place, London WC1A 1HU
Tel: 0207 034 9900
Email: enquiries@aoc.co.uk
Website: www.aoc.co.uk

Association of Governing Bodies of Independent Schools (AGBIS)

AGBIS supports and advises governing bodies of schools in the independent sector on all aspects of governance.
Registered charity No. 1108756
Association of Governing Bodies of Independent Schools, 3 Codicote Road, Welwyn, Hertfordshire AL6 9LY
Tel: 01438 840730
Email: office@agbis.org.uk
Website: www.agbis.org.uk

Association of Employment and Learning Providers (AELP)

AELP's purpose is to influence the education and training agenda. They are the voice of independent learning providers throughout England.
Association of Employment and Learning Providers,
2nd Floor, 9 Apex Court, Bradley Stoke, Bristol, BS32 4JT
Tel: 0117 986 5389
Email: enquiries@aelp.org.uk
Website: www.aelp.org.uk

The Association of School and College Leaders (ASCL)

Formerly the Secondary Heads Association, the ASCL is a professional association for secondary school and college leaders.
130 Regent Road, Leicester LE1 7PG
Tel: 0116 299 1122
Fax: 0116 299 1123
Email: info@ascl.org.uk
Website: www.ascl.org.uk

Boarding Schools' Association (BSA)

For information on the BSA see editorial on page 35

The British Accreditation Council (BAC)

The British Accreditation Council (BAC) has now been the principal accrediting body for the independent further and higher education and training sector for nearly 30 years. BAC-accredited institutions in the UK now number more than 300, offering everything from website design to yoga to equine dentistry, as well as more standard qualifications in subjects such as business, IT, management and law. As well as our accreditation of institutions offering traditional teaching, BAC has developed a new accreditation scheme for providers offering online, distance and blended learning. Some students may also look to study outside the UK at one of the institutions holding BAC international accreditation.
14 Devonshire Square, London, EC2M 4YT
Tel: 0300 330 1400
Email: info@the-bac.org
Website: www.the-bac.org

The British Association for Early Childhood Education (BAECE)

Promotes quality provision for all children from birth to eight in whatever setting they are placed. Publishes booklets and organises conferences for those interested in early years education and care. Registered charity Nos. 313082; SC039472
54 Clarendon Road, Watford, WD17 1DU
Tel: 01923 438 995
Email: office@early-education.org.uk
Website: www.early-education.org.uk

The Choir Schools' Association (CSA)

Represents 44 schools attached to cathedrals, churches and college chapels, which educate cathedral and collegiate choristers.
CSA Information Officer, Village Farm, The Street, Market Weston, Diss, Norfolk IP22 2NZ
Tel: 01359 221333
Email: info@choirschools.org.uk
Website: www.choirschools.org.uk

CIFE

CIFE is the professional association for independent sixth form and tutorial colleges accredited by the British Accreditation Council (BAC), the Independent Schools Council or the DfE (Ofsted). Member colleges specialise in preparing students for GCSE and A level (AS and A2) in particular and university entrance in general.
The aim of the association is to provide a forum for the exchange of information and ideas, and for the promotion of best practice, and to safeguard adherence to strict standards of professional conduct and ethical propriety. Further information can be obtained from CIFE:
Tel: 0208 767 8666
Email: enquiries@cife.org.uk
Website: www.cife.org.uk

Council of British International Schools (COBIS)

COBIS is a membership association of British schools of quality worldwide and is committed to a stringent process of quality assurance for all its member schools. COBIS is a member of the Independent Schools Council (ISC) of the United Kingdom.
COBIS, 55–56 Russell Square, Bloomsbury,
London WC1B 4HP
Tel: 020 3826 7190
Email: pa@cobis.org.uk
Website: www.cobis.org.uk

Council of International Schools (CIS)

CIS is a not-for-profit organisation committed to supporting its member schools and colleges in achieving and delivering the highest standards of international education. CIS provides accreditation to schools, teacher and leader recruitment and best practice development. CIS Higher Education assists member colleges and universities in recruiting a diverse profile of qualified international students.
Schipholweg 113, 2316 XC Leiden, The Netherlands.
Tel: +31 71 524 3300
Email: info@cois.org
Website: www.cois.org

Dyslexia Action (DA)

A registered, educational charity (No. 268502), which has established teaching and assessment centres and conducts teacher-training throughout the UK. The aim of the institute is to help people with dyslexia of all ages to overcome their difficulties in learning to read, write and spell and to achieve their potential.
Dyslexia Action Training and Guild, Centurion House, London Road, Staines-upon-Thames TW18 4AX
Tel: 01784 222 304
Email: trainingcourses@dyslexiaaction.org.uk
Website: www.dyslexiaaction.org.uk

European Association for International Education (EAIE)

A not-for-profit organisation aiming for internationalisation in higher education in Europe. It has a membership of over 1800.
PO Box 11189, 1001 GD Amsterdam, The Netherlands
Tel: +31 20 344 5100
Fax: +31 20 344 5119
Email: info@eaie.org
Website: www.eaie.org

ECIS (European Collaborative for International Schools)

ECIS is a membership organisation which provides services to support professional development, good governance and leadership in international schools.
24 Greville Street,
London, EC1N 8SS
Tel: 020 7824 7040
Email: ecis@ecis.org
Website: www.ecis.org

The Girls' Day School Trust (GDST)

The Girls' Day School Trust (GDST) is one of the largest, longest-established and most successful groups of independent schools in the UK, with 4000 staff and over 20,000 students between the ages of 3 and 18. As a charity that owns and runs a family of 26 schools in England and Wales, it reinvests all its income into its schools for the benefit of the pupils. With a long history of pioneering innovation in the education of girls, the GDST now also educates boys in some of its schools, and has two coeducational sixth form colleges. Registered charity No. 306983
10 Bressenden Place, London, SW1E 5DH
Tel: 020 7393 6666
Email: info@wes.gdst.net
Website: www.gdst.net

Girls' Schools Association (GSA)

For information on the GSA see editorial on page 36

The Headmasters' and Headmistresses' Conference (HMC)

For information on the HMC see editorial on page 37

Human Scale Education (HSE)

An educational reform movement aiming for small education communities based on democracy, fairness and respect. Registered charity No. 1000400
Email: contact@hse.org.uk
Website: www.hse.org.uk

The Independent Association of Prep Schools (IAPS)

For further information about IAPS see editorial on page 38

The Independent Schools Association (ISA)

For further information about ISA see editorial on page 39

The Independent Schools' Bursars Association (ISBA)

Exists to support and advance financial and operational performance in independent schools. The ISBA is a charitable company limited by guarantee. Company No. 6410037; registered charity No. 1121757
Bluett House, Unit 11–12 Manor Farm, Cliddesden, nr Basingstoke, Hampshire RG25 2JB
Tel: 01256 330369
Email: office@theisba.org.uk
Website: www.theisba.org.uk

The Independent Schools Council (ISC)

The Independent Schools Council exists to promote choice, diversity and excellence in education; the development of talent at all levels of ability; and the widening of opportunity for children from all backgrounds to achieve their potential. Its 1280 member schools educate more than 500,000 children at all levels of ability and from all socioeconomic classes. Nearly a third of children in ISC schools receive help with fees. The Governing Council of ISC contains representatives from each of the eight ISC constituent associations listed below. See also page 42.

Members:
Association of Governing Bodies of Independent Schools (AGBIS)
Girls' Schools Association (GSA)
Headmasters' and Headmistresses' Conference (HMC)
Independent Association of Prep Schools (IAPS)
Independent Schools Association (ISA)
Independent Schools Bursars' Association (ISBA)
The Society of Heads

The council also has close relations with the BSA, COBIS, SCIS and WISC.

First Floor, 27 Queen Anne's Gate,
London, SW1H 9BU
Tel: 020 7766 7070
Fax: 020 7766 7071
Email: research@isc.co.uk
Website: www.isc.co.uk

The Independent Schools Examinations Board (ISEB)

Details of the Common Entrance examinations are obtainable from:
Independent Schools Examinations Board,
Endeavour House, Crow Arch Lane, Ringwood BH24 1HP
Tel: 01425 470555
Email: enquiries@iseb.co.uk
Website: www.iseb.co.uk
Copies of past papers can be purchased from Galore Park: www.galorepark.co.uk

The Inspiring Futures Foundation (IFF)

The IFF provides careers education and guidance to schools and students. Professional support and training is available to school staff and our Futurewise programme provides individual, web-based, support for students and their parents. Career/subject insight courses, gap-year fairs and an information service are additional elements of the service.
Tel: 01491 820381
Email: helpline@inspiringfutures.org.uk
Website: www.inspiringfutures.org.uk

International Baccalaureate (IB)

For full information about the IB see full entry on page 387.

International Schools Theatre Association (ISTA)

International body of teachers and students of theatre, run by teachers for teachers. Registered charity No. 1050103
3 Omega Offices, 14 Coinagehall St,
Helston, Cornwall TR13 8EB
Tel: 01326 560398
Email: office@ista.co.uk
Website: www.ista.co.uk

Maria Montessori Institute (MMI)

Authorised by the Association Montessori Internationale (AMI) to run their training course in the UK. Further information is available from:
26 Lyndhurst Gardens, Hampstead, London NW3 5NW
Tel: 020 7435 3646
Email: schools@mariamontessori.org
Website: www.mariamontessori.org

The National Association of Independent Schools & Non-Maintained Schools (NASS)

A membership organisation working with and for special schools in the voluntary and private sectors within the UK. Registered charity No. 1083632
PO Box 705, York YO30 6WW
Tel/Fax: 01904 624446
Email: krippon@nasschools.org.uk
Website: www.nasschools.org.uk

National Day Nurseries Association (NDNA)

A national charity that aims to promote quality in early years. Registered charity No. 1078275
NDNA, National Early Years Enterprise Centre,
Longbow Close, Huddersfield, West Yorkshire HD2 1GQ
Tel: 01484 407070
Fax: 01484 407060
Email: info@ndna.org.uk
Website: www.ndna.org.uk

NDNA Cymru, Office 3, Crown House, 11 Well Street,
Ruthin, Denbighshire LL15 1AE
Tel: 01824 707823
Email: wales@ndna.org.uk

NDNA Scotland, The Mansfield Traquair Centre,
15 Mansfield Place, Edinburgh EH3 6BB
Tel: 0131 516 6967
Email: scot@ndna.org.uk

National Foundation for Educational Research (NFER)

NFER is the UK's largest independent provider of research, assessment and information services for education, training and children's services. Its clients include UK government departments and agencies at both national and local levels. NFER is a not-for-profit organisation and a registered charity No. 313392
Head Office, The Mere, Upton Park,
Slough, Berkshire SL1 2DQ
Tel: 01753 574123
Fax: 01753 691632
Email: enquiries@nfer.ac.uk
Website: www.nfer.ac.uk

Potential Plus UK

Potential Plus UK is an independent charity that supports the social, emotional and learning needs of children with high learning potential of all ages and backgrounds. Registered charity No. 313182
Room 5 The Mansion, Sherwood Drive, Bletchley, Milton Keynes, Buckinghamshire MK3 6EB
Tel: 01908 646433
Email: amazingchildren@potentialplusuk.org
Website: www.potentialplusuk.org

Round Square

An international group of schools formed in 1967 following the principles of Dr Kurt Hahn, the founder of Salem School in Germany, and Gordonstoun in Scotland. The Round Square, named after Gordonstoun's 17th century circular building in the centre of the school, now has more than 100 member schools. Registered charity No. 327117
Round Square, First Floor, Morgan House, Madeira Walk, Windsor SL4 1EP
Tel: 01474 709843
Website: www.roundsquare.org

Royal National Children's SpringBoard Foundation

On 1 July 2017 the Royal National Children's Foundation (RNCF) merged with The SpringBoard Bursary Foundation to create the Royal National Children's SpringBoard Foundation ('Royal SpringBoard'). The newly merged charity gives life-transforming bursaries to disadvantaged and vulnerable children from across the UK.
Buckingham Suite, 7 Grosvenor Gardens,
London SW1W 0BD
Tel: 020 3405 3630
Email: admin@royalspringboard.org.uk
Website: www.royalspringboard.org.uk

School Fees Independent Advice (SFIA)

For further information about SFIA, see editorial page 32

Schools Music Association of Great Britain (SMA)

The SMA is a national 'voice' for music in education. It is now part of the Incorporated Society of Musicians
Registered charity No. 313646
Website: www.ism.org/sma

Scottish Council of Independent Schools (SCIS)

Representing more than 70 independent, fee-paying schools in Scotland, the Scottish Council of Independent Schools (SCIS) is the foremost authority on independent schools in Scotland and offers impartial information, advice and guidance to parents. Registered charity No. SC018033
61 Dublin Street, Edinburgh EH3 6NL
Tel: 0131 556 2316
Email: info@scis.org.uk
Website: www.scis.org.uk

Society of Education Consultants (SEC)

The Society is a professional membership organisation that supports management consultants who specialise in education and children's services. The society's membership includes consultants who work as individuals, in partnerships or in association with larger consultancies.
SEC, Bellamy House, 13 West Street, Cromer NR27 9HZ
Tel: 0330 323 0457
Email: administration@sec.org.uk
Website: www.sec.org.uk

The Society of Heads

For full information see editorial on page 40

State Boarding Forum (SBF)

For full information about the SBF see editorial on page 35

Steiner Waldorf Schools Fellowship (SWSF)

Representing Steiner education in the UK and Ireland, the SWSF has member schools and early years centres in addition to interest groups and other affiliated organisations. Member schools offer education for children within the normal range of ability, aged 3 to 18. Registered charity No. 295104
Steiner Waldorf Schools Fellowship® Ltd, Suite 1, 3rd Floor, Copthall House, 1 New Road, Stourbridge, West Midlands, DY8 1PH
Tel: 01384 374116
Email: admin@steinerwaldorf.org
Website: www.steinerwaldorf.org

Support and Training in Prep Schools (SATIPS)

SATIPS aims to support teachers in the independent and maintained sectors of education. Registered charity No. 313688
West Routengill, Walden, West Burton, Leyburn,
North Yorkshire, DL8 4LF
Website: www.satips.org

The Tutors' Association

The Tutors' Association is the professional body for tutoring and wider supplementary education sector in the UK. Launched in 2013, they have over 850 members, including Individual and Corporate Members representing some 30,000 tutors throughout the UK.
Tel: 01628 306108
Email: info@thetutorsassociation.org.uk
Website: www.thetutorsassociation.org.uk

UCAS (Universities and Colleges Admissions Service)

UCAS is the organisation responsible for managing applications to higher education courses in England, Scotland, Wales and Northern Ireland. Registered charity Nos. 1024741 and SC038598
Rosehill, New Barn Lane,
Cheltenham, Gloucestershire GL52 3LZ
Tel: 0371 468 0 468
Website: www.ucas.com

UKCISA – The Council for International Student Affairs

UKCISA is the UK's national advisory body serving the interests of international students and those who work with them. Registered charity No. 1095294
Website: www.ukcisa.org.uk

United World Colleges (UWC)

UWC was founded in 1962 and their philosophy is based on the ideas of Dr Kurt Hahn (see Round Square Schools). Registered charity No. 313690.
UWC International, Third Floor, 55 New Oxford Street,
London, WC1A 1BS, UK
Tel: 020 7269 7800
Fax: 020 7405 4374
Email: info@uwcio.uwc.org
Website: www.uwc.org

World-Wide Education Service of CfBT Education Trust (WES)

A leading independent service which provides home education courses worldwide.
Waverley House, Penton,
Carlisle, Cumbria CA6 5QU
Tel: 01228 577123
Email: office@weshome.com
Website: www.weshome.com

Glossary

ACETS	Awards and Certificates in Education
AEA	Advanced Extension Award
AEB	Associated Examining Board for the General Certificate of Education
AEGIS	Association for the Education and Guardianship of International Students
AGBIS	Association of Governing Bodies of Independent Schools
AHIS	Association of Heads of Independent Schools
AJIS	Association of Junior Independent Schools
ALP	Association of Learning Providers
ANTC	The Association of Nursery Training Colleges
AOC	Association of Colleges
AP	Advanced Placement
ASCL	Association of School & College Leaders
ASL	Additional and Specialist Learning
ATI	The Association of Tutors Incorporated
AQA	Assessment and Qualification Alliance/Northern Examinations and Assessment Board
BA	Bachelor of Arts
BAC	British Accreditation Council for Independent Further and Higher Education
BAECE	The British Association for Early Childhood Education
BD	Bachelor of Divinity
BEA	Boarding Educational Alliance
BEd	Bachelor of Education
BLitt	Bachelor of Letters
BPrimEd	Bachelor of Primary Education
BSA	Boarding Schools' Association
BSc	Bachelor of Science
BTEC	Range of work-related, practical programmes leading to qualifications equivalent to GCSEs and A levels awarded by Edexcel
Cantab	Cambridge University
CATSC	Catholic Association of Teachers in Schools and Colleges
CCEA	Council for the Curriculum, Examination and Assessment
CDT	Craft, Design and Technology
CE	Common Entrance Examination
CEAS	Children's Education Advisory Service
CertEd	Certificate of Education
CIE	Cambridge International Examinations
CIFE	Conference for Independent Education
CIS	Council of International Schools
CISC	Catholic Independent Schools' Conference
CLAIT	Computer Literacy and Information Technology
CNED	Centre National d'enseignement (National Centre of long distance learning)
COBIS	Council of British International)

CSA	The Choir Schools' Association	INSET	In service training	PGCE	Post Graduate Certificate in Education
CST	The Christian Schools' Trust	ISA	Independent Schools Association	PhD	Doctor of Philosophy
DfE	Department for Education (formerly DfES and DCFS)	ISBA	Independent Schools' Bursars' Association	PL	Principal Learning
		ISCis	Independent Schools Council information service	PNEU	Parents' National Education Union
DipEd	Diploma of Education	ISC	Independent Schools Council	PYP	Primary Years Programme
DipTchng	Diploma of Teaching	ISEB	Independent Schools Examination Board	QCA	Qualifications and Curriculum Authority
EAIE	European Association for International Education	ISST	International Schools Sports Tournament	QCF	Qualifications and Credit Framework
ECIS	European Council of International Schools	ISTA	International Schools Theatre Association	RSIS	The Round Square Schools
EdD	Doctor of Education	ITEC	International Examination Council	SAT	Scholastic Aptitude Test
Edexcel	GCSE Examining group, incorporating Business and Technology Education Council (BTEC) and University of London Examinations and Assessment Council (ULEAC)	JET	Joint Educational Trust	SATIPS	Support & Training in Prep Schools/Society of Assistant Teachers in Prep Schools
		LA	Local Authority		
		LISA	London International Schools Association	SBSA	State Boarding Schools Association
		MA	Master of Arts	SCE	Service Children's Education
EFL	English as a Foreign Language	MCIL	Member of the Chartered Institute of Linguists	SCIS	Scottish Council of Independent Schools
ELAS	Educational Law Association	MEd	Master of Education	SCQF	Scottish Credit and Qualifications Framework
EPQ	Extended Project qualification	MIoD	Member of the Institute of Directors	SEC	The Society of Educational Consultants
ESL	English as a Second Language	MLitt	Master of Letters	SEN	Special Educational Needs
FCoT	Fellow of the College of Teachers (TESOL)	MSc	Master of Science	SFCF	Sixth Form Colleges' Forum
FEFC	Further Education Funding Council	MusD	Doctor of Music	SFIA	School Fees Insurance Agency Limited
FRSA	Fellow of the Royal Society of Arts	MYP	Middle Years Programme	SFIAET	SFIA Educational Trust
FSMQ	Free-Standing Mathematics Qualification	NABSS	National Association of British Schools in Spain	SMA	Schools Music Association
GCE	General Certificate of Education	NAGC	National Association for Gifted Children	SoH	The Society of Heads
GCSE	General Certificate of Secondary Education	NAHT	National Association of Head Teachers	SQA	Scottish Qualifications Authority
GDST	Girls' Day School Trust	NAIS	National Association of Independent Schools	STEP	Second Term Entrance Paper (Cambridge)
GNVQ	General National Vocational Qualifications	NASS	National Association of Independent Schools & Non-maintained Special Schools	SVQ	Scottish Vocational Qualifications
GOML	Graded Objectives in Modern Languages			SWSF	Steiner Waldorf Schools Fellowship
GSA	Girls' Schools Association	NDNA	National Day Nurseries Association	TABS	The Association of Boarding Schools
GSVQ	General Scottish Vocational Qualifications	NEASC	New England Association of Schools and Colleges	TISCA	The Independent Schools Christian Alliance
HMC	Headmasters' and Headmistresses' Conference			TOEFL	Test of English as a Foreign Language
HMCJ	Headmasters' and Headmistresses' Conference Junior Schools	NFER	National Federation of Educational Research	UCAS	Universities and Colleges Admissions Service for the UK
		NPA	National Progression Award		
HNC	Higher National Certificate	NQ	National Qualification	UCST	United Church Schools Trust
HND	Higher National Diploma	NQF	National Qualifications Framework	UKLA	UK Literacy Association
IAPS	Independent Association of Prep Schools	NQT	Newly Qualified Teacher	UKCISA	The UK Council for International Education
IB	International Baccalaureate	NVQ	National Vocational Qualifications	UWC	United World Colleges
ICT	Information and Communication Technology	OCR	Oxford, Cambridge and RSA Examinations	WISC	World International Studies Committee
IFF	Inspiring Futures Foundation (formerly ISCO)	OLA	Online Language Assessment for Modern Languages	WJEC	Welsh Joint Education Committee
IGCSE	International General Certificate of Secondary Education			WSSA	Welsh Secondary Schools Association
		Oxon	Oxford		

Index

Index